Individual Taxes

WORLDWIDE SUMMARIES
2004–2005

Individual Taxes

WORLDWIDE SUMMARIES
2004–2005

PRICEWATERHOUSECOOPERS

WILEY

John Wiley & Sons, Inc.

This book is printed on acid-free paper. ♾

Pricewaterhouse Coopers (*www.pwc.com*) is the world's largest professional services organization. Drawing on the knowledge and skills of more than 120,000 people in 139 countries, we build relationships by providing services based on quality and integrity.

Published by John Wiley & Sons, Inc., Hoboken, New Jersey.
Published simultaneously in Canada.

For general information on our other products and services, or technical support, please contact our Customer Care Department within the United States at 800-762-2974, outside the United States at 317-572-3993 or fax 317-572-4002.

Wiley also publishes its books in a variety of electronic formats. Some content that appears in print may not be available in electronic books.

For more information about Wiley products, visit our Web site at *www.wiley.com.*

ISBN 0-471-65391-8 (Set)
ISBN 0-471-65392-6 (Corporate Taxes)
ISBN 0-471-65393-4 (Individual Taxes)

Printed in the United States of America

10 9 8 7 6 5 4 3 2 1

Information Guide Series

This Guide is one of a series on business conditions in the countries in which PricewaterhouseCoopers firms have offices or carry out work, and is based on the latest available information from these offices.

To obtain a copy of a title in the Information Guide series, contact your local PricewaterhouseCoopers office, or call (800) 579-1646.

This series is available in print, on CD-ROM, and on the Internet at *www.pwc.com*

This Guide, *Individual Taxes—Worldwide Summaries,* supersedes the 2003–2004 edition.

PricewaterhouseCoopers Organization—Practice Firms Worldwide

To Our Readers:

I take great pleasure in introducing the 2004–2005 edition of the PricewaterhouseCoopers annual information guide, *Individual Taxes—Worldwide Summaries.* This edition has information on 111 countries and territories. All entries, unless otherwise stated, present tax rates and rules in effect at January 1, 2004.

Part of the PricewaterhouseCoopers information guide series, which also includes *Corporate Taxes—Worldwide Summaries,* this book exemplifies the breadth and depth of expertise offered by the worldwide PricewaterhouseCoopers network.

PricewaterhouseCoopers *(www.pwc.com)* provides industry-focused assurance, tax, and advisory services for public and private clients. More than 120,000 PricewaterhouseCoopers people in 139 countries connect their thinking, experience, and solutions to build public trust and enhance value for clients and their stakeholders. The tax practices in our worldwide network are able to provide a full range of services to meet the needs of our clients and their businesses.

PricewaterhouseCoopers refers to the network of member firms of PricewaterhouseCoopers International Limited, each of which is a separate and independent legal entity. Each of these firms is ready to help with your tax and business problems, wherever in the world you might need assistance. Don't hesitate to contact us.

Yours sincerely,

Paul Boorman
Global Tax Leader, PricewaterhouseCoopers

Foreword

This Guide has been prepared to provide a summary of basic information about individual taxes in 111 countries and territories. It is designed to outline briefly the individual tax rates and certain major features of the tax laws that affect individual taxation in the countries covered. For most countries, the tax summary is supplemented by a sample individual tax calculation to illustrate the basic rules.

In a guide of this nature it is not possible to provide detailed rules on which to base specific action. When more detailed information is required on a country, reference should be made to the specific laws, regulations and tax treaties of the country; and/or to tax advisers.

Unless otherwise indicated, the tax rates and rules in effect at January 1, 2004 have been used.

Table of Contents

PwC contact

For additional information on taxation in Antigua and Barbuda, contact:

Charles W. Walwyn
PricewaterhouseCoopers
11 Old Parham Road
P.O. Box 1531
St. Johns
Antigua, W.I.
Telephone: (268) 462 3000
Fax: (268) 462 1902
e-mail: charles.walwyn@ag.pwc.com

Significant developments

Unincorporated businesses are liable to a 2% tax on gross revenue greater than $50,000 per annum.

Territoriality and residence

Income from employment and investment income is tax-free for individuals who are resident in Antigua. Individuals are generally resident if their permanent place of abode is Antigua and they are physically present in Antigua for not less than 183 days in the income (calendar) year.

Temporary residents are taxed only on income arising in Antigua.

Permanent Residence Scheme/The purpose of this scheme is to offer permanent residence status to high net worth individuals wishing to establish residence and eventually domicile, for tax purposes, in a country that has no personal income tax, no capital gains tax and no inheritance tax.

Successful applicants will be issued with Permanent Residence Certificates that will enable them and their spouses to freely enter and leave Antigua without restriction. Applicants will not be granted an Antiguan passport, but could be considered for citizenship after seven years' residence.

Where a pension arises in a country with which Antigua has a double taxation treaty, that pension will be taxed at 5% and foreign tax deducted at source from the pension will be reclaimable.

Individuals who have been granted residence under the Permanent Residence Scheme pay an annual levy of US$20,000.

PricewaterhouseCoopers can act as agent for people wishing to take advantage of this scheme and will handle the application from start to finish.

Gross income

Employee gross income/Nonresidents and temporary residents are taxed on income arising in Antigua, including the value of benefits (i.e., houses, cars, and other benefits or allowances) received locally, whether or not in cash.

Capital gains and investment income/There is no separate capital gains tax, and capital gains are not included in or taxed as ordinary income. Nonresidents and temporary residents are taxable on investment income arising in Antigua.

Deductions

Personal allowances/Nonresidents and temporary residents are not entitled to claim any allowances in arriving at taxable income.

Tax credits

Relief from double taxation is given on Commonwealth income or in accordance with the provisions of a relevant treaty.

Other taxes

Unincorporated businesses and individuals carrying on any economic activity are required to pay tax monthly on gross income there from at the rate of 2% on income in excess of EC$4,167 per month. This does not apply to income received by an individual from employment.

Commission agents, estate agents and persons disbursing clients' funds pay the 2% tax on that portion belonging to the agent only.

Statutory payroll deductions/Statutory payroll deductions are as follows.

1. Social security:
   a. Employee portion—3% of chargeable income up to EC$4,500 per month;
   b. Employer portion—5% of chargeable income up to EC$4,500 per month.
2. Medical benefits:
   a. Employee portion—3.5% of chargeable income;
   b. Employer portion—3.5% of chargeable income.

   Chargeable income for the purpose of calculating social security and medical benefits amounts does not include most allowances.
3. Education levy:
   a. On the first EC$6,500 of chargeable income per annum—No deduction;
   b. On annual chargeable income between EC$6,500 to EC$60,000—2.5% deduction;
   c. On annual chargeable income for amounts in excess of EC$60,000—5% deduction.

   Chargeable income for the purpose of calculating the education levy does not include most allowances.

Tax administration

Returns/Nonresidents and temporary residents are required to file a tax return for income arising in Antigua. The tax year for individuals is the calendar year.

Payment of tax/Withholding tax is applicable on payments to nonresidents that may be regarded as income arising in Antigua, such as those listed below.

	%
Interest, rent, and annuities and other annual payments	20
Payments of a nature other than interest, rent, or annuities	25

Interest on bank deposits paid to a nonresident person is not subject to withholding tax.

At the time of writing, the Commissioner of Inland Revenue is seeking to assess withholding tax on dividends at a rate of 25%. This is the subject of an appeal.

Tax rates

There is a provision for tax on temporary residents of Antigua and Barbuda (defined as living in Antigua and Barbuda for less than 183 days). This tax is calculated on annual chargeable income using a sliding scale as follows:

Annual chargeable income		
From	To	Rate %
0	EC$ 500	2.5
EC$ 501	1,000	5.0
1,001	1,500	7.5
1,501	2,000	10.0
2,001	2,500	12.5
2,500	3,000	15.0
3,001	4,000	20.0
4,001	5,000	25.0
5,001	7,500	30.0
7,501	10,000	35.0
10,001	15,000	40.0
15,001	20,000	45.0
20,001	30,000	50.0
30,001		55.0

The tax is to be withheld by the employer from payment to the employee.

Exchange rate

Exchange rate of the Eastern Caribbean dollar is officially pegged at US$1 = EC$2.70.

Argentina

PwC contacts

For additional information on taxation in Argentina, contact:

Jorge San Martín
Lilian Falcon
Price Waterhouse & Co.
(Member Firm of PricewaterhouseCoopers)
Cerrito 268
1010 Buenos Aires, Argentina
Telephone: (54) (11) 4370 6700, 4381 8181/7373/7282
Fax: (54) (11) 4370 6800, 4383 6339, 4382 2793
e-mail: jorge.a.san.martin@ar.pwc.com
lilian.falcon@ar.pwc.com

Significant developments

Public Emergency Law No. 25.561 (Official Gazette January 7, 2002) and regulatory decrees have introduced important reforms to the exchange rate system, including exchange restrictions (restrictions for certain transactions in foreign currency and transferring funds abroad) and the abolition of the Convertibility Law (end of parity of the peso with the U.S. dollar) in favor of the establishment of a floating exchange rate for the peso in relation to the U.S. dollar. These measures have had an impact on the tax system.

Territoriality and residence

Individuals resident in Argentina pay tax on worldwide income.

Residence rules for income tax purposes are set out in the tax reform that was published in the Official Gazette on December 30, 1998 and are effective from fiscal year 1998. The definitions are as follows.

1. Residents:
   a. Argentine nationals living in Argentina;
   b. Argentine nationals working abroad during the first 12 months of living abroad (tax residence status is lost as from the first day of the 14th month), or who have obtained a permanent residence in a country other than Argentina (tax residence is lost as from the first day following the second month);
   c. Foreign nationals assigned to work in Argentina for more than five years;
   d. Foreign individuals—in general—residing in Argentina for more than 12 months (tax residence is acquired as from the first day of the 2nd month following).
2. Nonresidents:
   Foreign nationals assigned to work in Argentina for less than five years.
3. Foreign beneficiaries:
   a. Individuals working in Argentina on a temporary basis for less than six months in a calendar year;
   b. Argentine nationals residing abroad who do not qualify as residents;
   c. Foreign nationals residing abroad.

Except for the earned-income allowance, personal and family allowances are applicable only when the taxpayers and their families, if eligible, have been resident in Argentina for over six months of the tax year under consideration.

Foreign beneficiaries who earn income in Argentina through art or a profession are subject to income tax on these earnings at the rate of 24.5% (35% on assumed profit of 70% of gross income) to be withheld by the local payer.

Gross income

Employee gross income/All remuneration paid in cash or in kind, including allowances, reimbursements, or paid expenses (e.g., housing and cost-of-living allowances, school fees, tax reimbursements), is taxable without regard to length of residence or source of income.

Capital gains and investment income/There is no special tax on capital gains.

Except as described below, interest, rents, royalties, pensions, and annuities from Argentine and foreign sources are subject to income tax.

Interest on savings bank accounts and term deposits in Argentine banks, as well as government bonds, is exempt from income tax.

Dividends paid by foreign companies are treated as foreign-source income. They are taxable if distributed to residents, but are not taxable if the beneficiary is a nonresident.

The gain resulting from the sale of shares is not taxable.

Deductions

Business deductions/All losses and expenses incurred in obtaining and preserving taxable income are deductible, but living, personal, and family expenses are not deductible, except for Pension Fund and other social security contributions. In cases where fringe benefits include lump-sum allowances for travel, entertaining, and so on, only actual expenses incurred, supported by third-party vouchers, may be deducted from the related fringe benefit includable in taxable income.

Nonbusiness expenses/Mortgage and all other interest is not deductible, unless it relates to taxable income. Pension and other social security contributions; donations to tax-exempt charitable institutions up to a maximum of 5% of net income; local life and retirement insurance premiums and funeral expenses, up to a maximum established annually by the tax authorities; and contributions to third-party medical schemes, up to a maximum of 5% of net income, are deductible. Other medical expenses may be deducted up to a maximum of 40% of all corresponding invoices of the fiscal year, provided the deduction does not exceed 5% of net income.

***Personal allowances*/**Allowances in force for the year 2004 are shown below.

	Annual
	AR$
Basic	4,020
Spouse	2,400
Child (each)	1,200
Other admissible dependents (each)	1,200
Earned income allowance:	
Employees	18,000
Self-employed workers	6,000

The allowances are reduced in relation to the net income as follows:

Net income		% by which allowance is reduced
Over	Not over	
0	AR$ 39,000	0
AR$ 39,000	65,000	10
65,000	91,000	30
91,000	130,000	50
130,000	195,000	70
195,000	221,000	90
221,000		100

Tax credits

Tax credits are possible for income taxes paid abroad on foreign-source income.

Other taxes

***Social security taxes*/**Withholdings and contributions assessable on employee gross remuneration are as follows.

	Employer	Employee
	%	%
Pension Fund	10.17 or 12.71	7 or 11
Family Allowance Fund	4.44 or 5.56	—
Social Health	6	3
Social Services	2.39 or 2.73	3
Total social tax	23 or 27	13 or 17

The total employer social security rate of 27% is required from companies whose main activity consists of commerce or rendering services, provided their annual sales exceed AR$48,000,000. All other companies are subject to the 23% rate.

Decree 1676 (published on December 20, 2001) reduced the employee contribution to the pension fund from 11% to 5% for those employees who contribute to the individual capitalization account system administered by authorized private entities (AFJP—*Administradora de Fondos de Jubilaciones y Pensiones*). The reduced 5% rate has been increased to 7% and will increase gradually by 2% from July 1, 2004, and October 1, 2004, when the former 11% rate will again be applicable.

The Family Allowance Fund entitles an employee to receive a tax-free monthly allowance for his or her spouse and children, including the education of the latter, provided the employee's salary is not higher than AR$1,500.00. Self-employed persons are subject to pension fund contributions; the monthly payments range from AR$99.84 to AR$1,536.00. These contributions are adjusted annually.

The maximum remuneration subject to both employee and employer contribution is AR$4,800 per month. This amount is adjusted annually.

Depending on the location of the employee, a specific percentage of the social tax basis of the employer's contributions can be offset against the value-added tax (VAT) liability in its monthly VAT return. In Buenos Aires City no credit is available.

Professionals, researchers, scientists, and technicians contracted abroad to render services in Argentina for a term not exceeding two years and on a once-only basis may be excluded from the system at their own or their employers' request, provided the corresponding requirements are fulfilled.

Gross income tax/Gross income tax is a provincial tax applicable to self-employed individuals on gross earnings. The general tax rate is 3% in the Federal Capital, and similar rates are applicable in the different provinces. Professionals are exempt in the Federal Capital.

Tax on personal assets (wealth tax)/Individuals domiciled in Argentina are subject to an annual tax of 0.5% on their worldwide personal assets valued from AR$102,300 to AR$302,300 as at December 31, without consideration of liabilities. On assets with a total value of more than AR$302,300, the applicable tax rate is 0.75%. These taxable assets include, among other items, real estate, cars, shares held in foreign companies, and bank accounts. However, savings accounts at Argentine banks are exempt. Individuals domiciled abroad and working in Argentina for reasons duly proved for a period no longer than five years are assessable only on personal assets located in Argentina.

All taxpayers must file an annual tax return and pay the tax liability in April or May of every year, depending on whether they have or do not have shares in nonlisted corporations whose financial year-end is December, respectively.

Individuals living abroad who own assets located in Argentina must pay the corresponding tax in full and final settlement through a local representative. The tax rate is 0.75% on all assets. Tax is not levied where the total value of the assets does not exceed approximately AR$34,000.

From fiscal year 2002 shares held in Argentine companies are no longer included in the shareholder's wealth tax return. The company must determine wealth tax on all shares issued by them and owned by individuals residing in the country or abroad or owned by companies residing abroad. The wealth tax rate is 0.5% and is payable by the company to the tax authorities. However, reimbursement from the shareholders can be claimed.

Tax on bank account debits and credits/Debits and credits from bank accounts are subject to a tax at 0.6% (general tax rate) on the amount of the transaction. However the deposit and disposal of employment compensation and pension payments are tax exempt.

Local taxes on income/There are no local taxes on income payable in addition to the taxes mentioned above.

Tax administration

Returns/The earnings of each spouse (i.e., from employment, business activities, etc.) are assessable separately and individually.

Tax is assessable on individuals on a calendar-year basis. The general due date for filing is during the second or third week of April of each year.

Individual income tax returns are not required to be filed by employees who have no sources of income other than payroll compensation, since the tax should be duly withheld at source by the employer. However, the company should prepare an annual tax return reporting the annual remuneration, deductions and withholdings of each fiscal year; this is filed with the tax authorities only if the total tax liability has not been withheld. In addition, when annual net income is over AR$40,000, the employee is required to report his or her annual opening and closing net worth (locally and abroad) in a separate personal tax return for information purposes, which must be filed on June 16 of each year.

Self-employed workers (including members of boards of directors) must register with the tax authorities and file an annual income tax return. In addition, they are required to make advance payments on account of their income tax liability of the current year based on their income tax liability of the prior fiscal year.

Payment of tax/There is income tax withholding from salaries. Employers are required to withhold tax at the appropriate personal rates applied to the net taxable remuneration of each employee. Self-employed workers must pay the tax balance due subsequent to the filing of the respective tax return at the authorized banks.

Tax rates

The following individual income tax rates are as from January 1, 2000.

Taxable income		Tax on	Percentage
Over	Not over	Column 1	on excess
(Column 1)			
0	AR$ 10,000	—	9
AR$ 10,000	20,000	AR$ 900	14
20,000	30,000	2,300	19
30,000	60,000	4,200	23
60,000	90,000	11,100	27
90,000	120,000	19,200	31
120,000		28,500	35

INDIVIDUAL TAX CALCULATION

Calendar year 2004

Assumptions

Resident husband and wife, two children; one spouse earns all the income and is included on a local payroll; subject to Pension Fund contributions.

Tax computation

Gross income:		
Salary (including 13th salary)		AR$ 79,840.00
Interest income—Taxable (other than from bank time deposits, etc.)		8,500.00
Capital gain		1,800.00
Total gross income		90,140.00
Less—Capital gain (not subject to tax)		1,800.00
		88,340.00
Less—Deductions:		
Taxes on salary (social security taxes—13% up to a cap of 4,800 per month)	8,112.00	
Charitable contributions	1,200.00	
Medical scheme contributions (up to a maximum of 5% of net income) and other medical expenses (1)	4,011.40	13,323.40
		75,016.60
Less—Personal allowances:		
Spouse	1,680.00	
Children (two)	1,680.00	
Basic allowance	2,814.00	
Earned-income allowance	12,600.00	18,774.00
Taxable income		AR$ 56,242.60
Income tax		AR$ 10,235.80

Notes:

1. Maximum of 40% of invoices up to 5% of net income.
2. Exchange rate of the peso at December 31, 2003: US$1 = AR$2.88.

Australia

PwC contact

For additional information on taxation in Australia, contact:

Ann M. Previtera
PricewaterhouseCoopers
201 Sussex Street
Sydney, New South Wales 2000
Australia
Telephone: (61) (2) 8266 2946
Fax: (61) (2) 8266 5658
e-mail: ann.previtera@au.pwc.com

Significant developments

Personal income tax thresholds were lifted for 2003/2004, but Australia still has a comparatively high top personal rate (48.5% including the Medicare levy) applying at about one and one half times average earnings. As 2004 is an election year and there is a substantial federal budget surplus, promises of significant personal tax cuts are likely.

On December 8, 2003, the government abandoned a proposed tax exemption for certain foreign-source income of expatriates resident in Australia for less than four years because of Senate opposition to the legislation. The proposals included an exemption for their foreign-source income from assets and for withholding tax on interest payments for foreign liabilities.

A new Australia-U.K. tax treaty addresses the taxation of benefits from employee share options granted for employment in one country and exercised in the other and eliminates 10% interest withholding tax on interest payments by a resident borrower in one country to a financial institution resident in the other. A new protocol to the Australia-U.S. treaty has a similar provision regarding interest withholding tax.

Territoriality and residence

Australia taxes its resident individuals on a worldwide basis. Resident individuals are liable to Australian tax on income derived from all foreign sources, except for salary and wages derived in performing duties overseas for a continuous period of at least 91 days, provided these earnings are not exempt from tax in the foreign country in which they are earned. A tax credit is allowed for foreign taxes paid on taxable income derived from foreign sources (see "Tax credits" below).

Certain income is taxed as it accumulates in the case of investments in certain foreign entities (see "Tax credits").

Individuals are residents of Australia if they reside in Australia, and this includes the following.

1. Individuals whose domicile and permanent place of abode is in Australia.
2. Individuals who have actually been in Australia during more than one-half of the income year, unless the individual's usual place of abode is outside Australia and the individual does not intend to reside in Australia.

Persons coming to Australia to take up a contract of employment may be regarded as residents if they are to be in the country for more than six months. Citizenship and nationality do not determine liability to Australian income tax.

A nonresident individual is liable to Australian income tax only on income (other than interest, royalties, and dividends) derived from sources in Australia. Nonresidents are subject to withholding tax on (1) interest income paid to them by a resident, (2) dividend income from resident corporations, and (3) Australian-source royalties.

Under the Australian dividend imputation system, dividends paid out of Australian-taxed corporate income (franked dividends) entitle resident individuals to a rebate (and in some cases a refund) of the corporate tax and nonresidents to an exemption from dividend withholding tax (see "Capital gains and investment income").

Gross income

Employee gross income/Gross income of an employee includes cash remuneration arising from employment. Cash remuneration includes salaries, wages, commissions, bonuses, and allowances paid to employees. Employers are liable for a fringe benefits tax levied at 48.5% of the taxable value multiplied by a gross-up factor of the fringe benefits granted to employees. The gross-up factor is 2.1292 for "type 1 aggregate fringe benefits," broadly being fringe benefits where, subject to certain exceptions, the employer was entitled to an input tax credit for goods and services tax (GST). The gross-up factor is 1.9417 for other fringe benefits, which are referred to as "type 2 aggregate fringe benefits." Fringe benefits tax is deductible by the employer for income tax purposes. Benefits subject to fringe benefits tax are excluded from the employee's taxable income, but may be taken into account (reportable fringe benefits) when determining the employee's liability for tax surcharges such as the Medicare levy surcharge and the superannuation contributions surcharge and income-related obligations such as child support. If employee shares or share options are issued to an employee or associate at a discount to their market value, subject to an exemption for qualifying nondiscriminatory shares or options up to an annual threshold of A$1,000, the discount is included in the employee's assessable income, usually when restrictions on the shares cease or, in the case of options, on exercise. However, the employee may elect to be taxed for the income year when the shares or options are issued. There are complex issues regarding such elections, the value of the discount and where the shares or options relate to employment in more than one country.

Foreign nationals are generally taxable on salary and allowances relating to services performed in Australia, regardless of where payment is made and whether the income is remitted to Australia. Nonemployee resident taxpayers are subject to tax on noncash business benefits.

Resident individuals are subject to Australian tax on their overseas employment income, unless special exemption requirements are met (see "Tax credits"). However, tax treaties are in force with various countries, and provisions in those treaties may require a different tax treatment of certain employment income.

Capital gains and investment income/Capital gains tax applies to assets acquired on or after September 20, 1985. Capital gains made upon the realization of such assets are included in assessable income and are taxed at ordinary rates of tax. If the asset was acquired before 11:45 a.m. AEST on September 21, 1999 and was held for at least 12 months, the individual has a choice of including in taxable income 50% of the nominal gain (gross proceeds less costs not indexed for inflation) or 100% of the gain, allowing for the inflation indexing of costs up to September 30, 1999, but not beyond that date. If the asset was acquired on or after 11:45 a.m. AEST on September 21, 1999 and has been held for at least 12 months, 50% of the nominal gain (with no indexing of costs for inflation) is included in the individual's taxable income. Capital losses are allowable as deductions only against capital gains and cannot be offset against other income. In calculating capital losses, there is no indexation of the cost base.

Residents of Australia, including short-term residents, are liable for the tax on gains from the disposal of assets wherever situated, subject to a credit for foreign tax paid. Nonresidents are liable for tax on gains on the disposal of assets having a "necessary connection with Australia," defined broadly as including land or buildings situated in Australia, assets used in carrying on a business through a permanent establishment in Australia, shares in Australian private companies, interests in resident trusts, interests owned in partnership assets that have the necessary connection with Australia, and shareholdings of 10% or more in the issued capital of Australian public companies.

Where a nonresident becomes an Australian resident, capital assets owned by the nonresident (other than assets acquired before September 20, 1985 and assets having a "necessary connection with Australia") are deemed to have been acquired by the nonresident for a consideration equal to the market value of the assets at the time residence commences. Special provisions also apply where a resident individual ceases to be a resident, so that assets not having the necessary connection with Australia are deemed to be disposed of, unless an election to the contrary is made.

Resident individuals are taxable on foreign-source dividend, interest, and royalty income but are eligible for a credit for foreign taxes paid on such income (see "Tax credits" below).

A dividend imputation system designed to prevent the double taxation of Australian corporate profits distributed to individual shareholders applies to dividends paid out of Australian-taxed profits of resident corporations (franked dividends). Resident individual shareholders receiving franked dividends are entitled to a rebate of Australian corporate tax paid on the dividends. If a franking rebate exceeds the tax payable by a resident individual, the excess is refundable to the individual. Nonresident individuals receiving franked dividends are not entitled to a rebate but are exempt from withholding tax on the dividends, and they are exempt from withholding tax on unfranked dividends to the extent that the dividends are paid out of certain foreign-source dividend income and the company has specified an "Foreign Dividend Account declaration percentage" in relation to the dividend.

Nonresidents are not taxable on income from sources outside Australia. Australian-source unfranked dividend income, interest income, and royalty income are normally subject only to withholding tax. Other Australian-source income is taxable at personal rates applicable to nonresidents.

Deductions

Business deductions**/**To the extent these are not reimbursed, residents and nonresidents can deduct properly substantiated business expenses incurred in earning employment and other income, for example, business-connected travel expenses, automobile expenses, subscriptions to professional or trade organizations, and tax-agent fees. Expenses of a private or domestic nature are generally not deductible. Generally entertainment expenses are not allowable deductions.

Living-away-from-home allowances are subject to fringe benefits tax that is payable by the employer. A portion of living-away-from-home allowances in relation to the provision of accommodation and excess food costs is exempt from fringe benefits tax.

Certain relocation fringe benefits are exempt from fringe benefits tax. To the extent that a fringe benefit is exempt from fringe benefits tax, it will also usually be exempt from income tax. Employer-provided cars are taxed concessionally under fringe benefits tax rules.

Nonbusiness expenses/Gifts of A$2 or more to specified charities, cultural organizations, environmental organizations, and public institutions are deductible. A tax rebate is available at the rate of 20% of the excess of qualifying medical expenses over A$1,500. A 30% tax rebate is available for the cost of private health insurance premiums provided certain eligibility criteria are met.

Personal allowances/Residents receive the first segment of taxable income tax free. The tax-free threshold for the year ending June 30, 2004 is A$6,000 (see "Tax rates" below). Provided family income is below certain thresholds, a resident individual (or an individual in Australia with a special category visa or an approved visa for family tax benefit purposes) is entitled to family tax benefit Part A if he or she has a dependent child under 21 or a dependent full-time student aged 21 to 24 (who is not in receipt of youth allowance or a similar payment), but not a child above 16 receiving payments under a prescribed educational scheme. If a couple are both eligible, only one may claim. The benefit may be shared between eligible parents who are not a couple. Where family income is A$31,755 or less, the maximum family tax benefit Part A is payable, and reduces by 30 cents for each dollar above A$31,755 until the base rate for this benefit is reached. The base rate reduces by 30 cents for each dollar of family income over A$82,052 (plus A$3,285 for each family tax benefit child after the first) until the payment cuts out. The annual family income limits at which the family tax benefit Part A cuts out are: A$85,702 for a recipient with a dependent child under 18; A$86,956 for a recipient with a dependent child aged 18 to 24. These limits increase by A$6,935 for each additional family tax benefit child under 18 and A$8,188 for each additional family tax benefit child aged 18 to 24. These limits may be higher in certain cases for larger families or those receiving rent assistance.

The maximum annual rates of family tax benefit Part A are: for each child under 13—A$3,401.80; for each child 13 to 15—A$4,314.30; for each child 16 to 17—A$1,095; for each child 18 to 24—A$1,470.95.

The annual base rate of family tax benefit Part A is: for each child under 18—A$1,095; for each child 18 to 24—A$1,470.95.

In determining entitlement for the family tax benefit Part A, family income, known as "adjusted taxable income," includes taxable income, reportable fringe benefits, tax-free pensions and benefits, foreign income not taxed in Australia, and certain net rental property losses less payments to support a child from a previous relationship.

Where all or most of family income is earned by one person, family tax benefit Part B may be payable in addition to Part A. If the secondary earner's adjusted taxable income is A$1,825 or less, the maximum family tax benefit Part B is paid, regardless of the income of the primary earner. For each dollar above that limit, the payment reduces by 30 cents, cutting out when the secondary earner's annual income reaches A$11,559 if the youngest child is under 5, and A$8,614 if the youngest child is between 5 and 16, or from 16 to 18 and a full-time student. Regardless of their income, sole parents receive the maximum family tax benefit Part B.

Maximum annual rates of family tax payment Part B are: if the youngest child is under 5—A$2,920; if the youngest child is 5 to 15 or a full-time student of 16 to 18—A$2,036.70.

There are three choices as to the way in which the family tax benefit may be paid: as a direct payment from the Family Assistance Office; as a lump sum claim when filing an individual tax return; and as a reduction in pay-as-you-go (PAYG) withholding on salary income.

There is also a child-care benefit to help families with child-care costs where the care used is approved or registered.

Residents are entitled to specified rebates of tax, including a rebate set at a maximum of A$1,535 for the year to June 30, 2004 for a dependent resident spouse. The spouse rebate is subject to abatement for separate net income of the spouse, cutting out if this exceeded A$6,421 (in the year to June 30, 2004). In general, the dependent spouse rebate is not available to couples with children who are entitled to the family tax benefit Part B.

If a spouse's assessable income does not exceed A$10,800, a resident may make a maximum rebatable contribution of A$3,000 for the spouse (including a de facto) to a complying superannuation fund or retirement savings account (RSA) and obtain a maximum tax rebate of A$540 (the rebate is the amount of the contribution x 18%). The rebate is subject to abatement if the spouse's assessable income exceeds A$10,800, cutting out if this exceeds A$13,799. Other rebates include those for residence in isolated areas and certain lump sums received in arrears.

Nonresidents generally do not benefit from a tax-free threshold, nor do they qualify for the various rebates.

Tax credits

Australian-resident individuals are subject to Australian tax on their worldwide income, with credit allowed for foreign taxes paid on foreign-source income to the extent of Australian tax payable. However, an Australian resident deriving foreign salary and wage income from overseas employment during a continuous period of at least 91 days may be exempt from Australian tax on this income. For those taxpayers with exempt foreign-source income, a notional average rate of tax payable on the sum of exempt and nonexempt income is to be applied to the nonexempt component. For the purpose of calculating foreign tax credits, exempt foreign earnings are not to be aggregated with foreign income other than earnings.

Certain foreign noncomparably taxed income, which is generally sheltered in low-tax countries through foreign companies controlled by Australian residents and through trusts, may be attributed to Australian-resident controllers and taxed in Australia. Any income subject to taxation on attribution will be exempt from Australian tax when repatriated to Australia.

There are also measures to deal with passive foreign investment funds (FIFs), including interests in foreign companies, foreign trusts, and foreign life insurance policies. Essentially, and subject to important qualifications, the FIF rules tax increases or deemed increases in value and distributions from interests in offshore entities (wherever located), except for some categories that are specifically exempted. Investments in foreign companies listed on approved stock exchanges that are principally engaged in certain active businesses are exempt.

There are several other exemptions, including an exemption for life insurance policies held by natural persons giving life or life and disability coverage only. The FIF rules do not apply to visitors who have not applied for permanent residency and hold a temporary visa, broadly where the period covered by the visa and previous visas of which it is an extension does not exceed four years. Equivalent rules apply to New Zealand citizens.

Other significant items/Nonresidents are exempt from Australian tax on foreign-source income; therefore, no foreign tax credit is applicable.

Personal allowances (see above) generally take the form of tax rebates, which are available only to residents.

Other taxes

Social security taxes/There are no social security taxes; a 1.5% levy on taxable income is imposed on residents for the funding of a National Health Scheme (Medicare). A surcharge of 1% applies to high income taxpayers where the taxpayer and his or her dependants are not covered by a private health insurance fund registered in Australia.

Superannuation and retirement taxation/Employer supported and self-employed contributions to more than 100,000 complying superannuation entities and retirement savings accounts (RSAs) have a role in Australia similar to that of social security levies. The retirement benefits provided by these superannuation entities (which are independent of government, but have to comply with regulations so they are "complying") are in addition to the age pension which is provided by the Federal government and is means tested.

The rules regarding the taxation of superannuation are extremely complex and what follows is a brief summary of some highlights. Employers must contribute on behalf of their employees' superannuation an amount broadly equal to not less than 9% of their payroll, subject to exceptions, or be liable to a superannuation guarantee charge. It is usually tax effective, subject to certain limits, for employees to "sacrifice" salary to allow employer superannuation contributions on their behalf above this minimum. The maximum annual deductible contributions for employers per employee (for the year to June 30, 2004) are, based on the age of the employee: age 0 to 34—A$13,233; age 35 to 49—$A36,754; age 50 and over—A$91,149. The superannuation entity receiving employer contributions pays contributions tax of 15% on the amount of the contribution. In addition it is liable to a "surcharge" tax of an additional 14.5% for 2003/2004 (13.5% for 2004/2005 and 12.5 for 2005/2006) for contributions on behalf of employees whose adjusted taxable income exceeds certain limits. For the year to June 30, 2004 the full surcharge rate of 14.5% applies if adjusted taxable income equals at least A$114,981. Shading in applies if the employee's income is less than this amount and not less than A$94,690.

Complying superannuation funds pay tax of 15% on their earnings, except for venture capital franked dividends from a pooled development fund (PDF) which are not taxed, and tax on capital gains on assets acquired after 11:45 am AEST on September 21, 1999, and held for more than 12 months, which are effectively taxed at 10%. A similar treatment is available for capital gains on assets acquired before that time, or the fund may choose to pay tax of 15% on the capital gain less indexation for inflation to the earlier of the disposal date or September 30, 1999. For the year to June 30, 2004, the reasonable benefit limit (RBL) that an individual may accumulate for withdrawal as a lump sum in superannuation benefits (without paying excess benefits tax) is $A588,056, and the RBL is A$1,176,106 if at least half of the benefits are taken as a complying pension. Provided the individual is over 55, there is no tax on withdrawals from superannuation funds up to the first A$117,576 for components accumulated since June 1983. This is a lifetime threshold, indexed annually. Lump-sum withdrawals above this threshold, subject to the lifetime RBL, made by taxpayers over age 55 are taxed at 15%. Withdrawals exceeding the RBL, if previously subject to contributions tax, are taxed at 38%, and if not, are taxed at 47%. More concessional tax rules apply for components deemed to be pre-June 1983. A tax rebate of 15% applies for certain superannuation pensions and qualifying annuities paid to recipients over age 55.

Local taxes on income/There are no state or city income taxes.

Stamp tax (including Financial Institutions Duty)/All the states and territories of Australia impose stamp taxes at various rates on documents, such as mortgages and other secured interests, insurance policies, leasing transactions, and contracts effecting the transfer of unquoted marketable securities or real estate or interest therein. Because stamp tax is levied by the states and territories, the rates vary, depending on where the transactions are carried into effect.

Debits tax/The state governments impose a tax on most debits made to checking accounts kept with a bank. Certain debits and accounts are exempt from the tax. The tax is to be repealed on July 1, 2005. In New South Wales debits tax ceased on January 1, 2002.

Tax administration

Returns/A resident individual is required to file an income tax return where gross income exceeds the tax-free threshold (for the income year to June 30, 2004, A$6,000—see rate table below). A nonresident earning A$1 or more salary or wage income must file a return. There is no joint assessment or joint filing in Australia.

Employees and holders of certain investments must quote their income tax file number to their employer and/or relevant financial institution if they wish to prevent tax from being withheld (at the top marginal rate) on income paid to them.

Returns for individuals are filed on the basis of a fiscal year ending June 30; they are due for filing by the following October 31, unless an extension is approved.

Payment of tax/When salaries are paid by an Australian company or by a nonresident company from a base in Australia, PAYG tax installments must be withheld. PAYG tax must also be withheld from payments to contractors if an Australian Business Number (ABN) is not provided by the contractor and the payment amount disregarding GST exceeds A$50.

PAYG quarterly installments of tax calculated on certain income derived during the previous quarter are payable by certain individuals. The due dates for these quarterly payments are October 28, February 28, April 28, and July 28. The tax installments are based on the total of certain gross income such as fees for services, sales in carrying on a business, interest, dividends, and royalties derived during the previous quarter (but not salary or wages) multiplied by an installment rate provided by the Commissioner of Taxation to determine the tax payable. The individual may vary this installment rate, but if this is less than 85% of the rate that should have applied, a general interest charge will be payable. Individuals, companies and funds with an annual turnover of under A$1 million and taxpayers who are not registered for GST and their most recent "notional tax" is A$8,000 or more may choose to pay quarterly installments based on their "GDP-adjusted notional tax." If this method is chosen the installment payable will be based on the tax of a previous year adjusted for movements in Australia's GDP. Individuals whose notional tax amount is less than

A$8,000 pay a single annual installment. It has been indicated that if the balance of an individual's last assessment was less than A$250, the individual will be not subject to PAYG installment tax and need only pay tax on such income upon annual assessment.

Tax rates

For the year ending June 30, 2004/The following rates of tax apply to resident and nonresident individuals for the year ending June 30, 2004.

Residents

Taxable income Over (Column 1)	Not over	Tax on Column 1	Percentage on excess
0	A$ 6,000	—	0
A$ 6,000	21,600	—	17
21,600	52,000	A$ 2,652	30
52,000	62,500	11,772	42
62,500		16,182	47

Note:

Resident rates apply to a person who has been an Australian resident for tax purposes at any time during the income year and also to any nonresident in receipt of taxable Australian social security pensions.

Nonresidents

Taxable income Over (Column 1)	Not over	Tax on Column 1	Percentage on excess
0	A$ 21,600	—	29
A$ 21,600	52,000	A$ 6,264	30
52,000	62,500	15,384	42
62,500		19,794	47

INDIVIDUAL TAX CALCULATION

Year ending June 30, 2004 (current as at January 1, 2004)

Assumptions

Resident husband and wife; two children, one aged 4, the other aged 7. Neither the wife nor the children have any separate income. The husband and wife agree that the family tax benefit Part B is claimed through the tax system. Income includes salary of A$93,600, interest of A$5,000, long-term capital gain of A$2,000 (not taxable because asset was acquired prior to September 20, 1985), and gross foreign dividends of A$1,000 (on which foreign tax of A$150 is paid). The husband donates A$500 to a qualifying charity and has A$80 of employment-related deductions. The husband pays an annual premium of A$2,000 for private health insurance and seeks to claim the relevant rebate through the tax system.

Tax computation

Assessable income:		
Salary		A$ 93,600
Interest		5,000
Foreign dividend		1,000
		99,600
Less—Deductions:		
Gifts to qualifying charities	500	
Employment-related expenses (e.g., professional body subscriptions)	80	580
Taxable income		A$ 99,020
Tax thereon		A$ 33,346
Add—Medicare levy		1,485
		34,831
Less:		
Credit for foreign tax on dividends		(150)
Tax offset for private health insurance premium		(600)
Family tax benefit Part B		(4,957)
Tax payable		A$ 29,124

Note:

Exchange rate of the Australian dollar at December 31, 2003: US$1 = A$1.343.

PwC contact

For additional information on taxation in Austria, contact:

Friedrich Rödler
PricewaterhouseCoopers
Erdbergstraße 200
A–1030 Vienna, Austria
Telephone: (43) (1) 501 88 0
Fax: (43) (1) 501 88 601
e-mail: friedrich.roedler@at.pwc.com

Significant developments

The most important developments will occur with the enlargement of the EU by ten new member countries, as many of these new member states are next to Austria.

The old social security treaties will lose their validity, and the EU regulations regarding social security will come into force. The structuring of international assignments to these countries will change considerably. The legal provisions for immigration for the nationals of the new member countries will be amended to a large extent.

The discriminatory taxation of foreign investment funds and foreign capital income, such as interest and dividend income, was to a large extent abolished.

Regarding local employers taxes a relief for Austrian companies from contributions to family allowance fund took place for EU nationals assigned to Austria from EU countries and remaining under their home country social security scheme.

For 2005 a further tax reform is projected. It is intended to diminish labor costs and to render the Austrian income tax system less complicated.

Territoriality and residence

All persons resident in Austria are subject to Austrian income tax on their worldwide income, including income from trade or business, profession, employment, investments, and property. Nonresidents are taxed on income from certain sources in Austria only.

A person is generally regarded as resident with the establishment of a dwelling, an abode or, in any event, after a six-month stay in Austria. As of January 1, 2004, an Austrian dwelling will generally not create residence if it is not used for more than 70 days per calendar year and if the center of main interest for more than 5 years is allocated abroad.

Nationality is not in itself a criterion for determining residence or tax liability. However, it may serve as an indicator of residence in cases of doubt.

Gross income

Employee gross income/Income from employment includes all benefits in cash or in kind received by an individual from an employer and from third parties. Benefits in kind are valued according to specific rules, with some cases of global allocations (mainly cars). Company-provided housing is valued at 75% of the actual gross rent paid by the company; reimbursement for privately paid housing is fully taxable. Certain minor benefits in kind are tax exempt (e.g., the granting of company stock up to an annual limit of €1,460 per employee). Further tax-free amounts are available for nontransferable options exercised within seven years after grant. Reimbursement of an employee's actual relocation costs is tax exempt; lump-sum relocation allowances are tax exempt within certain limits. Reimbursement of tax costs is fully taxable.

Bonus payments (e.g., 13th- and 14th-month salaries (vacation and Christmas pay)) up to an annual amount equal to two average monthly salaries are taxed at a flat rate of 6%; the first €620 is tax free. Bonus amounts exceeding this ceiling are taxed at normal rates.

Nonresidents are subject to income tax on Austrian-source income at same rates as residents.

Special ruling for expatriates/With the aim of reducing taxes and facilitating payroll accounting for the rising number of foreign executives assigned to Austria, expatriates are granted a global allowance to cover housing allowances already in the current payroll accounting.

For the purposes of the directive, "expatriates" are individuals who have not been resident in Austria for the past ten years and who work temporarily for an Austrian employer (group company or permanent establishment for wage tax purposes) in Austria on behalf of a foreign employer. The work in Austria must not be planned to last more than five years, and employees must keep their residence in the home country.

Under the directive, the following foreign allowances paid to the expatriate by the employer can be considered tax-free directly in the current payroll accounting.

1. Expenses for moving:
   Lump-sum payments for moves due to assignments are tax-free up to 1/15 of annual gross salary.
2. Expenses for double household:
   Reasonable rental costs for a residence in Austria for the employee and family are tax deductible up to a monthly amount of €2,200.
3. Expenses for home leaves:
   If expatriates visit their foreign employer while on home leave, it is assumed that these costs represent expenses for a business trip and remain tax-free. No per diem allowances for travel to the parent enterprise and home leave can be claimed.

   In addition, home leave for the maintenance of the permanent residence is tax-free up to a monthly amount of €175 for the employee.
4. Expenses for education of children (school fees):
   If children of expatriates accompany their parents to Austria and must attend a private international school instead of a public school to continue their education, a monthly amount of €110 per child is tax deductible.

Additional special expenditures, business expenses, and extraordinary financial burdens can be considered in the annual tax return.

The employer must forward a written notification to the appropriate tax office at the beginning of the assignment and thereafter at the beginning of every calendar year, stating the names of the employees for whom the beneficial tax treatment is claimed, and must inform the tax authorities of their personal data, including addresses in Austria and in the foreign country.

Capital gains and investment income/In general, capital gains arising from nonbusiness activities are not taxed, subject to the following two exceptions.

1. Short-term capital gains—Profits on the sale of both Austrian and non-Austrian assets are considered "speculative" transactions and are subject to income tax at normal rates where the period between purchase and sale is not more than one year (real estate—10 years, in some cases 15 years; specific rules apply for sale of principal residence). Such profits totaling less than €440 are not taxable (tax exemption limit). Nonresidents are liable to tax only on "short-term" profits (10 years) from sales of Austrian real estate. Short term capital gains are taxed at normal income tax rates.
2. Sale of participations—Profits on the sale of holdings in corporations (in particular, AGs or Ges.m.b.H.s) are subject to income tax at reduced rates where the vendor has held at least 1% of issued share capital at any time within a period of five years preceding the date of sale. A deemed sale and taxable event arises if the individual gives up residence in Austria and if Austria is thereby losing the right to tax this income. Nonresidents are liable to tax on such profits if the company has its head office or a place of management in Austria.

Investment income comprises mainly dividends, profits from shares in silent partnerships and interest and income from investment funds.

Bank interest and interest on certain securities from Austrian sources received by Austrian residents are subject to withholding tax of 25%. Withholding tax settles the income tax liability on interest as well as inheritance tax on the source of interest. If an individual's average income tax rate is lower than 25%, a tax refund is available. Interest not subject to withholding tax (e.g., withholding-tax-exempt interest from abroad) is to be declared in the income tax return and is taxed at a special rate of 25% if received after March 31, 2003; in the case of inheritance, the special tax also settles the inheritance tax. Nonresidents are taxed on (except interest on bonds) if the underlying loan is secured by Austrian real estate.

Dividends received by Austrian residents and nonresidents are subject to a withholding tax of 25%, which settles the income tax liability; inheritance tax on the source of dividends is covered if less than 1% of issued share capital was held as participation. A refund is available if an individual's average tax rate, is below 25%. Dividends from abroad are to be declared in the income tax return and are taxed at the new special tax rate of 25% if received after March 31, 2003.

If the foreign dividends are not subject to a corporate tax burden comparable to the Austrian corporate tax, the foreign dividend will be subject to Austrian taxation with the normal progressive income tax rates (up to 50%).

For nonresidents, withholding tax on Austrian dividends represents the final tax burden. The provisions of applicable double taxation treaties must be observed.

For income from foreign investment funds special provisions and lump-sum taxation may apply (minimum taxation). The new income tax rate of 25% will apply to this income received after March 31, 2003.

If income from capital gains and investments is received from abroad, the relevant double taxation treaty is to be observed. As a general rule these treaties provide for taxation in Austria with tax credit for corresponding foreign taxes, if any.

Deductions

Business deductions/Expenses incurred in "acquiring, securing, and maintaining" income are deductible from the taxable income of the particular source of income concerned. All employees are entitled to a standard allowance of €132. Expenses in excess of this amount will be allowed if supported by receipts (e.g., office in home, continuing education; also, for short-term residents see the new directive described under "Gross income" above).

Nonbusiness expenses/Employee portions of mandatory contributions to Austrian and/or foreign social security are tax deductible.

Relief allowances are also available against taxable income if annual income does not exceed €50,900. This allowance includes sickness, life and accident insurance premiums; voluntary contributions to employer pension plans and/or state social security; expenses for the construction of a new house/apartment or renovation of housing space in Austria; and the purchase of certain shares and bonds. For these types of expenses, a standard allowance of €60 per year is granted, unless higher payments are substantiated. In the latter case, the deductible amount is limited to 25% of expenses up to €2,920 per year for single taxpayers and €5,840 per year for the sole earner of a married couple. For taxpayers with at least three children, the allowable expenses subject to the 25% limit are increased to €4,380 for single taxpayers and €7,300 for sole earners. Taxpayers who earn between €36,400 and €50,900 per year can claim only part of this allowance.

Church tax is deductible up to €75 (projected to increase for 2004 to €100), and charitable contributions to certain institutions are deductible up to 10% of the previous year's taxable income. Austrian tax adviser fees are fully deductible.

Exceptionally heavy financial burdens relief/Where taxpayers unavoidably incur exceptionally heavy financial burdens, they may claim an allowance against taxable income. Depending on the type of burden, this allowance may be claimed either in the amount of actual expenses (e.g., damage due to disaster) or to the extent that such expenses exceed a retention, that is, a certain percentage of income up to which no deduction is allowed (e.g., medical costs, funeral costs).

The retention percentage depends on the taxpayer's income and personal status, as follows.

Annual income		**Retention**
Over	**Not over**	**%**
0	€ 7,300	6
€ 7,300	14,600	8
14,600	36,400	10
36,400		12

The percentage is reduced by 1% for sole earners and for each dependent child.

Personal tax credits/Personal tax credits are available as follows.

	€
Basic—All taxpayers (1)	1,264.00
Employee (general) (2)	54.00
Employee transportation	291.00
Sole earners of married couples or, in case of at least one dependent child, single taxpayers and sole earners of unmarried couples (5)	364.00
Children (3):	
For each dependent child	610.80
Pensioners (4)	400.00

Notes:

1. The basic tax credit of €1.264 is granted pro rata for income up to an income of €35,511 per annum (p.a.). For income exceeding €35,511 p.a. no basic tax credit is available.
2. If income tax is withheld on salaries.
3. To be prorated according to months of eligibility.
4. Will be pro rata reduced to zero for income between €16,715 and €21,800 p.a.
5. The sole earner allowance is projected to increase depending on number of children for 2004. The planned increase is €130 for the first child, €175 for the second child, and €220 for each further child p.a.

Generally, personal tax credits are deductions from tax payable. By contrast, children's tax credits are paid to the taxpayer in cash, together with the family allowance (children subsidy, see note 5 under "Examples for monthly withholdings" below).

Foreign tax credits

Austria has entered into double taxation treaties with all major trading countries. Some of the treaties provide for elimination or partial elimination of double taxation by foreign tax credit (e.g., Canada, Italy, Japan, United Kingdom, United States). Under the majority of treaties, however, double taxation is avoided or partially avoided by an exemption-with-saving clause as to progression. As an exception to the rule, dividends and interest are usually fully taxable with a foreign tax credit.

Other taxes

Social security taxes/Monthly rates of compulsory (pretax) contributions in effect as of January 1, 2004 are shown below.

1. Pensions, sickness, unemployment, accident insurance, and certain minor contributions:

	Employer	Employee	Total
	%	%	%
Social security contribution rates (total)	21.85*	17.95*	39.80*
Social security categories:			
Sickness	3.70	3.70	7.40
Unemployment	3.00	3.00	6.00
Pension	12.55	10.25	22.80
Accident	1.40	—	1.40
Miscellaneous	1.20	1.00	2.20
Total	21.85	17.95	39.80

*On a maximum assessment basis (gross salary) of €3,450 per month and €6,900 p.a. for special payments (e.g., bonus payments such as 13th- and 14th-month salaries).

2. In addition, the employer is liable to the Family Burdens Equalization Levy at the rate of 4.5%, the municipal tax on payroll at the rate of 3% of monthly gross salaries and wages and, in the city of Vienna, a public transportation levy of €0.72 per week per employee. In addition, a contribution to the Chamber of Commerce is levied at a rate of approximately 0.40% of gross salaries paid.
3. Social security contributions on special payments are levied up to €6,900 per annum at a total rate of 38.3% (employer 21.35%; employee 16.95%).

   For certain family members (mainly spouses who are not educating or have not educated children for at least four years), an additional insurance contribution of 3.4% within the above-mentioned limits must be paid.
4. The employer must pay an additional contribution to an employee care fund at the rate of 1.53% on monthly gross salaries without limit for employments commencing as of January 1, 2003.

Austria has entered into agreements on social security with its major trading partners, under which, in most cases, it is possible for expatriates on temporary secondment from non-EU countries to apply for exemption from Austrian social security contributions for a certain period of time, provided home country social insurance continues. The Austrian social security authorities will ask for a home country certificate of coverage. For EU citizens, different rules apply (form E101).

Local taxes on income/There are no local income taxes for individuals.

Tax administration

Returns/Joint filing of income tax returns is not permitted. The tax year for individuals is always the calendar year.

Payment of tax/In general, income tax is withheld from salaries/wages, interest from Austrian banks and dividends (see “Capital gains and investment income” above). Income tax on other types of income is payable quarterly, with an annual return filing requirement.

Tax rates

Income tax/Tax rates in force as of January 1, 2002 are as follows.

Annual taxable income				
Over	**Not over**		**Percentage**	**Deduct progression**
(Column 1)				
0	€ 3,640	....	0	0
€ 3,640	7,270	....	21	€ 764.40
7,270	21,800	....	31	1,491.40
21,800	50,870	....	41	3,671.40
50,870		....	50	8,249.70

Notes:

1. Total income tax is reduced by the basic personal tax credit of €1264 (reduced by pro rata computation for certain categories—see above under "Personal tax credits, Note 1").
2. If the taxpayer is the sole earner of a married couple, income tax is reduced by another €364.

Payroll withholding tax/Assuming Austrian social security applies, wage tax and social security contributions are withheld as follows.

Examples for monthly withholdings:

(In euros)

Annual taxable salary		1/14th annual salary	Pretax monthly social security withholding	Monthly wage tax withholding
29,000	....	2,071.43	371.83	312.14
36,000	....	2,571.43	461.58	484.84
54,000	....	3,857.14	619.28	986.26
72,000	....	5,142.86	619.28	1,537.57

Notes:

1. Persons having employment income only are not obliged to file income tax returns. However, where such persons have incurred deductible business or nonbusiness expenses or did not have a constant salary for 12 months, a partial refund of taxes may be obtained by filing an income tax return.
2. The basic personal tax credit has been considered in the above calculation.
3. For the sole earner of a married couple, monthly tax amount withheld is reduced by €30.34.
4. Tax rates applicable to monthly salaries are based on the above-listed income tax rates.
5. For children, there is a tax-free subsidy p.a. ("family allowance") as follows:
   a. Basic amount:
      i. For children below the age of 3—€105.40 per month (p.m.)
      ii. For children between the age of 3 and 10—€112.70 p.m.
      iii. For children between the age of 10 and 19—€130.90 p.m.
      iv. For studying children between the age of 19 and 26 and orphans—€152.70 p.m.

b. Increase:

According to §8(3) Austrian Family burden equalization act the total family allowance is increased by the one time amount of €12.80 p.m., if family allowance is paid for at least two children.

c. Further increase:

If family allowance is paid for three children or more the allowance is increased for the third and each further child by €25.50 p.m each.

d. Increase for disabled:

Children subsidy for considerable disabled children is increased by €138.30 p.m.

e. Additional children surcharge:

An additional allowance where there are three or more children is granted. This allowance is given only when:

i. The family allowance for the children has been obtained;

ii. The household income for the calendar year does not exceed 12 times the monthly maximum basis of the mandatory social security for the previous year (i.e., in 2004 €40,320, which is the maximum basis for 2003).

The additional allowance amounts to €36.40 p.m. for the third and each additional dependent child.

Family allowances are granted even in the case where no income tax is payable.

Family tax credit is paid by the tax office in cash along with the children's tax credit (see "Personal tax credits" above).

As of January 1, 2002 *"Kinderbetreuungsgeld"* (maternity pay) is granted for all children born on or after January 1, 2002. A taxpayer entitled to the family allowance is eligible for maternity pay. This benefit, which amounts to €14.53 per day, is paid up to a maximum of 36 months, in general for 30 months. There is a limit for additional income, currently €14,600 per year, for the beneficiary.

6. The 13th- and 14th-month salaries are subject to social security deductions as described above (see "Social security taxes" above). The first €620 is tax exempt (see "Employee gross income" above); from the remaining amount, tax is withheld at a flat rate of 6%.

INDIVIDUAL TAX CALCULATION

Based on the law and tax rates in effect on January 1, 2004

Assumptions

Resident husband and wife, two dependent children; one spouse earns all the income; employment in Austria; Austrian employer, Austrian social security applies; interest from Austrian sources €11,250; dividends from abroad not subject to special tax rate (double taxation treaty country) €7,030; life insurance premiums of €7,300 per year.

Tax computation

Salary		€ 65,400
Less:		
Tax-favored portion (13th- and 14th-month salaries) ((65,400 ÷ 14) x 2)	9,343	
Social insurance contributions (12 x 619.28 for current salaries)	7,431	
Standard allowance—business expenses	132	16,906
		48,494
Interest income from Austrian bank deposits and bonds (gross): 11,250—withholding tax of 25% (see below)		
Add—Dividends from double taxation agreement (DTA) country (gross)		7,030
Taxable income		€ 55,524
Tax thereon at 50%	27,762	
Less—Progression	(8,250)	€ 19,512
Less—Personal allowances:		
Basic (1)	0	
Sole earner	364	
Employee	54	
Transportation	291	(709)
Income tax		18,803
Less—Tax credit according to DTA for foreign withholding tax on dividends (Assumption: 10% of 7,030)		(703)
		18,100
Add—Income tax on the 13th- and 14th-month salaries (6% of (9,343 – 620 free amount – 1,170 social security))		453
Add—Withholding tax on interest (25%)		2,813
Total income tax payable		€ 21,366

Notes:

1. Basic allowance of €1,264 after pro rata reductions for employees.
2. Exchange rate of the euro as of January 2, 2004: US$1 = €0.7942.

Azerbaijan

PwC contact

For additional information on taxation in Azerbaijan, contact:

Zaid S. Sethi
PricewaterhouseCoopers
The Landmark Building
96 Nizami str, 5th Floor
370010, Baku
Azerbaijan
Telephone: (994 12) 97 25 15
Fax: (994 12) 97 74 11
e-mail: zaid.sethi@az.pwc.com

Significant developments

New changes were introduced into the Tax Code and related legislation, effective from January 1, 2004. In particular, these changes include revision of the income tax rates.

Territoriality and residence

Persons actually staying in the territory of the Azerbaijan Republic for more than 182 cumulative days (regardless the duration of stay within a day) during a calendar year, and those working for a state service of the Azerbaijan Republic in a foreign country during a calendar year or within one calendar year, are considered resident. The stay of officials with a diplomatic or consular status, employees of international organizations or foreign nationals engaged in state service of foreign states, as well as their family members, will not be regarded as a period of stay in the territory of the Azerbaijan Republic unless such persons are engaged in entrepreneurial activities in Azerbaijan.

A physical person who stays either in the territory of the Azerbaijan Republic or in a foreign country for not more than 182 days will be considered a resident according to the criteria outlined below (in order of consideration).

1. Place of permanent residence.
2. Center of vital interests.
3. Habitual abode.
4. Citizenship of the Azerbaijan Republic.

Taxable income of a resident consists of worldwide income (i.e., income generated in and outside the Azerbaijan Republic). A nonresident's taxable income is that income generated solely from sources in the Azerbaijan Republic.

Gross income

The taxable base of residents is determined as the difference between gross income for a calendar year and expenses (or deductions).

Where income from employment has been taxed at source, no further income tax or deductions are calculated.

The taxable base for nonresident physical persons engaged in activity in the Azerbaijan Republic through a permanent establishment is the difference between gross income generated in a specific period from Azerbaijan sources with regard to the permanent establishment and the amount of expenses (or deductions) with respect to the generation of income during that period.

For nonresident physical persons engaged in activity in the Azerbaijan Republic unconnected with a permanent establishment, the taxable base is the income received from Azerbaijan sources.

Capital gains and investment income/Dividends and interest received by physical persons from resident enterprises are taxed at source at 10% and are not subject to further taxation. There is a moratorium on taxation of interest from banks and other credit organizations and dividends and interest from investment securities, effective until January 1, 2007.

Taxable benefits/The value of any of the following payments or benefits received in connection with employment is treated as taxable income.

1. Loans granted to a physical person at an interest rate that is lower than the interest rate at the interbank credit auction. The difference between the amount that would be paid under the interbank credit auction rate and the amount to be paid at the lower rate is taxable.
2. The assignment of goods (works, services) or gratuitous transfer thereof by an employer to an employee. Tax is levied on the difference between the value of these goods (works, services) based on their fair market value and the amount paid by the employee.
3. Any reimbursement of personal expenses to an employee.
4. The amount of any employee debt or obligation to the employer that is written off by the employer.
5. All insurance premiums paid by the employer, except the following types of insurance:
   a. All obligatory insurance;
   b. Voluntary medical insurance;
   c. All cumulative life insurance and pension insurance paid by the employer to Azerbaijan insurers under contracts of not less than five years;
   d. The difference between the insurance premiums and insurance payments.
6. The market value of other benefits, unless otherwise stipulated in normative acts.

Tax-exempt income/The following income is exempt from income tax.

1. Income of a diplomatic or consular employee who is not a citizen of the Azerbaijan Republic.
2. Income from the workplace of a person who is not a resident or citizen of the Azerbaijan Republic and who has lived less than 182 cumulative days in the territory of the Azerbaijan Republic during the tax year (if this income is paid by or on behalf of an employer who is not a resident of the Azerbaijan Republic and relates to activity not connected with a permanent establishment of the employer).
3. The value of gifts and financial aid:
   a. Financial aid for medical treatment or education received within a calendar year—Up to 1,000 times the conditional financial unit (currently AZM5,500 million);
   b. Financial aid received for medical treatment abroad—Up to 2,000 times the conditional financial unit;

c. Inheritances received—Up to 20,000 times the conditional financial unit.

The full value of gifts, financial aid, and inheritances received from the family members.

4. State allowances (except for allowances for temporary loss of labor capability), nonrefundable state fund transfers, state pensions, and state scholarships.
5. Individual one-off payments and financial aid from budget funds made on the decision of the respective executive authority.
6. Income derived from the sale of immovable property that has been the taxpayer's place of permanent residence for the last three years.
7. Income from the sale of movable tangible assets, except for precious stones and metals, precious stone and metal products, fine art, and antique items, as well as property used in the entrepreneurial activity of the taxpayer.
8. Compensation for damages.
9. Income received directly from production of agricultural products.
10. Alimony.
11. Payments of compensation nature, including monetary or in-kind allowance of military servants.
12. Entertainment, meal, accommodation, and other expenses of a social nature (not defined in the Tax Code).
13. Reimbursement of business expenses by the employer.
14. Other exemptions as provided.

Deductions

Dividends and interest received from resident enterprises and taxed at the source of payment in the Azerbaijan Republic are excluded from gross income.

Various deductions of up to 400 times the conditional fiscal unit may also be available (e.g., war veterans, invalids, persons with dependents, etc.).

Other taxes

Social security taxes/Effective January 1, 2003, social security taxes of 27% of an employee's gross income are payable by the employer. The employee is liable for a 2% social security contribution, which is withheld from salary. Entrepreneurs who are physical persons are liable to the social taxes at various rates based on activity type.

Withholding tax and rates/Withholding tax at the following rates is withheld from specified payments.

1. Dividends paid by resident enterprises—10%.
2. Interest paid by a permanent establishment of a resident or nonresident (or on behalf of such permanent establishment)—10%.
3. Rental fees for movable and immovable property, as well as royalties paid by residents or permanent establishment of nonresident (or on behalf of such permanent establishment) to physical persons—10%.
4. Withholding tax from rental fees and royalties received by physical persons may be credited against personal income tax liability on this income
5. Taxes deducted from incomes of nonresident physical persons not attributed to a permanent establishment (base) in Azerbaijan:

a. Payments in respect of leasing operations of resident enterprises, permanent establishments of nonresident enterprises (or on behalf of such establishment) or entrepreneurs, including financial leasing operations, as well as insurance payments under risk insurance or reinsurance agreements—4%;
b. Payments by a resident enterprise or a permanent establishment of nonresident enterprise for telecommunication or transport services during international communications or shipments between the Azerbaijan Republic or other states—6%;
c. Payments by a resident enterprise, permanent establishment of nonresident enterprise (or on behalf of such permanent establishment), or entrepreneur in connection with Azerbaijan source and the above-outlined other income (income from the assignment of goods, performance of works and provision of services, rental fees; income from immovable property in Azerbaijan, including income from the assignment of a participating share in such a property; income from the lease of movable property used in Azerbaijan; other income attributable to an activity in Azerbaijan)—10%.

Oil consortia and export pipeline tax regimes

The oil consortia and export pipeline tax regimes are two other types of tax regimes applicable in Azerbaijan. These regimes apply to all foreign investors involved in a production sharing agreement (PSA) or host government agreement (HGA) for construction of the export oil and gas pipelines, including foreign oil companies functioning as contractor parties and foreign-service companies providing services to the contracting parties or the operating company.

As of March 18, 2004 there are 23 ratified PSAs and two HGAs, and each of them provide different tax implications. However, the general concept of taxation in all of these agreements is same.

Under these regimes, expatriate employees that are tax resident in Azerbaijan are taxed only on income earned in connection with their employment in Azerbaijan. The PSAs and HGAs also generally exempt nonresidents from tax in Azerbaijan and define tax residents as those who spent more than 30 consecutive days or 90 cumulative days during a calendar year in Azerbaijan (in case of the PSAs) or more than 182 cumulative days during a calendar year in Azerbaijan (in case of the HGAs).

Employees who are Azerbaijan citizens are taxed in accordance with the statutory legislation of Azerbaijan.

Tax credits

The amount of income tax paid outside the Azerbaijan Republic on income not connected with an Azerbaijan source is accounted for at the time of payment of Azerbaijan income tax. The accounted amount may not exceed the tax amount computed under the effective Azerbaijan tax rates on such income.

Tax administration

Tax returns/The taxpayers listed below are liable for the filing of tax returns with tax authorities.

1. Resident physical persons having income that is not taxable at the source of payment should file a personal income tax return by April 15 of the year following the reporting year.

2. Nonresidents engaged in activity through a permanent establishment (base) must file by April 1 of the year following the reporting year or, if entrepreneurial activity has ceased, within 30 days of cessation.
3. Nonresidents with Azerbaijan-source taxable income that has not been taxed at source must file by April 1 of the year following the reporting year.

A nonresident taxpayer who has no permanent establishment (base) in Azerbaijan is entitled to a tax refund, which can be obtained by filing a declaration about such income before April 1 of the year following the reporting year.

A taxpayer may apply for a filing extension of the filing deadline, provided that taxes due have been paid. In this case, the filing date will be deemed to be extended for up to three months. The extension of the filing deadline, does not applies to the tax payment deadlines.

Payment of tax/Employer should transfer the withheld taxes on the same day of payment of income to its employee. Entrepreneurs shall be obliged to make current payments no later than the 15th day of the month following each calendar quarter.

Loss carry forward/The portion of expenses deductible from gross income generated from the entrepreneurial activity, which exceed said gross income, can be carried forward for a period of up to five years in equal installments or within 20% of profit of the current year.

Tax rates

Taxable monthly income		Tax on Column 1	Percentage on excess
From (Column 1)	To		
0	AZM 150,000	—	—
AZM 150,001	3,000,000	—	14
3,000,001		AZM 399,000	35

Taxable yearly income		Tax on Column 1	Percentage on excess
From (Column 1)	To		
Up to	AZM 1,800,000	—	—
AZM 1,800,001	36,000,000	—	14
36,000,001		AZM 4,788,000	35

Note:

Exchange rate of the Azerbaijan manat at March 18, 2004: US$1 = AZM4,927.

PwC contact

For additional information on taxation in the Bahamas, contact:

Kevin D. Seymour
PricewaterhouseCoopers
P.O. Box F 42682
Freeport, Grand Bahama, Bahamas
Telephone: (1) (242) 352-8471
Fax: (1) (242) 352-4810
e-mail: kevin.d.seymour@bs.pwc.com

Absence of taxation

Income tax is not imposed on individuals or corporations in the Commonwealth of the Bahamas.

Note

The Bahamian dollar (Bah$1.00) is at parity with the U.S. dollar.

Bahrain

PwC contact

For additional information on Bahrain, contact:

Elham Hassan
PricewaterhouseCoopers
BMB Centre, 4th floor
Diplomatic Area
P.O. Box 21144
Manama, Bahrain
Telephone: (973) 17 540554
Fax: (973) 17 540556
e-mail: elham.hassan@bh.pwc.com

Absence of taxation

Income tax is not imposed on individuals in Bahrain.

Note

Exchange rate (selling) of the dinar at January 1, 2004: US$1 = BD0.377.

PwC contact

For additional information on taxation in Barbados, contact:

R. Charles D. Tibbits
PricewaterhouseCoopers
The Financial Services Centre
P.O. Box 111
St. Michael, Bridgetown, Barbados, W.I.
Telephone: (1) (246) 431 2700, 436 7000
Fax: (1) (246) 431 1275, 429 3747, 430 9231
e-mail: charles.tibbits@bb.pwcglobal.com

General note

This entry is repeated from the 2003/2004 edition. For more up-to-date information consult the contact listed above or Jacqueline Collette at jacqueline.collette@us.pwc.com.

Significant developments

The basic rate of income tax has been reduced from 25% to 22.5%, with a further reduction to 20% planned for income year 2004. In addition, the government of Barbados has announced its intention to reduce the marginal rate of income tax to 37.5% for income year 2005, with a further reduction to 35% for income year 2006.

The maximum value of the taxable benefit for the provision of rent-free accommodation to an employee has been increased from Bds$14,400 to Bds$48,000 per annum.

Territoriality and residence

An individual who is both resident and domiciled in Barbados is taxed on worldwide income.

Individuals who are resident but not domiciled in Barbados are taxed on income derived from Barbados and on income from any other sources outside Barbados, to the extent that a benefit is received in Barbados.

An individual becomes resident by spending in the aggregate more than 182 days in Barbados in an income (calendar) year or by being ordinarily resident in Barbados in the relevant income year. An individual is considered to be ordinarily resident who has permanent accommodation available for personal use in Barbados and gives notice to the Commissioner of Inland Revenue of intent to reside in Barbados for a period of at least two consecutive income years. In calculating the number of days, the days of departure and arrival are included. Domicile is a question of intention, and long-term residence does not necessarily determine domicile. In general, a nonresident individual is not entitled to personal deductions against income and is taxed only on income arising in or remitted to Barbados.

Gross income

Employee gross income/Income includes salary, bonuses, commissions, and the value of all other benefits, whether or not in money, including housing. Cash housing allowances are treated as salary. The provision of rent-free accommodation gives rise to a taxable benefit to the employee up to a maximum of Bds$48,000 per year. There are special concessions for appropriately qualified foreign employees of corporations engaged in the international financial services sector, whereby up to 35% of their remuneration may be exempt from tax, if approved by the relevant government minister.

Capital gains and investment income/Barbados does not have a capital gains tax. Interest, dividends (except dividends received from local companies and those resident in certain other CARICOM countries), rents, royalties, professional fees, business profits, and annuities are all subject to tax, as is any type of investment income brought into Barbados by short-term residents. One-half of amounts received as royalties is exempt from tax.

Deductions

Business deductions/Where an individual is carrying on a trade, business, profession, or vocation, expenses are generally deductible if they are incurred for the purpose of producing assessable income for the enterprise. Employees may deduct only unreimbursed expenditures incurred for travel and entertainment in the performance of their duties. Depreciation of a motor vehicle is not deductible. Moving expenses to or from Barbados paid by an employer are not taxed.

Nonbusiness expenses/Deductions are allowed for the following:

1. Savings with a cooperative society (up to Bds$3,000 per annum after an initial period of two years).
2. Bonuses converted into shares of the employing company (up to a limit of the lesser of Bds$7,500 or 75% of the value of the bonus payable).
3. Bonuses paid by companies that do not offer shares to those employees converted into bonds, debentures, or stock of the Government of Barbados or invested in mutual funds (up to a limit of the lesser of Bds$7,500 or 75% of the value of the bonus payable).
4. Payments under deed of covenant (up to a limit of 10% of assessable income where payments are to a benevolent organization and 5% of assessable income where payments are to minors or incapacitated individuals).
5. Contributions to a registered retirement plan (up to a limit of the lesser of Bds$4,000 or 15% of assessable income); contributions to a registered retirement plan savings plan (up to a limit of the lesser of Bds$4,000 or 15% of assessable income). Where contributions are made to both a registered retirement plan and a registered retirement savings plan the combined contributions are limited to a maximum of Bds$6,000 or 15% of assessable income.
6. A housing allowance of Bds$3,500 for repairs, renovations, mortgage interest, and water- and energy-saving devices for residents of owner-occupied houses.
7. An additional housing allowance of Bds$2,500 for retrofitting an owner-occupied house with roof straps and window shutters.
8. Purchase of new shares in a public company and/or a mutual fund (up to a limit of Bds$10,000), and contributions to a venture capital fund (up to a limit of Bds$10,000).

Personal allowances/Residents of Barbados can claim the following allowances:

	Bds$
Individuals (Note)	15,000
Individuals over age 60 and in receipt of a pension (Note)	30,000
Individuals whose spouse had no income and who either fully supported or habitually lived with the spouse	3,000
Children (maximum of two)	1,000 each

Note:

No income tax is payable where a resident receives assessable income of less than Bds$15,000 (if a pensioner over age 60, Bds$30,000). Nonresidents are precluded from claiming any allowances or deductions in arriving at taxable income.

Tax credits

Relief for double taxation is given on Commonwealth income or in accordance with the provisions of any relevant double taxation treaty.

Full credit is given for tax withheld at source on dividends from preferred shares issued before January 1, 1975. Dividends on ordinary shares or preferred shares issued to individuals after January 1, 1975, paid to individuals out of pre–July 1992 retained earnings are grossed up by 15% and included in taxable income. A 15% dividend tax credit is permitted on this income. Those paid from post–July 1992 profits are subject to a final tax of 12.5%.

A credit for net foreign currency earnings is available on earnings from construction projects or professional services undertaken outside of the Caribbean Community (CARICOM). The credit varies depending on the percentage of foreign currency earnings to total earnings, but ranges from 35% to 93% of tax otherwise payable on such foreign currency earnings.

Local interest income is subject to a final tax of 12.5% when paid to resident individuals (15% when paid to nonresident individuals). Interest paid to pensioners aged 60 years and over is not subject to tax.

A reverse tax credit of Bds$500 per annum has been granted to any employed individual who is resident in Barbados and earns less than Bds$13,000 annually but not more than Bds$1,084 monthly.

Other taxes

National insurance and social security/The employee's share is 8.5% on earnings of up to a maximum of Bds$3,100 per month, with the employer paying 9.75%. Self-employed individuals make contributions quarterly of 13% on earnings of up to a maximum of Bds$3,100 per month.

Local taxes on income/There are no local taxes on income.

Tax administration

Returns/All individuals who carry on business (whether or not assessable income has been derived during the income year) or earn assessable income in excess of Bds$15,000 (in the case of pensioners over age 60, Bds$30,000) are required to file a separate income tax return. The tax year for individuals is the calendar year, and returns are filed by the following April 30.

Payment of tax/Income tax is normally withheld from salaries under the pay-as-you-earn (PAYE) system, and interest is payable to the taxpayer on overdue tax refunds. Individuals who have income from business or rents in excess of 25% of their total assessable income are required to make three prepayments of tax on June 15, September 15, and December 15, each representing 25% of the income tax payable on the proportion of such income to total assessable income for the previous income year.

Tax rates

Individual income tax rates are shown below.

Taxable income			
Over (Column 1)	Not over	Tax on Column 1	Percentage on excess
0	Bds$ 24,200	—	22.5
Bds$ 24,200		Bds$ 5,445	40.0

INDIVIDUAL TAX CALCULATION

Calendar year 2002

Assumptions

Resident husband (employed in the international financial services sector) and wife; one child aged 12 educated in Barbados, and one child aged 17 educated abroad; one spouse earns all the income; company provides rent-free accommodation and car.

Income tax computation

Salary (gross salary of 160,000 less 35%)		Bds$ 104,000
Car benefit (vehicle with value of 100,000)		10,000
Housing benefit (annual rental of 60,000, say)		48,000
		162,000
Less—Entertainment allowance (1)		7,800
Net employment income and total assessable income		154,200
Deductions:		
Pension contribution	4,000	
Donation under covenant	5,000	9,000
		145,200
Personal deductions:		
Personal	15,000	
Spouse	3,000	
Child (aged 12)	1,000	
Child (aged 17)	1,000	20,000
Taxable income		Bds$ 125,200
Income tax thereon		Bds$ 45,845
Less—Tax withheld from salary (PAYE)		(46,000)
Income tax refund		Bds$ 155

Notes:

1. The deduction of Bds$7,800 would not necessarily be automatically allowed. The taxpayer may be required to substantiate that the amount was expended on business entertainment.
2. Exchange rate of the Barbados dollar officially pegged at US$1 = Bds$2.00.

Belgium

PwC contact

For additional information on taxation in Belgium, contact:

Frank Dierckx
PricewaterhouseCoopers Tax Consultants sccrl-bcvba
Woluwedal, 18
B–1932 Sint-Stevens-Woluwe, Belgium
Telephone: (32) (2) 710 42 11, 710 43 24 (direct)
Fax: (32) (2) 710 42 99
e-mail: frank.dierckx@be.pwc.com

Significant developments

The information in this entry relates to tax year 2005 (calendar year 2004).

As from the income year 2004, statutory cohabitants are, from a Belgian income tax point of view, put in the same tax category as the married taxpayers.

Territoriality and residence

Belgium taxes its residents on their worldwide income irrespective of their nationality. Residents of Belgium are those who have established their domicile or their economic base in Belgium. Persons deemed to have done this are those who have registered in the population register of a commune in Belgium. The fiscal residence of married couples is determined by the place where the family is located. Nonresidents of Belgium are subject to income tax only on their income earned or collected in Belgium.

Within Belgium, nonresident status is granted to non-Belgian executives or specialists who "temporarily" work in Belgium for an international group. Those persons deemed to be nonresident are allowed tax concessions on the payment of certain allowances that are not taxable on the employee and are tax deductible for the employer. Furthermore, they are taxed on their Belgian-source income only.

Gross income

Employee gross income/Foreign executives or specialists working temporarily in Belgium and qualifying for nonresident tax status do not have to include in their gross taxable income reimbursements for additional expenses incurred from their transfer to or employment in Belgium. The additional expenses listed below may be reimbursed on the basis of actual amounts or by means of lump-sum allowances.

1. One-time moving expenses and the costs of setting up a house in Belgium.
2. Ongoing expenses, for example, cost-of-living, housing allowances, school fees, home leave allowance, travel expenses of children studying outside Belgium, exchange losses, and tax equalization.

Such additional expenses will be, within certain limits, exempt from tax to the extent that the total annual amount (excluding school fees and one-time expenses) does not exceed €11,250 (€29,750 in the case of executives working at a control and coordination office, research center, or scientific laboratory). Duties performed outside Belgium are proportionately exempted, but declaration must be made for total worldwide income earned within the employer's group.

Stock options are taxable at the time they are granted. The value of a stock option listed on a stock exchange is determined as the closing market price of the day preceding the offer of the option.

The value of a stock option not listed on a stock exchange is determined on a lump-sum basis and amounts to a certain percentage of the fair market value of the underlying shares increased by the discount, if any. This basic percentage is set at 15%, to be increased by 1% per year of option period exceeding five years.

Under certain conditions, the above percentages are reduced by 50%.

Capital gains and investment income/Capital gains and foreign-source investment income cashed outside the country are not taxable for nonresidents working in Belgium. Residents and nonresidents are, under certain conditions, taxed on capital gains realized on the sale of land as well as on the sale of buildings located in Belgium. Depending on the situation, this tax is levied either by means of a special levy (33%/16.5%) or through the application of professional withholding tax.

Deductions

Business deductions/Social security taxes are deductible. Employment-related expenses are deductible, provided they are substantiated; alternatively, standard deductions may be claimed up to a maximum of €3,050.

Nonbusiness expenses/The following nonbusiness expenses are deductible.

1. 80% of the support payments to near relatives or a separated spouse (nonresidents can deduct only payments made to residents of Belgium; however, there are some tax treaty exceptions).
2. Interest resulting from mortgage loans for real estate.
3. Charitable contributions to certain institutions to the extent of 10% of taxable income, with a maximum of €304,550 for tax year 2005.
4. 50% of the remuneration costs of domestic personnel (under certain conditions).
5. 100% of children's custody expenses, up to a maximum of €11.20 per day for children under three years old.

The following nonbusiness expenses give rise to a tax reduction, which is calculated on the basis of the average tax rate on the jointly taxable income, with a minimum of 30% and a maximum of 40%. (In some cases, it is calculated on the basis of the marginal tax rates.)

1. Life insurance premiums, with a maximum of €1,830.
2. Capital repayments of a mortgage loan, with a maximum of €1,830 (applicable together with the life insurance premiums).
3. "*Monory-bis*" deduction (acquisition of shares in employer company), with a maximum of €610.
4. Pension-savings contributions, with a maximum of €610.
5. Employee's contributions to group insurance.
6. Purchases (up to €2,200) of checks to be spent with local employment agencies.

To the extent that the tax reduction has been calculated in the way described above, and if certain other conditions are met, the proceeds of individual and group insurance and of the pension-saving plan will be taxed at a flat rate of 10%.

Personal allowances/Allowances deductible in determining taxable income are shown below. The incomes of a husband and wife are taxed separately.

Exempt income/The net taxable income of a taxpayer will be taxed at the rates detailed below (tax rates applicable for income year 2004). However, the following personal exemptions and exemptions for dependent children and other persons are granted.

1. €5,660 for each taxpayer.
2. For dependent children:

Number	Increase	Accumulated
	€	€
1	1,200	1,200
2	1,890	3,090
3	3,850	6,940
4	4,280	11,220

   For each dependent child after the fourth child, an additional €4,280 is deductible. A handicapped child is counted as two dependency deductions. For each child less than three years old on January 1 of the tax year, the above amounts are increased by €450, provided no children's custody expenses are deducted (see "Nonbusiness expenses" above).

3. For any other dependent person, an amount of €1,200 is deductible.

It must be stressed that the exemption takes place on the lowest part of income (at the lowest marginal tax rates).

The income of each spouse is taxed separately. Special rules exist when one spouse has no or low earned income, as noted below.

1. Only one spouse receives earned income:

   A splitting is applicable—An income equal to 30% of the net earnings of the spouse will be attributed to the spouse without earnings and taxed in that spouse's own name. Income that may be attributed to the nonearning spouse cannot exceed €8,160.

   If one of the spouses is self-employed or is engaged in a liberal profession and is effectively assisted by the other, an income equal to a maximum of 30% of the earning spouse's net earnings will be attributed to the assisting spouse if the net earnings of the latter do not exceed €10,600. The maximum of 30% can be exceeded, provided sufficient evidence of the real assistance of the helping spouse is given.

2. Both spouses receive earned income:

   The above regulations also apply where both spouses receive earned income if the earnings of one spouse exceed 70% of total earnings and the earnings of the other spouse do not reach €8,160. In this case, income may be attributed to the spouse earning less until 30% of total earnings and without exceeding the maximum of €8,160 is reached.

The exempt income, personal deductions and the attribution of income to the spouse are in principle applicable to residents and nonresidents, although for nonresidents these exemptions and deductions will be applicable only if they have a permanent home in Belgium during the entire taxable period to which the income relates, or if they receive earned income taxable in Belgium that represents at least 75% of their worldwide earnings.

Tax credits

Income from Belgian real estate and from a house that is occupied by and is the principal residence of the taxpayer is subject to a tax credit of 12.5% on the deemed rental value of the property owned.

Self-employed individuals earning business income or exercising a profession generating profits subject to the resident income tax can claim a tax credit of 10% of the difference between current year's equity (fiscal value of assets less debts) and highest equity of the three preceding tax years, up to a maximum of €3,750 per financial year.

Other taxes

Social security taxes/The employee's share of social security taxes is 13.07% of the total gross compensation; the employer's share varies around 34%. Social security taxes are deductible in determining taxable income. For foreign employees with short-term assignments in Belgium who continue to be subject to the social security schemes of their home country, an exemption from social security may be granted, depending on the nationality of the claimant. For foreign employees who are transferred to Belgium by a U.S. employer for a period not exceeding five years and who remain covered by the U.S. social security scheme, the Belgium/U.S. social security agreement provides for full exemption from Belgian social security taxes.

According to recent Supreme Court decisions, additional expenses reimbursed to foreign executives or specialists working temporarily in Belgium (see "Employee gross income" above) will be, within certain limits, exempt from social security taxes.

Special social security contribution/A special social security contribution is due from April 1, 1994, the amount varying between €9.30 and €60.94 per month. This contribution is collected by means of monthly deductions from net salary, although the final amount due will be determined through the tax return process on the basis of actual net taxable family income. The special social security contribution is not tax deductible. The maximum amount due by a family on a yearly basis amounts to €731.28.

Local taxes on income/For residents of Belgium, communal taxes are levied at rates varying from 0% to 9.5% of the income tax due. For nonresidents, a flat surcharge of 7% is due.

Tax administration

Returns/Spouses must file a joint tax return on their aggregated income (an exception is made for the year of marriage or divorce). The tax year relates to the income of the preceding calendar year.

Payment of tax/There is a compulsory income tax withholding from salaries (also for directors, now called "key men").

Professional withholding tax is indeed due under the following circumstances.

1. When remuneration is paid or attributed by Belgian residents, in Belgium or abroad, to Belgian residents or nonresidents.
2. When remuneration is paid or attributed by Belgian nonresidents if the remuneration concerned can be classified as professional expenses, that is, relating to income of the nonresident employer that is taxable in Belgium.

3. To calculate the withholding tax, employers may, on their own responsibility, take into account the special regulations that pertain to the taxation of both foreign executives and specialists working temporarily in Belgium (see "Territoriality and residence" above).

Tax rates

The minimum abatement is €5,660 for each taxpayer. This minimum abatement is increased for dependent children (see "Exempt income" above). The tax rate varies from 25% to 50%, excluding the communal tax. Tax rates for tax year 2005 are shown below.

Taxable income			
Over (Column 1)	Not over	Tax on Column 1 (Note)	Percentage on excess
0	€ 6,950	—	25.0
€ 6,950	9,890	€ 1,737.50	30.0
9,890	16,480	2,619.50	40.0
16,480	30,210	5,255.50	45.0
30,210		11,434.00	50.0

Note:

The tax in the third column must be increased by the additional communal tax (see "Local taxes on income" above).

INDIVIDUAL TAX CALCULATION

Tax year 2005 (calendar year 2004)

Assumptions

1. Foreign executive working temporarily in Belgium and fulfilling the required conditions to benefit from the special tax regime; married with two children; one spouse earns all the income.
2. Owner of a house in which the family is living; deemed net annual rental income has been fixed at €3,750. Since the taxpayer occupies the house, an abatement of €4,081 (increased by €340 for each dependent) is available. Since the income will be offset by the deduction of mortgage interest, the abatement will not be applied.
3. Gross compensation is deemed to include the reimbursement by the employer of certain exceptional expenses as provided for under the special tax regime and limited to €11,250, as well as the reimbursement of school fees for an amount of €6,500.
4. Services performed in Belgium during the year represent 75% of the total working days of the taxable period.
5. Deductible charitable gifts: €750.

Tax computation

Determination of taxable income

Real estate income		€ 3,750.00
Less—Mortgage interest		3,750.00
Net real estate income		€ 0.00
Total gross compensation		€ 70,000.00
Less:		
Nontaxable allowances	11,250.00	
School fees	6,500.00	17,750.00
Gross salary		52,250.00
Less—Social security taxes (13.07%) (1)		6,829.08
		45,420.92
Less:		
Exempt portion of salary for services performed outside Belgium (25% x 45,420.92)	11,355.23	
Standard deduction for business expenses	2,463.67	13,818.90
Taxable earned income		€ 31,602.02

Calculation of tax

	Taxpayer	Spouse
Taxable earned income	€ 31,602.02	
Attribution to spouse (30%, limited to 8,160)	—	€ 8,160.00
Less—Attribution to spouse	8,160.00	
Less—Itemized deductions (charitable contributions)	556.34	193.66
Net taxable income (2)	€ 22,885.68	€ 7,966.34
Income tax thereon	€ 8,138.06	€ 2,042.40
Less—Income tax on exempt income (3)	(2,277.50)	(1,415.00)
Income tax due	€ 5,860.56	€ 627.40

	Together
Total income tax	€ 6,487.96
Add:	
Communal tax of 7%	454.16
	6,942.12
Less—Creditable part of real estate tax	(468.75)
Income tax liability	€ 6,473.37

Notes:

1. Social security taxes have been calculated on the gross salary after deduction of the nontaxable allowances and school fees.
2. On the basis of a net taxable family income of €30,852.02 (€22,885.68 for the taxpayer and €7,966.34 for the taxpayer's spouse) the special social security contribution amounts to €350.25 (yearly basis).
3. Calculation of income tax on exempt income is as follows:

	Taxpayer €	Spouse €
Exempt income:		
Exemption for taxpayers	5,660.00	5,660.00
Exemption for dependent children	3,090.00	—
Total exempt income	8,750.00	5,660.00
Income tax	2,277.50*	1,415.00**

*6,950 at 25% and 1,800 at 30%.

**5,660 at 25%.

4. Exchange rate of the Euro on January 2, 2004: US$ 1 = €0.7942.

PwC contact

For additional information on Bermuda, contact:

Richard E. Irvine
PricewaterhouseCoopers
P.O. Box HM 1171
Hamilton HMEX
Bermuda
Telephone: (1) (441) 299 7136 (direct)
(1) (441) 295 2000 (general)
Fax: (1) (441) 295 1242
e-mail: richard.e.irvine@bm.pwc.com

Absence of taxation

Income tax and taxes on capital gains are not imposed on individuals in Bermuda.

Note

Exchange rate of the Bermuda dollar at January 1, 2004: US$1.00 = Bd$1.00.

Bolivia

PwC contact

For additional information on taxation in Bolivia, contact:

Rosa Talavera
PricewaterhouseCoopers S.R.L.
Avenida Mariscal
Santa Cruz & Yanacocha
Edificio Hansa, 19th Floor
La Paz, Bolivia
Telephone: (591) (2) 2408181 (ext. 101)
Fax: (591) (2) 211 2752
e-mail: rosa.talavera@bo.pwc.com

Significant developments

The rate for pension funds contributions has been reduced from 12.5% to 12.21%. The Housing Fund employee's contribution is no longer in force, effective November 2000.

Territoriality and residence

Bolivia taxes its citizens and residents on their Bolivian-source income only. Foreign-source income is not taxable in Bolivia. The Bolivian-source income of nonresident aliens is subject to Bolivian tax. Domicile and citizenship do not affect the tax base.

Gross income

Employee gross income/A resident is taxed on salaries, bonuses (except obligatory year-end bonus), profit participation, living allowances, housing allowances, tax reimbursements, benefits-in-kind, and any other form of income earned as an employee for work carried out in Bolivia. There are no concessions to short-term foreign residents. A nonresident is taxed on Bolivian-source earnings at the rate of 12.5% of gross income.

Capital gains and investment income/Investment income from a Bolivian source (except dividends paid to residents) is taxed as ordinary income. Capital gains are not subject to tax. Interest, dividends, and so on, earned in Bolivia by nonresidents are subject to a withholding tax of 12.5% when remitted or credited to a personal account. Investment income from outside Bolivia is not taxed in Bolivia.

Deductions

Business deductions/No business expenses may be deducted from income.

Nonbusiness expenses/A resident may deduct social security taxes paid. No other expenses are deductible.

Personal allowances/Residents are entitled to a basic deduction of two minimum salaries per month. As of December 31, 2003, the minimum salary was Bs440 per month.

Tax credits

All value-added tax (VAT) paid by individuals as part of the price of items for personal consumption is deductible from the personal income tax payable, provided the purchases are properly documented.

In addition to the tax credit for VAT, the law allows an additional tax credit equivalent to 13% of two minimum salaries per month.

Other taxes

Social security taxes/Pension funds are administered privately, and only employees contribute toward their retirement pension. The contribution rate is 12.21% of salary, with a ceiling of approximately US$3,367 per month. This payment is registered under individual accounts. As from November 2000, there is no longer an employee contribution to the official Housing Fund.

Local taxes on income/Other than the tax on salaries, there are no local taxes on income earned by employees. However, individuals that earn their income by performing independent activities (i.e., self-employed) or by investing in the financial markets are subject to a 12.5% annual income tax (see *Corporate Income Taxes—Worldwide Summaries, 2004–2005*). Banks or other financial institutions act as withholding agents on earnings from capital investment obtained by employees.

Tax administration

Returns/The employer submits a global tax return and withholds the tax on an employee's salary. No further tax-filing requirement exists for this tax. Individual taxpayers must submit tax returns on a monthly basis for VAT and transactions tax, and on an annual basis for income tax. There is no joint filing for husband and wife.

Payment of tax/Employers file and pay taxes withheld on behalf of their personnel. Investment and other income must be declared on an individual basis, and the related tax liability is paid by the taxpayer on an annual basis.

Tax rates

The tax rate is a flat 13% on salaries and 12.5% on other income.

INDIVIDUAL TAX CALCULATION

Income year 2003

(Taxes are liquidated on a monthly basis)

Gross income:		
Salary		Bs 336,000
Profit participation (one month's salary)		28,000
		364,000
Less—Nonbusiness deductions:		
Social security taxes—12.21% x 309,600 (60 x 440 x 12)		38,681
		325,319
Less—Personal deductions (Basic deduction, 12 x 880)		10,560
Taxable income		Bs 314,759
Tax payable—13% of 314,759		Bs 40,919
Less:		
Tax credit for VAT included in purchases (estimated)	29,000	
Tax credit—13% of two minimum salaries per month (13% x (12 x 880))	1,373	(30,373)
		Bs 10,546

Notes:

1. The year-end bonus, equivalent to one month's salary, is not subject to tax and therefore has not been included in the above computation.
2. Exchange rate of the boliviano at December 31, 2003: US$1 = Bs7.84.

PwC contact

For additional information on taxation in Botswana, contact:

Mr. D.K.U. Corea
PricewaterhouseCoopers
P.O. Box 1453
Gaborone, Botswana
Telephono: (267) 3952011
Fax: (267) 3973901

Significant developments

There have been no significant tax or regulatory developments regarding individual taxation in the past year.

Territoriality and residence

The Botswana tax system operates on a territorial basis, and income is taxable in Botswana if the source is within Botswana. Income for services performed outside Botswana is deemed to be from a Botswana source if the services are incidental to employment in Botswana.

To be a resident of Botswana for a tax year normally means the individual has a permanent place of abode in Botswana and is physically present in Botswana for not less than 183 days in that tax year or the previous tax year.

A resident is taxable on all income from a Botswana source in accordance with the tax rates. A nonresident is taxable on earned income in accordance with the tax rates, but pays withholding tax only at the rate of 15% for interest, dividends, commercial royalties, and management and consultancy fees, and at the rate of 10% on entertainment fees, where such income is of Botswana origin.

Gross income

Employee gross income/Expatriate employees are taxable on salary and on any overseas allowances, wherever payment is made. Living and housing allowances, tax reimbursements and the value of benefits, such as free accommodation and the use of motor vehicles, are included in taxable income. However, airfares and medical costs borne by the employer for the employee, spouse and dependent children and provided in the terms of the employee's contract are not taxable.

For individuals' contracts of employment signed on or after July 1, 1999, any gratuities paid are taxable to the extent of two-thirds of such gratuity. The remaining one-third is tax free. The percentage parameters are still 25% of gross salary for the first contract, 27.5% for the second contract, and 30% for the third and subsequent contracts. Contracts normally run two to three years.

The gross income of a resident citizen individual includes any interest or dividend income from an investment made outside Botswana. Interest income in such cases is included in the individuals' gross income and taxed accordingly. Dividend income from foreign source is taxes at 15%.

Capital gains and investment income/Capital gains on the disposal of immovable property and marketable securities (including shares in private companies) are taxable in Botswana if the source is in Botswana. For capital gains purposes, the cost of immovable property is adjusted to take account of inflation. For other gains, no inflation allowances are granted, but the taxable gain is set at one-half of the total gain. Capital gains for individuals are considered to be from a separate source and are taxed on the basis of Table VI of the Act (shown as Tax Rate Table III in this entry).

Interest income for any resident individual, accruing from any banking institution or building society in Botswana is exempt from tax up to a limit of P2,500.

Interest, dividends, commercial royalties, and management and consultancy fees payable by a Botswana resident to a nonresident are subject to withholding taxes of 15%. Similarly, entertainment fees are subject to a withholding tax of 10%. However, the double taxation agreements with the United Kingdom and South Africa exempt management and consultancy fees from the requirement to withhold taxes.

Deductions

Business deductions/No business-related expenses are deductible unless they are incurred as a condition of employment or for the purpose of producing the employee's income, such as in circumstances in which the expenditure can be shown to influence the level of the employee's income. An employee who is employed on a commission basis could be in this position. There are no standard or blanket deductions.

Nonbusiness expenses/Where a gratuity is not provided to the employee, contributions to an approved retirement benefit scheme are allowable up to a maximum of 15% of earned income.

Personal allowances/There are no personal allowances granted. All individual taxpayers are taxed under one of two tax tables (see "Tax rates" below).

Tax credits

A tax credit is granted unilaterally where amounts received by a Botswana resident have been subject to taxation in a foreign country and in cases where a double taxation agreement has been concluded. Botswana has double taxation agreements with Mauritius, South Africa, Sweden, and the United Kingdom. A tax credit is also granted where income from a source within Botswana has been subject to a withholding tax. The amount of the relief is limited to the lesser of the tax paid by deduction and that normally paid in Botswana on such income.

Other taxes

Social security taxes/There are no social security taxes or contributions.

Local taxes on income/There are no income taxes in addition to central government taxes.

Tax administration

Returns/All individuals are separately taxed, and separate filing of returns by husband and wife is required. The fiscal year, which ends on June 30, must be followed.

Payment of tax/A pay-as-you-earn (PAYE) system, under which income tax is withheld from remuneration payable to employees, is in operation.

Tax rates

For 2003/2004, as shown below.

Table I—Resident individual taxpayers

Taxable income Over (Column 1)	Not over	Tax on Column 1	Percentage on excess
0	P 25,000	—	0
P 25,000	43,750	—	5
43,750	62,500	P 938	10
62,500	81,250	2,813	15
81,250	100,000	5,625	20
100,000		9,375	25

Table II—Nonresident taxpayers

Taxable income Over (Column 1)	Not over	Tax on Column 1	Percentage on excess
0	P 43,750	—	5
P 43,750	62,500	P 2,188	10
62,500	81,250	4,063	15
81,250	100,000	6,876	20
100,000		10,625	25

Table III—Individuals in respect of net aggregate capital gains

Taxable income Over (Column 1)	Not over	Tax on Column 1	Percentage on excess
0	P 12,500	—	0
P 12,500	43,750	—	5
43,750	62,500	P 1,563	10
62,500	81,250	3,438	15
81,250	100,000	6,250	20
100,000		10,000	25

INDIVIDUAL TAX CALCULATION

For fiscal year ending June 30, 2004

Assumptions

Taxpayer is an expatriate employee who is resident in Botswana (tax rates from Table I).

Tax computation

Income tax

Salary		P 160,000
Overseas allowance		12,000
Interest received from South African source (excess over 2,500)		3,000
Motor vehicle benefit		2,750
Housing benefit		3,600
Taxable income		P 181,350
Income tax thereon		P 29,712
Less:		
PAYE paid	28,963	
Withheld from interest from South Africa	550	(29,513)
Balance of income tax payable		P 199

Capital gains tax

Income from sale of Botswana shares (50% of gain is taxable)	P 15,000
Capital gains tax payable	P 125

Note:

Exchange rate of the pula at February 25, 2004: US$1 = P4.7732.

PwC contact

For additional information on taxation in Brazil, contact:

Edmar A. Perfetto
PricewaterhouseCoopers Auditores Independentes
Centro Empresarial Água Branca
Avenida Francisco Matarazzo, 1400
Torre Torino
São Paulo, SP
Brazil
CEP 05001-903
Telephone: (55) (11) 3674 3722
Fax: (55) (11) 3674 2080
e-mail: edmar.perfetto@br.pwc.com

Significant developments

In May 2001, the Brazilian Central Bank (BACEN) published rules and requirements under which all residents of Brazil who have foreign-held assets and rights must file an information return with BACEN. For tax year 2004, taxpayers whose foreign assets amount to more than US$100,000 as at December 31, 2003 will be subject to this reporting requirement.

Decree 4.166, dated March 13, 2002, established that foreign residents that own assets and rights (like shareholders, owners of property in Brazil, etc.) have to register and obtain a taxpayer identification number (*Cadastro de Pessoas Fisicas*—CPF).

Territoriality and residence

Residents of Brazil are taxed on their worldwide income, and nonresidents are taxed exclusively at source on their Brazilian-source income. The source of income is determined by the place where the income payer is located, irrespective of where the work is performed.

Work permits and special visas are required for any alien intending to live and/or work in Brazil, whether for a short or a long period. Two types of visa may be granted in connection with work permits.

1. Permanent visas—Holders of permanent visas are considered residents as from the date of arrival in Brazil.
2. Temporary visas (valid only for up to two years)—Holders of temporary visas are also considered residents as from the date of arrival in Brazil, as long as they have an employment contract in Brazil. Otherwise, they will become tax residents as of their 184th day of presence in Brazil within any given 12-month period.

Gross income

Employee gross income/Taxable compensation includes everything that is either directly or indirectly connected with the work and/or assignment remuneration package, including salary, premiums, bonuses, allowances of any kind, tax reimbursements, club dues, and company-owned car.

Capital gains and investment income/In general, capital gains and investment income are computed as taxable income. However, in some circumstances certain transactions are tax-free or are taxed exclusively at source at lower rates.

Nontaxable income/Among other items of less importance, the following are free from any income tax.

1. Board, transportation, and special work uniforms or clothing supplied by the employer free of any charge or the difference between the amount charged and their market values.
2. Per diem allowances to cover room and board for working outside the county in which the company or office is based or in which the work is normally performed.
3. Labor indemnities, limited to the legal amounts, including indemnities for labor accidents for Brazilian legal purposes.
4. Contributions made by the employer to private social security programs in favor of the employee.
5. Reimbursement of relocation costs when moving to a different county at the request of the employer.

Deductions

Business deductions/Business expenses are not deductible.

Nonbusiness expenses/The following may be deducted from taxable income.

1. Alimony payments and/or pension contributions ratified by the Brazilian court.
2. Medical, dental, and hospital expenses, as well as payments to recognized Brazilian health insurance/medical-cost coverage programs.
3. Schooling expenses up to an annual limit of R$1,998 (approximately US$660) per student.
4. Social security contributions.
5. Contributions to Brazilian private pension funds (deduction subject to limitations).
6. Annual income up to R$12,696 relating to retirement or military pensions as from the year in which the taxpayer reaches 65 years of age.

Personal allowances/The taxpayer may deduct a flat allowance for each dependent in computing net taxable income. The allowance is R$1,272 (approximately US$424) per annum per dependent as from 2002.

Tax credits

Tax credits are available (within certain limits) with respect to income tax paid to countries with which Brazil has a ratified tax treaty or to countries that would render reciprocal treatment in relation to income taxes paid to the Brazilian government.

Other taxes

Social security taxes/Social security taxes are payable monthly at the rate of 7.65% to 11% of Brazilian-source salary income. However, the total contribution may not exceed R$264 (US$88) per month (based on January 2004 contributions).

Other taxes/Minor amounts are payable annually to applicable unions.

Tax administration

Returns/Residents must file a tax return annually. Since individual income tax is due and payable monthly, this return will account for only minor tax adjustments and will serve to list assets and liabilities.

Individuals receiving income or gains not subject to Brazilian withholding tax (i.e., alimony and/or pensions, rental income received from individuals, non-Brazilian-source income, capital gains on the sale of personal property, etc.) are subject to a special monthly income tax payment, which should be made by the last working day of the subsequent month. The tax is calculated on the basis of the normal tax table.

Spouses may elect to file tax returns jointly or separately. If filed separately, returns must allocate to each spouse income received jointly. Also, in the section pertaining to assets and liabilities, each spouse must show the corresponding items held individually. The value of jointly held assets/liabilities should be allocated according to ownership percentage or shown only on one spouse's return. The spouse not listing the jointly held assets/liabilities must declare that the items will be listed on the other spouse's tax return.

The head of a household may not treat as a dependent a spouse or any dependent who receives taxable income and pays tax accordingly.

Individuals resident or domiciled in Brazil must annually inform the Central Bank of the receivables of any nature, assets in currency, and assets and rights maintained abroad through a declaration. Individuals are exempt from the filing requirement as long as the total value of their assets on December 31 is less than US$100,000.

Payment of tax/Income tax is normally withheld at source, at rates varying from 0% to 27.5%, depending on the income bracket. The final liability is determined upon filing the tax return. Any difference between the amount as determined by the tax return and that withheld at source must be paid or is refunded to the taxpayer.

Tax rates

The following tax table is applicable to income tax payable in 2004 with respect to annual income earned during calendar year 2003, in Brazilian currency:

Taxable basis	Tax rate	Deductible portion
R$	%	R$
Up to 12,696*	—	—
From 12,696.01 to 25,380.00	15.0	1,904.00
More than 25,380.00	27.5	5,076.90

*Exempt.

Note:

These rates apply to all types of tax returns, that is, married individuals filing jointly or separately and single taxpayers.

INDIVIDUAL TAX CALCULATION

Fiscal year ending December 31, 2004 (tax year 2003)

Assumptions

1. Resident, married with two children (three dependents; wife takes classes); pays alimony to first spouse.
2. Income and gains in 2003 are as follows:

Brazilian-source salary income	R$ 110,000
Brazilian payroll withholding tax	20,854
Foreign-source income	80,000
Income tax paid to a foreign tax jurisdiction on foreign-source income	15,000
Short-term money market income—Brazilian-source	5,000
Withholding tax on short-term money market income	1,000
Capital gain—Profit on sale of property	5,000
Income tax on capital gain	750

Tax computation

Brazilian-source salary income		R$ 110,000
Foreign-source income		80,000
Short-term money market income—Brazilian source		5,000
Capital gain—Profit on sale of property		5,000
Gross income		200,000
Less—Income taxed only at source:		
Short-term money market income (1)	5,000	
Capital gain subject to special taxation (1)	5,000	10,000
Net taxable income before allowances and deductions		190,000
Less—Allowances and deductions:		
Social security contributions (2)	2,297	
Dependents (three)	3,816	
Medical expenses	1,500	
Alimony payments	10,000	
Schooling expenses (3)	5,994	23,607
Net taxable income		R$ 166,393
Income tax at 27.5%		R$ 45,758
Less—Amount deductible relating to lower tax brackets		(5,077)
		40,681
Less—Tax paid at source:		
On Brazilian-source salary income	20,854	
On foreign-source income	15,000	(35,854)
Net tax payable (4)		R$ 4,827

Notes:

1. Capital gains are taxed at the rate of 15% (definitive taxation), payable by the taxpayer up to the last working day of the subsequent month and taxation of variable income in the Brazilian market is taxed at 20% and is considered definitive taxation.
2. Employee's social security contribution for 2003: January to May—R$858.85; June to December—R$1,439.00.

3. Schooling payments are deductible regarding preschool, elementary, junior high, high school, college, and professional education of the taxpayer or his dependents.
4. Balance due is payable in full at the time of filing or, at the taxpayer's option, in up to six installments from April 30. Each installment may not be less than R$50. However, should the return show a balance due of less than R$100, this amount should be paid in one installment.
5. Exchange rate of the Real for January 2004: US$1 = R$2.87.

British Virgin Islands

PwC contact

For additional information on taxation in the British Virgin Islands, contact:

Meade Malone
Meade Malone & Co.
Geneva Place, 2nd Floor
333 Waterfront Drive
P.O. Box 3339
Road Town, Tortola
British Virgin Islands
Telephone: (1) (284) 494 4388, (1) (284) 494 4727 (direct)
Fax: (1) (284) 494 3088
e-mail: mwmabacus@surfbvi.com

Significant developments

There have been no significant tax or regulatory developments regarding individual taxation in the past year. For subsequent developments consult the contact listed above.

Territoriality and residence

A British Virgin Islands (BVI) resident is liable to income tax on worldwide income. A nonresident is liable for BVI income tax on BVI-source income only. The BVI Income Tax Ordinance defines a resident as "an individual resident in the Territory." There are no established criteria to determine whether a person is resident for this purpose. Factors taken into consideration in determining residency include the following.

1. An individual's immigration status.
2. How many days per year the individual is physically present in the BVI.
3. Where the individual's main place of residence can reasonably be said to be located.

Capital gains and investment income

Capital gains/There are no taxes on capital gains.

Dividends and interest/No withholding taxes are applied to dividends or interest, regardless of whether the taxpayer is resident or nonresident. Dividend and interest income is taxable to resident taxpayers as ordinary income, except dividends earned from companies registered in the BVI under the provisions of the Companies Act and bank deposit interest from banks registered in the BVI.

Deductions

Costs and expenses incurred in the production of income are deductible, but no personal allowances are granted.

Other taxes

There are no taxes on wealth, inheritance, or gifts.

Social security taxes/The employee and employer are taxed at 4% and 4.5%, respectively, on employee earnings up to a maximum of $23,400.

Withholding tax on rents and royalties/A withholding tax of 14% is payable on any rent, annuity, or other annual payment made to individual nonresidents (15% for companies). This requirement also extends to royalties.

Tax administration

Payment of tax/Employers must deduct income tax from employees' wages in accordance with the tax tables on a pay-as-you-earn (PAYE) basis. The tax withheld must be paid to Inland Revenue not later than 15 days after the end of the month in which the wages were paid. Late payments are subject to penalties ranging from 5% to 30%.

Tax rates

Resident individuals are subject to BVI income tax on their taxable income at the following rates.

Taxable income			
Over (Column 1)	Not over	Tax on Column 1	Percentage on excess
0	$ 7,500	—	—
$ 7,500	15,000	—	10
15,000	22,500	$ 750	15
22,500		1,875	20

Nonresident individuals are taxed on BVI-source income at the normal sliding-scale rates.

Note

The monetary unit is the U.S. dollar.

Brunei Darussalam

PwC contact

For additional information on taxation in Brunei Darussalam, contact:

Kin C. Lee
PricewaterhouseCoopers
No: 1: 4th Floor
Wisma Setia, Jalan Pemancha
Bandar Seri Begawan
Negara Brunei Darussalam
Telephone: (673) (2) 228593, 228595
Fax: (673) (2) 228594
e-mail: kin.chee.lee@bn.pwc.com

Absence of taxation

Legislation for the collection of personal income tax exists in Brunei, but at present this tax is waived.

Notes

Exchange rate of the Singapore dollar at February 1, 2004: US$1 = S$1.7004.

The Brunei dollar (B$) is interchangeable with the Singapore dollar (S$).

PwC contact

For additional information on taxation in Bulgaria, contact:

Irina Tsvetkova
PricewaterhouseCoopers Bulgaria
9–11 Maria Louisa Blvd
1000 Sofia, Bulgaria
Telephone: (359) (2) 91 003
Fax: (359) (2) 98 03 228
e-mail: irina.tsvetkova@bg.pwc.com

Significant developments

As from January 1, 2004, the nontaxable income level increased to BGL120 per month (BGL1,440 per year). The lowest tax rate is reduced to 12% (from 15%). New minimum and maximum monthly social security insurance bases have been set; the absolute minimum is BGL120 and the maximum is BGL1,200.

Territoriality and residence

Taxation of individuals' income in Bulgaria is based on their residence status. Bulgarian tax residents are taxed on their worldwide income. Nonresidents are taxed on their income from Bulgarian sources.

Irrespective of their citizenship, individuals are considered Bulgarian tax residents if they have a permanent domicile in the country (i.e., personal links such as a family or permanent home) or reside in the country for more than 183 days in any 365-day period, in which case the individual becomes a Bulgarian tax resident for the calendar year in which the 183rd day has expired.

If a double taxation treaty (DTT) is in place, the 183-day residency principle is applicable in accordance with the provisions of the treaty.

A foreign tax resident is any individual who is not a Bulgarian tax resident.

The law gives a broad definition of Bulgarian-source income. Generally, income from a Bulgarian source is all income received by an individual as a result of business activities performed in the country. Activities performed in the country are considered business activities if the individual either has a permanent establishment or a base in the country, or assigns or performs services in Bulgaria directly or through a procurator, a dependent agent or otherwise.

Any income derived as a result of performing work or rendering services in the country is deemed Bulgarian-source income, no matter where and by whom it is paid.

Investment income and professional income other than employment income are considered Bulgarian-source income if paid by a resident or by a permanent establishment of a nonresident entity in Bulgaria.

To be allowed to work in the country, expatriates need a work permit, which necessitates following a time-consuming procedure and submitting various documents to the labor authorities. A residence permit is issued to the expatriate on the basis of the work permit. No work permits are required for expatriates who are registered with Bulgarian courts as shareholders, directors, managers, procurators, or controllers of Bulgarian companies or registered with the Bulgarian Chamber of Commerce and Industry as heads of representative offices of foreign entities. Such individuals need a residence permit only.

Gross income

Individuals must pay personal income tax in accordance with the level of gross income.

Employee gross income/Taxable income from work on the basis of an employment contract includes the following.

1. Salary, wages, or any other remuneration for work performed, as well as any additional compensation for, for example, years of service, unhealthy work conditions, higher professional qualifications, cost-of-living adjustments, bonuses and premiums, and overtime pay.
2. All fringe benefits/benefits in kind provided by the employer or on the account of the employer.
3. Certain compensations received by the employee on the basis of the Labor Code (in general, for some cases of termination of the employment contract, unutilized paid leave, etc.).

The following income is not subject to taxation.

1. The value of free preventive food, antidotes and personal protection devices provided by the employer pursuant to the Labor Code and other laws.
2. The value of special work clothes and personal protective equipment, free work and representative clothes and uniforms provided by the employer pursuant to the Labor Code and other laws.
3. Business trip allowances and compensation for moving to another workplace, reassignment due to health reasons, noncompletion of work due to force majeure circumstances, and redundancy as provided under the Labor Code.
4. The value of any commuting fares provided by the employer free of charge.
5. Social expenses borne by the employer that are subject to taxation under the Corporate Income Tax Act.
6. Compensation for temporary work incapacity under the Mandatory Social Insurance Code.
7. The value of transport cards provided to the employees for the account of employer.

The loss carryforward facility is not applicable for individuals, except for sole traders.

No special concessions are granted to foreigners.

Capital gains and investment income/The concept of income globalization was introduced in Bulgaria as from January 1, 1998. Bulgarian tax residents (including expatriates who are considered Bulgarian tax residents) are taxed on capital gains and investment income realized from all sources during their period of residence. Foreign tax residents are taxed only on the capital gains and investment income derived from sources in Bulgaria.

Capital gains on the disposal or exchange of immovable and movable property as well as on the transfer of sole traders' enterprises are taxable on an annual basis (see the respective table). An exemption provided in respect to capital gains is discussed under "Tax exempt income" below.

The taxable base in the case of disposal or exchange of immovable property and means of transportation is the difference between the sale price and the higher of the actual and the adjusted purchase price of the property. For immovable property, the adjusted price is equal to the evaluation made for tax purposes; for cars, buses, trucks, and seat traction-engine vehicles, the adjusted price is their price in new condition adjusted by a depreciation coefficient; for other means of transportation, the adjusted price is their insurance value. The taxable base in all other cases of disposal or exchange of movable property is the difference between the sale price and the purchase price adjusted by the general index of consumer goods prices announced by the National Institute of Statistics.

The taxable base in transfers of sole traders' enterprises is the difference between the sale price specified in the purchase agreement and the net asset value of the sole trader.

Income from rent, annuities, and leases (except for rent from agricultural land) is subject to advance personal income tax at 15% and final tax on an annual basis. For tax purposes a statutory deduction of 20% of the gross income is available.

Personal income tax is not levied on dividends and liquidation proceeds paid by Bulgarian entities, which are taxed at 15% at source. The withholding tax is final. Dividends paid to Bulgarian tax residents by nonresidents who are not tax liable under the Bulgarian Corporate Income Tax Act are subject to a final personal income tax at 15% payable by the recipient.

Interest on deposits and accounts in local commercial banks and branch offices of foreign banks, mutual benefit funds, and savings and credit cooperatives; interest and discounts on state, municipal and corporate securities; moratorium interest on bond relations; income from investing insurance reserves of life insurance, marriage and child insurance; life insurance if related to an investment fund; income from investing assets of the voluntary pension insurance funds and interest on court-established receivables are exempt from taxation.

Other interest income is taxable at 20% final tax.

Royalties are taxed on an annual basis at the rates for taxation of nonemployment income (shown below).

Tax-exempt income/The most important kinds of tax-exempt income, in addition to those already mentioned, are listed below.

1. Capital gains on the sale or exchange of an apartment, house or villa, including the adjacent land, if it has been the principal residence of the seller for at least three years before the sale or the exchange.
2. Capital gains on the sale or exchange of up to two real estate properties that are not the principal residence of the seller, as well as agricultural and forest estates (no limit on number), if the period between the acquisition and the sale is more than five years.
3. Capital gains on vehicles acquired by the seller not less than one year before the sale.
4. Any other capital gains except those realized from sale of shares and share participation in companies, partnerships and other forms of joint ventures.
5. Amounts received as a result of making compulsory pension, health and social security contributions.
6. Compensation and other similar payments for certain types of physical injuries, death and occupational disease; property insurance; alienation of rights; losses; life insurance compensations and compensations from other personal insurance

made in the country when the insurance event occurs or the insurance term expires.

7. Income in cash or in kind received in accordance with the law as a social aid, and compensation for unemployment.
8. Aid received from social funds and organizations.
9. Stipends granted to Bulgarian tax resident individuals for education in Bulgaria and abroad.
10. Profits distributed in the form of new shares and company stock or in the form of an increase of the nominal value of already issued shares or stock.
11. Profits used for increasing the share capital of a company.
12. Inheritances and donations.
13. Gains from state lotteries, gambling, and other games of fortune.
14. Capital gains from shares in public companies and tradable rights in such shares realized on the regulated Bulgarian securities market.

Business income of individuals who perform certain business activities listed in the law and have a turnover for the previous year of not more than BGL50,000 (approximately US$31,600) is also exempt from personal income taxation (see "Business tax" below).

Tax regulations on specific types of income/The following basic types of income are also subject to personal income taxation (the list, however, is not comprehensive).

1. Income received by sole traders.
2. Income received by freelancers, individuals supplying personal services and artisans.
3. Income of managers, controllers, and members of management and supervisory boards.
4. Rental income.
5. Bonuses payable to managers or directors of companies in proportion to realized post-taxable profit, income or turnover.

Certain types of income, such as monetary and in-kind prizes from various competition events, compensations for lost profits and damages, taxable interest, sums received from voluntary pension, health, unemployment and life insurance coverage and income from incidental transactions are taxed at a flat rate of 20%. The tax is final.

Deductions

Business deductions/Individuals earning income other than employment income deduct pre-estimated expenses (not differentiated into business and other expenses) in calculating standard taxable income. For example, individuals working under individual services agreements (e.g., freelancers, civil contractors, notary officers, and physicians and dentists) in private practice may deduct 35% of their gross income before taxation; and individuals working under management services agreements (e.g., managers and members of management bodies) may deduct 10% of their gross income realized from management and supervisory activities. Sole traders determine their taxable base in accordance with the corporate profit tax regulations. Royalties are subject to 50% statutory deduction.

Nonbusiness expenses/Compulsory health, pension, unemployment, and other related contributions borne by individuals are tax deductible in full. Contributions paid by the employee under life insurance contracts and life insurance, if related to an investment fund, and personal voluntary health insurance contributions are deductible in total up to 10% of taxable income. The same limit for tax deductibility purposes applies to the total of personal voluntary pension and unemployment fund contributions. Personal income taxpayers, except for employees, may also deduct up to 10% of their taxable income for donations to various nonprofit organizations.

Personal allowances/There are no tax deductions for personal allowances for spouses or dependants. However, standard allowances for children, which are paid from the state budget, are not subject to personal income taxation.

Tax credits

Bilateral tax relief is granted in accordance with the provisions of the DTTs in force. Where no treaty protection is available, unilateral ordinary tax credit is granted, with the credit amount calculated separately for each source country ("per-country limitation").

Other taxes

Business tax/Individuals and legal entities who carry out certain commercial activities and have a total annual turnover of less than BGL50,000 (approximately US$31,600) for the previous year are liable for the so-called final license tax. The tax amount does not depend on realized income, but is a lump sum determined by law for each activity for different regions.

Social security contributions/The general rate of social security contributions is 36.7%, of which 27.7% is payable by the employer and 9% by the employee. The general rate of health insurance contributions is 6%, of which 4.5% is payable by the employer and 1.5% by the employee. As from January 1, 2004, new monthly insurance bases are in force, that is, new minimum and maximum insurance bases have been set. The minimum insurance base for freelancers is BGL200 (approximately US$126.40). For individuals working under employment agreements or as managers or controllers of companies, the minimum insurance base depends on the economic activity of the insurer as well as on the profession and grade of the insured person. The minimum base varies between BGL120 (US$75) and BGL730 (US$404). The maximum monthly insurance base is limited to BGL1,200 (US$758).

Local taxes on income/There are no local taxes on income.

Tax administration

Returns/In general taxpayers have to submit annual tax returns. Employees who work on the basis of an employment contract are not obliged to submit tax returns if their income is from employment only. However, tax resident individuals who have received only employment income from nonresident employers must file an annual tax return. For tax purposes, spouses are treated as separate taxpayers. No income splitting is allowed. The tax year is, without exception, the calendar year. Income is declared in the year in which it is received regardless of the year to which it relates.

The deadline for submission of tax returns is April 15 of the following year and the tax must be paid not later than 30 days as from the date of submission of the tax return. Individuals who file their tax returns and pay the annual tax by January 31 of the following year are entitled to 5% discount of the outstanding annual tax.

Individuals and legal entities liable to final license tax must file an annual tax return by January 31 of the current year. The license tax is payable in four equal installments.

Payment of tax/Personal income tax for employees is withheld by the employer from the gross remuneration on a monthly basis. The employer acts as an agent of the revenue authorities and transfers the tax due to the budget. Certain taxpayers who are not employees, such as sole traders, freelancers, managers, and controllers, must pay advance tax, either regularly (monthly/quarterly) or whenever income is received; where the income is paid by a Bulgarian entity, the advance tax must be withheld from the remuneration by the payer.

Tax rates

Employment income/The following tax rates, effective from January 1, 2004, apply to the monthly employment income.

Monthly taxable income		Tax on	Percentage
Over	Not over	Column 1	on excess
(Column 1)			
0	BGL 120	—	0
BGL 120	150	—	12
150	250	BGL 3.60	22
250	600	25.60	26
600		116.60	29

Nonemployment income/The following tax rates, effective from January 1, 2004, apply to the annual taxable income.

Annual taxable income		Tax on	Percentage
Over	Not over	Column 1	on excess
(Column 1)			
0	BGL 1,440	—	0
BGL 1,440	1,800	—	12
1,800	3,000	BGL 43.20	22
3,000	7,200	307.20	26
7,200		1,399.20	29

INDIVIDUAL TAX CALCULATION

Calendar year 2004

Assumptions

The taxpayer is a foreign citizen who has a work permit and works on the basis of an employment contract with a Bulgarian employer. She receives a gross salary of US$3,000 per month (approximately BGL4,746) as well as benefits in kind of US$1,500 (approximately BGL2,373).

Tax computation

	(Monthly basis)
Monthly salary	BGL 4,746.00
Monthly benefit in kind (accommodation)	2,373.00
Monthly gross income	7,119.00
Compulsory health, pension and unemployment contributions	126.00
Taxable base	BGL 6,993.00
Tax	BGL 1,970.57
Net monthly income	BGL 5,022.43*

*Approximately US$3,174.

Note:

Exchange rate of the lev at March, 10, 2004 is US$1 = BGL1.58226; €1 = BGL1.95583.

Cambodia

PwC contact

For additional information on taxation in Cambodia, contact:

Jean Loi
PricewaterhouseCoopers (Cambodia) Ltd.
124 Norodom Boulevard
Phnom Penh, Cambodia
Telephone: 855-23-218 086
Fax: 855-23-211 594
e-mail: jean.loi@kh.pwc.com

Significant developments

The rate of tax on salary for nonresidents increased from 15% to 20%.

Territoriality and residence

There is no personal income tax per se in Cambodia. Instead, a monthly salary tax is imposed on individuals who derive income from employment. General consulting income is excluded from salary tax but is subject to tax on profit (although rules exist that may deem certain consultants as employees).

Cambodian salary tax rules follow internationally familiar residency and source principles. A Cambodian resident's worldwide salary is subject to Cambodia salary tax, while nonresidents are taxed on Cambodian-source salary.

Residents are persons domiciled in or having a principal place of abode in Cambodia or are present in Cambodia for more than 182 days in any 12-month period.

Gross income

Employee gross income/A distinction is made between cash salary and fringe benefits.

Cash salary includes remuneration, wages, bonuses, overtime, and compensation paid for fulfilling employment activities. Employer-provided loans and advances are also considered cash salary.

Fringe benefits include the following.

1. Accommodation support, including payment of utilities and domestic helpers.
2. Education assistance (unless employment-related).
3. Provision of motor vehicles (presumably for private use).
4. Low-interest loans and discounted sales.
5. "Excessive or unnecessary" cash allowances, social welfare, and pension contributions.
6. Certain insurance support.
7. Entertainment or recreational expenditures (which may additionally be nondeductible to the provider for tax-on-profit purposes).

Exempt salary includes the following.

1. Certain redundancy payments.
2. Reimbursement of employment-related expenses.
3. Certain uniform entitlements.
4. Certain travel allowances.

5. Salaries of employees of approved diplomatic, international, and aid organizations.
6. Salaries of nonresidents where the salary cost is not deducted in Cambodia for tax-on-profit purposes.

Deductions

These are limited to small amounts for employee dependents and for repayment of employer loans or advances.

Tax credits

Taxes paid by resident taxpayers on foreign-source salary will be allowed as a credit against Cambodian salary tax on presentation of documentation confirming payment. The credit allowed is the lower of foreign tax paid or the proportion of salary tax on salary from all sources attributable to the foreign-source income.

Other taxes

Social security taxes and local taxes on income/There are no such taxes at present.

Tax administration

Returns/Employers must submit to the tax authorities, together with the payment of tax withheld, a monthly tax declaration for the withholding tax on salary. There is no employee annual return.

Payment of tax/Employers must deduct salary tax from employees' salaries in accordance with the tax tables on a pay-as-you-earn basis. The tax withheld must be paid to the tax authorities not later than 15 days after the end of the month in which the salaries were paid. Late payments are subject to penalties.

Tax rates

The monthly cash salary of residents is taxed at the following rates.

Taxable income		Tax on	Percentage
Over	**Not over**	**Column 1**	**on excess**
(Column 1)			
0	CR 500,000	—	0
CR 500,000	1,250,000	—	5
1,250,000	8,500,000	CR 37,500	10
8,500,000	12,500,000	762,500	15
12,500,000		1,362,500	20

Nonresidents are taxed at a flat rate of 20%, which constitutes a final tax.

Fringe benefits are taxable to the employer at a flat rate of 20% of the grossed up market value of the benefit.

INDIVIDUAL TAX CALCULATION

2003

Assumptions

1. Resident alien and spouse, two school-age children; husband earns all the income.
2. Annual gross salary of US$80,000; employer pays US$3,000 per month for accommodations. Calculations are in local currency.

Tax computation

Gross monthly income:	
Salary	CR 26,586,667
Allowable deductions:	
Wife and children	225,000
Net monthly taxable income	CR 26,361,667
Income tax assessment:	
Tax on first 12,500,000	CR 1,362,500
Tax on remaining 13,861,667	2,772,333
	4,134,833
Salary tax on fringe benefits:	
Accommodation (11,964,000 ÷ 0.8) x 20% (1)	2,991,000
Monthly salary tax payable	CR 7,125,833

Notes:

1. At December 15, 2003 exchange rate of US$1 = CR3,988.
2. Exchange rate of the riel at March 1, 2004: US$1 = CR4,125.90.

PwC contact

For additional information on taxation in Canada, contact:

Dave Black
PricewaterhouseCoopers LLP
Royal Trust Tower
Suite 3000, Box 82
Toronto Dominion Centre
Toronto, ON M5K 1G8 Canada
Telephone: (416) 365-2706
e-mail: dave.black@ca.pwc.com

General note

The following information is based on actual and proposed legislation as of January 1, 2004. It is assumed that the proposed legislation will become law.

Territoriality and residence

Individuals resident in Canada are subject to Canadian income tax on their worldwide income. Relief from double taxation is provided through Canada's international tax treaties and foreign tax credits and deductions for foreign taxes paid on income derived from non-Canadian sources. Nonresident individuals are subject to Canadian income tax on income from employment in Canada, income from carrying on a business in Canada and capital gains from the disposition of taxable Canadian property. Taxable Canadian property includes, among other things, real estate situated in Canada, both capital property and noncapital property used in carrying on a business in Canada and shares in Canadian resident corporations that are not listed on a stock exchange. In certain circumstances, shares in Canadian resident corporations that are listed on a stock exchange, shares in nonresident corporations and interests in nonresident trusts will be considered taxable Canadian property.

Individuals resident in Canada for only part of a year are taxable in Canada on their worldwide income only for the period during which they were resident.

Generally, an individual is resident in Canada for tax purposes if there is a continuing relationship between the individual and Canada. In determining an individual's residence, all of the relevant facts must be considered. Residential ties of particular significance include the maintenance of a dwelling place available for the individual's occupation and the residence of the individual's spouse and dependents. Secondary factors considered include social and business ties and personal property, including memberships in clubs and religious organizations, driver's licenses, vehicle registration, and medical insurance coverage. Citizenship, domicile, and residency under the tax laws of another country are not relevant. Ordinarily, individuals are considered to be resident where they maintain a fixed abode for themselves and their families. If an individual, who, as a matter of fact, is considered not resident of Canada, sojourns (i.e., is temporarily resident) in Canada for 183 days or more in a calendar year, the individual is deemed to be resident in Canada for that entire year.

Gross income

Employee gross income/Salaries, wages, commissions, directors' fees, and all other remuneration received by an officer or employee are included in income from employment. Canadian residents are taxable on worldwide income whether or not the income is remitted to Canada. Most fringe benefits received or enjoyed in connection with employment are also taxed as employment income. Foreigners working temporarily or permanently in Canada are eligible for special concessions for employment at a special work site or remote location. The rules may exempt from tax most amounts received as allowances for board and lodging, as well as transportation between the special work site and the employee's principal place of residence.

Capital gains and investment income/No special concessions are available to short-term residents with respect to the taxation of capital gains and investment income. Dividends from Canadian corporations are grossed up by one-quarter for inclusion in income. A tax credit may then be claimed for 16.67% of the dividend before the gross-up, which results in a net tax saving. Accrued interest income on most debt obligations must be reported annually.

Draft legislation that changes the tax treatment of interests held in foreign investment entities (FIEs) became effective for taxation years beginning after 2002. In general, taxpayers subject to the new rules must include in income either an inclusion based on a prescribed rate of interest, their share of the actual income, and capital gains of the FIE, or any change in the fair market value of the interest in the FIE from the previous year.

When capital property is sold at a profit in the year or a prior year, a reserve may be claimed on any proceeds that are not due until after the year-end. The reserve represents the portion of the gain related to the sale proceeds that are not due until after the end of the year. However, the reserve mechanism cannot be used to postpone gains for more than five years on most types of capital property. Amounts brought into income each year under the reserve mechanism are treated as capital gains. A reserve may not be claimed if the taxpayer was not resident in Canada at the end of the year or at any time in the immediately preceding year.

A lifetime capital gains exemption allows a Canadian resident individual to realize, tax-free, up to Can$500,000 in capital gains on the disposition of qualified farm property and shares of a qualifying small business corporation. An individual resident in Canada for only part of the year may be eligible to claim the exemption if that individual was a resident of Canada throughout the immediately preceding or following year.

A nonresident's Canadian-source passive income, such as interest, dividends, rents, and royalties, is subject to withholding tax of 25% (unless reduced by a treaty); such income is not subject to graduated rates. Alternatively, a nonresident can elect to be taxed at graduated rates on timber royalties or rental income from real property in Canada net of expenses.

Deductions

Business deductions/In computing income from employment, an individual may claim only very limited, specified deductions. Taxes and interest (except interest related to the earning of business and property income), most life insurance premiums, and casualty losses are not deductible. Allowable deductions in computing employment income include traveling and certain other expenses of officers or employees required as a condition of employment, as well as contributions to a registered pension plan of the employer, within certain limits.

Nonbusiness expenses/Deductible nonbusiness expenses include contributions to various registered savings plans, certain child care expenses, alimony and maintenance payments (if taxable to the recipient), eligible moving expenses for relocation within Canada (usually in connection with a change of employment). Draft legislation that applies to taxation years commencing after 2004 allows a loss from a property to be claimed only if there is a "reasonable expectation of profit" from that property. The new rules would apply to limit the deductibility of interest and other expenses.

Personal allowances/Personal allowances take the form of tax credits. The following credits apply for 2003.

Personal tax credits (1, 2)	Can$
Basic personal	1,241
Married (3)	1,054
Infirm dependents age 18 and over (3)	586
Disability (4)	1,005
Age—Persons age 65 and over (3, 4)	606

Other credits (2)	
Pension income	16% of eligible pension income (maximum credit is Can$160) (4).
Tuition fees	16% of eligible fees (minimum Can$100 per institution). Unused credits may be carried forward indefinitely (4).
Education	Can$64 per month for full-time students. Can$19 per month for part-time students. Unused credits may be carried forward indefinitely (4).
Interest on student loans	16% of the interest paid on loans under the Canada Student Loans Act and provincial student loan programs. Unused credits may be carried forward five years.
Medical expenses	16% of amount by which eligible expenses exceed lesser of Can$1,755 and 3% of net income (5).
Charitable donations	16% of the first Can$200 and 29% of the excess. Eligible donations are limited to 75% of net income. Unused donations may be carried forward five years (5).
Government pension plan and employment insurance plan contributions	16% of the lesser of the amount payable and the required premiums for the year (maximum credit is Can$419).

Notes:

1. Personal credits are fully indexed for inflation.
2. Any unused portion of the tax credits is not refundable.
3. The credit is reduced if the income of the individual, spouse, or dependent exceeds a threshold amount.

4. In some circumstances, the unused portion of the credit may be transferred to a spouse, parent, grandparent, child, grandchild, sibling, aunt, uncle, niece, or nephew.
5. One spouse may claim the other's medical expenses and/or charitable donations.

Tax credits

Personal allowances take the form of tax credits (see above).

Relief for foreign taxes in the Canadian system is accomplished through a tax credit and income deduction mechanism. If foreign taxes paid on property income (other than income from real property) exceed 15% of the income, the excess foreign taxes are not eligible for a Canadian foreign tax credit but rather become deductible from the property income. (This provision may have adverse implications for foreign citizens who have foreign property income and live in Canada.)

The overseas employment tax credit allows Canadian-resident individuals working abroad for more than six consecutive months to claim a tax credit if the overseas employment is for a specified employer in connection with contracts for certain defined activities (such as an engineering project). This maximum credit is equal to the employee's Canadian tax on Can$100,000 of qualifying overseas employment income.

Other taxes

Provincial taxes on income/In addition to the federal income tax, an individual who resides in or has income earned in any of the provinces or territories is also subject to provincial or territorial income tax. Except in Quebec, provincial and territorial taxes are calculated on the federal return and collected by the federal government. Rates vary among the jurisdictions and some provinces also impose surtaxes that may increase the provincial taxes payable. Provincial taxes are not deductible in computing taxable income.

Minimum income tax/In addition to the normal tax computation, individuals are required to compute an adjusted taxable income figure and include certain "tax preference" items that are otherwise deductible or exempt in the calculation of regular taxable income. If the adjusted taxable income exceeds the minimum-tax exemption of Can$40,000, a combined federal and provincial tax rate of about 25% is applied to the excess, yielding the Alternative Minimum Tax (AMT). The taxpayer then pays the greater of regular tax or the AMT. Taxpayers required to pay the AMT are entitled to a credit in future years when their regular tax liability exceeds their AMT level for that year.

Social security taxes/For 2003 Canadian resident employees are required to pay government pension plan contributions up to Can$1,801.80 and employment insurance premiums up to Can$819. A credit equal to 16% of the lesser of the amount payable and the required premiums for the year is allowed in computing the individual's federal taxes payable.

Self-employed persons contribute twice the employee's government pension plan contribution (up to Can$3,603.60 for 2003) and are permitted to deduct half of the contribution. The nondeductible half qualifies for a tax credit. Self-employed persons are not liable for employment insurance premiums.

Gift and inheritance taxes/There are no federal or provincial gift or inheritance taxes. However, all provinces and territories impose probate fees or administrative charges for probating a will.

Federal goods and services tax/The federal goods and services tax (GST) is levied at a rate of 7%. It is a value-added tax (VAT) applied at each level in the manufacturing and marketing chain and applies to most goods and services. However, the tax does not apply to sales of zero-rated goods or of tax-exempt supplies, such as basic groceries, healthcare services, educational services, and certain services provided by financial institutions.

Harmonized sales tax/New Brunswick, Newfoundland and Labrador, and Nova Scotia harmonized their sales tax systems with the GST and impose a single sales tax rate of 15%. The 15% rate includes an 8% provincial sales tax component and the 7% GST. It is imposed on essentially the same base as the GST.

Other provincial and local taxes/British Columbia, Manitoba, Ontario, Prince Edward Island, and Saskatchewan levy retail sales tax, at rates ranging from 6 to 10%, on most purchases. Alberta and the territories do not impose a retail sales tax. Quebec imposes a Quebec sales tax that is similar to the federal GST. Quebec's general rate of 7.5% applies to all taxable goods and services. Only Prince Edward Island and Quebec levy retail sales tax on prices that include the GST. As mentioned above, New Brunswick, Newfoundland and Labrador, and Nova Scotia levy a harmonized sales tax. Municipalities throughout Canada also levy property taxes. All provinces and territories impose land transfer taxes or registration fees on the purchase of real property within their boundaries.

Tax administration

Returns/In most cases, taxpayers must file tax returns on a calendar-year basis by April 30 of the following year. Married taxpayers file separately; joint returns are not allowed.

Payment of tax/Income tax is withheld from salaries. Any balance of tax owing is due April 30 of the following year. Individuals are required to pay quarterly installments if their tax payable exceeds amounts withheld at source by more than Can$2,000 (Can$1,200 for Quebec residents) in both the current and either of the two prior years.

Tax rates

Federal income tax/Federal rates are applied to taxable income. Personal tax credits, miscellaneous tax credits, and the dividend tax credit are subtracted from the result to determine basic federal tax.

2003 federal tax rates are given below.

Federal taxable income			
Over (Column 1)	**Not over**	**Tax on Column 1**	**Percentage on excess**
0	Can$ 32,183	—	16
Can$ 32,183	64,368	Can$ 5,149	22
64,368	104,648	12,230	26
104,648		22,703	29

In 2004, the lowest bracket will be $35,000, the middle bracket will be $70,000 and the highest bracket will be Can$113,804.

Provincial income taxes/All provinces and territories, compute income tax using "tax-on-income" systems (i.e., they set their own rates, brackets, and credits). However, except in Quebec, the federal definition of taxable income is used.

Combined federal/provincial effective top marginal tax rates for 2003 are shown below. The rates reflect 2003 budgets (provincial budgets are usually introduced in the spring of each year). The rates apply to taxable incomes above Can$104,648. They include provincial surtaxes, when applicable.

	Highest federal/provincial tax rate		
	Interest and ordinary income	Capital gains	Canadian dividends
	%	%	%
Alberta	39.0	19.5	24.1
British Columbia	43.7	21.9	31.6
Manitoba	46.4	23.2	35.1
New Brunswick	46.8	23.4	37.3
Newfoundland and Labrador	48.6	24.3	37.3
Northwest Territories	42.1	21.0	28.4
Nova Scotia	47.3	23.7	31.9
Nunavut	40.5	20.3	29.0
Ontario	46.4	23.2	31.3
Prince Edward Island	47.4	23.7	32.0
Quebec	48.2	24.1	32.8
Saskatchewan	44.0	22.0	28.3
Yukon	42.4	21.2	28.6
Nonresident	42.9	21.5	29.0

The following table shows the top provincial tax rates and provincial surtaxes. The provincial tax rates apply starting at the taxable income levels shown. Surtax rates apply to provincial tax above the surtax thresholds shown.

	Provincial tax		Provincial surtax	
	Top rate	Taxable income	Rate	Threshold
	%	Can$	%	Can$
Alberta	10.00	All (1)	N/A	N/A
British Columbia	14.70	88,260	N/A	N/A
Manitoba	17.40	65,000	N/A	N/A
New Brunswick	17.84	104,648	N/A	N/A
Newfoundland and Labrador	18.02	59,180	9	7,032
Northwest Territories	13.05	104,648	N/A	N/A
Nova Scotia	16.67	59,180	10	10,000
Nunavut	11.50	104,648	N/A	N/A
Ontario	11.16	64,871	20 (2)	3,747
Prince Edward Island	16.70	61,509	10	5,200
Quebec (3)	24.00	54,195	N/A	N/A
Saskatchewan	15.00	100,000	N/A	N/A
Yukon	12.76	104,648	5	6,000
Nonresident	13.92 (4)	104,648	N/A	N/A

Notes:

1. Alberta levies a single rate tax of 10% on taxable income.
2. Ontario also levies a 36% surtax on provincial tax exceeding Can$4,727. In 2004, Ontario's 20% surtax will be levied on provincial tax exceeding Can$3,856 and its 36% surtax will be levied on provincial tax exceeding Can$4,864. Plans to eliminate the 20% surtax and increase the remaining surtax to 56% were repealed.
3. Quebec has its own personal tax system, which requires a separate calculation of taxable income. In recognition of the fact that Quebec collects its own tax, for Quebec residents federal income tax is reduced by 16.5% of basic federal tax.
4. Instead of provincial tax, nonresidents pay an additional 48% of federal rates, so the rate shown is 48% of the top federal rate.

INDIVIDUAL TAX CALCULATION

Calendar year ending December 31, 2003

Assumptions

1. Resident husband and wife living in Ontario; two children (under 18); one spouse earns all the income.
2. Total remuneration of Can$110,000.
3. Capital gains of Can$16,000.
4. Foreign interest income of Can$5,000, from which Can$750 withholding has been deducted. Other interest income of Can$6,000.
5. All amounts are in Canadian dollars.

Tax computation

Income:		
Salary		Can$ 110,000
Interest		11,000
Taxable capital gain (one half of actual gain) (1)		8,000
Net income/Taxable income		Can$ 129,000
Income tax (see table above):		
Federal tax before credits		Can$ 29,765
Less—Personal credits:		
Basic	1,241	
Spouse	1,054	(2,295)
		27,470
Less—Other credits:		
Canada Pension Plan	288	
Employment insurance	131	(419)
Basic federal tax (BFT)		27,051
Less—Foreign tax credit:		
Lesser of (5,000 ÷ 129,000) x 27,2051 = 1,048 or 750		(750)
Federal income tax		26,301
Provincial (Ontario) income tax (2):		
Ontario tax	12,087	
Less—Personal credits:		
Basic	(473)	
Spouse	(402)	
Canada Pension Plan and Employment Insurance	(159)	
Basic Ontario tax	11,053	
20% surtax (20% x (11,053 – 3,747))	1,461	
36% surtax (36% x (11,053 – 4,727))	2,277	14,791
Total income tax (3)		Can$ 41,092

Notes:

1. Assuming the capital gains are not in respect of qualified farm property or shares of a small business corporation, a capital gains deduction is not available.
2. In Ontario, the following rates are applied to taxable income in 2003.

Taxable income: Over (Column 1)	Taxable income: Not over	Tax on Column 1	Percentage on excess
0	Can$ 32,435	—	6.05
Can$ 32,435	64,871	Can$ 1,962	9.15
64,871		4,930	11.16

Personal tax credits, miscellaneous tax credits and the dividend tax credit are subtracted from the result to determine basic Ontario tax. Ontario personal tax credit for 2003 for Government pension plan and Employment insurance premiums is equal to 6.05% (maximum credit is Can$159) of the lesser of the amounts payable and the required premiums for the year. Ontario surtaxes are not reflected in the Ontario tax rates and are added to basic Ontario tax.

3. The taxpayer does not have sufficient tax preference items to be liable for the minimum income tax.
4. Exchange rate of the Canadian dollar at December 31, 2003: US$1 = Can$ 1.2924.

PwC contact

For additional information on the Cayman Islands, contact:

David Walwyn
PricewaterhouseCoopers
P.O. Box 258 GT
Grand Cayman, B.W.I.
Telephone: (1) (345) 949 7000
Fax: (1) (345) 949 7352
e-mail: david.walwyn@ky.pwc.com

Absence of taxation

Income tax is not imposed on individuals in the Cayman Islands.

Note

Exchange rate of the Cayman Islands dollar is fixed at US$1 = CI$0.83.

Channel Islands, Guernsey (including Alderney)

PwC contact

For additional information on taxation in Guernsey, contact:

Tony Mancini
PricewaterhouseCoopers
P.O. Box 321
Le Truchot
St. Peter Port
Guernsey
Channel Islands, GY1 4ND
Telephone: (44) (1481) 727777
Fax: (44) (1481) 711075
e-mail: tony.mancini@uk.pwc.com

Significant developments

With effect from calendar year 2002 all income (other than trading profits arising to companies, individuals, or partnerships) is assessed on a current-year basis.

The Income Tax Authority has issued proposals regarding residency that aim to reduce the level of complexity and uncertainty that surround the current rules. The Authority deems that the present subjective tests should be replaced by an objective test based solely on the lengths of time spent in Guernsey or elsewhere. These proposals are expected to take effect from January 1, 2006.

Territoriality and residence

Individuals who are solely or principally resident in Guernsey are liable to tax on their worldwide income, while individuals who are resident but not solely or principally resident are taxable on Guernsey-source income and overseas income remitted to the Island. A person who is not resident in Guernsey is liable to tax on Guernsey-source income except bank-deposit interest, which by concession is exempt. Income from Guernsey exempt companies is not considered Guernsey-source income. Currently, a person who is on the Island for a period of 182 days or more in total in any year is resident for tax purposes.

Persons will be treated as principally resident if they are not solely resident but maintain their only residence on the Island. Becoming resident or principally resident can also be established in several other particular circumstances, such as whether the individual maintains accommodation in the island or spends more time on Guernsey than in any other country.

Gross income

Employee gross income/While treated solely or principally as a resident of Guernsey, an individual is assessable on the full amount of the emoluments of employment, no matter where the duties are performed. This will include certain benefits. Where a nonresident carries out any duties in Guernsey, the emoluments attaching to these duties are assessable in Guernsey.

Capital gains and investment income/There is no assessment on capital gains unless such gains result from a venture in the nature of a trade, in which case they are treated as income and liable to income tax at the rate of 20%.

A "dwellings profits tax" seeks to tax speculative short-term profits from residential property. The profit on disposal of any such property sold within 12 months of purchase is liable to tax at the rate of 100%.

Individuals who are treated as solely or principally resident are liable to tax at the rate of 20% on their worldwide investment income no matter where that income is paid. Nonresidents are liable to tax at 20% of their investment income arising in Guernsey. Guernsey bank deposit interest is by concession exempt from tax in the hands of nonresidents.

Deductions

Business deductions/There are no significant deductions allowable to the individual.

Nonbusiness expenses/Deductible nonbusiness expenses are listed below.

1. Interest paid to banks and similar financial institutions.
2. One half of life insurance premiums paid is allowable as a deduction, provided the following conditions are met:
   a. The premiums do not in aggregate exceed one-sixth of assessable income;
   b. The premium on each policy must be no more than 7% of the sum insured.
3. Pension contributions paid to approved schemes, subject to restrictions.
4. Certain annual payments such as alimony payments.

Personal allowances/Nonresidents are not entitled to Guernsey personal allowances. However, a resident of the United Kingdom or the other Channel Island can claim proportional allowances. Allowances for 2004 are as follows.

	£
Married allowance (Note)	15,450
Single allowance	7,725
Spouse's earned income allowance (maximum)	1,545

Note:

The married couples allowance is simply twice the personal allowance. There are no additional allowances available to married couples in Guernsey that are not available to two single individuals. The married allowance is reduced by the amount of the spouse's earned income allowance.

Other allowances exist for persons over age 65 and certain dependent relatives.

Tax credits

Foreign taxes on income, except income from a Jersey source or income from a U.K. source other than dividends or debenture interest, are not available as credits against the Guernsey tax liability. However, unilateral relief is given at either the rate of foreign tax or three-quarters of the effective rate of Guernsey tax, whichever is lower.

Other taxes

Social security taxes/Employees are subject to social security tax at the rate of 6.0% of their gross earnings up to a monthly earnings limit of £2,691.00. A self-employed person pays at the maximum rate of £65.20 per week.

Other taxes on income/No other taxes are levied on income.

Tax administration

Returns/The tax year is the calendar year, and the deadline for submission of returns is March 31 of the following year.

The income of a married woman who is living with her husband is deemed to be the income of the husband, subject to an election for separate assessment that does not affect total tax payable. A married woman is treated as living with her husband unless there is a permanent separation.

Payment of tax/Tax is due on June 30 and December 31 in the Year of Charge to which the income relates. However, tax is deducted from employee salaries and accounted for by the employer.

Tax rates

Tax is payable at the rate of 20% on net income after allowances.

INDIVIDUAL TAX CALCULATION

2004

Assumptions

Resident husband and wife, two children; one spouse earns all the income.

Personal tax computation

Salary		£ 70,000
Bank interest		10,000
Capital gain of 10,000—Exempt from tax in Guernsey		—
		80,000
Less—Charges on income		5,000
		75,000
Less—Allowances:		
Married couples allowance	15,450	
Life insurance premiums	750	16,200
Taxable income		£ 58,800
Tax payable—58,800 x 20%		£ 11,760

Note:

Exchange rate of the pound sterling at December 31, 2003: US$1 = £0.5602.

Channel Islands, Jersey

PwC contact

For additional information on taxation in Jersey, contact:

Jane Stubbs
PricewaterhouseCoopers
Twenty-Two Colomberie
St. Helier, Jersey
Channel Islands
Telephone: (44) (1534) 838200
Fax: (44) (1534) 838363
e-mail: jane.stubbs@uk.pwcglobal.com

General note

This entry is repeated from the 2003/2004 edition. For more up-to-date information consult the contact listed above or Jacqueline Collette at jacqueline.collette@us.pwc.com.

Significant developments

- Benefits in kind legislation will be effective from January 1, 2004.
- Tax filing deadlines and penalties are to be introduced and effective from January 1, 2004.
- Separate tax assessment for husband and wife from 2004.

Territoriality and residence

Individuals who are resident and ordinarily resident in Jersey are liable for tax on their worldwide income, while individuals who are resident but not ordinarily resident in Jersey are taxed only on Jersey-source income and overseas income that is remitted to Jersey. A person who is not resident in Jersey is liable for tax on Jersey sources of income, except bank-deposit interest, which by concession is exempt. Income from Jersey exempt companies is not considered Jersey-source income. Generally, the following establish an individual's residence for tax purposes:

1. Residence for a period of six months or more in total in any year.
2. Residence for more than three months per year on average over a period of four years.
3. Having accommodation available for that individual's use and visits to the Island for any length of time.

The concept of ordinarily resident is similar to that in the United Kingdom and is related, inter alia, to the place where the person is habitually resident.

Gross income

Employee gross income/ While a resident of Jersey, an individual is assessable on the full amount of the emoluments of employment, no matter where the duties are performed. Benefits are generally not taxable unless they can be converted to money or money's worth. Where a nonresident carries out any duties in Jersey, the emoluments attaching to these duties are assessable in Jersey.

Capital gains and investment income/There is no assessment on capital gains unless they result from a venture in the nature of a trade, in which case they are liable to income tax at the rate of 20%.

Residents are liable to tax at the rate of 20% on their worldwide investment income, no matter where that income is paid. Nonresidents are liable to tax at 20% on their investment income arising in Jersey unless their only Jersey source of investment income is bank-deposit interest, which by concession is exempt.

Deductions

Business deductions/There are no significant deductions allowable to individuals not engaged in a trade. Travel to and from work is not regarded as a business expense, nor are moving, motor, or entertainment expenses unless they were incurred wholly and exclusively for the purpose of the employment, trade, or profession.

Nonbusiness expenses/Deductible expenses are:

1. Interest paid to banks and similar financial institutions.
2. Premiums paid on a qualifying life insurance policy, subject to certain restrictions.
3. Pension contributions paid to approved schemes, subject to restrictions.
4. Annual payments.

Personal allowance/Nonresidents are not entitled to Jersey personal allowances. However, proportional allowances are available to Commonwealth or EU citizens in receipt of Jersey-source income.

Allowances for 2002 include:

	£
Earned income allowance—One-quarter of earned income (maximum) (1)	3,400
Married allowance	5,200
Single allowance	2,600
Child allowance (for each child)	2,500
Wife's earned income allowance (maximum) (2)	4,500
Higher child allowance for children in full-time further education	5,000
Additional child allowance for widow(er)s, etc.	4,500
Exempt income:	
Single person—Nil liability, up to	10,750
Married person—Nil liability, up to	17,250

Notes:

1. Joint income in cases of husband and wife.
2. In addition to earned-income allowance.

Other allowances exist for persons over the age of 65 and certain dependent relatives. Tax relief is also available for the cost of childcare.

Tax credits

Foreign taxes on income are not available as credits against the Jersey tax liability unless the income is Guernsey- or U.K.-source. (Tax on U.K. dividends and debentures is not creditable.) However, unilateral relief is given for foreign income taxes, which are deductible from the gross income as an expense.

Other taxes

Social security taxes/Employees are subject to social security tax at a rate of 6% of their gross earnings up to a monthly earnings limit of £2,754 for 2003 (maximum contribution per month £165.24). A self-employed person pays at a rate of 12.5% (subject to a maximum monthly contribution of £344.24).

Other taxes on income/None.

Tax administration

Returns/The tax year is the calendar year.

The income of a married woman living with her husband is deemed to be the income of the husband. A married woman is treated as living with her husband unless there is a permanent separation. From 2004, the previous concessionary form of separate tax assessment has been formulized subject to advance written request.

Payment of tax/Tax is due and payable on assessment, which is usually isused in the following year. There is no statutory withholding from payroll. Tax paid after a prescribed date (usually early in the December following the year of assessment) incurs a 10% surcharge.

Tax rates

Tax is payable at the rate of 20% on net income after allowances.

Alternative tax calculation/In Jersey, an alternative means of computing tax liability by reference to a marginal rate is undertaken automatically by the tax authorities. The taxpayer's liability is based on the lower of the tax paid at the 20% rate and tax calculated using the marginal rate. The method of computation is shown below.

INDIVIDUAL TAX CALCULATION

Tax year 2002

Assumptions

Resident husband and wife, two children; husband earns all the income.

Tax computation

Salary		£ 70,000
Bank interest (1)		10,000
Long-term capital gain—Not assessable		—
		80,000
Less:		
Mortgage interest	5,000	
Life insurance premiums	1,500	6,500
		73,500
Less:		
Earned income relief—Maximum	3,400	
Married allowance	5,200	
Child allowance (x 2)	5,000	13,600
Taxable income		£ 59,900
Tax thereon—59,900 x 20%		£ 11,980

Alternative tax calculation

Total gross income	A
(Including gross amount of Jersey income taxed at source—X)	
Less—Charges (e.g., loan/bank interest paid)	(B)
(Including gross amount of interest paid under deduction of Jersey tax—Y)	
Total net income	C
Exemption limit (2)	(D)
Excess income	E
Tax payable (E x marginal fraction) (3)	F
Less—Tax on income at source (X x 20%)	(G)
	H
Add—Retainable charges (Y x 20%)	I
Maximum tax payable (4)	J

Notes:

1. Interest is assumed to be received gross, which is the same as net of withheld tax where no tax credit is applicable. If a tax credit is applicable, it is restricted to the individual's net effective rate.
2. 2002 figures: Single, £10,750 (aged over 63, £12,000); married, £17,250 (aged over 63, £19,750). Wife's earned-income relief, child allowance, higher child allowance, and additional personal allowance should be added to exemption limits where appropriate.
3. Marginal fraction is 27% for 2002.
4. If the result above (J) is lower than the tax levied at 20% on income after allowances (see income tax computation above), then a relief is due.
5. Exchange rate of the pound sterling at December 31, 2002: US$1 = £0.6300.

PwC contact

For additional information on taxation in Chile, contact:

Julio Pereira G.
PricewaterhouseCoopers
Avda. Andrés Bello 2711
Cuarto Piso
Santiago, Chile
Telephone: (56) (2) 9400151
Fax: (56) (2) 9400503
e-mail: julio.pereira@cl.pwcglobal.com

General note

This entry is repeated from the 2003/2004 edition. For more up-to-date information consult the contact listed above or Jacqueline Collette at jacqueline.collette@us.pwc.com.

Significant developments

The reduction of personal income taxes approved in 2001 comes fully into force during 2003.

Territoriality and residence

Chile taxes its citizens resident or domiciled in Chile on worldwide income. Domicile is defined as physical presence with the intent to remain in the country. Residence is mere physical presence.

Foreigners working in Chile are subject to taxation only on their Chilean-source income during their first three years in Chile, after which worldwide income is taxed. In special cases, the three-year period can be extended.

Residence for tax purposes is acquired upon remaining six consecutive months in the country in one calendar year, or more than six months, whether consecutive or not, in two consecutive calendar years. If domicile is acquired before residence and the intention is to stay in Chile permanently or for a significant period of time, normal taxation applies as of the date of entry into the country. While residence is being acquired, when applicable, a flat 20% tax normally is levied.

Gross income

Employee gross income/Resident or nonresident foreigners are taxed on their salary, deducting social security contributions.

Such items as reimbursement of travel expenses and housing provided in the employer's interest, moving expenses and a reasonable relocation allowance are considered nontaxable income and are excluded from the tax calculation.

Such items as cost-of-living allowance, area allowances, car allowance, vacation travel expenses, and utilities are taxable.

Capital gains and investment income/There is no capital gains tax in Chile. Capital gains are taxed as normal income unless they are qualified by law as nontaxable income.

Investment income is also taxed as normal income. However, in the case of interest, only "real interest" is taxed, that is, interest effectively paid less cost-of-living increase. Certain gains on the sale of traded shares of Chilean corporations are tax exempt.

Deductions

Business deductions/In general, all expenses incurred that are in the employer's interest, provided they are duly documented, are deductible. Among these are travel and lodging expenses and documented entertainment. No blanket or standard deductions, such as representation allowances, are allowed.

Nonbusiness expenses/Except for social security contributions and a percentage of certain investments in shares and time deposits, no nonbusiness deductions are allowed.

Tax credits

The Income Tax Law allows a tax credit for taxes paid abroad by individuals domiciled or resident in Chile, provided there is a tax treaty in force with the foreign country. Personal allowances are in the form of a tax credit. No other tax credit is available.

Other taxes

Social security taxes/Foreign individuals may be exempt from local social security payments, provided they belong to a foreign social security entity covering at least pension, disability, illness, and death. Salaries are subject to social security contribution of 20%, up to an approximate amount of US$1,360 per month. The excess is not subject to contributions.

In practice, nonresidents normally would not be subject to social security contributions in Chile. However, if they were, the same description as for a resident foreigner would apply.

As noted above, social security contributions are deductible in determining taxable income.

Local taxes on income/There are no local income taxes to be paid, only central government taxes.

Tax administration

Returns/Yearly tax returns need not be filed if the employee receives only salary income. If taxable income from another source is received, such as interest income, a yearly return must be filed.

Husband and wife must file separate returns if each has separate income. The tax year and calendar year coincide. The calendar year is the period of 12 months that ends at December 31. The tax year is that in which taxes or part of them must be paid.

Payment of tax/In the case of employees, there is mandatory monthly withholding by the employer.

Tax rates

Second category tax rates/Tax rates applied to this category are shown below.

Tax units (1) Over	To	Factor	Deduction (2)
0	C$ 396,360	0.00	—
C$ 396,360	880,800	0.05	C$ 19,818.00
880,800	1,468,000	0.10	63,858.00
1,468,000	2,055,200	0.15	137,258.00
2,055,200	2,642,400	0.25	342,778.00
2,642,400	3,523,200	0.32	527,746.00
3,523,200	4,404,000	0.37	703,906.00
4,404,000		0.40	836,026.00

Notes:

1. The tax rates indicated are those for January 2003. The brackets in tax units vary monthly according to the cost-of-living variation. It is important to bear in mind that some rates for the Second Category Tax have changed. From calendar year 2003, the income from 90 to 120 monthly tax units will be subject to tax at a rate of 32%. Amounts from 120 to 150 tax units will be subject to tax at a rate of 37% and the income that exceeds 150 monthly tax units will be subject to tax at a rate of 40%.
2. As at January 1, 2003, the exchange rate was US$1 = C$718.73. A sample calculation for a monthly salary of US$4,000 for a single individual is:

US$4,000 x 718.73	C$ 2,874,920
Less—Social security	201,000
Taxable income	C$ 2,673,920
Income tax—2,673,920 x 0.32	C$ 855,654
Less—Fixed deduction	527,746
Income	C$ 327,908

Surtax/Surtax applies on a yearly basis when there has been no income subject to the monthly mandatory withholding tax or when part of the yearly income has not been subject to such withholding. To calculate the surtax, the rates for the Second Category Tax are used.

Nonresidents/While nondomiciled persons are acquiring residence in Chile for tax purposes (physical presence for six consecutive months), they are subject to a sole withholding tax of 20% in lieu of personal income taxes.

INDIVIDUAL TAX CALCULATION

Fiscal year 2003

Assumptions

Resident foreigner plus spouse and two children.

	C$
Gross compensation	40,000,000
Interest income	1,200,000

Tax computation

Second category tax

Salary per year	C$ 40,000,000
Monthly salary (40,000,000 ÷ 12)	C$ 3,333,333
Less—Social security (January 2002)	201,000
Taxable income	C$ 3,132,333
Income tax (3,132,333 x 0.32)	C$ 1,002,347
Less—Fixed deduction	(527,746)
Monthly income tax	C$ 474,601
Yearly income tax	C$ 5,695,212

Surtax

Second category income	C$ 37,588,000
Interest income	1,200,000
Surtax taxable income	C$ 38,788,000
Monthly surtax income (38,788,000 ÷ 12)	C$ 3,232,333
Surtax (3,232,333 x 32%)	C$ 1,034,347
Less—Fixed deduction	(527,746)
Monthly surtax	C$ 506,601
Yearly surtax (506,601 x 12)	C$ 6,079,212
Less—Second category tax	(5,695,212)
Surtax payable	C$ 384,000

Note:

Exchange rate of the peso at January 1, 2003: US$1 = C$718.73.

PwC contact

For additional information on taxation in the People's Republic of China, contact:

Cassie Wong
PricewaterhouseCoopers
18th floor, Beijing Kerry Centre
1 Guang Hua Lu
Chao Yang District
Beijing 100020
People's Republic of China
Telephone: (86) (10) 6561 2233
Fax: (86) (10) 8529 9000
e-mail: cassie.wong@cn.pwc.com

Significant developments

Starting from January 1, 2004, expatriates (excluding Hong Kong and Macau residents) commuting daily to and from China and Hong Kong/Macau may claim an individual income tax exemption in respect of the following reimbursement items obtained from their employers (including their affiliates) in relation to amounts spent in Hong Kong and Macau.

- Accommodation
- Meals
- Laundry
- Moving expenses
- Language training
- Children's education

For the exemption to be claimed, recognized written evidence must be provided for verification by the tax authorities in charge.

Territoriality and residence

Individuals who have a "place of abode" in China are subject to individual income tax on their worldwide income. For this purpose, "individuals having a place of abode" in China means those who maintain a place of residence in China because of their legal residence status, family, or economic ties.

Individuals who do not have a "place of abode" in China are taxed in accordance with their length of residency in China, as follows.

1. Nonresidents or resident foreign expatriates who reside in China for less than one year will be taxed only on their China-source income.
2. Foreign expatriates who reside in China for more than one year but not more than five years will be subject to tax on both their China-source income and their foreign-source income. However, upon application to and approval from the tax authorities, the taxation of foreign-source income can be limited to that received from Chinese enterprises, Chinese establishments, Chinese economic organizations, and Chinese individuals.
3. Foreign expatriates who reside in China for more than five consecutive years will be subject to tax on their worldwide income from the sixth year onward.

4. Foreign expatriates who travel in China and derive income from an overseas employer with no permanent establishment in China will be tax exempt if they do not physically stay in China, consecutively or cumulatively, for more than 90 days in a calendar year. The 90-day test is extended to 183 days if the individual is a tax resident of a country/region that has executed a taxation treaty/arrangement with China.

Gross income

Employee gross income/Salaries or wages of an individual include basic salary, bonus, foreign service premium, area allowance, cost-of-living allowance, housing allowance in excess of actual rental, local tax reimbursement, insurance and pension contributions, stock benefits, other cash benefit, and other benefits in kind discharging personal liabilities.

Other individual income/Taxable income also includes compensation for personal services, income from the publication of articles, royalties, interest, dividends, incidental income, and rentals.

Capital gains/Capital gains are treated as "other income" (see above) and are subject to tax in the same manner.

Real property gains tax/In addition to income tax, taxpayers are subject to a real property gains tax levied on gains from the transfer of real property. The rate of this tax ranges from 30% to 60%, depending on the size of the gain. This tax is in addition to any applicable income tax on such transfers. However, where an individual transfers the home (ordinary residential apartment), the gain is exempt.

Deductions

Business deductions and nonbusiness expenses/In calculating taxable income for wages and salaries, there are no allowances for actual business expenses. Specific deductions are given for income from compensation for personal services, that is, that of independent contractors; income from the publication of articles; royalties; or income from the lease of property.

1. If the amount received in a single payment is less than RMB4,000, a standard deduction of RMB800 is given.
2. If the amount received from a single economic transaction exceeds RMB4,000, a deduction equal to 20% of the payment is allowed.

Interest and dividends are taxed on the gross amounts received without deductions. For sales of property, the original value of the property and reasonable expenses incurred are deductible from the sales proceeds to arrive at the taxable income.

Personal allowances/All individuals are allowed a standard deduction of RMB800 per month from wages and salaries. The standard deduction for local Chinese individuals may be increased up to RMB1,600, depending on their place of work and return filed. Foreign expatriates, who include Hong Kong, Macau, and Taiwan residents, are given an additional allowance of RMB3,200 per month. Accordingly, the monthly deduction from wages and salaries available to such a foreign expatriate is RMB4,000.

Tax credits

Income tax paid to foreign countries for income earned abroad is allowed as a credit against China tax liability. The credit is limited to the amount of China tax on the foreign income. Documentary evidence of the tax payment to substantiate claims for foreign tax credits is required by the Chinese tax authorities.

Other taxes

Social security taxes/Social contributions to retirement funds, housing funds, and so on, which are mandatory for local employees, are usually not applicable to expatriates.

Local taxes on income/The local governments do not impose any tax on individual income.

Tax administration

Returns/Individuals are required to submit individual income tax returns to the Chinese tax authorities on a monthly basis and to make tax payments within seven days after the end of each month.

Payment of tax/The tax liability is assessed on income computed in renminbi (RMB). Foreign currencies are converted to renminbi according to the exchange rate quoted by the People's Bank of China.

Tax returns must be filed on a timely basis. Extensions to file may be granted under "special circumstances." A surcharge of 0.05% per day for all taxes, including individual income tax, will be assessed on delinquent payments pursuant to the law on the administration of tax collection that came into effect on May 1, 2001.

Withholding/When paying taxable income to an individual, the employer, unit or person making the payment is required, as the withholding agent, to withhold the individual income tax due.

Tax rates

Wages and salaries

Monthly taxable income		Tax	Quick
Not grossed up	Grossed up	rate	deduction
RMB	RMB	%	RMB
0–500	0–475	5	0
501–2,000	476–1,825	10	25
2,001–5,000	1,826–4,375	15	125
5,001–20,000	4,376–16,375	20	375
20,001–40,000	16,376–31,375	25	1,375
40,001–60,000	31,376–45,375	30	3,375
60,001–80,000	45,376–58,375	35	6,375
80,001–100,000	58,376–70,735	40	10,375
Over 100,000	Over 70,735	45	15,375

Where an individual's income tax liability is borne by the employer, the tax liability is calculated on an infinite gross-up basis (i.e., tax on tax).

Other income categories/A flat rate of 20% is applied on all other categories of income, that is, those included under "Other individual income" and "Capital gains" above. For independent contractors, if the income received for services performed is deemed to be too high, an additional tax will be assessed. For this purpose, a quantitative test will apply. In addition, a 30% tax reduction will be applicable to income from the publication of articles.

INDIVIDUAL TAX CALCULATION

Calendar year 2003

Assumptions

The individual is a foreign expatriate for income tax purposes. Monthly salary is US$7,000, and the income tax liability is not borne by the employer.

Tax computation

Monthly salary	US$ 7,000*
	RMB
Monthly income	58,100
Less—Personal allowance	4,000
Monthly taxable income	54,100
Tax at applicable rate of 30%	16,230
Less—Quick deduction	(3,375)
Monthly tax payable	12,855

*Assuming an exchange rate of US$1 = RMB8.3.

Note:

Exchange rate of the renminbi at January 1, 2004: US$1 = RMB8.2769.

PwC contacts

For additional information on individual taxation in Colombia, contact:

María Helena Díaz Méndez

Alexandra Gnecco
Calle 100 No. 11-A-35, Piso Tercero
Bogotá, Colombia
Telephone: (57) (1) 6340555
Fax: (57) (1) 6104626
e-mail: maria.helena.diaz@co.pwcglobal.com
alexandra.gnecco@co.pwcglobal.com

General note

This entry is repeated from the 2003/2004 edition. For more up-to-date information consult the contacts listed above or Jacqueline Collette at jacqueline.collette@us.pwc.com.

Significant developments

As from January 1, 2003, a new tax law is applicable in Colombia, which involves some changes regarding individual taxation. The information in this entry is current as of March 2003. For subsequent developments consult the contacts listed above.

Territoriality and residence

Colombia taxes its nationals and aliens as follows:

1. Alien residents are taxed on Colombian-source income. As from their sixth year of residence, alien residents are taxed on worldwide income.
2. Nonresident nationals and aliens are taxed on Colombian-source income.

For tax purposes, aliens become resident when they remain in Colombia for more than six months continuously or discontinuously within a tax year or when they complete this time period in the calendar year.

Nationals are considered residents if they maintain their family or their principal business site in Colombia.

Gross income

Employee gross income/An alien resident is taxed on salary earned for services provided in Colombia no matter where payment is made. Salary includes bonuses, living allowances, housing allowances, tax reimbursements, benefits in kind, and certain payments that must be made under Colombian labor law. All employees, including those who opt to receive an integral salary, that is, without the social benefits of a legal bonus and severance compensation, can treat at least 25% of the total annual labor payments or salary as exempt income. However, this exemption cannot be higher than COP$4,000,000 per month. Although some payments derived from a labor relationship may be agreed as not being salary, they are deemed to be taxable for income tax purposes.

Capital gains and investment income/An individual who is in Colombia for less than six years is taxed on Colombian-source capital gains and investment income.

Thereafter, the alien resident is taxed on worldwide capital gains and investment income.

Capital gains are taxed separately from ordinary income, but are taxed on the basis of the individual tax rates.

"Monetary correction" on savings accounts (an adjustment that savings and loan institutions credit to clients placed in certain types of savings or term-deposit accounts in order to compensate for inflation) is free of tax. The correction must be certified by the institution. Any additional yield recognized as interest is, however, taxable.

The inflation component of interest received on certain bonds by individuals not required to keep books of account, is not subject to income tax.

Domestic shareholders and individual foreign shareholders resident in Colombia are not subject to income tax on dividends or participations received from Colombian companies whose income has been taxed. However, individual foreign shareholders who are not resident in Colombia are subject to income tax at the rate of 7%, on dividends and participations received from Colombian companies whose income has been taxed.

Pension contributions/Mandatory contributions made to Colombian Retirement Pension Funds by an employee are not deemed to constitute income or capital gains for the employee and are therefore not part of the withholding tax base.

Similarly, voluntary contributions made by either the employee or the employer to these funds are not considered income or capital gains for the employee and are therefore not part of the withholding tax base, provided they, added to the mandatory contributions, do not exceed 30% of the employee's labor income. Notwithstanding the above, voluntary contributions will become taxable if they are withdrawn by the employee within five years of having been deposited in the fund.

Contributions made to foreign pension systems are deemed to be taxable for the expatriate or employee and are therefore part of the withholding income tax base.

Housing accounts/Also, deposits made to savings accounts to support the construction of housing are considered as nontaxable income, provided they do not exceed 30% of the employee's labor income and that the employee does not withdraw them before five years from the date of deposit. However, even if the deposit is withdrawn before five years, it would continue to be treated as nontaxable income if it is used to pay for new housing.

Benefits derived by making voluntary contributions and deposits to the above-mentioned saving accounts cannot be aggregated.

Deductions

Business deductions/Employees are not entitled to deduct business-related expenses from their compensation income.

Nonbusiness expenses/A resident alien can deduct from compensation mortgage interest paid in Colombia, up to a maximum of COP20,800,000 annually. Employees with annual income of less than COP77,700,000 may choose to deduct either mortgage interest or prepaid medical assistance and educational expenses.

Some donations are allowed as deductions, provided they are made to certain institutions dedicated to development of health, education, culture, religion, sports, scientific and technological research, ecology and the protection of the environment, or to social development programs of general interest. The amount of deduction for most of these donations is limited.

Personal allowances/There are no personal allowances.

Tax credits

A resident alien is not entitled to foreign tax credits.

Other taxes

Social security tax/Nonresident aliens should be affiliated with the Colombian Retirement Pension Funds if they are not covered in their native countries with a system equal to or better than Colombia's. The employee contribution rate is 3.375% of monthly salary for those assignees whose salary does not exceed four minimum salaries and 4.375% for those assignees who receive more than four minimum salaries. Employees earning more than 16 minimum salaries will also be obliged to contribute an additional percentage ranging between 0.2% and 1%. It is mandatory to be affiliated with the Welfare Security System, to which a supplemental 4% must be contributed.

Local taxes on income/There are no local taxes on individual income.

Tax administration

Returns/Any salaried taxpayer meeting the filing requirements for calendar year 2003 of income (COP60 million) or gross assets (COP150 million) must file a return. Taxpayers with only passive income must file a return for 2003 when income exceeds COP23.8 million or gross assets exceed COP150 million. Joint returns are not permitted. Income splitting is not allowed.

No taxable year other than the calendar year is permitted.

Payment of tax/There is income tax withholding from salaries. If a balance is payable by the taxpayer, it must be paid on the date for filing the return. Tax-filing season usually starts in April and ends in early June.

Tax rates

Individual income tax rates are voluminous; sample rates for calendar year 2003 are:

Taxable income		
Over	Not over	Income tax
COP 20,300,000	COP 20,500,000	COP 140,000
42,500,001	42,700,000	5,768,000
84,300,000		18,168,000

The excess over COP84,300,000 is taxed at the rate of 35%.

INDIVIDUAL TAX CALCULATION

Calendar year 2003

Tax computation

Total salary	COP	140,000,000
Less—Contributions made to a pension system that do not constitute income or occasional gain (1)		10,000,000
Net salary		130,000,000
Less—Exempt portion (25%)		32,500,000
Taxable salary		97,500,000
Less—Deductible interest income paid on mortgage (2)		4,000,000
	COP	93,500,000
Income tax:		
On 84,300,000	COP	18,168,000
35% on the excess of 9,200,000 x 35%		3,220,000
	COP	21,388,000
Capital gain obtained in the alienation of fixed assets held for more than two years	COP	9,800,000
Capital gains tax	COP	0

Notes:

1. This is the maximum mandatory contribution that would be made by the employee.
2. The maximum monthly amount allowed to be deducted corresponding to mortgage interest is COP20,800,000 (2003 threshold).
3. Exchange rate of the Colombian peso at January 1, 2003: US$1 = COP2,864.79.

PwC contact

For additional information on taxation in the Democratic Republic of Congo, contact:

Benjamin Nzailu Basinsa
PricewaterhouseCoopers
B.P. 10195
Kinshasa 1, D.R.C.
Telephone: MCI cardholders (243) (88) 44435, 40239
Fax: (243) (88) 00075
e-mail: bnzailu.pricewat@ic.cd

General note

This entry is repeated from the 2003/2004 edition. For more up-to-date information consult the contact listed above or Jacqueline Collette at jacqueline.collette@us.pwc.com.

Significant developments

There have been no significant tax or regulatory developments regarding individual taxation in the past year.

Territoriality and residence

Congo applies the rules of the territoriality of income. It taxes its citizens and aliens (residents and nonresidents) on income derived from professional, commercial, and employment activities carried out in Congo; from rental of real estate located in Congo; and from domestic investments. Foreign-source income is not taxable. The tax system is schedular.

Gross income

Employee gross income/The following items are included in taxable compensation: salary, living allowance, tax reimbursements, benefits-in-kind, and any other reimbursement of personal expenses, except medical expenses and reasonable housing and transportation allowances. Company-owned or company-leased housing may be provided to employees without being considered a taxable benefit, provided housing allowances or benefits-in-kind do not exceed 30% of gross salary. Nontaxable transportation allowances are fixed by reference to official public transportation prices.

The private use of company-owned or -leased vehicles is taxable. Moving and home-leave transportation expenses are nontaxable.

Family allowances are nontaxable to the extent that they do not exceed the legal limits. These are at present negligible. There are no special concessions for foreigners.

Capital gains and investment income/Capital gains are taxable at 40%.

Dividends and other profit distributions by domestic companies are subject to a final tax at the rate of 20%, which is withheld at source.

Rental income from real estate is subject to tax at 22% on gross income *(contribution sur les revenus locatifs)*. The main tax amount is withheld by the tenant when paying his or her rent (20% of the rent paid).

Deductions

Business deductions/Reimbursement of genuine business expenses is generally nontaxable.

Nonbusiness expenses/Expenses deductible by an employee are:

1. Medical expenses for employees and their dependents to the extent not reimbursed by the employer.
2. Pension and health plan contributions to a recognized scheme, provided these are payable under the terms of the employee's work contract.
3. Social security contributions.

Personal allowances/There are no personal allowances available, except for the family allowances mentioned above (see "Gross income"). Tax reductions are negligible.

Tax credits

No tax credits are available.

Other taxes

Social security taxes/All employees must contribute to a national pension scheme. Since August 20, 1992, the contributions have been fixed at 8.5% of the total gross remuneration; 5% is paid by the employer and 3.5% by the employee, based on gross remuneration less transport allocation, family allowance and housing allowance. These contributions are deductible in determining taxable income.

Local taxes on income/There are no income taxes payable in addition to central government taxes.

Tax administration

Tax returns and payment/Salaries and wages are subject to tax withholding at source, and employers are required to make annual tax returns for their employees prior to January 10 following the end of the fiscal year (December 31). Individuals with no sources of income other than wages and salaries need not file a tax return; this is the employer's responsibility. In all cases, income of spouses is combined.

Tax rates

The annual taxable income is subject to tax at graduated rates. For annual taxable income up to CDF2,331,600, the tax payable is CDF704,340. The excess over CDF2,331,600 is taxed at 50%. However, the total tax payable is limited to 30% of total taxable income.

End-of-career indemnities and indemnities paid by the employer (contractual or otherwise) following cessation of employment or on breaking a contract of employment are taxed separately at 10%.

For occasional workers, the rate for the calculation of tax on remuneration is fixed at 15%.

INDIVIDUAL TAX CALCULATION

Assumptions

Resident alien husband and wife, two children; one spouse earns all the income. The employer furnishes housing and a car and also reimburses medical expenses.

Tax computation

Basic salary		CDF 24,000,000
Overtime		2,000,000
Bonus		1,000,000
Compensation for inflation		2,000,000
Taxable salary		29,000,000
Add:		
Transport allowance	1,700,000	
Housing allowance	3,000,000	
Family allowance	800,000	5,500,000
Gross remuneration		34,500,000
Less:		
Transport allowance	1,700,000	
Housing allowance	3,000,000	
Family allowance	800,000	
Social security contribution (1)	1,015,000	
Legal family allowances	800,000	
Contributions to an outside recognized pension scheme	3,600,000	
Total deduction		10,915,000
Taxable income		CDF 23,585,000
Tax thereon:		
First 2,331,600 at graduated rates	704,340	
Remainder of 21,553,400 at 50%	10,626,700	CDF 11,331,040
Maximum tax payable (2)		CDF 7,075,500
Deduction for family expenses (6% on 430,100) (3)		(25,866)
Maximum tax payable		CDF 7,049,634

Notes:

1. 3.5% of gross remuneration less transport allocation, family allowance, and housing allowance.
2. The maximum tax payable is 30% of taxable income, or CDF6,989,694 in this calculation.
3. Deductions for family expense are calculated on the amount of tax on income between CDF0 and CDF1,686,000. The rate is fixed at 2% per person, limited to nine persons.
4. Exchange rate of the Congolese franc at December 31, 2002: US$1 = CDF385.

PwC contact

For additional information on taxation in Costa Rica, contact:

Gerardo Cásares Alvarado
PricewaterhouseCoopers
Edificio Price Waterhouse
Barrio Los Yoses
San José, Costa Rica
Telephone: (506) 224 15 55
Fax: (506) 253 4053
e-mail: gerardo.casares@cr.pwcglobal.com

General note

This entry is repeated from the 2003/2004 edition. For more up-to-date information consult the contact listed above or Jacqueline Collette at jacqueline.collette@us.pwc.com.

Significant developments

There have been no significant developments regarding individual taxation in the past year. The information in this entry is current as of January 2003. For subsequent developments consult the contact listed above.

Territoriality and residence

Income taxes on individuals in Costa Rica are levied on local income irrespective of nationality and resident status. For individuals domiciled in Costa Rica, any income obtained within the boundaries of Costa Rica is considered local income. For nonresidents in Costa Rica, any income derived from business, capital invested goods sold or services rendered within Costa Rica is considered of local source and therefore taxable. However, nonresidents are liable only for the applicable withholding taxes, depending on the nature of the local income.

Independent of nationality, an individual who is self-employed and has been living in Costa Rica more than six months of a taxable year and must file a regular income tax return is considered resident. This period may be shorter if the person is employed and subject to payroll withholding taxes.

Gross income

Employee gross income/Individuals domiciled in Costa Rica are taxed on salaries, commissions, fees, royalties, and any other form of remuneration for services rendered, plus any interest and rental income received from local sources. Any income earned abroad while in residence in Costa Rica is not taxable, as indicated above.

Individuals with a monthly salary of less than CRC296,000 and self-employed individuals with annual income of less than CRC1,316,000 are exempt from income taxes.

The reimbursement of personal living expenses and travel expenses for individuals not formally domiciled is not subject to taxes. This would include the reimbursement of similar expenses for the taxpayer's family. Certain expense allowances at the discretion of the tax authorities are not subject to taxation, nor are they deductible for the payer.

Capital gains and investment income/At present there is no capital gains tax on the sale of real estate or securities (Paragraph f) article 8 of the Costa Rican Income Tax Law).

Gains on the transfer of real estate are taxed at 1.51%.

The patrimony of commercial corporations (assets minus liabilities) is taxed at 0.1% for one year. This tax will be applied on the excess of CRC35,000,000.

Domiciled individuals are subject to a 16.5 tax on interest on bearer documents except for those bearer documents registered at the local stock exchange, in which case the tax is 8.8%. This tax is withheld at source of payment. Income on investments from a foreign source is not taxable.

Foreign-domiciled individuals are subject to withholding taxes at the rates shown below.

	%
Interest	16.5
Dividends	16.5
Directors' fees, etc.	16.5
Salaries	11.0
Fees	17.5

Because rental income denotes a permanent physical establishment in Costa Rica, the landlord must file a regular tax return indicating total income less permitted expenses; the net income is subject to tax at regular individual graduated rates.

Deductions

Business deductions/A domiciled individual, whether or not a national, whose only source of income is a salary for personal services cannot deduct business expenses, regardless of whether they are reimbursed or not. However, self-employed individuals and those whose source of income is from commissions (sales), fees, and so on, may deduct up to 25% of gross income as a deduction without itemizing expenses, or may elect to itemize the expenses incurred in producing the gross income. Itemized deductions must be substantiated to the authorities upon request.

Nonbusiness expenses/The amount of legal annual bonus (Christmas bonus) that does not exceed one-twelfth of net salary (which is one-thirteenth of gross salary) is exempt from income taxes.

Personal allowances/Individuals are permitted the tax credits shown below.

	Monthly	Annual
	CRC	CRC
Spouse	830	9,960
Child (each)	560	6,720

The child allowance is permissible only if the child is a minor, is unable to work, or is a university student under 25 years of age.

Tax credits

In accordance with Costa Rican legislation, there are no tax credits allowed to individuals for taxes paid to foreign governments.

Personal allowances take the form of tax credits (see above).

Other taxes

Social security taxes/An individual's share of social security taxes is 9% on total remuneration, which in the case of salary is deducted from the individual's payroll payment. Self-employed individuals' participation in the social security system can range from 9% to 15% tax on income.

Other taxes on income/None of the provinces or municipalities imposes any income taxes on individuals within its jurisdiction.

Tax administration

Returns/Only self-employed individuals who receive commissions, fees, royalties, or other forms of income for services rendered and those who receive interest or rental income from local sources must file a tax return that corresponds to a 12-month period ended on September 30. If both spouses earn income they must submit individual returns, in which case the personal child credit can be taken by only one of the spouses. The present legislation does not contemplate joint filing.

Payment of tax/Employees who receive salaries and other similar or complementary remunerations or benefits must pay a monthly income tax that is withheld by the employer from the monthly payroll. Individuals need not file an annual tax return for this type of income.

Self-employed individuals are required to make quarterly payments of estimated taxes, which are computed on the average of the last three fiscal years, and a final payment two and a half months after the end of the fiscal year.

Tax rates

Tax rates for self-employed individuals, based on annual taxable income, are:

Annual taxable income		Tax on	Percentage
Over	Not over	Column 1	on excess
(Column 1)			
0	CRC 1,316,000	—	0
CRC 1,316,000	1,965,000	—	12
1,965,000	3,278,000	CRC 77,880	13
3,278,000	6,569,000	248,570	24
6,569,000		1,038,410	30

Tax rates for employed individuals, based on monthly salary, are shown in the table below. Individuals who are both self-employed and employees may not take the CRC1,316,000 deduction.

Monthly taxable income		Tax on	Percentage
Over	Not over	Column 1	on excess
(Column 1)			
0	CRC 296,000	—	0.0
CRC 296,000	445,000	—	10.0
445,000	750,000	CRC 14,900	15.0
750,000	1,500,000	60,650	16.5
1,500,000		184,400	18.0

INDIVIDUAL TAX CALCULATION

Income year 2003

Gross income:		
Salary		CRC 12,220,000
Interest		300,000
Long-term capital gain		400,000
Total gross income		12,920,000
Less:		
100% of interest on which 8.8% is withheld at source	300,000	
Capital gain	400,000	
Legal annual bonus (Christmas bonus)	940,000	1,640,000
Taxable income		CRC 11,280,000
Monthly taxable salary		CRC 940,000
Monthly income tax		CRC 92,000
Less—Personal credits:		
Spouse	830	
Children (two)	1,120	(1,950)
Net monthly income tax		CRC 90,050
Annual income tax		CRC 1,080,600

Note:

Exchange rate of the colon at April 4, 2003: US$1 = CRC389.61.

Croatia

PwC contact

For additional information on taxation in Croatia, contact:

Iain McGuire
PricewaterhouseCoopers d.o.o.
Alexandera von Humboldta 4
10000 Zagreb, Croatia
Telephone: (385) (1) 63 28 888
Fax: (385) (1) 6111 556
e-mail: iain.mcguire@hr.pwcglobal.com

General note

This entry is repeated from the 2003/2004 edition. For more up-to-date information consult the contact listed above or Jacqueline Collette at jacqueline.collette@us.pwc.com.

Significant developments

The new General Tax Law, which sets a general legal framework for the tax system in Croatia, was introduced on January 1, 2001.

The Tax Advisory Law, which sets the framework for providing tax advisory services, was introduced on January 1, 2001.

The new Personal Income Tax Law was introduced on January 1, 2001. Amendments were introduced on January 1, 2003.

Territoriality and residence

Every domestic or foreign individual deriving income in the Republic of Croatia is defined as a taxpayer. In principle, all residents and persons temporarily resident or with their usual place of residence (physically present for more than 183 days in any period of two calendar years) within Croatia must pay tax in Croatia on their worldwide income. Individuals who are only temporarily resident in Croatia, or whose usual place of abode is abroad (foreign taxpayers) are liable to pay tax in Croatia on Croatian-source income.

When income is received from abroad, the recipient is required to self-assess tax, make a payment to the tax authorities within eight days of receipt and file a tax return at year-end.

Gross income

Tax is assessed on income derived by a taxpayer (salaries and pensions), income from independent activities (freelance work, crafts, agriculture, and forestry), income from property rights (e.g., rent or trade in real estate and certain intellectual property rights), and income from capital. In relation to rental income, expenses up to 30% of realized rent income is tax deductible. In the case of rooms, beds and flats rented to travelers for whom a tourist charge is paid, expenses incidental to realizing the income are determined to the value of 50% of realized revenue.

Compulsory social care contributions are not subject to income tax.

Tax concessions are provided to residents of special-interest regions. These reduce the tax rate applicable to residents living in these areas through higher personal allowances; income tax exemptions on income derived from agriculture and forestry; and higher depreciation rates for long-term capital invested in property.

Fringe benefits/Employers may give employees certain benefits that qualify as nontaxable. The following are the most significant:

1. Reimbursement of travel expenses (the real cost of traveling to work using public transportation).
2. Daily allowance for business trips in Croatia—Up to HRK170 per diem, plus travel and accommodation expenses.
3. Daily allowance for business trips abroad—The allowed sums as defined by a special decision (depending on the country), plus travel and accommodation expenses.
4. Reimbursement for use of employee's personal car for business purposes—Up to 30% of the price of gasoline per kilometer.
5. Cash granted to employees upon retirement—HRK8,000.
6. Disability benefit (HRK2,500), benefit upon the death of an employee (HRK7,500), or benefit upon the death of member of his or her immediate family (HRK3,000).
7. Bonuses (e.g., Christmas bonus) up to HRK1,000 p.a.
8. Loyalty bonuses to employees with 10 to 40 years of service—From HRK1,500 to HRK5,000.

If any of these benefits exceeds the quoted limit, the difference is considered to be salary and is taxable (employee and employer contributions, personal income tax, surtax).

Capital gains and investment income/The following gains are not subject to income tax:

1. Income in the form of interest on kuna or foreign currency savings accounts.
2. Interest from securities issued in accordance with a separate act.
3. Profit earned from the sale of financial property.
4. Profit shares from foreign companies that would, if they were resident taxpayers, be liable to pay profit tax.
5. Income realized from a joint business activity that is liable to profit tax abroad.

Profit tax election

Certain self-employed individuals may elect to pay profit tax and keep accounts in accordance with accounting standards instead of paying personal income tax.

Deductions

Business deductions/Certain business expenses paid to employees are not taxable (see above). Self-employed individuals can deduct business expenses that are necessary and connected to conducting their business activities. The list of nondeductible expenses is similar to that for profit tax purposes and includes entertainment expenses, excess travel allowances and 30% of the cost of business transport.

Nonbusiness expenses/These expenses are dealt with by the system of personal deductions set out below as well as within the corporate profit tax regime.

Personal allowances/An individual's taxable income is reduced by the following allowances:

1. Personal allowance (HRK1,500 per month).
2. Allowance for supporting a spouse and children—The taxpayer's personal allowance corresponds to a factor of 1. For every dependent, personal allowance is increased as follows:

	HRK per month
Dependent spouse (factor of 0.40)	600
First child (factor of 0.42)	630
Second child (factor of 0.59)	885
Third child (factor of 0.84)	1,260
Fourth child (factor of 1.17)	1,755
Fifth child (factor of 1.59)	2,385
Sixth child (factor of 2.09)	3,135
Seventh child (factor of 2.67)	4,005
Eighth child (factor of 3.34)	5,010
Ninth child (factor of 4.09)	6,135
Tenth child (factor of 5)	7,500

   For every additional child the factor is increased by an additional factor of 1.0, based on the personal allowance for the previous child.

3. Allowance for supporting disabled family members—If the taxpayer or a family member is disabled, the personal allowance factor is increased by 0.25.
4. Allowance for premiums paid for life insurance, additional health insurance, and voluntary retirement insurance amounts to factor of 0.8 of the personal allowance.
5. Domestic taxpayers are allowed an increased personal allowance for the following expenses:
   a. Expenses made for health care and orthopedic equipment, up to the amount of HRK12,000 per annum, if paid out of an individual's private funds;
   b. Loans and expenses incurred for the purchase or reconstruction of a house or a flat, up to the amount of HRK12,000 per annum;
   c. 50% of the contracted rent paid for housing, up to the amount of HRK12,000 per annum;
   d. Gifts in kind or in money made for cultural, educational, scientific, healthcare, humanitarian, sporting, religious, and similar activities up to 2% of the total receipts included in the annual tax return filed for the previous year.
6. Allowance for losses can be carried forward for up to five successive years.

Tax credits

Insofar as domestic tax rules give rise to double taxation, Croatia grants unilateral relief on a credit basis. Under the terms of an applicable treaty, relief is granted on the exemption basis in the case of the old Yugoslav double taxation treaties that are still in force and on a credit basis for new Croatian double taxation treaties.

Other taxes

***Social security taxes*/** Where income tax is due on salary from a full-time job, the pension contributions are deducted from the employee's tax base. Effective from January 1, 2003, the rate is 20%. The annual cap for calculating the pension contributions is HRK382,320.

In addition to this, an employer must make contributions, as follows:

1. Health care—15%.
2. Employment fund—1.7%.
3. Insurance against accidents at work—0.5%.

These contributions do not affect the tax base.

Foreigners employed by non-Croatian employers may be exempt from social security contributions, depending on whether Croatia has reciprocal social security agreements with the host country.

***Local taxes on income*/** Towns may levy surtax. For employees who live in towns where surtax is levied, the employer applies the surtax rate to the employees' income tax and deducts it from their salary. The majority of cities levy a surtax ranging from 1% to 18%.

Tax administration

The obligation to pay income tax arises when the taxpayer receives income. Payment is made either through payroll deductions or by advance tax payments.

***Deduction of tax on payment of salaries and pensions*/** On making every salary or pension payment, the employer (or pension payer) is obliged to calculate the amount of tax for each employee (recipient) and pay this into the prescribed accounts. The recipient receives a net salary payment (or pension).

***Advance tax payments*/** Self-employed persons and craftsmen make advance tax payments in accordance with their latest tax assessment. Persons engaged in agricultural activity pay tax quarterly on assessed cadastral income.

***Returns*/** At the end of the year, every taxpayer is obliged to submit a tax return to the appropriate branch of the tax administration. The tax return shows the difference between their tax liability and the amount of tax prepayments made in respect of the tax year. The taxpayer will be either entitled to a tax refund or will be required to make an additional tax payment.

A tax return is not required where the individual's only taxable income is from one employer.

Tax rates

The tax base is defined as gross salary less contributions and the employee's personal allowance. Income tax is levied at the following rates:

Income range (per month)	%
From HRK1,500 to HRK3,000	15
From HRK3,000 to HRK6,750	25
From HRK6,750 to HRK21,000	35
Over HRK21,000	45

INDIVIDUAL TAX CALCULATION

Calendar year 2003

Assumptions

Employee with a gross annual salary of HRK450,000 living in Zagreb with no dependents. This calculation uses the contribution rates effective from January 2003.

Employee tax computation

Gross annual salary	HRK	450,000
Less—Employee's contributions from gross salary:		
Pension (20 %)—Capped at annual base of HRK382,320		76,464
Gross salary reduced by contributions		373,536
Less—Personal allowance		18,000
Taxable base	HRK	355,536
Total tax payable	HRK	123,091.20
Surtax on tax payable (at 18%)	HRK	22,156.42
Net salary	HRK	228,288.38

Employer's contributions on gross salary

	HRK
Health (15%)	67,500
Insurance against accidents on work (0.5%)	2,250
Employment (1.7%)	7,650
Total employer's contributions	77,400

Note:

Exchange rate of the kuna at March 31, 2003: US$1 = HRK7.1650.

PwC contact

For additional information on taxation in Cyprus, contact:

Panikos N. Tsiailis
PricewaterhouseCoopers Cyprus
Julia House
3 Themistoclis Dervis Street
CY 1066 Nicosia, Cyprus
P.O. Box 21612, CY–1591 Nicosia, Cyprus
Telephone: (357) 22555000
Fax: (357) 22555001
e-mail: panikos.n.tsiailis@cy.pwc.com

Significant developments

There have been no significant tax or regulatory developments as regards individual income tax in the past year.

Residence and basis of taxation

Cyprus income tax is imposed on the worldwide income of individuals who are resident in Cyprus. An individual who spends more that 183 days in the year in Cyprus is considered resident in Cyprus in a tax year. Individuals who are not tax residents of Cyprus are taxed only on income accrued or derived from sources in Cyprus.

Gross income

Employee gross income/An alien employee who is tax resident in Cyprus is taxed in Cyprus on all remuneration, including benefits in kind such as free accommodation.

An employee is not taxed on reimbursements for travel and entertainment expenses.

Capital gains and investment income/Capital gains other than those from immovable property are not taxed in Cyprus. A 20% tax is imposed on gains arising from the disposal of immovable property in Cyprus or the disposal of shares of companies (other than companies whose shares are listed in any recognized stock exchange) that own immovable property. In the case of disposal of company shares, the gain is calculated exclusively on the basis of the gain from the immovable property. The value of the immovable property will be its market value at the time the shares were sold.

The taxable gain is the difference between the sale proceeds and the original cost of the property plus improvements as adjusted for inflation up to the date of disposal on the basis of the consumer price index in Cyprus. In the case of property acquired before January 1, 1980, the original cost is deemed to be the value of the property as at January 1, 1980 on the basis of the general valuation conducted by the Land Registry Office under the Immovable Property Law.

Pensions received from abroad up to C£2,000 are exempt. Any excess over C£2,000 is taxed separately at a fixed rate of 5%.

Interest and dividend income received by individuals are generally exempt from income tax but are subject to the defense contribution, which is imposed at 10% on interest income and 15% on dividend income.

Exempt income/The following income is exempt from tax.

1. A 20% exemption from tax (up to a maximum amount of C£5,000 annually) is provided on the remuneration earned from any office or employment exercised in Cyprus by an individual who was not resident of Cyprus before the commencement of employment in Cyprus. The exemption is provided for a period of three years starting from January 1 following the year of commencement of the employment.
2. Remuneration from salaried services rendered outside Cyprus for more than 90 days in a tax year to a non–Cyprus resident employer or to a foreign permanent establishment of a Cyprus resident employer is exempt from tax.
3. Profits from the sale of securities are exempt from tax. "Securities" is defined as shares, bonds, debentures, founders' shares, and other securities of companies or other legal persons incorporated in Cyprus or abroad and options thereon.
4. Social grants—The following three categories of grants are exempt from income tax:
    a. A grant of up to C£1,500 per annum granted to families for every child receiving full-time higher education in Cyprus (with certain restrictions) or full-time university education abroad;
    b. An annual grant for each dependent child of a family resident in Cyprus (subject to family income criteria);
    c. An annual grant of C£1,800 for blind persons.

Deductions

Business deductions/In general, any business-related expense (including contributions to trade unions or other professional bodies) is deductible, unless reimbursed. Expenses of traveling to and from work are not deductible.

Nonbusiness expenses/Subject to limitations, interest on housing loans, other interest, charitable contributions, social security contributions, and life insurance premiums are deductible.

Tax credits

Either through double taxation treaty or Cyprus unilateral relief, residents with foreign-source income are entitled to a credit equal to the income tax levied on that income in the foreign country. This credit cannot exceed the Cyprus income tax imposed on the same income.

Other taxes

Social security taxes/For 2004 the taxpayer's share of social security taxes is 6.3% of the first C£22,932 of salary.

Tax administration

Returns/Husbands and wives cannot file joint returns. Separate returns must be filed on a calendar-year basis.

Payment of tax/There is income tax withholding from salaries under the pay-as-you-earn system (PAYE). If a taxpayer has other income not subject to withholding, payments of estimated tax must be made in three equal installments on August 1, September 30, and December 31.

Tax rates

The following table lists the normal rates of taxation applicable to individuals.

Taxable income		Normal tax	Percentage
Over	Not over	on Column 1	on excess
(Column 1)	(Note)		
0	C£ 10,000	—	—
C£ 10,000	15,000	—	20
15,000	20,000	C£ 1,000	25
20,000		2,250	30

Note:

Foreign employees of international business entities (i.e., entities exclusively owned by aliens and deriving their income from activities carried on exclusively outside Cyprus) are entitled to the following tax advantages.

1. An international business entity's foreign employees working outside Cyprus are not subject to tax in Cyprus as they are not resident in Cyprus.
2. An international business entity's foreign employees are fully exempt from social insurance contributions.

INDIVIDUAL TAX CALCULATION

Calendar year 2004

Assumptions

Resident husband and wife; two children. One spouse earns all the income.

Income tax computation

Salary		C£ 42,000
Interest income		3,500
Dividend income		2,100
Capital gains		2,000
Total gross income		49,600
Less—Itemized deductions:		
Interest	3,500	
Dividends	2,100	
Capital gains	2,000	
Charitable contributions	300	
Subscriptions	700	8,600
Net income		41,000
Less—Social security contributions		1,444
Taxable income		C£ 39,556
Income tax thereon (see table above)		C£ 8,117

Defense contribution computation

Interest income—3,500 x 10%	C£ 350
Dividend income—2,100 x 15%	315
Defense contribution liability	C£ 665

Notes:

1. The income tax and defense contribution liabilities as calculated are discharged partly by withholding at source and partly by direct tax payments.
2. Exchange rate of the Cyprus pound at January 1, 2004: US$1 = C£0.4687.

PwC contacts

For additional information on taxation in the Czech Republic, contact:

Stephen Booth
Zuzana Vanecková
Antoni Turczynowicz
Lorenz Bernhardt
PricewaterhouseCoopers
Katerinská 40
120 00 Prague 2
Czech Republic
Telephone: (420) 251 151 111
Fax: (420) 251 156 111
e-mail: stephen.booth@cz.pwc.com
zuzana.vaneckova@cz.pwc.com
antoni.turczynowicz@cz.pwc.com
lorenz.bernhardt@cz.pwc.com

General note

Tax legislation and interpretations are still subject to relatively frequent changes. These amendments frequently occur without much prior notice and become effective immediately or even retroactively. Therefore, it is advisable to contact the experts listed above for up-to-date information.

Territoriality and residence

A resident of the Czech Republic is subject to tax on worldwide income, irrespective of whether the income is remitted to the Czech Republic.

An individual who spends at least 183 days in a calendar year or has a permanent place of abode in the Czech Republic is resident for tax purposes.

A nonresident is liable to tax on Czech-source income only, subject to double taxation treaties. Czech-source income includes income from work performed in the territory of the Czech Republic, even if just one day's duration, irrespective of the place of payment, if the employer is a Czech resident or has a permanent establishment in the Czech Republic. A nonresident is exempt from Czech tax on employment income resulting from work performed for a foreign employer resident abroad with no permanent establishment or deemed place of business in the Czech Republic as long as the time period related to the performance of the work does not exceed 183 days in a 12-month period.

Gross income

Employee gross income/The gross income of employees includes all wages, salaries, and bonuses paid and any benefits in kind (subject to minor exceptions) received as a result of employment. Benefits in kind are valued in principle at open-market values, although a fixed rate of 12% per annum of the purchase price is applied to cars provided by the employer unless the employee makes no private use of the car. The minimum benefit is CZK1,000 per month. The reimbursement of travel expenses in excess of fairly low statutory limits is also a taxable benefit to the employee. Certain nonmonetary educational, sporting, and health benefits are nontaxable. Temporary accommodation provided by an employer as a nonmonetary benefit is not taxable if arrangements are properly structured. An accommodation allowance is taxable.

Nonresident directors' fees and fees payable to nonresident members of other statutory bodies of Czech companies are subject to a withholding tax of 25%. No further tax is payable on this income. When paid to tax residents, directors' fees and fees to members of other statutory bodies of Czech companies are taxed under the payroll administration, using the progressive tax rates.

Capital gains and investment income/Capital gains form part of total income and are therefore subject to income tax at the taxpayer's marginal rate. Exemptions are available for gains arising on the disposal of assets that have not been used for commercial purposes and that have been held for certain minimum periods, as follows.

1. Securities—Held for more than six months.
2. Cars and certain other movable assets—Held for more than 12 months.
3. Real estate—Held for more than five years.

A gain on the sale of an apartment or house that has been the taxpayer's residence for at least two years before the sale is, subject to certain conditions, also exempt, as is a gain on the sale of property by the first owner in restitution.

A special withholding tax rate of 15% applies to income received by individuals from interest and other yields from savings on deposit accounts. Dividends (and other yields from securities or partnerships) from limited liability companies or limited partnerships, profit shares from silent partnerships, and interest from deposit certificates and bonds paid by a Czech resident entity to a resident or nonresident individual are all subject to withholding tax of 15%.

Dividends and interest received from foreign sources form part of an individual's taxable income only if the individual is considered Czech tax resident. Individuals can credit foreign tax paid on dividends and interest received from abroad against their Czech tax liability based on the relevant double taxation treaty. Credit relief is not given for the "underlying" tax, that is, tax imposed on the profits of the company from which a dividend is paid.

In respect of interest income paid within the EU, the rules of the savings directive must be followed.

Deductions

Business deductions/No deductions are available from income from employment. Sums received by way of reimbursement of expenses incurred in connection with employment are exempt from tax, provided they do not exceed the statutory limits. Private entrepreneurs may deduct ordinary business expenses.

Nonbusiness deductions/Necessary expenses incurred in the earning of income from sources other than trading sources can be deducted from the income earned. There are no standard deductions. For certain categories of income a fixed percentage of gross income can be claimed as a deduction instead of actual expenditures. Employees' mandatory social and health insurance contributions are deductible from employment income. Donations to Czech organizations for the purpose of financing science, education, culture, and so on, are deductible up to a maximum of 10% of total taxable income, provided the total value of the donations exceeds 2% of the tax base or is at least CZK1,000.

Personal allowances/A basic allowance of CZK38,040 per annum is available to all individuals. A further CZK21,720 per annum is available to taxpayers supporting their spouse in a joint home, provided the spouse's income is less than CZK38,040 per annum. An allowance of CZK25,560 per dependent child is available. Further allowances are available for students and disabled people. The allowances are deducted from the tax base. The interest paid on a mortgage loan or a loan provided from a housing savings plan can be also deducted from the tax base in a maximum amount of CZK300,000 per annum. Spousal and child allowances are available to all Czech tax residents, as well as to nonresidents whose Czech-source income is at least 90% of their worldwide income.

Tax credits

Based on Czech domestic tax legislation, when eliminating double taxation of income from abroad, the provisions of double taxation treaties concluded by the Czech Republic are to be followed.

Other taxes

Social security taxes/Health and social security contributions must be paid if an individual is employed by a Czech company. Secondees working in the Czech Republic for a foreign employers may also be subject to social security and health insurance contributions in the Czech Republic if the bilateral social security treaty or EU regulations so stipulate. For 2004, Czech health insurance and social security contribution rates are 12.5% (for the employee) and 35% (for the employer) of the employee's gross salary, with no ceiling. Entrepreneurs contribute a percentage of other income.

Social security contributions provide funding for three separate funds: pensions, unemployment benefits, and sickness, together with other benefits. Entrepreneurs can choose whether or not to contribute to the sickness fund.

Local taxes on income/There are no local taxes on income.

Tax administration

Returns/A tax return must be filed by March 31 following the calendar year-end. The deadline is extended to June 30 if the return is prepared and filed by an authorized tax adviser under a power of attorney, notice of which must be sent to the relevant tax authority on or before March 31. Husbands and wives must file separate returns.

A tax return need not be filed if all income received has been subjected to tax at source in the Czech Republic. This applies if employment income paid by a Czech employer through local payroll is the only source of income. Furthermore, a tax return need not be filed if income other than employment income does not exceed CZK6,000.

Payment of tax/Income tax is withheld monthly at source from income from employment for employees of a Czech company or branch and for employees of a foreign company assigned to work in the Czech branch of that foreign company. The Czech law also contains a deemed-employer rule whereby an employee of a foreign company who performs work for, and takes orders from, a Czech individual or Czech company may be seen as an employee for payroll withholding purposes irrespective of the legal employment arrangements. Unless the relevant double taxation treaty provides otherwise, nonresident individuals working in the Czech

Republic (e.g., consultants) who are not employees will be subject to 25% withholding by the Czech entity/person paying for the services.

Generally, individuals are responsible for making payments of tax in advance on the basis of prior-year liability. This also applies to the employment income of foreigners assigned to the Czech Republic by a foreign employer and whose salary is not subject to Czech payroll tax advance payments.

Tax rates

The 2004 tax rates are as follows.

Taxable income		Tax on	Percentage
Over	**Not over**	**Column 1**	**on excess**
(Column 1)			
0	CZK 109,200	—	15
CZK 109,200	218,400	CZK 16,380	20
218,400	331,200	38,220	25
331,200		66,420	32

INDIVIDUAL TAX CALCULATION

Calendar year ended December 31, 2004

Tax computation 1

Assumptions

The individual is a foreigner who is employed by a non–Czech-resident employer and who is assigned to work in the Czech Republic for a period of more than 183 days in a calendar year. The individual is married, supports a spouse and two children, and is considered to be a Czech tax resident. No social security contribution liability arises. Accommodation is provided directly by the employer.

Computation of tax

Income from employment:		
Salary	2,245,000	
Company car (12% of purchase price of 800,000)	96,000	CZK 2,341,000
Less:		
Personal allowance	38,040	
Spouse allowance	21,720	
Child allowance (2 children)	51,120	110,880
Taxable income		CZK 2,230,120
Rounding		CZK 2,230,100
Tax due (2,230,100 – 331,200) x 32% + 66,420		CZK 674,068

Tax computation 2

Assumptions

The individual is a foreigner who is employed by a Czech-resident employer. The individual is married, supports a spouse and two children, and is considered to be a Czech tax resident. The individual is liable to Czech social security and health insurance. Accommodation is provided directly by the employer. The individual keeps his main house abroad.

Computation of tax

Income from employment:		
Salary	2,245,000	
Company car (12% of purchase price of 800,000)	96,000	CZK 2,341,000
Less:		
Social security and health insurance (12.5% of salary)	280,625	
Personal allowance	38,040	
Spouse allowance	21,720	
Child allowance (2 children)	51,120	391,505
Taxable income		CZK 1,949,495
Rounding		CZK 1,949,400
Tax due (1,949,400 – 331,200) x 32% + 66,420		CZK 584,244

Note:

Exchange rate of the koruna at December 31, 2003: US$1 = CZK25.654.

Denmark

PwC contact

For additional information on taxation in Denmark, contact:

Poul-Erik Skou Larsen
PricewaterhouseCoopers
Strandvejen 44
DK-2900 Hellerup, Denmark
Telephone: (45) 39 45 39 45
Fax: (45) 39 45 99 87
e-mail: psl@pwc.dk

Significant developments

There have been no significant tax or regulatory developments in the past year.

Territoriality and residence

Danish tax legislation distinguishes between full and limited tax liability. The main criteria are residence, length of stay, place of work, employer's residence, and type of income, as described below. Citizenship does not affect Danish tax liability.

Individuals are subject to full tax liability when they (1) take up residence or (2) stay in Denmark without taking up residence when the stay exceeds six consecutive months interrupted only by short stays abroad (and then as from the day of arrival). An individual subject to full tax liability in Denmark is taxed on worldwide income and gains received or accrued.

Individuals are subject to limited tax liability on Danish-source income. Dividends are taxed separately.

Separate rules apply to contract labor and individuals participating in oil and gas exploration activities.

Gross income

Employee gross income/All remuneration from employment, whether in cash or in kind, is subject to tax when the employee has obtained a legal right to the remuneration, regardless of where payment is made and regardless of whether remitted. The liability extends to any living or housing allowance and any reimbursement of tax or other personal liability, whether paid directly to an employee or borne by the employer on the employee's behalf.

Payments to an employee for expenses of travel, entertainment, or any other service to be performed on behalf of the employer are taxable only to the extent that they are not actually expended in the performance of the service. Special rules apply for free housing provided by the employer and some work-related benefits in kind less than DKK4,900.

Capital gains and investment income/Taxable gains and investment income are added to taxable income. Certain allowances are available. Profit on the sale of a private house in which the owner has lived and that is situated on property having an area of less than, normally, 1,400 square meters is tax exempt. Gains on the sale of shares in a quoted company are exempt if the shares have been owned for at least three years and the shareholder's total shareholding of all quoted shares for at least three years has been worth less than DKK133,700 (DKK267,300 for a married couple). The limit is adjusted every year.

The taxable income of an individual subject to full tax liability includes interest, cash dividends, profits from gains on sale of shares owned less than three years, rents, royalties, professional fees, pensions, annuities, and alimony from all sources, wherever located, subject to any limitation that may be imposed under a tax treaty.

Dividends received from both domestic and foreign companies by resident individuals are subject to income tax. Dividends from domestic companies and gains on sale of shares owned at least three years of up to DKK42,400 (DKK84,800 for a married couple) are taxed at 28%. Dividends and gains on the sale of shares in excess of this amount must be reported and are taxed at a rate of 43%.

Exit taxation applies on shareholders leaving Denmark. However, the tax applies only if the shareholder has been subject to full Danish taxation for at least five years within the last ten years before the cessation of tax liability. The rules apply to both Danish and foreign shares. To avoid the burden of paying tax on an unrealized profit, permission can be obtained to postpone payment until the taxpayer has actually disposed of the shares.

Exit taxation also applies for individuals having options, bonds, certain pension plans, and so on. Special rules apply to counteract the avoidance of taxation by individuals leaving Denmark; (e.g., persons with limited tax liability and nontaxable persons who cancel a Danish pension scheme pay a special tax of 60% of the insurance value).

For the year in which tax liability ceases and the previous four years, supplementary taxation is also imposed in respect of extraordinary increases in payments to a pension scheme.

Deductions

Business deductions/An employee is entitled to deduct traveling expenses (in accordance with special rules), subscriptions to professional associations, necessary business literature, tools of trade, and so on (exceeding DKK4,900 per calendar year).

As per January 1, 2004, an employment allowance has been introduced for people engaged in active employment. The allowance amounts to 2.5% of the employment income; however, it cannot exceed DKK6,000. It is also possible to deduct travel expenses between home and work according to schematic rules. If the total distance per day is less than 25 kilometers, no deduction can be made.

Expatriates taking up temporary residence in Denmark may be granted an annual allowance for extra costs of living equal to the lesser of (1) DKK8,000 plus 5% of gross earned income or (2) 25% of gross earned income. This allowance is granted for the first two years; it will be granted only if an expatriate intends to stay in Denmark for no more than three years. It is also a condition that the assignee continues to be paid by the foreign employer.

Special tax legislation covers foreigners who sign contracts for work in Denmark after June 1, 1991. According to this legislation, they can apply for a tax of only 25% on gross income, provided they are tax resident, have a Danish employer, and their monthly income after ATP (*arbejdsmarkedets tillægspension*—the supplementary earnings-related pension scheme) and labor market contribution exceeds DKK56,000. However, taking into account the 9% labor market (i.e., social) contribution (see below), the amount before ATP and this 9% tax is DKK61,614. If the individual remains covered under another social security system during the stay in Denmark, this has an influence on the qualifying gross income. Special rules apply for researchers.

The tax rate of 25% applies for the first 36 months. The employee's stay in Denmark may be longer, but after the 36-month period the employee's income is taxed at ordinary rates.

In some cases, retroactive taxation with normal rates will come into play if the stay is prolonged.

Nonbusiness expenses/An individual subject to full tax liability can deduct all interest paid and contributions or premiums paid under certain pension schemes with a Danish pension fund or insurance company. Life insurance premiums paid to a foreign insurance company cannot be deducted, unless a tax treaty provides otherwise. Employee contributions to social security funds are withheld from salary payment and can be deducted, provided the requirements are fulfilled.

Personal allowances/A personal allowance of DKK36,800 is granted that has the effect of reducing income tax payable. The allowance is granted to each individual, but where a spouse cannot utilize the whole personal allowance, the balance is transferred to the other spouse.

With regard to individuals who are subject to limited tax liability, the personal allowance is granted only for salaries and pensions. A special allowance of DKK36,800 is granted for salaries subject to limited tax liability if the spouse is not entitled to a personal allowance.

Tax credits

An individual is entitled to deduct foreign income taxes paid or accrued on foreign-source income from the Danish tax payable up to a maximum of Danish tax paid on that part of the taxable income that is foreign-source income. Relief according to the double taxation treaties can be claimed if their provisions are more favorable.

Personal allowances take the form of tax credits.

Other taxes

Social security contributions/Social security contributions consist of labor market contributions (AM-*bidrag*/*arbejdsmarkedsbidrag*), special pension contributions (SP-*bidrag*/*særlig pensionsopsparing*), supplementary old-age pension contributions (ATP-*bidrag*), and work injury insurance.

The AM- and SP-*bidrag* to be paid by the employee is 9% of gross salary, and the ATP-*bidrag* to be paid by the employee is DKK895 per annum. The ATP-*bidrag* to be paid by the employer is DKK1,790 per annum. The work injury insurance is paid by the employer.

All social security contributions are tax deductible.

For banks and other financial institutions, a special payroll tax of 9.13% of gross salary must be paid.

Local taxes on income/County and municipal taxes are levied at flat rates. State and local taxes on income are not deductible for tax purposes.

Wealth tax/From 1997 the wealth tax has been abolished. However, individuals must still fill out asset explanations if requested by the tax authorities.

Real estate/Property value tax amounts to 1% of the market value of property up to DKK3,040,000 (2003) and 3% of the market value exceeding DKK3,040,000. However, if the property is purchased no later than July 1, 1998, a deduction is granted. Property value tax is charged on both Danish and foreign properties.

Tax administration

Returns/Husbands and wives file separate returns for the income year. Taxpayers receive a preprinted tax return in March, containing information that the tax authorities have already obtained from employers or financial institutions (for instance). If the tax return is not correct, it must be corrected, signed and filed no later than May 1.

Taxpayers with more complicated tax returns (most expatriates) must file tax returns no later than July 1.

The tax year for individuals is the calendar year.

When tax liability ceases as a result of leaving Denmark, an income tax return covering the period from the end of the last income year to the date tax liability ceases must be filed before the end of the calendar month following the month in which tax liability ceases. Postponements can normally be obtained upon application.

Payment of tax/There is income tax withholding from salaries (A-tax). For other types of income, an advance tax (B-tax) is paid in ten equal installments during the income year.

Tax rates

Tax rates in effect for calendar year 2004 are detailed below.

Personal income is taxed at a marginal rate up to 59%. Net capital income is taxed at a rate up to 59%, and negative net capital income and other allowances have a tax value of typically 32%, depending on local tax rates. People with independent businesses may choose a special tax system, whereby all business income is taxed at 30% as long as the income is kept in the business.

Income and allowances are divided into the three categories shown below.

1. Personal income (salary less pension contributions).
2. Capital income (interest income less interest expenses and net taxable capital gain).
3. Other allowances (also deductible in total taxable income).

Local income taxes are calculated on taxable income at flat rates ranging from 27% to 35%.

On income/State income tax is calculated as shown below.

1. Bottom tax—The aggregate of personal income and positive net capital income is taxed at 5.50%.

   Plus
2. Middle tax—The aggregate of personal income and positive net capital income in excess of DKK216,800 for a single taxpayer and DKK433,600 for a married couple is taxed at 6%.

   Plus
3. Top tax—The tax base for the top tax of 15% is the sum of all personal income and positive capital income. The tax is levied on the amount in excess of

DKK304,800. Unutilized portions of this amount cannot be transferred to the taxpayer's spouse.

The combined top marginal income tax rate cannot exceed 59%.

Income and expenses are annualized if the tax return covers a period shorter than one calendar year.

The tax rates for nonresidents subject to limited tax liability are identical to the state tax rates for resident individuals, together with a local tax rate of 32%. This gives a tax rate of 37.5% for salary income up to DKK216,800, 43.5% from DKK216,800 to DKK304,800, and 59% above DKK304,800.

On wealth/Wealth tax is no longer imposed.

INDIVIDUAL TAX CALCULATION

Calendar year 2004

Assumptions

A married couple with two children resident in Denmark in 2004. The husband, who earns all the income, is employed by a Danish employer. A composite local tax rate of 32.1% has been assumed. The employee is assumed to be covered by the Danish social security system. Total social security tax amounts to DKK895 per year plus the 9% social contribution withheld from the gross salary, all borne by the employee.

The tax consequences where the husband is temporarily employed by a Danish company are also indicated, assuming the employment conditions meet the requirements for the advantageous 25% taxation of gross income mentioned above.

Tax computation

Personal income

Salary and taxable benefits		DKK 1,000,000
Less:		
Social security taxes paid by employee	895	
Contribution to Danish pension scheme	24,000	
9% social contribution (on 975,105)	87,759	112,654
		DKK 887,346

Capital income (net)

Interest income	60,000	
Less—Interest expense	(30,000)	DKK 30,000

Other deductible expenses

Employment allowance	6,000	
Extra cost of commuting between home and place of work	10,000	DKK 16,000

Taxable income

Personal income	DKK 887,346
Capital income	30,000
Other deductible expenses	(16,000)
Taxable income	DKK 901,346

Taxes thereon

Taxable income (from above)		DKK 901,346
State income tax:		
Bottom tax—5.5% of personal and positive capital income	50,454	
Middle tax (6% of personal and capital income above 433,600)	29,025	
Top tax (15% of personal income plus capital income exceeding 304,800)	91,882	DKK 171,361
Less—Tax value of personal allowance for husband and wife—5.5% of 73,600		(4,048)
Total state tax		DKK 167,313
Local tax—32.1% of taxable income		DKK 289,332
Less—Tax value of personal allowance for husband and wife—32.1% of 73,600		(23,626)
Total local tax		DKK 265,706
Total tax payable		DKK 443,019
Social security tax paid by employee:		
ATP	895	
9% tax on salary	87,759	88,654
Social security tax paid for by pension funds (8% tax on ATP and pension contributions) (1)		1,992
Total tax expense (2)		DKK 523,665

Notes:

1. The 9% contribution is calculated on gross income. However, if the individual has a pension agreement with the employer, only 8% is withheld by the pension fund from the employee's pension contributions.
2. If the employee were covered by the 25% taxation of gross income, the total tax would be DKK221,836 plus social security charge of DKK895 plus 9% social security contribution of DKK87,759.
3. Exchange rate of the krone at December 31, 2003: US$1 = DKK5.9576.

PwC contacts

For additional information on taxation in the Dominican Republic, contact:

Freddy Perez
Ramón Ortega
Andrea Paniagua
PricewaterhouseCoopers
Lope de Vega esq. John F. Kennedy
Edificio Banco Nova Scotia, Third Floor
Santo Domingo, República Dominicana
Telephone: (809) 567 7741
Fax: (809) 541 1210
e-mail: freddy.perez@do.pwc.com
ramon.ortega@do.pwc.com
andrea.paniagua@do.pwc.com

Significant developments

There have been no significant tax or regulatory developments in the past year.

Territoriality and residence

The Dominican Republic follows a territorial concept for the determination of taxable income. Only Dominican-source income is subject to tax. Residents and nonresidents are taxed differently.

Persons are resident in the Dominican Republic if they live in the country for more than 182 days during a calendar year.

Gross income

Employee gross income/Broadly, the entire remuneration for personal services rendered in the Dominican Republic is subject to income tax. However, the employer is liable to pay tax (on a monthly basis) on compensation in kind, as set forth by the Tax Code. Such compensation includes, inter alia, housing, living allowances, and automobiles.

Capital gains and investment income/Capital gains are taxed at a rate of 25%. Interests from time deposits, savings accounts, and other sources that are received from financial institutions in the Dominican Republic are tax-exempt. Cash dividends to resident and nonresident individuals are subject to a withholding tax of 25%. Foreign investment and financial income of Dominican residents are subject to tax after the third year or taxable period of being considered as residents.

Deductions

Business deductions/In general, all expenses incurred in the production of taxable income are deductible.

Nonbusiness expenses/Nonbusiness expenses are not deductible.

Personal allowances/Residents are entitled to a standard deduction of DOP16,456 per month (DOP197,470 annually). Christmas bonuses are tax-exempt.

Other taxes

Social security taxes/A new Social Security Law was passed on May 9, 2001, and came into force in February 2003. The law introduces the following three insurance schemes.

1. Old-Age, Disability, and Survivorship Insurance.
2. Family Health Insurance.
3. Occupational Hazard Insurance.

Old-Age, Disability, and Survivorship Insurance replaces the former pension regime. It uses a capitalization system for dependent employees, whereby social security contributions are accumulated in individual accounts belonging to every affiliate. Those accounts will be managed by public and private entities called *"Administradoras de Fondos de Pensiones"* (AFPs).

The scope of the system covers legal residents in the Dominican Republic (nationals and foreigners) and Dominicans residing abroad.

Both the employer and the employee finance the system. The base contribution is 10% of the quotable salary of the employee, up to a ceiling of 20 minimum salaries in the case of pensions and 10 minimum salaries in the case of the family health insurance.

Law 87-01 provides a financing schedule for the next five years. For year 2004 the contributions are as follows:

1. Old-Age, Disability, and Survivorship Insurance—The employee's contribution amounts to 2.13%, with 5.37% to be contributed by the employer.
2. Family Health Insurance—The amounts to be contributed are 2.7% by the employee and 6.3% by the employer.
3. The Occupational Hazard Insurance—Totally covered by the employer, who pays an average contribution of 1.2% of the applicable wages.

All the aforementioned percentages are calculated on the quotable salary of the employee.

Contributions to the social security system (Pension Plans) came into force on May 9, 2003. Contributions to Occupational Hazard Insurance came into force on March 1, 2004. Contributions to Family Health Insurance are scheduled to come into force by April 1, 2004.

Technical education tax/A payroll-based contribution is imposed on employees and employers toward the financing of a program for the technical instruction and training of workers. The contribution of employers is 1% of total monthly payroll; for employees, it is 0.5% of bonuses received.

Other taxes on income/No other taxes are payable on income.

Tax administration

Returns/Spouses are required to file separate income tax returns covering their respective incomes. Income from property held in common is included in the return of the husband. Individuals are required to file a personal tax only when income from sources different from the salaries, wages, and bonuses (where the employer withholds tax) is received.

Payments of tax/Employers are required to withhold income tax on salaries, wages, and bonuses. Only a personal standard allowance of DOP197,470 yearly is allowed for withholding purposes. This standard allowance is adjustable per year based on the country's inflation.

Individuals and undivided estates advance income tax for the current year equal to 100% of the income tax calculated for the precedent fiscal year, to be distributed as follows: sixth month—50%, ninth month—30%, and twelfth month—20%. For income arising from trade activities, the payments are made following the mechanism applied to corporations.

Tax rates

Basic tax/Individuals pay tax on the excess of DOP197,470 received. Personal income is taxed at the following rates.

Taxable income		Tax on	Percentage
Over	Not over	Column 1	on excess
(Column 1)			
0	DOP 197,470	—	0
DOP 197,470	329,118	—	15
329,118	493,676	DOP 19,747.18	20
493,676		52,658.78	25

INDIVIDUAL TAX CALCULATION

Calendar year 2004; Income year 2003

Assumptions

Resident alien living in the Dominican Republic; husband and wife, two children; only one spouse is allowed to earn all the income.

Tax computation

Salary		DOP	900,000
Interest (other than nontaxable interest)			90,000
Christmas bonus			75,000
Total gross income			1,065,000
Less:			
Personal standard deduction	197,470		
Christmas bonus (maximum)	75,000		272,470
Taxable income		DOP	792,530
Income tax thereon		DOP	127,373

Note:

Official exchange rate of the peso at January 1, 2003: US$1 = RD$20.80.

PwC contact

For additional information on taxation in Ecuador, contact:

Luciano Almeida
Price Waterhouse & Co.
Carchi 702 y Av. 9 de Octubre. Third floor
PO BOX 09-01-5820
Guayaquil, Ecuador
Telephone: (593) (4) /228 1555
Fax: (593) (4) 239 3471
Quito, Ecuador
Telephone: (593) (2) 256 4142/223 2632
Fax: (593) (2) 2567 096
e-mail: luciano.almeida@ec.pw-co.com

Significant developments

A new tax table is in force for individual income tax calculation applicable for the fiscal year 2004.

Territoriality and residence

Ecuador currently taxes its citizens and foreigners mostly on their Ecuador-source income. Ecuador-source income is defined as any income derived from activities executed in Ecuador, regardless of where the income is received. It also includes income obtained abroad by Ecuador-resident individuals and corporations, whether local or foreign.

Foreigners are subject to tax on their Ecuador-source income regardless of their domicile or place of residence. Foreigners residing in Ecuador for a short period of time (less than six months) are subject to a flat 25% income tax on income received from local sources, which is withheld at source. Payments made to foreigners occasionally working in Ecuador, when not charged to an Ecuadorian company or branch of a foreign entity, do not give rise to income tax. Foreigners with resident visas are subject to income tax on any earnings and are not entitled to exclusion of income for periods of temporary absence from Ecuador.

Gross income

For personal income tax purposes, it is necessary to differentiate between two main contractual relationships that may exist between a company and a person: labor and professional fee-based relationships.

A labor relationship exists where a person provides personal and legitimate services to a company under the provisions of the Labor Code. The employee is then under a labor contract and included in the company's payroll, thus receiving a fixed monthly salary plus fringe benefits.

A professional fee-based relationship exists when an individual provides professional services to a company on a freelance basis or under a civil contract. This individual is not included in the company's payroll and is not subject to regulations established in the Labor Code. Usually this contractual relationship is used for independent contractors. Their remuneration will always be denominated as "fees."

Employee gross income/Residents (national or foreign) are taxed on their total labor compensation, net of social security contributions. Total compensation includes any payments in cash, kind or services made by the employer exclusive of certain few statutory social benefits. Allowances such as cost of living, car, vacation travel, housing, and utilities are considered taxable.

In cases where the employer pays personal income taxes and social security contributions on account of an employee (net salaries), the income tax liability on the net salary is added only once to the total income to arrive at a taxable base, and the social security deduction is not allowed.

Independent professional gross income/Residents (national or foreign) are taxed on the total fees invoiced. Under the new social security law, professionals will be required to pay social security contributions.

Capital gains and investment income/Occasional capital gains (defined as those obtained in the sale of real estate and stock transactions) are exempt from income tax. Other financial investment income forms part of an individual's taxable income. Dividends received from local corporations and interest received from savings account deposits are tax exempt.

Deductions

Business deductions/Expenses incurred in order to generate, maintain, or improve taxable Ecuadorian-source income are in principle deductible. For those individuals under a fee-based relationship, only business deductions can be justified.

Nonbusiness expenses/Social security contributions are the only deductions allowed against income arising from employment. Independent professionals are also allowed such deduction.

Personal allowances/An annual personal allowance of $7,200 is built into the current progressive tax table, which means that individuals pay income tax only on income over $7,200.

Tax credits

Credit is available for income taxes paid in another country on income generated abroad that is deemed taxable in Ecuador. The amount of tax credit allowed is limited to the amount equal to the Ecuadorian tax due on such income (a maximum of 25%).

Other taxes

Social security contributions/The current employee's personal contribution to the social security system is 9.35% of remuneration arising from employment (except certain statutory social benefits received). Special rates apply to employees working on special sectors of the economy. Social security contributions are deductible, except when borne by the employer.

Individuals under a professional fee-based relationship are required to pay social security contributions at the rate of 17.50%.

Local taxes on income/There are no local (provincial, county, or municipal) taxes on income.

Value-added tax/No VAT applies on employment services under a labor relationship. Personal services provided under a professional fee contract relationship are subject to VAT at 12%, which, when provided to companies, is subject to withholding by those companies.

Professionals are required to file VAT returns.

Tax administration

Returns/Annual tax returns need not be filed if the taxpayer's income does not exceed the taxable base (i.e., $7,200); the employer's annual withholding return is considered the employee's return in such cases. If taxable income is earned from other sources, or from more than one employer, the employer must consolidate both incomes in a single annual return.

Individuals who end their economic activity prior to the end of the fiscal year are required to file their corresponding income tax return upon termination of activity. Once this return is filed, the individual must cancel the Taxpayer Identification Number (TIN) connected with the activity within 30 days of termination.

The fiscal year is the calendar year.

Husbands and wives must file separate returns on their separate employment income. Other joint income, if any, must be split with each spouse declaring half.

Payment of tax/In the case of employees, there is mandatory monthly withholding by the employer as long as the total annual net income exceeds the taxable base of $7,200. Independent professionals are required to make advance tax payments equivalent to 50% of the previous year's tax less withholdings for that year. These tax advances payments are made in July and September.

Tax rates

The tax table applicable in Ecuador as of January 1, 2004 is as follows.

Taxable income		Tax on	Percentage
Over	Not over	base	on excess
(Base)			
0	$ 7,200	—	0
$ 7,200	14,400	—	5
14,400	28,800	$ 360	10
28,800	43,200	1,800	15
43,200	57,600	3,960	20
57,600		6,840	25

No other surtaxes or additional taxes apply.

INDIVIDUAL TAX CALCULATION

Calendar year 2004

Assumptions

Foreign person residing in Ecuador under labor relationship for an entire calendar year. Remuneration does not include Ecuadorian statutory social benefits. Taxpayer pays own social security contributions and income tax.

Tax computation

Remuneration		$ 60,000
—Statutory social benefits:		
Salary components ($8 per month)	96	
Christmas bonus (13th salary)	5,000	
Educational bonus (14th salary)	135	
Interest income in saving accounts (nontaxable)	1,000	
Capital gains, other than occasional	500	6,731
Total income		$ 66,731
Less:		
Exempt income	1,000	
Social security contributions (60,000 x 9.35%)	5,610	6,610
Taxable base (i.e., taxable work income)		$ 60,121
Income tax on first 57,600	6,840	
Income tax on excess at 25%	1,630	
Total income tax		$ 7,470
Less—Tax withheld by employer (estimate)		(7,042)
Tax due		$ 428

Reconciliation

Total income from all sources	$ 66,731
Total income tax	(7,470)
Total contributions to social security	(5,610)
Net income	$ 53,651

Notes:

1. At the moment that the company shares on its profits (statutory profit sharing) with its employee such profit sharing will become part of the person's taxable income.
2. The monetary unit is the U.S. dollar.

PwC contacts

For additional information on taxation in Estonia, contact:

Aare Kurist
Tax Department
AS PricewaterhouseCoopers
Pärnu mnt 15
10141 Tallinn, Estonia
Telephone: (372) (6) 141 800
Fax: (372) (6) 141 900
e-mail: aare.kurist@ee.pwc.com

Copies of all documents/inquiries to be sent to:

Cameron G. Greaves (TLS Baltic States Leader)
PricewaterhouseCoopers SIA
K. Valdemara 19
Riga, LV-1010, Latvia
Telephone: (371) 7094400
Fax: (371) 7830055
e-mail: cameron.greaves@lv.pwc.com

Significant developments

- According to a new amendment to the Income Tax Law, it is expected that the income tax rate (which is currently a flat 26%) will be reduced to 24% in 2005; to 22% in 2006; and to 20% in 2007.
- From January 1, 2004, certain foreign employment income derived by residents is exempt from taxation.

Territoriality and residence

An individual who is a resident of Estonia is liable to tax on worldwide income, irrespective of the origin of the income. Nonresidents are taxed on their Estonian-source income. Individuals are considered residents of Estonia if they have a permanent place of residence, their stay during any 12-month period is equal to or exceeds 183 days or they are Estonian public servants who are sent abroad on assignment. For the purposes of determining the number of days, any part of a day counts as a full day.

Gross income

Employee gross income/Taxable income includes employment and private business income and income from other sources. Income from other sources not exempt from taxation includes pensions and scholarships, alimony received, interest, royalties, rental income, foreign dividends, certain insurance proceeds, and gains from the disposal of assets. Taxable income also includes the income of a legal entity (controlled foreign corporation—CFC) located in a low-tax jurisdiction.

Certain state pensions, nonstate scholarships, gains from the sale of a resident taxpayer's own residential dwelling and the first sale of land acquired in the process of property reform, together with winnings from certain lotteries, among other items, are excluded from gross income. Benefits in kind (e.g., residential housing, company car) are taxable for the employer and are not included in the taxable income of the individual.

There are no special taxation rules for expatriates.

Exemption for foreign employment income and directors fees/Foreign employment income and directors' fees derived abroad by an Estonian resident are not subject to income tax in Estonia if all of the following conditions are met:

1. The individual has stayed abroad for employment purposes for at least 183 days during any 12-month period.

   and
2. Such income was taxable in the foreign country. The taxability of the income must be proven by a certificate stating the amount of the foreign income tax withheld or paid (even if such amount is nil).

Although some foreign employment income may end up not bearing any tax, it must be declared for information purposes in the recipient's resident Estonian individual income tax return.

Capital gains and investment income/Capital gains realized by resident individuals are generally taxed as ordinary income. However, the following gains are tax exempt for resident individuals:

1. Gains from the sale of a resident taxpayer's own immovable property, including any dwelling place that was used as a permanent or primary place of residence by the taxpayer until its sale or that has been transferred to the taxpayer's ownership through restitution of illegally expropriated property.
2. Gains from the sale of a resident taxpayer's own immovable property, including any dwelling place that has been transferred to the taxpayer's ownership through privatization with preemption (provided the immovable property is under two hectares).
3. Gains from the sale of a summer cottage or garden house, provided the taxpayer has owned it for more than two years and the size of the associated land is under 0.25 hectares.
4. Gains from the disposal of land granted as restitution to an individual in the course of property reform.

Gains derived by nonresidents from the disposal of property located in Estonia or registered in any Estonian register, as well as the disposal of rights in real estate, are generally subject to income tax at 26%. However, gains from the disposal of shares of Estonian corporate entities are subject to 26% Estonian tax only if the nonresident has disposed of 10% or more of the shares in the company and 75% of its assets are represented by real estate or buildings.

Dividends received by a resident are not taxed if they have been received from a company registered in Estonia. In addition, from January 1, 2004, the exemption on dividend income has been extended to dividends from foreign companies, if the underlying corporate tax has been paid or tax has been withheld from these dividends by the foreign company distributing them.

Interest from resident credit institutions and Estonian branches of nonresident credit institutions (from May 1, 2004, also from credit institutions resident in EU member states) is exempt from income tax. From May 1, 2004, interest paid to nonresidents (other than entities in low-tax jurisdictions) is expected to be exempt from Estonian withholding tax.

Deductions

Business deductions/Only business-related expenses for individuals engaged in business and registered as such with the tax authorities are deductible. These individuals must follow the cash basis in accounting for their income and expenditure.

Nonbusiness deductions/Alimony paid during the tax period can be deducted from taxable income, provided the alimony is taxable to the recipient under Estonian law.

Interest on a loan and/or a financial lease for the purpose of acquiring a single-residence building or apartment is deductible if paid to a resident credit institution or to an Estonian branch of a nonresident credit institution (from May 1, 2004, also to credit institutions resident in EU member states, as well as to financial institutions belonging to the same group) during the taxation period.

Residents have the right to deduct from their taxable income interest on student loans and the costs of their own or their under-26-year-old dependents' training in certified educational institutions (or alternatively, that of any under-26-year-old permanent resident of Estonia).

Residents may deduct from taxable income documented gifts and charitable contributions made to nonprofit associations and foundations listed by the government, to public universities and to cultural, sports, educational, or social security institutions belonging to the state or local authorities. Joining and membership fees of trade unions registered as nonprofit associations or foundations are deductible. The total deductions of such gifts, charitable contributions and joining and membership fees may not exceed 5% of the individual's income for the tax period after the deduction of other allowable expenses.

The deduction of interest, education expenses, charitable contributions, and trade union membership fees cannot exceed the lesser of (a) 50% of the taxable income for the tax year or (b) a fixed amount of EEK100,000 (EEK50,000 from January 1, 2005).

Premiums to certain annuity pension schemes and expenses incurred to buy the shares of approved resident pension funds may be deducted from taxable income. Such deduction is limited to 15% of income (after business deductions, if any) derived during the tax year.

Unemployment insurance contributions and contributions to compulsory accumulative pension schemes made during the tax year are deductible from the taxable income of a resident individual, without any limits.

General deduction/Annual income of up to EEK16,800 is not taxable. The annual tax-exempt basic allowance for resident individuals will be increased to EEK21,600 in 2005 and to EEK24,000 in 2006.

One of the resident parents with more than two children may take an additional general deduction (EEK16,800) for each additional child.

Starting from May 1, 2004, the deductions from taxable income allowed to residents will also become available to nonresident individuals who are tax resident in any EU member state, provided they derive at least 75% of their taxable income during the tax period from Estonia and submit a personal income tax return as an Estonian resident individual. Taxable income for the purposes of the preceding sentence will be deemed to be income before taking into account the deductions as determined under the laws of the respective EU member state.

Tax credits

For Estonian residents, income taxes paid abroad as final tax on income are allowed as a credit against national tax payable in Estonia. The tax credit is limited to 26% (it is expected that this limit will be reduced to 24% in 2005, 22% in 2006, and 20% in 2007) of the foreign income.

Other taxes

Social security taxes/Employers must pay social security contributions for their employees at a rate of 33%. Individuals engaged in business must make personal social security contributions.

Unemployment insurance/From January 1, 2002, both employers and employees are obliged to pay unemployment insurance contributions on employment income at the rates of 0.5% and 1%, respectively.

Compulsory accumulative pension scheme/Resident employees born after December 31, 1982 are obliged to join the compulsory accumulative pension scheme and make contributions at 2% from gross salary from July 1, 2002. For resident employees born before 1983 joining the pension scheme is voluntary, but after joining, it becomes compulsory and employees may not subsequently leave the scheme. In addition to the 2% contribution made by the employee, 4 percentage points of the social security contribution payable by the employer (33%) will be transferred to the employee's pension account. Both unemployment insurance contributions and contributions to compulsory accumulative pension scheme are withheld from employee's salary by the employer.

Local taxes on income/There are no local taxes on income.

Tax administration

Returns/A resident individual's annual tax return must be filed by March 31. Resident husbands and wives are treated as individual taxpayers, unless they apply to have their incomes combined. Residents are not required to file an annual tax return if they have received only employment income or health insurance benefits that have been subject to Estonian withholding tax at source.

A nonresident is obliged to file an income tax return generally by March 31 following the year of taxation on gains from the disposal of property and on certain types of income (wages, rent, royalties, interest, pensions, scholarships, awards, and benefits) when these have been received other than under deduction of withholding tax. Gains from the disposal of real estate, buildings, or apartments must be declared within one month of the transfer. Nonresidents are not required to submit tax returns for income that has been subjected to final withholding tax.

Payment of tax/Income from employment is subject to withholding tax. It is the employer's responsibility to withhold taxes and to transfer them to the local tax authorities without delay. The withholding calculation is based on the rates established for the taxation of annual income. The amount withheld is credited against the employee's annual tax liability.

Final income tax due must be paid by resident individuals to the tax authorities before July 1 following the year of taxation, except the income tax on gains from the disposal of property or business income, which is due by October 1 following the year of taxation.

A nonresident individual must pay final income tax due to the tax authorities along with the submission of the income tax return.

Tax rates

Individual income tax is levied at a flat rate of 26%. According to the new amendment to the Income Tax Law, it is expected that the income tax rate will be reduced to 24% in 2005; to 22% in 2006; and to 20% in 2007.

As noted above, annual income of resident individuals up to EEK16,800 is not taxable.

INDIVIDUAL TAX CALCULATION

Calendar year ending December 31, 2004

Assumptions

This calculation concerns a resident who has tax-exempt income of EEK16,800 per year (together, a married couple would have EEK33,600 of tax-exempt income).

Tax computation

Salary, premium, and other payments	EEK 1,100,000
Other income	20,000
Gross income	1,120,000
Less—Tax-exempt income:	
Nontaxable minimum income	16,800
Unemployment insurance contribution paid by employee	11,000
Income subject to income tax	EEK 1,092,200
Income tax payable	EEK 283,972
Less—Income tax withheld	(278,772)
Additional income tax due	EEK 5,200

Note:

Exchange rate of the Estonian kroon at December 31, 2003: US$1 = EEK12.41.

The kroon is pegged to the Euro at the rate: €1 = EEK15.64664.

Faroe Islands

PwC contact

For additional information on taxation in Faroe Islands, contact:

Ole Guldborg Nielsen
Rasmussen & Weihe
Statsautoriserað grannskoðarafelag, P/F
Á Gladsheyggi
P.O. Box 30
FO–110 Tórshavn
Faroe Islands
Telephone: (298) 35 17 00
Fax: (298) 35 17 01
e-mail: rasmussen@rasmussen.fo

Significant developments

Tax cuts have been made for resident individuals and will come into force from January 1, 2004.

Territoriality and residence

Faroese tax legislation distinguishes between full and limited tax liability. The main criteria are residence, length of stay, place of work, employer's residence, and type of income, as described below. Citizenship does not affect Faroese tax liability.

Individuals are subject to full tax liability when they (1) take up residence or (2) stay in the Faroe Islands without taking up residence when the stay exceeds six consecutive months interrupted only by short stays abroad (and then as from the day of arrival). An individual subject to full tax liability in Faroe Islands is taxed on worldwide income and gains received or accrued. Individuals are subject to limited tax liability on Faroese-situs services and other Faroese-source income. Dividends are taxed separately.

Separate rules apply to contract labor.

With the introduction of the Hydrocarbon Tax Act in 1999, special rules apply for individuals participating in oil and gas exploration activities. Foreign subcontractors (self-employed) and foreign employees engaged in hydrocarbon activities in Faroese territory are subject to pay a final tax of 35.5% (combined 35% tax rate and 0.5% social contributions).

Gross income

The taxable income of an individual subject to full tax liability includes rents, royalties, professional fees, pensions, annuities, and alimony from all sources (wherever located), subject to any limitation that may be imposed under a tax treaty.

Employee gross income/All remuneration from employment, whether in cash or in kind, is subject to tax when the employee has obtained a legal right to the remuneration, regardless of where payment is made and regardless of whether remitted. The liability extends to any living or housing allowance and any reimbursement of tax or other personal liability, whether paid directly to an employee or borne by the employer on behalf of the employee.

Payments to an employee for expenses incurred for travel, entertainment, or any other service to be performed on behalf of the employer are taxable only to the extent that they are not actually expended in the performance of the service. Special rules apply for free housing and other benefits in kind provided by the employer.

Capital gains and investment income/Capital gains and investment income are taxed separately and must be declared on a special self-assessment form. Gains on the sale of bonds and shares, options, debt, and dividends and on interest are not included in ordinary taxable income.

Profit on the sale of a private house owned for more than two years is normally tax exempt.

Capital gains, dividends, and interest are taxed at a fixed tax rate of 35%. Capital losses can only be deducted in the assessment of capital gain. Certain interim provisions apply for shares acquired before November 16, 2001, when the new legislation came into force.

For dividends from Faroese companies or interest from Faroese banks, the tax will be withheld by the company/bank.

Deductions

Business deductions/No business deductions are available to individuals. However, travel expenses will be (partly) reimbursed according to special rules. An application is necessary.

There are no special rules for expatriates taking up temporary residence in the Faroe Islands.

Nonbusiness expenses/An individual subject to full tax liability can deduct contributions or premium paid under certain pension schemes with a pension fund, a bank, or an insurance company. Employee contributions under certain pension schemes are withheld from salary payment and are not considered part of taxable income.

Mortgage or other interest is not deductible. However, according to special rules, part of mortgage interest can be reimbursed, provided the mortgage is obtained for private housing purposes. For 2003 the rate of reimbursement is 40%.

Personal allowances/Single individuals on old-age pension are eligible for an allowance, which is set up so that the basic pension amount will not be taxed. The basic pension amount for an individual in 2003 is DKK50,028. For married people, the basic pension amount is DKK39,756 each. There are also personal allowances for individuals with children under the age of 18. The child allowance ranges from DKK7,500 to DKK11,500 per child—the difference is due to the fact that the municipalities decide part of the child allowance. These allowances are deducted in figuring the computed tax.

Special provisions for fishermen/A special allowance is granted for fishermen. When computing the taxable income, 15% of income is deductible. However, this deduction must not exceed DKK75,000.

Tax credits

An individual is entitled to deduct foreign income taxes paid or accrued on foreign-source income from the Faroese tax payable up to a maximum of Faroese tax paid on the part of the taxable income that is foreign-source income. Relief according to double taxation treaties can be claimed if such provisions are more favorable.

Other taxes

Social security taxes/Social security taxes comprise contributions to a labor market unemployment fund (ALS—*Arbeiðsloysisskipanin*), supplementary old-age pension contributions (AMEG—*Arbeiðsmarknaðareftirlønargrunnur*), and contributions to a maternity fund.

The contributions paid by the employer are computed as a percentage of wages/ salaries and amount to 0.75% to ALS, 0.5% to AMEG, and 0.25% to a maternity fund. Employers are also required to hold accident insurance. All social security contributions are tax deductible for the employer.

The employee contributes 0.75% to ALS, 0.25% to the maternity fund, and 0.5% to AMEG. These employee contributions are nondeductible.

Banks and insurance companies must pay a special social tax of 5% of gross salary. Other value-added tax (VAT)–exempt businesses are taxed at 2.5%. This tax is not deductible.

Local taxes on income/Municipal taxes are levied at flat rates and vary between 13% and 22.5%. State and local taxes are not deductible for tax purposes.

Tax administration

Returns/Husbands and wives file separate returns for the income year. Taxpayers receive a preprinted tax return in February or March containing information that the tax authorities have already obtained from employers or financial institutions. If the tax return is not correct, it must be corrected, signed, and filed no later than March 15.

The tax year for individuals is the calendar year.

Postponements can be obtained upon application, but for no later than August 15.

A separate tax-return must be filed if any income has derived from capital gains.

Payment of tax/Any employer is obliged to pay out all wages and salaries through an authorized "payment office"—in reality, any bank, post office bank, or savings bank in the Faroe Islands. At the time of payment the tax will be computed and withheld. For other types of income, an advance tax is paid in 12 equal installments during the income year.

Tax rates

Tax rates for calendar year 2003 are detailed below.

Residents/Income taxes are assessed on the basis of a single annual tax return. Both the state and the municipality collect income taxes. The state taxes are progressive, with the following rates applied for taxable income in 2003.

Taxable income		Tax on	Percentage
Over	**Not over**	**Column 1**	**on excess**
(Column 1)			
0	DKK 21,000	—	0.0
DKK 21,000	65,000	—	8.0
65,000	120,000	DKK 3,520	19.0
120,000	160,000	13,970	23.5
160,000		23,370	37.0

In 2004 the first "level" of DKK21,000 will be raised to DKK22,000 and the highest "level" of DKK160,000 will be raised to DKK170,000. The first rate of 8% will become 7%, the rate of 23.5% will be 23.0%, and the top-rate of 37.0% will be reduced to 36.0%.

Municipal taxes are set each year by the various municipal authorities. In 2003 they varied between 13% and 22.5% and is calculated on taxable income in excess of DKK21,000 (for 2004 DKK22,000).

A special rule states that an individual can never pay more than 50% tax on his or her taxable income. Therefore, if an individual's tax is computed to be more than 50% of taxable income, the final tax will be lowered to 50% of taxable income.

Nonresidents/Nonresidents are taxed at 42% of any wage/salary/fee arising in the Faroe Islands, with no deductions. In addition, 0.5% social security (AMEG) must be paid.

Employees liable to taxation according to the Hydrocarbon Tax Act are taxed at a rate of 35% on wages and salaries for work performed in the Faroes (including Faroe Islands off-shore). The employee is also obliged to pay 0.5% to a pension fund, bringing the total tax up to 35.5%.

INDIVIDUAL TAX CALCULATION

Calendar year 2003

Assumptions

Individual receiving a salary of DKK1,000.000. Payment to a pension scheme of DKK43,500 (maximum yearly contribution for capital pension—for 2004 the maximum is raised to DKK44,100). Two children under the age of 18. The individual is situated in the Municipality of Tórshavn (capital of the Faroe Islands).

Tax computation

Salary		DKK	1,000,000
Less—Contribution to pension scheme			43,500
		DKK	956,500
Municipality tax:			
Taxable income	956,500		
Less—Fixed deduction (no municipal tax is imposed for taxable income below 21,0000)	(21,000)		
	935,500		
Municipality tax of Tórshavn (18.75%)	175,406		
Deduction for two children	(9,000)	DKK	166,406
Church tax (0.3% of 935,500) (voluntary)			2,807
State tax:			
Taxable income	956,500		
Tax on income up to 160,000	23,370		
Tax on income in excess of 160,000 (37.0%)	294,705		
Deduction for two children	(11,000)		307,075
Computed tax		DKK	476,288
Tax payable—The lower of:			
(1) 476,288 or (2) 956,500 x 50% = 478,250		DKK	476,288
Social security tax:			
Paid by the employer: 1.5% of 1,000,000		DKK	15,000
Paid by the employee—1.00% of 1,000,000 and 0.50% of 956,500		DKK	14,783

Note:

Exchange rate of the Danish krone at December 31, 2003: US$1 = DKK5.9576.

PwC contact

For additional information on taxation in Fiji, contact:

Jerome Kado
PricewaterhouseCoopers
Level 8, Civic Tower
262 Victoria Parade
(GPO Box 200)
Suva, Fiji
Telephone: (679) 313 955
Fax: (679) 300 981
e-mail: jerome.kado@fj.pwc.com

Significant developments

The government has increased the maximum marginal personal tax rate to 31% from the previously legislated 30%.

Widow and widower allowances have increased from F$1,000 to F$1,200.

Directors of companies in liquidation will be held liable for any outstanding tax liability of the company.

A Departure Prohibition Order process will be introduced which may be used by the tax office to prevent taxpayers from leaving the country without settling outstanding taxes.

Amendments to the antiavoidance provisions to further discourage tax avoidance.

Legislation has been introduced to effect the above and other proposed changes to the Fiji tax regime that were announced in the 2004 National Budget address. These changes are proposed to take effect from January 1, 2004.

Territoriality and residence

Residents/Resident individuals are liable to tax on taxable income accruing in or derived from Fiji or elsewhere. Pursuant to the ruling in a recent case, foreign income sourced from a nontreaty country is subject to income tax in Fiji, with credits available for tax paid on such income.

Residents are those who have been in Fiji during more than half the year, unless the Commissioner is satisfied that their usual place of abode is outside Fiji and that they do not intend to take up residence in Fiji. Persons domiciled in Fiji are also considered resident, unless their permanent place of abode is outside Fiji.

Nonresidents/Nonresidents are liable to tax only on taxable income accruing in or derived from Fiji.

Pensions received by nonresident pensioners from a Fiji source will not be taxed.

Foreign personnel/Income other than employment income is not subject to tax if one of the following applies.

1. It does not accrue in Fiji.
2. It is not derived from or received in Fiji by a person whose permanent place of abode is outside Fiji and who is in Fiji solely or mainly for the purpose of engaging in employment in Fiji under a contract of employment of not more than three years' duration.

Gross income

Employee gross income/A foreign person residing in Fiji solely or mainly for the purpose of engaging in employment is subject to tax on salary earned in Fiji regardless of where payment is made and regardless of whether it is remitted. Gross income includes wages, salaries, fees, and other emoluments, living allowances, housing allowances, tax reimbursements, and other benefits received from any office or employment. These allowances and benefits are explained below.

1. Housing—Where furnished accommodation is provided by an employer, an employee is treated as receiving a taxable benefit amounting to one-eighth (one-ninth where it is unfurnished) of basic emoluments, with a maximum benefit of $F12,000 ($F10,667 if unfurnished), unless the actual rent paid by the employer exceeds $F20,000 per annum, in which case the greater of 50% of the actual rent paid or one-eighth (one-ninth if unfurnished) of basic emoluments is deemed to be the benefit. Twice the amount of a rent contribution made by the employee may be offset against this benefit.
2. Cars—A fixed sum of $F1,800, $F2,000, or $F2,400 ($F1,350, $F1,500, or $F1,800 if the employee also owns a car), depending on engine capacity, is deemed to be the private benefit arising from the use of a company car. However, if the cost of the vehicle provided to the employee exceeds $F60,000, a sum of $F2,400 plus 10% of the cost in excess of $F60,000 is adopted, irrespective of the engine capacity (subject to reduction to 75% if the employee also owns a car).
3. Personal expenses of the employee borne by the employer. However, in the case of a foreigner recruited outside Fiji, passage costs borne by the employer or reimbursed to the employee for the employee and the employee's family for initial arrival and final departure, one return journey per annum for leave purposes and journeys made for urgent family reasons are not a taxable benefit to the employee. The exemption is limited to the cost of economy-class airfares using the most direct route between Fiji and the territory in which the employee was recruited. In all other cases, subsidized or free travel provided to employees is a taxable benefit.

Capital gains and investment income/There is no capital gains tax in Fiji. However, gains realized from the sale or other disposition of property acquired for purposes of resale or as part of a profit-making undertaking or scheme are taxable as ordinary income and are not treated as capital gains.

A full exemption from tax is available on dividends received by residents of Fiji from shares held in companies listed on the Suva Stock Exchange. This measure is aimed at encouraging a wider spread of ownership of capital and the development of the Stock Exchange as a vehicle for widespread share ownership.

For a foreign person who is resident in Fiji for tax purposes, income from Fiji sources, including interest, dividends, rents, and royalties, is subject to income tax at graduated rates. However, there is a concession for dividend income from Fiji-incorporated companies.

Income from interest, dividends, or royalties derived outside Fiji by a person resident in Fiji solely or mainly for the purpose of engaging in any employment under a contract of employment of not more than three years' duration is not subject to Fiji tax.

Deductions

Business deductions/In arriving at taxable income, deductions may be taken for expenses laid out wholly and exclusively for the purposes of deriving that income. Deductions are not available for personal or living expenses or for income taxes paid. However, reimbursements of relocation expenses and travel and automobile expenses for business purposes are not subject to tax.

Employee share scheme/From January 1, 2001, a maximum exemption of $F1,000 is allowable on the assessable value of the discount on any shares issued to employees under a "qualifying employee share scheme" as defined under the Fiji Income Tax Act.

Nonbusiness expenses/Deductions for nonbusiness expenses are minimal and are unlikely to be available to a foreign employee.

Personal allowances/Resident individuals, including those in Fiji for employment purposes, may claim the allowances listed below.

1. Wife allowance of $F1,200 if wife's income is not separately assessed.
2. Child allowance of $F500 each for the first two children and $F300 each for three additional children (allowances cover a maximum of five children).
3. Widow and widower allowances of $F1,200.
4. Life insurance premiums and approved retirement fund contributions up to $F1,500. From January 1, 2000 each spouse may claim $F1,500 for this allowance. Previously, this was limited to $F1,500 for a married couple.

The allowances are deducted for the purpose of determining taxable income.

Nonresidents may claim a portion of the allowance for a wife, the proportion being the same as that of their Fiji-source income divided by their worldwide income. Persons in Fiji for employment purposes for less than a full year may claim the allowances detailed above in proportion to either the period of their residence in Fiji or the period with respect to which they derive emoluments from their employment in Fiji, whichever is more favorable to the taxpayer.

Dividends/A deduction is available for dividends to the extent that they have been paid or credited from income that has been charged to tax. The deduction will not be allowed unless the taxpayer provides to the Commissioner a certificate issued by the company paying or crediting the dividends in accordance with the regulations.

Police vehicles/From January 1, 2004, a taxpayer who purchases and donates motor vehicles to the Fiji Police Force is entitled to a 150% deduction of the cost; provided the maximum cost of the vehicle claimed not exceed $F50,000.

Sports fund/From January 1, 2004, a 200% deduction is available to a taxpayer in respect of any cash donation made exceeding $F100,000 between April 1, 2004 and December 31, 2006 to a Sports Fund for the purposes of sports development in the Fiji Islands.

Tax credits

Tax credits apply to income derived from the countries with which Fiji has double taxation agreements—Australia, Japan, the Republic of Korea, Malaysia, New Zealand, Papua New Guinea, and the United Kingdom.

Other taxes

Resident interest withholding taxes/A withholding tax of 31% is deductible on payments or accrual of interest by banks and other financial institutions to resident depositors. However, this tax is not payable where the depositors provide the financial institutions with their tax identification numbers or where interest received does not exceed $F120.

Social security taxes/No social security taxes are imposed.

Land sales tax/Certain profits arising from the sale of land that are not subject to income tax may be liable to land sales tax at rates varying from 6.5% to 30%, depending on the level of profits.

Local taxes on income/There are no local taxes on income.

Fiji National Provident Fund/All employers must contribute an amount equal to at least 16% of the gross cash earnings of all employees to the National Provident Fund. The employer may deduct half of the required contributions from the employees' emoluments. Contributions up to 30% are allowed, and employers contributing above the basic minimum statutory contribution to the FNPF can now claim the excess as a deduction. Exemption maybe sought for nonresident employees, subject to certain conditions.

Tax administration

Returns/Husbands and wives are required to file joint returns, since the income of a married woman is treated, for income tax purposes, as her husband's, with the exception of profits or earnings from a wife's "personal exertion" that arise from a source not connected with any trade or business associated with her husband or from a company in which her husband has an interest. Where a wife has such unconnected personal exertion income, she may, by election, be assessed to tax in her own name on that income.

The taxable year for the individual is the calendar year.

A Departure Prohibition Order process will be introduced that may be used by the tax office to prevent taxpayers from leaving the country without settling outstanding taxes.

Payment of tax/There is income tax withholding from salaries. Generally, if taxpayers have sizable income not subject to withholding they will be required to make provisional payments of estimated tax in three installments.

Tax rates

Normal tax is assessed on taxable (chargeable) income, that is, total income less personal allowances. From January 1, 2004, where the taxable income of a resident exceeds $F20,000, normal tax is $F2,875, plus 31% of the taxable income in excess of $F20,000. In the case of nonresidents with taxable income in excess of $F20,000, normal tax is $F5,125, plus 31% of the taxable income in excess of $F20,000.

INDIVIDUAL TAX CALCULATION

Year ending December 31, 2004

Assumptions

Resident foreign husband and wife, two children; one spouse earns all income. Capital gains, being currently exempt from tax, have been excluded from the computation. Non-Fiji-source income being generally exempt, no tax credits are available against Fiji income tax liability.

Tax computation

Gross salary		$F 124,900
Add—Taxable benefits:		
Furnished housing	12,000	
Use of company car (1,800 to 1,999 cc)	2,000	14,000
		138,900
Interest on bank savings account—Self and wife		1,000
Total income		139,900
Deduct—Allowances:		
Wife	1,200	
Children (two)	1,000	
Life insurance and contribution to superannuation funds (maximum)	1,500	3,700
Taxable income		$F 136,200
Normal tax payable		$F 38,897

Note:

Exchange rate (bank selling) of the Fiji dollar at January 2, 2004: US$1 = $F1.7141.

PwC contact

For additional information on taxation in Finland, contact:

Mr. Kai Wist
PricewaterhouseCoopers Oy
P.O. Box 1015
FIN-00101 Helsinki, Finland
Telephone: (358) (9) 2280 1401
Fax: (358) (9) 2280 1240
e-mail: kai.wist@fi.pwc.com

Significant developments

Changes have been made to the social security legislation that widen the Finnish employer's liability to pay Finnish social security premiums on outbound assignees.

The income tax rates have been somewhat lowered.

Major changes to taxation of certain capital gains, especially dividends, will become effective in 2005.

Territoriality and residence

Finland taxes residents on their worldwide income. Residents are taxed according to progressive tax rates for national tax purposes and flat rates for municipal (and church and social security) tax purposes.

A nonresident alien, for example, one occasionally working in Finland, is taxed on Finnish-source income only. Tax treaties may provide, however, that under certain conditions even this income may not be taxed in Finland. Nonresidents are taxed at flat rates in accordance with the Nonresidents' Tax Act.

An expatriate regime provides a flat tax rate of 35% for those foreign employees whose work requires special knowledge. Other conditions are that monthly cash salary is at least €5,800 and that the length of the assignment is 6 to 24 months. The regime cannot be applied if the person has been resident in Finland within the last five years. The expatriate regime applies for a maximum of 24 months from the start of the assignment; after that period, the expatriate is taxed according to the normal rules.

Individuals are deemed to be resident in Finland if they have their permanent home or habitual abode in Finland or if they are present in Finland for a continuous period of more than six months. A temporary absence from Finland does not prevent a stay from being deemed continuous. Finnish citizens are considered resident in Finland for three full calendar years after they have left the country, unless they prove they had no essential connections therewith in the fiscal year in question. Residence may start or break off in the course of a year.

Gross income

Employee gross income/Taxable personal income of a resident employee includes, inter alia, wages and salaries in money and in kind, directors' bonuses, employee stock options, rental value of employee's free housing, pensions and annuities, living and housing allowances, car benefits, unemployment benefits, and capital gains (if taxable). The income is divided into earned income and capital income. Earned-income tax is imposed at progressive rates. Capital income is taxed at a flat rate of 29%. Dividends from publicly quoted shares and shares quoted on the Main List of the Helsinki

Exchange are taxed as capital income. Dividends from shares quoted on other lists of the Helsinki Exchanges and dividends from nonquoted shares are divided into capital income and earned income.

A nonresident alien is taxed only on Finnish-source income. Unless lower rates are provided in a tax treaty, the rates are 35% on salaries and pensions and 29% on dividends, interest, and royalties. In principle, no deductions are allowed against the aforementioned income. Tax is collected at source by withholding. Finnish-source income other than mentioned above is subject to income tax at flat rates of 35% (earned income) or 29% (capital income) unless a tax treaty provides otherwise.

Capital gains and investment income/Capital gains are fully taxable at a flat rate of 29%.

A gain from the sale of a home is exempt from taxation if the house or apartment has been the taxpayer's home for at least two years continuously during the period of ownership.

Interest income from deposits in Finnish bank accounts and Finnish bonds is subject to tax at source at a flat rate of 29%. This tax is final.

Deductions

Business deductions/Expenses incurred in acquiring or maintaining taxable income are, in principle, deductible items. The maximum allowance for travel expenses to and from work is €4,700, with an own-risk share of €500. Generally, only travel expenses incurred though the least expensive means of transportation (public transportation: train, bus, streetcar, or ship) are deductible. Other deductions for earning income may include expenses for professional literature, own tools, and so on, against original payment receipts. Moving, automobile, and entertainment expenses are generally not deductible.

A standard deduction of €620 from salary income is granted if actual business expenses are below that amount.

Nonbusiness expenses/The following deductions are available.

1. Pension premiums—Mandatory pension premiums are wholly tax deductible for both national and municipal tax purposes (see the calculation below). The deductibility of voluntary pension premiums is limited.
2. Unemployment insurance premiums—Mandatory unemployment insurance premiums are deductible for both national and municipal tax purposes (see the calculation).
3. Interest—Interest expenses from certain loans are deductible when calculating capital income.

Tax credits

For their period of residence, Finnish residents can credit national taxes paid abroad as final tax on income against national tax payable in Finland on the same income.

Other taxes

Social security taxes/A sickness insurance premium of 1.5% is paid on income for municipal taxation. This premium is not tax deductible.

In addition, a pension insurance premium of 4.6% and the unemployment insurance premium of 0.25% are withheld from the employee's salary. These premiums are deductible in the employee's taxation.

Local taxes on income/Municipal tax is levied at flat rates on taxable income. This tax rate varies between 16% and 20.0%, depending on the municipality.

Church tax/Church tax is paid by members of the Evangelic Lutheran and Orthodox churches in Finland at flat rates on the taxable income as determined for municipal tax. Rates vary between 1% and 2.25%.

Wealth tax/A wealth tax is levied on net wealth exceeding €185,000. The amount of the tax is €80 on wealth of €185,00 and 0.9% on the excess.

Nonresidents pay wealth tax in Finland on net wealth exceeding €135,000. The percentage is the same as for residents, that is, 0.9%.

Tax administration

Returns/Spouses file separate returns; joint filing or income splitting is not possible. Individuals file returns on a calendar-year basis by the end of January each year, unless they belong to the so-called tax proposal system in which case the due date is in mid-June. The tax year is the calendar year.

Nonresident aliens generally do not file any tax return because the final tax is withheld at source from their Finnish-source income. For income other than salary, pension, dividends, interest, or royalties (e.g., rental income), a tax return must be filed in accordance with the general procedures.

Payment of tax/There is preliminary income tax withholding from salaries and the other most usual types of income, for example, pensions, remuneration, and dividends. Generally, if taxpayers have income not subject to withholding (e.g., salary paid from abroad), they will be required to make monthly payments of estimated tax.

Tax rates

Employment income/National taxation rates are as follows.

Taxable income			
Over (Column 1)	**Not over**	**Tax on Column 1**	**Percentage on excess**
€ 11,700	€ 14,500	€ 8	11
14,500	20,200	316	15
20,200	31,500	1,171	21
31,500	55,800	3,544	27
55,800		10,105	34

Capital income/The tax rate on capital income is a flat tax rate of 29%.

Other national and municipal taxation/In addition to the above-mentioned national tax, the taxpayer must pay municipal, church, and national pension and sickness insurance premiums (see "Other taxes" above). Church tax is included, since it applies to foreigners if they are members of the Evangelic Lutheran and Orthodox churches or the Finnish German church.

INDIVIDUAL TAX CALCULATIONS

Calendar year 2004

Assumptions

Resident alien living in Helsinki, married, two children (ages 6 and 10). One spouse earns all the income. Covered by the Finnish social security system. Resident, with Finnish social security.

Tax calculation

Income

Cash salary		€ 73,500
Fringe benefits		1,500
Total salary income		75,000
Deductions:		
Standard deduction	620	
Daily travel costs between home and work	0	
(the amount exceeding 500, maximum 4,700)	0	
Business deductions (amount exceeding 590)	0	
Compulsory pension insurance (4.6%)	3,450	
Compulsory unemployment insurance (0.25%)	188	
Voluntary pension insurance contribution	0	4,528
		€ 70,742

Taxable income	Municipal income tax	National income tax
Earned Income	€ 70,742	€ 70,742
Less—Earned income deduction (over 6 months)	1,135	
Less—Basic deduction (12 months)	0	
Taxable earned income	€ 69,607	€ 70,742

Capital income

Capital gains		€ 10,000
Rental income		5,000
Total capital income		15,000
Deductions from capital income:		
Expenses (e.g., safe deposit)	100	
Interest on home or study loans	7,500	7,600
		€ 7,400

Taxes

Municipal tax	€ 12,181
Church tax	696
Sickness insurance premium	1,044
National income tax	15,185
Tax on capital income	2,146
Deductions from taxes:	
Deficit compensation (29% of interest, if the amount of interest expenses exceeds the amount of capital income)	0 (1)
Total tax on income	€ 31,252

Notes:

1. Interest expenses did not exceed the amount of capital Income; thus, no deficit compensation will be granted.
2. Exchange rate of the euro at March 18, 2004: US$1 = €0.8144.

PwC contact

For additional information on taxation in France, contact:

Jean-Luc Pierre
Landwell & Associés
32, rue Guersant 75833 Paris Cedex 17
Telephone: (33) 1 56 57 83 92
Fax: (33) 1 56 57 49 51
e-mail: jean-luc.pierre@fr.landwellglobal.com

Significant developments

The finance act of 2004 has substantially amended the taxation of corporate dividends in France. The dividend tax credit (avoir fiscal) will no longer be granted in respect of dividends paid to individuals from January 1, 2005. Avoir fiscal will be replaced by a 50% relief on dividends received from French companies and companies located in a tax treaty country.

Moreover, the finance act for 2004 has reformed the taxation of capital gains on real estate.

Territoriality and residence

Individuals, whether French or foreign nationals, who have their tax domicile in France are generally subject to personal income tax on worldwide income unless excluded by a tax treaty. Individuals who are not domiciled in France (nonresidents) are subject to tax only on their income arising in France or, in certain instances, on imputed income.

Under domestic law, an individual is considered to be domiciled in France if at least one of the four criteria listed below is met.

1. The habitual abode of the person or family is in France.
2. France is the principal place of sojourn (more than 183 days in a calendar year).
3. Professional activities are carried out in France.
4. France is the center of economic interests.

Under bilateral tax treaties concluded with France, tax domicile is first determined under the law of the country that asserts the power to tax. If the individual is considered to be resident under the laws of two countries, the treaty provides "tie-breaker" provisions to determine the country of residence. These tie-breaker tests generally include as criteria, in order of importance, permanent residence, center of personal and economic relations, habitual abode, and, if none of the foregoing tests is determinative, the decision of the competent authorities.

Gross income

Employee gross income/Unless expressly excluded by tax treaty as subject to tax in another country or by domestic law, compensation earned in France and abroad by a resident is subject to French income tax, regardless of where payment is made and whether it is remitted.

Compensation includes both salary and cash allowances (e.g., cost-of-living, hardship, schooling, and home-leave allowances and income tax reimbursements) but excludes social security and pension contributions made to French and qualified foreign plans. Business expense reimbursements are not taxable. Special concessions may be made to foreign nationals on short- or long-term assignments not exceeding six years. Exceptions may also be created either under tax treaties or pursuant to agreements negotiated with the French tax authorities for employees of headquarters operations located in France. Special relief also exists for one-time moving premiums.

Capital gains and investment income/Unless exempt under a tax treaty, capital gains arising from the sale of real property are taxable, but the tax base is reduced on the basis of the holding period. The sale of a principal residence is tax exempt.

Capital gains arising from the sale of quoted or unquoted securities, as well as of shares in SICAV (*Societé d' Investissement a Capital Variable*) and FCP (*Fonds Commun de Placement*), are subject to a 16% rate (plus 10% social surcharges) where the proceeds of such sales exceed €15,000 (2004 income).

Taxable investment income consists of total income from dividends and interest actually or constructively received in a calendar year, adjusted for any related tax credits, less related investment expenses (e.g., brokers' and management fees).

For French-source dividends paid until December 31, 2004, individuals must add back to the cash dividend the tax credit recognized on the dividends paid by French companies, but they are entitled to deduct the tax credit from net tax payable on all income. For dividends paid from January 1, 2005, the dividend tax credit will no longer be granted. It will be replaced by a 50% relief on dividends received from French companies as well as from companies located in a tax treaty country.

Moreover, for dividends received from tax treaty countries, the gross dividend (i.e., cash dividend received plus any withholding tax) is taxable, but a tax credit against total income is recognized.

For dividends received from nontax treaty countries, no tax credit is allowed, but only the net cash dividend is taxable. In addition to income taxes, dividend income is subject to social surcharges of 10%.

Net French-source interest income may be included in an individual tax return with other investment income; alternatively, for certain types of securities, the taxpayer may elect to have interest income taxed at flat tax rates that range from 16% to 60% (plus 10% social surcharges, depending on the nature of the underlying investment). Interest paid by a foreign company to persons having their tax domicile in France must be included in taxable income. Such interest is grossed up to include any tax credit granted pursuant to a tax treaty. All taxable interest income is also subject to 10% social surcharges.

For more details on the social surcharges and their applicability to capital gains and investment income, see below.

Deductions

Business deductions/Employees may elect either a standard 10% business expense deduction (limited to €12,648 on 2003 income) or itemized business expenses. Journalists benefit from an income tax exemption for the first €7,650 of their income.

Nonbusiness expenses/Residents may deduct their French social security, unemployment contributions, and pension contributions from gross income. Unless otherwise provided by treaty, optional contributions to foreign pension plans are not deductible.

Employees are entitled to a further 20% deduction, limited to €23,180 (2003 income).

Taxpayers may be entitled to one or more of the tax credits or general deductions shown below.

1. Limited tax credits are available for major repair expenses on principal residences, insurance premiums, charitable contributions, domestic employees, students, and child care.
2. General deductions are available for support and alimony payments.

Tax credits

Unless specifically excluded by treaty, foreign-source income is taxable in France. Residents are entitled to tax credits for withholding tax paid on certain types of income from other tax treaty countries. For dividends paid until December 31, 2004, residents are also entitled to a tax credit (*avoir fiscal*) equal to 50% of the cash dividends paid by French companies. For dividends paid from January 1, 2005, the dividend tax credit will no longer be granted. The tax credit will be replaced by a 50% relief on dividends received from French and also from companies located in a tax treaty country. Moreover, foreign-source income exempt from French tax by virtue of a tax treaty is added to income taxable in France, either to determine the French tax rate applicable to income taxable in France (exemption with progression) or to calculate gross French tax liability, from which tax paid abroad is deducted (tax credit system), depending on the applicable tax treaty.

Other taxes

Social security taxes/For 2004, the employee's share of social contributions represents approximately 18% to 23% of salary. (See also "Nonbusiness expenses" above)

Wealth tax/Wealth tax is assessed on individuals whose net wealth as at January 1, 2004, exceeds €720,000. Wealth tax rates range from 0.55% on net wealth between €720,000 and €1,160,000 to 1.8% on net wealth in excess of €15 million. French residents are subject to wealth tax on worldwide assets, while the tax base for nonresidents is limited to assets situated in France.

Wealth tax returns for calendar year 2003 must be filed by June 15, 2004. The tax is payable upon filing of the return.

Local taxes/Private occupiers of French real estate pay a local tax, known as habitation tax. Tax revenues go to some of the local government bodies (in descending order of geographical size, the departments, and communes). The tax is based on the assessed value of real estate.

Tax administration

Returns/Husbands and wives must file joint returns. Separate filing status is not permitted, except under strictly limited circumstances. French residents' income tax returns are based on calendar-year income and must be filed by March 1 of the following year (however, by April 5, 2004, for 2003 calendar-year income). The total taxable income is divided into the number of shares ("parts") that reflects the taxpayer's marital status and number of dependents. Children under 18 years of age and disabled children of all ages can be claimed as dependents.

Children from the ages of 18 to 21, as well as children from the ages of 21 to 25 who are full-time students, can upon request be claimed as dependents. The tax benefit or dependent children is limited in most cases to a maximum of €2,086 (limit) for each of the first two children and €4,172 for each additional child.

Payment of tax/There is no income tax withholding from salaries, except for nonresidents deriving income from employment and professional activities in France. For nonresidents, tax at flat rates of 0%, 15%, and 25% is withheld at source. An annual income tax return is required if the income subject to withholding tax falls into the 25% withholding tax bracket.

Taxpayers must pay their current year's taxes in one of two ways: in two installments and a final payment, with each installment equal to one-third of the previous year's tax liability and the final payment equal to the excess of the actual tax liability over the two installment payments; or in monthly installments. Foreign nationals working in France for the first time normally pay their tax in September of the year following their arrival. Thereafter, they follow the standard system.

Tax rates

Tax rates for the tax year ending December 31, 2003 are as follows.

Taxable income		
Over	Not over	Tax rate
		%
0	€ 4,262	0.00
€ 4,262	8,382	6.83
8,382	14,753	19.14
14,753	23,888	28.26
23,888	38,868	37.38
38,868	47,932	42.62
47,932		48.09

Social surcharges/Social surcharges are applicable to various kinds of income. The total social surcharges on interest, dividends, and capital gains for 2004 are as shown below.

	%
General social contribution	7.5
Social tax	2.0
CRDS contribution	0.5
Total	10.0

The general social and CRDS contributions are discussed below.

General social contribution/A social contribution (*contribution sociale généralisée*—CSG) of 7.5% on employee compensation and investment income must be paid by all French-resident individuals. As a "universal" charge, it applies to all forms of gross income, including the following.

1. Employee compensation, including benefits in kind and stock option gains.
2. Pensions.
3. Income earned from independent services.
4. Investment income, including rental income, dividends, interest, and capital gains (as discussed under "Social surcharges" above).

The CSG is not deductible if assessed on income or capital gains taxed at a flat rate. 5.1% within the 7.5% overall rate is tax deductible if the general social contribution is assessed on income or capital gains taxed at graduated rates. The total 7.5% contribution is withheld directly by employers from salary. Special rules apply to foreign-source employee compensation. A separate tax bill is issued for CSG on investment income, based on the individual's annual tax return.

Contribution for reimbursement of the social debt/Since February 1, 1996, a social tax of 0.5% called the CRDS (*contribution au remboursement de la dette sociale*) has been levied on ail French residents on most categories of income (including foreign-paid compensation) and is also not deductible for fax purposes. This additional surtax is expected to remain in force for 18 years.

INDIVIDUAL TAX CALCULATION

2003

Assumptions

Resident employee, married with two children under age 18 (one in middle school (*college*) and one in high school (*lycée*)). The employee earned €121,960 net income in 2003, received €3,050 in U.K. dividend income, paid €1,525 of qualified life insurance premiums, and made support payments to his parents (in financial need) of €2,287, for which he has the receipts. He sold listed shares for €53,357 and realized a €2,134 net capital gain.

Tax computation

Net salary (after deduction of social security)		€ 121,960.0
Less—Standard deductions:		
Business expense deduction—10% (maximum 12,437)	12,196.0	
Standard deduction—20% (maximum 22,780)	21,953.0	34,149.0
Taxable salary		87,811.0
Add:		
U.K. dividends	3,050.0	
Less—Withholding tax: 15%	(457.5)	
Net amount	2,592.5	
Tax credit—17,000 x 18%	467.0	3,059.5
Total taxable income		90,870.5
Less—Support payments to parents		2,287.0
Taxable income after deductions		€ 88,583.5
Tax thereon:		
Income tax on 88,583.5 (3 shares) (1)		€ 19,835.0
Tax on capital gains (16% x 2,134)		341.5
Total income and capital gains tax		20,176.5
Less:		
Life insurance payments (total – 1,525; maximum allowed—910 (610 + 150 per child) x 25%)	227.5	
Student reduction (61 for middle school, 153 for high school)	214.0	(441.5)
Net tax due before tax credits		19,735.0
Social tax on dividends and capital gains—2% x (3,059.5 + 2,134)		104.0
General social contribution—7.5% x (3,059.5 + 2,134) (2)		389.5
CRDS—0.5% x (3,059.5 x 2,134)		26.0
Less—Tax credits on dividends		(467.0)
Total net income tax		€ 19,787.5

Notes:

1. The method of calculating a household's income tax liability is first to calculate the tax for two shares and then to calculate the tax for the actual number of shares, including the children. If the difference between the two calculations exceeds €2,086 (2003 income) for each of the first two children or €4,172 for each additional child, then the maximum tax reduction per child is limited to €2,086 for each of the first two children and €4,172 for each additional child. If the amount per child is less than €2,086 for each of the first two children or €4,172 for each additional child, the actual amount is used in the calculation.

2. The general social contribution rate applicable to gross income is 7.5%. An additional CRDS tax of 0.5% is also payable on this amount, as well as on taxable income after deductions.
3. Exchange rate of the Euro at January 2, 2004: US$1 = €0.79.

Germany

PwC contact

For additional information on taxation in Germany, contact:

Petra Peitz-Ziemann
PricewaterhouseCoopers GmbH
Marie-Curie-Str. 24-28
D–60439 Frankfurt (Main), Germany
Telephone: (49) (69) 9585 6586
Fax: (49) (69) 9585 6107 (Zentrale)
Fax (49) (69) 9585 6723
e-mail: petra.peitz-ziemann@de.pwc.com

Significant developments

Since January 1, 2002, only 50% of dividends paid to resident individuals has to be recognized as taxable income, albeit with no corporation tax imputation credit attached to the dividend.

As a result of the German tax reform, the top marginal tax rate was reduced and currently amounts to 45% for 2004. Including the 5.5% solidarity surcharge, this leads to a combined top marginal rate of 47.475%. The top marginal tax will be further reduced to 42% for 2005 and thereafter. The 5.5% solidarity surcharge will most likely stay in place and must be considered accordingly.

For 2004, the employee monthly contribution to social security and unemployment taxes is limited to a maximum of €669 for an annual maximum of €8,034.

As of January 1, 2004, the employee monthly contribution to old-age medicare insurance is limited to a maximum of €30.

Territoriality and residence

All resident individuals are taxed on their worldwide income. Generally, individuals are deemed to be resident if they are physically present in Germany for more than six months in any one calendar year or for a consecutive period of six months over a year-end. Nonresident individuals are taxed (usually by withholding) on German-source income only.

Contrary provisions in double taxation treaties override German national law unless the latter is more favorable (from the German tax point of view only) to the taxpayer.

Nationality is not of itself a criterion for determining residence or tax liability, although it may serve as an indicator of residence in (unusual) cases of doubt.

Gross income

Employee gross income/Taxable compensation includes all remuneration, allowances and benefits in kind given to or provided for an employee. Benefits in kind are valued, in principle, at cost to the employer, although there are some cases of global allocations (mainly cars), mostly for administrative simplicity. Certain minor benefits in kind (such as annual employee outings) are not taxed. Reimbursement of an employee's relocation costs to Germany is not a taxable benefit, provided certain (basically adequate) limits are observed. There are no special concessions for foreigners.

Capital gains and investment income/Long-term capital gains are tax-exempt, while 50% of short-term gains totaling more than €511 are added to an individual's taxable income. The time limits for long-term gains are 10 years for land and buildings and 12 months for securities and other assets.

Special rules apply to the taxation of capital gains from the sale of a significant interest (1% or more) in a business.

Investment income (i.e., interest and dividends) is part of an individual's total income for tax purposes. It qualifies for an "Investor's allowance" of €1,370 per taxpayer and a global deduction of €51 for related expenses, but otherwise does not lead to any special concessions. These amounts are doubled in the case of married taxpayers filing jointly.

If worldwide interest and dividend income exceeds the above-mentioned investor's allowance, interest, and surcharge withholding tax of 26.375% is automatically withheld at source. The withholding tax is treated as a payment on account of the final income tax liability.

From January 1, 2002, only 50% of dividend income is taxable under German income tax law.

Short-term capital gains and investment income from abroad are taxed under normal German rules, subject to the provisions of the relevant double taxation treaty. If, under the treaty, they cannot be taxed in Germany, they are taken into account when determining the tax rate to be applied to taxable income.

Deductions

Business deductions/Various properly documented and necessarily incurred business expenses may be deducted by an individual unless they are reimbursed by the employer. This includes the cost of traveling to and from work, business literature, business subscriptions, and professional dues. There is a blanket employee allowance for business deductions of €920 per annum. To the extent actual employment-connected expenses exceed the lump sum of €920, they are deductible if they can be substantiated.

Nonbusiness expenses/Social security contributions and insurance premiums can be deducted up to specified limits. Mortgage interest is deductible but only against income from the property. Tax advisers' fees are fully deductible, as is church tax (see "Church tax" below). Contributions to German charities and certain international charities are deductible up to 5% of adjusted gross income. For contributions for scientific purposes, the percentage is increased by another 5%. Contributions to political parties up to a total of €1,600 per annum are also deductible (€3,200 for married taxpayers filing jointly).

Personal allowances/The allowances shown below are deductible in computing gross income.

	Per annum €
Child allowance—Per child registered in Germany	3,648
Additional special allowance to dependent children under 16 years of age	2,160
Employee allowance	920

An educational allowance of €924 per child is allowed for dependent children registered in Germany but attending school away from home.

There are also a number of other specific allowances and reliefs, for example, for the elderly and the disabled.

Tax credits

Foreign withholding taxes on passive income from abroad are usually credited against the applicable German income tax unless the relevant tax treaty specifies otherwise. No credit is given for underlying income tax, and unused credit cannot, for passive income, be carried forward or applied to income from a third country.

Other taxes

Social security taxes/The employee's portion of German social tax contributions (social security and unemployment tax) is limited to €669 per month on amounts up to €5,150 per month) for a maximum annual contribution of €8,034. The employer must contribute an equal amount. Contributions covering sickness insurance are not compulsory for employees earning over €3,488 monthly.

An old-age medicare insurance contribution is payable by the employee and the employer in equal amounts. The employee contribution is limited to €30 per month (0.85% on amounts up to €3,488 per month).

Social security contributions and insurance premiums are deductible from adjusted gross income up to specified limits.

Church tax/Members of officially recognized churches pay church tax as a surcharge on their income tax. The rates are either 8% or 9%, depending on the German state where the individual is resident.

Income tax surcharge/To improve the economic situation and infrastructure in the five new eastern states of Germany, the German government is levying a 5.5% income tax surcharge for an indefinite period. The surcharge is imposed as a percentage on all individual income taxes.

Local taxes on income/There are no local taxes applicable to employees.

Tax administration

Returns/Resident husbands and wives file joint returns unless they are legally separated or one spouse requests otherwise. The income is split for all purposes, including the calculation of allowances. The tax year is the calendar year.

Payment of tax/Payment of tax on salary and employment benefits is by withholding. The amounts withheld are treated as a payment on account of the final income tax liability. If taxpayers have other income, they will usually be asked to make quarterly payments on account, on the basis of final liability as determined by the most recent final assessment.

Tax rates

2004

Single taxpayer

Taxable income From	To	Tax rate
0	€ 7,664	—
€ 7,665	52,152	At geometrically progressive rates starting at 16% rising to 45%

(The tax on income above €52,152 can be calculated by multiplying the income by 45% and reducing this figure by €8,845.)

Married taxpayer

Taxable income From	To	Tax rate
0	€ 15,328	—
€ 15,329	104,304	At geometrically progressive rates starting at 16% rising to 45%

(The tax on income above €104,304 can be calculated by multiplying the income by 45% and reducing this figure by €17,690.)

2005

Single taxpayer

Taxable income From	To	Tax rate
0	€ 7,664	—
€ 7,665	52,152	At geometrically progressive rates starting at 15% rising to 42%

(The tax on income above €52,152 can be calculated by multiplying the income by 42% and reducing this figure by €7,914.)

Married taxpayer

Taxable income			
From	To		Tax rate
0	€ 15,328		—
€ 15,329	104,304		At geometrically progressive rates starting at 15% rising to 42%

(The tax on income above €104,304 can be calculated by multiplying the income by 42% and reducing this figure by €15,828.)

INDIVIDUAL TAX CALCULATION

Calendar year 2004

Assumptions

Resident husband and wife, no religious affiliation, two children under 16 years of age.

Tax computation

Annual gross salary	100,000	
Less—Employment allowance or higher itemized business expenses	920	€ 99,080
Interest income (1,000)	1,000	
Dividend income (5,000, of which 50% is taxable)	2,500	
Less—Investor's allowance	(2,740)	760
Short-term capital gain	300	
(under de minimis amount €511, therefore ignored)	(300)	0
		99,840
Less:		
Lump sum for social security and life insurance premiums	4,002	
Tax advisor's fee	1,500	5,502
Less—Child allowances (two)		11,616
Taxable income		€ 82,722
Income tax at joint return rates		€ 20,172
Less—Withholding tax on German investment income in excess of tax-free amounts		(75)
		20,097
Surcharge		1,105
Total tax payable		€ 21,202

Note:

Exchange rate of the Euro at February 23, 2004: US$1 = €0.79960.

PwC contact

For additional information on taxation in Ghana, contact:

Charles Egan
PricewaterhouseCoopers
PMB CT 42
Cantonments, Accra, Ghana
Telephone: (233) (21) 506217/8
Fax: (233) (21) 506216
e-mail: charles.a.egan@gh.pwcglobal.com

General note

This entry is repeated from the 2003/2004 edition. For more up-to-date information consult the contact listed above or Jacqueline Collette at jacqueline.collette@us.pwc.com.

Significant developments

There have been no significant tax or regulatory developments as regards individual taxation in the past year.

Territoriality and residence

Ghana taxes its resident individuals on any of the following income accruing in, derived from, brought into, or received in Ghana:

1. Gains or profits from trade, business, profession, or vocation.
2. Gains or profits from any employment, including any allowances or benefits paid in cash or given in kind to or on behalf of an employee other than in respect of medical or dental cost, or any passage from or to Ghana.
3. Dividends.
4. Any charge or annuity.
5. Royalties, premiums, and any other profits arising from property, including rents from immovable property, except with the first five years of completion of the property.
6. Receipts including royalties or periodic or deferred payments of any kind derived from any transaction wherever and whenever made, affecting directly or indirectly, and/or from any natural resources in Ghana, and notwithstanding whether the receipts are paid within or outside Ghana.

An individual is resident for tax purposes if that individual is one of the following:

1. A citizen of Ghana and present in Ghana for a period or periods equal in total to 183 days or more in any year beginning January 1.
2. An employee or official of the government of Ghana posted abroad during the year.
3. A Ghanaian who is temporarily absent from Ghana for a period not exceeding 365 continuous days, where that Ghanaian has a permanent home in Ghana.

Nonresidents are liable to Ghanaian income tax at the rate of 20% on any income derived in Ghana from any trade, business, profession, or vocation or which derives from an employment exercised in Ghana. This rate applies to income earned by a nonresident individual who has stayed in Ghana for a period or periods amounting to less than 183 days in a particular year.

Gross income

Employee gross income/Total emoluments paid to an employee or on the employee's behalf are included in the chargeable income of the employee for any year of assessment. All fixed cash allowances for housing and entertainment are taxable, but reimbursements for expenses actually incurred exclusively on behalf of and for the benefit of the employer are not taxable to the employee.

Chargeable income also includes any benefit derived from the use of a motor vehicle, furnishing, or accommodation provided by the employer. There are no concessions for foreigners.

Capital gains and investment income/A capital gains tax is payable by every person on any capital gains accruing or derived from the realization of any chargeable asset, including buildings of a permanent or temporary nature; business and business assets, including goodwill; land other than agricultural land; any right or interest in, to, or over any stocks and shares; and any assets declared as chargeable by a legislative instrument. The applicable rate is 10% on gains in excess of GHC500,000, regardless of the period for which the asset was held prior to disposal.

Withholding tax on interest income for individuals has been abolished.

Nonresidents are subject to a final withholding tax of 10% on any dividend income paid to them by a resident.

Deductions

Business deductions/Expenses of a private or domestic nature are generally not deductible. For all individuals other than employees, all outgoings and expenses incurred wholly, exclusively, and necessarily, in the production of the income that is subject to tax are deductible. These include:

1. Interest on money borrowed and employed in acquiring the income.
2. Rent payable on land or buildings occupied for the purpose of acquiring the income.
3. Repairs and maintenance expenses for premises, plant, machinery, and so on, employed in acquiring the income.
4. Local rates and taxes on premises.
5. Bad debts.
6. Losses incurred in a mining, export manufacturing and farming enterprises.

No blanket or standard deductions are allowed.

Nonbusiness expenses/Apart from social security contributions, qualifying insurance premiums, and donations, no nonbusiness expenses are deductible, and no standard deductions are allowed.

Personal allowances/The tax-free threshold from January 1, 2001, is GHC1,200,000. In addition, there is an allowance of GHC300,000 for a married man, a married woman maintaining her husband and household, and an unmarried man or woman with two or more dependent children. Disabled persons (self-employed or employees) are allowed a tax-free deduction of 25% of the assessable income from any business or employment accruing to them. There is an old-age relief of GHC300,000, deductible from the total income of a self-employed individual or employee who is more than 60 years old. A children's education relief of GHC240,000 per child in a registered secondary school in Ghana is granted. This is restricted to three children and is claimable by one parent only. Persons who support aged relatives are granted a relief of GHC200,000 in respect of each, for a maximum of two such relatives. A relief of GHC500,000 is given in the case of professional, technical, or vocational training. All residents are entitled to these reliefs.

Tax credits

There are no tax credits available to short-term residents.

For both residents and nonresidents who have had tax withheld from any income received by them, there is a tax credit against their tax payable to the full amount of any such tax withheld.

Other taxes

Social security taxes/Social security contributions are 5% and 12.5% of basic salary for employees and employers, respectively. They are deductible for tax purposes. 2.5% of each employee's total monthly contributions are allocated as a contribution to the National Insurance Scheme.

Local taxes on income/There are no local income taxes.

Tax administration

Returns/There is no joint filing for husband and wife. A tax year other than the calendar year is not permitted.

Payment of tax/Every employer is required to make monthly deductions of tax from the total emoluments of each employee in accordance with regulations made under the law.

Tax rates

The following rates of tax are in effect from January 1, 2001:

Chargeable income		Tax on Column 1	Percentage on excess
Over (Column 1)	Not over		
0	GHC 1,200,000	—	0
GHC 1,200,000	2,400,000	—	5
2,400,000	5,400,000	GHC 60,000	10
5,400,000	24,000,000	360,000	15
24,000,000	48,000,000	3,150,000	20
48,000,000		7,950,000	30

The above rates are applicable only to residents.

INDIVIDUAL TAX CALCULATION

Year ending December 31, 2003

Assumptions

Resident husband and wife; two children in approved educational institution. (Neither the wife nor the children have any separate income.) Husband is provided with fully furnished accommodations and use of an official car with driver and fuel. Income includes salary of GHC131,200,000 (equivalent of approximately US$19,294 at GHC6,800 = US$1) and GHC500,000 gross interest.

Tax computation

Basic salary		GHC 131,200,000
Less—Employee's contribution to social security fund (5% of basic salary)		6,560,000
		124,640,000
Add:		
Rent element (15% of basic salary)	19,680,000	
Car element (15% of basic salary) (1)	3,600,000	23,280,000
		147,920,000
Less—Reliefs:		
Married	300,000	
Children's education	480,000	780,000
Chargeable income		GHC 147,140,000
Tax thereon:		
On first 48,000,000	7,950,000	
On remaining 99,140,000 at 30%	29,742,000	
Tax payable		GHC 37,692,000

Notes:

1. Restricted to GHC300,000 per month, that is, GHC3,600,000 per year.
2. Exchange rate of the cedi at March 5, 2003: US$1 = GHC8,500.00.

PwC contact

For additional information on taxation in Greece, contact:

Dimitris Varvaritis
PricewaterhouseCoopers Business Solutions SA
268 Kifisias Avenue
152 32 Halandri
Athens, Greece
Telephone: (30) (210) 6874 548
Fax: (30) (210) 6874 444
e-mail: diimitris.varvaritis@gr.pwc.com

Significant developments

There have been no significant tax or regulatory developments regarding individual taxation.

Territoriality and residence

Subject to relevant tax treaty provisions, income tax is payable by all individuals earning income in Greece, regardless of citizenship or place of permanent residence. Permanent residents are taxed on their worldwide income. Individuals residing in Greece under certain circumstances indicating intent to remain permanently are considered permanent residents.

Gross income

Employee gross income/Nonresident aliens are taxed on salary earned for work performed in Greece, regardless of where payment is made and regardless of whether it is remitted. They are not taxed to the extent their compensation relates to services performed outside Greece.

All fringe benefits are normally considered taxable income to the employee. However, company-provided housing and furniture given to executives could be considered in the tax courts as nontaxable income. Similarly, tuition for children could also be considered nontaxable income.

Capital gains and investment income/Dividends paid to shareholders are not taxed. Dividends are always taxed at the time of distribution in the name of the distributing company. Dividends and capital gains from Greek or European mutual funds are tax exempt income from foreign (outside the EU) mutual funds is subject to a 20% withholding tax at the time of payment by the intermediary bank and such tax payment terminates any income tax liability for such income.

Interest on deposits of any kind with local banks is subject to a 15% income tax withheld at source. Interest on government treasury bills and bonds issued after 1998 is subject to a 10% income tax withheld at source. Interest earned on any deposits in other than in euros with banks operating in Greece is not taxed if the beneficiary of such income is a foreign resident.

Gains on the sale of shares listed on the Athens Stock Exchange are taxed at source. Gains from the sale of shares listed on a foreign stock exchange or other internationally recognized exchange are also exempt from capital gains tax.

Deductions

Business deductions/As a general rule there are no business deductions allowable to the employee, because business-related expenses would be reimbursed by the employer.

Nonbusiness expenses/Deductible nonbusiness expenses must be supported by original related tax documents.

Taxpayers (only Greek tax residents) enjoy various deductions based on their expenditures as follows.

1. Deduction from taxable income of life insurance premiums and medical insurance coverage of the taxpayer and his/her family up to €1,000.
2. Deduction from taxable income of the compulsory contributions to social security funds, with no ceiling applicable.
3. Deduction from taxable income of the donations to the Greek state, municipalities, communities, churches, charities, religious and educational institutions, athletic associations, and qualifying institutions supporting the arts, up to a maximum of 10% of declared income.

Personal allowances/No allowances are available for individual taxation.

Tax credits/The amount of tax computed on the basis of the scale shown under "Tax rates" below is reduced by the following tax credits:

1. Tax credit of maximum €150 on the rent expenditure for the main residence of the taxpayer and family. The tax credit is calculated on the rent expenditure ceiling up to €1,000 at a rate of 15%.
2. Tax credit of maximum €150 on the rent expenditure for the housing of the taxpayer's children in their place of study, given that the relevant educational institutions are qualified. As above, the tax credit is calculated on the rent expenditure ceiling up to €1,000 at a rate of 15%.
3. Tax credit of maximum €100 on the expenditure for private lessons or tuition fees for any educational level for the taxpayer or for each child.
4. Tax credit of 15% on the expenditure for medical and hospitalization expenses of the taxpayer and his/her dependants. The amount of tax credit cannot exceed €6,000.
5. Tax credit of 15% on mortgage loan interest for the acquisition of a first residence depending on the year the loan was granted.
6. Tax credit of 15% on specific family expenses. The amount of tax credit cannot exceed €75.

Income tax paid in a foreign country is deductible from Greek tax but only on reported income earned abroad and up to the applicable Greek income tax.

Other taxes

Social security taxes/Employee contributions to social security are computed at the rate of 16.0% on monthly gross salary, currently up to a salary limit of €2,058.25 (effective January 1, 2004), 14 times annually. As from January 1, 1993, the ceiling does not apply to those employees who are insured for the first time with social security funds in Greece. However, the social security ceiling is valid for the following, inter alia, persons.

1. Greek and foreign persons who have been insured up to December 31, 1992, in any EU member state.
2. Those persons who have been insured before January 1, 1993, in countries with which Greece has signed a social security totalization treaty, or with which there is a treaty signed but not yet ratified, or with which a treaty has been initialed.

Employee social security contributions are withheld by the employer.

Social security payments are deductible in determining net taxable income as shown in the tax calculation.

Share transfer tax/A 5% transfer tax is levied when individuals and sole traders (Greek or foreign) transfer shares not listed on the Athens Stock Exchange. The tax of 5% is calculated on the real value of the shares transferred as defined by a Ministry of Finance Circular, and the relevant liability is borne by the seller.

A 0.3% tax is imposed on sales of shares listed on the Athens Stock Exchange or a recognized foreign exchange. This tax is calculated on the value of shares sold as shown in the statement prepared by the brokerage company and is borne by the seller (individuals, regardless of citizenship or place of permanent residence) of the shares.

Local taxes on income/No local taxes on income are imposed.

Tax administration

Returns/Married couples are obligated to file a joint tax return, but the income of each spouse is taxed separately. However, the taxable income of one spouse from a business that is financially dependent on the other spouse is added to the taxable income of the other spouse. No taxable year other than the calendar year is permitted.

Payment of tax/Income tax is withheld from salaries. Taxpayers that generate income other than employment income pay 55% of their current year's tax liability as a tax advance for the following year's taxation.

The withholding tax on salaries, pensions, and wages is calculated on the amount of monthly salary after being reduced by the employee share of social security contributions, multiplied by 14 (12 monthly salaries, plus monthly salary for Christmas bonus, one-half monthly salary for Easter bonus, and one-half monthly salary for vacation bonus). This amount constitutes the employee's annual net salary before income tax. The annual withholding income tax is calculated on the basis of the personal income tax scale shown below (see "Tax rates" below), after being adjusted with the increases provided for dependent children also referred to in "Tax rates." The actual amount of tax withheld is the tax calculated with the application of the tax scales and is reduced by 2.5%

Annual income tax withholding on salaries, wages, and pensions is set off against the final income tax assessed on the basis of the individual income tax return. Any amounts withheld in excess of the annual income tax assessed are refunded.

Tax rates

Income tax on individual net income and on the corresponding nontaxable amount is calculated according to the table below.

Taxable income		Tax on Column 1	Percentage on excess
Over (Column 1)	Not over		
0	€ 8,400	—	0
€ 8,400	13,400	—	15
13,400	23,400	750	30
23,400		3,750	40

Income tax on individual net income from salaries and /or pensions is calculated according to the table below.

Taxable income		Tax on Column 1	Percentage on excess
Over (Column 1)	Not over		
0	€ 10,000	—	0
€ 10,000	13,400	—	15
13,400	23,400	510	30
23,400		3,510	40

In addition, taxpayers (resident in Greece) with taxable income from dependent personal services (salaries, wages, and pensions) enjoy a tax benefit (increase of the upper limit of nontaxable income) according to the number of dependent children as follows:

1. €1,000 increase of the nontaxable bracket for one dependent child, that is, €11,000.
2. €2,000 increase for two dependent children, that is, €12,000.
3. €10,000 increase for three dependent children, that is, €20,000.
4. When there are more than three dependent children, the tax benefit for each additional child beyond the third increases the nontaxable bracket by €1,000, that is, €21,000.

Nonresident individuals who are not Greek tax residents and earn income from sources located in Greece are liable to 5% income tax on the amount of the first bracket of the tax scale. EU residents who derive more than 90% of their total income from Greece are eligible for the tax-free bracket.

INDIVIDUAL TAX CALCULATION

Calendar year 2003

Assumptions

Resident alien husband and wife, two children; wife without taxable income, "old" employee for social security calculations (insured before January 1, 1993)

Tax computation

Gross income:		
Salary		€ 80,000.00
Interest on government bonds		600.00
Interest on bank deposits		600.00
Total gross income		81,200.00
Less—Interest on government bonds and bank deposits		1,200.00
Adjusted gross income		80,000.00
Less—Social security payments		4,195.45
Net income		75,804.55
Less—Deductions:		
Life insurance premiums	840.00	
Donation to nonprofit organization	300.00	1,140.00
Taxable income		€ 74,664.55
Corresponding tax		€ 23,715.82
Less—Tax credits:		
Medical expenses (actually paid 1,000) x 15%	150.00	
Private lessons expenses (actually paid 1,000) x 10%	100.00	
Annual family expenses (actually paid 3,000) x 15% (limited to 75€)	75.00	(325.00)
Income tax liability		23,390.82
Plus—Withholding tax on interest from bank deposits		90.00
Plus—Withholding tax on interest on government bonds		60.00
Total income tax liability		€ 23,540.82

Note:

Exchange rate of the Euro at January 2, 2004: US$1 = €0.7942.

Guatemala

PwC contacts

For additional information on taxation in Guatemala, contact:

Oscar Cordon
Edgar Mendoza
PricewaterhouseCoopers
Edificio Tívoli Plaza
6a Calle 6-38, Zone 9
Guatemala City, Guatemala
Telephone: (502) (2) 345-080
Fax: (502) (2) 331-8345
e-mail: oscar.cordon@gt.pwc.com
egdar.mendoza@gt.pwc.com

Significant developments

The information in this entry is current as of January 2004. There have been no significant tax or regulatory developments in the past year. For subsequent developments, consult the contacts listed above.

Territoriality and residence

Guatemala taxes its citizens and resident or nonresident individuals on their compensation attributable to services rendered in Guatemala and on other Guatemalan-source income.

Gross income

Employee gross income/Nonresident aliens are taxed on salary earned for work done in Guatemala, regardless of where payment is made and regardless of whether it is remitted. They are not taxed to the extent that their compensation relates to services performed outside Guatemala. Quantifiable fringe benefits, such as housing allowance, living allowance, house, tax reimbursement, and the like, are considered taxable income.

Capital gains and investment income/Guatemalan-source capital gains are taxed at a flat rate of 10%. Capital gains and investment income from outside the country are not taxed by Guatemala. Capital losses can be netted only against capital gains.

Nonresidents/A nonresident alien's income from a Guatemalan source is subject to income tax withholding at varying rates.

1. Interest—10%, except when the related foreign-exchange proceeds are sold directly into the Guatemalan banking system, and they are paid to a financial or banking institution.
2. Dividends—10%, except when taxpayers have paid corporate income tax.
3. Salaries—10%.
4. Rents, royalties, professional fees, and technical services—31%.

Deductions

All individuals, including resident aliens, can deduct the following in determining taxable income.

1. Personal deduction: Q36,000.
2. Social security contributions (4.83% of salary).
3. Life insurance premiums.
4. Medical expenses (excluding medicine).

Tax credits

An income tax credit is granted for value-added taxes (VATs) paid on goods purchased and services contracted for one's exclusive personal use. The law permits a credit for up to 12% of total income; it is possible to use 100% of this credit. Resident aliens cannot take income taxes paid to foreign countries or governmental units as a credit against their tax liability in Guatemala.

Other taxes

Social security taxes/The taxpayer's share of social security taxes is 4.83% of compensation, without a maximum limit.

Other taxes on income/Interest income earned by domiciled persons is subject to a flat 10% withholding tax.

Tax administration

Returns/Husbands and wives cannot file joint returns. The tax year for individuals runs from July 1 to June 30.

Payment of tax/Income tax must be withheld from salaries; rentals; royalties; fees for technical, professional, or scientific activities; or any kind of individual services.

Tax rates

Taxable income		Tax on	Percentage
Over	Not over	Column 1	on excess
(Column 1)			
Q 0	Q 65,000	0	15
65,000	180,000	Q 9,750	20
180,000	295,000	32,750	25
295,000		61,500	31

INDIVIDUAL TAX CALCULATION

Tax year ending June 30, 2004

Assumptions

Resident alien husband and wife; two children; one spouse earns all the income. Individual tax amounts are in local currency.

Tax computation

Gross taxable income:		
Salary		Q 120,000
Incentive bonus		864
		120,864
Deductions:		
Personal deduction	36,000	
Insurance premiums	6,000	
Social security	5,800	47,800
Net taxable income		Q 73,064
Income tax assessment:		
Fixed tax on 65,000	9,750	
On excess (20% of 8,064)	1,613	Q 11,363
Less—Value-added tax credit (1)		(14,504)
Tax to be paid		Q 0.00

Notes:

1. The law permits a credit for VAT paid up to 12% of total income; it is possible to use 100% of this credit. To claim it, the taxpayer must have supporting documents, such as invoices.
2. Exchange rate of the quetzal at January 1, 2004: US$1= Q8.228.

PwC contact

For additional information on taxation in Guyana, contact:

Ronald M. Alli
Jack A. Alli Sons & Co.
145 Crown Street
Queenstown, Georgetown, Guyana
Telephone: (592) (22) 62904, 66532, 37005-7
Fax: (592) (22) 53849
e-mail: ronald.alli@jaasco.com

Significant developments

Self-employed individuals who have annual turnover of less than G$10 million have their taxable income ascertained by a presumptive method using factors such as size of business premises, number of employees, assets used in business, education, training and years in practice, etcetera, and specifying standard deductions for each category. The Commissioner-General may require an individual submitting a presumptive tax return to also submit a regular tax return; such an individual will be subject to the higher tax.

Effective September 1, 2003, professional services tax on specified individuals is applicable.

Effective January 1, 2004, minimum tax is applied to self-employed individuals whose annual turnover is less than G$10 million.

Territoriality and residence

Income is taxable when it accrues in or is derived from Guyana, whether or not the individual is resident in Guyana. Earned income derived from sources outside Guyana is taxable only if it is received in Guyana by a resident individual. Unearned income derived from sources outside Guyana is taxable, whether received in Guyana or not, on individuals who are ordinarily resident or domiciled in Guyana, but is taxable on a resident who is not ordinarily resident or domiciled in Guyana only if it is received in Guyana.

Individuals are resident in Guyana if they reside there permanently or, being in Guyana, intend to reside there permanently, except for such temporary absence as the Commissioner of Inland Revenue may deem reasonable and not inconsistent with the claim of such individuals to be resident in Guyana.

An individual who resides in Guyana for more than 183 days in a calendar year is considered as resident for tax purposes.

Gross income

Employee gross income/An employee is taxed on income received for services performed in Guyana whether or not the income is received in Guyana. Employment compensation includes all benefits and allowances derived from employment, except allowances for medical or dental expenses or for a passage to or from Guyana and allowances for subsistence, travel, company car, entertainment, security, or expense if explained to the satisfaction of the Commissioner.

Capital gains and investment income/Residents and nonresidents are subject to capital gains tax on net gains derived from Guyana, except for capital gains on the disposal of shares or stock in public companies, which are exempt from taxation for any person. Residents who are ordinarily resident or domiciled in Guyana are also subject to capital gains tax on gains arising outside of Guyana, while residents who are not ordinarily resident in Guyana or domiciled therein are subject to tax only to the extent the gain is received in Guyana.

Capital gains tax is chargeable at the rate of 20% on gains exceeding G$1,000 where disposal of the assets occurs within 1 to 25 years of their acquisition. Short-term gains (arising within 12 months) are subject to tax as ordinary income. Gains on disposal of assets occurring more than 25 years after acquisition are exempt from taxation. There are certain minimal exemptions on disposal of personal assets. The market value at January 1, 1991 of assets held prior to that date is taken into consideration when computing capital gains.

Investment income arising outside of Guyana to a nonresident is not taxable in Guyana. A resident who is not ordinarily resident or domiciled in Guyana is taxable only to the extent that such income is received in Guyana.

Tax at 20% is withheld from gross distributions and bank interest arising in Guyana to nonresidents and from bank interest in Guyana to residents. Such income, unless an election is made, is exempt from further taxation on residents. Certain categories of taxpayers are exempt from taxation on bank interest. Residents are exempt from income tax/withholding tax on dividends received from a resident company.

Tax at 20% is withheld from discounts earned on treasury bills.

Taxpayers who are working painters, sculptors, or authors are assessed over a two- or three-year period on income arising from the sale of work, depending on the period of production.

Deductions

Business deductions/Generally, all outgoings and expenses incurred wholly and exclusively in the production of income are deductible. However, for nonresidents, certain expenses are not allowable, for example, property rental expenses.
In circumstances where expenses and consequently profits cannot be readily ascertained, the Commissioner (or a judge on appeal) may determine a fair and reasonable percentage of turnover of the business done by a nonresident person in arriving at taxable income.

Nonbusiness expenses/Expenses of a private, domestic, or capital nature are expressly excluded from deduction. Personal expenses, including home mortgage and improvement interest, life insurance and superannuation premiums, and charitable donations, are no longer deductible.

Personal allowances/A basic allowance of G$240,000 is deductible in determining taxable income. The allowance is prorated according to the individual's earning period.

Tax credits

Credit is granted to residents for taxes paid in foreign countries in accordance with the relevant double taxation treaties. Where no treaties currently exist, there are provisions for the unilateral granting of relief from double taxation.

Other taxes

Social security taxes/There is a social security tax, referred to as "national insurance contributions," which is deducted at source and to which employees contribute 4.8% (5.2% effective April 1, 2004) of their gross wages and employers contribute 7.2% (7.8% effective April 1, 2004) of their employees' gross wages. There is a maximum total rate of G$10,103 (G$10,607 effective from February 1, 2004 and G$11,491 effective from April 1, 2004) per month for monthly incomes in excess of G$84,188 (G$88,396 effective February 1, 2004).

Professional services tax/Effective September 1, 2003, specified professionals are required to collect and remit to the Guyana Revenue Authority a professional services tax of either 5% or 10% (depending on type of services, as set out in the First Schedule of the Tax Act). The imposition of this tax has been challenged by certain professional groups.

Effective January 1, 2004, specific individuals are required to pay a prescribed annual fee between G$75,000 and G$250,000, depending on their profession as set out in the First Schedule of the Tax Act.

Other/Other taxes are levied in the form of local rates on property, customs and excise duties, and consumption tax on certain goods, as well as property tax on the net asset worth of taxpayers.

Tax administration

Returns/Tax returns must be filed in specified form by April 30 of the year following the calendar year-end or accounting year-end. Tax returns are filed for income earned in a calendar year (which coincides with the tax year), except in the case of a sole trader or a partnership where filing is done according to the accounting terminal date approved by the Inland Revenue.

Each individual is required to file a separate return.

Payment of tax/There is payroll withholding of income tax under the pay-as-you-earn (PAYE) system. Withholding tax is deducted at source on bank interest paid to residents and on gross distribution, bank interest, and other specified payments made to nonresidents. Income tax on other income is paid in quarterly installments in the year in which the income arises.

Any shortfall of taxes deducted at source or paid in quarterly installments should be met by April 30 following the year of income.

Tax rates

Income tax on an individual's chargeable income is payable at the rate of 20% on the first G$110,000. Chargeable income over G$110,000 is taxed at the rate of 33 1/3%. There are special rates applicable to income arising from gold and diamond mining.

Withholding tax is payable at rates of 20% on gross distributions, dividend payments, 20% on other specified payments made to nonresidents, 0% on commercial bank interest and discounts earned on treasury bills paid to residents. Dividends received by a resident from a resident company are exempt from income tax/withholding tax.

Double taxation treaties may reduce the rate of withholding tax applied.

Minimum tax/A self-employed individual whose turnover for the performance of services is less than G$10 million must pay a minimum tax of 2% of annual turnover in lieu of regular income tax if the regular income tax is less than 2% of annual turnover in any year of assessment.

INDIVIDUAL TAX CALCULATION

Year of income 2003/Fiscal year 2004

Income tax

Assumptions

1. Resident alien with employment income of G$7,980,800, maintaining a nonworking spouse and two children in Guyana and earning interest from a savings account with a local bank.
2. Resident alien pays mortgage interest for property acquired in country of origin. Interest is not an allowable deduction in Guyana.
3. Resident alien pays life insurance premiums for self in country of origin. Life insurance premiums are not allowable deductions in Guyana.

Tax computation

(Calculations are based on rates effective for year to December 31, 2003)

Salary		G$ 7,980,800
Bank interest	12,870	
Less—Withholding tax deducted at source	(2,574)	
Bank interest received	10,296	
Less—Amount exempt from further taxation	(10,296)	—
Short-term capital gains		2,000
		7,982,800
Less—Personal allowance		240,000
Taxable income		G$ 7,742,800
Income tax on taxable income of 7,742,800		G$ 2,566,267

Capital gains tax—Long-term gain

Assumptions

Individual alien considered a resident of Guyana disposes of land and building used as residence acquired in July 1984 at a cost of G$750,000 and sold in September 2003 for G$2,000,000, with a market value of G$1,500,000 at January 1, 1991. Legal expenses incurred on the sale of the property: G$1,200.

Tax computation

Cost of land and building	G$ 750,000
Proceeds of sale of land and building	G$ 2,000,000
Market value of land and building at January 1, 1991	1,500,000
Gain	500,000
Less—Legal expenses	1,200
Net gain	G$ 498,800
Capital gains tax on 498,800 at 20%	G$ 99,760

Note:

Exchange rate of the Guyanese dollar at December 31, 2003: US$1 = G$195 at Bank of Guyana or G$200 at the Cambios.

PwC contact

For additional information on taxation in Honduras, contact:

Jorge Alberto Fú Padgett
PriceWaterhouseCoopers Honduras
Colonia Loma Linda Norte
Bloque F—Calle
Diagonal Coma No. 1
Tegucigalpa, Honduras
Telephone: (504) 231 19 11, 238 87 08/239 87 09
Fax: (504) 31 19 06
e-mail: jorge.fu@hn.pwc.com

Significant developments

This information is current as of 2004. There have been no significant developments as regards individual taxation in the past year.

Territoriality and residence

Honduras taxes its citizens and residents on their worldwide income. The highest marginal rate is 25%.

Nonresidents are taxed on their compensation attributable to services performed in Honduras regardless of where payment is received. Nonresidents are taxed at a 35% flat rate.

Gross income

Employee gross income/Nonresident aliens are taxed on salary and other income earned from sources located within Honduras. They are not taxed to the extent their compensation relates to services performed and compensated outside Honduras.

Total compensation includes any payments in cash or kind. Allowances such as cost of living, vehicles, housing, and utilities are considered taxable.

Capital gains and investment income/A nonresident alien is taxed on Honduran-source capital gains in the taxable year in which the gain occurs.

Nonresident alien's income from Honduras-source interest, dividends, rents, and royalties is subject to 5%, 0%, 30%, and 25% tax, respectively, usually withheld at source, and such income is not thereafter subject to graduated rates.

If aliens are resident, in principle they are taxed on worldwide income at graduated rates.

Deductions

Business deductions/Resident aliens can deduct properly documented expenses incurred in the practice of a liberal profession such as medical, dental, and health-related expenses up to an amount equal to L.20,000 annually.

Nonresident aliens have no business deductions.

Nonbusiness expenses/Resident and/or nonresident aliens cannot deduct nonbusiness expenses.

Personal allowances/Resident aliens cannot claim personal allowances, but the first L.70,000 of income is not taxable. Nonresidents cannot claim any personal allowances (also see "Territoriality and residents" above.)

Tax credits

Income taxes paid to foreign countries can no longer be deducted from taxable income of resident aliens.

Other taxes

Social security taxes/The maximum social security tax is L.2,016 per annum, or 3.5% on the first L.4,800 of monthly income. The excess over L.4,800 is tax exempt.

Other taxes on income/A minor personal municipal tax on an individual's income is imposed at the following rates:

From	To	Rate
0	L. 500,000	.30/000
L. 500,001	10,000,000	.40/000
10,000,001	20,000,000	.30/000
20,000,001	30,000,000	.20/000
30,000,001		.15/000

Tax administration

Returns/Annual returns are not required to be filed by employed resident aliens as the tax liability is paid via withholding tax, an adjustment is made through the payroll at the year end to ensure that the correct amount of tax has been paid for the individual.

Nonresident alien taxpayers usually do not file returns.

Payment of tax/Tax is withheld at source from payroll income. A taxpayer who is a proprietor is not subject to withholding but will be required to make quarterly payments of estimated tax.

Tax rates

Tax rates for fiscal year 2004 are as follows.

From	To	%
0.00	L. 70,000	0*
L. 70,001	100,000	10
100,001	200,000	15
200,001	500,000	20
500,001		25

*Tax free.

INDIVIDUAL TAX CALCULATION

2004

Gross income:	L.	450,000
Less—Standard deductions		20,000
Taxable income	L.	430,000
Tax thereon (1)		
First 70,000 x 0%		—
Next 30,000 x 10%	L.	3,000
Next 100,000 x 15%		15,000
Next 230,000 x 20%		46,000
Total tax liability	L.	64,500

Notes:

1. According to tax schedule for 2004.
2. Exchange rate of the lempira at February 28, 2004: US$1 = L.18.00.

Hong Kong

PwC contact

For additional information on taxation in Hong Kong, contact:

Rod Houng-Lee
PricewaterhouseCoopers
21/F Edinburgh Tower
The Landmark
15 Queen's Road Central
Hong Kong
Telephone: (852) 2289 2472
Fax: (852) 2810 9888
e-mail: rod.houng-lee@hk.pwcglobal.com

Significant developments

The following salaries tax measures proposed by the former Financial Secretary in his 2003/2004 budget speech delivered on March 5, 2003 were enacted into law and became effective in 2003/2004:

- Increases in salaries tax rates in 2003/2004 and 2004/2005.
- Increases in the maximum standard rate of tax from 15% to 15.5% in 2003/2004 and 16% in 2004/2005.
- Narrowing of the salaries tax bands in 2003/2004 and 2004/2005.
- Removal of the exemption for holiday warrant and passage.
- Increase in the maximum limit for deduction of donations to approved charities from 10% to 25% of the income of the tax year.

Territoriality and residence

Residence, domicile, and citizenship are not relevant to tax liability, except for the purpose of the People's Republic of China (PRC) double taxation arrangement (see "Tax credits" below), where the term "resident" is used. All individuals, resident or nonresident, are subject to tax on Hong Kong-source employment income, Hong Kong income from an office and Hong Kong pensions, as shown below.

1. Hong Kong employment income—Whether a person has a Hong Kong employment is usually determined by whether that person has entered into a contract of employment with a Hong Kong employer or Hong Kong-resident company. If the source of employment income is in Hong Kong, all the income is taxable, unless all of the services were rendered outside Hong Kong for a particular year of assessment. However, to provide unilateral relief for Hong Kong-source employment, income referable to services rendered outside Hong Kong will not be taxed in Hong Kong if the employee is liable to and has paid tax similar in nature to Hong Kong tax in the territory where the services are rendered.
2. Non–Hong Kong employment income—The Inland Revenue Department usually accepts that a person has a non–Hong Kong employment where three factors are present:
    a. The employer is resident outside Hong Kong;
    b. The contract of employment was negotiated and entered into, and is enforceable outside Hong Kong; and
    c. The employee's remuneration is paid outside Hong Kong.

For a non–Hong Kong employment, only the income attributable to services rendered in Hong Kong is taxable. If all of the services for a year of assessment are rendered outside Hong Kong, salaries tax is not payable in Hong Kong. A person with a non–Hong Kong employment who only renders services in Hong Kong during visits not exceeding a total of 60 days in a tax year is treated as if no services were rendered in Hong Kong in that year. Income from an office and pensions do not qualify for the apportionment basis and exclusion of income under the "visits not exceeding 60 days" rule.

3. Income from an office (such as directors' fees)—The source of such fees is determined by reference to where the company is managed and controlled.
4. Pensions—Pensions are taxable if the funds out of which the payment is made are situated in Hong Kong.

Gross income

Employee gross income*/*Taxable income includes any wages, salary, leave pay, fees, commissions, bonuses, gratuities, perquisites, and allowances, subject to certain exemptions.

1. Benefits in kind. If the employer has sole and primary liability for payment of benefits, and no other person including the employee acts as surety in respect of the liability, the employee will generally not be taxed, except in two situations:
   a. If the benefit is capable of being converted into money by the employee; or
   b. If the employer pays any amount in connection with the education of a child of an employee or holiday journey of an employee.
2. Cash allowances for holiday warrants, insofar as used for travel and transportation of personal effects for such travel, are exempt.
3. Free housing or rental refunds are taxed only on the rental value computed as a percentage of total income, as follows:

	%
Hotel, one room	4
Hotel, not more than two rooms	8
Other accommodation	10

4. Any sum received by way of commutation of pension under a recognized occupational retirement scheme upon death, incapacity, retirement, or termination of service is exempt, with certain exceptions where there is a termination of service of less than ten years with an employer. Any sum received by way of commutation of pension under the Pensions Ordinance is exempt.
5. There are no special concessions for foreigners or short-term residents, except that an employee engaged in a non–Hong Kong employment will not be subject to salaries tax on income from services rendered in Hong Kong during visits not exceeding a total of 60 days in the basis period for a year of assessment.

Capital gains and investment income*/*All capital gains, dividends, and interest on bank deposits are not taxable in Hong Kong.

Deductions

Business deductions*/*Expenses are allowable insofar as they are incurred wholly, exclusively and necessarily in the production of income subject to salaries tax. In practice, very few expenses meet these requirements. Some travel expenses (excluding private travel expenses, e.g., home to place of work) and entertainment expenses may qualify for deduction. There are no blanket or standard deductions. A deduction is allowed for self-education expenses paid up to a maximum of HK$40,000.

Nonbusiness expenses/"Concessionary deductions" are available in respect of approved charitable donations, home loan interest, elderly residential care expenses, and contributions to recognized retirement schemes.

1. Charitable donations made in cash to approved charities are allowable when the aggregate is not less than HK$100. The allowance for donations is restricted to 25% of the income of the tax year. For 2002/2003, the restriction was 10%.
2. From 1998/1999 onward, home loan interest paid is deductible for five years of assessment (proposed to be extended to seven years in the 2004/2005 budget). The place of residence must be situated in Hong Kong. For 2001/2002 and 2002/2003, the maximum deductible is HK$150,000. For 2003/2004 onward, the maximum deduction will be HK$100,000.
3. Elderly residential care expenses paid to a residential care home in respect of a parent or grandparent of a taxpayer or spouse are deductible up to a maximum of HK$60,000 per year for each parent or grandparent.
4. Contributions to recognized retirement schemes, including the Mandatory Provident Fund, are deductible up to a maximum of HK$12,000 per year.

Personal allowances/Allowances are granted as listed below for the taxpayer, spouse (provided the individual was married at any time during the tax year and, in the case of a wife living apart from her husband, provided he was maintaining or supporting the wife), unmarried children under the age of 25 years (provided children aged 18 to 24 are receiving full-time education), children over the age of 18 physically or mentally incapacitated for work, disabled dependents eligible to claim a disability allowance from the Hong Kong government, and the taxpayer's or spouse's parents or grandparents maintained by the taxpayer if the parents or grandparents are ordinarily resident in Hong Kong and are aged 60 or more or eligible to claim a disability allowance from the Hong Kong government.

Amounts for 2002/2003, 2003/2004, and 2004/2005 are shown on the following page.

	2002/2003 HK$	2003/2004 HK$	2004/2005 HK$
For a single person (Note)	108,000	104,000	100,000
For a married couple (Note)	216,000	208,000	200,000
Child allowances:			
First	30,000	30,000	30,000
Second	30,000	30,000	30,000
Third to ninth (each) (Note)	15,000	30,000	30,000
Dependent parent or grandparent allowance (each)	30,000	30,000	30,000
Dependent parent or grandparent living together with taxpayer (each)	60,000	60,000	60,000
Dependent brother or sister allowance	30,000	30,000	30,000
Single parent allowance (for single parent with sole or predominant care of a child)	108,000	104,000	100,000
Disabled dependent allowance	60,000	60,000	60,000

Note:

If a married couple both have income liable to salaries tax, they are taxed as two single persons. The married allowance is given only if one spouse has no income liable to salaries tax, where the married couple have elected for joint assessment to salaries tax or where an election has been made for personal assessment.
A couple must state which spouse will claim the child allowance.

Mandatory Provident Fund

Hong Kong's Mandatory Provident Fund (MPF) system came into operation on December 1, 2000. The MPF is designed to provide a formal, compulsory system of retirement protection by way of a privately managed contribution scheme. All benefits derived from mandatory contributions must generally be preserved until the contributor reaches the prescribed retirement age of 65.

An employee is required to contribute 5% of his/her monthly income and the employer must match this amount. The maximum level of income for contribution purposes is HK$20,000 (approximately US$2,564) per month, so the maximum mandatory contribution for each of the employee and employer is HK$1,000 (US$128) per month.

Employees' mandatory contributions are tax deductible up to a limit of HK$12,000 (US$1,538) per annum. Employers' MPF contributions are tax deductible to the extent that they do not exceed 15% of each employee's yearly emoluments.

Exemption from the MPF system is provided for some very limited categories of employees, including a person from overseas who enters Hong Kong for employment for not more than 13 months or who is a member of a provident, pension, retirement, or superannuation scheme (however described) of a place outside Hong Kong.

Tax credits

In practice, few foreign tax credits apply. However, an arrangement has been entered into between the PRC and the Hong Kong Special Administrative Region for the avoidance of double taxation of income. The arrangement applies in Hong Kong in respect of income derived in any year of assessment commencing on or after April 1, 1998. Where a resident of Hong Kong derives income from Mainland China, the amount of tax paid in the PRC in respect of that income is allowed as a credit against any Hong Kong tax imposed on that resident in respect of the same income. However, the amount of credit is not to exceed the amount of Hong Kong tax computed in respect of that income.

Hong Kong has entered into a tax treaty with Belgium. However, the procedures to bring the treaty into force have not yet been completed. Once it enters into force, a foreign tax credit relief will be available to a resident of Hong Kong in respect of Belgian tax paid on income derived from Belgium.

Other taxes

Hong Kong has no social security taxes or other taxes on income and no wealth tax, gift tax, or inheritance tax. Estates of deceased persons are subject to estate tax, but not on property situated outside Hong Kong. There are no local taxes.

Tax administration

Tax returns/Returns are filed in specified forms on the basis of a tax year ending March 31. Although husbands and wives who each have taxable earnings are required to file separate salaries tax returns, they may elect for joint assessment if such an election would result in reduced total salaries tax liability.

Payment of tax/There is no withholding on wages and salaries, with the exception that an employer is under an obligation to withhold any payment to an employee who is about to leave Hong Kong other than on a normal business trip.

Provisional salaries tax is a prepayment during the current year of the salaries tax payable in respect of income being earned during that year. It is based on the salaries tax payable for the previous year. It is credited against the salaries tax finally assessed for the current year. This assessment will also include a charge of provisional salaries tax for the following year.

Tax rates

For 2002/2003

Net taxable income		Tax on	Percentage
Over	Not over	Column 1	on excess
(Column 1)			
0	HK$ 35,000	—	2
HK$ 35,000	70,000	HK$ 700	7
70,000	105,000	3,150	12
105,000		7,350	17

The maximum tax, however, is limited to tax at the standard rate (15%) on the net assessable income (after any business deductions) less concessionary deductions but without the deduction of personal allowances.

For 2003/2004

Net taxable income				
Over	Not over		Tax on Column 1	Percentage on excess
(Column 1)				
0	HK$ 32,500	....	—	2.0
HK$ 32,500	65,000	....	HK$ 650	7.5
65,000	97,500	....	3,087	13.0
97,500		....	7,312	18.5

The maximum tax, however, will be limited to tax at the standard rate (15.5%) on the net assessable income (after any business deductions) less concessionary deductions but without the deduction of personal allowances.

For 2004/2005

Net taxable income				
Over	Not over		Tax on Column 1	Percentage on excess
(Column 1)				
0	HK$ 30,000	....	—	2
HK$ 30,000	60,000	....	HK$ 600	8
60,000	90,000	....	3,000	14
90,000		....	7,200	20

The maximum tax, however, will be limited to tax at the standard rate (16%) on net assessable income (after any business deductions) less concessionary deductions but without the deduction of personal allowances.

INDIVIDUAL TAX CALCULATION

Year of assessment 2003/2004

Assumptions

1. The individual is employed by a non–Hong Kong employer under an overseas employment contract and is required to travel extensively to other areas. The remuneration has been paid outside Hong Kong.
2. The individual is married and has two children. Wife does not work.
3. Salary calculation—Year of assessment 2003/2004. Income based on the year April 1, 2003 to March 31, 2004. Provisional tax payable for the year of assessment 2004/2005.
4. Accommodation provided by employer is rent-free.
5. Days spent out of Hong Kong on business—120.
6. Children's education expenses paid by employer: HK$80,000.
7. Perquisites capable of being converted into money, for example, a gift of a car: HK$100,000.
8. Perquisites not capable of being converted into money (not taxable): HK$8,000.
9. Interest income (not taxable): HK$10,000.
10. Long-term capital gain (not taxable): HK$60,000.
11. Approved charitable donations: HK$2,000.

12. The individual is a member of an overseas retirement scheme and is not required to join Hong Kong's MPF scheme.

Salaries tax computation

Base salary		HK$ 620,000
Add:		
Perquisites—Education expenses	80,000	
Other taxable perquisites	100,000	180,000
		HK$ 800,000
Portion of income attributable to time spent in Hong Kong		
800,000 x (245 ÷ 365) (1)		HK$ 536,986
Rental value of residence:		
(10% of 800,000 = 80,000 x (245 ÷ 365))		53,698
Assessable income		590,684
Less—Concessionary deductions:		
Approved charitable donations		2,000
Net assessable income after concessionary deductions		588,684
Less—Personal allowances (2):		
Married allowance	208,000	
Children (two)	60,000	268,000
Net chargeable income		HK$ 320,684
Salaries tax liability for year of assessment 2002/2003 (3, 4):		
32,500 at 2%	650	
32,500 at 7.5%	2,437	
32,500 at 13%	4,225	
223,184 at 18.5%	41,289	HK$ 48,601
Less—Provisional tax previously paid, say		(42,656)
Additional tax due 2003/2004		5,945
Provisional tax payable for year of assessment 2004/2005		54,937
Total tax due		HK$ 60,882

Notes:

1. If the individual in this case had signed a contract of employment with a Hong Kong company and thus had a Hong Kong employment, his/her gross income of HK$800,000 would be fully taxable and not be apportioned.
2. Personal allowances are not apportioned.
3. If the individual's net assessable income after concessionary deductions had been HK$2,010,167 or above, it would be taxed at the standard rate of 15.5%.
4. For 2004/2005, if the individual's net assessable income after concessionary deductions is $1,570,000 or above, it would be taxed at the standard rate of 16%.
5. Provisional tax payable for year of assessment 2004/2005.

	HK$	HK$
2003/2004 net assessable income after concessionary deductions		588,684
Less—Personal allowances		
Married allowances	200,000	
Net children (two) provisional chargeable income	60,000	260,000
		328,684
Provisional tax payable:		
30,000 at 2%		600
30,000 at 8%		2,400
30,000 at 14%		4,200
238,684 at 20%		47,737
		54,937

6. Exchange rate of the Hong Kong dollar at January 1, 2004: US$1 = HK$7.80.

Hungary

PwC contact

For additional information on taxation in Hungary, contact:

Paul Grocott
PricewaterhouseCoopers Kft
Wesselényi u. 16.
H–1077 Budapest, Hungary
Telephone: (36) (1) 461 9260
Fax: (36) (1) 461 9110
e-mail: paul.grocott@hu.pwc.com

Significant developments

- As from January 1, 2003, the health care contribution is no longer payable on dividends subject to 35% personal income tax.
- As from January 1, 2003, stock option schemes are classified on the basis of the relationship between the provider and the beneficiary (e.g., employment) instead of the former classification as fringe benefits.
- The special Hungarian fringe benefit taxation (where the tax on benefits is paid by the employer) has been significantly limited; as a result, the tax on certain noncash benefits must now be paid by the employee.
- As of May 1, 2004, EU regulation No. 1408/71 will come into force. As a result, many foreigners, who have not been paying Hungarian social security contributions, may have to start contributing.

Territoriality and residence

Hungarian personal income tax is assessed on the following.

1. Domestic-source income.
2. Foreign-source income, provided the individual is resident in Hungary.

Income originating in Hungary or taxable in Hungary by virtue of an international agreement or other reciprocal arrangement is considered domestic-source income, even if it is paid from abroad. Income paid from abroad will be liable to tax whether or not this income has been transferred or brought into the country.

Individuals are resident in Hungary if they have their permanent home, center of vital interests or habitual place of staying in Hungary.

Gross income

Employee gross income/The gross income of employees includes all cash remuneration and most personal expenses (overseas allowances, insurance, pension, tax reimbursement, tax equalization payments, etc.) paid by the employer. Housing can still be provided tax free by either the foreign or the Hungarian company, provided certain conditions are met.

Fringe benefits (e.g., home leave) are taxable to the employer at a flat rate of 44%. Where the fringe benefits tax cannot be levied by the Hungarian tax authorities (e.g., where the company providing or paying for the benefit is an overseas company), the benefit will be treated as compensation taxable to the individual. Similarly, where a noncash benefit does not qualify as a fringe benefit, then the value of this benefit will be taxable to the employee.

Capital gains and investment income/Capital gains on the sale of real estate, investments, and certain high-value items are taxed at a flat 20% rate. Interest income is effectively zero-rated in most cases. Dividend income from Hungarian companies is taxed at flat rates of 20% or 35%, depending on the ratio of the dividend distribution to the shareholders' equity in the company. For dividend income from abroad, the flat rate is 20%. This can be reduced by credit for any foreign taxes withheld. However, there is a minimum Hungarian tax of 5% on dividends from nontreaty countries.

In most cases, taxes on capital gains are paid by withholding. In all cases they are the final tax burden.

Capital gains realized on the Budapest Stock Exchange are taxed at zero rate; furthermore, as of May 1, 2004, capital gains realized on some EU exchanges will also be taxed at zero rate.

Deductions

Business deductions/Fees for membership in professional associations and trade unions are deductible from employment income.

Nonbusiness expenses/None.

Personal allowances/A few personal reliefs are available in the form of tax rebates. These are generally of little relevance to expatriates on medium-term assignments, partly because of lower limits in most cases and partly because of direct links to Hungarian institutions. Examples include life insurance, building society savings schemes, university (but not school) fees for dependents, child allowance, charitable donations, and repayment of mortgage.

There was also a tax-deferral scheme for the encouragement of portfolio investments in Hungarian shares, which was discontinued as of 2004.

An individual may determine that up to 1% of net tax payable be paid to a listed Hungarian charity and another 1% to a registered Hungarian church rather than to the tax office.

Tax credits

If a double taxation treaty does not apply, Hungarian residents are taxed at marginal rates on foreign-source income, but credit is given for foreign taxes paid. The credit may exceed neither 90% of the foreign tax paid abroad, nor the Hungarian personal income tax calculated applying an average tax rate (which is determined by dividing the calculated tax by the consolidated tax base). Most treaties provide for an exemption with progression rather than a credit for active income (e.g., from second employment).

Other taxes

Social security taxes/The individual's share of social security contributions is a flat 12.5% of gross salary (health care contribution—4% (no cap); pension contribution—8.5% (capped at income of HUF 5,305,000/year)). An additional 1% of gross salary must be contributed as employees' unemployment contribution (no cap). Foreign individuals are exempt from mandatory social security contributions but not from the 1% employees' unemployment contribution. 25% of the pension contribution paid is no longer deductible from the calculated tax as of 2004.

Social security contribution at the rate of 29% and employers' unemployment contribution at a rate of 3% of gross salary (no cap) are payable by Hungarian employers. Fringe benefits are subject to either the 29% employers' social security contribution or an 11% health tax where there is no insurance (e.g., employment) relationship. In the absence of a mandatory insurance relationship, neither 29% employers' social security contribution nor 11% health tax contribution should be paid in respect of any remuneration paid by a foreign company or a partially or wholly foreign-owned entity to a foreign individual.

Other contributions (training fund) are 1.5% of the total salary paid to all employees, including foreign individuals.

There are social security agreements in force between Hungary and Austria, Bulgaria, Croatia, the Czech Republic, Germany, Poland, Romania, Russia and the other members of the Commonwealth of Independent States, the Slovak Republic, Slovenia, Switzerland, and Yugoslavia. As of May 1, 2004, EU regulation No. 1403/71 will come into force; as a result, Hungary will have a regulation on social security in common with all the EU member and EEA (European Economic Area) states.

Withholding taxes/For resident individuals, withholding tax rates are as follows.

1. Dividends—20%, or 35% on dividends of more than 30% of the shareholders' equity.
2. Interest—Generally nil.
3. Royalties—Royalties are taxed at normal rates, although in most instances only a portion of the income is subject to tax.

Local taxes on income/Local authorities have the right to levy certain minor taxes.

Tax administration

Returns/Returns must be filed for each tax year (i.e., the calendar year) by April 20 of the following year.

Returns need not be filed where the individual does not have taxable income or where the individual's only taxable income is from a sole Hungarian employer. At the taxpayer's option, this can be extended to successive employments, provided appropriate details are given to the employer by January 15 of the following year. In this case the employer may file on behalf of the employee.

Individuals must file separate returns; there is no joint filing for husband and wife.

Payment of tax/Income tax is withheld from salaries and most investment income. For other income, individuals must pay income tax themselves. Taxpayers with income not subject to withholding generally must make quarterly payments. Employers are required to notify the tax office of total pay, benefits, and expenses paid or reimbursed (employment income).

Tax rates

With effect from January 1, 2004, the tax rates are as follows.

Taxable income		Tax on Column 1	Percentage on excess
Over (Column 1)	Not over		
0	HUF 800,000	—	18
HUF 800,000	1,500,000	HUF 144,000	26
1,500,000		326,000	38

INDIVIDUAL TAX CALCULATION

Calendar year 2004

Assumptions

Expatriate employee with salary from foreign employer and benefits as shown, and with foreign investment (dividend) income. Not subject to Hungarian Social Security.

Tax computation

Income tax

Gross salary	HUF 21,955,200
Add—Other cash allowances paid by the Hungarian disburser directly to the foreign individual	3,600,000
Less—Housing invoiced to and paid directly by the foreign individual, limited to the amount received in respect of the housing	2,500,000
	23,055,200
Add:	
Insurance premiums paid by employer (e.g., life insurance, savings type)	500,000
School fees	1,000,000
Total income taxable at scale rates	HUF 24,555,200
Tax due:	
On the first 1,500,000	HUF 326,000
On the remaining 23,055,200 at 38%	8,760,976
Total Hungarian income tax borne on aggregated income	HUF 9,086,976

Tax on dividends

Foreign dividend	HUF 500,000
Tax liability on dividend (20%)	HUF 100,000

Note:

Exchange rate of the forint at December 31, 2003: US$1 = HUF207.92.

PwC contact

For additional information on taxation in India, contact:

Nityanand Gupta
PricewaterhouseCoopers Pvt. Ltd.
Sucheta Bhawan (Gate no. 2, IInd Floor)
11-A, Vishnu Digamber Marg
New Delhi-110 002, INDIA.
Tel: 0091 11 23232916
Fax: 0091 11 23210594, 96
e-mail: nityanand.gupta@in.pwc.com

Significant developments

1. The surcharge has been increased from 5% to 10% for individuals whose taxable income exceeds Rs.850,000. For individuals with taxable income below Rs.850,000, there in no surcharge.
2. Dividend income on shares from domestic companies and income in respect of units of specified mutual funds and of the Unit Trust of India is exempt from tax in the hands of recipients.
3. Capital gains arising from the transfer of specified listed shares acquired on or after March 1, 2003 and before March 1, 2004 are exempt from tax, provided the shares are held for a period of 12 months or more before its transfer. (The Finance Minister in his Interim Budget Speech on February 3, 2004, has indicated that the exemption will be extended for a further period of three years, but this has not yet been legislated.)

Territoriality and residence

Residents are taxed on their worldwide income. Nonresidents are taxed only on income that is received in India or that accrues or is deemed to accrue in India. A person not ordinarily resident is taxed like a nonresident but is also liable to tax on income accruing abroad if it is from a business controlled in or a profession set up in India.

A person is resident if present in India (1) for 182 days or more in a year or (2) for 60 days or more in a year and 365 days or more during the preceding four years. Individuals fulfilling neither of these conditions are nonresidents. A resident who remained in India for 729 days or less during the preceding 7 years or who was nonresident in 9 out of 10 preceding years is not ordinarily resident. (The rules are slightly more liberal for persons of Indian origin residing abroad and visiting India or for Indian citizens leaving India for employment abroad.)

Gross income

Employee gross income/An individual's entire remuneration (including benefits in kind valued as per the tax rules) received from an employer is taxable. The tax paid by the employer on nonmonetary perquisites provided to the employee is not taxable in the hands of the employee.

The government of India has issued guidelines regarding employees' stock option plans or schemes. If the employer's stock option plan and scheme is in accordance with government guidelines, the taxable event will occur only at the time of sale of shares. Otherwise the benefit is taxable at the time of exercise. Concessional treatment is accorded to provision of housing, car, leave passage within India, reimbursement of medical expenses, and certain retirement benefits.

A foreign employee of a foreign enterprise who is not present in India for more than 90 days in a year is not taxed on remuneration received from the foreign employer for services performed in India, provided the foreign enterprise is not engaged in any trade or business in India and provided the remuneration is not deductible in computing the employer's taxable income in India. In a treaty situation, the 183-day rule applies.

Specified income of a foreign citizen or a not ordinarily resident person is exempt from tax if that person is engaged with the approval of the prescribed authority to render technical services under an agreement entered into by an international organization with the government of India and funded by the government of a foreign state.

Capital gains and investment income/Residents are taxed on capital gains and investment income irrespective of place of accrual. Nonresidents and persons not ordinarily resident pay tax only on capital gains and investment income accruing in India or received in India. Capital gains on assets held for over three years (one year in the case of shares or units) are considered as long-term capital gains. Long-term capital gains are determined after adjusting costs by prescribed inflation factors and are taxed at 20% plus surcharge, if applicable. Other capital gains are aggregated with ordinary taxable income, which is taxed at the applicable rates. In the case of nonresidents, capital gains on the transfer of shares or debentures in Indian companies are computed (without adjustment for inflation factors) in the foreign currency in which the shares or debentures were acquired, and the capital gains reconverted into Indian rupees are taxed.

Long-term capital losses can be set off only against long-term capital gains. Short-term capital losses can be set off against long-term as well as short-term capital gains.

In the case of nonresident Indians the rate is 10% (plus surcharge, if applicable) on long-term capital gains arising on sale of specified assets purchased in foreign currency, computed without any adjustment in respect of inflation factors.

In respect of long-term capital gains arising on sale of securities listed in India, taxpayers have the option to choose to pay 10% plus surcharge, if applicable, on the capital gain amount computed without adjustment for inflation. Income from specified investments is exempt, up to certain limits.

Deductions

Business deductions/In computing the taxable income from salaries, a standard deduction equal to the lesser of 40% of salary or Rs.30,000 is allowed to all employees drawing salary of Rs.500,000 or less. For employees drawing salary of more than Rs.500,000, the deduction is Rs.20,000. No other deduction is available for business-connected expenses, unless a special allowance is specifically granted to meet certain specified employment-related expenses (conveyance in performance of duties, cost of travel on tour or transfer, etc.). Such allowances are exempt to the extent of actual expenses incurred, and only the balance, if any, is taxable.

Nonbusiness expenses/No deductions are available from salaries for interest or taxes. Deductions up to certain limits are allowed for approved charitable contributions, retirement benefit funds, medical insurance premiums and, to a very limited extent, children's education/hostel allowance received from the employer.

Personal allowances/There are no personal allowances apart from the standard deduction mentioned above, professional tax (see below) and a limited deduction for certain allowances in connection with a posting in specified hilly, border, remote, or tribal areas.

Tax credits

Tax rebate/A rebate equal to 30% for individuals having total gross total income not exceeding Rs.100,000, 20% for individuals having gross total income Rs.150,000 or less, and 15% for individuals having gross total income of more than Rs.150,000 but less than Rs.500,000 is allowed on specified investments. These investments include amounts paid for life insurance premiums, specified schemes, contributions to specified provident funds, long-term investments, amounts spent on construction/ purchase of a residential house or repayment of certain loans, tuition fees for full-time education of two children (limited to Rs.12,000 per child) and subscriptions to specified infrastructure bonds, among other items. The rebate is allowed from the gross tax up to a maximum of Rs.20,000 (Rs.15,000 if gross total income is more than Rs.150,000 and less than Rs.500,000), out of which the rebate in excess of Rs.14,000 (Rs.10,500 where gross total income is more than Rs.150,000 and less than Rs.500,000) must be out of investment in infrastructure bonds. No rebate is allowed for individuals having gross total income more than Rs.500,000. Tax rebates cannot exceed the gross tax payable.

A woman resident in India and below the age of 65 years is entitled to a further rebate of an amount equal to 100% of income tax or Rs.5,000, whichever is less. An individual resident in India and above the age of 65 years is entitled to a further rebate of an amount equal to 100% of income tax or Rs.20,000, whichever is lower.

Foreign taxes paid/Only residents are allowed credit against their Indian tax liability for income tax paid abroad on income arising abroad (limited to the Indian tax on the doubly taxed income).

Other taxes

Social security taxes/There are no social security taxes.

Local taxes on income/Professional taxes imposed by certain states are minimal and are deductible in computing taxable income.

Tax administration

Returns/Husbands and wives file returns separately. Joint filing is not permitted. For tax purposes, the year ends on March 31.

Payment of tax/Income tax is withheld from salaries at the time of payment. If the taxpayer has other taxable income, then the taxpayer must pay advance tax on the basis of estimated income.

Tax rates

Income tax is calculated at graduated rates. On income of Rs.150,000, the tax is Rs.19,000, and income in excess of Rs.150,000 is taxed at 30%. Long-term capital gains are taxed at 20% (10% in the case of securities listed in India).

For individuals whose taxable income exceeds Rs.850,000, the tax amount calculated in the manner prescribed above is increased by a surcharge of 10% of the tax liability.

INDIVIDUAL TAX CALCULATION

Year ended March 31, 2004

Assumption

The taxpayer is a not ordinarily resident alien.

Tax computation

Salary		Rs. 3,500,000
Add:		
Value of accommodation provided (10% of 3,500,000)	350,000	
Value of car/chauffeur provided (1,600/600 per month)	26,400	376,400
		3,876,400
Less—Standard deduction		20,000
		3,856,400
Add:		
Interest accruing in India	20,000	
Short-term capital gain accruing in India	24,000	
Long-term capital gain accruing in India (1, 2)	35,000	79,000
		3,935,400
Less—Contribution to approved charities (10,000 at 50%)		5,000
Taxable income		Rs. 3,930,400
Gross tax (excluding tax on long-term capital gains)		Rs. 1,142,620
Less—Tax rebates:		
Contribution to provident fund	350,000	
Infrastructure bonds purchased	20,000	
	370,000	
Rebate allowable: (3)		0
Tax payable		1,142,620
Add—Tax on long-term capital gains (10.5%) (2)		3,500
		1,146,120
Add—Surcharge (5% of 1,146,120)		114,612
Total tax payable		Rs. 1,260,732

Notes:

1. 500 shares of Company X (assumed to be listed) sold in financial year 2003/2004 (purchased in financial year 1991/1992 at Rs.10 per share) at Rs.80 per share. Cost inflation index: 1991/1992—199; 2003/2004—463. Taxable long-term capital gain (after applying indexation methodology): 40,000 minus (500*10*463/199) = 28,367. Tax thereon @ 22% = 6,240.
2. Capital gains arising on sale of long-term listed securities can be taxed at a reduced rate of 11% but without indexation adjustment benefits, at the option of the taxpayer.
3. No tax rebate is allowed if individual gross total income is more than Rs.500,000.
4. Exchange rate of the rupee at January 1, 2004: US$1 = Rs.45.69.

Indonesia

PwC contact

For additional information on taxation in Indonesia, contact:

Firdaus Asikin
Tax Partner to Kantor Akuntan Publik
Drs Hadi Sutanto & Rekan
Gedung PricewaterhouseCoopers
Jalan HR Rasuna Said Kav. C-3
Kuningan
Jakarta 12940, Indonesia
Telephone: (62) (21) 521 2901–6
Fax: (62) (21) 521 2911–2
e-mail: firdaus.asikin@id.pwcglobal.com

General note

This entry is repeated from the 2003/2004 edition. For more up-to-date information consult the contact listed above or Jacqueline Collette at jacqueline.collette@us.pwc.com.

Significant developments

Indonesia is slowly recovering from the severe economic crisis that began in 1997 and subsequent political turmoil. A new government was democratically elected in 1999 followed by a couple of cabinet reshuffles up to the end of 2000. Heavy reliance on support from the International Monetary Fund, the World Bank, and other international financial institutions for the survival of its economy still continues.

Territoriality and residence

Resident individuals are, by law, taxed on worldwide income, whether or not remitted to Indonesia. A resident taxpayer is an individual who is present in Indonesia for more than 183 days during any 12-month period or has the intention to reside in Indonesia.

A nonresident is taxed on compensation received for work performed or utilized in Indonesia, regardless of where payment is made, at a rate of 20% (constituting a final tax). However, if the cost of this compensation is not borne by an Indonesian entity, this compensation is, in practice, not taxable in Indonesia. In addition, residents of tax treaty countries on short-term assignment in Indonesia may be protected from Indonesian tax where certain conditions are satisfied.

Gross income

Employee gross income/"Income" is widely defined to include almost any increase in economic prosperity. Resident taxpayers are not normally taxed on compensation received in kind (e.g., housing, cars) for work or services performed. Cash allowances for home-leave travel, education and similar costs are taxable in full to the individual taxpayer. Benefits in kind paid by certain tax-exempt, deemed-profit-basis or nontaxpayer entities are taxable.

Capital gains and investment income/Capital gains, excluding gains from sales of land and/or buildings and from sales of certain shares, form part of an individual's taxable income. Capital gains are taxable as income at the individual income tax rates.

Individuals who sell land and/or buildings valued at more than Rp60,000,000, or less than Rp60,000,000 but have an income of more than the PTKP (pendapatan tidak kena pajak; nontaxable income) threshold, should pay income tax (a final tax) on the gross amount of the sales transaction. The tax rate is 5%.

Sales of shares listed on an Indonesian stock exchange are subject to final withholding tax of 0.1% of the gross sales consideration. An additional final tax of 0.5% applies to the share value of founder shares at the time an initial public offering takes place, irrespective of whether the shares are held or sold. Shareholders can elect not to pay this tax; in this case, the actual gain will be subject to normal tax at the time the shares are sold.

Investment income, excluding interest on savings schemes, is also included as part of an individual's taxable income. Interest income on time deposits with Indonesian banks or their overseas branches as well as interest income on time deposits placed through Indonesian branches of foreign banks (in any currency) are currently taxed at a final flat preferential rate of 20%. Interest on bonds listed on Indonesian stock exchanges continues to be subject to final withholding tax at 15%.

Deductions

Business deductions/A specific tax exemption or concessional deduction covering approved business and occupational expenses is granted, amounting to 5% of the gross income up to a maximum of Rp1,296,000 per annum.

Nonbusiness expenses/Contributions to a pension fund approved by the Minister of Finance are recognized as allowable deductions. Other nonbusiness expenses, such as income taxes, mortgage interest, and charitable contributions, are not tax deductible.

Personal allowances/The annual personal allowances shown below are available. These allowance amounts came into effect in 1999 and are valid for the 2002 tax year.

	Rp
Taxpayer	2,880,000
Wife	1,440,000
Dependents (maximum three), each	1,440,000
Occupational expenses 5% of gross income, max	1,296,000

These personal allowances take the form of deductions; they are not available to nonresident taxpayers.

Tax credits

A credit is granted for tax paid or due abroad in connection with income received or accrued abroad. The tax credit is calculated at the rate this income would have been taxed had it been earned and taxed in Indonesia, unless the amount of tax paid or due abroad is lower.

Other taxes

Social security taxes/Indonesia does not have a comprehensive social security system. However, the Worker's Social Security Act (Jamsostek) encompasses occupational accident security, death security, old-age security, and health maintenance security, and operates as follows.

Employers are responsible for full contributions to occupational accident security, death security and health maintenance security funds. The contribution for old-age security is borne jointly by the employer and the employee; at 3.7% and 2% of monthly pay, respectively. Employee contributions to Jamsostek are collected by the employer through payroll deductions.

There are five major classifications under the occupational accident security component, with rates ranging from 0.24% to 1.74% of monthly pay, depending on the employer's type of business.

Death security contributions are made at 0.30% of monthly pay.

Health maintenance security is payable by the employer under Jamsostek if the company does not have in place an existing health scheme for employees that meets the government's minimum standard. The contribution amounts are 6% of monthly pay for married employees and 3% of monthly pay for single employees, subject to a maximum of Rp60,000 per month for married employees and Rp30,000 per month for single employees.

Expatriates are not required to participate in Jamsostek.

Fiscal exit taxes/This tax (Rp1 million per exit from Indonesia by plane, Rp500,000 by ship, or Rp200,000 by land) is payable by most residents and, by law, represents a prepayment of the personal income tax liability. Where the tax is borne by a company for its employees' business trips, the tax is considered a prepayment of the company's income tax liability. In most other circumstances, this tax becomes a cost unless the individual files personal income tax returns (see "Tax administration"). There are a number of exemptions to the payment of fiscal exit tax, including children below the age of 12.

Other taxes on income/There are no other taxes on income.

Tax administration

Individual taxpayers with income of more than the nontaxable threshold are required to register with the Indonesian Tax Authorities to obtain a personal tax identification number (*Nomor Pokok Wajib Pajak* [NPWP]) and to file annual individual tax returns (there are some exceptions) within three months of the end of the tax year (which is the calendar year).

In mid-2000, the Indonesian tax authorities issued a new ruling regarding individual taxation, under which expatriate tax residents are required to register and file tax returns on their worldwide income. Effective from January 1, 2001, the requirement also applies to national Indonesian tax residents.

Payment of tax/An employer is responsible for the deduction of taxes from its employees' earnings and for the remittance of those taxes to the tax authorities. In addition, at the end of the calendar year, the employer is obliged to recalculate the income taxes of its employees. If it appears that the total amount of taxes paid monthly during the year is less than the total tax payable, the balance must be paid by the following March 25 at the latest.

Individual taxpayers are also required to pay monthly tax installments on their income unless their only income originated from employment and the income tax thereon has been accounted for correctly by their employer. In this case, the income tax withheld by their employer from the employment income will constitute a tax credit against the overall income tax liability declared in their individual tax returns.

Tax rates

The rates applied to taxable income, effective as of January 1, 2001 and are still applicable for 2002, are shown below.

Individual tax rates/For resident individuals (general), the following tax rates apply:

Taxable income	Rate	Tax
	%	Rp
On the first Rp25,000,000	5	1,250,000
On the next Rp25,000,000	10	2,500,000
On the next Rp50,000,000	15	7,500,000
On the next Rp100,000,000	25	25,000,000
Over Rp200,000,000	35	

Tax on severance payments/Severance payments are taxed separately at the following rates:

Taxable income	Rate	Tax
	%	Rp
On the first Rp25,000,000	—	Nil
On the next Rp25,000,000	5	1,250,000
On the next Rp50,000,000	10	5,000,000
On the next Rp100,000,000	15	15,000,000
Over Rp200,000,000	25	

INDIVIDUAL TAX CALCULATION

Calendar year 2002

Assumptions

Resident taxpayer and wife with two children; salary is paid on a gross basis (1).

Tax computation

Gross wages paid in 2002		Rp 600,000,000
Employer's contribution for Jamsostek (0.54%) (2)		3,240,000
Capital gains (domestic) on sales of assets other than land, buildings, or shares		30,000,000
		633,240,000
Less—Allowable deductions:		
Taxpayer	2,880,000	
Wife	1,440,000	
Children (two)	2,880,000	
Business expenses	1,296,000	
Employee contribution to Jamsostek (2%)	12,000,000	20,496,000
Net paid taxable income		Rp 612,744,000
Income tax thereon:		
On first 25,000,000	1,250,000	
On the next 25,000,000	2,500,000	
On the next 50,000,000	7,500,000	
On the next 100,000,000	25,000,000	
On remainder (412,744,000)	144,460,400	Rp 180,710,400
Payable thus:		
Income tax withheld on wages received		Rp 171,250,000
Balance payable		9,460,400
		Rp 180,710,400

Notes:

1. To apply the above calculations to an expatriate living in Indonesia, omit the employer and employee contributions to Jamsostek.
2. The employer's contribution to Jamsostek consists of the occupational accident security contribution of 0.24% and the death security contribution of 0.3%.
3. Exchange rate of the Indonesian rupiah at December 31, 2002: US$1 = Rp8,940. The exchange rate has varied significantly in recent years. The official rates published weekly by the Tax Office are used in computing taxable income.

PwC contact

For additional information on taxation in Iran, contact:

Abbas Hoshi
Hoshiyar/Behmand & Co.*
130, Ghaemmagham Farahani Avenue
P.O. Box 15815-1619
Tehran, Iran
Telephone: (98) (21) 8305391–4, 8844684, 8843704–5
Fax: (98) (21) 8844685
e-mail: hb-ir-pwc@dpi.net.ir
a.hoshi@behmandhoshi.com
(Fax is also recommended.)
Web site: www.behmandhoshi.com

*A cooperative firm of PricewaterhouseCoopers in Iran.

General note

This entry is repeated from the 2003/2004 edition. For more up-to-date information consult the contact listed above or Jacqueline Collette at jacqueline.collette@us.pwc.com.

Significant developments

A new tax law was approved in February 2002, based on which the salary tax rate has been decreased. This new tax rate is applicable on salary income earned from February 17, 2002.

Territoriality and residence

All Iranians residing in Iran are subject to tax on their worldwide income. Iranians resident abroad and foreigners resident in Iran are subject to national taxes on income earned in Iran. Iranian nationals are considered resident in Iran if they have a place of residence in Iran or have resided for a total of more than six months in Iran during any one year.

In computing worldwide income, an Iranian resident in Iran must include the net amount of income received abroad or remitted from abroad. This implies that relief for tax paid in other countries is given by deducting this tax from gross income.

A foreign national resident in Iran will be subject to tax only on income earned in Iran, and not on worldwide income.

In the case of income earned from sources in Germany, France, South Africa, and a few of the new republics in Central Asia with which there are double taxation treaties, either such income is excluded from income tax or the gross amount will be taken as income and tax paid at source will be taken as an advance payment. General rules of 183-day residence and the taxpayer's not being subject to the other country's tax apply in Iran.

Foreign nationals who work in Iran and have obtained a work permit are treated as resident. The resident permit is issued accordingly.

Foreign currency transfer/An expatriate working in Iran as an employee of a registered company or branch is allowed to transfer net salary abroad in foreign currency purchased from official money dealers, owners of funds resulting from export activities or transferred from foreign-source funds (such funds should be kept in an Iranian bank account) and even from Iranian commercial banks (since July 2001).

Gross income

Employee gross income/Taxable income is deemed to include, for both foreigners and Iranians, all of their income (as limited above), together with free housing (as explained below), cost-of-living allowances or other cash payments, tax payments made by the employer on behalf of the employee, bonuses (less Rls1,450,000 per month, and a free car (as explained below).

Nonpecuniary benefits liable to salary tax are assessed and computed as noted below.

1. Free housing:
   a. Furnished—Equal to 25% of salary;
   b. Unfurnished—Equal to 20% of salary and taxable recurring compensation after the relevant deduction, if any.
2. Allocated car with driver—Equal to 10% (without driver, equal to 5%) of salary and taxable recurring compensation after the relevant deduction, if any.
3. Such other nonpecuniary award as may, at the proposal of the Ministry of Finance and with the approval of the Council of Ministers, be considered as benefits received—An amount equal to the cost price incurred by the payer.

There are no concessions to foreigners working in Iran on a short-term or a long-term basis.

Note: The employer of an expatriate employee is required to provide the Tax Office with the employee's salary agreement, the amount of which should not be less than the deemed taxable salary of US$1,000 to US$7,000 per month (depending on the job description and nationality of the employee). However, in practice, the expatriate's salary agreement is not sent to the Tax Office, and in this case taxable salary is assessed on a deemed-salary rather than on a reported-salary basis. The arbitrary amount of the salary subject to income tax is determined by the Tax Office for each year, on the basis of the expatriate's nationality and the nature of the assigned job (which is specified in the work permit). The employers' decision not to send the salary agreement is mostly because the actual salary package is usually more than the deemed salary (as stated in the table).

Capital gains and investment income/Capital gains and income from investments are taxable and the related tax is withheld at source. For a short-term resident, this income is subject to income tax in Iran, provided the capital asset or investment has been acquired/made and reported during the stay in Iran and provided the income is realized during this period.

Deductions

An annual basic deduction of Rls17,400,000 (Rls1,450,000 per month) is allowed. The basic annual deduction will be increased at the beginning of each Iranian year—March 20—based on the inflation rate.

Business deductions/There are no specific business deductions except for family medical expenses of employees working in underdeveloped areas (the list of which is announced by the Planning and Management Organization), which are subject to a 50% discount on the tax amount applicable to the salary income.

Personal allowance/Personal, spouse, or dependent allowances are not available.

Tax credit

Since the withholding tax on salary is calculated on an annual income basis, and filing an annual personal tax return is no longer a tax requirement, withheld tax constitutes a final tax. There are no available tax credits thereon.

Other taxes

Social security taxes/The social security organization provides coverage in the following cases for laborers and employees falling within the regulations:

1. Accidents at work and occupational diseases and their consequences.
2. Ordinary accidents and illnesses, pregnancy, and childbirth.
3. Disability.
4. Retirement.
5. Death.

An insured person has the right to benefit from family assistance. Members of the insured person's immediate family can benefit from this law in respect of illness.

All employers are required to arrange for the insurance of their workers, irrespective of the type of employment or contract or the method of payment of wages or salary (cash or otherwise). The social security organization may insure the self-employed or employees and owners of enterprises in accordance with special regulations for all or certain of the cases enumerated in this law, but any insurance of domestic servants and occasional workers is dependent on mutual agreement between the employer and the employee.

Insurance contributions are to be made at a rate of 27% of salary and other regular compensation—7% payable by the employee (usually withheld from the monthly salary) and the balance of 20% at the employer's expense. The monthly ceiling of the salary and wages subject to this contribution starting from March 20, 2002 basic salary was Rls67,900 per day (Rls2,037,000 per month) and from September 22, 2002 was increased to Rls3,000,000 monthly. A new ceiling, to be announced, will be effective from March 21, 2003. Expatriates working in Iran are subject to the above-mentioned regulation, except in the cases described below:

1. If there is a contract or agreement between the Iranian government and the government of the concerned country, the terms of this contract should be observed.
2. If the employee provides the Iranian social security organization with a legal certificate that confirms that the employee is insured with the social security organization of the home country or any other country for the period that the employee is working in Iran, the employee is exempt from payment of a social security premium for that period.

Unemployment insurance charges/An unemployment charge equal to 3% of salary, subject to a social security premium, is levied. The charges are payable directly by the employer. The Social Security Organization is in charge of collecting this amount through the monthly payroll submitted by the employer.

Ministry of Labor charges/All expatriates' salaries (except in a few cases) are subject to a fixed charge equal to 30% (according to the Annual Budget Law) of salary (to be determined on a deemed basis) plus 3% on employment charges (which is calculated on the maximum salary subject to the social security deduction). This is payable to the Ministry of Labor by the employer. Salary is determined on an arbitrary basis and is equivalent to US$1,000 to US$7,000, depending on the expatriate's nationality and job title. The reduction of these charges is now under review by the government.

Local taxes on income/There is no local income tax.

Property tax/According to the new tax law property tax is no longer assessed on the assets of an individual.

Tax administration

Returns/In Iran, there is no aggregation of the incomes of a husband and wife for determining total taxable income. Tax is payable by each individual on the basis of that individual's income. The taxable year is the year ended March 20.

Payment of tax/According to the new tax law, tax is withheld at source and individuals are no longer required to file annual tax return. An individual who has a business practice is required to keep financial records and also file an annual tax return. Such individual's income is subject to tax rate as stated in Article 131 (15 to 35%).

Foreigners' tax procedure/Expatriates are allowed to work in Iran under the conditions established by the Ministry of Labor. A work permit and a residence permit are issued on the basis of the request of either the Iranian company or the government offices that have contracted with the foreign company. If the work visa is issued, the employee should obtain the work permit, which is valid for 1 to 12 months. The company (or branch) in Iran is responsible for payment of the related salary tax, and the expatriate employee will be able to obtain an exit visa upon providing the authorities with the salary tax clearance (in the form of clearance against payment of taxes or issuance of a guarantee letter by the employer accepting the responsibility of payment of taxes). If the expatriate is also a branch manager or the managing director of a company, an additional branch or company corporate tax clearance is also necessary.

In the case of expatriate employees employed by a government office, a guaranteed letter (accepting the tax responsibility) issued by the employer is sufficient to issue the clearance letter (which is necessary to get an exit visa).

Individuals who stay in Iran for less than one year (as defined for Iranian tax purposes) and pay income tax for a period of assignment in Iran of more than the income tax due for their part-year stay are allowed to claim a credit for the extra taxes (according to the new tax law), but the tax procedure has not yet been announced.

Tax rates

The tax rates shown below are according to Article 131.

Income tax/Individuals are taxed at rates varying between 15% to 35%, as shown below:

Taxable income			Tax on	Percentage
Over	Not over		Column 1	on excess
(Column 1)				
0	Rls 30,000,000	....	—	15
Rls 30,000,000	100,000,000	....	Rls 4,500,000	20
100,000,000	250,000,000	....	18,500,000	25
250,000,000	1,000,000,000	....	56,000,000	30
1,000,000,000	....	....	281,000,000	35

Salary withholding tax/Tax is withheld from wages and salaries at progressive rates; the first annual salary of Rls15,600,000 is exempt, and the extra amount up to Rls42,000,000 is subject to a 10% tax. The excess of this amount is subject to tax rates according to Article 131, as follows:

Taxable income			Tax on	Percentage
Over	Not over		Column 1	on excess
(Column 1)				
0	Rls 17,400,000	....	—*	—
Rls 17,400,000	59,400,000	....	—	10
59,400,000	117,400,000	....	Rls 4,200,000	20
117,400,000	267,400,000	....	15,800,000	25
267,400,000	1,017,400,000	....	53,300,000	30
1,017,400,000	....	....	278,300,000	35

*Exempt.

Exchange rate

Effective March 21, 2002, one unique exchange rate, the market rate, is in use. Exchange rate of the rial at January 1, 2003: US$1 = Rls7,978.00.

Ireland, Republic of

PwC contact

For additional information on taxation in Ireland, contact:

Colm Kelly
PricewaterhouseCoopers
Wilton Place
Dublin 2, Ireland
Telephone: (353) (1) 6789999
Fax: (353) (1) 6626616
e-mail: colm.Kelly@ie.pwc.com

Significant developments

The information in this entry is current as of January 2004. For subsequent developments consult the contact listed above.

Territoriality and residence

Irish income tax is imposed on the following.

1. The worldwide income of an individual resident and domiciled in Ireland.
2. Income arising in Ireland and the United Kingdom and foreign income remitted to Ireland of an individual resident but not domiciled in Ireland.
3. Income arising in Ireland of an individual not resident in Ireland.

The following two rules determine the tax residence position of an individual for 2004.

1. An individual who is present for 183 days or more in Ireland during a tax year (ending December 31) is resident for that year.
2. An individual who is present for 280 days in aggregate in Ireland between that year and the preceding year will be resident for that year, provided more than 30 days are spent in Ireland in each year.

For tax residence purposes, "present" means present in Ireland at midnight.

Additional rules apply in relation to ordinary residence, which may affect the scope of income within the charge to Irish tax.

Gross income

Employee gross income/Expatriate employees regarded as resident but not domiciled in Ireland, will be liable to Irish tax on that portion of their foreign salary that they remit to Ireland, together with any benefits in kind (such as a house or car) or allowances that are provided to them by their foreign employer. The remittance basis does not apply to income from the United Kingdom. If, in addition, the individuals are in receipt of salary, benefits or allowances from an Irish-affiliated company, these items are fully taxable.

Capital gains and investment income/A single rate of 20% applies to most capital gains (excluding certain interests in funds and life insurance policies where the rate of 23% applies). In computing capital gains on assets acquired before January 1, 2004, the base cost is indexed by reference to the level of Irish inflation during the period of ownership and up to December 31, 2002 only. Thereafter, indexation does not apply. Annual chargeable gains of up to €1,270 for an individual are exempt from capital gains tax. This exemption is not transferable between spouses.

A nondomiciled Irish resident individual is liable to Irish capital gains tax on the full amount of gains arising in Ireland or the United Kingdom and on that portion of foreign gains that is remitted to Ireland.

Income tax on interest paid on normal deposit accounts held by Irish resident individuals in banks and other financial institutions is confined to the standard rate of tax (20% from January 1, 2004) and is deducted at source. Individuals who are both nonresident and nonordinarily resident and who make a relevant declaration can receive deposit interest gross.

Investment income of a nondomiciled person arising outside Ireland and the United Kingdom is taxed only to the extent that it is remitted to Ireland.

Deductions

Business deductions/Individuals may claim a deduction for expenses incurred wholly, exclusively and necessarily in the course of their employment. These expenses would include travel costs when the employment requires absence from home, as well as reasonable maintenance expenses for such absences. Expenses incurred traveling to and from work are not deductible. There are no standard deductions.

Cross-border relief/A separate tax relief can be claimed by Irish residents who commute to work in connection with an employment held outside Ireland. It applies where an individual commutes daily or weekly to work outside Ireland (in a country with which Ireland has a tax treaty) for a minimum period of 13 consecutive weeks in a tax year. The relief is given by reducing the tax otherwise payable by the proportion that the income from the qualifying employment bears to the total income.

Nonbusiness expenses/The principal nonbusiness expenses that may be deducted are interest on loans for investments in certain private trading or rental companies. Other expenses that may be deducted, subject to certain limitations, are retirement annuity premiums for self-employed individuals and employees in nonpensionable employment. Contributions to revenue-approved pension schemes are allowable deductions for employees. Personal medical and certain dental expenses can also be claimed as a deduction, subject to certain conditions. Employers who do not provide employees with access to an occupational pension scheme must provide access to a Personal Retirement Savings Account (PRSA). Employers are not obliged to contribute to a PRSA but must provide the facility for pension contributions to be deducted directly from the employee's salary and transmitted to the PRSA provider.

There are no standard deductions.

Tax relief is available for donations by individuals to certain approved bodies (charities/educational establishments).

Tax relief is granted at source at the standard rate of 20% in respect of mortgage interest and medical insurance premiums paid to authorized insurers.

Personal tax credits/Tax credits are available at the standard rate of tax. For 2004 the main personal tax credits are €1,520 single, €3,040 married, and €1,820 widowed. A home carer credit of €770 is available to married couples where one spouse works in the home caring for a dependent person. Certain income restrictions apply.

No child credit is available except for incapacitated children, for whom the credit is €500. Individuals are entitled to a pay-as-you-earn (PAYE) credit of €1,040 if they have employment income from which income tax is deducted at source.

Additional credits may be available (e.g., for rent paid, etc.).

Tax credits on dividends/Dividend withholding tax applies to dividends and other distributions made by Irish resident companies. The standard rate of income tax is withheld on these dividends. Exemptions apply in the case of certain categories of individuals who are neither resident nor ordinarily resident.

Other taxes

Social security taxes/The individual's share of pay-related social insurance (PRSI) contributions is 6% (4% plus 2% health levy) on the first €42,160 of income and 2% on earnings in excess of €42,160. The first €127 per week of earnings is exempt from PRSI contributions but not the health levy. The PRSI contribution rate for employers is 10.75% for 2004. For self-employed persons and certain directors a rate of 5% applies to all income.

From January 1, 2004, all benefits in kind (noncash remuneration) provided to an employee are subject to both employer and employee PRSI. The taxable benefit is treated as "notional pay" from which employee PRSI must be deducted. There are special rules to be applied in calculating notional pay.

Local taxes on income/There are no local taxes on income in Ireland.

Tax administration

Tax year/The Irish tax year is aligned with the calendar year.

Returns/In the absence of an election to the contrary, the incomes of a husband and wife are aggregated, and the income tax is assessed on and paid by the higher earner. Either spouse may elect to be taxed as a single person. Income of children is not generally aggregated with that of the parents, although there are provisions for this in certain cases. Tax returns are made for the tax year and must be filed by October 31, following the tax year-end.

Payment of tax/Income tax is withheld from all salaries paid from Irish pay points. From January 1, 2004, all benefits in kind (noncash remuneration) provided to an employee is subject to PAYE. The taxable benefit is treated as "notional pay" from which PAYE must be deducted. There are special rules to be applied in calculating the notional pay.

For other income, a system of self-assessment applies, and payment is made in two installments. Preliminary income tax for any year is due and payable by October 31 in that year. The balance of any income tax due for that year is payable by the following October 31. The revenue authorities retain the power to raise assessments as necessary. The revenue authorities now have a power of attachment whereby they can seize assets of defaulters.

For the tax year 2004, where chargeable gains are realized in the period January 1, 2004 to September 30, 2004, the capital gains tax is due for payment by October 31, 2004. Where chargeable gains are realized in the period October 1, 2004 to December 31, 2004, the tax is due for payment by January 31, 2005.

Any income tax due on exercise of stock options in the tax year 2004 must be paid by the employee within 30 days following the exercise.

The employer is responsible for accounting for the PAYE and PRSI due on notional pay to the revenue authorities and, generally, the PAYE and PRSI must be deducted from the employee's income at the same time. Special rules apply in certain circumstances.

Tax rates—Full tax year

Single or widowed person—No dependent children

Taxable income: Over (Column 1)	Taxable income: Not over	Tax on Column 1	Percentage on excess
0	€ 28,000	—	20
€ 28,000		€ 5,600	42

Single or widowed person—Dependent children

Taxable income: Over (Column 1)	Taxable income: Not over	Tax on Column 1	Percentage on excess
0	€ 32,000	—	20
€ 32,000		€ 6,400	42

Married couple—One income

Taxable income: Over (Column 1)	Taxable income: Not over	Tax on Column 1	Percentage on excess
0	€ 37,000	—	20
€ 37,000		€ 7,400	42

Married couple—Two incomes

Taxable income: Over (Column 1)	Taxable income: Not over	Tax on Column 1	Percentage on excess
0	€ 56,000	—	20
€ 56,000		€ 11,200	42

Note:

To the extent that there is only one earner between a married couple, the lower rate tax band that applies to the earning spouse is limited to €37,000. This is €9,000 higher than that available to a single person but potentially €19,000 less that would be available to a couple who are both income earners.

INDIVIDUAL TAX CALCULATION

Tax year 2004 (January 1, 2004 to December 31, 2004)

Assumptions

Irish-resident, non–Irish-domiciled husband and wife, two children; one spouse who is employed by an Irish company earns all the income.

Tax computation

Salary		€ 61,000
Dividend from Irish company—Gross		€ 2,500
Total gross income		€ 63,500
Capital gain (after relief for personal annual exemption)		€ 5,000
Taxable income		€ 63,500
Income tax thereon(see table above):		
37,000 @ 20%	7,400	
26,500 @ 42%	11,130	
		€ 18,530
Less—Tax credits:		
Personal credit	3,040	
PAYE credit	1,040	
Home carer credit	770	
Dividend withholding tax (2,500 at 20%)	500	(5,400)
Net income tax liability		€ 13,180
Capital gains tax (5,000 at 20%)		€ 1,000

Notes:

1. Other payments:

	€
Pay-related social insurance (rate 4%)*	1,510
Levies (rate 2%)	1,270
Total	2,780

*The 4% of PRSI is calculated on earnings up to a ceiling of €42,160. Once the ceiling has been reached, no further contributions are payable. In addition, the first €550 of earnings each month are exempt. Therefore, in the above scenario the individual will take eight months to reach the threshold and the PRSI calculation will be as follows:

€42,160 – (€550 x 8 months) x 4% = €1,510

2. Exchange rate of the euro at January 2, 2004: US$1 = €0.79.

PwC contact

For additional information on taxation in the Isle of Man, contact:

David Churcher
PricewaterhouseCoopers
Sixty Circular Road
Douglas, Isle of Man
Telephone: (44) (1624) 689689
Fax: (44) (1624) 689600
e-mail: david.churcher@iom.pwc.com

Significant developments

There have been no significant tax or regulatory developments in the past year although significant changes to Isle of Man tax legislation are currently under consideration.

Territoriality and residence

Residents/Individuals who are resident in the Isle of Man are liable to tax on their worldwide income from all sources. Generally, a person present on the Island for six months or more in the tax year is regarded as resident. However, individuals may be judged to be resident with less than six months' presence in one year, depending on such factors as the maintenance of a home available for their use on the Island and the purpose of their visits to the Island and abroad.

By concession, an individual who has accommodation available for use in the Island is not treated as resident if visits to the Island in any two consecutive years of assessment do not exceed four months in aggregate. Individuals falling within the concession will be liable to Isle of Man income tax on local source income in the same manner as a person who is not resident.

Nonresidents/A nonresident is liable to tax on income arising or accruing from any source whatsoever in the Island, with the exception of bank interest, building society interest, and dividends paid by certain companies included in a list held by the Treasury for this purpose. New legislation is currently being considered which will entitle a nonresident to a personal allowance. In order to claim the maximum allowance a return of income will be required. Individuals will then be entitled to a proportion of the single person's allowance (but not less than £2,000) based on the ratio of their Manx-source income to their total world income. Where nonresidents do not submit a return of their total world income they will be entitled to a fixed deduction of £2,000. The computation for this purpose will exclude any source that is exempt from income tax in the Isle of Man.

International limited partnerships/A limited partner in an international limited partnership is not liable to income tax on income received from that partnership as long as the partnership has been granted a "certificate of status" as an international limited partnership.

Gross income

Employee gross income/A resident is assessable on income from employment (including most benefits), wherever carried out. There is no remittance basis of assessment. A nonresident is assessed on income from employment carried on in the Isle of Man.

Capital gains and investment income/There is no capital gains tax in the Isle of Man. Similarly, there are no death or estate duties or capital transfer, gift or wealth taxes.

Investment income is charged to tax as follows.

1. For a resident, on income from any source inside or outside the Island.
2. For a nonresident, on income arising in the Island, at the prevailing higher rate of income tax (see "Tax rates" below). However, by extrastatutory concession, the Treasury will take no action to pursue the liability to income tax on bank interest, building society interest, and dividends paid by certain companies to nonresidents.

Deductions

Business deductions/Business deductions are applicable to individuals only for disbursements or expenses incurred wholly and exclusively in acquiring the income on which income tax is payable. They would include travel expenses, professional expenses, and a proportion of household expenses. The expense of traveling to and from work is not deductible. There are no standard deductions.

Nonbusiness expenses/Deductible nonbusiness expenses are as follows.

1. Interest paid by a resident on any mortgage or loan, provided, in most cases, that the lending institution is based in the Isle of Man. If interest is paid at more than a reasonable commercial rate, the excess is not deductible.
2. Pension contributions paid to approved superannuation funds.
3. Within certain limits, 50% of the annual amount of life insurance premiums.
4. Charitable covenants to charities and certain covenanted educational payments.

Personal allowances/Nonresidents are not generally entitled to personal allowances, and all of their taxable income is taxed at the prevailing higher rate. However, a nonresident subject to deduction of tax under the ITIP (Income Tax Installment Payments) scheme would be granted a portion of the single person's allowance.

Allowances for 2004/2005 are as follows.

	£
Single person	8,225
Married couple (combined allowance—totally transferable)	16,450
Single parent (entitled to single parent benefit)	5,630*
Blind person/Disabled person	2,530*

*Paid in addition to a single person allowance.

Tax credits

Foreign tax credits are available under the United Kingdom/Isle of Man treaty. The treaty does not cover dividends or debenture interest. U.K. personal allowances may be given under U.K. legislation to Isle of Man residents, provided a claim is made to the U.K. authorities. The Island does not have a treaty with any other country. Where no bilateral agreement exists, Isle of Man residents paying or liable to pay foreign tax (other than U.K. tax covered by the treaty) as well as Isle of Man tax on income arising outside the Island are entitled to relief from Isle of Man tax on the lesser of the marginal amount or the amount of foreign tax on which the deduction is claimed. The marginal amount is calculated as the difference between (1) the tax on the total amount including foreign taxed income and (2) the tax on total income excluding the foreign income in respect of which the relief is to be allowed. This is known as unilateral relief.

Other taxes

Social security taxes/No national insurance contributions are payable where earnings are less than £91 per week. Above this limit, 10% is paid by employees on earnings up to a limit of £670 per week, giving a maximum contribution of £2,698 per annum (on a salary of more than £31,720 per annum). National insurance contributions are not payable on the benefit of cars and car fuel provided by employers.

Self-employed persons earning £4,745 or more per annum pay a flat-rate contribution of £2.05 per week. In addition, there is a contribution of 8% of profits between £4,745 and £31,720 per annum. Therefore, the maximum additional contribution is £2,158 (on earnings of more than £31,720 per annum). This additional contribution is allowable in full for tax purposes.

Other taxes on income/There are no other taxes on income. Other taxes are raised in the form of customs and excise duties on certain goods and through value-added tax on the purchase of most goods and services.

Tax administration

Returns/The tax year runs from April 6 to April 5. Tax returns must be filed before June 30 for total income of the preceding tax year. Legislation should be introduced during 2004 to extend the filing date to October 5, 2004.

A wife's separate income is deemed to be her husband's for income tax purposes, and such income must be recorded on the husband's tax return. Husband and wife can elect to be taxed separately.

Payment of tax/An employee's tax and national insurance contribution are deducted by the employer under the ITIP system, and the employer is accountable to the Assessor each month for the amounts due. Income tax (other than that paid under the ITIP system) is payable on or before January 1 for the year ending on the following April 5 (i.e., on income of the current tax year). There are special rules for taxation of nonresident individuals or individuals who commence or cease residence in the Isle of Man.

Tax rates

A standard rate of 10% is charged on taxable income of resident individuals up to £10,000 for single persons and £20,000 for married couples. A higher rate of 18% is charged on taxable income exceeding the standard rate limits. The nonresident tax rate is 18% on total taxable income.

INDIVIDUAL TAX CALCULATION

Tax year 2003/2004

Assumptions

Resident husband and wife, two children; one spouse earns all the income.

Tax computation

Salary		£ 50,000
Interest (1)		10,000
Capital gains—Not assessable		—
		60,000
Less:		
Mortgage interest	5,000	
Life insurance premiums (50% of 1,500)	750	
Charitable covenants	1,000	6,750
		53,250
Less—Personal allowance		16,450
Taxable income		£ 36,800
Tax thereon:		
First 20,000 at 10%	2,000	
Balance of 16,800 at 18%	3,024	
Total tax due (2)		£ 5,024

Notes:

1. Interest and dividends paid by Isle of Man companies are paid gross to residents.
2. Manx effective rate (5,024 ÷ 60,000) x 100 = 8.37%.
3. Exchange rate of the pound sterling at December 31, 2003: US$1 = £0.5602.

PwC contacts

For additional information on taxation in Israel, contact:

Gerry Seligman
Shlomi Zehavi
Vered Kirshner
Kesselman & Kesselman
Trado Tower, 25 Hamered Street
P.O. Box 452
Tel-Aviv 61003
Telephone: (972) (3) 795 4555
Fax: (972) (3) 795 4506
e-mail: gerry.seligman@il.pwc.com
shlomi.zehavi@il.pwc.com
vered.kirshner@il.pwc.com

Significant developments

Pursuant to the tax reform legislation of 2003, personal income tax rates on an individual's income from employment are being reduced over a phase-in period through 2007. Effective January 1, 2004, the government has further accelerated the implementation of the rate reductions and widening of the tax brackets.

Effective July 1, 2003, a new levy is imposed on employers who have foreign residents employed in Israel. The levy is 8% of the employee's monthly compensation.

Territoriality and residence

Israeli tax residents are taxable on their worldwide income.

Nonresident individuals are subject to income tax on Israeli-source income and to capital gains tax on capital gains from assets situated in Israel (see "Capital gains and investment income" below). Sourcing rules determine when income is to be regarded as being from an Israeli source.

The Income Tax Ordinance (ITO) defines an Israeli tax resident as a person whose center of life is in Israel. Various factors are analyzed in determining where the individual's center of life is located. Additionally, the following is a "days test" that serves as a presumption in determining the individual's "center of life" (this presumption is refutable by the taxpayer as well as by the tax authorities).

1. Any individual who has been present in Israel during a certain tax year for 183 days or more, shall be presumed to have his or her center of vital interests in Israel in that tax year.
2. Any individual who has been present in Israel during the tax year for 30 days or more, and a total of 425 days or more during the current tax year and the two previous tax years (in aggregate), shall be presumed to have his or her center of vital interests in Israel in such tax year.

The ITO defines a nonresident taxpayer as being anyone other than a person resident in Israel.

Should an individual be deemed to be an Israeli resident while at the same time resident of another country, the tie-breaker tests set out in the applicable treaty will determine in which country the individual will be viewed as resident. Generally, the treaties focus on factors relating to where the person's permanent home is maintained, in which country the person's personal and economic relations are closest ("center of vital interests" test) and in which country the person is a national.

Gross income

Employee gross income/All remuneration derived from employment, including allowances paid to an employee for cars, clothes, transport, professional literature, and the like, are taxed as ordinary income.

In the case of loans to employees where the interest rate charged is less than the rate of increase in the consumer price index (CPI) (with an addition of 4% annual interest), the interest differential will be taxed as ordinary employment income.

The prescribed value of the regular use of a company car is considered to be income of the employee.

For employee stock options granted before January 1, 2003, determination and taxation of the benefit arising from the exercise of a right or of an option at a price below the market value of the shares will be either at exercise in the case of a nonqualified plan or will be deferred to sale in the case of a qualified plan.

With respect to nontraded options for traded shares granted after January 1, 2003, the tax reform legislation provides for the deferral of the taxation event to the date of realization of the shares. The gains derived from the realization of the shares will be taxable as regular employment income, or as capital gains depending upon the taxation route selected by the employer. Detailed rules are applicable.

The only benefits that are exempt from tax are employers' contributions to further education funds and their contributions to approved pension and benefit schemes (subject to certain requirements and maximum levels of contribution).

Special deductions for qualifying expatriates/A nonresident employee who is granted "Foreign Expert" status would be entitled to deduct from Israeli taxable income the following items for a period not exceeding 12 months of employment in Israel.

1. Documented rent and certain utilities (gas, water, electricity) costs or accommodation expenses. The employee should retain a copy of rental contracts, hotel bills, and utility charges.
2. Daily living expenses—These expenses are limited to the lower of (i) NIS260; or (ii) according to Israeli tax authority guidelines up to 50% of the employee's gross remuneration. This deduction is only for the actual days that the employee is physically present in Israel. The employee will need to record the days in and out of Israel so that this deduction may be claimed for tax purposes.

"Foreign Expert" status is granted to a nonresident who while abroad has been invited by an Israeli individual or by an Israeli resident entity (not being a manpower company or temporary agency) to perform services in his area of expertise for the inviting party and has received approval from the Ministry of Labor and Social Welfare. Additional qualifying conditions apply. New regulations, setting out the terms and conditions for granting foreign expert status, are expected to be issued in the near term. Further, it is expected that such regulations will provide conditions that would further reduce the population of foreign resident employees who would qualify to be granted such status.

"Approved specialists" (nonresidents approved by the director of the Investment Center at the Ministry of Industry and Trade), provided they are experts who possess skills not readily available locally, are taxed at a maximum rate of 25% on their earnings for a period of three years, with a possible extension of up to a further five years. They are also entitled to the benefits available to foreign experts in the first 12 months. Approval is generally given on income up to US$75,000 per annum.

Capital gains and investment income/Capital gains tax is generally payable on capital gains by residents of Israel on the sale of assets (irrespective of the location of the assets) and by nonresidents on the sale of:

1. Assets located in Israel.
2. Assets located abroad that are essentially a direct or indirect right to an asset or to inventory or that are an indirect right to a real estate right or to an asset in a real estate association located in Israel. Taxation will apply only in respect of that part of the consideration that stems from the above property located in Israel.
3. Assets that are a share or the right to a share in an Israeli entity.
4. Assets that are a right in a foreign resident entity that is essentially a direct or indirect right to property located in Israel. Taxation will apply only with respect to that part of the consideration that stems from the property located in Israel.

Capital gains realized by a nonresident from the sale of assets may qualify for treaty exemption depending upon the particular circumstances and the provisions of the applicable treaty. When assets are attributable to an Israeli permanent establishment or are real estate rights, treaty exemption will generally not be available.

For the purposes of assessing tax, the capital gain is generally calculated in local currency terms, and provisions exist for segregating the taxable gain into its real and inflationary components. The inflationary amount is equal to the original cost of the asset less depreciation (where applicable) multiplied by the percentage increase in the Israeli consumer price index from the date of acquisition of the asset to the date of its sale. This component of the inflationary amount is exempt to the extent it accrued after January 1, 1994 and is generally subject to tax at the rate of 10% for the component accrued before then.

A nonresident who invests in taxable assets with foreign currency may elect to calculate the inflationary amount in terms of the foreign currency originally invested. Under this option, in the event of a sale of shares in an Israeli resident company, the inflationary amount attributable to exchange differences on the investment is always exempt from Israeli tax.

In the case of a disposal of shares by individuals (with some exceptions) special provisions would apply to such part of the "real gain" that is attributed to the seller's share of retained profits. Generally, the seller's proportionate part of retained profits will be taxed as if this amount had been received as dividends immediately before the sale (i.e., at a general rate of 25%). However, the proportionate part of the retained profits that is attributable to the period up to December 31, 2002, will be subject to tax at the rate of 10%.

The share of retained profits is the amount of gain equal to the proportional part of the retained profits of the company that the seller of the shares would have rights to by virtue of those shares. Profits for this purpose are generally defined as financial statement profits available for distribution which accumulated over the period from the end of the tax year prior to the year of acquisition of the shares to the end of the tax year prior to the year of sale, provided that profits accumulated prior to January 1, 1996 are not to be included. The amount of the profits is not to exceed the amount of income taxed in the above-mentioned period, less the taxes thereon, any dividend distributed therefrom and losses that have accumulated in the company that have not been offset with the addition of tax-exempt income. A nonresident is not exempt from tax on this type of inflationary amount.

The real gain accrued at the sale of an asset purchased on or after January 1, 2003 is taxed at an applicable 25% rate. Real gains derived from the disposal after January 1, 2003 of an asset purchased prior to this date will be subject to capital gains tax at a blended rate. The ordinary individual tax rate (determined in accordance with the individual's marginal tax rate in the range of 30% to 49%) will be applied to the gain amount that bears the same ratio to the total gain realized as the ratio the holding period commencing at the acquisition date and terminating on January 1, 2003 bears to the total holding period. The remainder of the gain realized will be subject to capital gains tax at the beneficial 25% rate.

Special tax rates apply to assets purchased prior to April 1, 1961. With effect from the beginning of 2005, these special tax rates will be increased by 1% in each tax year until the tax rate on the real gain reaches a rate of 25%.

In the case of traded securities of Israeli corporations (with some exceptions), as of January 1, 2003, Israeli resident individuals who are not engaged in a business of trading securities will be subject to tax at 15% rate on realized capital gains (or 25% if they elect to deduct interest expenses). Non-Israeli residents will generally continue to be exempt from tax on capital gains derived from the sale of shares traded on the Tel-Aviv Stock Exchange (TASE).

An Israeli capital gains tax exemption is also available to foreign residents, irrespective of whether or not the foreign resident is a resident of a country with which Israel has concluded a treaty for the avoidance of double taxation, upon the disposal of an interest in a nontraded "research and development intensive company" (as defined by Israeli tax regulations) where such interest was acquired through an allotment of shares as from 2003.

Special provisions of the law apply to the sale of securities that were acquired prior to their listing on such an exchange. Israeli resident individuals who dispose of foreign securities that are listed for trading on overseas exchanges are generally liable to Israeli tax of 35% of the capital gain arising thereon, calculated in terms of the foreign currency invested. As of January 1, 2007, a tax rate of 15% will generally apply.

Capital losses generated in 1996 and onward can be carried forward indefinitely, while capital losses generated in the tax year prior to 1996 can be carried forward over the next seven years.

Until the end of 2006, capital losses from securities traded on the TASE may be set off only against capital gains from securities traded on the same stock exchange and capital losses from the sale of foreign securities can be offset only against gains from the sale of foreign securities. As of the year 2007 capital losses from the sale of securities traded on TASE or on a foreign stock exchange can be offset against each other.

Exit tax/Under the new exit tax provisions introduced by the tax reform legislation, individuals that cease to be Israeli tax residents are deemed to have disposed of all of their capital assets, including options or shares received from employers, on the day immediately preceding their exit date and are consequently subject to capital gains tax. The taxation is generally deferred until the actual sale of the assets. Exemptions under the exit tax provisions for certain capital assets are available under the provisions of the law.

Dividends/Dividends from resident companies are generally subject to 25% withholding tax (15% for dividends distributed from approved enterprises), which represents the final tax to the individual. Dividends received from foreign nontraded companies are liable to a maximum tax of 25%. Interest and dividends derived from foreign securities are currently taxed at a rate of 35%. Commencing in 2007, interest and dividends attributed to foreign securities will be subject to 15% and 25% tax, respectively.

Deductions

Business deductions/Business expenses deductible from business-source income must be incurred wholly and exclusively during the tax year for the purposes of producing this income. Employees are entitled to relatively few deductions. However, subsistence expenses if required to travel out of town and subsistence expenses abroad may be deducted.

Self-employed individuals are subject to special rules for determining the deductibility of expenditure on the maintenance of private and small commercial vehicles, as well as other expenditures such as telephone costs when the business is conducted from the taxpayer's house.

Nonbusiness expenses/Contributions to an approved provident fund and a training fund are deductible up to predetermined limits for the self-employed and certain employees. Mortgage interest and medical expenses are not deductible. Charitable contributions are not deductible, but a tax credit may be allowed (see below).

Personal allowances/Residents are entitled to personal tax credits against their tax liabilities according to their status. At January 2004 each point is worth NIS178 per month, resident individuals being entitled to a minimum of 2.25 points. Additional points are granted for, among other items, dependent children, new immigrants and single-parent families.

Tax credits and deductions are granted for certain payments for life insurance premiums and payments to provident and pension funds.

Tax credits

Israeli residents are entitled to relief from double taxation under unilateral domestic relief provisions or under applicable tax treaties. Detailed rules apply.

Foreign residents are not entitled to personal tax credits or unilateral tax relief on foreign income. However, in circumstances where it can be shown that the amount of tax payable in Israel exceeds the amount of tax credit available in the home country on specific Israeli-source income, the Minister of Finance is permitted to order a total or partial tax reduction.

Donations to recognized public institutions entitle the taxpayer to a tax credit of 35% from donations that in aggregate are not less than NIS370, provided the donations do not exceed 30% of annual taxable income or NIS2,120,000, whichever is less. These amounts apply for 2003 and are expected to be updated for 2004. Excess donation amounts can be carried forward for three years under certain circumstances.

Personal tax credits are available; see "Personal allowances" above.

Other taxes

Social security taxes/Employees' National Insurance contributions are 1.40% on the first NIS3,482 of income per month and 5.58% on the difference between NIS3,482 and the maximum monthly compensation amount of NIS34,820. The employers' contribution is 5.93% up to the maximum monthly compensation amount of NIS34,820. Contributions for nonresidents are funded by the employee at 0.17% and 0.69% in accordance with the above limits and by the employer at a single rate of 0.84%.

National Health Insurance premiums/Health Insurance premiums are levied at 3.10% on the first NIS3,482 and 4.8% on the difference between NIS3,482 and the maximum monthly compensation amount of NIS34,820. Nonresidents are not subject to National Health Tax.

Special detailed rules and rates regarding National and Health Insurance apply to irregular salary payments, the self-employed, and to other sources of income generated by an Israeli resident (i.e., rent, interest, dividends, pension, etc.). Capital gains are not subject to National and Health Insurance contributions.

Local taxes on income/There are no local taxes on income.

Land appreciation tax/Capital gains on real estate are assessed to land appreciation tax. The law relates to any real estate in Israel, including houses, buildings, and anything permanently fixed to land; real estate rights and leases for 25 years or more. Tax calculations closely follow the calculation of tax on capital gains (see below). The tax rate on the real gain is reduced from the marginal individual tax rate (up to 49%) to 25% on assets that were purchased after November 7, 2001. Regarding assets purchased prior to November 7, 2001, the reduced tax rate will be applicable only to the gain accumulated after November 7, 2001. The gain will be attributed to the period commencing on November 7, 2001 in accordance with the ratio of the holding period after this date to the entire holding period.

The purchaser of real estate is subject to acquisition tax at the rates of 0.5% to 5%.

Sales tax/Sales tax at the rate of 2.5% is applicable to the sale of most real estate rights. The sales tax does not apply to certain types of apartments (residential dwellings) that are classified as inventory. Sales tax will not apply to sales of real estate purchased after November 7, 2001. Certain other exemptions will be available.

Tax levy on employment of foreign residents/Effective July 1, 2003, a new levy is imposed on employers who have foreign residents employed in Israel. The levy is 8% of the employee's monthly compensation, and is paid to the income tax authorities on a monthly basis as part of the monthly withholding tax filing reporting. It is neither a tax deducted from the employee income nor a corporate tax, but is a separate levy to be borne by the employer. There are some exceptions, which principally apply to health care providers and residents of neighboring countries and territories.

Tax administration

Returns/A resident taxpayer whose income consists solely of earnings from employment is generally not required to file a tax return where tax is withheld at source from his wages and at the prescribed levels from other specified sources (e.g., rental, dividend, interest, and capital gains), unless the taxpayer meets one of the following exceptions, in which case he would be required to file a tax return (certain further exceptions may also be applicable).

1. Wages exceed NIS530,000.
2. Income from another source (e.g., interest and dividends) exceeds NIS270,000 (out of which the proceeds from the sale of foreign traded securities does not exceed NIS55,000) or 50% of employment income, whichever is lower.
   or
3. The taxpayer is the owner of any foreign assets or the holder of deposits with a foreign banking institution, with a value of US$100,000 or more.
4. The taxpayer is the settlor or beneficiary of a truct during the tax year.
   or
5. The taxpayer received a distribution from a trust of more than NIS100,000.

It should be noted that the amounts and conditions above may still be modified for the year 2003.

Married couples are permitted to file separate or joint returns. In the latter case, a separate calculation may still be obtained for tax on income from personal exertion in any business or vocation or from employment, provided the income is from independent sources.

Tax returns are filed on a calendar-year basis.

Payment of tax/Payroll withholding of income and social tax is statutory, irrespective of the residence of the employer or employee. In general, withholding taxes in respect of salary payments effected from the 14th day of one month to the 13th day of the following month are payable on the 15th day that following month.

Self-employed individuals are generally required to make monthly or bimonthly advance tax payments, usually based on a percentage of turnover.

Tax rates

Income tax is calculated at graduated rates, as follows (2004 annual estimate, subject to possible future adjustment including for inflation in the course of the year).

Annual taxable income		Accumulated tax on Column 1	Percentage on excess
Over (Column 1)	**Not over**		
0	NIS 37,800	—	10
NIS 37,800	49,560	NIS 3,780	17
49,560	132,480	5,779	27
132,480	236,520	28,168	43
236,520	409,680	72,905	45
409,680		150,827	49

A minimum tax rate of 30% generally applies to certain classes of passive income not derived from business or employment.

Most types of interest, dividends and capital gains have varying, fixed rates of tax set in the Income Tax Ordinance (See "Capital gains and investment income" above).

INDIVIDUAL TAX CALCULATION

Tax year 2004 (estimate)

Assumptions

Resident husband and wife, two children; wife has no taxable income.

Tax computation

Salary		NIS 300,000
Interest on unlinked deposits		40,000
Bank interest on foreign deposit		40,000
Profit on sale of Tel Aviv Stock Exchange–quoted securities (purchased after January 1, 2003)		20,000
		400,000
Less:		
Interest on unlinked bank deposits (taxed at a reduced tax rate)	80,000	
Profit on quoted securities (taxed at a reduced tax rate)	20,000	100,000
		300,000
Less—Personal contribution to provident fund		5,580
Net income		NIS 294,420
Tax according to tax tables		NIS 98,960
Add:		
Interest on unlinked deposits taxed at 10%	4,000	
Interest on foreign deposit taxed at 15%	6,000	
Profit from sale of TASE-quoted securities taxed at 15%	3,000	13,000
		111,960
Less:		
Personal tax credits (2.25 points as resident, 1 point for wife not working)—3.25 x 178 x 12	6,942	
Donations—5,000 x 35%	1,750	
Provident fund contribution	1,395	(10,087)
Total income tax liability		NIS 101,873

Note:

Average exchange rate of the new shekel in 2003: US$1 = NIS4.55.

PwC contact

For additional information on taxation in Italy, contact:

Luca Barbera
International Assignment Solutions
Pirola Pennuto Zei & Associati
Via Vittor Pisani, 19
20124 Milan, Italy
Telephone: (39) (02) 66995481
Fax: (39) (02) 66995460
e-mail: luca.barbera@studiopirola.com

Significant developments

There is no longer any tax credit mechanism applicable to Italian dividends distributed starting from January 1, 2004. Dividends derived from nonqualified shareholdings are subject to a flat substitute tax equal to 12.5%; if they derive from qualified shareholdings, they are subject to progressive tax rates on 40% of their total amount.

The tax regime for capital gains derived from the disposal of shares has been modified with effect from January 1, 2004. Shareholders are subject to a separate tax of 12.5% on capital gains deriving from the disposal of nonqualified shareholdings. Capital gains deriving from qualified shareholdings are included in the taxpayer's personal taxable income for an amount equal to 40% of the total gain and are subject to the taxpayer's marginal tax rates.

Major changes are to be implemented in the future. In particular, Proxy Law no. 80 of April 7, 2003 has stated some principles that should have an impact on Italian income tax rates, which are due to be reduced (to 23% on income up to €100,000 and 33% on income exceeding that limit).

Territoriality and residence

Individuals are considered to be resident in Italy if, for the greater part of the fiscal year (i.e., for more than 183 days), they are registered with the Registry of the Resident Population (*Anagrafe*); or have their residence or domicile (principal place of business and interests) in the territory of the state.

The exemption from tax on income deriving from employment activities performed abroad has been abrogated as of January 1, 2001. Double taxation may be mitigated through the application of a tax credit.

The taxation of employment income deriving from an activity performed abroad is now applicable as follows.

1. Italian tax residents working abroad are taxed on income, wherever produced, on the basis of the "world wide taxation" principle.
2. In respect of Italian resident employees working abroad for more than 183 days in a 12-month period, in a permanent and coordinated way and having the working activity performed abroad as the only object of the work relationship, the taxable basis is now determined on the basis of "figurative salaries" (*retribuzioni convenzionali*), based on the employees' level and sector of activity. Figurative salaries are capped, despite the actual income received by the employee.

Figurative salaries do not apply for social security purposes if there is a social security agreement in force with the other country.

An antiabuse rule provides that Italian citizens who move to countries considered as "tax havens" (these are determined through a decree of the Ministry of Finance), are deemed to be resident in Italy even if they cancel with the Registry of the Resident Population, unless otherwise proven by the individuals.

The main income tax levied on individuals is the personal income tax (IRPEF—*Imposta redditi persone fisiche*).

Gross income

Employee gross income/Taxable salary includes all compensation (money or benefits in kind) and emoluments received in relation to employment, including any received as a share of profits or through subsidy or an act of generosity.

Out-of-town travel indemnities exceeding €46.48 per day in Italy or €77.47 per day abroad are included in taxable income if no meal and accommodation costs are reimbursed.

Some fringe benefits are taxable on a lump-sum basis, such as housing, loans, or a company car.

Transfer indemnities are taxed at 50% of their amount, on an amount that cannot exceed €1,549.37 for transfers inside the national territory, and €4,648.11 for transfers outside the national territory.

Note that this kind of taxation is valid only for the first year.

There are no special concessions to foreigners on calculating taxable income.

Capital gains and investment income/For individuals, capital gains are normally taxable, even if not arising from speculative intent or by way of a business.

There are no taxes on capital gains deriving from the following.

1. The sale of real estate used as principal residence if owned for more than five years.
2. The sale of real estate, even if owned for less than five years, if it has been used as principal residence for most of the period of ownership.

Changes in dividends and capital gains tax will be in force starting from January 1, 2004.

<u>2003 tax year</u>: Capital gains tax on securities is levied at a flat rate of 12.50% where the shares sold or transferred do not exceed 2% of voting rights or 5% of capital in the case of listed shares or 20% of voting rights or 25% of capital in the case of other participation (nonqualified shareholdings); and 27% where the shares sold or transferred exceed the above limits (qualified shareholdings).

<u>2004 tax year</u>: Shareholders are subject to a separate tax of 12.5% on capital gains deriving from the disposal of nonqualified shareholdings. Forty percent of the total capital gains deriving from qualified shareholdings are included in the taxpayer's personal taxable income and are subject to the taxpayer's marginal tax rates. Capital gains arising from the disposal of shares in a blacklisted company (e.g., a tax-haven) are fully subject to tax at individual marginal tax rates.

If the stocks are included in a so-called managed saving (*risparmio gestito*), dividend income is not subject to withholding tax. Such dividends are included in the profit (or loss) of said *risparmio gestito,* which is taxable at a 12.5% rate.

The tax credit mechanism is no longer applicable to Italian dividends distributed starting from January 1, 2004. Dividends derived from nonqualified shareholdings are subject to a flat substitute tax equal to 12.5%; if they derive from qualified shareholdings, they are subject to progressive tax rates on 40% of the total amount.

Dividends distributed by a foreign entity and paid through a resident broker are subject to a withholding tax at the rate of 12.50%. Starting from fiscal year 2004 the 12.5% flat tax is applied on the net dividend received (net of foreign withholding tax provided by the relevant tax treaty). When a nonresident broker is used, these dividends are included in the Italian tax return and taxed at a 12.5% flat rate.

Deductions and tax credits

Business deductions/There are no special deductions for business related expenses. Starting from January 1, 2001, self-employment income arising from the activities of managing directors, auditors, contractors, directors, and accountants is treated as employment income and therefore benefits from the same tax credits as employment income. Income from patents, trademarks, and so on, gives the right to a 25% deduction.

Some business-related expenses are not included in taxable income.

Nonbusiness expenses/Allowable deductions from taxable income include medical expenses related to handicaps, social security contributions and charitable contributions to the Roman Catholic Church; the principal residence income (i.e., figurative income) is totally deductible from the taxpayer's aggregate income.

For mortgage interest (up to €3,615.20), medical expenses (over €129.11), and insurance premiums (for the part of the premium related to the risk of death, disability or nonself-sufficiency, up to €1,291.14), a tax credit is allowed equal to 19% of the total amount of the expenses for fiscal years 2003 and 2004. Starting from January 1, 2001, it is possible to deduct the contributions paid to certain kinds of pension funds; such deduction is allowed up to 12% of gross income (gross of tax credits), limited to €5,164.57.

Employment income tax credits starting from January 1, 2003/For fiscal year 2003 (and 2004) an employee is entitled to the following tax credit:

Income range (In €)	Tax credit (In €)
27,000–29,500	130
29,500–36,500	235
36,500–41,500	180
41,500–46,700	130
46,700–52,000	25

Self-employment income tax credits starting from January 1, 2003/Starting from January 1, 2003, tax credits for self-employed workers (prorated for a calendar year) are as follows:

Income range (In €)	Deduction (In €)
25,500–29,400	80
29,400–31,000	126
31,000–32,000	80

Personal allowances/Personal allowances are granted in the form of tax credits.

1. The tax credit for dependent spouse who earns less than €2,840.51 per annum is as follows:

Taxable income		2004
Over	Not over	tax credit
0	€ 15,494.00	€ 546.18
€ 15,494.00	30,987.00	496.60
30,987.00	51,646.00	459.42
51,646.00		422.23

2. Amount of dependent children deduction for 2004 tax year (same as those for 2003 tax year):
   a. €516.46 where:
      i. Income is less than €36,152 and with one dependent child;
      ii. Income is less than €41,317 and with two dependent children;
      iii. Income is less than €46,481 and with three dependent children;
      iv. Four dependent children.
   b. €303.68 for the first child if income is less than €51,646;
   c. €336.73 for second and subsequent children where income is less than €51,646;
   d. €285,08 for each child where income is higher than €51,646.
3. Dependent children in the absence of a spouse—equal to dependent-spouse deduction.
4. Any other dependent with an income lower than €2,840.51—same as for dependent children.
5. Dependent children less than three years old: add €123.95 each to the normal deduction.
6. The deduction for children younger than three years old is not applicable if the €516.46 deduction applies.

Tax credits

Taxes paid abroad as a tax on income included in the Italian taxable base are allowed as a credit against personal income tax. Taxes withheld at source are deductible from total taxes due. Taxpayers are entitled to a refund should the taxes withheld exceed the final tax due.

Other taxes

Social security contributions/Participation in the Italian social security scheme is compulsory for virtually all salaried employees and wage earners. An Italian employer must therefore register with the Italian Social Security Administration (INPS).

Social security contributions are due from both the employee and the employer. Only the workers' charges are considered in the following discussion.

INPS contributions to be paid by employees (white-collar workers and cadres) are about 10% of their gross annual compensation.

For fiscal year 2004 social security contributions due from managers and executives (i.e., *dirigenti*) are as described below.

Commercial agreement...........	8.89% (INPS) on income up to a ceiling of €37,883 and 9.89% on income over €37,883. If the manager has contributed to the mandatory social security scheme only starting from January 1, 1996, INPS contributions are due only up to €82,401. *plus* 1% (*Fondo Mario Negri,* a pension fund) on a notional remuneration of €59,225 per annum of gross income, and €129.11 per annum as professional training charges, *plus* 1.95% (FASDAC—*Fondo Assistenza Sanitaria Dirigenti Aziende Commerciali*—a separate supplementary medical care plan) on a notional remuneration of €44,194 per annum of gross income, *plus* €1,394 (PREVIR—*Associazione Antonio Pastore*—an entity consisting of a combination of insurance and investment). Not compulsory.
Industrial agreement...............	8.89% (INPS) on income up to a ceiling of €37,883 and 9.89% on income over €37,883. If the manager has contributed to the mandatory social security scheme only starting from January 1, 1996, INPS contributions are due only up to €82,401, *plus* A flat contribution of €610.45 (FASI), plus €206.58 for the first inscription, *plus* PREVINDAI (*Fondo di Previdenza a Capitalizzazione per I Dirigenti di Aziende Industriali*—an additional pension fund) as follows: • *Dirigenti* enrolled before April 28, 1993—3% up to a maximum annual earning of €100,709.10; 4% starting from a maximum annual earning over €100,709.10 up to €139,443.36, • *Dirigenti* enrolled after April 28, 1993—3% up to an annual earning of €85.215

Self-employed individuals not covered by a mandatory pension fund must register with a special "pension fund" (so-called separate management—*gestione separata*). The contribution is equal to 17.80% of the fees up to €37,883.00 and to 18.80% of the fees up to €82,401.00 (contribution ceiling, annually revised, of €80,391 for 2003 and of €82,401.00 for 2004). Two-thirds of the total amount is the contractor's share, and one-third is the self-employed individual's share.

Also see "Nonbusiness expenses" above.

IRAP/This tax (*imposta regionale sulle attività produttive*) is applicable on productive activity exercised in any of the 20 Italian regions. IRAP has replaced, inter alia, local tax on income (ILOR—*l'imposta locale sui redditi*).

Taxpayers for IRAP purposes are, among others, self-employed individuals, nonresident taxpayers who exercise business activities in Italy through a permanent establishment, and partnerships.

Briefly, the IRAP taxable base is the difference between compensation received and directly related business expenses (depreciation of tangible and intangible assets included). Personnel and interest costs are nondeductible.

The IRAP tax rate is fixed at 4.25%.

Additional income taxes/There are two additional income taxes in force: a "regional additional tax" (ranging from 0.9% to 1.4%), and a municipal additional tax (up to 0.5%). Both these additional taxes are regulated under IRPEF rules.

Note that, even if the regional additional tax ranges from 0.9% to 1.4%, regions can decide to adopt a higher rate or to fix special criteria to determine the rate applicable.

Below is the list of the regions that have significantly different 2003 regional tax rates:

1. Lombardia:
   a. 1.2% on income up to €15,493.71;
   b. 1.3% on income from €15,493.71 up to €30,987.41;
   c. 1.4% on income exceeding €30,987.41.

   The rate remains equal to 0.9% for income deriving only from pension and main residence.
2. Marche:
   a. 0.9% on income up to €15,493.71;
   b. 1.91% on income from €15,493.71 up to €30,987.41;
   c. 3.60% on income from €30,987.41 up to €69,721.68;
   d. 4% on income exceeding €69,721.68.
3. Piemonte:
   a. 0.9% on income up to €10,329.14;
   b. 1.4% on income exceeding €10,329.14.
4. Umbria:
   a. 0.9% on income up to €10,329.14;
   b. 1.1% on income exceeding €10,329.14.
5. Veneto:
   a. 1.2% on income up to €10,329.14;
   b. 1.3% on income from €10,329.14 up to €15,493.71;
   c. 1.4% on income from €15,493.71 and €69,721.68;
   d. 1.9% on income exceeding €69,721.68.

   The tax rate is equal to 0.9% for families with an income not exceeding €30,987.41 and a disabled family member.

Further increases of regional and municipal tax rates have been frozen starting from January 1, 2003.

Tax administration

Returns/2003 returns must be filed by July 31, 2004 (or October 31, 2004 in case of electronic filing). The tax year for individuals is the calendar year.

Payment of tax/An income withholding tax is imposed on salaries on the basis of the tax rates applicable to the annual employment income. For tax year 2003 the estimated payment due is 98%. The on-account payment is payable in two installments: 40% of 98% in May/June 2004 and 60% of 98% in November 2004. The balance is due when the annual tax settlement is submitted.

Tax rates

Tax rates for 2003 and 2004 for the normal computation of IRPEF are determined on a graduated scale, as shown below.

Taxable income		
Over	Not over	Rate
(Column 1)		(%)
0	€ 15,000	23
€ 15,000	29,000	29
29,000	32,600	31
32,600	70,000	39
70,000		45

The tax rates above do not include regional tax (ranging from 0.9% to 1.4%) or municipal tax (up to 0.5%).

Starting from year 2003 new rules are in force regarding a "no-tax area" for the calculation of individual income tax.

No-tax area	Applicable to	Total
In €		In €
3,000	Any taxpayer	3,000
4,500	Employees	7,500
4,000	Pensioners	7,000
1,500	Self-employed workers	4,500

The no tax area decreases when the income increases. It is no longer available for income exceeding €33.500.

In order to calculate pro rata application of the no-tax area, the formula is as follows:

$$\frac{€26{,}000 + \text{Applicable no tax area*} + \text{Other applicable deductions} - \text{Total income} - \text{Dividend tax credit**}}{€26{,}000}$$

If the above ratio is:

a. Equal to or higher than 1, the deduction is fully applicable;
b. Equal to or lower than 0, the deduction is not applicable;
c. Between 0 and 1, the deduction applies following the above ratio (rounded to the first four decimals).

The 2003 Italian Financial Act introduced the so-called *clausola di salvaguardia* ("safeguard clause"). This clause states that in case the tax calculated with the 2003 tax rates is higher than the tax calculated with the 2002 tax rates, it will be possible for the taxpayer to calculate the 2003 tax due using the 2002 tax rates.

*The no tax area should not be taken into consideration for Regional tax and Municipal tax purposes.

**The dividend tax credit is no longer applicable on dividends distributed starting from fiscal year 2004.

INDIVIDUAL TAX CALCULATION

Income 2003 year (2004 tax return)

Assumptions

Husband (employee), dependent wife and two children. Employment income of €90,000; mortgage interest for main residence of €3,600 net income of owner's home of €0.

Tax computation

Gross employment income		€ 90,000.00
Less—Social security contributions (10%)		9,000.00
Taxable income		€ 81,000.00
Gross income tax		€ 28,162.00
Less—Personal allowances/Tax credits:		
Dependent spouse	422.23	
Dependent children (two)	570.16	
Employment tax credit	—	
Mortgage interest (19% of €3,600)	684.00	(1,676.39)
Net income tax		26.485.61
Additional regional income tax (up to 1.4% of taxable income) (1)		1,087.52
Additional municipal income tax (up to 0.5% of taxable income) (2)		405.00
Total income taxes due		€ 27,978.13

Notes:

1. The regional tax ranges from 0.9% up to 1.4% of taxable income, therefore the amount of this tax depends on the place where the individual is located or performs work.
2. Municipal tax ranges from 0% to 0.5% of taxable income; therefore the presence and the amount of this tax depends on the place where the individual is located or performs work.
3. Exchange rate of the Euro at January 2, 2004: US$1 = €0.79.

PwC contact

For additional information on taxation in the Ivory Coast, contact:

Dominique Taty—Associate Partner
Fidafrica (member of PricewaterhouseCoopers)
Immeuble Colina, 2nd Floor, Bd Roume Plateau
01 BP 3173
Abidjan 01, Côte d'Ivoire
Telephone: (225) 20 22 25 88
Fax: (225) 20 22 23 75
e-mail: d.taty@ci.pwcglobal.com

General note

This entry is repeated from the 2003/2004 edition. For more up-to-date information consult the contact listed above or Jacqueline Collette at jacqueline.collette@us.pwc.com.

Significant developments

This entry is updated as of March 31, 2003. There have been no significant tax or regulatory developments in the past year.

Territoriality and residence

The Ivory Coast taxes residents on their worldwide income.

Individuals resident in the Ivory Coast are subject to specific direct income tax, depending on the kind of revenue earned, and to general revenue tax (IGR—*L'Impôt Général sur le Revenu*).

Gross income

Employee gross income/Four taxes presented below are withheld from taxable gross income (strikethrough: as defined below). Taxable gross income is also the basis for calculation of taxes paid by the employer (tax on salaries and a social security contribution).

Taxable income includes all cash remuneration, including living allowances, housing allowances, bonuses, and social contributions paid by the employer. However, social contributions are not taxable if they do not exceed both 10% of total gross income and CFAF3,600,000 a year, and a transportation allowance is not taxable if the amount does not exceed CFAF19,000.

In-kind benefits, such as housing, electricity, water, and air conditioning, are taxed according to a schedule of deemed values. Reimbursements of business expenses are not taxed up to an amount that equals 10% of taxable cash income plus reimbursements.

There are no allowances for short-term residents.

Expatriate tax concessions/Holiday fare of an expatriate and expatriate's family paid by the employer is not taxable.

Reimbursements paid after leaving the country are not reported, to the extent that these reimbursements are not paid by the local employer.

Capital gains and investment income/Capital gains are not taxable, except for certain gains arising from the sale of shares.

Deductions

Business deductions/Individuals may take a standard 15% IGR deduction on their gross income for business-related expenses, such as travel fees, representation costs, and business materials. The deduction is applied to the adjusted gross income, derived by first calculating the 20% general deduction, described below, and deducting IS (salary tax—*L'impôt sur les traitements et salaires*) and CN (national contribution—*Contribution Nationale*) taxes.

Nonbusiness expenses/A general or standard deduction of 20% is applied to gross taxable income and is the highly recommended tax choice for resident aliens. See "Tax rates" below for the formula used to apply this deduction.

Although the deduction of specific nonbusiness expenses is permitted under tax law, the practice rarely is used, since the results usually are less favorable than the result from taking the standard deduction.

Specific nonbusiness deductions include:

1. Interest on loans and debts.
2. Mandatory payment of freely paid arrears on rents.
3. Maintenance or alimony payments.
4. Life insurance premiums paid to an insurance company, up to 6% of the taxable income before deduction of the premiums.
5. Voluntary payments to a retirement account with concurrent life insurance, up to 6% of the net income with a ceiling of CFAF200,000, increased by CFAF40,000 for each dependent child.
6. Direct and equivalent taxes, including the general revenue tax (the effective IGR rate adjusted accordingly).
7. 50% of monetary gifts made to recognized athletic associations, up to 5% of the declared gross income.

Personal allowances/The number of a taxpayer's dependents does not affect IS (salary tax), CN (national contribution), CNS (contribution nationale de solidarité—solidarity contribution), or CNPS (social security) but is reflected in the progressive IGR schedule.

IGR allowances are based on deductions ratios called "parts" that relate to the taxpayer's family status. Unmarried taxpayers may deduct one part, married taxpayers may deduct two parts, and taxpayers may add one-half part for each dependent child, up to a maximum per family of five parts. See also "Individual tax calculation" below.

Tax credits

No tax credits are granted. However, the tax obligations of nonresidents may be affected by a tax treaty in effect between the Ivory Coast and the country where the taxpayer is resident. The Ivory Coast has such treaties with Belgium, Canada, France, Germany, Italy, Norway, Switzerland, and the United Kingdom. Tax credits and requirements are specified by the treaty.

Social taxes paid to the home country by expatriates are not creditable against Ivory Coast taxes.

Other taxes

Social taxes/Employers must contribute to the social security system (CNPS—*Caisse Nationale pour la Prévoyance Sociale*). The employer also pays 8% of the taxable salary to the CNPS Retirement Fund, of which 4.8% is the employer's contribution and 3.2% is withheld from the employee's salary up to a monthly ceiling of CFAF1,647,315.

Other taxes/None.

Tax administration

Returns/Employers must calculate and withhold taxes due by employees, and they must file monthly salary tax returns for both employee tax and the employer's payroll tax. Adjustment declarations are filed annually by April 30. Employees are not required to file individual tax returns unless they work for more than one employer or they work for an employer that is not established in the Ivory Coast. Returns must be filed on a calendar-year basis.

A husband and wife are taxed separately. The husband's salary is taxed under the head-of-household category, with the relevant deductions for dependents. The wife's salary is taxed as an unmarried taxpayer without dependents. Husband and wife, however, may also file jointly.

Payment of tax/Taxes, including withholding taxes, are remitted by the 15th of each month for the preceding month.

Tax rates

1. Salary tax (IS):
   1.5% of 80% of gross income (GI).
2. National contribution (CN):
   80% of gross income taxed at progressive rates from 1.5% to 10%, based on varying tax brackets as shown below.
   Formula: CN = 80% x GI x (Rate) – (Variable)

Taxable base		Rate	
Over	**Not over**	**of tax**	**Variable**
0	CFAF 600,000	Nil	CFAF Nil
CFAF 600,000	1,560,000	1.5%	9,000
1,560,000	2,400,000	5.0%	63,600
2,400,000		10.0%	183,600

3. General income tax (IGR):
   Taxable base:
   The taxable base (T) is derived as shown below, and includes a 15% deduction.
   Formula: IGR = (T/N x (rate) – V) x N, where:

   T = [GI x 80% – (IS + CN)] x 85%

   GI = Gross income

   IS = Tax on salary

   CN = National contribution

   V = Predetermined variable

   N = Number of parts

Taxable base	Net tax	–	Variable	x	Number of parts
	Tax thereon				
From 0 to 300,000		Nil			
300,001 to 547,000	(R x 10/110	–	27,273)	x	N
547,001 to 979,000	(R x 15/115	–	48,913)	x	N
979,001 to 1,519,000	(R x 20/120	–	84,375)	x	N
1,519,001 to 2,644,000	(R x 25/125	–	135,000)	x	N
2,644,001 to 4,669,000	(R x 35/135	–	291,667)	x	N
4,669,001 to 10,106,000	(R x 45/145	–	530,172)	x	N
Over 10,106,000	(R x 60/160	–	1,183,594)	x	N

4. Solidarity contribution (CNS):
   1% of gross income.
5. Social security contribution (CNPS):
   3.2% of gross income, without any deduction, up to a monthly ceiling of CFAF1,647,315.

INDIVIDUAL TAX CALCULATION

Assumptions

Resident alien, married, two children; employer classified in highest-risk category for CNPS Workmen's Compensation Fund.

Tax computation

Annual base salary		CFAF 40,000,000
Taxes withheld from salary:		
Salary tax (IS) (40,000,000 x 80% x 1.5%)	480,000	
National contribution (CN) (40,000,000 x 80% x 10%) – 183,600	3,016,400	
General income tax (IGR)—Taxable base [(40,000,000 x 80%) – (480,000 + 3,016,400) x 85%] = 24,228,060 24,228,060 ÷ 3 = 8,076,020		
IGR—Tax [(8,076,020 x 31%) – 530,172] x 3	5,920,183	
Solidarity contribution: (40,000,000 x 1%)	400,000	
CNPS Retirement Fund	632,569	
Total tax and social security		CFAF 10,449,152
Net income		CFAF 29,550,848
Employers contributions:		
Local payroll tax	4,800,000	
Family Allowance Fund	48,300	
Workmen's compensation	42,000	
Retirement Fund	948,853	
Total employer contributions		CFAF 5,839,153

Notes:

Exchange rate of the CFA franc at January 1, 2003: US$1 = CFAF625.50.

Parity remains fixed between the CFA franc, used in 14 French-speaking African countries and the Euro zone. The rate is CFAF655.95 = €1. The convertibility of the CFA franc continues to be assured, as long as transfers are made through banking channels.

Jamaica

PwC contact

For additional information on taxation in Jamaica, contact:

Eric A. Crawford
PricewaterhouseCoopers
Scotiabank Centre
Duke Street
Kingston, Jamaica
Telephone: (1) (876) 922 6230
Fax: (1) (876) 967 1949
e-mail: eric.crawford.jm@pwc.com

Significant developments

There have been no significant tax or regulatory developments in the past year.

Territoriality and residence

In general, Jamaica taxes its citizens and residents on their worldwide income. A nondomiciled individual working in Jamaica is taxed on the compensation attributable to the Jamaican services and other Jamaican-source income.

Individuals are treated as being resident in Jamaica for a tax year if they satisfy any one of several conditions.

1. They spend at least six months in Jamaica in the tax year or visit Jamaica with the intention of remaining there permanently and have actually been in the island for six months in the tax year.
2. They (or their spouses) have a place of abode available for their use in Jamaica, and they visit the island at any time during the tax year, no matter how short the stay.
3. They habitually visit Jamaica for substantial periods. The Commissioner of Income Tax would probably regard periods totaling three months as substantial and visits occurring in four consecutive years as habitual.

An individual not domiciled in Jamaica is taxable in Jamaica on any Jamaican-source income and, where resident, on remittances of foreign income to the island.

Gross income

Employee gross income/An individual resident but not domiciled in Jamaica is taxed on the emoluments (salary, living allowances, benefits in kind, cars, etc.) paid for work done for or on behalf of Jamaica, regardless of where payment is made and regardless of whether the emoluments are remitted to Jamaica. Income for services rendered outside Jamaica is not taxed if the services are not related to Jamaica.

Benefits, whether in cash or kind, payable for services rendered are taxable. Accommodation is ascribed a maximum taxable value of 15% of total taxable emoluments/other than the value of the accommodation. If the cost or market value of the accommodation exceeds other emoluments, the value is 15% of the average of other emoluments including those paid by connected parties and annual cost/market value of the accommodation.

The taxable benefit arising from the private use of a company car ranges from J$30,000 to J$140,000 and is determined by reference to the cost, the age, and the relative percentage of private and business use.

Persons to whom allowances for laundry and uniforms (up to a specified limit) can be paid tax-free must be designated by the Commissioner of Income Tax.

Tax reimbursement is exempt from tax, provided it does not exceed the excess of Jamaican taxes paid over the tax liability on the same amount of income in the recipient's home country.

Capital gains and investment income/No tax is levied on capital gains. There is, however, a tax of 7.5% of the consideration paid on the transfer of certain assets, for example, land and company securities (including stock). The tax is limited to 37.5% of the capital gain. Resident individual recipients of unfranked dividends and interest are subject to 25% withholding tax at source (corporate recipients, 33 1/3%). Franked income is distributions received by a corporate body subject to income tax that is resident in the island and from which distribution tax has been deducted at source.

An individual resident but not domiciled in Jamaica is taxed in Jamaica on investment income arising outside Jamaica to the extent that the income is remitted to Jamaica.

Dividends from listed companies/Between the period June 1, 2000 and April 1, 2001, dividends paid by a Jamaican corporation whose shares are quoted on the Jamaican Stock exchange were taxed at the rate of 20%. Since April 1, 2001, similar dividends have been taxed at the reduced rate of 10% and are now taxed at the rate of 0% from April 1, 2002.

The rate of tax on dividends from unlisted companies remains at 25% for individuals.

Long-term savings accounts/Certain categories of interest income earned on long-term savings accounts (LSAs) were made tax exempt. These are the following.

1. Interest paid or credited in respect of investments or deposits made by individuals with prescribed persons if:
   a. The deposit remains for a minimum of five years without any withdrawal from the principal sum invested;
   b. The deposit or investment (other than interest accrued or credited) does not exceed J$1million dollars in any year;
   c. The account is not transferable, except on the death or bankruptcy of the depositor or investor;
   d. Not more than 85% (75% after July 2001) of the interest accrued in any year is withdrawn during that year.
2. Benefits derived from investments in certain life insurance policies may also be exempt from income tax if specified criteria are satisfied.

Deductions

Business deductions/To the extent not reimbursed, individuals (resident or nonresident) can deduct all expenses that are incurred wholly and exclusively by them in earning their income, for example, business-related travel, automobile, and entertainment expenses. Expenses for travel to and from work are not deductible. There are no standard deductions or deductions for expenses that are wholly personal.

Nonbusiness expenses/Social security and superannuation contributions to approved pension schemes are deductible in determining taxable income, as is interest paid in acquiring income. Approved charitable contributions, restricted to 5% of taxable income, are also deductible.

There are no standard deductions.

Relief is not available for medical expenses, insurance premiums, and mortgage interest paid on a local dwelling unless rented

Personal allowances/There are no personal allowances.

Tax credits

Foreign tax paid on income that is not taxed in Jamaica is not available as a credit against the individual's Jamaican tax liability on other income.

Other taxes

Withholding tax/Prescribed persons are required to withhold tax at source at a rate of 25% on interest income paid or credited on investment instruments (subject to any lower rate as prescribed in a double taxation treaty). "Prescribed persons" are entities defined as such and include: the Accountant General, any bank operating under the Banking Act or the Bank of Jamaica Act; any institution operating under the Financial Institutions Act; any building society; any society registered under the Cooperative Societies Act, licensed securities dealers; societies registered under the Industrial and Provident Societies Act (unless certain conditions are met); the Ministry of Finance; life insurance companies; companies registered under the Companies Act in which the government, or an agency of the government holds more than 50% of the ordinary shares and which issues interest bearing securities; issuers of commercial paper; unit trust management companies; and any person connected with any of the persons mentioned above.

Social security taxes/Effective October 1, 2003 there was an increase in the insurable wage ceiling under the National Insurance Act, resulting in a new maximum of J$240.50 per week or J$12,500 per annum.

Other taxes on income/The National Housing Trust Contributions and Education Tax, which are payroll taxes, are each payable by employees at the rate of 2% on taxable compensation for employment in the island. They are not deductible for income tax purposes. Both these taxes are payable by the employer at the rate of 3%. Expatriate employees are entitled to claim a refund of their National Housing Trust contributions when leaving the island permanently.

Concessionary loans/There is a taxable benefit on loans made to employees, as well as directors, of specified financial institutions where the interest on those loans is at less than market value. Market value is prescribed by the Minister of Finance and is currently 18%. The taxable benefit is treated as an emolument for the purposes of income tax and is subject to pay-as-you-earn (PAYE) regulations. Tax is not payable in respect of the benefit derived from certain types of loans where the aggregate amount loaned for the purposes specified does not exceed J$1.5 million.

Tax administration

There are six taxation departments.

1. Tax Administration Services Department (TASD)—deals with administrative issues.
2. Taxpayer Audit and Assessment Department (TAAD)—deals with the audit and assessment functions of income tax, general consumption tax (GCT/VAT), stamp duty, and transfer tax.

3. Taxpayer Appeals Department (TAD)—processes appeals to decisions made by tax commissioners.
4. Revenue Protection Department (RPD)—investigates customs breaches and fraudulent acts in respect of the various tax Acts.
5. Inland Revenue Department—deals with all compliance and tax collection functions.
6. The Customs Department.

Returns/Husbands and wives generally file separately and must elect in writing to be jointly assessed. Such a choice is unlikely to be beneficial.

The income tax year runs from January 1 to December 31. Taxpayers normally file their returns on a calendar-year basis, but a fiscal-year basis may be approved by the Commissioner of Income Tax.

Payment of tax/There is withholding of income tax from salaries. If withholding is not possible, for example, because the employer is not resident in Jamaica, the taxpayer will be required to make payment of estimated tax in quarterly installments. Income tax returns must be filed by March 15th in the year following the year of assessment.

Tax rates

The rates shown below are applied to taxable income for 2003.

Taxable income	%
On first J$120,432	Nil
On excess over J$120,432	25

INDIVIDUAL TAX CALCULATION

Calendar year 2003/2004

Assumptions

Resident, non–Jamaican-domiciled married man.

Tax computation

Salary		J$ 3,200,000
Car benefit (scale rate) (1)		40,000
Housing accommodation—15% of $3,240,000 (2)		486,000
		3,726,000
Less:		
National insurance contributions (social security)	12,250	
Superannuation contributions	320,000	332,500
		3,393,500
Add:		
Bank deposit interest (net 24,000 + 8,000 tax withheld)	32,000	
Dividends received from listed companies	10,000	
Capital gains (exempt)	0	42,000
		3,435,500
Less—Approved charitable donations (3)		91,286
Taxable income		J$ 3,344,214
Tax payable:		
On first 120,432	0	
On dividends from listed company 10,000 at 0%	0	
On remaining 3,223,782 at 25%	805,946	J$ 805,946
Less—Credit for tax deducted from local bank interest and dividends		(8,000)
Net tax payable		J$ 797,946

Notes:

1. Assume car purchased in 1994 costing J$500,000, having under 50% private use. If the annual value of accommodation is greater than other emoluments, then the benefit assessed is 15% of ($3,240,000 + annual value) ÷ 2.
2. Annual value is less than other emoluments in this instance.
3. Limited to 5% of statutory income.
4. Exchange rate of the Jamaican dollar at December 31, 2003: US$1 = J$60.4153.

PwC contact

For additional information on taxation in Japan, contact:

Hiroyuki Suzuki
PricewaterhouseCoopers
Zeirishi—Hojin ChuoAoyama
Kasumigaseki Bldg. 15F
2-5, Kasumigaseki 3 chome
Chiyoda-ku
Tokyo 100-6015, Japan
Telephone: (81)(3) 5251 2400
Fax: (81)(3) 5251 2424
e-mail: hiroyuki.suzuki@jp.pwc.com

Significant developments

During 2003, in order to stimulate the Japanese stock market, there have been further tax revisions in respect of capital gains arising from sales of shares and dividends; this follows the revisions made in 2002. There have also been minor revisions to personal allowances, that is, the concept of the special allowance for a spouse has been changed. Social security taxes have been changed significantly from April 1, 2003.

Territoriality and residence

Nonresident taxpayers are taxed only on their Japan-source income. Nonpermanent resident taxpayers are taxed on Japan-source income plus that part of non–Japan-source income that is paid in or remitted to Japan. Permanent resident taxpayers are taxed on their worldwide income. Expatriate taxpayers are generally classified as nonpermanent resident taxpayers for the initial 60 months of residency, unless their Japan assignment period is limited to less than 12 months (if limited to less than 12 months, they are classified as nonresident). After the first 60-month period, the expatriate becomes a permanent resident taxpayer.

Gross income

Employee gross income/Salary, foreign-service premiums, cost-of-living allowances, tax reimbursements, and other benefits in kind (except for certain tax-exempt items) are classified as taxable remuneration (employment income). Japan-source employment income is remuneration earned for services rendered in Japan, regardless of when or where the remuneration is paid.

Reasonable relocation expenses, including expenses for a spouse and children, that are borne by the employer, do not constitute taxable income. A reasonable amount of airfare for home leave, including airfare for family members traveling together with the employee, is not taxable. Where an employer provides housing, the amount of the taxable benefit is determined on a formula basis and, provided the housing arrangements are structured properly, generally is less than actual rent. In the case of housing provided for a director (a board member) of a domestic or foreign company, the taxable value would generally be 50% (35% if it can be substantiated that the house is also used for business purposes by the employer) of the actual rent. However, if the housing provided by the company is considered too luxurious, the market rent is taxable.

For directors and employees, income arising from the exercise of stock options is generally taxed when exercised. However, income arising from certain qualified stock options is not taxable when exercised but taxed as capital gains when the stocks given by exercising the options are transferred if certain conditions are met.

Capital gains and investment income/Capital gains are, in principle, aggregated with other income after deductions for necessary expenses and after a statutory deduction of a maximum of ¥500,000. If the transferred assets were owned for more than five years, the gain is regarded as a long-term capital gain, and the taxable basis is reduced to 50% of the net capital gain.

Special taxation measures may be applicable to the taxation of capital gains derived from a transfer of real property (land, building, and structures).

Capital gains arising from sales of certain designated securities (including shares in corporations, convertible debentures, etc., but excluding bonds and/or ordinary corporate debentures, etc.) are taxed separately from other income at a flat rate of 26% (combination of national tax of 20% and local inhabitants tax of 6%). However, in the case of capital gains realized on the transfer of listed securities through designated securities companies, the tax rate is reduced to 10% (combined 7% national tax and 3% local inhabitants tax) during the period from January 1, 2004 to December 31, 2007; a rate of 20% (combined 15% national tax and 5% local inhabitants tax) will be applicable afterward. Also, a taxpayer may opt to be taxed on capital gains at 10% until December 31, 2007 (and 20% afterward) through withholding and have this be the final tax on the gains, provided certain listed shares are sold through special securities company accounts.

Capital losses arising from a transfer of listed shares thorough designated securities companies on or after January 1, 2003 can be carried forward for three years.

Under the following conditions, capital gains from the transfer of listed shares may be exempt from income tax.

1. The shares must be acquired during the period from November 30, 2001 to December 31, 2002.
2. The shares must be transferred thorough designated securities companies (but not through special securities company accounts).during the period from January 1, 2005 to December 31, 2007.
3. The total acquisition cost must not exceed ¥10 million.

Interest on bank deposits and/or certain designated financial instruments is taxed separately from other income and is subject to 20% withholding tax (a combination of national tax of 15% and local inhabitants tax of 5%).

Dividends are, in principle, taxed in aggregate with other income. When a dividend is derived through a payment administrator in Japan, 20% withholding income tax is levied. However, the withholding tax rate is reduced to 10% (a combination of national tax of 7% and local inhabitants tax of 3%) during the period from January 1, 2004 to March 31, 2008. In the case of dividends derived from listed shares or certain other dividends paid through administrators in Japan, the taxpayer can opt to have taxation on the dividends completed through withholdings for national income tax purposes. For local inhabitants tax purposes, any dividend is subject to comprehensive taxation and thus is taxed in aggregate with other income afterward. A nonresident's income from Japan-source interest, dividends, rents, and royalties is generally subject to tax at a 20% rate (15% in the case of interest on bank deposits and/or certain designated financial instruments) or lower treaty rates through withholding tax at source.

Deductions

Business deductions/Business expenses are generally not tax deductible against employment income. An employer's reimbursements of business expenses, such as moving, travel, and entertainment expenses, do not constitute taxable income to the employee, provided the expenses are required for the employer's business.

Instead of a tax deduction for (unreimbursed) business expenses, a permanent and/or nonpermanent resident employee can deduct an earned income relief, computed by applying an appropriate rate to gross employment income as follows. (The minimum standard deduction is ¥650,000 or gross employment income, whichever is lower).

Gross employment income			
Over	**Not over**	**Standard deduction**	**Percentage on excess**
(Column 1)		(On Column 1)	
¥ 1,625,000	¥ 1,800,000	¥ 650,000	40
1,800,000	3,600,000	720,000	30
3,600,000	6,600,000	1,260,000	20
6,600,000	10,000,000	1,860,000	10
10,000,000		2,200,000	5

A self-employed taxpayer is allowed to claim a tax deduction for business expenses, provided it can be substantiated that the expenses are necessary.

Nonbusiness expenses/Interest, including mortgage interest, is not tax deductible. Japanese social security contributions are fully deductible. Medical expenses (irrespective of where they were paid), charitable contributions designated by the Ministry of Finance in Japan and insurance premiums paid in Japan are tax deductible, with certain limitations.

Personal allowances/Permanent and nonpermanent resident taxpayers are entitled to a personal allowance (¥380,000 for national income tax purposes, ¥330,000 for local inhabitants tax purposes) for themselves, for their dependent spouses and for each of their dependents. In the case of a nondependent spouse, a special allowance can be taken, depending on the spouse's income (maximum ¥380,000 and ¥330,000 for national income tax purposes and local inhabitants tax purposes, respectively) by taxpayers whose income amount does not exceed ¥10 million. Also, an additional special allowance (¥250,000 and ¥120,000 for national income tax purposes and local inhabitants tax purposes, respectively) may be claimed for a dependent aged 16 to 22.

In general, a nonresident is not permitted any of these deductions.

Tax credits

Resident taxpayers can credit foreign income taxes against their Japanese national tax and local inhabitants tax liabilities (with certain limitations) for non–Japan-source income taxed in Japan. A nonresident is not entitled to a foreign tax credit.

Withholding tax on Japan-source dividends is generally creditable against a resident's annual tax liability. A special deemed tax credit is available in addition to the tax withheld on dividends received from domestic companies for both national tax and local inhabitants tax purposes.

Fixed-percentage reduction/As a permanent measure for tax reduction, the Japanese government has granted each taxpayer a fixed-percentage reduction.

1. National tax—For national income tax purposes, the tax due is reduced by 20% (the maximum reduction is ¥250,000 per year).
2. Inhabitants tax—Local inhabitants tax due is reduced by 15% (maximum reduction is ¥40,000 per year).

Other taxes

Social security taxes/An employee whose salaries or bonuses including fringe benefits are paid in Japan by a local employer, which includes a Japanese branch of a foreign corporation, is generally liable to pay a share of social security premiums. The employee's share consists of the following contributions.

	Standard premiums on monthly salary	Standard premiums on bonuses
Health insurance	4.1% (Maximum ¥40,180 per month)	4.1% (Maximum ¥81,000 per payment
Long-term care insurance	0.445% (Maximum ¥4,361 per month)	
Welfare pension	6.79% (Maximum ¥42,098 per month)	6.79% (Maximum ¥101,850 per payment)
Unemployment insurance	0.7%	0.7%
Total	12.035%	11.59%

In the case of an expatriate, the above total rate for monthly premiums will be reduced to 11.335%, since enrollment in an unemployment insurance program generally is not required. This is because an expatriate will not be unemployed in Japan, since the company guaranteed to employ the expatriate as a condition for obtaining a working visa and the expatriate will return to the home country upon termination of the assignment in Japan. In this case, the employee's maximum share of monthly premiums is limited to ¥86,639. As noted above, the Japanese social security contributions are deductible for a resident employee.

Totalization agreements/Designed to avoid overlaps in social security enrollment, the social security agreement between Japan and Germany became effective as of February 1, 2000, and that between Japan and the United Kingdom became effective as of February 1, 2001. The agreements between Japan and the United States has been signed on February 19, 2004 and will enter into force on the first day of the third month following the month in which the parties have completed an exchange of certain diplomatic notes to notify that the respective statutory requirements have been fulfilled.

The agreement between Japan and France is now under negotiation.

Local taxes on income/Japanese local governments (prefectural and municipal governments) levy local inhabitants tax on taxpayers' previous year's income if they are residents of Japan as of January 1 of the current year. For inhabitants tax purposes, an equalization "per capita" tax is also assessed, at a minimum rate of ¥3,000 and a maximum rate of ¥4,000 per annum, depending on the locality in which the taxpayer resides. Local inhabitants tax is not deductible.

If taxpayers engage in their own business, a business enterprise tax will be levied on their business income by the local prefectural government. Business enterprise tax is deductible for calculation of business income.

Tax administration

Returns/Joint tax returns are not permitted in Japan. The tax year is the calendar year for all resident-status individuals, and a taxpayer is required to file a national tax return by March 15 of the following year.

If a taxpayer's income consists only of employment income from one employer that does not exceed ¥20 million in a year, the payer of the income makes a so-called year-end adjustment on the employment income, and if total income other than employment income is ¥200,000 or less, the employee is not required to file an income tax return.

Payment of tax/If salary is paid in Japan by a local employer, including a Japan branch of a foreign corporation, monthly withholding of both national and local income taxes is required. The tax due on overseas payments of salary is payable when the tax return is filed, rather than through payroll withholding. Provisional payments of national tax are required in July and November if the previous year's final tax liability with adjustments based on the current tax rates (after the deduction of withholding tax) is ¥150,000 or more.

Tax rates

National tax

Taxable income		Tax on	Percentage
Over	Not over	Column 1	on excess
(Column 1)			
0	¥ 3,300,000	—	10
¥ 3,300,000	9,000,000	¥ 330,000	20
9,000,000	18,000,000	1,470,000	30
18,000,000		4,170,000	37

Local inhabitants tax/Combined prefecture and municipal taxes are applied at the rates shown below.

Taxable income		Tax on	Percentage
Over	Not over	Column 1	on excess
(Column 1)			
0	¥ 2,000,000	—	5
¥ 2,000,000	7,000,000	¥ 100,000	10
7,000,000		600,000	13

Nonresidents/A nonresident's Japan-source compensation (employment income) is subject to a 20% national income tax on gross compensation.

INDIVIDUAL TAX CALCULATION

Calendar year 2003

Assumptions

1. Nonpermanent resident taxpayer with a wife (no income) and two children who are younger than 15 years old.
2. Remuneration is fully paid in Japan or, if partly paid outside of Japan, no business days were spent outside of Japan during the taxable year.
3. Interest on bank deposit in Japan: ¥100,000 (1).
4. Capital gain on sale of shares in foreign company and which is not derived through a securities company in Japan: ¥500,000 (2).
5. There is no remittance of money from abroad to Japan during the taxable year.

Tax computation

Gross remuneration		¥ 10,000,000
Less—Earned income relief:		
Up to 6,600,000	1,860,000	
10% of excess	340,000	2,200,000
Taxable income		¥ 7,800,000

	National tax	Inhabitants tax
Income as above	¥ 7,800,000	¥ 7,800,000
Deductions:		
Basic exemption	380,000	330,000
Dependent spouse	380,000	330,000
Other dependents (two)	760,000	660,000
Social insurance premium paid (3)	1,196,699	1,196,699
Taxable basis (rounded)	¥ 5,083,000	¥ 5,283,000
Income taxes:		
330,000 plus 20% on excess over 3,300,000	¥ 686,600	—
20% on interest income of 100,000 (1)	15,000	¥ 5,000
100,000 plus 10% on excess over 2,000,000	—	428,200
Equalization per capita tax (maximum)	—	4,000
Special tax reduction (4, 5)	(137,320)	(40,000)
Total taxes	¥ 564,200	¥ 397,200

Notes:

1. Taxation of interest on bank deposits is fully settled by the withholding of tax at source at a rate of 20% (combined national tax at 15% and local tax at 5%).
2. Foreign-source capital gain derived by a nonpermanent resident taxpayer is not taxable unless it is remitted to Japan.
3. The social insurance premiums paid of ¥1,196,699 would be calculated provided that the gross remuneration of ¥10 million consists of equalized 12 months' salaries and two bonuses equal to four months' salary.
4. For national tax purposes—20% of ¥686,600 or ¥250,000, whichever is lower.
5. For inhabitants tax purposes—15% of ¥433,200 or ¥40,000, whichever is lower.
6. Exchange rate of the yen at December 31, 2003: US$1 = ¥107.53 (TTM).

PwC contacts

For additional information on taxation in Kazakhstan, contact:

Courtney Fowler
Natalya Revenko
Michael Wagner
Tatiana Gorbacheva
PricewaterhouseCoopers
29/6 Satpaev Avenue, 3rd Floor
Almaty 480070, Kazakhstan
Telephone: (7) (3272) 980448
Fax: (7) (3272) 980252
e-mail: courtney.fowler@kz.pwc.com
natalya.revenko@kz.pwc.com
mike.wagner@kz.pwc.com
tatiana.gorbacheva@kz.pwc.com

Significant developments

With effect from January 1, 2004, an employer is generally liable to pay social tax at a regressive rate from 21% to 7% of gross remuneration of all employees (i.e., both local and expatriate), with a lower regressive rate from 11% to 5% applying to expatriate employees classified as administrative-management and engineering-technical personnel.

Effective from January 1, 2004, the monthly amount of employment income subject to obligatory pension contributions is capped at KZT495,000, or approximately US$3,557 at the current exchange rate, resulting in a maximum monthly pension contribution of approximately US$356 per individual.

Kazakhstan administrative legislation establishes severe penalties for an under-statement of an individual income tax liability. In particular, if the actual income tax differs from the assessed advance payments by more than 10%, a penalty of 70% of the amount of the actual income tax based on the final Individual Income Tax Declaration in excess of the estimated amount declared in the Statement/Calculation of Estimated Annual Individual Income Tax.

Territoriality and residence

In general, expatriate individuals are classified as residents and are subject to taxation on their worldwide income if they meet either of the following physical presence tests:

1. Physical presence in Kazakhstan for at least 183 days in any consecutive 12-month period ending in a tax period (e.g., 2003).

   or

2. The sum of the following formula is at least 183: Total number of days present in Kazakhstan in 2003 plus one-third the number of days present in 2002 plus one-sixth the number of days present in 2001.

If they do not meet the aforesaid residency tests, nonresidents are subject to taxation on their Kazakhstan-source income only.

Gross income

Employee gross income/All types of direct and indirect income are included in taxable compensation. There are no concessions for short-term residents.

Capital gains and investment income/Capital gains are generally taxed as regular income. Capital gains from the sale of a share participation in a resident legal entity are taxed at a reduced rate of 15%, which is withheld at source.

Deductions

Business deductions/There are no business deductions allowed for employees. An individual registered as an entrepreneur may claim business deductions.

Nonbusiness expenses/There are no deductions for nonbusiness expenses.

Personal allowances/These allowances take the form of deductions (currently approximately US$79) per dependent per year and are allowed only for local employees. Foreign individuals are not eligible for the personal allowance deductions.

Tax credits

Certain groups of taxpayers are allowed a tax credit for foreign taxes paid, limited to the amount of Kazakhstan tax due on that income.

Other taxes

Social tax/With effect from January 1, 2004, social tax is payable at a regressive rate from 21% to 7% of gross remuneration of all employees (i.e., both local and expatriate), with a lower regressive rate from 11% to 5% applying to expatriate employees classed as administrative-management and engineering-technical personnel.

Obligatory pension contributions/Obligatory pension contributions are borne by Kazakhstan citizens and permanently resident foreign citizens at a rate of 10% of their gross income. This does not normally apply to expatriates on temporary assignment to Kazakhstan.

Starting January 1, 2004 monthly income subject to obligatory pension contributions is capped at the threshold of approximately US$3,557 per month (at exchange rate of Kazakhstan tenge to U.S. dollar effective on the date of this writing). Monthly gross income exceeding this threshold is subject to obligatory pension contributions totaling 10% of the threshold, or approximately US$356.

Additional local taxes on income/There are no additional local taxes on income.

Tax administration

Kazakhstan applies three basic tax administration procedures:

1. Withholding at source of payment, whereby tax agents who pay income are obliged to compute and withhold individual income tax from actual income and pay tax to the tax authorities on the individuals' behalf;
2. Advance payments by tax agents (shadow withholding), whereby tax agents are obliged to estimate income tax from expected income payments to individuals and make monthly advance payments on the individuals' behalf;
3. A self-assessment system whereby all taxpayers who have taxable income (in the absence of a tax agent) are required to submit a Statement of Estimated

Annual Individual Income Tax prior to January 20 of the current calendar year detailing both the estimated annual taxable income and the estimated annual amount of tax due.

In addition, expatriates are required to submit annual tax declarations detailing both the actual annual income and the income tax due on or before March 31 of the year following the completed tax year.

If an expatriate departs Kazakhstan during a tax year, his or her tax declaration is due not later than ten days prior to the departure.

Tax rates

2003/The 2003 individual tax rates were graduated, with indexed brackets taxed at rates ranging from 0% to 30% as follows.

Taxable income		Tax on	Percentage
Over	Not over	base	on excess
(Base)			
0	KZT 156,960	—	5
KZT 159,960	418,560	KZT 7,848	10
418,560	6,278,400	34,008	20
6,278,400		1,205,976	30

2004/The 2004 individual tax rates are graduated, with indexed brackets taxed at rates ranging from 5 to 20% as follows.

Taxable income		Tax on	Percentage
Over	Not over	base	on excess
(Base)			
0	KZT 165,420	—	5
KZT 165,420	441,120	KZT 8,271	8
441,120	2,205,600	30,327	13
2,205,600	6,616,800	259,709	15
6,616,800		921,389	20

INDIVIDUAL TAX CALCULATION

Assumptions

1. Nonresident.
2. Annual salary—US$80,000.
3. Bonuses—US$2,000 (Kazakhstan-source income).
4. Living allowance—US$1,000 (Kazakhstan-source income).
5. Personal exemptions—none.
6. No tax credits or nonbusiness expenses.
7. Tax is paid by the individual.

Tax computation for 2003

	Total for the year	
Salary	US$	80,000
Bonuses		2,000
Living allowance		1,000
Total income	US$	83,000
Exchange rate—US$1 to KZT		151.00
Total amount of income	KZT	12,533,000
Less—Allowable deduction (1)		41,456
Taxable income	KZT	12,491,544
Tax thereon	KZT	3,069,919
Less—Tax paid		(2,814,092)
Tax due	KZT	255,827

Notes:

The annual allowable deduction per person for the year 2003 is KZT10,464.

Tax computation for 2004

	Total for the year	
Salary	US$	80,000
Bonuses		2,000
Living allowance		1,000
Total income	US$	83,000
Exchange rate—KZT/US$		139.15
Total amount of income	KZT	11,549,450
Less—Allowable deduction (1)		0
Taxable income	KZT	11,549,450
Tax thereon	KZT	1,907,919
Less—Tax paid		(1,736,206)
Tax due	KZT	171,713

Notes:

1. Effective January 1, 2004, nonresidents are not allowed deductions.
2. Exchange rate (National Bank of Kazakhstan) of the tenge on March 1, 2004: US$1 = KZT139.15.

PwC contacts

For additional information on taxation in Kenya, contact:

Shaira Adamali
Gavin McEwen
PricewaterhouseCoopers
The Rahimtulla Tower
Upper Hill Road
P.O. Box 43963
00100 Nairobi, Kenya
Telephone: (+254) (20) 285000
Fax: (+254) (20) 285001
e-mail: shaira.adamali@ke.pwc.com
gavin.t.mcewen@ke.pwc.com

Significant developments

With effect from January 1, 2003, all individuals liable to tax are required to file self-assessment returns within six months of the tax year-end. Previously, this requirement did not apply to individuals whose only source of income was employment income that had been taxed through the payroll under the pay-as-you-earn (PAYE) system and the correct tax liability had been deducted and paid. The first tax year this applies to is the year ended December 31, 2002; the self-assessment tax returns are due by June 30, 2003.

As of June 12, 2003 noncash benefits provided to employees are to be taxed at the higher of cost and fair market value. Previously the taxable benefit value was the higher of cost and the Commissioner's prescribed rate, where applicable. The Commissioner of Income Tax has still, however, retained some limited powers to prescribe rates at which benefits are taxed for benefits where it is difficult if not impossible to determine the cost or fair market value.

From January 1, 2004 the maximum tax-free lump-sum payments from registered pension schemes and provident and retirement benefit funds has been increased to KShs480,000.

The taxation of pension payments and withdrawals from provident and retirement benefit funds in excess of the above amounts has also changed from January 1, 2004. Payments to individuals on the occasions noted below and payments/with-drawals of members of a scheme for less than 15 years are to be taxed differently.

Payment/withdrawals on retirement from registered schemes on the following occasions are to be taxed at the individual rates of tax and the tax so calculated is to be the final tax:

- Attainment of 50 years of age or above.
- Member of a registered scheme for 15 years or more.
- Retirement due to ill-health.

The individuals who will benefit under this change are those who continue to receive other taxable income after such a payment/withdrawal is received.

Territoriality and residence

Kenyan residents and citizens are subject to Kenyan income tax on their worldwide earned income. Residence is defined as either having a permanent home in Kenya and being present in Kenya for any period of time in a tax year, or spending 183 days or more in Kenya in any one tax year or an average of more than 122 days over 3 consecutive tax years.

Gross income

Employee gross income/Nonresident employees are taxable only on their income earned from within Kenya or derived from Kenya. Residents are taxed on worldwide earned income, regardless of source. Income of an individual for tax purposes includes all payments made by an employer to an employee. This includes salaries, wages, bonuses, and fringe benefits received or enjoyed by virtue of employment.

Noncash benefits usually give rise to taxable income at the higher of cost to the employer and fair market value (see above), although some benefits are taxed at standard amounts (see below).

1. Housing:

   For employees other than directors with gross emoluments of less than KShs50,000 per month, the taxable housing benefit is computed at 15% of gross salary plus benefits (10% for agricultural employees residing on a plantation or farm). For employees earning above KShs50,000 per month and whole time serve directors, the housing benefit is the higher of the actual rent paid or, where the premises are owned by the employer, the fair rental market value of the premises. However, for nonwhole time service directors, the taxable housing benefit is the higher of 15% of the gains or profits from employment excluding the value of those premises or the rent paid by the employer if paid under an agreement made at arm's length with a third party. A whole time service director is defined as 'a director of a company who is required to devote substantially the whole of his time to the service of that company in a managerial or technical capacity and is not the beneficial owner of, or able, either directly or through the medium of other companies or by any other means, to control more than 5% of the share capital or voting power of that company.'

2. Company cars:

   Motor vehicles supplied by the employer are assessed at the higher of 2% per month of the cost of the vehicle or prescribed standard rates.

3. Fringe benefit tax:

   Interest-free or low-interest loans granted to employees prior to June 11, 1998, are taxed on an imputed interest benefit of the lower of 15% or rates prescribed by the Commissioner. For loans granted, or whose terms were varied, after June 11, 1998, the tax burden has been shifted to the employer.

   Interest-free or low-interest loans provided by an employer to an employee after the above-mentioned date are subject to fringe benefit tax (FBT). The FBT is calculated using the 91-day Treasury bill rate, representing the market lending rates, less the interest charged to the employee. The current 91-day Treasury bill rate is 1% per annum. The benefit is then taxed using the resident corporate tax rate, currently 30%. The FBT does not constitute an assessable benefit on the employee; it represents an added cost to the employer. This cost is not allowable for corporation tax purposes and must be paid even if the employer does not pay corporation tax (i.e., is in a tax loss position). The tax must be paid by the employer together with the monthly PAYE payments on or before the ninth day of the month following the payroll month.

4. School fees:

   Education fees borne by the employer may not be taxed on the employee, except where the employer has tax-exempt status. If, however, the employee is not taxed on the benefit received, the fees will not be an allowable expense for the employer.

5. Other prescribed benefit rates:

Communal electricity, for example, from a generator	KShs1,500 per month
Communal water, for example, from a borehole	KShs500 per month
Furniture	12% of original cost per annum
Telephone	30% of annual bills

Where a contract of employment states that remuneration should be paid free of all taxes, the amount received by the employee is deemed to be net income, and the figure is grossed up to determine the tax liability.

All benefits should be taxed along with salaries, wages, and bonuses under the pay-as-you-earn (PAYE) system.

Capital gains and investment income/Capital gains tax is not currently imposed in Kenya.

Income from dividends within Kenya is subject to withholding tax of 5% for residents and this is a final tax. Kenya-source interest income is subject to a general withholding tax of 15% for residents. However, different withholding rates apply as follows, depending upon the kind of financial instruments.

	%
Housing bonds	10
Bearer instruments (other than government bearer bonds and treasury bills)	25
Any other interest	15

Withholding tax on interest income is the final tax.

The nonresident withholding tax rates on interest and dividends are 15% and 10%, respectively, and this represents the total tax liability. The tax withheld on payments to unit trusts is 15% for interest and 5% for dividends, and this represents the final tax.

Lower rates may apply where there is a double taxation treaty in force.

Exempt income includes interest on tax reserve certificates and from savings accounts with the Kenya Post Office Savings Bank.

Deductions

Business deductions/An individual may claim a deduction for any expense incurred wholly and exclusively in the production of employment income. Reimbursements of business expenses such as entertainment, travel, and car expenses are not part of taxable income. Airfares and moving expenses paid to expatriate employees, recruited outside Kenya and who are in Kenya solely to perform their duties, are not taxable. Leave passages for such employees are also not taxable.

Nonbusiness expenses/Reimbursed medical insurance or medical expenses are not normally taxable.

Relief of up to KShs17,500 per month is given for contributions to registered pension funds or provident funds. The employee is entitled to claim this deduction in preference to the employer.

Interest payments on loans borrowed for the purposes of improvement, construction, or purchase of residential premises are deductible, subject to a limit of KShs100,000 per annum.

First-time buyers saving for the purchase of a residential property can be eligible for a tax deduction of the lower of actual savings payments made and KShs4,000 per month. This deduction can be claimed providing the funds are deposited with an approved Institution under the 'Registered Home Ownership Savings Plan in the qualifying year. Such deductions are available for a period of ten years providing that when the funds are deducted and remitted for the relevant fund by an individual's employer.

With effect from January 1, 2003, resident individuals are entitled to insurance relief of the lower of 15% of premiums paid and KShs3,000 per month. Relief is given as a credit against tax payable. The following conditions must be fulfilled in order to qualify.

1. The individual has paid for life insurance for himself or his dependants where the insurance secures a capital sum payable in Kenya.
2. An individual's employer has paid for the above and the individual has been taxed on the value of the benefit received.
3. The insurance policy must be one taken out after January 1, 2003.

Premiums paid for education policies with a maturity period in excess of ten years also qualify as part of the above.

Special deduction/Under certain circumstances, expatriates may claim a one-third deduction from taxable income if they are employed by a regional office that carries on no business in Kenya and if they are absent on business for at least 120 days in any tax year.

Home-ownership savings plan/First-time buyers of houses can obtain a special KShs480,000 deduction, provided the following conditions are met.

1. The deduction is limited to KShs48,000 per year for each of ten consecutive years.
2. The amount must be deposited with prescribed financial institutions.
3. The funds must be withdrawn at the end of the tenth year and, within one year of withdrawal, applied only toward the purchase of a house.

Any income earned on the funds in this ten-year period is also tax free, subject to all conditions being met.

Personal allowances/Allowances are minimal, amounting to KShs12,672 per annum for all individual taxpayers, and applied as credits against the tax liability.

Tax credits

Relief is given for double taxation only where a treaty exists. Available personal allowances are in the form of tax credits. However, with effect from January 2002, Kenyan citizens chargeable to tax in Kenya on employment income accrued in or derived from another country are eligible for a tax credit against Kenyan tax in respect of the tax they pay on the same income in the other country.

Other taxes

Social security taxes/Every employee must contribute to the National Social Security Fund. The contribution is 5% of salary, subject to a maximum of KShs200 per month. The employer makes a corresponding contribution. Overseas personnel who are expected to be employed for less than three years can sometimes claim exemption if they can show that they contribute to a similar scheme in their home country. To do this they must complete an S.F.7 form and produce evidence of contributing to an overseas social security scheme.

Hospital insurance/Employees earning over KShs1,000 per month must contribute approximately 2% of their salaries to the National Hospital Insurance Fund, subject to a maximum of KShs320. An individual can be exempt from making contributions if the individual's spouse is making contributions to the fund.

Airport tax/The airport tax paid by air passengers is collected at the time of ticket purchase.

Tax administration

Returns/Wives with income from employment, self-employment, or certain professions can opt to file separate self-assessment returns from their husbands. A wife's income from employment (or self-employment in certain professions) is taxed at special rates equal to the normal basic rates of tax. This has the effect of separating the income of husband and wife so that lower rates apply to both.

Self-assessment returns must be filed by June 30 in the year following the year of income. The year of income is a calendar year. Any balance of tax due must be paid by April 30 in the year following the year of income.

Payment of tax/The majority of tax on employees is paid by withholding from salaries and benefits in the form of PAYE. Any further tax liability is based on self-assessment, and it must be paid by April 30 following the year of income to which the liability relates. An individual (other than one whose total taxable income has been subjected to tax at source) whose tax liability exceeds KShs40,000 per annum is required to pay four installment taxes by April 20, June 20, September 20, and December 20.

The installment tax payable on each due date is 25% of the lower of 110% of tax assessed in the prior year or the taxpayer's estimate of the current year's tax liability.

Tax rates

The rates applied to taxable income from January 1, 2004, are shown below.

Taxable income			
Over (Column 1)	Not over	Tax on Column 1	Percentage on excess
0	KShs 116,160	0	10
KShs 116,160	225,600	KShs 11,616	15
225,600	335,040	28,032	20
335,040	444,480	49,920	25
444,480		77,280	30

The above rates also apply to a wife's employment income and self-employment income from certain professions.

As shown above, the maximum rate of 30% is charged on income in excess of KShs444,480 (approximately US$5,841 using an exchange rate of US$1:KShs76.10).

INDIVIDUAL TAX CALCULATIONS

Year 2004

I—Resident Kenya citizen

Assumptions

Resident Kenya citizen, married with two children. Gross income of husband is KShs5,840,000; of wife, KShs800,000. Benefits provided to the husband by his employer include an 1,800 cc motor vehicle (cost, KShs1,000,000) and a telephone (annual bill of KShs12,000); wife receives no benefits. Received bank deposit interest of KShs70,000 and dividend income of KShs40,000 and paid mortgage interest of KShs120,000 on owner-occupied property. Made capital gains of KShs500,000 on sale of residential property.

Tax computation

Husband

Gross income		KShs 5,840,000
Add—Benefits at standard rates:		
1,800 cc motor vehicle (1)	240,000	
Telephone	3,600	243,600
Total		6,083,600
Add—Bank deposit interest (2)		Nil
		6,083,600
Less—Mortgage interest (maximum deduction)		100,000
Taxable income		KShs 5,983,600
Tax thereon:		
On first 444,480 of taxable income	77,280	
On remaining 5,539,120 at 30%	1,661,736	1,739,016
Less—Personal relief		(12,672)
Tax payable (3)		KShs 1,726,344
Dividend income—Gross		KShs 40,000
Tax on dividend income—Deducted at source (final tax)		KShs 2,000
Interest income—Gross		KShs 70,000
Tax on interest income—Deducted at source (final tax)		KShs 10,500
Capital gain on sale of property		KShs 500,000
Tax on gain		KShs Nil

Wife

Gross income		KShs 800,000
Tax thereon:		
On first 444,480	77,280	
On remaining 355,520 at 30%	106,656	183,936
Less—Personal relief		(12,672)
Tax payable		KShs 171,264

Total liability to taxation

Total tax liability:	
Husband	KShs 1,726,344
Wife	171,264
	KShs 1,897,608

Notes:

1. Car benefit is the higher of KShs86,400 or 24% per annum of capital cost.
2. Withholding tax borne at source represents final tax.
3. Credit for tax deducted under the PAYE system to be given against total liability, as above.

II—Expatriate employed by a regional office

Assumptions

Expatriate employed by a regional office; married with two children; gross income KShs3,600,000. Business travel, excluding leave, totals 140 days. Benefits provided by employer include a 1,800 cc motor vehicle (cost, KShs1,500,000), a telephone (annual bill KShs12,000), housing, and furniture (original cost KShs40,000). Housing cost to the employer is KShs1,000,000 per year. This calculation only applies where certain conditions have been met.

Tax computation

Gross income		KShs 3,600,000
Add—Benefits at standard rates:		
1,800 cc motor vehicle (1)	360,000	
Telephone	3,600	
Furniture	4,800	
Housing at cost	1,000,000	1,368,400
		4,968,400
Less—Regional deduction (4,968,400 x 33.333%)		1,656,117
Taxable income		3,312,283
Tax thereon:		
On first 444,480	77,280	
On remaining 2,867,803 at 30%	860,341	KShs 937,621
Less—Personal relief		(12,672)
Tax payable (2)		KShs 924,949

Notes:

1. Car Benefit is the higher of KShs86,400 or 24% of capital costs.
2. Credit for tax deducted under the PAYE system to be given against total liability, as above.
3. Exchange rate of the Kenya shilling at January 1, 2004: US$1 = KShs76.10.

Korea, Republic of

PwC contact

For additional information on taxation in Korea, contact the following tax partner of the member firm, Samil Accounting Corporation:

Ando Yun
Samil Accounting Corporation
Kukje Center Building, 5th F #191
2-ka Han-Kang-Ro
Yong-San-ku Seoul 140-702
Korea
Telephone: (82) (2) 709-0551
Fax: (82) (2) 796-7027, 790-1507
e-mail: ando.yun@kr.pwcglobal.com

General note

This entry is repeated from the 2003/2004 edition. For more up-to-date information consult the contact listed above or Jacqueline Collette at jacqueline.collette@us.pwc.com.

Significant developments

There have been no significant tax or regulatory developments regarding individual taxation in the past year. The information below is current as of January 2003. For subsequent developments consult the contact listed above.

Territoriality and residence

All individuals in Korea are classified for income tax purposes, as listed below:

1. Citizen—Korean national.
2. Resident—Non-Koreans having a domicile or residence within Korea for one year or more, individuals having an occupation that would generally require them to reside in Korea for one year or more, or individuals whose families accompany them to Korea and who retain substantial assets in Korea. Generally, residency is determined on a "facts and circumstances" test, evaluated on an individual basis.
3. Nonresident—An individual who is not deemed to be a resident.

Korean citizens and individuals considered as residents for tax purposes are subject to Korean income tax on worldwide income. An expatriate who is deemed to be a nonresident is taxed only on Korean-source income. A nonresident is not allowed all the personal deductions granted to residents, except for a basic deduction of W1 million and additional personal deduction of W1 million.

Gross income

Employee gross income/Individual income can be categorized as taxable, nontaxable, or tax-exempt. Taxable income includes global income, capital gains, forestry income, and severance pay, each of which is subject to tax on a unique tax rate structure. There are certain elements of income on which the government has waived its taxing rights, whether or not an application for exemption is filed by an individual. There are other items of income for which a taxpayer can submit an application for tax.

Global income is subject to global taxation and includes earned income (salaries, wages, bonuses, and other amounts received for personal services rendered), interest income, dividend income, rental income, personal business income, temporary property income, pension income, and other income (prize winnings, royalties, rewards, etc.).

Korean tax law segregates earned income into Class A or Class B income, depending on the income source.

1. Class A earned income—Employment income received from a domestic (Korean) corporation or a Korean branch office of a foreign corporation for services rendered in Korea. Such income is subject to payroll withholding taxes by the employer on a monthly basis.
2. Class B earned income—Employment income received in foreign currency from a foreign corporation outside Korea. However, even if foreigners who work in Korea are paid their wages overseas, the wages are considered Class A earned income rather than Class B earned income where the wage is deducted as an expense in calculating the taxable income of a permanent establishment of the foreign corporation in Korea. The employer is not required to withhold Korean taxes at the time of payment of Class B income; however, the individual is required to declare this income annually and pay income taxes thereon on a voluntary basis. Alternatively, an individual may elect to pay Class B income taxes through a licensed taxpayers' association, which collects and remits such taxes on a monthly basis. Taxpayers who join such an association are eligible to receive a 10% reduction in the amount of income tax payable.

Capital gains and investment income/Gains arising from the disposal of capital assets are included in an individual's taxable income but are taxed separately from global income. Certain capital gains are specifically exempt from tax. These include gains from certain transfers of farmland and other real estate; gains from the transfer of one house, including land, per household; and gains from the transfer of listed stock (corporate equity share certificates). However, exceptionally, when the total stake of a shareholder together with any related parties in a listed company exceeds 3% and total market value is W10 billion or more, the capital gains are taxed at the rate of 22% (if the holding period is less than one year, 33% would be applied). If the stake is in a small- and medium-sized company, the gains are subject to tax at 11%.

Gains from the disposal of foreign assets are taxable where the transfer is made after January 1, 1999 and the transferor has been a Korean resident for five years or more at the time of sale.

Capital losses are deductible only against capital gains. Unused losses may not be carried forward. Interest income earned on other than National Savings Association deposits and dividend income received from both domestic and foreign corporations are taxable. Most interest and dividend income earned from Korean sources is subject to 16.5% tax withholding at source. Resident taxpayers are required to include any interest and dividends received from non-Korean sources in global income and to pay taxes thereon at basic global tax rates (discussed below).

Nontaxable income/The following elements of employee income are nontaxable:

1. Housing and related costs paid by an employer directly to a landlord on behalf of an expatriate employee. However, utility costs paid by an employer are taxable to the employee.
2. Reimbursement of business expenses, including social membership costs and entertainment expenses incurred by an employee for business purposes.

3. Cost of an automobile and driver and related maintenance and insurance expenses provided by an employer, provided the automobile is registered in the name of the employer and the driver is on the employers' payroll register.
4. Reimbursement of operating costs for a personal automobile used for business purposes, up to W200,000 per month.
5. Relocation and moving expense reimbursements.
6. Reasonable amounts of employer-reimbursed home-leave travel expenses for expatriate employees.

Special exclusion for overseas expatriate allowances/Overseas service allowances received by expatriates employed in Korea in excess of the regular salary they would be paid while working in their home country, such as cost-of-living allowances, hardship provisions, housing, transportation, education, utilities, domestic help, and security services, can be excluded from taxable income. The total amount of such allowances considered to be nontaxable is limited to 40% of an expatriate's monthly base salary.

Tax-exempt income/Individuals can request tax-exempt treatment for certain types of income (specified below) by submitting through their employer an application to the appropriate tax authorities.

1. Wages and various allowances received by a foreigner providing services under a high-technology inducement contract prescribed under the Foreign Investment Promotion Law, for a period of five years from the acceptance date of the technical service agreement.
2. Wages received by a qualified foreign technician/engineer providing services in Korea to a domestic entity under an engineering technology inducement agreement under the Engineering Technology Promotion Law (of which consideration amounts to US$300,000 or more) for five years from the date the expatriate commences rendering services in Korea.
3. Wages received by a foreign technician with five or more years' work experience at mining, construction, manufacturing, or certain technology-intensive industries or having a bachelor's degree and three or more years' working experience at these industries.
4. Wages and salaries received by a foreign researcher working in a qualified research center.

Deductions

Business deductions/All business-related expenses, such as moving expenses, travel expenses, automobile expenses, and certain amounts of entertainment expenses, are tax deductible. Alternatively, reimbursements for such expenses can be claimed by the business as deductible expenses and need not be included in the individual's taxable income.

Nonbusiness expenses/Certain other allowable deductions are outlined below (applicable to salary income earner only):

1. An earned-income deduction is allowed for salary or wage earners as follows:
   a. Entire income up to W5 million;
   b. 45% of the income from W5 million up to W15 million;
   c. 15% of the income from W15 million up to W30 million;
   d. 10% of the income from W30 million up to W45 million;
   e. 5% of the income in excess of W45 million.

2. A deduction for certain insurance premiums paid by an individual and other dependents, up to a maximum of W1 million.
3. A deduction for medical expenses incurred by a taxpayer, up to a maximum of W5 million, to the extent that the expenses exceed 3% of total earned income. However, medical expenses paid for parents aged 65 or over and living together with the taxpayer and for the handicapped are not subject to the above W5 million limit.
4. A deduction for all of an employed taxpayer's own education expenses (including graduate school fees). Other education expenses within certain limits incurred by a taxpayer's dependents are deductible (W5 million for each dependent attending university, W2 million for each dependent attending elementary school, middle school or high school, W1.5 million for each dependent attending preschool).
5. A deduction for certain types of charitable contributions, generally up to a maximum of 10% of gross global income after the earned income deduction described above.
6. A deduction of W6 million (maximum) for wage earners who do not own a home or who are owners of a house of a certain size and who subscribed to a particular savings program for home ownership.
7. In lieu of one of the deductions listed above (except for the earned income deduction), a standard special deduction of W600,000 is available.
8. A deduction for expenditure paid by credit cards, up to 20% of the amount in excess of 10% of earned income. This deduction is limited to a maximum of W5 million.

Personal deduction/Korean tax law provides all resident taxpayers with the following personal deductions from individual taxable income:

1. A basic deduction of W1 million per year.
2. A deduction of W1 million for a spouse who lives with the taxpayer and who has income of less than the W1 million.
3. A deduction of W1 million for each eligible dependent who lives with the taxpayer and has income of less than the W1 million.
4. An additional deduction of W1 million for each handicapped person in the taxpayer's household. The handicapped person may be the taxpayer, spouse, or other dependent. To qualify for the deduction, the spouse and/or dependent are not permitted to have income in excess of W1 million.
5. An additional deduction of W1 million for each taxpayer, spouse, or dependent aged 65 or over in the taxpayers' household. To qualify for this additional deduction, the spouse or other dependent should not have income in excess of W1 million.
6. An additional deduction of W500,000 for a woman householder with dependents.
7. An additional deduction of W500,000 for a woman salary earner in the case of a two-earner married couple.
8. An additional deduction of W500,000 per child for a working woman who has children under the age of six.
9. In cases where there is only one family member (including the taxpayer) qualified for personal deduction, an additional deduction (in respect of small number of eligible persons) of W1 million and W500,000 for two family members (including taxpayer) who qualify for personal deduction is available in addition to the deductions listed above.

Nonresidents of Korea are only allowed to claim the personal deduction noted in (1) and (9).

Exception from income deductions/A person who files separately (i.e., chooses to pay a flat rate of withholding at source, and does not include such income in the global return) for interest income, dividend income, pension income, or other income that is subject to separate taxation will not be eligible for the basic deduction, additional deduction or any other deductions.

Tax credits

Certain tax credits against the global income tax are available to resident taxpayers. These include:

1. A tax credit for Class A and Class B wages (up to a maximum of W400,000 per year):
   a. Where the calculated tax amount is W500,000 or less, the credit is the amount of the calculated amount multiplied by 45%, that is, W225,000;
   b. Where the calculated tax amount is more than W500,000, the credit is W225,000 plus 30% of the calculated tax amount in excess of W500,000.
2. A tax credit of 10% of the income tax for Class B wage earners who voluntarily report their monthly earnings and pay monthly income taxes through a licensed taxpayers' association.
3. A tax credit of 19% of certain dividends received by each shareholder against the individual income tax calculated on the global income increased by 19% of dividends received.
4. A tax credit for foreign income taxes paid abroad by Korean residents, up to a limit of the amount of Korean income taxes before the foreign tax credit times the ratio of foreign-source income to worldwide total taxable income. Any excess over the maximum allowable credit may be carried forward for five years. Alternatively, foreign tax paid can be deducted from taxable income.

Other taxes

Minimum tax/A minimum tax, with exceptions, will be calculated at the greater of 40% of income tax liability before exemptions or actual tax after exemptions. The minimum tax is applied to business income of a resident individual and Korean-source business income of a nonresident individual, but it is not applied to employment (earned) income.

Social security taxes/Under the national pension program, companies are required to contribute an amount equal to 4.5% of employee salaries to the national pension fund. Employees are also required to contribute an amount equal to 4.5% of their salaries. The employee contributions to the national pension program are tax deductible. This national pension contribution is capped at a monthly salary of W3,600,000. Thus, the maximum monthly pension contribution to be paid by an employee is W162,000.

There is also a severance pay system that requires no employee contribution. Severance pay, or retirement income, is taxed separately from global income.

Local taxes on income/Besides the basic income tax (which is paid to the national tax office), there is also a local residence tax surcharge, which is paid to the city or province that is the domicile of the taxpayer. The residence tax is calculated as 10% of the basic income tax liability.

Tax administration

Returns/A tax return must be filed by taxpayers who have both of Class A and Class B income or Class B income if not declared through a licensed taxpayers' association. Taxpayers must file returns for the calendar year during May (before May 31) of the following year or prior to leaving Korea permanently. There is generally no provision for filing joint tax returns under Korean tax law.

Payment of tax/A taxpayer who receives only Class A and/or retirement income is generally not required to file an annual tax return. The employer is required to withhold income taxes at source on a monthly basis and to finalize the employee's tax liability and issue a final tax settlement certificate not later than the end of February of the following tax year. The employer is not required to withhold Korean taxes at the time of payment of Class B income; however, the individual is required to declare this income annually and pay income taxes thereon on a voluntary basis. Alternatively, the individual may elect to pay Class B income taxes through a licensed taxpayers' association, which collects and remits such taxes on a monthly basis. Taxpayers who join such an association are eligible to receive a 10% reduction in the amount of income tax payable. A member firm of PricewaterhouseCoopers in Seoul, the Samil Accounting Corporation, operates such an association (Samil Taxpayers' Association).

Tax rates

Effective from January 1, 2002, individual income tax rates on global income range from 9% to 36%. The top marginal tax rate, including the residence surcharge (see below), is 39.6% on taxable income in excess of W80 million.

Basic global income tax/The following tax table summarizes the basic global tax rates applicable for the income received from January 1, 2002 and thereafter.

(In W '000s)

Annual taxable income			
Over (Column 1)	Not over	Tax on Column 1	Percentage on excess
0	W 10,000	—	9
W 10,000	40,000	W 900	18
40,000	80,000	6,300	27
80,000		17,100	36

Residence tax surcharge/A residence tax surcharge is assessed at a rate of 10% of the income tax liability.

INDIVIDUAL TAX CALCULATION

Calendar year 2003

Assumptions

Resident alien husband and wife, two children under the age of 20; one spouse earns all the income.

Tax computation

Salary		W 40,000,000
Overseas allowances		26,000,000
Gross income		66,000,000
Less—Exclusion for overseas allowances (1)		16,000,000
Adjusted gross income		50,000,000
Less:		
Earned income deduction	13,500,000	
Standard deduction	600,000	
Basic exemption	1,000,000	
Spouse exemption	1,000,000	
Dependent exemption (1,000,000 x 2)	2,000,000	18,100,000
Taxable income		W 31,900,00
Income tax		W 4,842,000
Less—Income tax credit (2)		(400,000)
		4,442,000
Residence tax (10% of income tax)		444,200
		4,886,200
Less—Tax payable through payroll tax withholding or with return		(3,480,000)
Total tax payable		W 1,406,200

Notes:

1. Computed as 40% of base salary.
2. A tax credit of up to a maximum of W400,000 per year is available related to income tax.
3. Exchange rate (base rate) of the won at December 31, 2002: US$1 = W1,200.4.

PwC contacts

For additional information on taxation in Liechtenstein, contact:

Werner Schmid
Victor Meyer
PricewaterhouseCoopers AG
Stampfenbachstrasse 73
8035 Zurich, Switzerland
Telephone: (41) (1) 630 11 11
Fax: (41) (1) 630 41 15
e-mail: werner schmid@ch.pwc.com
victor.meyer@ch.pwc.com

Significant developments

There have been no significant tax or regulatory developments in the past year.

Territoriality and residence

Individuals are regarded as resident in Liechtenstein if they are residing within Liechtenstein with the intention of staying there permanently. In addition, individuals are deemed to be resident for tax purposes if they are residing in the country and performing a gainful activity (employed or self-employed).

An individual not engaged in a gainful activity becomes subject to income tax after a continued stay of six weeks with their own accommodation or three months without having their own accommodation (rental or property).

In principle, tax is levied on the resident taxpayer's worldwide earned income and net wealth. There are important income items that are exempt from income tax, as described below.

Gross income

Employee gross income/An employee resident in Liechtenstein for tax purposes is taxed on any salary and any other monetary benefits (including reimbursements of living expenses) received from the employer, regardless of where the work has been performed, where payment is made or whether it is remitted.

Capital gains and investment income/Any capital gains are included in the determination of gross income, except for those realized on the sale of real estate that are subject to the Liechtenstein real estate profits tax.

Income from investments (mainly dividends, interest, rental income) is exempt from income tax, provided net wealth tax has been paid on the underlying assets.

Deductions

Business deductions/Individuals with income from employment are entitled to a deduction, generally CHF1,500, as compensation for outlays relating to employment, such as travel to and from work and extra costs for outside meals.

Nonbusiness expenses/Deductible expenses include premiums for life, sickness, and accident insurance up to a maximum of CHF5,000 per married couple, CHF2,500 per single taxpayer, and CHF1,500 per child; contributions to pension funds up to 12% of taxable income and all social security contributions required by law; the cost for higher education for children up to CHF12,000 per child; and medical expenses, as well as expenses for dentistry borne by the taxpayer up to CHF6,000 per person.

Personal allowances/Personal allowances, deductible in determining taxable income, are granted as follows. See also "Tax credits" below.

	CHF
Taxpayers without own household	2,400
Taxpayers with own household but without children	4,800
Taxpayers with own household and with dependent children	6,000
Allowance per child	6,000
Allowance per person for private capital gains	5,000
Allowance in the amount of the effective contribution per person whom the taxpayer is legally required to support, other than children	No limit

Tax credits

Apart from those deriving from the double taxation treaty with Austria, there are no foreign tax credits available. For couples, total income and wealth tax is reduced by one-third for a tax amount of up to CHF2,897, by 30% for a tax amount of more than CHF2,897, and by 28% for a tax amount of more than CHF3,549, with a minimum of CHF550 and a maximum of CHF5,500. Single mothers and fathers can deduct one-half of the above-mentioned reduction.

Other taxes

Social security taxes/For 2002 the employee's share of social security contributions (old-age and dependent pension schemes, disability insurance) is 4.4% with no upper limit; the employer pays an additional 6.936%, including contributions to the family compensation fund and administration costs. For self-employed taxpayers, social security contributions are assessed on a progressive scale with a maximum of 11.336%. Unemployment insurance amounts to 0.25% on the first CHF97,200 of the gross wage (see also "Nonbusiness expenses" above).

Other taxes on income/There are no other taxes on income.

Wealth tax/Wealth tax is levied on the net assets of the taxpayer. All assets of the taxpayer, including domestic real estate, investments in securities, cash, time deposits, precious metals, and all other personal property, are included in the determination of net assets. Related liabilities, such as mortgages and other borrowings, may be deducted. Assets are, in general, assessed at their approximate fair market value. (The related unrealized gains or losses are not included in taxable income.) Additionally, the first CHF70,000 for a single taxpayer (CHF140,000 for a married taxpayer) of the taxpayer's net assets are tax deductible.

Tax administration

Returns/Spouses living together are taxed jointly on their combined income and assets. Returns must be filed annually, normally by late April. Employees must enclose a certificate of remuneration issued by the employer(s). Taxpayers are obliged to file their returns on a calendar-year basis.

Payment of tax/A wage tax withholding from salaries is levied on the employer, provided that the employer is domiciled in Liechtenstein. The tax payable by the individual based on the annual invoice is reduced by the withholdings already made by the employer. The balance is payable within 30 days after receipt of the assessment and invoice, respectively. On salaries of employees with a nonresident employer, no wage tax withholding is levied.

Tax rates

Individual income tax rates are determined not only by taxable income but also by taxable wealth (see "Individual tax calculation" below).

Basic tax rates/The basic tax rates are specified below.

	Tax rate
	%
On income	1.080
On wealth	0.054

Communal tax/The communes levy a communal tax of 200% of the national tax (Balzers 180%, Mauren 190%, Schaan 170%, Vaduz 160%); the top income tax rate is thus 17.01% (Balzers 15.88%, Mauren 16.44%, Schaan 15.37%, Vaduz 14.74%), and the top wealth tax is 0.8505%.

Surcharge/The following surcharges on the basic tax on income and wealth are levied and result, in total, in the national tax due.

From CHF	To CHF	Surcharge %	From CHF	To CHF	Surcharge %
	214	0	1,112	1,146	215
214	225	5	1,146	1,180	220
225	237	10	1,180	1,216	225
237	248	15	1,216	1,253	230
248	261	20	1,253	1,284	235
261	274	25	1,284	1,316	240
274	287	30	1,316	1,349	245
287	300	35	1,349	1,382	250
300	314	40	1,382	1,417	255
313	328	45	1,417	1,453	260
328	342	50	1,453	1,489	265
342	358	55	1,489	1,526	270
358	374	60	1,526	1,564	275
374	391	65	1,564	1,603	280
391	409	70	1,603	1,635	285
409	427	75	1,635	1,668	290
427	447	80	1,668	1,702	295
447	464	85	1,702	1,736	300
464	483	90	1,736	1,770	305
483	502	95	1,770	1,806	310
502	522	100	1,806	1,842	315
522	543	105	1,842	1,879	320
543	565	110	1,879	1,916	325
565	588	115	1,916	1,955	330
588	611	120	1,955	1,974	335
611	636	125	1,974	1,994	340
636	661	130	1,994	2,014	345
661	684	135	2,014	2,034	350
684	708	140	2,034	2,055	355
708	733	145	2,055	2,075	360
733	758	150	2,075	2,096	365
758	785	155	2,096	2,117	370
785	812	160	2,117	2,306	375
812	841	165	2,306	2,495	380
841	870	170	2,495	2,657	385
870	900	175	2,657	2,873	390
900	931	180	2,873	2,981	395
931	960	185	2,981	3,089	400
960	988	190	3,089	3,197	405
988	1,018	195	3,197	3,305	410
1,018	1,049	200	3,305	3,413	415
1,048	1,080	205	3,413	3,521	420
1,080	1,112	210	3,521		425

INDIVIDUAL TAX CALCULATION

National and communal tax for tax year 2002

Assumptions

1. Married man with two children, resident in Vaduz.
2. Employment income of CHF175,400 net of social security contributions.
3. Compensation as director of CHF2,500.
4. Securities and savings accounts total of CHF140,000; income thereon of CHF7,000.
5. Capital gains on security transactions of CHF20,000.
6. Insurance premiums for life insurance of CHF2,500; surrender value of CHF15,000.
7. Motorcar with market value of CHF25,000.
8. Living in own apartment; assessed value of CHF180,000, mortgage of CHF100,000, mortgage interest of CHF6,000.

Determination of taxable income

Gross income:		
Income from employment		CHF 175,400
Compensation as director		2,500
Income from securities and savings accounts		7,000
Capital gains on security transactions		20,000
		CHF 204,900
Less—Tax-exempt income—Income from securities and savings accounts		7,000
Total gross income		197,900
Less—Deductions:		
Income-connected expenses	1,500	
Insurance premiums, say	2,500	
Cost for children's higher education (maximum, 2 x 12,000)	24,000	
Medical and dental expenses, say	3,650	
Mortgage interest (not allowed as deduction)	—	31,650
Net income		166,250
Less—Personal allowances:		
For taxpayer having own household	6,000	
Allowance for children (2 x 6000)	12,000	
Allowance for capital gain (4 x 5,000)	20,000	38,000
Taxable income		CHF 128,250

Determination of taxable wealth

Year ended December 31, 2002

Assets:		
Apartment		CHF 180,000
Securities and savings accounts		140,000
Surrender value of life insurance		15,000
Household effects (33% of insurance value), say		50,000
Car		25,000
Total assets		CHF 410,000
Less—Liabilities:		
Mortgage		100,000
Net assets		310,000
Less—Allowances:		
Increase in wealth during the year (capital gain)	20,000	
Tax exemption	140,000	160,000
Taxable wealth		CHF 150,000

Tax computation

National tax:		
1.08% on taxable income of 128,250	1,385	
0.054% on taxable wealth of 150,000	81	CHF 1,466
Progression surcharge according to table—165%		2,419
		3,885
Less—Allowance for couples (33.33% of 3,885)		(1,295)
Total national tax		2,590
Communal tax—160% of national tax		4,144
Total income and wealth tax		CHF 6,734

Notes:

1. The unit of local currency is the Swiss franc.
2. Average exchange rate of the Swiss franc for the tax year 2002: US$1 = CHF1.55563.

PwC contact

For additional information on taxation in Luxembourg, contact:

Michiel Roumieux
PricewaterhouseCoopers
400, route d'Esch
B.P. 1443
L–1014 Luxembourg
Telephone: (352) 49 48 48 1
Fax: (352) 49 48 48 2900
e-mail: Michiel.Roumieux@lu.pwc.com

Significant developments

For significant developments, refer to the above contact.

Territoriality and residence

Individual income tax is levied on the worldwide income of individuals residing in Luxembourg, as well as on Luxembourg-source income of nonresidents. Generally, an effectively used abode in Luxembourg or a stay in Luxembourg in excess of six consecutive months entails residence, even if the period overlaps two fiscal years or is interrupted by short absences.

Gross income

Employee gross income/Income from employment includes all benefits in cash and in kind received by an individual. If an employer provides a house or apartment to an employee, the monthly benefit in kind is valued at 25% of its unitary value, with a minimum of three-quarters of the rent effectively paid by the employer. If the employer also makes available the furniture contained in the accommodation, the value of the benefit in kind is increased by 10%. If the employer pays electricity and other charges, these must be added to the benefit at their nominal value. If the employee rents a house or an apartment and pays the rent, reimbursement of the rent by the employer is taxed entirely as a benefit.

The monthly benefit in kind arising from the private use of a company car corresponds to private mileage multiplied by the car's kilometer cost. This evaluation can be replaced by a lump-sum evaluation method, according to which the monthly taxable fringe benefit corresponds to 1.5% of the full purchase price (including options and value-added tax (VAT)) of the new car.

A number of items are exempt from tax, such as debtor-interest savings on a reduced- or nil-interest loan granted by the employer (within certain limits) and additional salary for overtime payments, up to a certain limit and under certain conditions. Under specific limits and certain conditions, moving expense reimbursements are tax exempt. Nonresidents are taxed on salaried income if their occupation is exercised in Luxembourg or if their salary is paid from Luxembourg. Tax treaties generally grant exemption if the nonresident stays for less than 183 days in the calendar year and if the remuneration is paid and borne by a party in the other country.

Capital gains and investment income/Capital gains derived from the disposal of movable properties are subject to Luxembourg progressive income tax rates (0% to

38.95%), provided the holding period does not exceed six months and to the extent that the total capital gains exceed €500.

If movable properties are disposed of more than six months following their acquisition, capital gains are not taxed unless the individual holds an important participation. Capital gains derived from the disposal of an important participation are taxed as extraordinary income at half the average combined tax rate (maximum 19.475%).

A participation qualifies as important when the individual taxpayer (together with his or her household) holds or has held, directly or indirectly, more than 10% of the corporate capital over the five years prior to the date on which the shares are disposed of.

Capital gains on buildings and land (regardless of the holding period) are taxed as extraordinary income at one-quarter of the average global tax rate (maximum 9.737%). The first €50,000 (doubled for married taxpayers taxable jointly) realized over a ten-year period on cumulative capital gains resulting from the sale of immovable property (regardless of the holding period) and important participations (held for more than six months) is tax exempt. In the case of a capital gain on a building acquired through direct inheritance, an additional allowance of up to €75,000 may be granted under specific conditions. Capital gains on the sale of a main residence are exempt from taxation.

For long-term capital gains (holding period of more than six months for movable property and two years for immovable property), the acquisition price is adjusted by taking account of inflation coefficients.

Capital losses can be offset only against capital gains in the same year.

Gross income from capital and investments is included in taxable income. An exemption of €1,500 is granted on portfolio income (dividends and interest). It is doubled in the case of collectively taxed spouses. Half of the dividend income received is tax exempt if paid by a qualifying company.

Deductions

Business deductions/Income-related expenses are normally deductible. Employees benefit from minimum standard deductions of €540 for job-related expenses. These deductions are doubled if the spouse is also employed. If expenses for tools, specific work clothes, and so on, exceed the minimum, the actual expenses may be deducted. Commuting expenses between home and place of work are tax deductible, with a minimum yearly amount of €396 and a maximum of €2,970 per year.

A minimum lump-sum allowance of €25 is deductible from income from capital and investments. The minimum lump-sum allowance is doubled in the case of collectively taxed spouses if both earn income from capital and investments. Actual expenses exceeding this lump-sum allowance can be deducted. Nonresidents can deduct only expenses related to income subject to Luxembourg taxation.

Nonbusiness expenses/For residents, certain premiums paid for life, sickness, accident, disability, and third-party liability insurance are deductible, up to €672 increased by the same amount for jointly taxable spouses and each dependent child. This allowance is increased for a one-time premium for death insurance subscribed to assure the reimbursement of a loan taken out for the purchase of a house. The related tax deduction varies with the age of the taxpayer. Under specific conditions insurance premiums paid within the context of a private pension scheme qualifying under Luxembourg tax law are also tax deductible. Based on the taxpayer's age, the maximum tax deduction varies from €1,500 to €3,200. The deduction applies to each spouse, provided both are covered by a private pension insurance contract.

Certain contributions to savings and home-loan associations are deductible up to €672 increased by the same amount for jointly taxable spouses and each dependent child. Interest arising on a loan contracted to purchase a car, furniture, and so forth, is deductible up to €672 increased by the same amount for jointly taxable spouses and each dependent child. A minimum standard deduction of €480 is granted for the above expenses; it is doubled if the spouse is also employed.

Employee's contributions to a qualifying employer-provided pension scheme are tax deductible up to a limit of €1,200 per year. Compulsory Luxembourg and foreign legal social security contributions covered by a social security treaty, as well as donations to qualifying institutions under certain conditions and limits, are also deductible.

Nonresident employees may deduct compulsory social security contributions and contributions to an employer-provided supplementary pension scheme, as well as the flat allowance of €480.

Personal allowances/Residents may deduct extraordinary charges for sickness, accidents, living costs of parents, and so on, to the extent that they exceed a certain percentage of their taxable remuneration. In addition, specific deductions are also available, notably for kindergarten costs and domestic help. A salaried-income-related allowance of €600 is granted to residents, as well as to nonresidents. This deduction is doubled if the spouse also is employed.

Jointly taxable spouses who both exercise a professional activity taxable in Luxembourg benefit from a lump-sum allowance of €4,500.

Within specific conditions, residents who acquire newly issued shares in Luxembourg based companies can deduct the underlying acquisition up to €500 for 2004 (doubled for married taxpayers who are taxable jointly). To qualify for the underlying deduction, the individual must notably hold the shares for at least the subsequent four fiscal years (calendar years) following the year of acquisition.

Nonresident taxpayers/If at least 90% of the professional income of a nonresident is taxable in Luxembourg, the taxpayer may opt to be treated as a resident for tax purposes, thus benefiting from the same deductions and allowances as a resident. The tax rate applied to Luxembourg-source income is then determined on the basis of the taxpayer's household total worldwide professional income.

Tax credits

Foreign income received by residents that is subject to a tax equivalent to Luxembourg income tax and is not exempted by a double taxation agreement is granted a tax credit; any nonimputable tax in excess is deductible as a tax-deductible expense.

Other taxes

Social security taxes/Compulsory social security contributions for employees are listed below.

1. For sickness: 2.65% of gross periodic remuneration, limited to an annual ceiling of €84,177.60.

2. For pension: 8% of gross remuneration, limited to an annual ceiling of €84,177.60.

Certain multilateral and bilateral social security agreements protect the interests of temporarily resident employees.

Employees subject to Luxembourg social security contributions are subject to the so-called dependency contribution on their gross professional income, reduced by €4,208.88 per year. Net portfolio income and taxable capital gains of Luxembourg resident taxpayers are also subject to the dependency contribution. The dependency contribution rate amounts to 1% (flat rate).

Wealth taxes/Wealth taxes are assessed on resident taxpayers' worldwide taxable wealth and on nonresident taxpayers' Luxembourg taxable wealth. Taxable wealth corresponds to the gross value of the elements comprising wealth, less qualifying deductions. Wealth taxes are assessed at a flat rate of 0.5% of the global taxable wealth value.

Tax administration

Income tax returns/The total income of husband and wife and the nonsalary income of minor children forming part of the household are aggregated for purposes of the annual tax computation. Combined assessments are due in principle if the spouses are not separated on the basis of a legal or judicial dispensation. The fiscal year corresponds to the calendar year. Note that all taxpayers are not authorized to file an income tax return.

Payment of income tax/Payroll income taxes are withheld by the employer on a monthly basis and may be regularized depending on the circumstances through an annual tax return or an annual adjustment (*décompte annuel*).

Wealth tax returns/An individual's wealth tax is determined on the basis of a specific tax return. An assessment of the taxpayer's taxable wealth takes place, in principle, every three years at a predetermined valuation date. Where the taxpayer's taxable wealth changes significantly between two valuation dates, a new evaluation is made for the next predetermined valuation date.

Payment of wealth tax/Wealth taxes are payable upon the issue of the tax assessment by the tax authorities and then subsequently by quarterly tax advances.

Income tax rates

Tax is calculated in accordance with a graduated table, ranging from 8% on taxable income in excess of €9,850 to 38% on income in excess of €34,500 for 2004. A solidarity tax of 2.5% of taxes is added. Married nonresident taxpayers who are not separated are put into Tax Class 2 (generally the tax class for resident spouses living together) if they are taxable in Luxembourg for more than 50% of the professional income of their household. If both spouses derive professional income taxable in Luxembourg, the application of Tax Class 2 leads to a combined assessment. Married nonresident taxpayers living together who do not comply with the above 50% condition are put into the higher intermediary Tax Class 1a.

The following tables show taxes for taxable salaried income between €20,000 and €155,000. (Taxable salary income equals gross salary income minus all qualifying standard deductions under Luxembourg income tax law.)

Single taxpayer (class 1)
Single taxpayer with dependent children (class 1a.x)

(In Euros)

Taxable salaried income	Income tax				
	Single (S) (Class 1)	**Single: special rate** (Class 1a)	**S + 1 Child (C)** (Class 1a.1)	**S + 2 C** (Class 1a.2)	**S + 3 C** (Class 1a.3)
20,000	1,390	61	—	—	—
38,700	7,217	6,057	5,135	4,212	3,290
58,000	14,734	13,575	12,652	11,730	10,807
77,400	22,290	21,131	20,208	19,286	18,363
96,700	29,808	28,648	27,726	26,803	25,881
116,000	37,325	36,166	35,243	34,321	33,398
135,500	44,920	43,761	42,838	41,916	40,993
155,000	52,515	51,356	50,434	49,511	48,589

Married taxpayer (class 2)
Married taxpayer with dependent children (class 2.x)

(In Euros)

Taxable salaried income	Income tax			
	Married (M) (Class 2)	**M + 1 Child (C)** (Class 2.1)	**M + 2 C** (Class 2.2)	**M + 3 C** (Class 2.3)
20,000	41	—	—	—
38,700	2,527	1,605	682	—
58,000	7,373	6,451	5,528	4,606
77,400	14,434	13,511	12,589	11,666
96,700	21,951	21,028	20,106	19,183
116,000	29,468	28,546	27,623	26,701
135,500	37,064	36,141	35,219	34,296
155,000	44,659	43,736	42,814	41,891

INDIVIDUAL TAX CALCULATION

Year 2004

Assumptions

Collectively taxed spouses with two children who reside in Luxembourg during the entire year 2004. They have the following income.

1. One spouse receives a salary.
2. Both spouses earn dividend and interest income from Luxembourg.

The standard deductions are exceeded because of the following.

1. They live in the countryside at a distance of some 20 kilometers from the workplace of the salaried spouse.
2. They pay debtor interest on a loan taken out for the purchase of a car and computer equipment, as well as life, sickness, and personal liability insurance premiums.

3. They make donations to qualifying institutions.
4. They invest in shares in qualifying companies.

Tax computation

Determination of taxable income

Salary		€ 90,000
Less:		
Standard deduction	540	
Deduction for travel between home and work	1,980	2,520
		87,480
Income from securities:		
Dividends	2,000	
Interest	2,000	
Less:		
Exemption on income from securities	(3,000)	
Exemption of half of dividends	(1,000)	0
Net income		87,480
Less:		
Maximum deduction for debtor interest on a consumer loan	2,688	
Maximum deduction for insurance premiums	2,688	
Compulsory social security on salary (dependency contribution not included)	8,965	
Donations	250	14,591
Taxable income		72,889
Less:		
Qualifying shares acquisition	1,000	
Standard salaried income allowance	600	1,600
Adjusted taxable income		€ 71,289

Determination of tax

Adjusted taxable income rounded		€ 71,250
Tax on ordinary income (tax class 2.2)		€ 9,945
Solidarity tax (9,660 x 2.5%)		249
Total income tax		10,194
Less:		
20% withholding taxes on dividends from Luxembourg	400	
Tax withheld on salary	12,680	13,080
Tax to be reimbursed by the tax authorities		€ 2,886

Summary of income tax and social security charges

Social security contributions (employee's part)	€ 8,965
Dependency contribution	€ 858
Income taxes	€ 10,194

Note:

Exchange rate of the Euro at March 12, 2004: US$1 = €0.8210.

PwC contact

Christina Lam
Lowe Bingham & Matthews—PricewaterhouseCoopers
Sociedade de Auditores
Avenida Doutor Mario Soares
Bank of China Building
28/F, Unit C, Macau
Telephone: (853) 7995 111 (Macau); (852) 2289 8888 (Hong Kong)
Fax: (853) 7995 222 (Macau); (852) 2810 9888 (Hong Kong)
e-mail: christina.wc.lam@hk.pwc.com

Significant developments for 2004

The Macau Professional Tax Regulation was amended on July 31, 2003, with retrospective application from July 1, 2003. The amendments mainly cover the following:

Assessment of taxable income

1. The nontaxable income amount has increased from MOP85,000 to MOP95,000 per annum.
2. The tax progressive rate has been reduced from the range of 10% to 15% to 7% to 12%.
3. Taxable income is based on 75% of total assessable income.
4. No stamp duty on tax amount is levied.
5. Nontaxable income has been amended to include some more items.

In addition, certain groups of taxpayers who were previously excluded under the old professional tax system, will now be included under the new tax system. These include:

1. Civil servants.
2. Religious workers.
3. Teachers and trainees and part-time workers who are above 60 years old.

Double Tax Arrangement between People's Republic of China and Macau, Special Administrative Region (SAR)

The Arrangement between the Mainland and Macau SAR for Avoidance of Double Taxation on Income and Prevention of Tax Evasion (Macau Tax Arrangement) was signed on December 27, 2003 in Macau. Unlike the Tax Arrangement between the Mainland and Hong Kong Special Administrative Region for Avoidance of Double Taxation on Income (HK Tax Arrangement) signed in 1998, the Macau Tax Arrangement is a comprehensive version covering the various types of income in respect of the PRC Individual Income Tax, Foreign Investment Enterprises (FIE) and Foreign Enterprises Income Tax and Local Income Tax.

Territoriality and residence

Residence and/or domicile are irrelevant for Macau individual tax purposes. Individual tax is levied and payable only where Macau-source income is earned. Earnings of salaried employees and self-employed persons are taxed under the professional tax regulations. Income of all entities (i.e., companies, partnerships, sole proprietors, etc.), including individuals who receive income derived from commercial activities in the territory, is subject to Complementary Tax.

Certain overseas personnel who hold key managerial positions and are seconded to an approved offshore institution established in Macau may enjoy an exemption from professional tax for the first three calendar years of their employment.

Unless otherwise stated, the information below relates to the regulations applicable to professional tax.

Professional tax is payable by anyone receiving income from services performed in Macau irrespective of the following.

1. Where the income was received.
2. The number of days spent in Macau.
3. Whether the recipient is a resident or not.

   and

4. Whether the recipient is paid in money or in kind. Where income other than cash is received, the Macau tax bureau may assess the value on benefits so received.

Gross income

Employee gross income/Employee gross income comprises the items shown below.

1. Salary, overtime, commission, and bonuses, but not lump-sum payments on retirement;
2. Passages for holidays.
3. Other benefits in kind not in connection with employment.
4. Other allowances paid by the employer (other than reimbursements of expenses incurred on behalf of the employer) are also subject to professional tax.

Capital gains and investment income/Gains and investment income are tax exempt (i.e., not subject to either professional or complementary tax) with the exception of dividends received from local corporations, which are subject to complementary tax, either at corporate or shareholders' level.

Deductions

Business deductions/Business deductions are applicable only to self-employed individuals (i.e., business or professional income), whose income is taxed under the professional tax regulations.

For salaried employees, there are no provisions in the tax regulations for business deductions.

Nonbusiness expenses/None.

Personal allowances or subsidies/The following examples of allowances or subsidies can be claimed as nontaxable items in determining taxable income for professional tax purposes:

1. Personal allowance of MOP95,000 per annum or MOP7,916 per month; the personal allowance is MOP120,000 for employees over 65 years old and for those who are disabled with proven incapacity above 60%.
2. Medical allowances claimed with relevant documents supported.

3. Allowances up to the limit of those applying to civil servants are granted:
   a. Family allowance (wife and parent—MOP170/month, children aged under 18 or under—MOP220/month).
   b. Marriage allowance (MOP2,300).
   c. Birth allowance (MOP2,300).
   d. Living allowance (MOP1,000/month).
   e. Rental allowance (ranging from MOP3,500 to MOP12,000 depending on the size of the rented property).
   f. Death allowance (6 times the basic salary).
   g. Funeral allowance (MOP2,700).
   h. Transportation of remains allowance (ranging from MOP47,000 to MOP200,000 depending on the location).
   i. Safety allowance in compensation for hardship and unsafe conditions (e.g., police, guards).The maximum amount is MOP30,000 per annum.
   j. Benefit-in-kind (e.g., car, driver and mobile phone, etc.), subject to further instructions on the computation basis for benefit-in-kind to be issued by the Macau Tax Bureau.
   k. Reimbursed entertainment and travel expenses.
   l. Reimbursed transportation expenses, daily allowance, and travel allowance for business trips, up to the limit of those applying to civil servants.
   m. Compensation for termination of employment in accordance with the statutory limit, provided that the employment relationship will not be reinstated within the next 12 months.
   n. Compensation in lieu of mandatory holidays or benefits in accordance with the Macau Labour Law.

Other taxes

Apart from professional and complementary taxes, there is also a social security fund contribution. The total contribution of MOP45 per month is payable. For resident employees, the employer contributes two-thirds of the amount (i.e., MOP30) whereas the employee contributes one-third of the amount (i.e., MOP15). For nonresident employees, the employer will be responsible for the full payment.

Tax administration

Returns/Husbands and wives are taxed separately in Macau on a calendar-year basis.

Payment of tax/For salaried individuals only, this is similar to the pay-as-you-earn (PAYE) system used in other countries. The employer is obliged to collect the amount of professional tax payable from its employees each month and remit such payments to the Macau Tax Bureau before the 15th of the month following the quarter-end for local resident employees. Monthly remittance is required for nonresident employees.

Tax rates

Professional tax/The professional tax rates are progressive and cumulative up to a maximum rate of 12%.

Assessable income			Tax on Column 1	Percentage on excess
Over (Column 1)	Not over			
0	MOP 95,000	....	—	—
MOP 95,000	115,000	....	—	7
115,000	135,000	....	MOP 1,400	8
135,000	175,000	....	3,000	9
175,000	255,000	....	6,600	10
255,000	375,000	....	14,600	11
375,000		....	27,800	12

Complementary tax/Complementary tax rates range form 2% to 15% if income is below MOP300,000. If income exceeds MOP300,000, the tax is 15%. (Tax rates from 2% to 15% are applied with complicated adjustments.)

Professional tax liability is calculated separately from complementary tax liability.

A surcharge (stamp duty) of 5% on the complementary tax payable is also levied.

INDIVIDUAL TAX CALCULATION

July 1, 2003

Assumptions

Taxpayer, married with two children, both less than seven years old.

Tax computation

Calculation of professional tax payable

Salary, overtime, commissions, and bonuses		MOP 640,000
Less:		
Personal allowance	95,000	
Family allowance, including allowances for children (MOP 170 + MOP 220 + MOP 220) x 12	7,320	102,320
		537,680
Taxable income		
Less—25%		134,420
		MOP 403,260
Tax thereon:		
On first MOP 375,000		MOP 27,800
On remainder—28,260 at 12%		3,392
		31,192
Less—25% (1)		7,998
		MOP 23,394

Calculation of complementary tax payable

Income from a commercial activity	MOP 320,000
Deductions	0
Taxable income	MOP 320,000
Tax thereon—320,000 at 15%	MOP 48,000
Surcharge (stamp duty)—48,000 at 5%	2,400
Complementary tax payable	MOP 50,400

Amount of tax payable

Professional tax and surcharge	MOP 23,394
Complementary tax and surcharge (stamp duty)	50,400
	MOP 73,794

Notes:

1. A one-off 25% reduction applied to the tax payable was granted by the Macau Chief Executive for year 2004.
2. Exchange rate of the Macau Pataca at December 31, 2003: US$1 = MOP7.9977.

Malaysia

PwC contacts

For additional information on taxation in Malaysia, contact:

Chuan Keat Khoo
Peter K. S. Chow
PricewaterhouseCoopers
Wisma Sime Darby, 11th Floor
Jalan Raja Laut
50350 Kuala Lumpur, Malaysia
Telephone: (60) (3) 2693 1077
Fax: (60) (3) 2693 0997
e-mail: chuan.keat.khoo@my.pwc.com
peter.chow@my.pwc.com

Significant developments

With effect from tax year 2004, resident individuals remitting income from overseas are exempt from income tax on the income remitted.

Territoriality and residence

An individual, whether tax resident or nonresident in Malaysia, is taxed on any income accruing in or derived from Malaysia. The status of individuals as residents or nonresidents determines whether or not they can claim personal allowances and the benefit of graduated tax rates. Resident status is determined by reference to the number of days an individual is present in Malaysia. Generally, an individual who is in Malaysia for a period or periods amounting to 182 days or more in a calendar year will be regarded as a tax resident.

Basis of assessment/Assessment of income is on a current-year basis. An individual is taxed on income from nonbusiness sources for a year of assessment on a calendar-year basis. Business sources of income are assessed for a year of assessment on the basis of the financial/accounting year ending on a day in that particular year of assessment.

Gross income

Employee gross income/An employee is taxed on employment income earned for work performed in Malaysia, regardless of where payment is made. Employment income includes salary, allowances, perquisites, benefits in kind, tax reimbursements, and rent-free accommodation provided by the employer.

Medical benefits, as well as child care benefits provided by the employer, are not taxable. Leave passages, restricted to one overseas trip (up to a maximum amount of RM3,000) and three local trips per year, are also tax exempt in the hands of the employee. Cars or other household items provided for private use are valued at prescribed rates that are lower than the actual cost incurred by the employer. Rent-free accommodation provided by the employer is valued at the lower of 30% of the employee's total cash remuneration or the actual rental value. Gifts of new computers by employers are not deemed benefits in kind and hence not taxable.

Short-term visiting nonresident employees are not subject to tax on income from employment exercised in Malaysia if the period of employment does not exceed 60 days in a calendar year. If the period of employment straddles two calendar years, they are exempt if the total period of their employment over the two years does not exceed 60 days.

Expatriates working in operational headquarters and regional offices in Malaysia are taxed only on the portion of chargeable income attributable to the number of days they are in Malaysia.

Capital gains and investment income/Capital gains on the disposal of real property (including shares in a real property company—RPC) situated in Malaysia, are subject to real property gains tax (RPGT). The tax is levied at rates ranging from a maximum of 30% (for assets held for less than two years) to 0% (for assets held for more than five years). Capital losses on the sale of real property (other than losses on the disposal of RPC shares) are available for computation of relief, which is allowed as a deduction against total tax assessed on taxable gains arising on the sale of real property in the same year. (A real property company is a controlled company that owns real property or RPC shares with a defined value of not less than 75% of its total tangible assets.) Other capital gains are not subject to tax.

An individual who is not a citizen or a permanent resident in Malaysia is subject to real property gains tax on gains arising from the disposal of real property or RPC shares on or after October 17, 1997 at a rate of 30% on disposals within five years and at 5% on disposals after five years.

Gains from the disposal of properties between June 1, 2003, and May 31, 2004, are exempt from RPGT.

Interest received by a resident individual is subject to income tax at a flat rate of 5%. Interest received on deposits for a period of 12 months or more is tax exempt. Interest received from certain types of bonds or securities is also exempt from tax.

Interest paid to a nonresident individual by commercial or merchant banks or finance companies operating in Malaysia is exempt from tax.

Deductions

Business deductions/Employees are allowed a deduction for any expenditure incurred wholly and exclusively in the performance of their duties, but no allowance is given for tax depreciation. Expenses of a private or domestic nature are expressly excluded from deduction; for example, the cost of traveling to and from a place of employment is not deductible.

Nonbusiness expenses/Nonbusiness expenses, for example, domestic or household expenses and taxes, are not deductible. Mortgage interest incurred to finance the purchase of a house is deductible only if income is derived from the house. Donations to approved funds and subscriptions to associations related to the individual's profession are deductible.

Personal allowances/A resident individual receives a personal deduction of RM8,000, and an allowance of RM3,000 for a spouse if the individual's income is aggregated with the spouse's income. Where income of the individual is separately assessed from the income of the spouse, each person is eligible for personal relief of RM8,000, but spouse allowance (of RM3,000) would not be available.

A child allowance of RM1,000 for each child under 18 years of age is also available. This allowance may be increased to up to two or four times the normal deduction where certain conditions are satisfied. Instead of the normal child relief, an allowance of RM5,000 is granted for each physically or mentally handicapped child. Child relief can be claimed by a wife whose income is assessed separately from her husband's. Additional deductions of RM5,000 (personal relief) or RM2,500 (spouse) will be granted if the individual or spouse is disabled.

Medical expenses incurred for the individual's parents qualify for deduction, but this deduction is limited to a maximum of RM5,000. An additional amount of up to RM5,000 is given for medical expenses for self, spouse, or child on treatment of a serious disease (e.g., AIDS, leukemia). This amount includes medical examination fees of up to RM500 incurred for self, spouse, or child. A wife who is assessed separately on her income is also eligible for these deductions.

Expenses of up to RM5,000 incurred for the purchase of disability-supporting equipment for the individual's own use if the individual is a disabled person, or for the use of a spouse, child, or parent who is disabled, would be allowed as a deduction.

Contributions to approved pension/provident funds and annual premiums for insurance policies taken out by a resident employee on that employee's own life, a spouse's life or jointly are allowed, subject to a limit of RM5,000. An additional amount of up to RM3,000 is given for premiums for insurance on education or for medical benefits incurred for the individual, spouse, or child. Similar relief subject to limits of RM5,000 and RM3,000 is also given for contributions/premiums incurred by a spouse, where the spouse's income is separately taxed. An additional amount of up to RM1,000 is also given for premiums on an insurance for annuity benefits.

A deduction limited to a maximum of RM5,000 is allowed for fees paid for a course of study in Malaysia undertaken to acquire technical, vocational, or industrial, scientific, technological skills up to tertiary level. A deduction of up to RM500 is given for purchase of books, journals, magazines, and other similar publications for purpose of enchancing knowledge.

Personal allowances are deducted in arriving at chargeable income of the resident individual.

Tax credits

A tax resident is entitled to claim foreign tax credits against Malaysian tax. Where a treaty exists, the credit available is the whole of the foreign tax paid or the Malaysian tax levied on the foreign-source income, whichever is lower. In the absence of a tax treaty, the credit due is restricted to one-half of the foreign tax paid.

Other taxes

There are no social security taxes or local taxes on income.

Real property gains tax/Real property gains tax is imposed at rates from 0 to 30% on gains arising from the disposal of real property (which includes the disposal of shares in a real property company) situated in Malaysia (see "Capital gains and investment income" above).

Tax administration

Self-assessment for individuals/From the year of assessment 2004, self-assessment for individuals will be implemented. Under the self-assessment system (SAS), the responsibility for correctly assessing a person's tax liability is transferred from the Inland Revenue Board (IRB) to the taxpayer.

The return form for the year of assessment 2004 will be issued to individual taxpayers in January 2005 or earlier and will be due for submission not later than April 30, 2005. The amount of tax payable for the year must be self-computed, and the return form is deemed to be a notice of assessment upon submission, for which tax is due and payable.

Returns/Up to the year of assessment 2003, returns were filed jointly by a married couple in the name of the husband. From assessment year 2004, separate returns will be issued to each spouse. The income of a wife who is living with her husband is assessed separately from that of the husband. However, a wife who is a resident or a Malaysian citizen can elect to be taxed jointly with her husband. A husband who has no income may also elect to be assessed jointly with his wife under the wife's name.

Returns for assessment year 2004 must be submitted to the IRB by April 30, 2005.

Payment of tax/Tax payments by employees are collected through compulsory deductions from salary. All deductions are made on a pay-as-you-earn (PAYE) basis. Under the SAS, tax for a year of assessment is due and payable on April 30 of the year following that year of assessment (the "due date"), for example, tax payable for year of assessment 2004 is due and payable on April 30, 2005. Therefore, if tax deemed assessed on an individual upon the submission of his return for that year of assessment exceeds the total amount deducted from the individual's salary, the difference must be paid on or before the due date.

Tax rates

The following are the rates applicable to resident individual taxpayers.

Taxable income		Tax on	Percentage
Over (Column 1)	Not over	Column 1	on excess
RM 50,000	RM 70,000	RM 3,475	19
70,000	100,000	7,275	24
100,000	150,000	14,475	27
150,000	250,000	27,975	27
250,000		54,975	28

A nonresident individual is taxed at a flat rate of 28% on total taxable income.

INDIVIDUAL TAX CALCULATION

Year of assessment 2004

Assumptions

Resident employee and wife, two children; one spouse earns all the income.

Tax computation

Gross income:		
Salary		RM 200,000
Interest (18,640) (1)		—
Total gross income		200,000
Less—Approved donations		1,000
		199,000
Less—Personal exemptions:		
Self and wife	11,000	
First child (over 18 and attending university)	1,000	
Second child (under 18)	1,000	
Medical expenses for parents (maximum)	5,000	
Life insurance premiums and provident fund contributions (maximum)	5,000	
Premiums on education/medical insurance (maximum)	3,000	
Purchase of books for enhancing knowledge (maximum)	500	26,500
Taxable income		RM 172,500
Income tax at joint return rates (see table above)		RM 34,050

Notes:

1. Nonexempt interest received from banks and finance companies is subject to a withholding tax of 5%, which is a final tax. No further tax is payable thereon.
2. The exchange rate of the ringgit is fixed at: US$1 = RM3.80.

PwC contacts

For additional information on taxation in Malta, contact:

Dr. Antoine Fiott
Dr. Neville Gatt
PricewaterhouseCoopers
167 Merchants Street
Valletta VLT03
Malta
Telephone: (356) 21 247000
Fax: (356) 21 244768
e-mail: antoine.fiott@mt.pwc.com
neville.gatt@mt.pwc.com

Significant developments

1. The standard value-added tax (VAT) rate was increased by 3% to 18% as of January 1, 2004. Amendments have been made to align Maltese VAT law with EU legislation. These will come into force on May 1, 2004.
2. The exemption from tax on capital gains on transfers of inherited immovable property has been removed.
3. The beneficial tax regime that applied for investment services companies/insurance managers and their expatriate employees will no longer apply for companies obtaining their investment services license under the Investment Services Act after October 1, 2003. In respect of companies that held an investment services license before the said date, the tax benefits continue to apply (both in respect of the company and the expatriates) up to a date that has yet to be determined.
4. A new provision enables the Finance Minister to make rules for the implementation of any EU Directive relating to any matter that affects the operation of the Income Tax Acts.
5. Consistent with previous years, a further liberalization of exchange controls has been effected.

Territoriality and residence

Malta taxes individuals who are both domiciled and ordinarily resident in Malta on their worldwide income. Any person who is not ordinarily resident or domiciled in Malta is taxable only on income arising in Malta and on any foreign income remitted to Malta. A nonresident individual is taxed only on income arising in Malta. There are few specific rules relating to residence, ordinary residence, domicile, locality of income, or the remittance of income to Malta. Persons are usually held to be domiciled in a country where they actually have their permanent home. The locality where income arises is determined in accordance with the category of income concerned; different criteria may apply to different sources of income. Persons are considered to be ordinarily resident in Malta when they are so resident in the ordinary or regular course of their lives. The remittance of income to Malta is a question of fact.

Gross income

Employee gross income/Gains or profits from employment with a Maltese employer are usually fully taxable, including the value of "any benefit provided by reason of any employment or office." Remuneration received for services rendered outside Malta by persons not domiciled or not ordinarily resident in Malta should not be liable to tax in Malta. Apportionment is resorted to where necessary. All rewards for services rendered, including fringe benefits and benefits in kind, are taxable, although some exemptions are provided. Taxable benefits include living allowances, housing allowances, tax reimbursements (grossed up), use of car, paid vacation trips, and stock options.

Fringe benefits/Fringe benefits regulations provide the valuation criteria for fringe benefits and the instances in which a fringe benefit is deemed not to arise.

Three main categories of fringe benefits are identified by the regulations.

1. Category 1—Use of motor vehicles:

   The valuation of a fringe benefit arising on the use of a car would be calculated on the basis of three elements, that is, the car use value, the maintenance value, and the fuel value. The car use value is equivalent to 17% of the car value or to 10% of the car value if the car is more than six years old. In respect of both the maintenance and fuel value, the basis of valuation is in each case 3% of the car value if the latter does not exceed Lm12,000 and 5% of the car value in any other case. The fringe benefit is equal to the aggregate of these three elements multiplied by a percentage signifying the private use of the car. The private use percentage varies depending on the respective car value and may go up to 60%.

   The private use element (i.e., the taxable element) of a car cash allowance is 50% of the allowance if the allowance is Lm1,000 or less, or the cash allowance less Lm500 if the allowance exceeds Lm1,000.

   The following are not deemed to constitute a fringe benefit:

   a. The use of a vehicle (value not exceeding Lm7,000) by a salesperson or a support person who is not a company official, as authorized by the Commissioner of Inland Revenue;
   b. The use of a company van.

2. Category 2—Use of other assets, including accommodation:

   Use of immovable property/accommodation involves a chargeable fringe benefit of 5% of the higher of the market value and the original cost of the immovable property. No fringe benefit is deemed to arise in certain situations, for example, use of an official residence by the holder of public office, temporary accommodation for security purposes, and so on. The cost of making the immovable property available for use by the employee (such as water, electricity, ground rent, redecoration, repairs and maintenance, and professional fees) is also a fringe benefit.

   The fringe benefit on the use of other assets (other than immovable property and motor vehicles) stands at 12% of the higher of the market value and the original cost of the asset. The original cost is reduced by 40% in the case of assets that are owned for more than six years. Use of computers, related equipment and internet connection service is not considered a fringe benefit.

3. Category 3—Other benefits:

   The value of other fringe benefits is the actual cost to the employer of providing the fringe benefit or the market value thereof. This category of fringe benefits includes, among other items, beneficial loan arrangements (with an interest rate below 8%), share option schemes, reimbursement of private expenses, discounted goods and services, free or subsidized meals, and gifts. Valuation criteria differ according to the type of benefit with the possibility of a partial or a full exemption in certain cases.

Telephony services, computer equipment, recreational and child-minding facilities, health insurance (subject to some restrictions), certain awards, and certain training courses, among other items, provided to employees are not considered to be fringe benefits.

Capital gains and investment income/Tax on capital gains is imposed on any gain realized on the transfer of immovable property (real estate), shares and other securities (excluding certain securities listed on a stock exchange recognized under the Financial Markets Act and investments that yield a fixed rate of return), business, goodwill, copyright, patents, trade names, and trademarks. Gains from the transfer of other assets fall outside the scope of the tax. The rate of tax is the marginal rate of tax applicable to the particular taxpayer. Gains arising outside Malta and derived by a person who is either not domiciled or not ordinarily resident in Malta or is a returned migrant who qualifies for a reduced rate of income tax are not subject to tax even if remitted to Malta.

Subject to the applicable statutory requirements, nonresidents are exempt from tax on any interest, discount, premium or royalties, and capital gains from specified sources, for example, disposal of units in collective investment schemes and of shares or securities in companies satisfying certain conditions.

A final withholding tax system operates for certain types of investment income (see "Tax administration, Payment of tax" below), paid by certain payers to specified categories of (Maltese-resident) recipients. The investment income provisions charge to tax investment income received by certain resident collective investment schemes and tax resident investors on gains realized on disposal of units in funds investing a certain level of their assets outside Malta.

Deductions

Business deductions/Certain allowances are available for business-related expenses in the case of persons exercising a trade, business, profession, or vocation. These include, inter alia, scientific research, bad debts, and losses carried forward. To be deductible, expenses of an employee must be incurred wholly and exclusively in the production of the income and must be necessarily incurred. Where the employer reimburses employees for expenses incurred on the employer's behalf, no tax liability should arise in the hands of the recipients unless a gain or profit accrues to them from the arrangement.

Nonbusiness expenses/Alimony payments paid by a taxpayer to an estranged spouse are allowed as a deduction, while the receipt of the alimony is taxable in the hands of the recipient. The receipt of a payment for the maintenance of children is not taxable in the hands of the estranged spouse and not deductible in the hands of the person making the payment. A deduction is allowable in respect of private school fees (capped at a maximum amount). No other nonbusiness expenses are allowed.

Personal allowances/No personal allowances by way of credits or deductions are granted.

Tax credits

There are no special credits for short-term residents. Income taxes paid abroad on income that becomes taxable in the hands of a Maltese resident may qualify for a credit if a double taxation treaty has been concluded with the relevant country or under the unilateral relief provisions of Maltese law.

Other taxes

Social security taxes/For employees who do not earn more than Lm6,748 per annum, the employer and the employee each pay social security tax of 10% of salary. Employees earning in excess of Lm6,748 contribute Lm12.98 per week (the same amount is contributed by the employer). Self-employed persons who earn less than Lm6,748 pay a flat contribution percentage of 15% on net income. Those earning in excess of Lm6,748 contribute Lm19.47 per week.

Local taxes on income/There are no local or municipal taxes in Malta.

Other taxes/Other taxes imposed include customs and excise duties on certain goods; a tax on air travel; VAT on the importation and purchase of most goods and services; and stamp duty on certain documents and transfers, including transfers of immovable property and marketable securities; and issues and renewals of insurance policies. Stamp duty is also imposed on transmissions by death of immovable property and shares in Maltese companies.

Tax administration

Returns/Returns are filed on a calendar-year basis. Husband and wife are jointly responsible for filing tax returns, and spouses must choose which of them is to be registered as the taxpayer. The election of a "responsible spouse" remains effective for five years. The responsible spouse may elect to have the tax on the other spouse's earned income computed separately. If a separate computation is chosen, husband and wife are assessed separately at single taxpayer rates. Unearned income is assessable in the hands of the spouse earning the higher level of income.

The tax return, together with a self-assessment, must be submitted by the end of June of the year following the basis tax year. Under certain conditions, a taxpayer may file a declaration instead of a full tax return, in which case this should be filed by the end of April of the year following the basis year. Penalties are incurred on late filing of returns. The self-assessment is deemed to represent the correct tax position, and unless the Commissioner of Inland Revenue disagrees with the self-assessment, an assessment will not be raised.

Payment of tax/Income tax is withheld from salaries (including taxable fringe benefits) under the Final Settlement System (FSS), which in most cases equals the individual's total tax liability. Where income is not subject to the FSS (e.g., self-employed persons), the taxpayer is required to make three payments in the basis tax year under the provisional tax (PT) system. The PT payments based on the last self-assessment filed by the individual and payments are divided into three installments of 20%, 30%, and 50%, respectively. The tax liability that is still due at the tax return date after deducting all tax credits must be settled immediately with the submission of the return. Interest at 1% per month is charged on any unpaid tax.

Provisional tax is also payable at 7% on the selling price of certain assets disposed of on account of tax imposed on capital gains. A final withholding tax of 15% is imposed on specified types of investment income (e.g., banking interest paid to Maltese residents), and on income from most part-time work. Taxpayers may opt out of these schemes, in which case tax on such income will be charged at normal rates.

Tax rates

Income is taxable at graduated rates. For year of assessment 2005 (year of income 2004), in the case of single individuals (including married individuals opting for separate computation) there is a tax liability of Lm805 on the first Lm 6,750 of income. Married individuals will be liable to Lm1,267 tax on the first Lm10,000 of income. For amounts exceeding these thresholds, the tax rate is 35% for both single and married individuals. The single rates apply also to married couples opting for a separate computation. Subject to certain conditions, the married rates also apply to single parents, widows/widowers and separated parents.

Tax rates for basis tax year 2004 are as follows.

Married resident taxpayers

Taxable income			
Over (Column 1)	Not over	Tax on Column 1	Percentage on excess
0	Lm 4,300	—	0
Lm 4,300	6,000	—	15
6,000	7,250	Lm 255	20
7,250	8,500	505	25
8,500	10,000	817	30
10,000		1,267	35

Single resident taxpayers (or married couples opting for a separate computation)

Taxable income			
Over (Column 1)	Not over	Tax on Column 1	Percentage on excess
0	Lm 3,100	—	0
Lm 3,100	4,100	—	15
4,100	5,000	Lm 150	20
5,000	6,000	330	25
6,000	6,750	580	30
6,750		805	35

A tax regime exists for foreign individuals who acquire, subject to certain conditions, a Maltese residence permit. In the case where the permit is acquired on or after 1988, it entitles the holder to a flat tax rate of 15% on all income (including income and capital gains arising in Malta and foreign-source income remitted to Malta), subject to a minimum annual tax liability of Lm1,800. Where the residence permit was acquired prior to 1988, the holder is taxed at 15% on all income (including income and capital gains arising in Malta and foreign source income remitted to Malta) over Lm2,500 for married taxpayers, and 15% on income over Lm1,800, subject to a minimum tax liability of Lm1,000 per annum.

The tax rate of 15% is also extended to returned migrants. In this case a tax-free bracket applies on annual income not exceeding Lm1,800 for single taxpayers and Lm2,500 for married taxpayers. A minimum tax liability of Lm1,000 per annum is payable.

Nonresident individuals (married or single)

Taxable income Over	Not over		Tax on Column 1	Percentage on excess
(Column 1)				
0	Lm 300		—	0
Lm 300	1,300		—	20
1,300	3,300		Lm 200	30
3,300			800	35

INDIVIDUAL TAX CALCULATION

Year of assessment 2005 (year of income 2004)

Assumptions

Resident married expatriate employed by a Maltese company.

Tax computation

Gross income:		
Salary (including value of fringe benefits		Lm 29,500
Foreign interest remitted		2,000
Capital gains arising in Malta		2,500
Total gross income		34,000
Less—Expenditure necessarily incurred in producing the income		3,500
Total taxable income		Lm 30,500
Tax thereon:		
On the first 10,000	1,267	
On balance of 20,500 at 35%	7,175	
Total tax liability		Lm 8,442
Less:		
Tax withheld by deduction from salary	7,500	
Provisional capital gains tax	700	(8,200)
Net tax payable		Lm 242

Note:

Exchange rate of the lira at December 31, 2003: US$1 = Lm0.3767.

PwC contact

For additional information on taxation in Mauritius, contact:

N. M. Robert Bigaignon
PricewaterhouseCoopers
Cerné House, 6th Floor Chaussée
Port Louis, Mauritius
Telephone: (230) 212 5011, 208 8036, 208 8038
Fax: (230) 208 8037
e-mail: robert.bigaignon@mu.pwc.com

Significant developments

The government introduced two new schemes: the Integrated Resort Scheme (IRS), and the Scheme to attract Professionals for Emerging Sectors (SAPES) to attract foreign professionals and high net worth individuals who are looking for a new country of residence. The schemes provide a number of incentives including the right to buy immovable property in Mauritius.

Territoriality and residence

Individuals, irrespective of nationality, deriving income from sources within Mauritius are subject to Mauritian income tax on all such income, whether or not they are resident. Income derived by a resident noncitizen from outside Mauritius is exempt from tax.

Resident individuals are subject to Mauritian income tax on their worldwide income from all sources. However, earned income derived from outside Mauritius is taxable only to the extent that it is received in Mauritius. Credits are available for foreign taxes paid on income derived from foreign sources. Income from employment duties performed in Mauritius is deemed to have been derived from Mauritius, even if the related remuneration is received outside Mauritius.

An individual is resident in Mauritius in an income year in the following cases.

1. The individual's domicile is in Mauritius, unless his or her permanent place of abode is outside Mauritius;
2. Presence in Mauritius in that income year and the two preceding income years is for an aggregate period of 270 days or more;

   or
3. Presence in Mauritius is for a period of or periods amounting in the aggregate to at least 183 days in that income year.

Gross income

Employee gross income/All income derived from employment exercised in Mauritius is liable to tax in Mauritius, regardless of where payment is made or who the employer is. Employment income includes salary, wages, leave pay, overtime pay, perquisites, allowances, bonuses, gratuities, commissions, compensation for loss of office, tax borne by employer, pensions, retiring allowances, annuities, all benefits in kind, and reward or remuneration in relation to employment. Passages by sea, air, or land between Mauritius and another country provided under a contract of employment are not considered as income from employment.

Benefits in kind include the annual value of residential accommodation, use of cars, free meals, and full board provided for employees, as well as pecuniary liabilities of employees that are borne or reimbursed by the employer. Most benefits in kind are valued at standard scale rates that are usually less than the actual cost to the employer. For example, the benefit of rent-free unfurnished accommodation does not normally exceed 10% of assessable emoluments. For furnished accommodation, the corresponding percentage is 12.5%. For cars, the yearly benefit is a fixed sum of Rs12,000, but it may be higher for expensive cars. These rates, which date back to 1979, are expected to be revised soon.

Expatriate employees and qualifying Mauritian employees of a bank holding a Category 2 Banking License, a company holding a Category 1 Global Business License (formerly offshore bank or offshore company), or a company operating in the freeport zone or Information and Communication Technology (ICT) sector or conducting any business approved by the Financial Services Commission such as actuarial services or investment management and advisory services are entitled to a deduction from their tax bill of 50% of the income tax payable by them on emoluments derived from such entities. A similar deduction of 50% is allowable to expatriate employees and qualifying Mauritian employees of a pioneer-status enterprise, an export enterprise, a company engaged in electronics and high-technology activities, a company holding a regional headquarters certificate, or a company engaged wholly in the management of a venture capital fund, provided the number of employees entitled to the deduction does not exceed two for each company. In neither case may the period of exemption exceed in aggregate four income years for each enterprise or company.

Income derived by a nonresident expatriate from consultancy services or training provided in Mauritius, other than under a contract of employment, is free of income tax, provided the period during which the services are rendered does not exceed 183 days in a fiscal year. The income of nonresident expatriates who are engineering and support service personnel required by a pioneer-status enterprise or a company engaged in electronics and high-technology activities for the installation and maintenance of equipment and training of local staff is also exempt from income tax. Director's fees payable to a nonresident director of a resident company are free of tax.

Capital gains and investment income/There is no capital gains tax in Mauritius. Where individuals enter into a series of purchases and resales of property, the tax authorities may take the view that they are carrying on a trade and assess them to tax accordingly. Income derived from dealings in units and securities is, however, exempt from tax. Capital gains received by a resident or nonresident from outside Mauritius are not taxable.

Investment income derived from outside Mauritius is taxable in a resident recipient's hands whether or not it is received in Mauritius. However, a tax credit in respect of foreign tax paid on such income is allowable against Mauritius tax computed with reference to that income. This normally nullifies any tax incidence in Mauritius on foreign income.

Deductions

Business deductions/Where an individual derives income from a trade, business, profession, or vocation, deductions are allowed for all outgoings incurred wholly and exclusively in the production of the assessable income, including capital allowances on qualifying assets. Land and nonindustrial buildings do not qualify for capital allowances, with the exception of school buildings and consulting rooms of medical practitioners. An individual may also claim a deduction for any fees or expenses payable to a recognized institution for education or training, subject to a maximum of Rs50,000. Unauthorized deductions include all expenditure of a capital, domestic, or private nature; expenditure relating to exempt income; all taxes; any reserve or provision (e.g., reserve for doubtful debts); gifts and donations; and entertainment expenses.

Employees are allowed a deduction for expenses necessarily incurred in the performance of their duties. A very restrictive interpretation of the term "necessarily incurred in performing the duties" is adopted by the tax authorities, and in practice few claims are admitted. Moving expenses are not allowable. Expenses incurred by members of professional bodies in respect of continuing professional education and membership fees are allowable, subject to a limit of Rs30,000.

Nonbusiness expenses/Deductions may be claimed for mortgage interest or interest on loans raised on the security of a life insurance policy or of a standing crop or on the pledge of shares or debentures, provided the loan is taken for the acquisition of property for residential purposes or for financing the tertiary education of the taxpayer's children. Interest paid to a nonresident that is not assessable to Mauritian tax on the interest received is normally not allowable. The deduction in respect of interest incurred is limited to Rs250,000 (Rs125,000 per working spouse).

Medical expenses, contributions to medical schemes and contributions to the National Pension Fund are allowable, with certain restrictions, as personal reliefs and deductions in determining chargeable income.

Relief by way of a deduction is given for life insurance premiums and certain investments, such as the acquisition of units or shares issued by tax incentive companies or companies listed on the stock exchange. With regard to the investments, the deduction is limited to 40% of the amount invested or Rs50,000, whichever is less. Any amount in excess of Rs50,000 is deductible in the two succeeding income years, subject to a maximum of Rs50,000 in any income year.

Taxes are not allowable as a deduction, and there are no standard deductions other than the personal reliefs and deductions enumerated below.

Personal allowances/Resident individuals may claim the following reliefs and allowances that are deductible from their total net income to arrive at the income chargeable to tax.

	Rs
Basic personal deduction	75,000
Deduction for dependent spouse, that is, a spouse who has no income or whose income for the income year does not exceed Rs55,000	60,000
Additional allowance if individual, spouse, or any dependent child is permanently disabled	50,000
Dependent unmarried children (limited to 3 in number):	
Under 18 or, if 18 or over, receiving full-time instruction at an educational institution or being unemployed	25,000
Receiving full-time instruction at the University of Mauritius, attending a course at a polytechnic or at an appointed educational institution providing tertiary education in Mauritius or serving under articles of indenture overseas	50,000

	Rs
Receiving full-time instruction at a university outside Mauritius or attending a course at a polytechnic outside Mauritius	100,000
If child is attending a course at the Industrial and Vocational Training Board or at a state-owned or -approved technical school	50,000
If child is over 18 and handicapped	50,000
Retirement pension relief—100% of pension, subject to a maximum of	75,000
Alimony and maintenance paid to a spouse in accordance with a court order	Amount paid
Emoluments relief—15% of emoluments, subject to a maximum of	125,000
Agricultural income relief—15% of agricultural income, subject to a maximum of	100,000
Contributions to prescribed funds or schemes such as superannuation funds or schemes, civil service Family Protection Scheme and the National Pensions Fund	Amount paid
Premiums on life insurance policy	(Note)
Premiums on retirement annuities allowable to self-employed persons or persons who derive income from nonpensionable offices	(Note)
Premiums on personal pension schemes	(Note)
Contributions to approved medical schemes	(Note)
Medical expenses incurred in a health institution or hospital for self, spouse, or dependent children—75% of difference between expenses incurred and amounts reimbursed, subject to a maximum of:	
Treatment in Mauritius	20,000
Treatment outside Mauritius	30,000
Contributions to retirement savings schemes, subject to a maximum of	50,000

Note:

Deductions for contributions to medical schemes, premiums on personal pension schemes, or retirement annuities are limited in the aggregate to 20% of net income. Life insurance premiums are deductible, subject to a maximum of Rs80,000 per year.

A nonresident individual is not entitled to any personal allowances or deductions other than emoluments relief, agricultural income relief, and pension relief. A nonresident citizen of Mauritius may, however, claim the basic personal deduction.

Tax credits

The following reliefs are allowable by way of deduction from tax payable.

On income tax payable by an expatriate or qualifying Mauritian employee of a company holding a Category 1 Global Business License or a bank holding a Category 2 Banking License (formerly an offshore company or offshore bank), a company operating in the freeport zone or ICT sector or conducting any business approved by the Financial Services Commission on emoluments derived from such entities.	50% of tax otherwise payable
On income tax payable by an expatriate or qualifying Mauritian employee of a pioneer-status enterprise, an export enterprise, a company engaged in electronics and high-technology activities, a company holding a regional headquarters certificate, or a company engaged wholly in the management of a venture capital fund, provided the number of employees entitled to the deduction does not exceed two for each company.	50% of tax otherwise payable

Unilateral foreign tax credit is allowed for foreign taxes paid, limited to Mauritius tax referable to the relevant foreign income subject to tax. Foreign tax credit available under a tax treaty will be allowed if it is more favorable.

Other taxes

Social security taxes/Contributions to the National Pensions Fund are payable by the employer at 6% and by the employee at 3% of cash remuneration up to a maximum remuneration of Rs6,765 monthly. Monthly contributions for remuneration exceeding Rs6,765 are made at the standard flat rates of Rs406.00 for the employer and Rs203.00 for the employee. In addition, employers are required to contribute 2.5% of remuneration, subject to a maximum of Rs169.00 per month per employee and to pay a monthly levy of 1% of basic salaries and wages of every employee.

Local taxes on income/There are no local taxes on income in Mauritius.

Tax administration

Returns/Income tax returns are filed on prescribed forms for a year of assessment ending June 30 on the basis of the income earned during the preceding income year ended June 30. With the approval of the Commissioner of Income Tax, a self-employed taxpayer may file a tax return relating to a 12-month period ending on a date other than June 30 in the preceding year.

Every individual taxpayer is required to file on or before September 30 following the end of the income year an annual return on a prescribed form, disclosing income from all sources as well as full particulars of deductions, allowances, and tax credit reliefs claimed.

A married woman is assessed separately from her husband with regard to all income derived by her. She is entitled to claim all personal reliefs and deductions available to an individual taxpayer, including deductions for children. However, the number of children for whom deductions may be claimed is limited to three per married couple.

Payment of tax/Under the pay-as-you-earn (PAYE) system, income tax is withheld from wages and salaries on a noncumulative basis, and a final adjustment is made at the end of the income year when the taxpayer files the annual return of income. If tax is underpaid under the PAYE system, the unpaid balance becomes payable on or before September 30 following the end of the income year. If tax is overpaid, a refund of the excess tax is made to the taxpayer, normally within three months from the date of filing of the annual return of income. Tax withheld under PAYE from the emoluments of expatriate pilots and flight engineers approved by the Minister of Finance is deemed to be a final tax.

Under the current payment system (CPS), self-employed individuals must pay tax on their business income semiannually. The first payment is due on March 31 in the income year and is based on income for the preceding period from July 1 to December 31. The second and final payment and the annual tax return are due on September 30 following the income year.

Tax rates

Income tax is calculated at graduated rates as shown below.

Chargeable income				
Over (Column 1)	Not over		Tax on Column 1	Percentage on excess
0	Rs 25,000	....	—	15
Rs 25,000	....		Rs 3,750	25

INDIVIDUAL TAX CALCULATION

Year of assessment 2004/2005 (income for the year ending June 30, 2004)

Assumptions

The employee is resident in Mauritius but domiciled in Australia, is married and has two unmarried children, ages 16 and 19. The latter is receiving full-time instruction at a university in Australia. A furnished house is provided by the employers, who pay an annual rent of Rs120,000 plus all electricity, telephone, and gas bills. The employers also provide a new automobile of 1,800 cc that they purchased for Rs900,000. The employee has not derived any income from Australia.

Tax computation

Salary		Rs 1,080,000
Yearly December gratuity		90,000
Electricity, telephone and gas bills		48,000
Car benefit		12,000
Housing accommodation		120,000
Total income from employment		1,350,000
Add:		
Interest on bank savings account	12,000	
Less—Exemption	(75,000)	—
Total gross income		1,350,000
Less—Emoluments relief		125,000
		1,225,000
Less—Personal reliefs and deductions:		
Basic personal deduction	75,000	
Wife	60,000	
One child aged 16	25,000	
One child aged 19 attending university overseas	100,000	
Contribution to National Pensions Fund	2,436	
Contribution to approved medical scheme	5,000	
Life insurance premiums paid	15,000	282,436
Chargeable income		Rs 942,564
Tax payable:		
On first 25,000	3,750	
On remaining 917,564 at 25%	229,391	
Tax payable		Rs 233,141

Notes:

1. Tax is withheld from the salary of the employee under the PAYE system. Any tax underpaid will become payable on or before September 30, 2004; any tax overpaid will be refunded by the tax authorities within three months from the date the annual return of income is filed.
2. Exchange rate of the rupee at December 31, 2003: US$1 = Rs26.30.

Mexico

PwC contacts

For additional information on taxation in Mexico, contact:

Claudia Campos
Jeff Tollers
PricewaterhouseCoopers
Mariano Escobedo No. 573
Col. Rincón del Bosque
11580 México, D.F.
Telephone: (52) 5 2 63 57 74 (Campos)
(52) 5 2 63 57 70 (Tollers)
IAS fax: (52) 5 2 63 86 76
e-mail: claudia.campos@mx.pwc.com
jeff.tollers@mx.pwc.com

Significant developments

Some very significant changes in income taxation for individuals are being phased in. From 2001 to 2005, the top tax rate is being reduced from 40% to 32%. Starting in 2002 and 2003, some items of investment income that were formerly tax exempt or subject to a final withholding at source are now included in the annual tax return. There are also some additional personal deductions, and a new requirement to report certain nontaxable items for informational purposes only.

Territoriality and residence

Resident individuals are subject to Mexican income tax on their worldwide income, regardless of their nationality. Nonresidents, including Mexican citizens who can prove residence for tax purposes in a foreign country, are taxed only on their Mexican-source income.

For 2004, the definition of "tax resident" has changed. The federal Tax Code provides that a person is resident of Mexico when he establishes a home in Mexico. If the individual has a home in another country, then the individual is a resident in the country where he has his center of vital interests. A person is considered to have his center of vital interests in Mexico if either (1) more than 50% of his income comes from Mexican sources in the calendar year or (2) Mexico is the primary place of his professional activities.

Notice of termination of tax residency/Starting in 2004, taxpayers are now required to file a notice of termination of tax residency within 15 days of terminating residency.

Gross income

Employee gross income/Income from personal services (earned income) includes salaries, commissions, and allowances of all types, including those for housing, living expenses, education, foreign service, tax reimbursements, and employer profit-sharing distributions.

Fringe benefits such as "social welfare benefits" may be considered as totally or partially exempt income if the employer satisfies certain eligibility requirements (e.g., nondiscrimination). However, the exempt amount of social welfare benefits is limited to the equivalent of one annual minimum wage (Ps16,513 for 2003) once the employee's salary (together with these benefits) exceeds the equivalent of seven times the minimum wage.

The personal use of an employer-provided automobile is usually not considered to represent additional taxable income to the employee. However, the employer's deductibility of automobile costs and expenses is subject to certain limitations, concerning mainly the maximum value of the vehicle. A per diem rate for business travel is treated as a taxable allowance unless supported by third-party receipts for travel expenses that are limited to lodging, meals, and transportation. Travel expenses are subject to certain maximum limits for domestic and foreign travel and are deductible (and thus not imputed as income to the employee) only when incurred outside a 50-kilometer radius from the employer's base.

Living expense reimbursements, including housing and rental allowances, are generally taxable to the employee, even if paid directly to third parties.

Reimbursements of expenses of a spouse or dependents usually represent taxable income to the employee.

Nonresidents' wages, salaries, and other remuneration for personal dependent services rendered in Mexico are taxed on the basis of income received in a 12-month fiscal year, as follows.

Cumulative income		
Over	**Not over**	**%**
0	Ps 125,900	Exempt
Ps 125,900	1,000,000	15
1,000,000		30

The rates are applied to the cumulative income as it is earned over a 12-month period, whether or not the period coincides with a calendar year.

The tax rate applicable to independent personal services performed by a nonresident in Mexico is a flat 25%. Fees paid to nonresident members of boards of directors or advisory boards (regardless of where the services are performed) are taxed at a flat 25%.

However, no tax is imposed when the compensation (other than board of director fees) is paid by a nonresident of Mexico (even if not subject to tax) who does not have in Mexico any kind of establishment to which the services relate, provided always that the individual is physically present in Mexico less than 183 days (consecutive or not) in any 12-month period. A nonresident who has become subject to the nonresident tax on service income continues to be subject to tax until it is shown that the nonresident has been out of Mexico for at least 183 consecutive days. Under some circumstances, tax treaties exempt Mexican-source income paid by a nonresident of Mexico to a resident of a treaty country.

The tax, when applicable, is withheld if the income is paid by a resident (or a nonresident with a permanent establishment in Mexico). Otherwise, the tax is payable on a monthly basis by the individual earning the Mexican-source income, generally by the 17th day of the following month.

Capital gains and investment income/Gains on the disposition of real property or shares of capital stock receive favorable income tax treatment in that historical costs (converted to pesos) may be adjusted (increased) for inflation (on the basis of the number of months the asset had been held). In the case of shares of capital stock of a Mexican corporation, the adjustment also includes amounts intended to partially cover net retained earnings, whether capitalized or not. The resulting net gain for tax purposes is taxed under a formula favorable to the taxpayer, depending on the number of years the asset was held before sale. Gains on sales of securities through the Mexican Stock Exchange, provided the securities are classified as available to the general public, are exempt from tax. Shares of Mexican companies traded abroad in authorized exchanges (e.g., ADRs (American Depository Receipts)) are also exempt when determined by the Mexican Ministry of Finance to be placed among the general investing public.

Gains from the sale of the taxpayer's principal residence are exempt.

Persons considered as residents of Mexico are taxed on their worldwide capital gains, whereas nonresidents are subject to Mexican tax only on gains arising from sales of real property located in Mexico (including shares of foreign companies holding a significant amount of Mexican real property) or nonexempt sales of shares of Mexican companies, regardless of where the sale takes place.

Residents are required to include investment income received during the year in their annual returns, except for the previously mentioned exempt capital gains. Interest from the Mexican banking system, except for certain exempt accounts with small balances, is subject to withholding, and is includable in the annual tax return 2003. Except for certain transitional provisions, interest paid on most Mexican government obligations is taxable starting in 2003.

Interest on bank accounts, bonds, and other debt obligations issued by nonresidents remains fully taxable, and includes adjustments for inflationary losses and exchange gains and losses with respect to the principal.

Starting in 2002, resident individuals must include in taxable income dividends received from Mexican corporations (grossed up for the corporate income tax paid by the corporation) in their individual income tax returns and claim the underlying corporate income tax paid as a credit against their personal tax liability. This "deemed paid" credit system allows individual taxpayers to compute their tax on dividends at their own personal tax rate, which may be lower than the corporate tax rate of 33% in 2004. (Note: The corporate tax rate is also being gradually reduced, staying in step with the reduction in the individual tax rates so that the corporate rate is always the same as the highest individual marginal tax rate).

Starting in 2003, an individual can set up a trust for educational purposes and the trust income will not be taxable.

Taxable investment income includes income earned (even if not distributed) by investments of any kind located in countries considered to be tax havens in proportion to the ownership percentage of the resident taxpayers. If the taxpayer does not have effective control of the administration of the tax haven investment or the total amount of the investments are maintained at less than Ps160,000, the income need not be recognized until it is received.

Residents are also required to file a separate report with the tax authorities by February 28 of each year regarding their direct and indirect investments during the previous calendar year in countries considered to be tax havens. Failure to file the information report may subject the resident individual to severe penalties, including a prison sentence. Prior to 2002 if the total tax-haven investments were maintained at less than Ps160,000, the report was not required, but starting in 2002 all such investments must be disclosed.

Nonresidents are subject to withholding taxes on Mexican-source interest income at rates varying from 0% to 35%, depending on several factors. Other types of Mexican-source income (including rents and royalties) are also subject to withholding taxes when paid to a nonresident. In the case of dividends and other corporate distributions, there is no tax withheld on the dividend, and no further tax is imposed on the nonresident investor/shareholder.

Tax treaties may reduce or eliminate tax withholding to nonresidents, and the treaty provisions should be analyzed accordingly, depending on the country of residence of the individual receiving Mexican-source income. See the PricewaterhouseCoopers publication *Corporate Taxes—A Worldwide Summary 2004–2005* for details on treaty countries and rates.

Deductions

Employees are allowed to exclude an amount equal to 30 days' minimum wages if they receive a year-end bonus, 15 days' minimum wage each if they receive a vacation bonus or employees' participation in profits, and up to 5 times the daily minimum wage per week of overtime, with certain limitations. These exclusions are taken into account by the employer when calculating the income tax withholding.

Business deductions/Employees are allowed no business-related deductions, but employer reimbursements of properly supported business-related moving and traveling expenses are not taxable to the employee.

Nonbusiness expenses/Resident taxpayers are allowed to deduct unreimbursed medical, dental, or funeral expenses for themselves and their dependents, as well as certain charitable contributions. Health insurance premiums are deductible, and home mortgage interest (adjusted for inflation) are also deductible.

Contributions to certain special private retirement accounts and voluntary contributions to the retirement accounts of the Mexican Social Security system are also deductible, limited to an amount equal to five minimum wages per year (about Ps82,563 in 2004). Withdrawals from these plans become taxable income.

There are no standard deductions (except that an individual may deduct an amount equal to 35% of gross rental income—instead of actual expenses and depreciation of the property).

Tax credits

Residents may credit against their Mexican tax liability, subject to limitations, foreign income tax paid on foreign-source taxable income.

On a monthly basis, a credit on salary also reduces the tax liability by up to Ps1,157. Higher benefits are provided to employees with an income of under four minimum wages per year. However, this credit is lost if an annual tax return is filed.

A nonrefundable low-income tax credit designed to reduce the tax burden of taxpayers with lower incomes is also granted. This credit, which can be as high as Ps36,244 in 2003, is phased out if the taxpayer's employer provides tax-exempt benefits to its employees.

Other taxes

Social security taxes/Employee contributions to the Mexican Social Security Institute are withheld at source. The employer also makes contributions. Both contributions are calculated at varying rates and subject to various limits based on multiples of the minimum wage.

The maximum annual contribution for employees is about US$1,150. The employer's maximum annual contribution is about US$6,300, excluding occupational risk premiums, which vary, depending on the activity of the employer. These maximum contributions apply to employees earning more than approximately US$36,000 per year or US$3,100 per month.

Local taxes on income/Most Mexican states levy a relatively low rate of tax on salaries (but not on income in general), which in most cases is payable by the employer. The Federal District imposes a 2% payroll tax, but it is payable by the employer and constitutes a tax-deductible expense for it.

Tax administration

Returns/All residents receiving income during the calendar year are required to file an annual tax return no later than April 30 of the succeeding year, except in certain cases, such as when an individual earns Mexican bank interest only of up to Ps$100,000 per year—or when the taxpayer's only income consists of salaries paid by a single Mexican employer and the salary is less than about Ps$300,000 per year. In this latter case, if the taxpayer was employed through December 31, the employer computes the final tax liability and makes an adjustment in the employee's withholding; no return is required (unless requested otherwise by the employee, to claim personal deductions or other credits, in which case the employee is personally responsible for filing the annual tax return). Although joint returns are not allowed new miscellaneous rules allow a married couple to have the highest income earner report all investment income. Personal service income should be declared by the spouse earning it, because income splitting is not allowed. In addition, see "Capital gains and investment income" above regarding the obligation to file an annual tax-haven investment information report by February 28, irrespective of the need to file an annual tax return. Residents receiving only compensation income will be required to file an annual income tax return if total compensation is more than Ps$300,000, compensation was paid by more than one employer, or compensation was paid by a foreign employer.

Under the current miscellaneous rules, most taxpayers must file their annual tax returns electronically.

Information disclosures/Under certain circumstances, individuals are required to report six nontaxable items on their annual tax returns, for informational purposes only: loan proceeds, prizes, gifts, inheritances, proceeds from the sale of a personal residence, and travel expense reimbursements. Although disclosed on the return, these items remain nontaxable. If these items are not disclosed, the result could be a loss of their tax-exempt status.

Payment of tax/Tax is payable upon filing the return. The full tax on salary income and certain interest and dividend income is withheld at source. However, in the case of salaries received by resident individuals from nonresident employers (and nonresident employees subject to the nonresident tax on salaries discussed above), Mexican law requires the filing of monthly estimated tax returns to pay an amount equal to the tax withholdings applicable to these wages. The monthly returns are generally due by the 17th day of the following month, and are usually filed electronically.

Tax rates

Effective calendar year 2004

Taxable income		Basic tax	
Over	Not over	Tax on Column 1	Percentage on excess
(Column 1)			
Ps 0.01	Ps 5,153.22	0.00	3.00
5,153.23	43,739.22	Ps 154.56	10.00
43,739.22	76,867.80	4,013.10	17.00
76,867.81	89,355.48	9,645.12	25.00
89,355.49	106,982.82	12,767.04	32.00
106,982.83		18,407.70	33.00

Notes:

1. The above brackets are effective for calendar year 2004.
2. A tax rate reduction is being phased in by eliminating the highest tax brackets, leaving the following as the highest tax rates:

Year	Highest marginal rate
	%
2002	35
2003	34
2004	33
2005	32

3. As mentioned earlier, in addition to the low-income credit discussed below, an additional credit on salary is allowed on a monthly basis.

Low-income credit on annual return/A nonrefundable credit of up to 50% of the tax on lower incomes based on the tax rate schedule, designed to reduce the tax burden of taxpayers earning lower incomes, is granted. The credit is reduced proportionately for higher levels of income and phased out if taxpayers receive tax-exempt fringe benefits from their employer. At year-end, the employer computes the amount of the credit, and the employees claim it in their personal returns.

The following table is used to compute the preliminary amount of credit. The portion of the preliminary credit that is noncreditable because of nontaxable fringe benefits is equal to twice the percentage that nontaxable income is of total remuneration. Thus, when the nontaxable portion reaches 50% of total remuneration, no credit is allowed. This ratio is computed by the employer on a company wide basis (not for each employee separately).

The following table shows the rates for computing the preliminary annual low-income tax credit.

Lower limit	Upper limit	Credit on tax on lower limit	% of credit on marginal tax
Ps 0.01	Ps 5,153.22	Ps 0.00	50
5,153.23	43,739.22	77.22	50
43,739.23	76,867.80	2,006.58	50
76,867.81	89,355.48	4,822.20	50
89,355.49	106,982.82	6,383.46	50
106,982.83	215,769.06	9,203.70	40
215,769.07	340,081.74	23,563.74	30
340,081.75		36,243.54	0

INDIVIDUAL TAX CALCULATION

2004

Assumptions

1. Resident alien who earns a salary, with wife and two children.
2. Wife and children have no income.
3. Husband's income is as follows.

	Ps
Salary, allowances, and bonus	1,000,000
Nontaxable fringe benefits	100,000
Investment income from abroad, on which a foreign tax of 30% (Ps16,500) was paid to the foreign country on a nonresident basis	55,000
Long-term capital gains on sales of shares in Mexican stock market (exempt)	30,000

4. Allowable deductions include the following.

	Ps
Medical expenses	54,000
Charitable contributions	30,000
	84,000

5. Companywide nontaxable benefits are equal to 10% of total remuneration. The nonallowable portion of the low-income credit is therefore 20%.

Tax computation

Income:		
Salary, allowances, bonus, and fringe benefits		Ps 1,100,000
Less—Earned-income exclusions:		
Nontaxable fringe benefits	100,000	
Excludable portion of Christmas bonus	1,357	
Excludable portion of vacation premium	678	102,035
Taxable earned income		997,965
Add—Foreign-source investment income		55,000
		1,052,965
Deduct:		
Medical expenses	54,000	
Charitable contributions	30,000	84,000
Taxable income		Ps 968,965
Tax thereon		Ps 302,862
Less—Tax credits:		
Low-income credit (80% of 36,243.54)		(28,995)
		273,867
Less—Foreign tax credit (1)		(2,964)
Net tax liability		Ps 270,903

Notes:

1. The foreign tax credit allowed is the lesser of the foreign tax paid on the foreign-source income (limited to the equivalent of the foreign taxes paid on a nonresident basis) or the foreign tax credit limitation (as in this example), which (under current law) is computed by applying the annual tax tables to the foreign-source income by itself, as follows.

Foreign source income	Ps 55,000.00
Less—Lower limit	43,739.22
Excess	Ps 11,260.78
Times tax rate (17%)	
Income tax	Ps 1,914.33
Plus—Tax on lower limit	4,013.10
Total tax	5,927.43
Less—Low income tax credit	2,963.16
Total foreign tax limitation	Ps 2,964.27
Foreign tax paid	Ps 16,500.00

2. Exchange rate of the peso at April 2, 2004: US$1 = Ps11.196.

Mozambique

PwC contact

For additional information on taxation in Mozambique, contact:

M. Isabel Fernandes
PricewaterhouseCoopers
Rovuma Carlton Hotel
Centro de Escritórios, 3º andar, 1
Maputo, Mozambique
Telephone: (258) (1) 307620
Fax: (258) (1) 307621
e-mail: maria.isabel.fernandes@mz.pwc.com

Significant developments

As of the beginning of 2003, Mozambique has been going through a major tax reform, which consists in the replacement of the existing individual income tax and in the strengthening of the tax administration by improving collection procedures and increasing enforcement capacity. Since January 1, 2003, a new Code on Individual Income Tax (CIRPS—*Código do Imposto Sobre o Rendimento das Pessoas Singulares*) has come into force.

Territoriality and residence

Residents are taxed on their worldwide income. Nonresidents are taxed on income arising in Mozambique.

Taxpayers are deemed to be resident if they have been in Mozambique for more than 180 days in a calendar year in which income arises or for less time if, on December 31, they occupy a residence under circumstances indicating intent to continue occupancy on a regular basis. Members of the crew of a vessel or of an airplane registered in Mozambique are also regarded as residents.

Gross income

Employee gross income/Remuneration is defined in the individual income tax code and covers all payments in connection with work carried out in Mozambique, regardless of where payments is made or its nature (salaries, wages, earnings, rewards, percentages, commissions, partnership earnings, allowances or bonus, attendance fees, emoluments, participation in penalties/fines, other accessory remunerations, and any type of remuneration in general).

Travel and accommodation paid by the employer not connected with the functions of the employee and taxes and other legal costs due by the employee and paid on his or her behalf by the employer are also considered employment income for tax purposes.

All fringe benefits in cash or in kind, including housing allowances and the use of company-paid houses and vehicles, are also taxable pursuant to the law.

Capital gains and investment income/Gains resulting from the following are considered capital gains.

1. The transfer of rights regarding immovable property and similar acts.
2. The transfer of shareholding and other securities.
3. The selling of intellectual and industrial property and know-how.

4. The transfer of contractual positions or other rights inherent in contracts regarding immovable property.

   and

5. Net income from operations in regard to financial instruments.

Interest and other remuneration from capital; interest and premiums on write-down or disposal of securities; interest on shareholders' loans and profits not distributed to shareholders; income from shareholdings; income from intellectual property and from know-how if not earned by the original owner are also treated as investment income.

There are no deductions on capital gains and investment income.

Capital gains are treated in one of two ways:

1. 50% of the positive or negative balance resulting from the onerous transfer of rights or contractual positions regarding immovable property and intellectual and industrial property, including know-how, is taxable.
2. In the case of gains or losses resulting from the onerous transfer of shareholding, the percentage of the value to be considered for tax purposes is proportional to the time the taxpayer has held the shareholding, namely:
   a. 75% of value if held for up to 12 months;
   b. 60% of value if held between 12 and 24 months;
   c. 40% of value if held between 24 and 60 months;
   d. 30% of value if held for more than 60 months.

Most capital gains and investment income are taxed through withholdings by the paying entity at 20%. Income from debit bonds as well as swap operations is taxed at 10%. Interest paid on bank deposits to individuals by Mozambican resident credit institutions is currently tax-exempt. Resident individuals earning income arising from bonds (nominative/bearer), shares and swaps from resident entities may opt to add this income to global individual income and have it taxed as such.

Deductions

Business deductions/The reimbursement of car expenses is not taxed if they are duly supported and if the car is under the employer's name. Otherwise, the mileage allowance must be reasonable, and the rate cannot be higher than the one applied to public officers.

Business expenses incurred by a sole trader or partnership in connection with a commercial, industrial, or agricultural activity are deductible against corresponding income under corporate tax rules.

Income from real estate is reduced by maintenance and support expenses incurred on the immovable property. No documentary proof is needed, provided the amount of such expenses does not exceed 30% of the immovable property income earned. Should the maintenance and support expenses exceed the stipulated limit, all maintenance and support expenses may also be deducted, provided the taxpayer presents supporting documentation for the total costs incurred.

Income from real estate is also reduced by interest paid to Mozambican credit institutions and by the municipal tax on real estate.

Nonbusiness expenses/Gross income from employment is reduced by the following expenses.

1. Contributions to the social security system and mandatory contributions of public officials.
2. Contributions to unions.
3. Compensation paid by the employer to the employee in lieu of notice for unilateral termination of work contract.
4. Pensions paid under a court order and duly supported.
5. Deductions related to the individual and family status of the taxpayer:
   a. MZM600,000 for single or legally separated taxpayers;
   b. MZM480,000 for each married or nonlegally separated taxpayer;
   c. MZM200,000 for one dependent; MZM300,000 for two dependents; and MZM400,000 for three or more dependents;
6. Deductions for the avoidance of international double taxation.

Personal allowances/The only personal allowances are pensions, maintenance, and alimony paid by the taxpayer (ruled by a court decision). Pensions up to MZM168 million per year are not taxed. Pensions in the amount exceeding the annual limit are taxed on the total amount earned (where the taxpayer earned exclusively pension income). However, the tax payable cannot be higher than the amount that exceeds the nontaxable limit.

Tax credits/Tax credits are available for taxes paid on foreign-source income in order to avoid international double taxation.

Other taxes

Social security taxes/Social security contributions are payable monthly on all salaries, wages, regular bonuses, or other regular income, excluding meal subsidies. The employer contributes an amount equal to 4% of monthly salary and the employee contributes 3% of monthly salary. The employer withholds employees' contributions.

Local taxes on income/None.

Tax administration

Returns/The tax year is the calendar year.

A taxpayer with income only from employment and pensions must file tax returns from January to March of the year following the tax year. In all other cases, tax returns must be filed from January to April of the year following the tax year.

Married couples file a joint tax return. Income of joint filers is not split but is divided by 2 for the purpose of assessment of the tax rate, or 1.85 if one of the spouses earns income equal or higher than 95% of the combined income of the couple. The computation is then multiplied by 2.

Payment of tax/Remuneration from employment is taxed at source through application by the employer of a standard tax table. Tax deducted at source is adjusted on the basis of the annual return. Special rules apply to independent work income, capital gains, investment income, and real estate income.

Tax rates

Earned income tax/The following are the general rules on employment income.

Annual income (MZM)	Rate (%)	Deduction (MZM)*
To 28,000,000	10	—
From 28,000,001 to 112,000,000	15	1,400,000
From 112,000,001 to 336,000,0000	20	7,000,000
From 336,000,001 to 1,008,000,000	25	23,800,000
Above 1,008,000,000	32	94,360,000

*Amount deductible after applying rate to whole amount.

Special rates apply to capital gains and investment capital income, as discussed above.

INDIVIDUAL TAX CALCULATION

Year ending December 31, 2003 (calendar-year basis)

Assumptions

Married couple resident in Mozambique for the entire year of 2003, with two children under 21; one spouse earns all income, which comprises salary, interest on term deposit and capital gain on the sale of a house.

Tax computation

Earned income:		
Salary	MZM	155,000,000
Capital gain on sale of house		200,000,000
Interest on term-deposit account—12,000,000 (1)		Nil
		355,000,000
Deduct:		
Social security contributions		4,650,000
50% of capital gain		100,000,000
Assessable income		250,350,000
Less—Minimum amount not taxable		(24,000,000)
Taxable income	MZM	226,350,000
Split income (coefficient to split income—1.85)	MZM	122,351,351
Tax thereon (20%)	MZM	24,470,270
Amount deductible		7,000,000
Gross tax due	MZM	17,470,270
Gross up by factor of 2	MZM	34,940,540
Less—Deductions from gross tax due:		
Married couple		(960,000)
Two dependents		(300,000)
		33,680,540
Less—Tax withheld on account of salary tax payable (2)		(36,735,000)
Tax recoverable	MZM	3,054,460

Notes:

1. Interest earned by individuals on term deposit account is not taxable.
2. Assume 23.7% monthly.
3. Exchange rate of the metical at December 31, 2003: USD$1 = MZM23,821.68.

Namibia, Republic of

PwC contact

For additional information on taxation in Namibia, contact:

Albè Botha
PricewaterhouseCoopers
P.O. Box 1571
Windhoek, Namibia
Telephone: (264) (61) 2841000
Fax: (264) (61) 2841260
e-mail: albe.botha@na.pwc.com

Significant developments

Namibia now has a system of self-assessment.

The following information on taxation in Namibia is accurate as of January 1, 2004. The 2004/2005 budget amendments are not included. For subsequent developments, refer to the contact above.

Territoriality and residence

The general rule is that tax is payable only on income derived or deemed to be derived from sources within Namibia.

The most important "deemed Namibian sources" relate to the following.

1. Interest (taxable in the hands of residents on a worldwide basis).
2. Income derived outside Namibia in the course of a trade conducted in Namibia.
3. Royalty and similar payments in respect of the use of intellectual property in Namibia.

Otherwise, residence, domicile and citizenship are not normally relevant, and there are no special concessions for nonresidents unless a tax treaty applies. Namibia has treaties with France, Germany, India, Mauritius, Romania, Russia, South Africa, Sweden, and the United Kingdom.

Gross income

Employee gross income*/*Gross income includes all receipts in respect of services rendered, in cash or in kind, in particular the following.

1. Salaries and fees.
2. Deemed value of accommodation provided by employer.
3. Deemed value of the use of a company motor vehicle.
4. All cash allowances and subsidies, subject to deductions for business expenses.

The principal exemptions are as follows.

1. Under certain conditions, the remuneration of heads of foreign governments and U.N. employees stationed in Namibia is exempt from taxation.
2. Relocation expenses paid by the employer are not taxed as fringe benefits in the employee's hands.
3. Where an approved scheme by the Receiver of Revenue is established for the provision of employee housing, the taxable fringe benefit arising from provision of accommodation, housing allowances, or mortgage interest subsidies is reduced by at least one-third, provided the annual remuneration of the employee

exceeds N$30,000. If not, a formula is used if the remuneration of the employee exceeds N$15,000 but not N$30,000.

4. Employer contributions to approved retirement funds and medical aid schemes (private health insurance) are not taxable in the hands of employees.

Capital gains and investment income/The general rule is that capital gains are not taxable and capital losses are not deductible in the calculation of taxable income. Capital receipts are not defined by statute. Profits on the realization of assets are likely to be treated as exempt if the assets are income producing. Profits on assets acquired with the intention of resale at a profit are generally taxable as income. Duration of ownership and the intentions of the taxpayer at the time of acquisition are also relevant, but there is no prescribed holding period.

Dividends are exempt from taxation (with the exception of local building society dividends). Interest is normally taxable on a worldwide basis; broadly speaking, however, a temporary resident is taxed only on locally sourced interest, that is, interest earned overseas on foreign capital is exempt. The first N$500 of interest from Namibian financial institutions, in respect of a natural person, is exempt. As a result of the source rules and the exempt status of dividends, few items subject to foreign tax are liable to Namibian taxation. There is no general unilateral provision for relief from double taxation, although a specific provision prevents double taxation of royalties.

Deductions

Business deductions/There are no standard deductions for employees for business expenses. Travel, entertainment, and motor vehicle expenses are potentially deductible, but the onus is on the employee to prove they were incurred in the production of taxable income. Where allowances are provided by the employer, this onus is more readily discharged, but the deduction cannot normally exceed the allowance.

Nonbusiness expenses/An employee may deduct contributions of up to N$30,000 per annum to an approved pension, retirement annuity, provident, or educational policy fund registered in Namibia.

Domestic mortgage interest is not deductible. There are minor deductions for donations to educational institutions.

Personal allowances/There are no personal allowances.

Other taxes

Namibia has no gift tax, estate duty, or capital transfer tax.

Social security/Namibia has a limited social security system. The Maternity Leave, Sick Leave and Death Benefit Fund became operational in 1996, and membership is compulsory for all employees. It is funded by employer and employee contributions of 0.9% of salary, with a maximum contribution of N$27 per month each.

Enabling legislation provides for the following three additional funds, which are not yet operational.

1. National Medical Benefit Fund.
2. National Pension Fund.
3. Development Fund.

Membership in the Medical Benefit and Pension Funds will not be required if employees are members of approved schemes provided by employers. The

Development Fund (to provide training and employment schemes, student funding, etc.) is not expected to be funded by dedicated contributions.

Workmen's compensation/Under the Workmen's Compensation Act, employers are required to contribute to a fund that provides cash benefits for industrial injury, disability, and death. Contribution rates vary according to inherent occupational risk, from less than 1% in most low-risk commercial/administrative occupations to 8% for high-risk sectors (drilling, tunneling, and rock-blasting). Employees whose annual remuneration exceeds N$38,000 are normally excluded from coverage.

Tax administration

Returns/The tax year runs from March 1 to February 28/29 of the following year. Tax returns must normally be filed within four months from the end of the financial year.

Namibia has a system of self-assessment, which must include a computation of the taxpayer's taxable income and tax payable, and the payment of tax due on the income so computed.

The final payment of tax must be made within four months of financial year-end. Interest at 20% per annum is levied on any late payments.

Husbands and wives submit separate tax returns and are taxed separately.

Payment of tax/Pay-as-you-earn (PAYE) tax is withheld from an employee's salary by the employer and must be remitted to the revenue authorities monthly. Any individual who earns income in excess of N$5,000 (e.g., interest or profit from trade) that is not subject to PAYE is required to register as a provisional taxpayer.

Provisional taxpayers are required to submit half-yearly estimates of their income at end-August and end-February each year and pay the applicable taxes thereon. The taxpayer is required to effect payment based on actual figures and is no longer able to estimate payment based on the amount of the last assessed year.

Tax rates

Personal income tax rates for the year ended February 28, 2002 are as follows.

Taxable income		Tax on	Percentage
Over (Column 1)	Not over	Column 1	on excess
0	N$ 24,000	—	0
N$ 24,000	40,000	—	17.5
40,000	80,000	N$ 2,800	29.5
80,000	200,000	14,600	34.5
200,000		56,000	35.0

INDIVIDUAL TAX CALCULATION

Year ending February 28, 2002

Tax computation

Salary		N$ 280,000
Add—Fringe benefits:		
Use of company motor vehicle costing 100,000 (1)	18,000	
House provided by employer, in Windhoek (2)	21,600	
Entertainment allowance	12,000	51,600
		331,600
Deduct:		
Pension contribution (Namibian-registered fund)	14,000	
Entertainment expenses	11,600	25,600
		306,000
Add:		
Interest from Namibian bank	4,500	
Less—Standard exemption	(500)	4,000
Taxable income		N$ 310,000
Income tax:		
On 200,000		N$ 56,000
On 110,000 at 35%		38,500
Total income tax payable		N$ 94,500

Notes:

1. Car benefit calculated at 1.5% per month of cost of vehicle to employer.
2. Assuming three bedrooms and two reception rooms. Rates vary according to location and number of rooms.
3. Exchange rate of the Namibian dollar at March 18, 2004: US$1 = N$6.70. The Namibian dollar trades at par with the South African rand.

PwC contacts

For additional information on taxation in the Netherlands, contact:

Louis de Vries
PricewaterhouseCoopers
De Entree 201
1101 HG Amsterdam Z-O
The Netherlands
Telephone: (31) (20) 568 72 45
Fax: (31) (20) 568 65 64
e-mail: louis.de.vries@nl.pwc.com

Knowledge managers
Muriël Schoenmakers
Telephone: (31) (20) 568 6325
Fax: (31) (20) 568 5975
e-mail: muriël.schoenmakers@nl.pwc.com

Manon Ultee
Telephone: (31) (10) 407 5744
Fax: (31) (10) 407 5720
e-mail: manon.ultee@nl.pwc.com

Significant developments

There have been no significant tax or regulatory developments in the past year.

Territoriality and residence

The Netherlands taxes its residents on their worldwide income; nonresidents are subject to tax only on income derived from specific sources in the Netherlands (mainly income from employment, director's fees, business income, and income from Dutch immovable property).

Article 4 of the General Taxation Act prescribes that the facts and circumstances determine an individual's residence. In case of a dispute the Dutch tax courts will examine the durable ties of a personal nature with the Netherlands.

Gross income

Box 1—Employee gross income and primary residence/Income from current or past employment, self-employment, and the deemed rental income from the taxpayer's primary residence is assessed in box 1. Mortgage interest payments in relation to the financing, renovation or maintenance of the primary residence may be deducted from box 1 income.

All benefits in kind are, in principle, considered as taxable income. Such benefits include accommodation allowances, private use of the company car, home-leave allowances, and pre- and post-assignment bonuses. Employer-paid reimbursement of relocation costs relating to the acceptance of a new employment and employer contributions toward approved pension schemes are not taxable.

Costs relating to the assignment to the Netherlands incurred by a foreign employee may be reimbursed tax-free. These so-called extraterritorial costs include all costs that the employee would not have incurred had he or she not been assigned to the Netherlands. Double housing costs, cost-of-living allowances, language courses, and so on, qualify as extraterritorial costs.

If certain conditions are met (see "30% ruling" below), a foreign employee working in the Netherlands may be granted a tax-free allowance amounting to 30% of the income from current employment (the so-called 30% ruling). The tax-free 30%

allowance is intended to cover all extraterritorial costs. If the foreign employee benefits from the 30% ruling, extraterritorial costs may not be reimbursed tax-free in addition to the 30% tax-free allowance.

Nonresident employees are taxed on salary earned for employment activities performed inside the Netherlands. If the employment is exercised for a Dutch employer, the work is deemed to be performed in the Netherlands, unless the employment is fully exercised outside the Netherlands or unless the salary earned in connection with foreign duties is taxed abroad. As a general rule a statutory director of a Dutch company is subject to Dutch taxation irrespective of the country where the duties relating to the directorship are actually performed. An exception is made only if a double taxation treaty stipulates otherwise. Box 1 income is taxed at progressive rates up to a maximum of 52%.

Box 2—Income from substantial interest/A Dutch resident who, alone or together with a spouse or other close relatives, holds at least 5% of the shares of a company or who holds rights to acquire a 5% interest in a company has a so-called substantial interest. The benefits derived from this substantial interest are taxable in box 2. These benefits include dividends and the gain on the sale of one or more of the shares or rights. Taxation in box 2 will apply only to a nonresident who holds a substantial interest in a Dutch-based company. All box 2 income is taxed at a flat rate of 25%.

Box 3—Income from savings and investments/Income from investments (e.g., dividends and interest) is as such not taxable. However, the net assets (assets minus debts) of an individual are deemed to generate a fixed return on investment of 4% per year. This fixed return is taxed in box 3. All net assets that are not intended for daily use and that are not taxed in box 1 or box 2 belong to the box 3 taxable base. For Dutch residents, part of the taxable base is exempt and several specific deductions apply.

Nonresidents are subject to taxation only on the net value of a limited number of Dutch assets, including the following.

1. Dutch real estate not used as the primary residence.
2. Profits rights unrelated to shares or an employment.

Capital gains and investment income/For residents and nonresidents, capital gains and investment income as such are not taxable, except as detailed for box 2 and box 3 above.

Deductions

Box 1—Business deductions/The following deductions may be claimed relating to employment income when filing a Dutch tax return.

1. A fixed annual amount for commuting by public transport.
2. A fixed daily deduction for sailors.

30% ruling/As stated above, foreign employees qualifying for the 30% ruling may receive a tax-free allowance amounting to 30% of their income from current employment. To qualify for the 30% ruling, the foreign employee should have specific expertise that is not or scarcely available on the Dutch labor market. The employee should have at least 2.5 years of relevant (international) working experience.

The 30% ruling may apply for a maximum period of 120 months. Under the provisions of the 30% ruling, employees who are, based on facts and circumstances, considered as resident taxpayers may opt to be treated as partial nonresidents. Partial in this respect implies that they are treated as residents for box 1 and as nonresidents for box 2 and box 3 purposes. The 30% ruling must be applied for within four months of starting the Dutch employment. If not applied for within this time, the ruling, if granted, will not apply retroactively as of the beginning of the Dutch employment, but only as of the month following the month in which the application was filed. The 30% ruling may, in principle, only be applied if the employee is included in a Dutch wage tax administration.

Nonbusiness deductions/Residents (and partial nonresidents) are entitled to claim deductions mainly relating to their personal or family circumstances: child care expenses, maintenance payments to a former spouse (alimony), expenses arising from sickness or disability, educational expenses, support payments to children, weekend expenses of disabled children, charitable donations, and losses of specified venture capital investments (deductions for certain expenses are capped or subject to thresholds).

Life annuity premiums are tax deductible only if the taxpayer can prove an insufficiency in the pension rights/pension capital built up to date.

Levy rebates/Resident and partial nonresident taxpayers are entitled to so-called levy rebates. Except for the general levy rebate, several levy rebates, depending on the personal situation of the taxpayer can be claimed (children levy rebate, single parent levy rebate, etc.). The levy rebates cannot be transferred to the taxpayer's partner. The rebates reduce the amount of tax due and can therefore be considered as tax credits. There are several tax levy rebates varying from as less as €110 to €1,825. The levy rebates consist of a part relating to and reducing the amount of income tax due and a part relating to and reducing the amount of national insurance tax due. The income tax part is granted only to taxpayers who reside in the Netherlands for the whole year (or to nonresident residing in a country that concluded a tax treaty including a nondiscrimination clause). The national insurance tax part is only granted to taxpayers covered under the Dutch social security system.

Election to be treated as a resident taxpayer/The taxation of nonresidents is limited to specific sources of Dutch income, and only a few deductions may be claimed. Nonresidents may therefore opt to be treated as resident taxpayers, which enables them to claim levy rebates and other deductions that are available only to residents and partial nonresidents.

Worldwide income of a nonresident taxpayer who elects to be treated as a resident taxpayer is taken into account, and a relief for double taxation, mostly based on the exemption-with-progression method, will be granted for all items of income that are, based on the tax treaties, not allocated to the Netherlands. Opting to be treated as a resident is a possibility only for residents of most of the countries that have concluded tax treaties with the Netherlands.

Tax credits

Only residents and most partial nonresidents are entitled to relief from double taxation under unilateral relief provisions or under tax treaties.

Other taxes

Social security/Employee insurance contributions and national insurance tax are levied on residents and nonresidents under a number of different regulations.

Under the national insurance tax regulations, tax is levied on income up to a maximum of €29,543. At present, the tax is capped at €9,571 per annum. From this amount several levy rebates may be deducted varying from €107 to €1,770.

Under the employee insurance regulations, contributions are levied on income up to a maximum of €43,754. The contribution rate depends on the line of industry the employee belongs to, but on average the contributions are capped at €1,656 for the employee and €4,468 for the employer.

In addition, employees earning less than €29,606 a year are compulsory covered by the state medical plan. In this case fixed health insurance premiums are due by the employee amounting to at maximum €370 per annum as well as additional variable premiums. The employer contributions amount to a maximum of €1,998.

Local taxes on income/There are no local taxes on income.

Tax administration

Returns/If both husband and wife are resident taxpayers, they are taxed separately for their business income, employment income, pension income, and other periodic payments less premiums for life annuities and for certain other periodic payments. Spouses and persons living as a joint household for at least six months in a calendar year can choose to whom of both they want to allocate the following income or deductions for Dutch income tax purposes: the taxable income from the primary residence, childcare expenses, the taxable income from a substantial interest (box 2), the fixed return of box 3, and the nonbusiness deductions relating to the taxpayers' personal circumstances.

Tax returns must be filed after each calendar year, in principle, before April 1.

Payment of tax/If an employee is on a Dutch payroll, wage tax will be withheld from his salary. Generally speaking, if taxpayers have sizable income that is not subject to wage tax withholding, they may be required to make advance payments of estimated additional income tax.

Tax rates

Calendar year 2004

Box 1 income

Taxable income		Tax on	Percentage
Over	Not over	Column 1	on excess
(Column 1)			
0	€ 16,265*	—	1.0
€ 16,265	29,543*	€ 162	7.95
29,543	50,652	1,217	42.00
50,652		10,082	52.00

*In the first and second bracket of box 1, national insurance tax is levied at a rate of 32.40%.

Box 2 income/Box 2 income is taxed at 25%.

Box 3 income/Box 3 income is taxed at 30%.

INDIVIDUAL TAX CALCULATION

Calendar year 2004

Assumptions

The taxpayer is a foreign national residing in the Netherlands and benefiting from the 30% ruling; spouse and two dependent children under 12 years of age. The husband is the sole earner. Salary is paid from a Dutch payroll. The taxpayer owns a mortgaged home in the Netherlands and has requested that the Dutch Revenue consider him a partial nonresident taxpayer.

Tax computations

Box 1

Worldwide gross income:		
Gross Dutch salary	52,500	
30% tax-free allowance	22,500	
Total gross income		€ 75,000
Taxable salary		€ 52,500
Less—Employee insurance contributions		1,656
		50,844
Less—Balance of imputed income from primary residence in the Netherlands less the mortgage interest paid		12,500
Taxable income		€ 38,344
Calculated tax	4,912	
Less—Levy rebates	(98)	€ 4,814
Calculated national insurance tax	9,571	
Less—Levy rebates	(3,164)	€ 6,407
Amounts due/paid:		
Income tax	4,814	
National insurance tax	6,407	
Employee insurance contributions	1,656	
Total withholdings		€ 12,877
Net income		€ 62,123

Box 2*

	€
Capital gain on sale of 10% of shares in a foreign company	50,000
Dividends from Dutch company	2,000
Calculated tax for resident	13,000
Calculated tax for partial nonresident	500

*For box 2 partial nonresidents (a provision under the 30% ruling) are taxable only on Dutch-source income.

Box 3*

	€
Average value of summer house abroad	€ 300,000
Average balance savings account	20,000
Taxable income	11,054
Calculated tax for resident (not taking into account a possible relief for double taxation for the taxable income from the summer house abroad)	3,316
Calculated tax for partial nonresident	0

*For box 3 partial nonresidents (a provision under the 30% ruling) are taxable only on Dutch-source income.

Note:

Exchange rate of the Euro on January 2, 2004: US$1 = € 0.7942.

PwC contact

For additional information on taxation in the Netherlands Antilles, contact:

Peter Bolwerk
Steve Vanenburg
PricewaterhouseCoopers N.A.
Julianaplein 38
Curaçao, Netherlands Antilles
Telephone: (599) (9) 4300000
Fax: (599) (9) 4611119
e-mail: peter.j.bolwerk@.anpwc.com
steve.r.vanenburg@.anpwc.com

Significant developments

New Fiscal Framework/On December 29, 1999 the Parliament of the Netherlands Antilles has approved three tax bills, which are known as the New Fiscal Framework (NFF), published under P.B. 244, 245, and 246.

The principal reasons for the enactment of the NFF are the objective of the government to part from its tax-haven image and to revitalize its financial services industry. The main elements of the NFF with regard to individuals are, among others:

1. Income Tax Ordinance:
   a. Introduction of deemed income provisions;
   b. Amendment of the substantial interest provisions.
2. Introduction of a dividend withholding tax of 10%. This tax will only take effect on a date that will be announced in a separate Ordinance, but that is not expected to happen in the near future.

Turnover tax/In Curacao and Bonaire turnover tax is levied on the provision of services and deliveries by entrepreneurs and companies. A limited number of services and deliveries are exempt. “Services” does not include advisory and management services provided to or by offshore companies and offshore banks.

An entrepreneur liable to the turnover tax must file a declaration with the Tax Inspectorate before the 16th day of the following month at the Tax Collector’s office. The rate amounts to 5%.

Territoriality and residence

An individual’s specific circumstances determine residence for tax purposes. These circumstances include permanent home, habitual stay, and center of economic and social interest. Residents are taxed on worldwide income, while nonresidents are taxed only on certain specified income generated within the Netherlands Antilles. Individuals are taxed from their date of arrival. Accordingly, there is no significance as to the timing of arrival.

Gross income

Residents/Gross income of residents includes gains, profits, and income derived from the sources below.

1. A business or profession.
2. Employment.

3. Proceeds from immovable property.
4. Net income from capital.
5. Certain periodic receipts.
6. Net income from capital.

Deemed income/For the individual income tax purposes, a resident taxpayer can be taxed on deemed annual income from capital if he owns shares in a Netherlands Antilles Exempt Company, or shares, membership rights or an interest in a nonresident company ("foreign investment company"), the activities of which, on a consolidated basis, mainly consist of lending, portfolio investments, and similar activities.

Resident taxpayers are obliged to include the fair market value of such Exempt Company or foreign investment company in their annual taxable income. An amount equal to 4% of the fair market value of the shares, membership rights or interest at the beginning of the year will be considered as taxable income each year.

In case the actual income received exceeds the deemed amount, this income actually received does not have to be included in the taxable income rather than the amount of the deemed income.

The deemed income provision will also apply to the value of receivables on, profit sharing certificates in, and rights in an Exempt Company or in a foreign investment company.

Substantial interest/A substantial interest exists if a resident taxpayer owns at least 5% of the shares in a resident or nonresident company, the capital of which is divided into shares or if a qualifying nonresident tax payer owns at least 5% of the shares in such a domestic company. The gain realized on the alienation of the shares is subject to income tax. The gain is defined as the difference between the sales price and the historic acquisition price of the shares.

Residents/The termination of the residency of a taxpayer, other than by death, will also be considered as an alienation of shares. Upon the taxpayer's emigration, the tax administration will impose a preserving assessment for the accrued capital gain (although not yet realized). If certain conditions are fulfilled, deferral of payment of this tax can be obtained. The tax due becomes payable if the shares are sold within a period of ten years after the emigration. If the shares are not sold within this ten-year period the debt will be forgiven.

Retirees/Legislation regarding the so-called pensionado arrangement has been enacted whereby (retired) individuals who meet certain requirements may opt to be taxed at low rates. To apply for this tax incentive, the individual should not have been a Netherlands Antilles resident in the five years before taking up residence in the Netherlands Antilles. Furthermore, the qualifying pensioner/retiree must be at least 50 years of age, and must own and use a house in the Netherlands Antilles with a value of at least Naf450,000.

There are at present two retiree incentives: one that qualifies for applicability of the TAK (tax agreement for the Kingdom of the Netherlands), and one that does not. The pensioner/retiree may opt to pay one of the following.

1. A flat 10% tax rate on foreign income (minus allowable deductions) (TAK remains applicable);
   or

2. A fixed annual tax of approximately Naf261,100 (TAK is not applicable).

Nonresidents/Individuals living in the Netherlands Antilles for more than one year are generally considered residents. Residents are taxed on their worldwide income. Individuals not residing in the Netherlands Antilles are subject to individual income tax on their net income from certain specified sources in the Netherlands Antilles. The following are the more important sources of such income.

1. A business or profession carried out within the Netherlands Antilles personally or through a permanent representative or proxy holder. An exemption can be granted if the practice is of a temporary nature or lasts less than three consecutive months.
2. Employment. Individuals who work for a period of less than three months may request an exemption, although in practice such requests are usually not granted.
3. Acting as a director of a company established in the Netherlands Antilles.
4. Immovable property (within the Netherlands Antilles).
5. A mortgage on immovable property
6. Under circumstances income from a Netherlands Antilles Company in which a substantial interest is held.

Substantial interest/Dividends and interest from shares belonging to a substantial interest as well as capital gains upon the sale of such shares received by a nonresident shareholder within ten years after his migration from the Netherlands Antilles are subject to income tax. With respect to the determination of the amount of the capital gains derived from a substantial interest, the acquisition price for shares and profit sharing certificates in a resident company is established at the historic acquisition price.

With regard to the acquisition price of shares and profit sharing certificates in a nonresident company of an individual who immigrates to the Netherlands Antilles the acquisition price, is as a general rule, established at the fair market value.

Capital gains and investment income/Capital gains and losses arising from the sale or exchange of private assets are exempt from taxation. If private assets are employed as capital of a business, the capital gains and losses form part of personal taxable income. Also, capital gains realized on the sale of shares are taxed if the seller has a "substantial interest" (i.e., at least a 5% shareholding) in the company. Shares held by the spouse will be taken into consideration in determining whether the 5% shareholding criterion has been met. If the seller does not have a "substantial interest," but one of their (grand)children or the (grand)parents have a "substantial interest," shares of the seller are considered to be a "substantial interest." The gain is subject to a reduced rate of tax applicable to nonrecurring items of income. Liquidating dividends are taxable to the extent that they exceed paid-in capital.

If a person has a "substantial interest" or is considered to have one, then a receivable on the company is also considered a substantial interest.

Deductions

Business deductions/To the extent they are business-related and not reimbursed, an individual can deduct such items as moving expenses, travel expenses, entertainment expenses, and automobile expenses.

Expatriate exemptions/The Netherlands Antilles have regulations in place for expatriate income taxes. Fringe benefits (wages in kind) are tax exempt insofar they are less than NAf15,000 per year. Under certain conditions, the provisions can be applied for two periods of five years

Expatriates in the Netherlands Antilles are those employees who prior to the employment in the Netherlands Antilles resided for a period of at least five years in a foreign country, who are working in the offshore financial industry, the tourism industry, telecommunications industry, airline industry, the oil industry, or at universities, and who are staying in the Netherlands Antilles on a temporary basis. The employee must contribute specific expertise to the company. This expertise can be proven in two ways.

1. The employee must have completed studies at an institution of higher education or academic institution and have at least three years' working experience.
2. The employee must have at least five years' working experience and have a salary of at least NAf100,000. In order to qualify, the "specific expertise" should not be readily available in the local labor market.

The following salary elements are, among others, not included in the taxable salary.

1. Compensation for educational costs at the international or Dutch school on Curaçao or an equivalent school abroad, up to a maximum of NAf25,000 per child annually.
2. Social security premiums paid abroad if they are intended as an old-age provision.
3. Travel and moving expenses in relation to the immigration and repatriation of the employee and family, including hotel room costs, with a certain maximum.
4. Settling-in allowance of the lesser of two months' salary or NAf12,000.
5. Car rental expenses during the first two months after the arrival, up to a maximum of NAf2,700.

Nonbusiness expenses/Subject to limitations, a resident taxpayer can deduct charitable contributions, medical expenses, life insurance premiums, and savings plan payments. In addition, a resident taxpayer can deduct interest (with certain limits), pension plan contributions, social security premiums, and alimony.

Personal tax credits/Personal tax credits exists to the following amounts:

	%
Basic tax credit for every taxpayer	1,531
Additional credits:	
For married taxpayer with nonworking spouse	1,021
For taxpayers aged 60 and older	408
For children, depending on age, study, and place of residence	109 to 1,089

Tax credits

Tax credits are generally not allowed unless provided for by a specific tax treaty. Foreign taxes can be deducted from gross income.

Other taxes

Social security taxes/As of 2004 (income year 2004) the employee's share of taxes for old-age pension, widows and orphans is 5% of a maximum of US$26,100 gross wages. The employer contributes 6%. Amounts over this are not charged. Expatriates may be exempt from this tax.

Coverage for workers earning up to US$25,600 is compulsory. Contributions are 2.1% for the employee, 8.3% for the employer.

Contributions for accident insurance amount to 0.5% to 5%, depending on employment on a maximum salary of US$25,600.

The *Algemene Verzekering Byzondere Ziektekosten* (AVBZ) is a national social insurance from which the entire population of the Netherlands Antilles can derive rights. The AVBZ guarantees, among other benefits, medical care to persons suffering from a chronic disease or a mental or physical disorder. The premium charged to create the necessary funds amounts to, in general, 2% of taxable income, with a maximum charge of US$3,784 per year. The employer's share amounts to 0.5% of the employee's income, with a maximum of US$946 per year. Individuals qualifying for minimum income of US$2,921 (unmarried) or US$3,314 are charged at the rate of 1%.

Old-age pensioners are taxed at a rate of 1.5%.

Dividend withholding tax/Dividend tax is not applicable.

Inheritance and gift taxes/Gifts and receipts from an estate of an Antillean resident are taxable. Nonresidents owning real estate in the Netherlands Antilles are also subject to these taxes. The rates (2% up to 24%) depend on the amounts received and the relationship of the beneficiary to the deceased or the donor. Gifts and receipts from estates of a nonresident shareholder of a Netherlands Antilles company are not subject to Antilles estate and gift taxes.

Land and property taxes/The transfer of Netherlands Antilles–located immovable property is subject to a 4% transfer duty. A land tax is levied on real estate located in the Netherlands Antilles at an annual rate of 0.5% on the value of undeveloped land and 0.6% of the value of developed land. The 15% island surcharge also is applicable.

Taxes on capital/No capital duties are levied in the Netherlands Antilles. There is no net wealth tax for individuals or companies

Tax treaties

As part of the Kingdom of the Netherlands, the Netherlands Antilles is party to a federal tax agreement with the Netherlands and Aruba (TAK). Subject to this treaty, dividends, interest, and royalties paid out to a Netherlands Antilles recipient may qualify for reduced rates of withholding taxes in the subject countries. For an individual recipient, the Dutch withholding tax amounts to 15%.

Tax administration

Returns/Tax returns are filed on a calendar-year basis. Each spouse is taxed individually on his or her personal income (e.g., income derived from a business, a profession, or employment). Nonpersonalized income is, in principle, included in the taxable income of the spouse with the higher personal income.

Payment of tax/The Netherlands Antilles employs the pay-as-you-earn (PAYE) system, so tax is withheld from salaries.

Tax rates

Progressive rates are levied on taxable income. In addition, an island surcharge is levied on the amount of tax due. The maximum rate amounts to 57.2%.

Special reduced rates of tax apply to certain nonrecurring items of income, for example, liquidation proceeds from a company at a maximum of 39% and dividends from or capital gains on the sale of "substantial share interests" at 32.5%.

A dividend withholding tax has been introduced as of January 1, 2000. However, the provisions will become effective at a later date, but that is not likely to happen in the near future. Salaries and wages are subject to tax withholding at source. Provisional assessments can be issued during a fiscal year. Any additional tax is payable upon receipt of an assessment. Netherlands Antilles tax relief may be obtained for specific sources of foreign income.

Tax rates effective for the year 2004 are as follows.

Taxable income		Tax on	Percentage
Over (Column 1)	Not over	Column 1	on excess
0	NAf 25,100	—	15.6
NAf 25,100	36,100	NAf 3,915	23.4
36,100	47,740	6,492	32.5
47,740	63,360	10,271	39.0
63,360	106,920	63,363	46.8
106,920		36,749	57.2

INDIVIDUAL TAX CALCULATION

Calendar year 2004

Assumptions

Resident married taxpayer with two children (under 16 years old).

Tax computation

Gross income:		
Salary		NAf 160,000
Interest		14,000
Capital gain		5,000
Total gross income		179,000
Less—Tax-exempt capital gain		5,000
Adjusted gross income		174,000
Less—Itemized deductions:		
Interest	5,000	
Social security	2,500	
Alimony	8,000	15,500
Taxable income		NAf 158,500
Income tax before credits		NAf 66,252
Tax credits:		
Basic tax credit	1,531	
For nonworking spouse	1,021	
Plus two children's' credits (2 x 109)	218	
Total tax credits		(2,770)
Income tax		NAf 63,482

Note:

Exchange rate of the Netherlands Antilles guilder at January 1, 2004: US$1 = NAf1.768.

PwC contact

For additional information on taxation in New Caledonia, contact:

Jeanroger Vallé
PricewaterhouseCoopers
10 rue Jules Garnier
Nouméa, New Caledonia
Telephone: (687) 28 66 67
Fax: (687) 28 53 21
Mail address: B.P. 4213
98847 Nouméa Cedex
New Caledonia
e-mail: nccontacts@nc.pwc.com
Att: Jeanroger Vallé

Significant developments

There have been no significant taxation or regulatory developments as regards individual taxation in the last year.

Territoriality and residence

Resident individuals are subject to New Caledonian income tax on their worldwide income except as indicated in the provisions of the tax treaty between France and New Caledonia and except foreign income subject to income tax in the country of source (although such foreign income is used to compute the effective tax rate applicable to the income taxable in New Caledonia).

Nonresident individuals are subject to New Caledonian income tax on their local-source income. A 25% notional tax rate is applied to these revenues.

In accordance with the Territorial Tax Code, the following persons would be considered resident.

1. Individuals who have established their home or are present for more than 183 days each year in the territory.
2. Individuals who exercise their profession in New Caledonia, unless they demonstrate it is only on a limited basis.
3. Individuals who maintain the center of their economic interests in New Caledonia.

Gross income

Employee gross income/Income from personal services (cashed income) includes salaries, commissions, and allowances of all types, including those for housing, living expenses, and tax reimbursements, as well as cashed participations of employees in profits.

Benefits are free of tax except for benefits derived from the use of company housing or a company car. For these benefits, valuation is not challenged if it is equal to at least the following.

1. 12% of gross salary for housing.
2. XPF3,000 monthly per horsepower for a company car.

Airline fares paid by the company are not considered benefits.

No concessions are available for short-term residents.

Capital gains and investment income/Capital gains are generally tax exempt for individuals unless they result from the sale of a personal business or practice. Gross dividends received from New Caledonian companies are subject to withholding at source of 13.25%. This is a final tax. Net interest income (i.e., after deduction at source of 8% withholding tax) received from deposits with local banks or from shareholders' loans in local companies, at up to an officially published rate, is also exempt from income tax.

All other investment income, including capital gains on capitalization bonds held for less than eight years, is subject to tax. The withholding tax collected locally or in France (double taxation treaty) gives the right to a tax rebate.

Deductions

Business deductions/Individuals are allowed to deduct an amount equal to 10% of their net salary (within an XPF800,000 limit) as a standard business deduction. However, they may elect to justify actual costs.

Other deductions/There is a standard deduction of 20% of salary revenue net of the business deduction (i.e., only 80% of salary revenue net of business deduction is retained for purposes of calculating income tax). This deduction is limited to XPF1,800,000.

In addition, the following expenses are deductible.

1. Social security contributions.
2. Life insurance premiums, within an annual XPF275,000 limit.
3. Mortgage interest for a principal home, limited XPF500,000 limit, or with no limit, depending on the date of the loan.
4. Certain investment incentives, within an annual XPF1 million or XPF1.5 million limit.
5. Alimony (no limit) paid to a divorced spouse.
6. Superannuation contributions, within an annual limit of approximately XPF2.9 million (employer and employee contributions).
7. Salaries and related charges paid for domestic help, within a limit of XPF800,000.

Personal allowances/Tax is calculated on a family basis. The family includes self, spouse, and dependents. All income earned by the family is aggregated and then divided by the following, according to the status of the individual shown.

1. Bachelor, divorced, or widowed, without dependents—1.0.
2. Married with no dependents—2.0.
3. Widowed with one or more dependents—1.5.

This number is then increased by the following.

1. 1.0 per disabled child or child completing studies in France or abroad.
2. 0.5 per any other dependent child.
3. 0.5 per dependent parent.

The divided revenue is used for the scale calculation. The income tax charge determined is then multiplied by the number.

Tax credits

A standard rebate of 10% of tax, up to a limit of XPF100,000, is granted to resident taxpayers. No specific credits are available to short-term residents.

Other taxes

Social security taxes/Compulsory social security taxes are levied; the employee contribution equals 12% of gross salary within a monthly limit of approximately XPF252,000 to XPF388,500. A compulsory additional retirement fund contribution also applies.

Local taxes on income/There are no local income taxes payable in addition to central government taxes.

Tax administration

Returns/The tax year is the calendar year. Joint filing for prior-year revenue of husband and wife must be completed by April 1 each year. An additional month is allowed for individuals declaring business revenues on a nonstandard basis.

Payment of tax/There is no payroll withholding of income tax. Tax is payable by three installments: the first and second installments for year n tax are payable by March 31 of year $n + 1$ and July 31 of year $n + 1$ and are each equal to one-third of the year $n - 1$ income tax charge. The balance is generally claimed in October of year $n + 1$.

Tax rates

The tax rates applicable to the share of taxable income are as follows.

Taxable income*		Tax on	Percentage
Over	Not over	Column 1	on excess
(Column 1)			
0	XPF 1,000,000	—	0
XPF 1,000,000	1,300,000	—	5
1,300,000	1,600,000	XPF 15,000	10
1,600,000	2,200,000	45,000	15
2,200,000	2,800,000	135,000	20
2,800,000	4,500,000	255,000	30
4,500,000		765,000	40

*Total assessable income less deductions divided by the number that is a function of the number of dependents and of marital status.

INDIVIDUAL TAX CALCULATION

Based on the law and tax rates in effect at December 31, 2003

Assumptions

1. Resident who earns a salary, with wife and two children (number of shares: 2 + 0.5 + 0.5 = 3).
2. Wife and children have no income.
3. Husband's income is as follows.

	XPF
Net salary, allowances and bonuses (after compulsory contributions and superannuation contributions within the limits allowed by the Tax Code)	8,000,000
Housing benefit (12% of salary)	960,000
Other income	350,000
	9,310,000

4. Allowable deductions include the following.

	XPF
Domestic help	400,000
Mortgage interest of XPF1,000,000, limited to	500,000
	900,000

Tax computation

Determination of taxable income

Salary, allowances and bonuses		XPF 8,000,000
Fringe benefits		960,000
		8,960,000
Loss:		
Business deduction	800,000	
Standard deduction	1,632,000	2,432,000
		6,528,000
Other income		350,000
		6,878,000
Deduct:		
Salaries paid to domestic help	400,000	
Mortgage interest	500,000	900,000
Taxable income		XPF 5,978,000
Income per share (5,978,000 ÷ 3)		XPF 1,992,000

Determination of tax per share

On the first 1,600,000	XPF 45,000
On the remaining 392,000 at 15%	58,800
	XPF 103,800

Determination of total tax payable

Tax per share (103.800) x 3	XPF 311,400
Less—10% standard tax rebate	(31,140)
Tax payable	XPF 280,260
Rounded to	XPF 280,200

Note:

Exchange rate (selling) of the Pacific franc at January 1, 2004: US$1 = XPF100.
The Pacific franc is pegged to the Euro at €1 = XPF119.33.

New Zealand

PwC contacts

For additional information on taxation in New Zealand, contact:

Julia C. Hoare
PricewaterhouseCoopers
Private Bag 92162
Auckland, New Zealand
Telephone: (64) (9) 355 8000
Fax: (64) (9) 355 8001
e mail:julia.hoare@nz.pwc.com

Significant developments

In 2003 the New Zealand and Australian governments introduced new elective rules that allow trans-Tasman groups of companies to attach both imputation credits (representing New Zealand tax paid) and franking credits (representing Australian tax paid) to dividends paid to shareholders.

In 2003 the New Zealand government passed legislation that introduced progressive tax rates for employer contributions to superannuation funds and a new deferred deduction rule targeting arrangements that offer investors tax deductions greater than the amounts they have invested.

The government is proposing to exempt from New Zealand tax particular types of foreign-source income derived by migrants and returning expatriate New Zealanders for a period after their arrival in New Zealand. The proposals as currently drafted are targeted at employees, although the scope may be extended to include other migrants. Legislation is unlikely to be introduced until late 2004.

In 2003 the government proposed a new tax payment regime, which, if implemented, will change the frequency and timing of provisional tax payments. One of the proposals, a 6.7% discount on tax payable on a new business's first year income, is likely to be introduced in April 2004. The other proposals may be included in legislation to be introduced in late 2004.

Territoriality and residence

A resident of New Zealand is subject to tax on worldwide income. A nonresident is subject to tax only on income from sources in New Zealand.

Residence is determined by the following tests.

1. Permanent place of abode:
   Persons are deemed residents of New Zealand if they have a permanent place of abode in New Zealand, notwithstanding that they may also have a permanent place of abode outside New Zealand.
2. 183 days' presence:
   Persons are deemed residents of New Zealand from the date of their arrival in New Zealand if they are personally present in New Zealand for a period or periods exceeding in total 183 days in any 12-month period.

Employment and self-employed income earned in New Zealand by nonresidents is taxable unless the nonresidents' exemption or a double taxation agreement exemption applies.

Nonresidents' exemption/A nonresident's personal services income earned in New Zealand is exempt from New Zealand tax if all the following conditions apply:

1. The visit (or visits) of the nonresident do not exceed a period or periods of 92 days in total in the income year.
2. The nonresident is liable for income tax on New Zealand–source income in their country of residence.
3. The services are performed on behalf of a person who is not resident in New Zealand.

This exemption does not apply to public entertainers, such as performing artists and professional athletes. They are subject to a maximum 20% withholding tax.

Special rules apply to nonresident contractors. Withholding tax is required to be deducted from payments to nonresident contractors who do not hold valid certificates of exemption. The tax withheld is an interim tax credited against the taxpayer's ultimate income tax liability. From December 1, 2003, nonresident contractors who are present in New Zealand for less than 92 days in any 12-month period and eligible for total relief under a double taxation agreement no longer have to apply for a certificate of exemption.

Double taxation agreements/Although the terms of treaty articles vary, generally remuneration derived by a nonresident employee from personal services performed in New Zealand is not taxable in New Zealand if all the following conditions apply.

1. Recipient is present in New Zealand for not more than 183 days in any 12-month period.
2. Remuneration is paid by or on behalf of a nonresident employer.
3. Remuneration is not borne by a permanent establishment (branch) or a fixed base that the employer has or is deemed to have in New Zealand.

Gross income

Employee gross income/A resident is taxed on salary, wages, bonuses, tax reimbursements, allowances, and retirement gratuities received in cash, regardless of where payment is made. Nonresidents are taxed only to the extent their employment income is earned in New Zealand (i.e., services are performed in New Zealand), regardless of where payment is made and whether it is remitted to New Zealand. Allowances paid in cash that are no more than a reimbursement of expenses incurred within employment are generally not taxable. The benefit arising from the use of an employer-provided motor vehicle, a low-interest loan or discounted goods or services is not taxable to the employee, but the value of a benefit from the provision of shares or options, lodging or housing by an employer is taxable to the employee. Other benefits provided to an employee in a nonmonetary form are generally not taxable in the employee's hands (see "Fringe benefit tax" below).

Resident individuals are subject to New Zealand tax on their overseas income. A credit is available for foreign tax paid on that income up to the level of New Zealand tax payable.

Capital gains and investment income/There is no capital gains tax. However, the income tax legislation specifically includes various forms of gain that would otherwise be considered a capital gain within the definition of "income." Gross income includes gains on the sale of real estate in certain circumstances and on personal property where the taxpayer acquired the property for resale, or deals in such property, or where a profit-making purpose or scheme can be deemed or imputed. Gains on financial instruments are taxable when realized or when the instruments are deemed to have been disposed of. Above certain threshold limits, such gains are taxable on an accrual (yield-to-maturity) basis, which may include unrealized gains.

Rent derived from property is gross income. Deductions are allowed for expenses incurred in deriving the rental income.

New Zealand residents holding a 10% or greater interest in a controlled foreign company (CFC) include in their taxable income the income (calculated under New Zealand tax rules) of the CFC multiplied by the percentage their interest represents in the company.

A foreign investment fund (FIF) regime applies to nonexcepted interests in foreign investment funds. Resident holders of such interests are taxed on the change in value of the interest over the income year, together with distributions received. Generally, income from interests in CFCs and FIFs resident in the following countries is excluded: Australia, Canada, Germany, Japan, Norway, the United Kingdom, and the United States. No distinction is made between passive and business income.

Officials have proposed significant changes to the taxation of offshore portfolio investments and the FIF regime. Any changes are unlikely to be enacted before 2005.

Investment income derived by a nonresident from a New Zealand source is taxable in New Zealand, but where that person is a resident of a country that has a double taxation agreement with New Zealand, the tax on dividends and interest income is generally limited to 15% or 10% of that gross income under the provisions of the treaty. The foreign investor tax credit (FITC) regime effectively eliminates nonresident withholding tax (NRWT) on fully imputed dividends paid by a New Zealand company to a nonresident. The FITC regime provides that total New Zealand tax paid on a nonresident investor's earnings through a New Zealand company can be limited to 33% (the company tax rate). It does not operate by exemption from NRWT. Rather, where a dividend is imputed, the paying company qualifies for a reduction in its income tax if it pays a supplementary dividend. The combination of reduced income tax plus NRWT on both dividends can result in a total New Zealand tax on the earnings of only 33%.

Deductions

Business deductions/No deduction is allowed for expenditure to gain income from employment. Deductions are available for expenditure incurred in deriving gross income (other than employment income) or in carrying on a business. Subject to certain exemptions, entertainment expenditure is only 50% deductible.

Nonbusiness expenses/No deduction is permitted for medical, superannuation, or insurance contributions.

Personal allowances/Common rebates include the following.

	Maximum rebate
	NZ$
Child taxpayer rebate	156
Charitable donation rebate	630
Housekeeper rebate	310

In addition, tax credits for family assistance are available. These credits are aimed at low- and middle-income families. They are generally paid in fortnightly installments with any under or overpayment being calculated annually. Amounts received are not taxable.

Tax credits

Tax credits are available for the following.

1. Tax withheld at source:
   a. Deduction from employee wages;
   b. Installments (provisional tax) paid by business taxpayers;
   c. Resident withholding tax (RWT) on interest and dividends paid to residents;
   d. Nonresident withholding tax on interest, dividends, and royalties where the withholding tax is not a final tax.
2. Tax paid by a CFC on the income that is attributed to New Zealand shareholders.
3. Foreign tax paid on foreign-source income derived by a resident (up to the level of New Zealand tax payable).
4. Imputation credits. To avoid double taxation of income derived by a corporation, the tax it pays on its income is imputed to the shareholder. Where a dividend is accompanied by an imputation credit, tax is payable on the gross dividend (dividend received plus imputation credits), with the imputation credits available to offset the tax. Imputation credits cannot be utilized by nonresident shareholders. However, dividend withholding payment credits, which arise from a withholding tax on foreign dividends received by resident corporations, can be utilized by nonresidents.
5. See also "Personal allowances" above for permitted rebates.

Other taxes

Accident insurance/A statutory-based scheme of accident insurance is funded in part by premiums payable by employers and employees. Premiums paid by employers (including the self-employed) fund insurance for work-related accidents. Premiums are payable at a rate set for the industrial category on leviable earnings up to a maximum of NZ$87,185 per employee.

Nonwork accident insurance is funded by premiums paid by employees and the self-employed. The premium is a flat NZ$1.20 per NZ$100, including goods and services tax (GST), on taxable earnings up to a maximum of NZ$88,728. The maximum levy is therefore NZ$1,064.

Fringe benefit tax/Employers are subject to a tax-deductible fringe benefit tax (FBT) on the value of noncash fringe benefits provided to their employees. Employers can elect to pay FBT at flat rates (64% on attributed benefits; 49% on pool benefits, i.e., those benefits that cannot be attributed to a particular employee) applied against the value of the benefit, or can attribute fringe benefits to individual employees and pay

FBT based on each employee's marginal tax rate. Under the attribution option, the applicable FBT rate depends on the net remuneration (including fringe benefits) paid to the employee. The attribution calculation treats the fringe benefit as if it were paid in cash and calculates FBT as the notional increase in income that otherwise would have arisen. The multirates are as follows.

Net remuneration	**FBT rate**
	%
NZ$8,075 or less	17.65
NZ$8,076 to NZ$30,590	26.58
NZ$30,591 to NZ$45,330	49.25
More than NZ$45,330	63.93

Fringe benefits include cars available for private use, loans at below prescribed interest rates, contributions to medical insurance schemes and contributions to foreign superannuation schemes. Employers' contributions to an approved superannuation fund (excludes foreign schemes) are subject to a withholding tax of 33%. Fringe benefit tax is also applicable to benefits received by an employee from a third party where there is an arrangement between the employer and the third party, and where the benefit would be subject to fringe benefit tax if it had been provided by the employer.

The government has undertaken a review of FBT and proposed significant changes, particularly in relation to the treatment of motor vehicles and car parks. Any changes are expected to be introduced in 2005.

Goods and services tax/A form of value-added tax, GST, applies to most supplies of goods and services. The narrow category of exempt supplies includes financial services. The rate applied to taxable supplies is 12.5% or 0%. The 0% rate applies to only a few supplies, including exports. Two significant changes were enacted in 2003: a "reverse charge" mechanism that requires the self assessment of GST on the value of services imported by some GST registered persons and the zero rating of financial services supplied to other registered businesses.

Superannuation fund withdrawal tax/An effective tax of 5% applies to amounts withdrawn from superannuation funds, to the extent the withdrawals include the return of superannuation contributions made by an employer on an employee's behalf after April 1, 2000. The tax also applies to withdrawals of earnings derived after April 1, 2000 on employer contributions.

Tax administration

Returns/The New Zealand tax year ends on March 31. Returns (if required) must be filed by July 7 each year, depending on the income type and/or the country of source. Individuals file separate returns. There is no provision for joint returns for husband and wife. Failure to file a return (if required) may result in prosecution and penalties. There is no requirement to file a return for most individuals who earn only employment income, or income where tax is deducted at source at the appropriate rate.

Payment of tax/With the exception of employee shares/options income, employment income (source deduction income) is subject to income tax under a pay-as-you-earn (PAYE) system. If tax on nonsource deduction income exceeded NZ$2,500 in the prior year, provisional tax payments are required during the year, generally on the basis of the prior year's tax uplifted by 5%. Provisional tax is generally paid in advance in three installments. New rules allow taxpayers to pool their provisional tax payments with those of other taxpayers through an arrangement with a commercial intermediary. Tax pooling allows underpayments to be offset by overpayments within the same pool and vice versa. The new rules apply from April 1, 2003.

Any balance of tax (terminal tax) payable arising from the filing of a return to March 31 is generally not due for payment until the following February 7 (for those linked to a tax agent, terminal tax is due on April 7). Tax not paid by the due date is subject to an initial late payment penalty of 5%, plus an incremental penalty of 1% per month until the tax is paid. The initial late payment penalty is staggered so that 1% will apply on the day after due date and a further 4% applies if the tax is still outstanding after seven days.

Where provisional tax paid is less than the amount of income tax deemed due on that installment date, interest is imposed. Where provisional tax is overpaid, interest is payable to the taxpayer. The interest expense is deductible for tax purposes to business taxpayers, and interest earned on overpaid terminal tax is gross income for tax purposes. Interest rates effective from November 8, 2001 are 11.93% on underpayments and 4.83% on overpayments.

Tax rates

Year ending March 31, 2004

Taxable income		Tax on	Percentage
Over (Column 1)	**Not over**	**Column 1**	**on excess**
0	NZ$ 38,000	—	19.5
NZ$ 38,000	60,000	NZ$ 7,410	33.0
60,000		14,670	39.0

INDIVIDUAL TAX CALCULATION

Income year 2004 (year ending March 31, 2004)

Assumptions

Salary earner (resident).

Tax computation

Gross salary		NZ$ 153,000
Add:		
Housing benefit (1)	5,000	
Cost-of-living allowance (1)	5,000	
Taxable reimbursement	5,000	
Foreign-source interest	3,100	18,100
Taxable income		NZ$ 171,100
Tax thereon		NZ$ 57,999
Plus ACC (accident compensation) levy		1,064
		59,063
Less—Rebates:		
Deductible donations to New Zealand charities (33%)		(630)
		58,433
Less:		
Tax and ACC withheld from salary	57,820	
Foreign tax credit	310	(58,130)
Tax to pay		NZ$ 303

Notes:

1. Depending on the individual's specific circumstances, housing and other allowances may be able to be paid tax free.
2. Exchange rate of the New Zealand dollar at December 31, 2003: US$1 = NZ$1.52896.

PwC contact

For additional information on taxation in Norway, contact:

Tore Østebrød
Advokatfirmaet PricewaterhouseCoopers DA
Karenslyst allé 12
0245 Oslo, Norway
Telephone: (47) 95 26 06 76
Fax: (47) 24 06 26 76
e-mail: tore.ostebrod@no.pwc.com

Significant developments

There have been no significant tax or regulatory developments regarding individual taxation in the past year.

Territoriality and residence

Norway taxes its residents on their worldwide income and capital. Nonresidents working in Norway are taxed on their compensation attributable to Norwegian sources. Resident status is obtained when an alien intends to reside in Norway other than temporarily. A stay of more than six months is always considered to be residence.

Gross income

Employee gross income/Nonresident aliens are taxed on salary earned for work performed in Norway, irrespective of where payment is made or whether it is remitted. Compensation relating to work performed outside Norway is not taxed. All benefits paid by the employer (e.g., living allowances, housing allowances, tax reimbursements, paid vacation, travel costs for nonbusiness visits to the employee's country of origin) are subject to tax.

Capital gains and investment income/Capital gains on portfolio investments are taxed at a flat rate of 28%. Norwegian real estate capital gains are always taxable, regardless of residence.

Dividends received by domestic shareholders from domestic companies are subject to income tax at the rate of 28%. Such shareholders are, however, given a credit for tax paid by the distributing company, with the effect that they pay zero tax.

Foreign-source dividends received by a domestic shareholder are taxed as ordinary income unless otherwise decreed in the relevant tax treaty. Foreign withholding tax is credited against Norwegian tax.

A withholding tax of 25% is levied on dividends paid by a Norwegian company to nonresident aliens. The withholding tax can be reduced by the relevant tax treaty.

Deductions

Business deductions/If not reimbursed, an alien (resident or nonresident) can deduct all business-connected expenses. These expenses comprise such items as moving expenses, traveling expenses, and automobile expenses. Entertainment expenses will not be allowed as a deduction. In practice, this will apply only to individuals who are not employed, for example, consultants.

Nonbusiness expenses/An alien (resident or nonresident) can deduct mortgage and other interest expenses (limitations may exist for interest on foreign loans, for nonresidents etc.), expenses incurred in producing income, private pension premiums (maximum NOK40,000), alimony, and commuting expenses in excess of NOK9,200. In addition, a minimum allowance (minimum, NOK4,000; maximum, NOK47,500) can be claimed as a deduction. An alien who intends to be in Norway for less than four years can elect to take a standard deduction instead of itemized deductions. The standard deduction is calculated as 15% of gross taxable income (earned income only). If the standard deduction is elected, only the minimum allowance and contributions to company pension schemes may be deducted.

Personal allowances/No personal allowances can be claimed when calculating net income subject to tax.

Tax credits

Resident aliens can take income taxes paid to a foreign country as a credit against their tax liability (subject to limitations and tax treaty conditions). In practice, this applies only to income earned in nontax-treaty countries and to dividends. A nonresident alien would not be entitled to a foreign tax credit.

Other taxes

Social security taxes/The taxpayer contributes to the social security system through a social security tax, which is calculated on gross salary income (including benefits-in-kind) at a rate of 7.8%. The employer pays an additional 14.1% of the employee's gross income as a contribution to the social security scheme. A solidarity tax of 12.5% on gross income is payable on income (salary-related) in excess of 16G (one G is at present NOK56,861).

Local taxes on income/See "Tax rates" below.

Tax administration

Returns/Joint filing with income splitting is not permitted. If both spouses have earned income, each files a separate return and is taxed in Class 1 as a single taxpayer. Otherwise, they file one return and are taxed in Class 2 as a married couple. Tax returns must be filed on a calendar-year basis. A tax return (PSA) is to be completed by the end of April. In the PSA, all available details have been imposed by the tax authorities, and the taxpayer must check the return carefully and delete or add items in accordance with the facts.

Payment of tax/There is income tax withholding from salaries. Generally, if taxpayers have sizable income not subject to withholding, they will be required to make quarterly payments of estimated taxes.

Tax rates

Local taxes on income/All municipalities are separate taxing authorities and impose a local tax at an aggregate rate of 28% on taxable income in excess of NOK65,800 for a married person whose spouse is not working (Tax Class 2). This band is NOK32,900 for a single person or married couple where both are working (Tax Class 1).

Top tax/An additional tax (state tax) on salary income, including benefits in kind, is assessed. For Class 2 taxpayers, top tax is 13.5% of earned income between NOK378,600 and NOK906,900 and 19.5% in excess of NOK906,900. For Class 1 taxpayers the tax free band is NOK354,300, increasing to 19.5% on income in excess of NOK906,900.

INDIVIDUAL TAX CALCULATION

Fiscal 2004

Assumptions

Resident alien husband and wife; one spouse earns all of the income.

Tax computation

Gross income:		
Salary		NOK 1,000,000
Interest		60,000
Dividends from abroad		10,000
Gain on sale of shares		30,000
Total gross income		1,100,000
Less (choosing the 15% standard deduction):		
Minimum allowance	47,500	
15% standard deduction on 1,000,000	150,000	
Contribution to pension scheme (paid by employee)	18,900	216,400
Taxable income		NOK 883,600
Income tax:		
Local tax (municipal tax)—28% of (883,600 – 65,800)		NOK 228,984
Social security		78,000
Top tax—13.5% of (906,900 – 378,600)		71,320
Top tax—19.5% (1,000,000 – 906,900)		18,154
		396,458
Less—Withholding tax on foreign dividend (25%)		(2,500)
Income tax for married couple		NOK 393,958

Note:

Exchange rate of the krone at December 31, 2003: US$1 = NOK6.675.

Oman

PwC contact

For additional information on Oman, contact:

Jeffrey Todd
PricewaterhouseCoopers
Hatat House, Suites 205–210
(P.O. Box 3075, PC112)
Ruwi, Sultanate of Oman
Telephone: (968) 56 37 17
Fax: (968) 56 44 08
e-mail: jeff.todd@om.pwc.com

Absence of taxation

Income tax is not imposed on individuals in Oman.

Note

Exchange rate of the Omani rial at December 31, 2003: US$1 = RO0.385.

PwC contact

For additional information on taxation in Pakistan, contact:

Syed Shabbar Zaidi
A.F. Ferguson & Co.
State Life Building 1-C
I.I. Chundrigar Road
Karachi 74000 Pakistan
Telephone: (92) (21) 242 6682-6, 2426711-5
Fax: (92) (21) 241 5007, 242 7938
e-mail: s.m.shabbar.zaidi@pk.pwc.com

Significant developments

The Income Tax Ordinance, 2001 has been promulgated in Pakistan, effective from July 1, 2002. The following information on taxation in Pakistan is according to that new law and is accurate as of January 31, 2004.

Territoriality and residence

Liability to tax varies according to the tax residential status of the individual in the tax year (July to June). Individuals are resident in Pakistan in a tax year if they are in Pakistan for a period amounting in all to 182 days or more, or are employees or officials of the Federal or Provincial Government of Pakistan. Individuals who do not qualify as residents are assessed as nonresidents.

Residents are taxed on worldwide income, except where under a double taxation treaty the income earned outside Pakistan is not taxable in Pakistan. A foreign tax credit is allowed in Pakistan for tax paid abroad on foreign-source income. This relief is allowed at the lower of tax at the average rate of tax in Pakistan and the foreign income tax paid. Foreign-source income of a resident, who is not a citizen of Pakistan, is exempt if the individual is resident only by virtue of employment and presence in Pakistan does not exceed three years. This exemption does not apply in the case of income from a business established in Pakistan and foreign-source income that is brought into or received in Pakistan.

A nonresident is taxed only on Pakistan-source income.

Gross income

Employee gross income/Salary is Pakistan-source income and is taxable in Pakistan if it results from employment exercised in Pakistan or if it is paid by or on behalf of the Federal Government, a Provincial Government or a local authority in Pakistan. Salary is the amount received by an employee from an employment, whether of a revenue or capital nature. It can include leave pay, payment in lieu of leave, overtime, bonuses, commissions, fees, gratuities, work condition supplements, monetary and nonmonetary perquisites, any allowance except that solely expended in the performance of employee's duties of employment, profits in lieu of or in addition to salary, pension, annuity, and tax reimbursements. In addition, amounts or perquisites paid or provided by an associate of the employer, a third party under an arrangement with the employer or an associate of the employer, a past employer, or a prospective employer or payments to an associate of the employee are also to be considered as salary. The extent of taxability and exclusions from income of some perquisites are discussed under "Deductions" below.

Capital gains and investment income/Capital gains on the sale, exchange or transfer of movable capital assets are taxable. However, exemptions apply to movable property held for personal use (excluding certain items like jewelry, paintings, etc.), shares of public companies and modaraba certificates. Capital gains tax does not apply to stock-in- trade. Capital gains, other than on statutorily depreciable assets, realized within one year of acquisition are fully taxed; after one year, 75% of such gains are taxed and 25% are exempt.

All cash dividends are to be taxed at the rate of 10% as a separate block of income. Stock splits are not considered as income.

Capital gains and investment income earned outside Pakistan are not taxable in the case of nonresidents.

Employees share scheme/The value of a right or option to acquire shares under an employees share scheme is not chargable to tax. However, when an employee is issued shares under the scheme, the value of resulting benefit is taxed as "salary" income.

Deductions

The following deductions are allowed.

1. Utilities—Reimbursement for utilities or a utilities allowance is exempt from tax up to 10% of basic salary.
2. Medical allowance or reimbursement is exempt upto 10% of basic salary.
3. Rebate at the average rate of tax is allowed on donations made to approved nonprofit organizations on the lower of donation value and 30% of the individual's taxable income.
4. Personal expenditure on medical services incurred by a resident individual are allowed as a deduction from total income, provided the expenditure is supported by documentary evidence. The allowance, however, is not to exceed lower of PRs30,000 and 10% of basic salary.

Tax credits

A foreign tax credit is granted for foreign tax paid on income accrued outside Pakistan, as outlined above under "Territoriality and residence" above.

Other taxes

Social security taxes/No social security tax is payable in Pakistan.

Local taxes on income/The only significant tax on salaries is federal income tax.

Tax administration

Returns/All taxpayers must file returns separately. Joint returns cannot be filed. Employees are required to file their returns only on a fiscal-year basis (July to June). Every resident taxpayer whose last declared or assessed income is more than PRs200,000 is required to file a wealth statement along with the return of income; the Commissioner can also require any person to furnish this statement.

Payment of tax/There is income tax withholding from salaries. The amount to be withheld is arrived at by applying to the salary paid the average rate of tax on the estimated income of the employee for the fiscal year.

Tax rates

Where total income includes agricultural income up to PRs80,000 of total income

Taxable income		Tax on	Percentage
Over (Column 1)	Not over	Column 1	on excess
0	PRs 80,000	—	—
PRs 80,000	150,000		7.5
150,000	300,000	PRs 5,250	12.5
300,000	400,000	24,000	20.0
400,000	700,000	44,000	25.0
700,000		119,000	35.0

Where agricultural income comprises more than PRs80,000 of total income

Taxable income		Tax on	Percentage
Over (Column 1)	Not over	Column 1	on excess
0	PRs 150,000	—	7.5
PRs 150,000	300,000	PRs 11,250	12.5
300,000	400,000	30,000	20.0
400,000	700,000	50,000	25.0
700,000		125,000	35.0

Rebate/A rebate, based on the amount of income tax liability calculated before the rebate, is allowable. The amount ranges from 5% (if salary is in excess of PRs1 million) to 70% (where salary is between PRs60,000 to PRs80,000).

INDIVIDUAL TAX CALCULATION

Income year ended June 30, 2003

Assumptions

An expatriate considered resident for Pakistan tax purposes earns the income. There are no special exemptions for marital status or children.

Tax computation

Basic salary		PRs 2,400,000
Rent paid by the employer in respect of accommodation provided to the employee		120,000
Utility allowance	300,000	
Less—Exemption (up to 10% of basic salary)	(240,000)	60,000
Addition for company-maintained car (1)		60,000
Adjusted salary income		2,640,000
Additional income:		
Dividends	5,000	
Long-term capital gain (75% of which is taxable)	50,000	55,000
Taxable income		PRs 2,695,000
Tax on dividend income (PRs5,000 @ 10%)		PRs 500
On balance of PRs2,690,000		815,500
		816,000
Less—Rebate @ 5%		(40,800)
Total tax payable		PRs 775,200

Notes:

1. Amounting to 5% of the employer's cost of acquiring car and for its running costs (partly used for business purposes and partly for private).
2. Exchange rate of the rupee at March 31, 2004: US$1 = PRs59.593.

PwC contact

For additional information on taxation in Panama, contact:

Antonio E. Latorraca
PricewaterhouseCoopers
Samuel Lewis Avenue & 55 East Street
Obarrio, Panama
(P.O. Box 6-4493
El Dorado, Panama)
Telephone: (507) 206-9200
Fax: (507) 264-5627
e-mail: antonio.latorraca@pa.pwc.com

Significant developments

Value-added tax (VAT) paid during the fiscal year in the acquisition of goods and services can now be applied as a direct credit against income tax.

Territoriality and residence

Panama's tax system is based on a territorial concept of income. Citizens and residents are taxed on income earned from Panama sources. Nonresidents are taxed only on income from Panama sources, and the tax on any type of income paid to a nonresident must be withheld by the payer. Citizens, residents, and nonresidents are not taxed on exempt income (i.e., interest on Panamanian government securities and interest on savings accounts and time deposits maintained with banks established in Panama).

According to this territorial principle of taxation, compensation received in respect of duties performed wholly overseas will not be subject to Panama individual income tax. The system for determining this exempt income is to consider income related to the days spent outside Panama on job-related duties as foreign source, so that it is not liable to tax.

Gross income

Employee gross income/An employee is taxed on compensation earned for work done in Panama, regardless of where payment is made or received.

Compensation includes salary, premiums, profit distributions, living allowances, housing allowances, tax reimbursements, benefits in kind, house, car, retirement benefits, and any other compensation in kind. There is no concession to a foreign employee.

Capital gains and investment income/Capital gains on the sale of real estate located in Panama and on securities not registered with the National Securities Commission are taxable.

Capital gains arising from the sale of real estate are subject to a specific tax rule. Capital gains from the sale of shares, bonds, and other securities represent an integral part of the taxpayer's gross income, unless these securities are exempt.

Investment income from a Panama source, such as dividends, is subject to a 10% withholding tax. However, dividends on bearer shares are subject to 20% withholding tax.

Deductions

Business deductions/Unreimbursed items such as moving expenses, business-connected travel expenses, and business entertainment expenses are not deductible against the employee's compensation income.

A fixed allowance (representation expenses) can be given to employees as a part of salary. This allowance is considered to be gross taxable income, and the taxpayer may deduct 25% of this allowance as expenses up to a maximum of B/. 6,000 per year. Representation expenses are not subject to social security and educational insurance taxes for either the employee or the employer.

Nonbusiness expenses/Interest paid on mortgage loans for homes or for home improvements on residences located in Panama is deductible; the maximum deduction allowed is B/.15,000 annually, provided the interest payment does not classify as preferential interest for new homes. Interest paid on loans for financing education is deductible if duly documented. The educational insurance tax (see below) is deductible. Medical expenses are deductible, provided they were incurred in Panama and are duly documented. Donations to local educational and charitable institutions are deductible, provided the deductions are authorized by the law establishing such institutions or by the Income Tax Department. Dues paid to nonprofit associations or organizations in Panama are also deductible expenses. Contributions to private funds (savings and/or retirement) are deductible from income tax up to 10% of total gross income for the period.

Personal allowances/An individual who is not married is entitled to a personal exemption of B/.800; married couples filing a joint return are entitled to an exemption of B/.1,600. An additional exemption of B/.250 is granted for each dependent. These exemptions are applicable in determining taxable income.

Value-added tax/50% of total VAT paid during the fiscal year on the acquisition of goods and services can be applied as a direct credit against income tax, up to 10% of income tax payable.

Tax credits

No tax credits are allowed for income taxes paid to foreign countries.

Other taxes

Social security taxes/Social security tax is assessed at a rate of 7.25% on wages and other compensation paid, including compensation-in-kind. However, compensation-in-kind from the employer is subject to social security tax. There is no maximum limit on the taxable amount.

Educational insurance tax/Educational insurance tax is assessed at the rate of 1.25% on salaries and wages paid to be withheld by the employer. On income not subject to withholding tax, such as benefits in-kind, the employee will be required to pay tax of 2.75% on the income tax return. There is no maximum limit on the taxable amount.

Local taxes on income/There are no local taxes on income.

Tax administration

Returns/Husbands and wives can file joint returns. Joint filing is not advantageous if both spouses earn separate income, because the tax rates are graduated. The only advantage of filing a joint return for a couple with a single source of taxable income is that in a joint return, there is an exemption of B/.1,600, while in a single return, the exemption is B/.800.

All taxpayers, except employees having only one source of income from wages, salary, or other remuneration for personal services and whose monthly income tax is deducted by the employer, must file a tax return on a calendar-year basis.

Employees having only one source of income from personal services who want to take advantage of nonbusiness expenses must file a tax return. Employees who receive representation expenses are also required to file a tax return.

Tax returns and estimated income for the current year must be filed on forms prescribed and supplied by the Income Tax Department.

Payment of tax/There is income tax withholding from wages, salaries, and other remuneration for personal services.

The total amount of the taxpayer's estimated income tax is payable annually in three equal installments on June 30, September 30, and December 31. If the estimated amount paid exceeds the actual amount computed at the end of the year, the excess is applied against the current year's estimated income tax or against taxes due in subsequent years. If there is still an overpayment after applying the excess to the estimate for the current year, a refund may be obtained, provided the tax authorities determine that no additional tax is due.

Tax rates

Taxable income		Tax on	Percentage
Over	Not over	Column 1	on excess
(Column 1)			
B/. 3,250	B/. 4,000	B/. 130	4.0
4,000	6,000	160	6.5
6,000	10,000	290	11.0
10,000	15,000	730	16.5
15,000	20,000	1,555	19.0
20,000	30,000	2,505	22.0
30,000	40,000	4,705	27.0
40,000	50,000	7,405	30.0
50,000	200,000	10,405	33.0
200,000		59,905	30.0

INDIVIDUAL TAX CALCULATION

Calendar year 2004

Assumptions

Resident married taxpayer with four children.

Tax computation

Basic Salary		US$ 80,000
Less—Deductions:		
Charitable contributions	500	500
		79,500
Less—Personal exemptions:		
Joint return	1,600	
Children (250 x 4)	1,000	
Interest on mortgage	15,000	
Educational tax withheld and paid (80,000 x 1.25%)	1,000	18,600
Net taxable income		US$ 60,900
Tax thereon:		
On first 50,000		US$ 10,405
On remaining 10,900 at 33%		3,597
		14,002
Less—VAT deduction (1)		(1,400)
Tax payable		US$ 12,602

Notes:

1. Corresponding to the 50% of total VAT paid during the year on the acquisition of goods and services, limited to 10% of income tax payable.
2. Exchange rate of the balboa at January 1, 2004: US$1 = B/.1.00.

PwC contacts

For additional information on taxation in Paraguay, contact:

Daniel O. Elicetche
E. Rubén Taboada
PricewaterhouseCoopers
General Díaz 521
6 Piso, Edificio Internacional Faro
Asunción, Paraguay
Telephone: (595) (21) 445 003
Fax: (595) (21) 444 893
e-mail: daniel.o.elicetche@py.pwc.com
ruben.taboada@py.pwc.com

Note

The following information on taxation in Paraguay is accurate as of December 31, 2003. For subsequent developments, refer to the contact above.

Absence of taxation on income or earnings

Income tax is not imposed on individuals in Paraguay.

At present there is a proposed law before the Paraguayan Congress that establishes some changes to the tax system. The proposal includes a personal income tax with a rate of 10%. This new tax would be imposed on income from personal services on a dependent and nondependent employment relationship basis and realized capital earnings, if they exceed a minimum established amount.

Exchange rate

The free market exchange rate (applicable for any kind of transaction) of the guaraní at December 31, 2003: US$1 = PYG6.170.

Peru

PwC contacts

For additional information on taxation in Peru, contact:

Rudolf Röder
Monica Nieva
Walter Aguirre
PricewaterhouseCoopers
Canaval y Moreyra 380, Floor 19
Lima 27, Peru
Telephone: (511) 2116500
Fax: (511) 4422073
e-mail: rudolf.roeder@pe.pwc.com
monica.nieva@pe.pwc.com
walter.aguirre@pe.pwc.com

Significant developments

There have been no significant tax or regulatory developments regarding individual taxation in the past year.

Territoriality and residence

For income tax purposes, individuals are classified as domiciled and nondomiciled, depending on if they are Peruvian nationality individuals residing permanently in Peru or foreign individuals who have resided in Peru for a continuous period of two or more years. Temporary absences of up to 90 days in the taxable year do not interrupt the continuity of such residence. Domicile is lost after two years of residency abroad or when the individual obtains a resident visa in another country and has left Peru, or has a labor contract to work abroad for a period of not less than one year.

In general, changes in the domiciled or nondomiciled status of an individual will become effective for tax purposes only as of the next calendar year.

A domiciled individual is liable for Peruvian tax with respect to his or her worldwide income, whereas a nondomiciled individual is liable to tax only with respect to Peruvian income.

Gross income

Employee gross income/Gross income from employment consists of salaries, bonuses, housing, school allowances, and, in general, any payment in cash or in kind earned by an employee in Peru, regardless of nationality, length of residence in Peru and whether the remuneration is earned or paid outside Peru.

Foreigners receive the same tax treatment as Peruvians, without any special concessions; however, moving costs and accommodation expenses during the first three months after arrival in Peru, as well as the cost of home-leave fares, are not deemed taxable income. Severance indemnities in the amounts provided by law and indemnities for vacations not taken that are paid to terminated employees are excluded from income tax.

Capital gains and investment income/Peruvian-source interest, rentals, royalties, and capital gains are subject to general income tax and must be computed to determine the individual's taxable income.

Dividends and profits distributions are subject to a withholding of 4.1% upon distribution.

Deductions

Business deductions/Peruvian legislation allows companies to pay directly or to reimburse business expenses incurred by executives. Consequently, deductions for moving, travel, automobile, and other expenses are not permitted to individuals. Likewise, under certain conditions, donations can be deducted.

Nonbusiness expenses/Individuals who obtain income other than remuneration are entitled to certain deductions in accordance with the type of income obtained. In the case of rentals, they can deduct 20% of the income. In the case of royalty payments, they can deduct 10% of gross royalties received. Independent professionals can deduct 20% of gross revenues up to a limit of 24 tax units, (this deduction is not applicable to the fees received by company directors, proxies, executors among others).

Personal allowances/Domiciled individuals who receive income from employment or independent professional income are entitled to a total deduction equivalent to seven tax units (UIT) from their gross income. For year 2004, one tax unit is equivalent to S/.3,200 (approximately US$915).

Tax credit

Subject to certain limits established by law, taxpayers may claim a credit for income taxes paid abroad.

Other taxes

Social security taxes/The social welfare fund comprises the Pension Fund (National Pension Fund or Private Pension Fund) and the Health System. With regard to the Pension Fund, the employee must choose between the National and Private Funds.

Extraordinary Solidarity Tax/Extraordinary Solidarity Tax (*Impuesto Extraordinario de Solidaridad*—IES) must be paid by the employer, at a rate of 1.7% of employee remuneration. Independent professionals are liable for the IES at the 1.7% rate.

The social security and IES rates will be applied to the employee's monthly salary as follows.

	Employer	Employee
	%	%
National Pension Fund	—	13
Private Pension Fund	—	12*
Health System	9	—
Extraordinary Solidarity Tax	1.7	—

*Each pension fund will charge an insurance and commission rate of approximately 4%, resulting in a total contribution of approximately 12%.

The employee's contributions are not deductible in determining taxable income.

Local taxes on income/Income tax is the only tax assessable on income. There are no state or municipal income taxes.

Peru

Tax administration

Returns/Income tax returns must be generally filed by the first week of April. Late filing is subject to fines; late payment is subject to moratorium interest. Individuals earning only income from employment are not obliged to file tax returns.

Payment of tax/Income tax on remuneration must be withheld. It must be paid on account on a monthly basis. Any balance due must be paid by individuals according to the rules established by the tax administration.

Tax rates

Income tax rates are as shown below. A 7 UIT deduction is available.

Taxable amount*	Tax rate
	%
Up to 27 UIT(S/.86,400)	15
From 27 to 54 UIT (S/.86,401 to 172,800)	21
Over 54 UIT (S/.172,801)	30

*For year 2004, one tax unit is equivalent to S/. 3,200 (approximately US$915).

INDIVIDUAL TAX CALCULATION

Calendar year 2004

Assumptions

1. Resident Individual domiciled taxpayer.
2. Salary: US$100,000.
3. Exchange rate of the nuevo sol: US$1= S/.3.50.

Tax computation

Gross income		S/. 350,000
Actual deduction (7 UIT) (1)		22,400
Taxable income		S/. 327,600
Income tax thereon		
15% on first 27 UIT	12,960	
21% on 27 to 54 UIT	18,144	
30% on income over 54 UIT	46,440	
		S/. 77,544

Notes:

1. Under Peruvian legislation, there are no additional deductions or allowances for marital status and children.
2. Exchange rate of the nuevo sol at January 1, 2004: US$1 = S/.3.463.

PwC contact

For additional information on taxation in the Philippines, contact:

Tammy H. Lipana
PricewaterhouseCoopers Philippines
29th Floor Philamlife Tower
8767 Paseo de Roxas
1226 Makati City, Philippines
Telephone: (63) (2) 845 27 28, (63) (2) 459 2001 (direct)
Fax: (63) (2) 845 28 06
e-mail: tammy.lipana@ph.pwcglobal.com

Significant developments

Effective January 1, 2004, the withholding tax rate on professional fees, talent fees, and so on, for services rendered by individuals has been changed to 5% of gross income exceeding P720,000 for the year and 10% for lower amount.

In 2003, value-added tax (VAT) was imposed (after five years of deferment) on sale of services by persons engaged in the practice of a profession or calling and professional services rendered by general professional partnerships; entertainers, radio and television broadcasters and choreographers; musical, radio, movie, television, and stage directors; professional athletes; and customs, real estate, stock and immigration and commercial brokers. Beginning January 1, 2004, however, the services of the following individuals are VAT exempt:

1. Medical doctors duly registered with the Professional Regulation Commission.
2. Lawyers duly registered with the Integrated Bar of the Philippines.

Tax treaties with the following countries came into force or were renegotiated with Bahrain, Bangladesh, the Czech Republic, Sweden, and Vietnam.

Territoriality and residence

The Philippines taxes its resident citizens on their worldwide income. Nonresident citizens and aliens, whether or not resident in the Philippines, are taxed only on income from sources within the Philippines.

A resident alien is an individual who is stateless or is a national of another country and who lives in the Philippines with no definite intention as to length of stay, but who is not a mere transient or sojourner. An expatriate working in the Philippines on a contract for an indefinite period potentially falls into this category.

Most expatriates will be classified as nonresident aliens, because their contract will be for a specified period of engagement. A nonresident alien individual who comes to the Philippines and stays there for more than 180 days during any calendar year will be deemed a nonresident alien engaged in trade or business in the Philippines. If the aggregate stay in the Philippines during any calendar year does not exceed 180 days, the individual may be deemed a nonresident alien not engaged in trade or business in the Philippines.

Expatriates assigned in the Philippines for a definite period are generally regarded as nonresidents engaged in trade or business in the Philippines.

Gross income

Employee gross income/An alien, whether resident or not, is taxed on compensation income earned from services rendered in the Philippines regardless of where payment is made and whether it is remitted into the Philippines. The nonresident alien is not taxed on compensation income from services performed outside the Philippines. Employee gross income, from the point of view of a non-resident alien engaged in trade or business in the Philippines, includes all payments for services rendered in the Philippines, such as salaries and bonuses.

Social security contributions and union dues paid by employees are not included in gross income and are exempt from taxation.

Fringe benefits tax/Fringe benefits furnished to managerial and supervisory-level employees by the employer are subject to a final fringe benefits tax (FBT) of 32% (in general) on the grossed-up monetary value of the benefits. Managerial employees are those who may mandate and execute management policies to hire, transfer, suspend, lay off, recall, discharge, assign, or discipline employees. Supervisory employees are those who effectively recommend such managerial actions if the exercise of authority on behalf of the employer is not merely routine or clerical in nature but requires the use of independent judgment. The FBT is a final tax payable on a calendar quarterly basis by the employer and deductible as part of fringe benefit expense. Benefits subject to FBT are no longer included in employees' taxable income.

The grossed-up monetary value of a fringe benefit is determined by dividing the actual monetary value of the benefit by 68%. It represents the whole amount of the income realized by the employee, which includes the net amount that has been received plus the amount of FBT due from the employee but paid by the employer.

"Fringe benefits" are defined as any goods, services or other benefits furnished or granted in cash or in kind by an employer to an individual employee, except rank and file employees such as, but not limited to, the following.

1. Housing.
2. Expense account.
3. Vehicles of any kind.
4. Household personnel (e.g., maid, driver).
5. Interest on a loan at less than the market rate (currently set at 12%) to the extent of the difference between the market rate and the actual rate granted.
6. Membership fees, dues, and other expenses borne by the employer for the employee in social and athletic clubs and similar organizations.
7. Expenses for foreign travel.
8. Holiday and vacation expenses.
9. Educational assistance to the employee and dependents.
10. Premiums for life insurance, health and other nonlife insurance, and similar amounts in excess of what the law allows.

The monetary value of benefits in the form of motor vehicles used for both personal and business purposes and housing is equal to 50% of the lease payment or the depreciation value of the property, whichever is applicable. However, if the housing unit is situated in or adjacent (within 50 meters) to the business premises, the benefit is not taxable. Likewise, a motor vehicle used normally for business purposes is not taxable.

The following fringe benefits are not taxable.

1. Fringe benefits required by the nature of or necessary to the trade, business, or profession or for the convenience or advantage of the employer.
2. Benefits authorized by and exempted from tax under special laws.
3. Employer contributions for the benefit of the employee to retirement, insurance, and hospitalization benefit plans.
4. Benefits given to rank and file employees, whether or not granted under a collective bargaining agreement. However, these are subject to withholding tax on compensation, unless otherwise tax exempt.
5. De minimis (small value) benefits as defined in the rules and regulations.

Valuation of fringe benefits/In general, if a fringe benefit is granted in money or directly paid for by the employer, the value of the fringe benefit is the amount granted or paid for. If furnished in property and ownership thereof is transferred to the employee, the value of the fringe benefit is the fair market value of the property as determined by the Commissioner of Internal Revenue, pursuant to his power to prescribe real property values. If the fringe benefit is granted or furnished by the employer in the form of a property but ownership is not transferred to the employee, the value of the fringe benefit is equal to the depreciation value of the property.

Taxation of expatriates/Expatriates employed by certain entities or industries enjoy certain tax concessions. These expatriates include alien executives of offshore banking units, service contractors and subcontractors engaged in oil exploration activities, and regional headquarters and regional operating headquarters of multinational companies. They are taxed at 15% on their gross compensation income. The applicable FBT rate is also 15%. The grossed-up monetary value is determined by dividing the actual value of the benefit by 85%.

The FBT imposed on fringe benefits enjoyed by nonresident aliens not engaged in trade or business within the Philippines is 25% of the grossed-up monetary value of the fringe benefit. The grossed-up monetary value is determined by dividing the actual value of the benefit by 75%.

Capital gains and investment income/Nonresident aliens are taxed on Philippine-source capital gains, irrespective of their period of stay in the Philippines. The rates are 0.5% of the gross sales for those shares of stocks listed and traded in the stock exchange; 5% on the first PHP100,000 and 10% on the excess of the net capital gains for unlisted shares of stock; and 6% of the higher of the gross sales price or fair market value of real property sold, withheld at the time of sale. Capital losses are deductible only from capital gains. In computing net capital gains or losses from other capital assets, only 50% of the gain or loss is to be taken into account if the capital asset has been held for more than 12 months; otherwise, 100% of the gain or loss is to be considered.

A nonresident alien is also taxed on Philippine-source investment income such as interest, dividends, and royalties at the rate of 20% (for those engaged in trade or business in the Philippines) or 25% (for those not engaged in trade or business in the Philippines) final tax (or a lower treaty rate). The tax is withheld at source, and the income is no longer subject to the graduated rates.

Resident aliens are taxed on their Philippine-source income at graduated rates. However, Philippine-source interest and royalties are taxed at 20%. Interest on residents' deposits under the expanded foreign currency deposit system (FCDU) accounts is taxed at 7.5%, while interest on long-term deposits or investment in the form of savings, common or individual trust funds and other investments evidenced by certificates, and so on, is exempt from tax, subject to certain conditions. Interest income on FCDU accounts of nonresidents is tax exempt. Royalties on literary works and musical compositions are subject to a final tax of 10%. Dividend income received from a domestic corporation is taxed at 10%.Tax rates for capital gains from shares of stock and real property are the same as those for nonresident aliens.

Deductions

Business deductions/Aliens, whether residents or not, who are receiving only salary or compensation income are not allowed any deduction against such income.

In the case of individuals engaged in business or the practice of a profession, the following expenses are allowed as deductions from gross income.

1. All ordinary and necessary expenses paid or incurred during the taxable year in connection with the trade, business, or profession, including raw materials, supplies and direct labor.
2. Wages and other forms of compensation for personal services actually rendered, including the grossed-up monetary value of fringe benefits and travel expenses incurred in the pursuit of the trade or profession.
3. Business rentals.
4. Interest paid or incurred within a taxable year in connection with the conduct of a taxpayer's profession, trade or business, less an amount equal to a certain percentage of the interest income subject to final tax.
5. Entertainment, amusement, and recreation expenses, not to exceed the following ceilings:
   a. 0.50% of net sales for taxpayers engaged in sale of goods or properties; or
   b. 1% of net revenue for taxpayers engaged in sale of services, including professionals and lessors of properties.
6. Taxes.
7. Losses.
8. Bad debts.
9. Depreciation.
10. Charitable and other contributions, subject to certain limitations.
11. Research and development expenditures.

In lieu of these allowable deductions, an individual other than a nonresident alien may elect a standard deduction not exceeding 10% of gross income.

Nonbusiness expenses/Home mortgage interest, medical expenses, contributions, and other personal expenses cannot be claimed as deductions for income tax purposes. However, social security contributions are excluded from gross income.

Personal allowances/Resident aliens and, subject to certain conditions, nonresident aliens engaged in trade or business in the Philippines, are allowed a personal exemption of PHP20,000 if single, PHP25,000 if head of the family and PHP32,000 if married. An additional exemption of PHP8,000 for each dependent child (not to exceed four dependents) is allowed to married individuals. These personal and additional exemptions take the form of deductions instead of tax credits.

A family with gross income of not more than PHP250,000 for the year may deduct premium payments for health/hospitalization insurance up to a maximum of PHP2,400.

Tax credits

Aliens deriving income from foreign sources are not allowed a tax credit for foreign income taxes against Philippine income tax.

Other taxes

Social security taxes/The maximum annual social security and Philhealth contribution payable by a taxpayer for 2004 is PHP8,250.

VAT/A 10% VAT is imposed on services performed in the exercise or practice of profession or calling, except on services rendered by doctors and lawyers, and professional services rendered by general professional partnerships; entertainers, musical, radio, movie, and television and stage directors; and professional athletes, as well as services rendered by customs, real estate, stock, immigration, and commercial brokers. The VAT is based on the gross receipts representing the contract price, compensation, service fee, rental, or royalty, including the amount charged for materials supplied with the services and deposits and advanced payments actually or constructively received during the taxable period/quarter for the services performed or to be performed for another person, excluding VAT.

Local taxes on income/The local governments are not authorized to impose any tax on income.

Tax administration

Returns/For tax purposes, a husband and wife must file one consolidated income tax return, but the tax is computed separately. Income that cannot be definitely attributed or identified as exclusive income of either spouse is divided equally between them. Generally, this results in lower combined tax liability than when the tax is jointly computed.

Substituted filing of returns is mandatory for all qualified employees. Substituted filing is applicable when the employer's annual return of withholding tax on compensation and final tax (BIR Form 1604CF) may be considered as the "substitute" income tax return of its employees inasmuch as the information provided in his or her Certificate of Income Tax Withheld (BIR Form 2316) would exactly be the same information contained in Form 1604CF.

Substituted filing, however, will not apply to nonresident aliens engaged in trade or business in the Philippines.

All individual taxpayers who do not qualify for substituted filing are required to file their returns on a calendar-year basis. The return must be filed on or before April 15 of the succeeding year.

Payment of tax/Generally, the income tax withheld from the salaries or compensation of aliens, resident or not, is equal to their final tax liability on such compensation. If not, the balance must be paid at the time the return is filed. In certain cases, income tax liability may be paid in two equal installments.

Tax rates

Rates of tax on income of aliens, resident or not, depend on the nature of their income—that is, compensation income, income subject to final tax or other income (see below).

Compensation/For resident aliens and nonresident aliens doing business (as earlier defined) and receiving compensation income, the tax rates are as follows.

Taxable income		Tax on	Percentage
Over	Not over	Column 1	on excess
(Column 1)			
0	PHP 10,000	—	5
PHP 10,000	30,000	PHP 500	10
30,000	70,000	2,500	15
70,000	140,000	8,500	20
140,000	250,000	22,500	25
250,000	500,000	50,000	30
500,000		125,000	32

For example, the tax due on a taxable compensation income of US$25,000 (PHP1,389,650) is US$7,370 (PHP 409,688).

Business income/For an individual, whether citizen or resident alien, who is self-employed or practices a profession, the tax rates are the same as above. An individual with a taxable compensation income of US$25,000 and a taxable business or professional income of US$25,000 will have a total taxable income of US$50,000 (PHP2,779,300) and will pay a total individual income tax of US$15,370 (PHP854,376).

In the case of nonresident aliens not doing business in the Philippines, the tax rate is a flat 25% of the gross income received from all sources within the Philippines.

Income subject to final tax/This is usually on passive investment income. For resident and nonresident aliens engaged in trade or business in the Philippines, the maximum rate is 20%; for nonresident aliens not engaged in trade or business in the Philippines, the rate is a flat 25%. (See also under "Capital gains and investment income" above.)

INDIVIDUAL TAX CALCULATION

Calendar year 2004

Assumptions

1. Resident alien husband and wife with two dependent children.
2. Salary and allowances of husband arising from employment: salary of PHP600,000; living allowances of PHP100,000; housing benefits (100%) of PHP300,000.
3. Teaching salary of wife: PHP50,000.
4. Gross dividend income from investment in shares of stock of a domestic corporation of PHP10,000 (from 2003 profits).
5. Interest of PHP20,000 on peso bank account.
6. Capital gain on sale of shares of PHP5,000.
7. Taxes withheld by employer of husband at PHP173,640 and by employer of wife at PHP1,300.

Income tax computation

	Husband	Wife
Gross income (1):		
Salary	PHP 600,000	PHP 50,000
Living allowances	100,000	—
Housing benefits (300,000) (2)	—	—
	700,000	50,000
Deductions:		
Personal exemption	32,000	32,000
Additional exemption for dependent children (3)	16,000	—
	48,000	32,000
Net taxable income	PHP 652,000	PHP 18,000
Tax due:		
On first 500,000	PHP 125,000	
On remainder of 152,000 at 32%	48,640	
On first 10,000		PHP 500
On remainder of 8,000 at 10%		800
	173,640	1,300
Less—Tax withheld by employer per Form 2316 (4)	(173,640)	(1,300)
Net tax due	PHP 0	PHP 0

Notes:

1. The following items were not included in the income tax return because they are subject to final tax.

	PHP
Interest on peso bank account	20,000
Capital gain on sale of shares	5,000
Dividend income	10,000
Housing benefits	300,000

   The final tax of 10% on dividends applies to income earned on or after January 1, 1998. Income that is part of retained earnings as of December 31, 1997, even if declared or distributed as dividends on or after January 1, 1998, is not subject to final tax.

2. Housing benefits are subject to FBT, payable by the employer. Under the FBT regulations, such benefits are taxable to the extent of 50% of the rentals for the house or living quarters used by the employee and paid by the employer if the lease contract is in the name of the employer.

   To compute the FBT due, 50% of the rental payment is grossed-up before applying the 32% tax. Thus, the grossed-up value of PHP150,000 is PHP220,588, and the tax payable is PHP70,588.

3. The additional exemption for dependent children is to be claimed by the husband unless he explicitly waives his right in favor of his wife.
4. For individuals receiving salary and other allowances from one employer only, the tax due is usually equal to tax withheld, since the employer is required to compute and withhold the total tax due on the employee's compensation earned during the year, using the annual graduated income tax table, before paying the last payroll for the year.
5. The above individual tax calculation also applies to nonresident aliens engaged in trade or business in the Philippines for their Philippine-source income, except that personal exemptions are allowed only under certain conditions.
6. Exchange rate of the Philippine peso at December 30, 2003: US$1 = PHP55.5860.

PwC contact

For additional information on taxation in Poland, contact:

Piotr Kowalski
PricewaterhouseCoopers Warsaw
Al. Armii Ludowej 14
00-638 Warsaw, Poland
Telephone: (48) (22) 523 4000
Fax: (48) (22) 523 4040
e-mail: piotr.kowalski@pl.pwc.com

Significant developments

Beginning from January 1, 2004, it is possible to use a preferential 19% taxation with respect to the revenues derived by individuals conducting certain business activities. To benefit from this preferential tax treatment, the individual should conduct the business activity and meet all the conditions as described in the Polish personal income tax act (PIT Act). However, opting for preferential taxation may involve some difficulties, such as the arduous administrative obligations and procedures necessary to start and run one's own business activity and lack of possibility to file a joint married tax return.

Territoriality and residence

Polish personal income tax law regulating the scope of one's tax liability in Poland was changed as of January 1, 2003. Previous criteria for determining an expatriate's tax liability (i.e., the length of stay in Poland in a given calendar year or employee's contractual arrangements) are no longer used. The amended regulation makes the tax obligation in Poland dependent only on whether an individual has a place of residence in Poland within the meaning of the Polish Civil Code and international tax regulations. An individual who is found to have a place of residence in Poland is subject to worldwide taxation in Poland (i.e., in accordance with the so-called unlimited tax liability principle) regardless of whether this person spends less than 184 days in Poland or is employed directly by a Polish company (established with foreign participation). In consequence, not only employment income is subject to taxation in Poland, but also any other private income derived in Poland or abroad (such as bank interest, dividends, exercise of stock options, rental income), unless international double taxation treaties limit the right of Poland to tax such income. Moreover, such a person is not able to take advantage of the preferential taxation on certain types of income (e.g., board fees). A person who is considered not to have a place of residence in Poland will be subject to Polish taxation on a limited basis, that is, only on income derived for work performed in Poland or from sources located in Poland (any other income derived from non-Polish sources will not be subject to tax in Poland). Moreover, such a person will be able to take advantage of the preferential taxation on certain types of income (e.g., director's fees).

Gross income

Employee gross income/Employee gross income includes basic pay, overtime pay, supplemental pay, awards and bonuses, compensation for unused holiday or vacation time, all other monetary amounts, and benefits in kind, as well as all other services obtained without payment. Income from each source is defined as the surplus generated in a tax year of revenue over the costs of obtaining that revenue. If, in a given tax year, losses from any source of income (with a few exceptions) exceed the taxpayer's total income from all sources, the taxpayer has the right to carry forward each source's loss by deducting this loss over the next five years from income derived from the same source. The deduction cannot exceed 50% of total amount of loss in any of the given five years. For individuals liable to Polish tax only on Polish-source income, earnings from some sources are taxed at a flat rate of 20% unless a bilateral tax treaty between Poland and the individual's country of residence states otherwise. These types of earnings are as follows.

1. Earnings from copyrights and other intellectual property rights such as trademarks, patents and designs, including proceeds of sale.
2. Income from the transfer of technology.
3. Income received from another party for the use of industrial, commercial, or scientific equipment.
4. Income received from another party for information and expertise in the fields of industry, commerce, or science.
5. Income from work in the fields of art, literature, science, education, journalism, and athletic activities, including income from participation in artistic, scientific, and cultural competitions (independent work).
6. Income from work commissioned by national or local government authorities or administrative bodies or by the courts or the prosecutor's office (in particular, that of expert witnesses in all types of legal and administrative proceedings) and income received as a fee for participation in commissions established by local government bodies.
7. Income received as fees for membership on boards of directors, supervisory boards, committees, and other decision-making bodies of legal entities.
8. Income from rendering personal services on the basis of a specific work contract or self-employment contract concluded with a legal entity, an entity without legal personality or a business, as long as these services are not business services offered by the individual contractor to the public.
9. Income received from activities performed personally under management or similar contracts.

Capital gains and investment income/Income from the sale of real property is taxed separately at the rate of 10% if the sale is not carried out within the scope of regular economic activity and occurs within five years from the end of the tax year in which the purchase of the property took place (with certain exceptions, for example, when revenue from the sale of real property is spent for living accommodation of the taxpayer) or if a special tax relief was claimed, the sale occurs within ten years. Income from the sale of objects (i.e., chattels) is taxed at the progressive tax rates if the sale occurs within six months from the date of acquisition. Interest income from the granting of a loan is taxed at 19%, except where the granting of loans is the object of regular economic activity. Dividends from joint stock companies and shares in profits of limited liability companies are distributed from the net after-tax profit of a company. Income from sale of shares and dividend income as well as undistributable retained earnings sourced in Poland, are not aggregated with income from other sources. This type of income is taxed at 19%.

Tax-exempt income/Approximately 100 types of income are tax exempt. The most important are as follows.

1. Monetary damages received on the basis of administrative law, civil law, and other legal acts (with certain exceptions).
2. Receipts from property insurance and personal insurance claims (with certain exceptions).
3. Money won in legally registered games of chance and lotteries.
4. Income of individuals if that income derives from funds established by international financial institutions or from resources allocated by other countries on the basis of agreements concluded between the Council of Ministers of Poland (or a Ministry with the consent of the Council of Ministers) and those institutions or countries.
5. Cash equivalents provided to employees when they need to use their own tools, goods, and equipment to perform work.
6. Reimbursement of an employee's costs for relocation to another place of employment and reimbursement for the costs of settling in the new place (up to 200% of the monthly salary due to the employee in the month of transfer).
7. Limited daily allowances and other amounts due to employees for the duration of business trips.
8. Additional pay granted to employees temporarily transferred to work away from home and other benefits granted according to the principles and limits outlined in the rules for state employees.
9. Value of expenses covered by an employer for employees staying in hotels for employees and in quarters rented from private persons for the purpose of collective lodging of employees, up to PLZ500 per month.

Deductions

Business deductions/There is a standard annual deduction for employees equal to PLZ102.25 per month.

Nonbusiness expenses/The employee's portion of social security contributions is deductible from gross income before tax. Health insurance contributions are also deductible.

Personal allowances/For 2004 there is a personal allowance of PLZ530.08 for all taxpayers.

Tax credits

A taxpayer's income originating abroad, if subject to Polish taxation (not exempt from taxation in Poland under an agreement for the avoidance of double taxation), is accumulated with income earned from work in Poland, and the tax is calculated on this sum according to the tax table. Income tax is then reduced by the amount of tax paid outside Poland. This tax credit may not exceed the tax calculated on total income multiplied by the proportion of income arising outside Poland to total income (unless a relevant double tax treaty provides otherwise).

Other taxes

Social security taxes/Until the end of 1998 the employer was subject to the entire obligation for Polish social insurance. From January 1, 1999, following the reform of the Polish social security system, the obligatory social security contribution has been divided between the employer and the employee. Contributions to pensions and disability insurance are paid by employer and employee on total gross compensation until such cumulated compensation exceeds the contribution cap, which is set at 30 times the national average monthly salary estimated for a particular year (for 2004 the cap is set at PLZ68,700—approximately US$17,800). When the individual's cumulative income reaches the cap limit, contributions are no longer paid to pensions and disability insurance either by the employee or the employer. Contributions to sickness (employee) and accident insurance (employer) as well as the Labor Fund and Guaranteed Benefits Fund (employer) are paid without a cap limit on total gross salary.

The contribution rates are as follows.

	Contribution amount	Paid by
Pensions and disability insurance	16.26% of total gross salary (up to the cap)	Employer
	16.26% of total gross salary (up to the cap)	Employee
Sickness insurance	2.45% of total gross salary	Employee
Accident insurance (Note)	0.97% to 3.86% of total gross salary	Employer
Labor Fund	2.45% of total gross salary	Employer
Guaranteed Benefits Fund	0.15% of total gross salary	Employer

Note:

Beginning from January 2003, the accident insurance rate generally depends on the number of employees:

1. Nine or fewer employees—1.93%.
2. More than nine employees—The rate depends on the type of economic activity and ranges from 0.97% to 3.86%.

The amount of the contribution paid by the individual is deductible from gross income before tax unless the income on which the social security contributions were calculated is exempt form personal taxation.

Foreign individuals engaged with a Polish entity under an employment contract are generally subject to security contributions, unless an exemption is provided under an applicable totalization agreement (this may, however, change on the day Poland accedes to the European Union, i.e. as of May 1, 2004). However, according to the law there are some social security exemptions, including those listed below.

1. Service contracts if the individual is already subject to mandatory social security contribution from another source and the service contract is concluded with another entity than the regular contract of employment and work under service contract is not provided for the former employer.
2. Management board fees.
3. Some benefits set out in the decree of the Minister of Labor and Social Policy of December 18, 1998 concerning "detailed rules of setting the assessment base for pensions contributions."

Health insurance/A new regulation with respect to health insurance (i.e., the Common Insurance in National Health Fund Act) is effective as of April 1, 2003.

Polish nationals who are subject to social security insurance are mandatorily subject to national health insurance; alternatively, they can voluntarily participate in the state health insurance scheme. Foreign individuals are subject to obligatory health insurance only if they are subject to Polish social insurance and if they are residing in Poland on the basis of a visa with work permit or residence card or temporary residence card. Foreign individuals not referred to above are neither obliged nor entitled to participate (i.e., voluntarily) in the national health insurance system, unless an appropriate international agreement provides otherwise.

The monthly contribution rate for health insurance is 8.25% of the assessment base. This rate is to be increased over the next three years to 8.5% in 2005, 8.75% in 2006, and finally to 9% in 2007. In the case of obligatory participation, this is equal to the individual's gross income diminished by the social security contributions. In the case of voluntary participation, the amount of the assessment base is declared by the insured individual but cannot be lower than the average national salary as published from time to time. As of January 1, 2003, 7.75% is deducted from the individual's Personal Income Tax (PIT) and the remaining 0.5% is paid directly from individual's net income. As of April 1, 2003 members of supervisory boards who receive remuneration for performing these duties are subject to mandatory health insurance. The entity providing the remuneration is obliged to register the member for health insurance, calculate the appropriate contribution, deduct it from the board member's income, and pay it to the Polish Social Security Institution (*Zaklad Ubezpieczeń Spolecznych*—ZUS).

Tax administration

Returns/Employers are obliged to prepare for each employee an information return showing the cumulative yearly amount of income received by the employee under his or her Polish employment contract and the tax advances withheld by employer on the income. The information should be prepared and submitted to the employee well as to the relevant tax office by the end of February following the year the income was received. Based on the information issued by the employer the employee files an annual tax return.

In principle, the taxpayers must file tax returns with the tax office, stating income earned in the given year. The annual tax returns must be filed before April 30 following the close of the fiscal year for which they are made, and differences between advance payments and the taxpayer's actual tax liability must be settled by this deadline. In some cases, employers may be asked by their employees to prepare annual tax reconciliations on their behalf. In such a case excess withholdings are credited against the taxpayer's March advance tax payment.

Husbands and wives are treated as individual taxpayers unless they apply to have their incomes combined. This is permitted only when the spouses are married throughout the given tax year, are subject to the marital property law, and are liable to Polish tax on their worldwide income.

Payment of tax/Individuals who derive income from an employment contract, a commission contract or a retirement or disability pension will have tax withheld from sums due to them. The standard procedure is to withhold the full amount of tax due (at 19%, 30%, or 40%) from a taxpayer's monthly income. 19% is withheld monthly if income does not exceed PLZ37,024; 30% if income is between PLZ37,024 and PLZ74,048; and 40% thereafter (for 2004). The rate of withholding depends on the cumulative income earned from the start of the year to the month preceding the month for which the tax is withheld. Income is understood to include all revenues obtained by an employee in a given month less PLZ102.25 (standard monthly deduction from earnings in 2004).

As of January 1, 2003, Polish entities are subject to a new obligation for submitting information to the tax authorities where: (1) nonresident natural persons perform work on their behalf (provide services), and at the same time (2) if the fee due to the said foreign individuals for the services provided is paid out by foreign entities. The obligation will arise, if (1) under double taxation treaties, the situation could have an impact on the tax obligation arising or on the amount of tax liability of the recipients of the fee and (2) the foreign entity either directly or indirectly participates in the management or control of the entity that is subject to the obligation to inform, or holds at least 5% of the voting rights in the capital of that entity. If these conditions are met, Polish entities will be obliged, without being requested by the tax authorities, to amass, draw up and submit information on fees paid to foreign nationals for services rendered to them.

Tax rates

Annual taxable income		Tax on	Percentage
Over	Not over	Column 1	on excess
(Column 1)			
0	PLZ 37,024	—	19
PLZ 37,024	74,048	PLZ 6,504.48*	30
74,048		17,611.68	40

*The personal allowance of PLZ530.08 has been deducted.

INDIVIDUAL TAX CALCULATION

Calendar year 2004

Assumptions

The taxpayer is nonresident and arrived in Poland for a temporary stay and thus has limited tax liability to Polish taxation in 2004. The taxpayer is employed under a Polish employment contract.

Tax computation

Annual salary		PLZ 234,400.00
Interest on savings		2,200.00
Benefit in kind—Accommodation		46,800.00
Income originating abroad		43,500.00
Long-term capital gain (originating abroad)		5,900.00
		332,800.00
Less—Income taxed at the flat rate:		
Interest on savings (1)	2,200.00	
Less—Income not subject to taxation in Poland:		
Income originating abroad	43,500.00	
Long-term capital gain	5,900.00	51,600.00
Annual gross income		281,200.00
Less:		
Pension and disability insurance contribution (16.26% of gross income, up to the cap)	11,170.62	
Sickness insurance contribution (2.45% of gross income)	6,889.40	
Standard deduction	1,227.00	19,287.02
Annual taxable income		PLZ 261,912.98
Health insurance contribution (8.25% of gross income less social security contributions)	21,709.05	
Nondeductible part of health insurance contribution (0.5% of gross income less social security contributions)	1,315.70	
Total annual tax due		PLZ 92,757.68
Less—Deductible part of health insurance contribution (7.75% of gross income less social security contributions)		(20,393.35)
Tax annual tax due after deduction of health insurance contribution		PLZ 72,364.30

Notes:

1. The taxpayer would have to pay a 19% flat rate tax on interest on savings: Interest on savings = PLZ2,200.00; flat 19% = PLZ418.00, unless the relevant provisions of double tax treaty provides otherwise.
2. Average exchange rate of the zloty at March 16, 2004: US$1 = PLZ3.8544.

Portugal

PwC contact

For additional information on taxation in Portugal, contact:

John Duggan
PricewaterhouseCoopers
Edificio Caravelas
Rua Dr. Eduardo Neves, 9 - 5°
1069-053 Lisbon, Portugal
Telephone: (351) 21 791 4020
Fax: (351) 21 791 4030
e-mail: john.duggan@pt.pwc.com

General note

The information below is current as of January 2004. For subsequent developments consult the contact listed above.

Significant developments

The legislation for 2004 has not brought about any significant changes.

Territoriality and residence

Residents in Portugal for tax purposes are taxed on their worldwide income at progressive rates varying from 12% to 40%. Nonresidents are liable to income tax only on Portuguese-source income, which includes not only that portion of remuneration that can be allocated to the activity carried out in Portugal but also remuneration that is borne by a Portuguese company or permanent establishment. Nonresidents are taxed at a flat rate of 25% on their taxable remuneration.

A person who spends more than 183 days in aggregate in Portugal during the calendar year is deemed to be resident in Portugal for tax purposes. Alternatively, persons who have maintained a residence suggesting a habitual residence in Portugal as of December 31 are deemed to be residents, even if they have spent less than 183 days in Portugal during a calendar year.

If a transfer of tax residence by a Portuguese national to territories with a more favorable tax regime occurs, the Portuguese national is deemed to be tax resident in Portugal not only for the tax year of transfer, but also for the following four years, unless it can be proved that the change of residence is for a relevant reason, namely an assignment from a company domiciled in Portugal to that territory for a specific period of time.

It should be noted that residence status applies for an entire tax year, which is the calendar year. Split-year residence is not possible under domestic law.

Married couples are deemed to be resident taxpayers if one spouse is resident for tax purposes in Portugal.

Taxable income

Employment income/Employment income/remuneration is specifically defined in the personal income tax code and covers all payments in connection with work carried out in Portugal, such as salary, bonuses, commissions, tax reimbursements, redundancy payments, pensions, allowances (e.g., cost-of-living and housing allowances), and benefits in kind (e.g., company cars), regardless of where the payment originates.

Domestic and foreign travel allowances in excess of those permitted to employees of state departments are also taxable as employment income.

Mileage and lunch allowances are not taxable within the thresholds established for employees of state departments.

Benefits in kind/In general, benefits in kind provided by an employer are subject to income tax at the employee level. There are specific provisions on taxation of employer-provided housing or housing allowances, use and acquisition of company cars and share plans.

The taxable benefit from the use of a company car corresponds to 0.75% of the acquisition cost of the car, multiplied by the number of months of use of the car. If the company car is then acquired by the employee, a further benefit in kind will correspond to the difference (if positive) between the market price of the car and the total amount already taxed as a benefit in kind to the employee as a result of using the car. The market price corresponds to the difference between the acquisition price and the product derived from that value and a depreciation factor published by the relevant authorities.

Pensions/The first €8,121.00 of pension income is tax exempt, unless the total income exceeds a certain limit (approximately €72.842,44 for 2003), in which case, the exemption is reduced by the excess.

Termination of employment/Redundancy payments are taxable on the portion that exceeds one and a half times the average remuneration paid during the last 12 months of service, multiplied by the number of years of service, unless a new employment contract or service contract is made with the employer or a related person within 24 months from the date of termination of the employment contract.

Capital gains and investment income/Capital gains derived from the sale of shares held for more than 12 months are exempt from personal income tax. If the shares were held for less than 12 months, the capital gains arising from the disposal of those shares will be liable to taxation at a flat rate of 10%.

Fifty percent of capital gains arising from the sale of real estate by tax residents in Portugal is taxed at progressive rates varying from 12% to 40%. The gain may be wholly or partially exempt if the property being sold is the taxpayer's primary residence and the sale proceeds, reduced by the value of any outstanding loans relating to the purchase of the property being sold, are reinvested in the acquisition, improvement or construction of another primary residence in Portugal within two years from the sale or during the 12 months before the sale.

Capital gains earned by nonresidents that are not borne by a permanent establishment in Portugal are fully taxable at a flat rate of 25% (with an exception for capital gains on the disposal of shares, which are taxed as mentioned above).

Fifty percent of dividends paid by companies that have a permanent establishment in Portugal to resident individuals are liable to Portuguese personal income tax and disclosed on the annual tax return. A 15% withholding tax applies to those dividends paid by resident entities. This tax can be set off against the individual's tax liability.

Dividends paid by companies that are not resident in Portugal are liable to income tax and should be fully disclosed on the annual tax return. A credit against the Portuguese tax liability is available for the lower of the tax paid in the foreign country on those dividends or the amount of tax payable in Portugal on that income. For dividends paid by countries with which Portugal has signed a double taxation treaty, the tax credit should not exceed the percentage established in the treaty.

Should these dividends be paid through a paying agent in Portugal, a 20% final tax will be deducted, unless the dividends are paid to an investment fund in Portugal.

Interest income arising from current or saving accounts on Portuguese banks is taxed at 20% for both residents and nonresidents.

Business and professional income/Income from a commercial, industrial, or agricultural activity and income from a sole trader (including scientific, artistic, or technical services) or from intellectual rights (when earned by the original owner) may be taxed either in accordance with a simplified regime or based on the taxpayer's accounts. The simplified regime will apply only to taxpayers who, not having opted for organized accounts, have a turnover lower than €149,739.37 or a gross business and professional income lower than €99,759.58. Under this simplified regime, the above income is taxed on 0.20 of sales of products or 0.65 of income arising from other business and professional services, with a minimum taxable income of €3,125. This option might be taken even if the period of three years under the simplified regime is not yet complete.

Deductions

Maintenance and repair expenses may be deducted against rental income, to the extent that they are dully documented. Municipal property tax paid with regard to the rented property may also be deducted against the rental income.

Union fees (in the part that does not constitute a direct contribution for health, education, elderly support, home, insurance, or social security benefits) may be deducted against employment or pension income. The deduction is 150% of total fees, up to a limit of 1% of the taxpayer's gross employment or pension income.

Alimony payments or other amounts defined by court order are deductible.

Tax credits

The following tax credits are available for 2004 against the amount of tax due by an individual.

1. Personal tax credits:
   a. Single person—€219.36;
   b. Married couple (husband and wife)—€365.60;
   c. Per dependent child—€146.24;
   d. Per ascendant—€201.08;
   e. Single parents—€292.48.

   The above tax credits are increased by 50% for individuals with proven disabilities, except for ascendants.
2. Health expenses:
   a. A tax credit of 30% of nonreimbursed health expenses, if properly documented, including health expenses (exempt from VAT, or subject to VAT at a rate of 5%) incurred by the taxpayer and his/her spouse and dependents, expenses incurred by the taxpayer's ascendants with an income lower than the national minimum wage (€365.60 per month) and interest on loans made to bear such expenses;

b. A tax credit of 30% of all other health expenses resulting from a medical prescription is also available, with a limit of €55.59 or 2.5% of those expenses (whichever is higher).

3. Education expenses—30% of all education expenses up to a limit of €584.96. This limit is increased by €109.68 for each dependent where the number of dependent studying children is three or more.
4. Housing interest or rent—30% of interest or capital repayments on loans made for acquisition of principal private residences or rental of a permanent house, limited to €538.55. This tax credit is not available if the loans were granted by entities that are resident in territories with a more favorable tax regime (as defined by the Portuguese tax authorities) and that do not have a permanent establishment in Portugal to which that income may be recharged.
5. Life insurance premiums—25% of premiums with a limit of €55.99 for a single person and €111.98 for married couples.
6. Health insurance premiums—25% of premiums, limited to €74.65 for a single person and €149.31 for married couples. These limits are increased by €37.38 for each dependent child.
7. Contributions to individual retirement saving plans (*Plano Poupança Reforma*—PPR), educational plans (*Plano Poupança Educação*—PPE) or individual retirement/educational plans (PPR/E)—25% of the such contributions with a limit of €661.41 per taxpayer, or 5% of the total taxable income, if lower. These limits may be increased by 5% for taxpayers between 35 and 50 years old, and 10% for taxpayers younger than 35 years old.
8. Payments to *Planos Poupança em Acções* (special saving plans in shares in Portugal)—7.5% of the such payments limited to €199.95 per taxpayer, on the condition that no reimbursements are made within six months after the payments.
9. Annual deposits in *Contas Poupança-Habitação* (savings accounts used to fund housing acquisition and maintenance)—Credit of 25%, limited to €575.57.
10. Acquisition of new equipment for the utilization of renewable energy or consumption of natural gas—30% of the total costs of acquisition of such equipment or other complementary equipment defined on the tax legislation, limited to €714.
11. Acquisition of personal computers, hardware or software—25% on the acquisition expenses, limited to €182.97.
12. Expenses of lawyers and other legal services—20% of expenses, limited to €139.71.
13. Fees and expenses paid to retirement homes in respect of parents and grandparents whose income does not exceed the national minimum salary (€365.60 per month)—25% with a limit of €315.67. The combined amount of credits for education and retirement home expenses is limited to €710.97.
14. VAT incurred with services of food and beverage, repair of domestic furniture, of the house, and repair of vehicles (in this last case, if the service was provided by individuals or companies subject to the simplified regime of taxation)—25% of the VAT with the limit of €50.
15. Donations to the central or local government or any government agency or body, donations to a church, religious institution, charity, museum, school, library, or

other recognized social welfare or cultural entity—Tax credit of 25%, limited to 15% of the individual's income tax liability.

16. International double taxation—Tax credits are available for foreign taxes paid on foreign-source income.

Other taxes

Social security/Individuals are subject to social security contributions on their gross income at 11%. These contributions cover family, pension, and unemployment benefits. An employed individual is entitled to an earned income deduction of 72% of the annual national minimum salary (€3,158.78), or of the actual social security contributions, whichever is higher.

Foreign residents may be exempt from social security in Portugal if they contribute to a compulsory social security system in an EU country or a country that has a bilateral social security agreement with Portugal.

In addition to social security contributions at a general rate of 23.75%, employers must make contributions to an insurance for occupational accidents. These contributions vary according to work and risk classification.

Members of statutory boards of companies are subject to different social security rates (10% with respect to employee contributions, and 21.25% for employer contributions). The contributions of members of statutory boards are based on their effective remuneration but subject to a monthly minimum and maximum income level of €365.60 and €4,387.20, respectively (for 2004).

Self-employed individuals are subject to a social security scheme that enables them to choose between two available schemes and the level of income on which contributions are paid.

1. Compulsory contribution scheme, subject to a 25.4% rate.
2. Extended contribution scheme, subject to a 32% rate.

Self-employed individuals are entitled to select the monthly income level on which social security contributions are paid, which may vary between €365.60 (national minimum salary for 2004) and €4,387.20 (12 times the national minimum wage). The selected level of income must be communicated to the Social Security authorities. Upon default, it will be based on the minimum level of income or on the last reported level under the earlier scheme.

Local taxes/Municipal property tax is charged on the registered value of real estate.

Tax administration

Tax returns/Individuals that have earned only employment income and/or pensions must file tax returns by March 15 of the year following the tax year in question, in all other cases, returns must be filed by April 30 of the following year. The tax year is the calendar year.

Married couples file joint returns. Income is divided by two to determine the tax rate. The resulting tax liability is then doubled, regardless of the earnings ratio. The same procedure applies to nonmarried couples living together at the same tax address in Portugal for at least two years who opt to be taxed as married couples.

Payment of tax/Portugal uses a PAYE (pay-as-you-earn) system, adjusted by tax return filing. Additional payments or refunds are made based on the tax returns filed.

Tax rates

Resident income tax rates

Taxable income	Tax rate	Deductible amount
(In euros)	(%)	(In euros)
Up to 4,266.00	12	0
From 4,266.00 to 6,452.00	14	85.32
From 6,452.00 to 15,997.00	24	730.51
From 15,997.00 to 36,792.00	34	2,330.23
From 36,792.00 to 53,322.00	38	3,801.83
Over 53,322.00	40	4,868.30

As described above, special rates apply to capital gains and investment income.

INDIVIDUAL TAX CALCULATION

Calendar year 2004

Assumptions

1. Resident foreigner and spouse, with two dependent children under 18.
2. One spouse without income.
3. The proceeds on the sale of a property are not reinvested in another private residence in Portugal.
4. Election to waive Portuguese social security contributions.

Tax computation

	€	€
Earned income:		
Salary		70,000.00
Tax withheld (assume 28.5%)	19,950.00	
Capital gain on sale of house (reduced price index because owned for more than two years)		10,000.00
Interest on saving account (1)		2,000.00
Tax withheld at 20%	400.00	—
		82,000.00

	Option A (Note 1)	Option B (Note 1)
Taxable income:		
Salary	70,000.00	70,000.00
Capital gains (2)	5,000.00	5,000.00
Interest on saving account (1)	2,000.00	—
Deduction—Social security (3)	3,158.78	3,158.78
	73,841.22	71,841.22
Split income (coefficient to be used: 2)	36,920.61	35,920.61
Tax rate	38%	34%
Deductible amount	3,801.83	2,330.23
Tax on declared income	20,456.44	19,765.55
Tax credits:		
Married personal credit	365.60	365.60
Children personal credit (4)	292.48	292.48
School expenses (5)	584.96	584.96
Health expenses (6)	150.00	150.00
Tax withheld on interest on savings account (1)	400.00	—
Tax withheld on account on salary	19,950.00	19,950.00
Refund on tax paid	1,286.60	1,577.48
Net income (7)		
(Total income – tax withheld + refund on tax paid)	57,936.60	56,627.48

Notes:

1. Taxpayers may opt to declare the interest on savings accounts and, therefore, to consider the tax withheld on that interest at a 20% tax rate, as a payment on account. Option A reflects this scenario. In Option B, this has not been done.
2. As mentioned, on the basis that the proceeds on the sale of the property were not reinvested in another private residence in Portugal, only 50% of the capital gains on the sale are taxed as regular income.
3. Because social security is waived, the deduction is limited to the standard employment income deduction.
4. €146.24 per dependent child for 2004.
5. Limit for 2004.
6. 30% on the assumed amount of health expenses (€500).
7. Exchange rate of the euro on January 2, 2004: US$1 = €0.7942.

PwC contact

For additional information on taxation in Puerto Rico, contact:

Marta Acevedo
PricewaterhouseCoopers LLP
Banco Bilbao Vizcaya Tower, Suite 900
254 Muñoz Rivera Avenue
Hato Rey, Puerto Rico 00918
Telephone: (1) (787) 772-7929
Fax: (1) (787) 766-1094
e-mail: marta.acevedo@us.pwc.com

Significant developments

There have been no significant development as regards individual taxation in the past year.

Territoriality and residence

All bona fide residents of Puerto Rico (regardless of citizenship) are subject to Puerto Rico income tax on their worldwide income at graduated rates. Generally, a bona fide resident for income tax purposes is a person residing in a "bona fide" dwelling in Puerto Rico for a period of 183 days or more. Nonresident individuals are taxable only on their income from sources within Puerto Rico and on gross income effectively connected with the operation of a trade or business within Puerto Rico.

Gross income

Employee gross income/In general, all compensation for personal services rendered within Puerto Rico, of whatever kind and in whatever form or place paid, is includable in gross income. If services are paid for with property other than money, the fair market value of the property is included in gross income. Other compensation, such as housing allowances, school allowances, cost-of-living allowances, and tax reimbursements, is also generally includable.

Capital gains and investment income/Resident individuals are subject to tax at the graduated rates on net income from capital gains, interest, dividends, rents, and distributions of partnership profits from sources within and without Puerto Rico. Puerto Rico's tax laws accord favorable tax treatment to long-term capital gains versus ordinary income by allowing the excess of net long-term capital gains over net short-term capital losses to be taxed at a fixed 20% rate (10% in some instances). Otherwise, the taxpayer may opt to include this gain as part of gross income in the income tax return for the year in which the gain is recognized and pay a tax in accordance with normal tax rates.

Interest income received from banks and thrift institutions in Puerto Rico, to the extent it exceeds an annual exclusion amount of $2,000, is eligible for a flat 17% tax in lieu of taxation at graduated rates, provided the payer is authorized in advance to withhold the 17% at source.

Dividends received from Puerto Rican corporations, as well as from foreign corporations that have derived 80% or more of their gross income during the preceding three-year period from Puerto Rican sources, other than dividends paid from certain tax-exempt income, are eligible for a flat 10% tax in lieu of taxation at graduated rates, provided the tax is withheld at source, as generally required by law.

Nonresidents engaged in a trade or business in Puerto Rico (i.e., performing services within Puerto Rico) are taxed on their net income from Puerto Rican–source capital gains and investment income at the same rates as resident individuals.

Nonresident U.S. citizens not engaged in a trade or business in Puerto Rico are subject to Puerto Rican taxes on net income from Puerto Rican–source capital gains, interest, dividends, rents, and distributions of partnership profits at the same rates as resident individuals. Nonresident aliens not engaged in a trade or business within Puerto Rico are subject to Puerto Rican taxes on the gross income from such sources at a flat rate of 29%, or at a higher graduated rate if that rate exceeds the flat rate of 29%, except that the flat 10% tax rate is applicable to certain dividends, as described above for resident individuals.

Deductions

Business deductions/Resident individuals can deduct, to the extent not reimbursed, ordinary and necessary business expenses in connection with a trade or business, subject to a limitation of $1,500 or 3% of adjusted gross income (AGI) from salaries, whichever is less. In the case of married persons living together who opt to file separate returns, the limitation would be $750 or 3% of AGI from salaries, whichever is less, for each. Nonresident individuals can deduct such expenses to the extent they are connected with income that is effectively connected with the operation of a trade or business within Puerto Rico.

Nonbusiness expenses/The law provides an option to itemize deductions or to claim a standard deduction. The standard deduction for 2004 is $3,150 for married individuals filing a joint return, $2,100 for single individuals and married individuals living separately, $2,730 for heads of households, or $1,575 for married individuals filing separate returns.

Resident individuals can deduct as itemized deductions property tax on residential property (only on the principal residence), fees paid on automobile license plates, casualty losses to the taxpayer's principal residence, and, subject to limitations, mortgage interest, rent paid on a house constituting the taxpayer's principal residence, certain costs for the education of dependents in elementary or secondary schools (including interest paid on student loans at university level), medical expenses, charitable contributions, interest paid on student loans, and childcare expenses.

Additional deductions (that can be claimed even if the taxpayer elects to claim the standard deduction) include, subject to certain limitations, interest on an automobile loan, contributions to IRA accounts, contributions to government pension plans, two wage earners' deductions, and deductions for veterans, young people who work, and ordinary and necessary expenses.

Nonresident U.S. citizens are allowed to deduct most of the nonbusiness deductions in the same proportion that Puerto Rican–source AGI bears to total AGI from all sources.

Nonresident aliens are generally not allowed any of the nonbusiness deductions listed above.

Personal allowances/Resident individuals and nonresident U.S. citizens are allowed as a deduction a personal allowance of $1,300 if single or married not living with spouse, $3,000 (per couple) if married and filing a joint return or head of household, or $1,500 if married and filing a separate return. In addition, a $1,600 allowance is allowed for dependents.

No personal allowances are granted to nonresident alien individuals.

Tax credits

A foreign tax credit is available to all individuals (both U.S. citizens and aliens) resident in Puerto Rico. However, for aliens, there is a requirement that the foreign country of citizenship must grant a similar credit to U.S. citizens residing in that country.

Taxpayers whose only source of income consists of salaries under $10,000 are granted a credit equal to their tax liability.

Starting in 2004, taxpayers whose only source of income includes wages, salaries, and pensions within a range of $10,000 to $50,000 will receive a tax credit ranging from $50 to $250.

Other taxes

Social security taxes/The U.S. social security combined tax rate of 7.65% applies in Puerto Rico in the same manner and uses the same wage base and tax rates as in the United States. For 2004, the old-age, survivors, and disability insurance (OASDI) rate of tax is 6.2% of the taxable wage base of $87,900. The Medicare rate of 1.45% applies to all wages paid. For self-employed individuals, the rates are 12.4% of self-employment income up to the base of $87,900, and 2.9% on total self-employment income, respectively. (No deduction of this amount is permitted in determining AGI for Puerto Rico income tax purposes.)

Local taxes on income/Other than the municipal license tax on gross business income of a sole proprietor, there are no local taxes on individual income.

Tax administration

Returns/Husbands and wives living together may elect to file separate or joint returns. There are different tax rate schedules for each case. Taxpayers may file their returns on a calendar- or fiscal-year basis.

Resident individuals must file a Puerto Rico return if gross income for the taxable year exceeds the personal exemptions and standard deductions allowed. Nonresident U.S. citizens must file a Puerto Rico return if their Puerto Rican-source income exceeds the personal exemptions, unless the tax has been fully paid at source. Nonresident aliens must file a Puerto Rico return for their Puerto Rican-source income regardless of the amount, unless the tax on such income has been fully paid at source.

Tax returns are due by the 15th day of the fourth month following the close of the taxable year in the case of residents and nonresident U.S. citizens, and by the 15th day of the sixth month following the close of the taxable year for nonresident aliens.

Payment of tax/Wages and salaries of resident individuals are subject to withholding tax. Generally, if taxpayers have sizable income not subject to withholding tax, they will be required to make quarterly payments of estimated tax. Any income taxes due after estimated payments are to be paid in full on or before the 15th day of the fourth month following the close of the taxable year (April 15 for calendar-year individual taxpayers).

Tax rates

Rates in effect for taxable year 2004 are as follows.

1. Married person living with spouse and filing a joint return, married person not living with spouse, single person, head of household, estate, or trust:

Taxable income			
Over (Column 1)	Not over	Tax on Column 1	Percentage on excess
0	$ 2,000	—	7.0
$ 2,000	17,000	$ 140	10.0
17,000	30,000	1,640	15.0
30,000	50,000	3,590	28.0
50,000		9,190	33.0

2. Married person living with spouse and filing separate return:

Taxable income			
Over (Column 1)	Not over	Tax on Column 1	Percentage on excess
0	$ 1,000	—	7.0
$ 1,000	8,500	$ 70	10.0
8,500	15,000	820	15.0
15,000	25,000	1,795	28.0
25,000		4,595	33.0

Alternative minimum tax/Taxpayers with AGI of $75,000 or more are subject to an alternative minimum tax at the following rates:

1. Over $75,000 but not over $125,000—10%.
2. Over $125,000 but not over $175,000—15%.
3. Over $175,000—20%.

Additional tax/Taxpayers with taxable income in excess of $75,000 are subject to a 5% additional tax on the excess; for married individuals living with their spouse and filing separate returns, the additional tax will be 5% on the excess over $37,500. This additional tax is limited in 2004 to $7,310 ($3,655 if married filing separately) plus 33% of the taxpayer's personal exemption and credits for dependents.

INDIVIDUAL TAX CALCULATION

Year ending December 31, 2004

Assumptions

The taxpayer is a resident of Puerto Rico for the entire year 2004, married and living with spouse and two children, filing a joint return, and electing the optional 17% withholding tax on certain interest income.

Tax computation

Gross income:		
Salary		$ 80,000
Interest from Puerto Rican banks	8,000	
Less—Annual exclusion	(2,000)	
	6,000	
Less—Amount subject to optional 17% withholding tax (see below)	(6,000)	—
Gain on sale of stock (held more than six months)		5,000
Total gross income		85,000
Less—100% of capital gain		5,000
Adjusted gross income		80,000
Deductions (itemized):		
Mortgage interest	5,500	
Real estate tax on personal residence	500	
Charitable contributions (excess over 3% of AGI)	700	6,700
		73,300
Personal allowances:		
Married, living with spouse	3,000	
One university student	1,600	
One nonuniversity student	1,600	6,200
Taxable income		$ 67,100
Income tax:		
On first 50,000		$ 9,190
On remainder (17,100) at 33%		5,643
Tentative regular tax liability		$ 14,833
Alternative minimum tax (10% of AGI)		$ 8,000
Regular tax liability		$ 14,833
Optional 17% withholding tax on interest (17% of 6,000)		1,020
Alternative tax on long-term capital gain (20% of 5,000)		1,000
Total tax liability		$ 16,853

Note:

The monetary unit is the U.S. dollar.

Romania

PwC contacts

For additional information on taxation in Romania, contact:

Ron Barden
PricewaterhouseCoopers Romania
Opera Center
1–5 Costache Negri Street
Sector 5 Bucharest
Romania
Phone: (40) (1) 202 8500
Fax: (40) (1) 202 8700
e-mail: ron.barden@ro.pwc.com

Significant developments

Starting January 1, 2004, the Fiscal Code governing the tax legislation for individuals has entered into force.

Territoriality and residence

The Fiscal Code maintains the principle of worldwide taxation of income earned by Romanian individuals domiciled in Romania, except for salary income obtained from abroad in connection with their activities carried out across the border. Romanian individuals domiciled abroad and foreign individuals who earned Romanian-source income are taxable in Romania only to the extent their income is earned through a fixed base or during a physical presence generally exceeding 183 days in any 12-month period.

Income is considered as deriving from a Romanian source if the place of origin of the income of the natural person or the place where the income is earned is situated in the Romanian territory, irrespective of where it is paid.

Individuals may be exempt from individual income taxation under the regulations of applicable international conventions for the avoidance of double taxation between Romania and their country of residence.

Foreign citizens that fulfill the criterion of fiscal residency during three consecutive years will be subject to worldwide income taxation in Romania starting with the fourth year. The three years will be counted starting in 2004.

Work permits

1. Work visas and work permits are issued for foreign individuals who intend to be employed in Romania based on a Romanian employment contract.
2. Work visas are granted by the Romanian diplomatic offices in the countries where the foreign individual is domiciled, based on a certificate that can be obtained from the Romanian Ministry of Labor.
3. Work permits are granted by the Romanian Ministry of Labor, based on the work visa and an extensive set of documents to be provided by the foreign individual.
4. No work permits are required for foreign individuals seconded to perform activities in Romania while not concluding a Romanian labor agreement.
5. Work permits are generally issued for six months with the possibility for six months extensions.

Gross income

Employee gross income/Employee gross income includes basic pay, overtime pay, supplemental pay, awards and bonuses, compensation for unused holiday or vacation time, and all other monetary amounts and benefits in kind, as well as other services obtained without payment. The income from each source is defined as the total amount of revenues received during a month, irrespective of the period in which it was generated.

Salary tax continues to apply to salary income (at a top marginal rate of 40% for amounts exceeding approximately US$385 per month).

Income tax applies to income resulting from salaries; a freelance profession; rental of real estate; copyrights; agricultural activities (in agricultural associations without legal personality); independently organized art, entertainment or sports; prizes; and pensions. Individual income taxes also apply to any gains, interest and other earnings of a permanent or casual nature.

Certain sources of income are exempt from individual income tax, for example, income obtained by foreign consultants from programs approved by the Romanian government with other governments or international government or nongovernmental organizations.

Benefits in kind are basically taxable at their market value; the private use of company cars is generally taxable at 1.7% on a monthly basis of vehicle value proportionately divided by the private mileage covered.

The value of in-kind benefits is assessed and is taxed in the month they are received. Tax settlement is made at the same time with payment of last salary rights pertaining to the respective month.

According to Romanian law, there are no concessions for short-term residents.

Capital gains and investment income/Capital gains are taxed at 1%. The 1% tax is a withholding tax and is considered a final tax. According to the Romanian legislation, the capital gain represents the positive difference between the selling price and the purchase price per types of securities, minus the applicable commissions and the nominal value. Tax is to be withheld by the buyer.

Dividends are subject to a 5% withholding tax.

Individual income tax of 1% is calculated on interest and withheld by the bank at the moment it is registered in the current account or in the deposit account (when capitalized) or at repurchase of deposit certificates.

The interests related to state bonds, current account deposits, as well as to bonds of the municipality, of the National Housing Agency and of other entities issuing bonds regarding the construction of houses is exempt from taxation.

Interests related to deposits with the mutual aid house shall be assimilated to the interests related to sight deposits and are not taxable.

The tax rate applicable to interest income is 1%, which is calculated, withheld, and paid by the payer of interest on a monthly basis.

Nonresidents/Nonresidents are subject to the following withholding taxes unless a bilateral tax treaty between Romania and the individual's country of residence states otherwise.

1. 5% on interest.
2. 15% on dividends.
3. 15% on commissions on commercial transactions.
4. 15% on revenues from technical assistance, expertise, training, and other services.
5. 15% on royalties obtained through concession of patents, licenses, trademarks, and other intellectual rights.

Tax-exempt income/The most important types of tax-exempt income are specified below.

1. Income from the sale of movable and immovable assets, sponsorship, inheritance, and donations.
2. Compensation from collective dismissals.
3. Compulsory social security contributions are deductible in the computation of the salary tax for the primary, as well as for the secondary position.
4. Reimbursement of an employee's relocation expenses, according to specific legislation, if the transfer is in the company's interest.
5. Per diems granted to employees on business trips.
6. A personal deduction (granted only to Romanian individuals).
7. Income of foreign individuals performing consultancy activities in Romania, within international free finance agreements concluded or guaranteed by the government with other governments or international governmental or non-governmental bodies.
8. Interest on state bonds, current account deposits, as well as bonds issued by the National Housing Agency.
9. Granting and vesting in stock option plans are nontaxable events.
10. Pensions up to ROL8 million (US$237) monthly.

Deductions

Personal allowances/There is a personal deduction of ROL2 million (approximately US$59) and a professional deduction of ROL300,000 (approximately US$9) per month.

Other taxes

Social security contributions

Employer:	
Social Security	Between 22–32% depending on work conditions (capped at 5 average national salaries)
Health Fund	7% (not capped)
Unemployment Fund	3% (not capped)
Solidarity Fund	2% (not capped)
Chamber of Labor Commission	0.75%, 0.25%
Employee:	
Social Security	9.5% (capped at 5 average national salaries)
Health Fund	6.5% (not capped)
Unemployment Fun	1% (not capped)

The average gross national salary for 2004 is estimated at ROL7,682,000 (approximately US$227).

Foreign citizens working in Romania on the basis of a work permit and a labor contract registered with the Labor Office are considered Romanian employees (whether or not they are deemed to be resident in Romania) and are liable for Romanian social security contributions and the Unemployment Fund contribution.

A foreign citizen who is not resident in Romania and is not employed or paid by an employer who has a permanent establishment in Romania has no liability to pay social security contributions and no requirement to prove payment of social security contributions in another territory.

Tax administration

Returns/The income tax is deducted from an employee's salary and paid by the local employer through a bank payment order at the time monthly salaries are paid. There is no requirement for individuals to submit tax returns if they are receiving only salary income form the same employer during the year. For these individuals the employer has the obligation to register with the Romanian Tax Authorities (RTA) a fiscal form.

For Romanian individuals receiving income other than salary a global individual income tax return must be submitted to the RTA by May 15 of the following year.

The following individuals domiciled in Romania are among those who must submit individual income tax returns:

1. Romanians working or seconded abroad.
2. Romanians who have two jobs at any one time.
3. Romanians who receive interest and/or dividends and/or rental income from abroad.
4. Independent consultants.

A foreign citizen working in Romania on a foreign employment contract must file a tax declaration letter within 25 days following the month to which the payment relates. The Romanian beneficiary of the foreign employee's services must file a monthly notification letter within 15 days from the start date of the assignment. The expatriate may appoint a fiscal representative to observe the tax compliance rules for the period(s) the expatriate is not in the country. The fiscal representative and the expatriate can be held jointly responsible for failure to observe the tax compliance rules.

Husbands and wives are treated as individual taxpayers; the concept of income splitting does not exist in the Romanian legal system.

Penalties for late submission of tax declarations amount up to ROL100 million.

In addition to the global individual income tax declaration, taxpayers must submit special declarations for income obtained from abroad, income obtained from independent activities, incomes obtained from ceding the usage of goods (e.g., leasing of property or machinery), and so on.

For income that has borne final tax at source (i.e., from dividends, transfer of shares, interest, other income, and pensions), the payer of the income and therefore of the tax (by withholding) must submit an informative declaration.

Tax registration/The following classes of individuals and legal entities obtaining income from activities rendered in Romania must register with the Romanian Tax Authorities to obtain a tax number (fiscal code) and a tax certificate.

1. Romanian individuals without domicile in Romania and foreign individuals who obtain income from activities carried out in Romania must submit a tax

registration declaration within 30 days of obtaining the fist Romanian sourced income.

2. Individuals who carry out commission, mandate, representation, royalty, or other similar contracts must register within 30 days from the beginning of the activity.

The Romanian tax authorities must be informed within 30 days of any change in the data.

Payment of tax/Individuals whose income derives from an employment contract, a commission contract or a retirement or disability pension will have tax withheld from the sums due them. The standard procedure for a local employment contract is to withhold the full amount of tax due (at the levels shown below) from the employee's monthly income.

In the case of a foreign employee who is paid in hard currency, the calculation of tax due is made by translating the monthly gross income into lei at the official exchange rate of the last day of said month, and the taxes will be calculated and paid from this amount.

Late payment penalties currently amount to 0.06% per day, with an additional 0.5% for each month of delay.

Tax rates

Annual rates/For the year 2004 the maximum marginal rate of 40% is applied to annual income in excess of ROL156 million (approximately US$4,617).

Annual income		Tax on	Percentage
Over	Not over	Column 1	on excess
(Column 1)			
0	ROL 28,800,000	—	18
ROL 28,800,000	69,600,000	ROL 5,184,000	23
69,600,000	111,600,000	14,568,000	28
111,600,000	156,000,000	26,328,000	34
156,000,000		41,424,000	40

Monthly rates/For the year 2004, the maximum marginal rate of 40% is applied to monthly income in excess of ROL13 million (approximately US$385).

Monthly income		Tax on	Percentage
Over	Not over	Column 1	on excess
(Column 1)			
0	ROL 2,400,000	—	18
ROL 2,400,000	5,800,000	ROL 432,000	23
5,800,000	9,300,000	1,214,000	28
9,300,000	13,000,000	2,194,000	34
13,000,000		3,452,000	40

INDIVIDUAL TAX CALCULATION

2004

Assumptions

The taxpayer is nonresident, arrived in Romania for a temporary stays (over 183 days in any 12-month period) and is employed by a foreign employer.

Tax computation

Monthly basis (assuming the expatriate has only a foreign employment agreement)

	ROL
Monthly gross income	73,000,000
Tax on salary	27,452,000
Net monthly income	45,548,000

Annual income

	ROL
Annual gross income	876,000,000
Tax on salary	329,424,000
Net monthly income	546,576,000

Note:

Exchange rate of the lei (National Bank of Romania rate) at April 20, 2004: US$1 = ROL33,788.

Russian Federation

PwC contact

For additional information on taxation in the Russian Federation, contact:

Russell Lambert
PricewaterhouseCoopers
Kosmodamianskaya Nab. 52, Bld. 5
115054 Moscow, Russia
Telephone: (7) (095) 967 6000
Fax: (7) (095) 967 6001
e-mail: russell.lambert@ru.pwc.com

Significant developments

The following information on individual taxation in the Russian Federation is accurate as of March 15, 2004. For subsequent developments, refer to the contacts above.

Territoriality and residence

For both Russian and foreign individuals, tax residence in Russia is determined by the number of days in the calendar year in which a person is present in Russia. For personal income tax purposes, an individual is considered resident if physically present in Russia for 183 or more days in a calendar year (days of arrival and departure are counted as one day).

Russian residents are liable to tax on their total worldwide income received in a calendar year. Nonresidents are taxed on income received from sources in Russia. Some tax treaties provide for periods of exemption from Russian taxation on the Russian-source income of nonresidents. Consequently, the details of any applicable tax treaty should always be examined before commencing work in Russia.

Income from Russian sources is determined as income received from property located in Russia, remuneration for activity performed in Russia, dividends received from Russian legal entities, and so on. The most important change in the definition of the Russian-source income provides that income received for work in Russia is subject to Russian personal income tax even if it is paid by a foreign legal entity from abroad.

Gross income

***Employment income*/**All income received in the course of a calendar year from employment is subject to personal income tax. This includes all earnings, bonuses, and other forms of payment or remuneration in cash or in kind. For expatriates, taxable income includes allowances paid to employees living in Russia and compensation for school fees, food, travel by employees and their families on holiday, and other nonbusiness purposes. Benefits in kind are taxed at their monetary equivalent (market price).

***Capital gains*/**There is no separate capital gains tax. Instead, gains from the disposal of property and assets are subject to income tax at the normal rate. The taxable amount is calculated as the difference between sale proceeds and historical cost or application of a statutory exemption. The statutory exemption is provided for all property sold during a calendar year and is limited to RUB1 million in the case of real estate and RUB125,000 for other property. Proceeds received from the sale of property are fully excluded from taxation if the property is owned for five years (immovable) and three years (other). This statutory exemption does not apply to gains on assets disposed of in the course of entrepreneurial activities. Additionally, the legislation sets special rules for transactions with securities.

Other taxable income/Other types of income taxable in Russia are as follows:

1. Interest income from deposits outside Russia.
2. Dividends on shares
3. Income from leasing property, both in Russia and abroad.
4. Royalties from the creation, publication, performance, and use of works of literature, art, and science, as well as from inventions, discoveries, and industrial prototypes (subject to deductions).
5. Interest and gains from deposits in banks and other credit institutions in Russia (above set limits).
6. Material benefits (i.e., in the form of savings, for example, where interest paid for a loan extended by the employer to an employee is lower than the market rate).

Nontaxable income/The following income is not taxable:

1. Reimbursement by an employer for expenses arising from a work-related change of domicile and relocation allowances within set limits.
2. Payments by an employer in compensation for injury or damage to health incurred in the performance of employment duties.
3. Severance gratuities payable upon dismissal (limits may be applicable).
4. Business travel expenses within limits.

Deductions

Nonbusiness expenses/Donations to qualifying charities are deductible from taxable income (within limit of 25% of the individual's income).

Expenditures incurred by an individual on the acquisition or construction of an apartment or house and payment of interest on mortgage loans are allowed as a deduction of up to RUB1 million plus the full amount of interest. This is a once-in-a-lifetime exemption.

Personal allowances/Individuals are granted a deduction of RUB400 per month for the taxpayer and RUB300 per month for a child or a dependent. These deductions are provided until the individual's cumulative annual income reaches RUB20,000.

Individuals can also deduct from taxable income costs of their own and their children's education in Russian-licensed institutions, medical services (for themselves and close relatives), and medicine. The limit on each type of deduction is RUR38,000.

Tax credits

Residents of Russia are entitled to credits against their Russian tax liabilities if provided by a relevant double taxation treaty. The credit cannot exceed the amount of tax payable in Russia.

Other taxes

Social security taxes/The following social security taxes are payable.

1. Unified Social Tax (UST)—All Russian and foreign legal entities registered in Russia are required to make UST payments with respect to their employees and contractors. Remuneration, bonuses, and other income paid in cash and in kind

accrued by an employer in favor of employees, as well as remuneration paid under civil law contracts for provision of works/services, and copyright agreement, is included in the taxable base. The tax is calculated for each individual. The UST is the liability of the employer only; employees are not liable to make any social security contributions.

The maximum UST contribution is 35.6%. Regressive tax rates are applied if certain requirements are fulfilled. The actual rate depends on the volume of the annual wage/salary of the employee:

a. Not more than RUB100,000—35.6%;
b. From RUB100,001 to RUB300,000—RUB35,600 + 20% of the amount exceeding RUB100,000;
c. From RUB300,001 to RUB600,000—RUB75,600 + 10% of the amount exceeding RUB300,000;
d. More than RUB600,000—RUB105,600 + 2% of the amount exceeding RUB600,000.

Starting from January 1, 2003, UST is paid with respect to foreign nationals in full in accordance with the rates stated above.

2. Statutory pension contributions—In addition to UST, all Russian and foreign legal entities registered in Russia are required to make statutory pension contributions to the State Pension Fund with respect to their Russian employees. Such contributions are fully deductible against UST. Russian pension contributions are not mandatory for foreign employees temporarily residing in Russia under Russian law. Only foreign employees having residence permits are eligible for pension and social reimbursements from the Russian state pension system.

   The base for statutory pension contributions is similar to the base for UST. For Individual entrepreneurs the base is equal to the income related to the entrepreneurial activity, excluding related expenses.

   Tax rates depend on age and gender of employees and also on the amount of tax base and are divided into insurance and investment portions.

3. Statutory accident insurance—Employers are also obliged to pay an obligatory contribution of insurance against accidents at work and professional diseases. The rate of this contribution varies from 0.2% to 8.5% of the wage fund, depending on the type of activity of the employer.

Gift and inheritance tax/Gift and inheritance tax is payable by Russian and foreign citizens on transfers of assets located in Russia, whether by way of gift or inheritance. Rates go up to 40%, depending on the value of the transfer and the relationship of the transferor and transferee. Transfers from one spouse to another are exempt.

Property tax/Property tax is imposed on property located in Russia and owned by Russian and foreign citizens, subject to double tax treaties provisions. The tax applies to buildings, houses, and apartments and is levied at the rate of 0.1% to 2% of the value of the property.

Transport tax/Transport tax is imposed on cars, motorcycles, buses, vans, planes, helicopters, yachts, boats, ships, and other water, air, and land transport registered in Russia and owned by Russian and foreign individuals. Fixed rates (per unit of horse-power, gross ton, or unit of transport), which are differentiated based on the engine capacity, gross tonnage and type of transport, are applied. The actual rates in regions may be subject to the maximum five-fold increase/decrease by legislative bodies of Russian Federation constituents. Reporting and payment rules are established by the regional legislative authorities (e.g., in Moscow reporting and payment shall be made on an annual basis by January 20 following the reporting year).

Tax administration

Returns and payment/Tax in respect of employment earnings and certain other payments must be deducted at source by the entity making the payment. This includes tax on income from the performance of labor under civil law contracts. Individuals receiving income from foreign sources and some other types of income from which tax is not withheld at source are responsible for the declaration of taxable income and payment of Russian tax.

Declarations of income must be submitted no later than April 30 following the reporting year. The tax payment is generally due no later than July 15 of the year following the reporting year. Tax overpaid may, at the taxpayer's request, be either refunded or credited against future liabilities.

A declaration of actual income received during the period of stay in Russia must also be made one month prior to permanent departure from Russia. Joint returns for a husband and wife are not permitted. There is no provision for a taxable year other than the calendar year.

Tax rates

Income tax is payable in rubles at the rates applicable to certain income categories. Earnings in foreign currency are converted into rubles at the exchange rate of the Central Bank of the Russian Federation on each date income is received. The tax rate is 13% for all types of income received by residents, except those listed below.

1. Dividends received by tax residents are taxed at 6%. There is a special offset mechanism for dividends paid out by group companies to its shareholders.
2. The tax rate of 35% is established in respect of certain types of income:
   a. The value of any awards and prizes received during contests, games, and other events conducted for the purpose of advertising goods, work, and services, in excess of the set limits.
   b. Insurance payments under voluntary insurance agreements in excess of the set limits.
   c. Interest income on deposits in Russian banks in excess of the amount calculated based on the Central Bank current interest rate on ruble deposits during the period for which the interest is accrued and 9% annual interest on foreign currency deposits.
   d. Amounts of interest on the taxpayer's borrowed funds in excess of the limits.
3. The tax rate is established at 30% in respect of any income received by individuals that are nonresidents of the Russian Federation for tax purposes.

Exchange rate issues

Foreign income is convertible into rubles for tax calculation purposes at the exchange rate quoted by the Central Bank of the Russian Federation, effective on the date of receipt of the income. Tax payments are to be made in rubles only and only through individual accounts.

Exchange rate of the ruble at March 12, 2004: US$1 = RUB28.5083;
€1 = RUB35.0053.

St. Lucia

PwC contact

For additional information on taxation in St. Lucia, contact:

Richard N. C. Peterkin
PricewaterhouseCoopers
PricewaterhouseCoopers Centre
Pointe Seraphine
P.O. Box 195
Castries, St. Lucia, W.I.
Telephone: (1) (758) 452 2511
Fax: (1) (758) 452 1061
e-mail: richard.n.peterkin@lc.pwc.com

Significant developments

There have been no significant tax or regulatory developments in regard to individual taxation in the past year.

Territoriality and residence

St. Lucia income tax is imposed on the following.

1. Income of an individual ordinarily resident in St. Lucia that accrues to the individual directly or indirectly from all sources whether in or outside St. Lucia.
2. Income of an individual resident but not ordinarily resident in St. Lucia that accrues to the individual directly or indirectly from all sources in St. Lucia and income accrued from sources outside St. Lucia to the extent that the income is remitted to St. Lucia.
3. Income arising in St. Lucia to a nonresident, and income accrued from sources outside St. Lucia to the extent that the income is received in St. Lucia.

An individual is regarded as resident in St. Lucia if one of the following applies.

1. The individual's permanent place of abode is in St. Lucia and the individual is physically present for some period of time in the income year.
2. The individual is physically present in St. Lucia for not less than 183 days in the income year.
3. The individual is physically present in St. Lucia for a continuous period of less than 183 days in the year of income but is resident in the immediately preceding or succeeding year of income.

Gross income

Employee gross income/Employees resident in St. Lucia are taxed on their salary and on the value of any allowances or benefits, whether in cash or otherwise, received from an employer. Taxable benefits include employer-provided automobile and housing (except where representative occupation can be established) but do not include travel and entertainment allowances where the employee substantiates expenditure in the performance of duties to the extent of the allowances.

Capital gains and investment income/Capital gains are not taxable to individuals ordinarily resident in St. Lucia. Investment income in the form of dividends and bank interest from corporations or banks in St. Lucia is exempt from income tax. For individuals not ordinarily resident in St. Lucia (i.e., those present for a short term), such income, if arising outside St. Lucia, is taxable only to the extent that it is remitted to St. Lucia.

Deductions

Business deductions/Employees may deduct expenses incurred wholly and exclusively in the performance of the duties of their employment, but only to the extent that these expenses are not reimbursed by the employer.

Nonbusiness expenses/Nonbusiness expenses are not deductible.

Personal allowances/In determining chargeable income, a resident individual, upon due claim, is allowed the following deductions.

	EC$
Personal allowance	16,000
Spouse allowance	1,500 (1)
Maintenance or alimony (under court order)	Full amount
Child allowances	1,000–2,000
Deduction for higher education	5,000
Deduction for life insurance, other retirement benefits:	
Premiums paid in St. Lucia (maximum)	8,000
Premiums paid outside St. Lucia (maximum)	3,000
Owner-occupied property:	
Mortgage interest (maximum)	15,000
Property taxes	Actual
Insurance premiums	Actual
Upkeep and maintenance	Actual
Donations to charitable, religious, educational institutions (under deed of covenant for at least three years)	(2)
Medical expenses	Actual
Purchase of shares in building or cooperative societies	Up to 5,000
Interest on student loans	3,000
Purchase of shares in a public and private company registered in St. Lucia	5,000
Registered Home Ownership Savings Plan	6,000
Purchase of a solar water heater	6,500
Approved pension funds established in St. Lucia	Full amount
Dependent relative allowance	350

Notes:

1. Reduced dollar-for-dollar to the extent the spouse's assessable income exceeds EC$1,500.
2. Actual, but may not exceed 25% of assessable income.

Tax credits

A tax credit for foreign tax paid is granted where income accrues to a resident in St. Lucia when that income has been taxed in another country with which there is no treaty or where the income is not covered by the applicable treaty. This credit is the lesser of the tax payable in the other country or the tax charged in St. Lucia.

Other taxes

Social security taxes/The individual's share of National Insurance Scheme contributions (for retirement, sickness, and disability benefits) is 5% of gross salary up to a maximum contribution of EC$250 per month (i.e., on a monthly salary of EC$5,000).

Local taxes on income/There are no other taxes on income.

Tax administration

Returns/Separate returns are required from married persons where the other spouse has income in that spouse's own name. For employed persons, the taxable year is the calendar year.

Payment of tax/There is withholding of tax from salaries. Employed persons must file returns within three months of the end of the income year, and any additional tax assessed is payable upon filing.

Tax rates

Tax rates on chargeable income from January 1, 2003 are as follows.

Taxable income		Tax on	Percentage
Over	Not over	Column 1	on excess
(Column 1)			
0	EC$ 10,000	—	10
EC$ 10,000	20,000	EC$ 1,000	15
20,000	30,000	2,500	20
30,000		4,500	30

INDIVIDUAL TAX CALCULATION

Assumptions

1. Married person resident in St. Lucia with two children; one child attends a university overseas; spouse has no assessable income.
2. Employment income: EC$150,000, net of National Insurance contributions.
3. Director's fees: EC$6,000.
4. Bank interest received: EC$12,000 (bank in St. Lucia).
5. Dividend income received: EC$8,000.
6. Mortgage interest paid: EC$18,000.
7. Life insurance premiums: EC$9,000. (Insured amount: EC$250,000).
8. Capital gain on sale of investments: EC$60,000.

Tax computation

Gross income:		
Income from employment		EC$ 150,000
Director's fees		6,000
Bank interest received		12,000
Dividends received		8,000
Capital gain on sale of investments		60,000
		236,000
Deduct—Tax-exempt income:		
Bank interest	12,000	
Dividends	8,000	
Capital gain	60,000	80,000
		156,000
Less—Allowances:		
Personal allowance	16,000	
Spouse allowance	1,500	
Child allowance (1 x 1,000)	1,000	
Child higher education allowance (1 x 5,000)	5,000	
Life insurance premiums (restricted)	8,000	31,500
		124,500
Less—Owner-occupied property expenses:		
Mortgage interest (maximum)	15,000	
Property taxes (say)	2,000	
Insurance premium (say)	1,500	
Upkeep and maintenance (say)	1,000	19,500
Chargeable income		EC$ 105,000
Tax thereon:		
On the first 30,000		EC$ 4,500
On the remaining 75,000 at 30%		22,500
		EC$ 27,000

Note:

Exchange rate of the Eastern Caribbean dollar at January 1, 2004: US$1 = EC$2.670.

Saudi Arabia

PwC contact

For additional information on taxation in Saudi Arabia, contact:

Sami B. Al Sarraj
Al Juraid & Company
10th Floor, North Tower
King Faisal Foundation Bldg.
P.O. Box 8282
Riyadh 11482, Saudi Arabia
Telephone: (966) (1) 465 4240
Fax: (966) (1) 465 1663
e-mail: salsarraj@aljuraid.com

Absence of taxation

Income tax is not imposed on individuals in Saudi Arabia.

Note

Exchange rate of the Saudi Riyal at January 1, 2004: US$1 = SR3.75.

PwC contact

For additional information on taxation in Singapore, contact:

Jenny Goh
PricewaterhouseCoopers Services Pte Ltd.
8 Cross Street
#17-00 PWC Building
Singapore 048424
Telephone: (65) 6236 3388
Fax: (65) 6236 3715
e-mail: jenny.goh@sg.pwcglobal.com

Significant developments

Certain changes were announced in the 2004 Singapore Budget, including the following.

1. Despite a reduction in the corporate tax rate (from income year 2004), the top marginal personal tax rate for a tax resident remains at 22%.
2. All foreign-source income received in Singapore by a resident individual will be exempt from tax with effect from income year 2004.
3. Certain Singapore-sourced investment income from financial instruments received by individuals is exempt from tax from income year 2004.

Territoriality and residence

Income is taxable when it accrues in or is derived from Singapore, whether or not the individual is resident in Singapore. Income derived from sources outside Singapore is taxable only if it is received in Singapore by a resident individual. However, all income remitted into Singapore is exempt from tax with effect from income year 2004. Prior to this year, only certain income remitted into Singapore may be exempt from tax—for example, Not Ordinarily Resident (NOR) individuals can remit their overseas income relating to pre-arrival in Singapore free of tax during the qualifying NOR period.

Individuals are resident in Singapore if they reside there except for such temporary absence therefrom as may be reasonable and not inconsistent with a claim to be resident in Singapore. Individuals who are physically present or who exercise an employment (other than as a director of a company) in Singapore for 183 days or more during the year preceding the year of assessment are treated as resident for that year of assessment. As a concession, an expatriate who stays in Singapore for a consecutive period spanning three calendar years (not necessarily three complete calendar years) is considered a resident. Resident individuals are entitled to certain personal allowances and are subject to graduated tax rates ranging from 0% to 22%. Nonresident individuals are not entitled to any personal allowances and are subject to tax at the corporate rate of 20% (with effect from income year 2004). As a concession, their employment income is taxed at the higher of 15% or the graduated resident rates with personal allowances. This concession does not apply to nonresident directors.

Gross income

Employee gross income/If the employment is exercised in Singapore, employment income is treated as earned there and is therefore taxable in Singapore. The countries of the employer, of payment and of the beneficiary of the services are generally irrelevant in determining the country of source of employment income.

Employment income includes salaries, bonuses, allowances, perquisites, and benefits in kind. Certain benefits in kind are accorded preferential rates, which are less than the actual cost to the employer. The benefit of housing accommodation is normally calculated as the lesser of 10% of the assessable emoluments (including gains from stock options) and the annual (rental) value of the property, less the rent paid by the employee. Furniture and fittings provided are taxable at prescribed rates. By concession, only 20% of the cost of one home-leave passage in respect of the employee and spouse, and two trips for qualifying children, is assessed on the expatriate. The amount of tax borne by the employer is treated as additional income of the employee.

Short-term visiting employees are not subject to tax on income from an employment exercised in Singapore if the employment does not exceed 60 days. This exemption, however, does not apply to a public entertainer or to a company director.

Area representatives of nonresident companies who reside in and use Singapore as a base for activities extending to other countries are assessed on the remuneration relating to the time actually spent in Singapore or on the remuneration received in Singapore, whichever is greater.

NOR individuals will be accorded the following favorable tax treatment during the qualifying period subject to the fulfillment of certain conditions.

- Exemption for income earned prior to Singapore assignment and remitted to Singapore. With the new foreign-source income exemption for Singapore residents (as highlighted above), this may no longer be an attractive tax incentive for NORs.
- Exemption on employer's contribution to nonmandatory overseas pension or social security funds, subject to limitations.

  and
- Time apportionment of Singapore employment income, subject to a minimum of 90 business days outside of Singapore and a minimum 10% tax.

All retirement benefits other than CPF (Central Provident Fund) benefits, including gratuities and pensions, are generally taxable; partial exemption may be possible in specified cases. CPF is the national pension scheme in Singapore. The scheme is only available to Singapore citizens and permanent residents and it provides a lump sum at the normal retirement age, consisting of past contributions made at prescribed rates by the employee and the employer, as well as interest thereon. However, CPF contributions made under certain circumstances are deemed to be part of employment income, which is taxable.

Another retirement scheme is the SRS (Supplementary Retirement Scheme). However, the withdrawals from this scheme may be fully taxable or 50% taxable, depending on whether certain conditions have been fulfilled.

Capital gains and investment income/There is no capital gains tax in Singapore. Where an individual enters into a series of capital transactions, however, the tax authorities may take the view that the individual is carrying on a business and assess that person to income tax accordingly.

Income from interest, dividends, rents, royalties, and so on, derived from Singapore is taxable whether or not the individual is resident in Singapore. However, certain types of interest received by a nonresident individual are exempt from income tax, such as interest on deposits with banks and on qualifying debt securities. Investment income derived from sources outside Singapore is taxable in the hands of resident individuals only if it is received in Singapore.

For the period January 1, 2003, to December 31, 2004, interest received by resident individuals on amounts exceeding S$100,000 will be exempt from tax if they are derived from standard savings, current and fixed deposit accounts in Singapore. However, if they are POSB (Post Office Savings Bank) savings deposits, the exemption will also apply to interest earned from deposits on the first S$100,000. With effect from January 1, 2005, the exemption will be extended to all interest income earned in any standard savings, current and fixed deposit accounts in Singapore.

With effect from June 1, 2003, foreign dividends, foreign branch profits and foreign service income remitted to Singapore will be exempt from tax if the highest corporate tax rate in the foreign jurisdiction is at least 15%. From income year 2004, the exemption is extended to all foreign-source income of a Singapore resident individual. In addition, certain Singapore-source investment income from financial instruments received by individuals is exempt from tax with effect from income year 2004.

Deductions

Business deductions/Where an individual carries on a trade, business, profession, or vocation, deductions are allowed for all outgoings and expenses incurred wholly and exclusively in the production of the income being assessed, including capital allowances (fiscal depreciation) on most fixed assets except for land and nonindustrial buildings.

Nonbusiness expenses/An individual can deduct annual subscriptions paid to professional institutes or societies in which membership is generally required as a condition of employment. Interest expense may be deductible, provided it is incurred wholly and exclusively in the production of income. Mortgage interest is, therefore, deductible only where the property concerned yields income. A deduction may also be claimed for donations to approved charities. This includes donations made in the form of cash, artifacts, shares that are listed on the Singapore Exchange and unit trusts readily marketable in Singapore, and land and buildings to approved. Such approved donations will qualify for double deduction unless certain naming rights are attached to the amount donated.

No deductions are allowed for medical expenses or for any other personal or household expenditure.

Singapore citizens and permanent residents are allowed deductions against their taxable income for contributions made to the CPF or an approved pension/provident fund but subject to the following limits.

1. Contributions made up to the limit prescribed in the CPF Act.
2. For a self-employed individual, the deduction for contributions made is restricted to the lesser of S$21,780 (S$19,800 for income year 2005) or 33% of assessable business income, whichever is lower.

Life insurance premium is deductible, but subject to certain conditions; the total deduction (i.e., contributions to the CPF and life insurance premium) is restricted to S$5,000.

A deduction for SRS contributions of up to 15% (for Singapore citizens and permanent residents) and up to 35% (for foreigners) of income can be claimed against the income earned in the year in which the contributions are made (subject to income capping rules similar to CPF income capping rules).

Personal allowances/For year of assessment 2005 (income year 2004) the following amounts are deductible from the assessable income of a resident individual to arrive at the income subject to tax.

1. Self—Nil.
2. Wife allowance—S$2,000.
3. Handicapped spouse allowance—S$3,500 for the maintenance of a handicapped spouse whose income does not exceed S$2,000 for the year.
4. Earned income allowance—Lesser of actual earned income or S$1,000 if age is under 55; increased for individuals who are 55 and over or are handicapped.
5. Child allowance:
   a. Qualifying child relief for individuals having up to four children under the age of 16 years or in full-time education—First, second, and third child, S$2,000 each; fourth child, S$2,000 only if born after 1987;
   b. Handicapped child—S$3,500;
   c. Enhanced child relief for better-educated working mothers—The child relief for each of the first four children is equal to the normal child relief plus a percentage of the mother's earned income, subject to a maximum. For a child 12 years and above on the first day of the income year, the percentages applicable for the first, second, third, and fourth child are 5%, 10%, 15%, and 15%, respectively, with a maximum for each child of S$10,000 including reliefs claimed under (a), (b), and (c) above. For a child under 12 years of age on the first day of the income year, the respective percentages for the first, second, third, and fourth child are 5%, 15%, 20%, and 25%, with a maximum for each child of S$15,000 including reliefs claimed under (a), (b), and (c) above. Relief is available for a fourth child only if born after 1986. As a fourth child born in 1987 does not qualify for normal child relief, the increased or enhanced child relief is given at S$1,500 plus the applicable percentage of the mother's earned income.

      Reliefs claimed under (a), (b), and (c) may be apportioned and claimed as agreed between a husband and wife. The total relief claimed by husband and wife must not exceed the maximum claim available for each child. This option of a split claim is not available for the fourth child if born in 1987.
   d. A S$20,000 one-time tax rebate against either or both parents' tax liability plus a tax rebate at 15% of the mother's earned income against her tax liability is available for a third child born after 1986 and a fourth child born after 1987 if the child and the elder siblings are all Singapore citizens. The 15% tax rebate is restricted to S$20,000 in respect of the third child and S$40,000 in respect of the fourth child born on or after April 1, 2001.

      For a second Singaporean child born after 1989 to a mother under 31 years of age, a one-time special rebate against either or both parents' tax liability, depending on the mother's age, is available as follows.

Age of mother	Tax rebate
	S$
Below 28 years	20,000
Below 29 years	15,000
Below 30 years	10,000
Below 31 years	5,000

The special tax rebates must generally be used up within seven or nine years. Divorcees are able to continue claiming the unabsorbed tax rebate.

6. Aged dependent relief:
   a. Aged parent or grandparent maintained by taxpayer—S$3,500.
   b. Aged parent or grandparent living with taxpayer—S$5,000.
   c. Aged dependent's income must not exceed S$2,000 per annum.

   An additional S$3,000 will be added to the above dependent relief if the parent or grandparent is handicapped.
7. Delivery and hospitalization expenses—An amount not exceeding S$3,000 for a fourth child born after 1987.
8. Educational expenses—Course fees (including tuition and examination fees) not exceeding S$3,500 relating to approved academic, professional, or vocational qualifications. Fees for courses, seminars, and conferences to nonapproved courses can be included as long as they are relevant to the taxpayer's new occupation and the career change is made within two years of assessment of the completion of these nonapproved courses.
9. Foreign maid levy—Twice the amount of levy imposed on one maid is deductible against the earned income of a married woman or of a divorced or separated woman with dependent children living with her in the same household.
10. Reservists—S$1,500 or S$3,000 for those who have completed or performed national service. A relief of S$750 each will also be given to Singaporean parents and wives of reservists against their own income.

Additional allowances are granted for dependent great-grandparents and handicapped siblings, as well as for topping up CPF accounts of parents' and nonworking spouse's (aged 55 years and above deriving income of not more than S$2,000).

Tax credits

For treaty countries, credit for all or part of the foreign tax against the tax assessed on the foreign income in Singapore may be granted. For nontreaty countries, unilateral tax credits are given for foreign tax paid on dividend income, royalties, employment income and director's fees derived therefrom, and all service fees received from any country. Tax deducted at source from a Singapore dividend is available as a credit against any Singapore tax payable or, if no tax is payable, as a refund. However, Singapore dividends paid under the one-tier taxation system is exempt from tax.

Other taxes

Social security taxes/CPF contributions are payable in respect of Singapore citizen and permanent residents only. With effect from October 1, 2003, the employer contributes 13% and the employee contributes 20% of ordinary wages paid in cash (e.g., monthly salary), up to a maximum contribution of S$780 (S$715 from January 1, 2004) and S$1,200 (S$1,100) per month, respectively, and 13%/20% of additional wages (e.g., year-end bonus), up to a maximum contribution as follows.

1. Prior to January 1, 2004;
   a. The actual additional wages if the annual ordinary wages is not more than S$72,000 and the total wages is not more than S$100,000;
   b. The difference between S$100,000 and annual ordinary wages if the total wages exceed S$100,000 but the annual ordinary wages are not more than S$72,000; or
   c. 40% of annual ordinary wages if total wages exceed S$100,000 and annual ordinary wages exceed S$72,000.
2. From January 1, 2004:
   a. The actual additional wages if the annual ordinary wages is not more than S$66,000 and the total wages is not more than S$93,500;
   b. The difference between S$93,500 and annual ordinary wages if the total wages exceed S$93,500 but the annual ordinary wages are not more than S$66,000; or
   c. The lower of S$27,500 or the actual additional wages if annual ordinary wages exceed S$66,000.

The above CPF contribution caps will be further reduced from January 1, 2005 onward, in line with the ordinary wage ceiling reduction targeted to take effect from that date.

No CPF contributions are required for foreign nationals.

See also “Employee gross income” and “Nonbusiness expenses” above.

The contribution rate caps for contributions made to the SRS scheme are as follows.

	%
Singapore citizens or permanent residents	15
Foreigners	35

Unlike CPF, this is a voluntary scheme, and employers are not allowed to contribute. The maximum amount to be contributed is subject to income capping rules that are similar to CPF income capping rules.

Local taxes on income/There are no other taxes on income in Singapore.

Tax administration

Returns/Each taxpayer is required to make an annual return of income and of such particulars as may be required to determine the personal allowances due. A wife can elect to be separately assessed on her income. In such a case, she can choose to file a return separate from her husband’s. The tax return must be filed on a calendar-year basis and must be submitted by April 15.

Payment of tax/The tax assessed is payable within one month of the date of the assessment whether or not a notice of objection to the assessment has been lodged with the tax authorities. The notice of objection must be lodged within 30 days of the date of the notice of assessment, failing which the assessment will be treated as final.

In the case of an employee, the tax authorities will upon application generally allow the payment of tax by monthly installments with no interest, using the giro system.

Tax rates

Residents/A resident individual's taxable income (after setoff of personal allowances) is subject to income tax at progressive rates. Current rates for year of assessment 2004 (income year 2003) are shown below.

Taxable income Over (Column 1)	Taxable income Not over	Tax on Column 1	Percentage on excess
0	S$ 20,000	—	0
S$ 20,000	30,000	—	4
30,000	40,000	S$ 400	6
40,000	80,000	1,000	9
80,000	160,000	4,600	15
160,000	320,000	16,600	19
320,000		47,000	22

Nonresidents/Nonresident individuals are taxed at 20%, except that Singapore employment income is taxed at a flat rate of 15% or at resident rates with personal reliefs, whichever yields a higher tax. A nonresident director's remuneration does not qualify for the reduced rate, and tax at 20% must be deducted from remuneration paid to a nonresident director.

INDIVIDUAL TAX CALCULATION

Income year 2004 tax liability (year of assessment 2005)

Assumptions

The employee is a foreign national resident in Singapore, his wife does not earn any income, and they have two children under the age of 16.

Tax computation

Salary and allowances		S$ 150,000
School fees		15,000
Benefits in kind:		
Home-leave passage—20% of 11,500	2,300	
Furniture, refrigerator, air conditioners, stove, and fans at nominal rates, plus (estimated) utilities	6,900	9,200
		174,200
Value of unfurnished accommodation—Lesser of annual rent paid by employer (say 72,000) and 10% of assessable emoluments (174,200)		17,420
		191,620
Investment income:		
Bank interest income	500	
Dividends—Singapore (assuming a one-tier exempt dividend)	—	500
Assessable income		192,120
Deduct—Personal allowances:		
Earned income	1,000	
Wife	2,000	
Children	4,000	(7,000)
Taxable income		S$ 185,120
Tax thereon:		
Tax on first 160,000		S$ 16,600
Tax on balance—25,120 at 19%		4,772
Total tax payable		S$ 21,372

Note:

Exchange rate of the Singapore dollar at February 1, 2004: US$1 = S$1.7004.

PwC contact

For additional information on taxation in the Slovak Republic, contact:

Joe Kerrane, Tax Partner
PricewaterhouseCoopers Tax, k.s.
Hviezdoslavovo namestie 20
815 32 Bratislava
Slovak Republic
Telephone: (421) (2) 5441 41 01
Fax: (421) (2) 5441 41 02
e-mail: joe.kerrane@sk.pwcglobal.com

General note

This entry is repeated from the 2003/2004 edition. For more up-to-date information consult the contact listed above or Jacqueline Collette at jacqueline.collette@us.pwc.com.

Significant developments

Significant changes to the tax legislation were introduced in the Slovak Republic on January 1, 2003, especially relating to value-added tax (VAT). The legislation may be subject to frequent amendments and official interpretation as the market economy develops. It is therefore advisable to contact PwC Bratislava for up-to-date information.

Territoriality and residence

A resident of the Slovak Republic is subject to tax on worldwide income, irrespective of whether the income is remitted to the Slovak Republic.

An individual who spends more than 183 days in a calendar year or holds a residence permit or has a permanent place of abode in the Slovak Republic is resident for tax purposes.

A nonresident is liable to tax on Slovak-source income only, subject to relief available under an applicable double taxation treaty. Slovak-source income includes income from work performed in the territory of the Slovak Republic, irrespective of the place of payment or if the employer is a Slovak resident.

Gross income

Employee gross income/The gross income of employees includes all wages, salaries, and bonuses paid and any benefits in kind (subject to minor exceptions) received as a result of employment. In principle, benefits in kind are valued at open-market values, although a fixed rate of 12% per annum of the purchase price is applied to cars provided by the employer, unless the employee is not entitled to private use of the car. The reimbursement of travel expenses in excess of fairly low statutory limits is also a taxable benefit to the employee.

Fees payable to members of statutory bodies of Slovak companies are taxed under the payroll administration using progressive tax rates. Employers must keep Slovak payroll records.

Capital gains and investment income/Capital gains form part of total income and are therefore subject to income tax at the taxpayer's marginal rate. Exemptions are available for gains that arise on the disposal of assets that have not been used for commercial purposes and have been held for specified minimum periods, as follows:

1. Securities held for more than 36 months.
2. Cars and other movable assets held for more than 12 months.
3. Real estate held for more than five years.

Subject to certain conditions, a gain on the sale of an apartment or a house, provided that it has been owned by the taxpayer and has been the taxpayer's residence for at least two years before the sale, as well as a gain on the sale of property by the first owner after restitution are also exempt from personal income tax.

Interest earned on Slovak savings deposits is subject to a final withholding tax of 15%. Dividends received from Slovak companies are also subject to final withholding tax at the rate of 15%.

Interest, dividends, and other investment income received from foreign sources are added to total taxable income and taxed at a progressive rate. Credit relief is available for foreign taxes paid on such income (see "Tax credits").

Foreigners who are not tax residents in the Slovak Republic are not liable to tax on investment income received from foreign sources.

Deductions

Business deductions/No deductions are available from income from employment. Sums received by way of reimbursement of expenses incurred in connection with employment are exempt from tax, provided they do not exceed the statutory limits. Private entrepreneurs may deduct ordinary business expenses.

Nonbusiness deductions/In certain cases necessary expenses incurred in the earning of income from nonbusiness sources can be deducted from the income earned (i.e., rental income). There are no standard deductions. For certain categories of income, a fixed percentage of gross income can be claimed as a deduction instead of actual expenditures. Employees' social and health insurance contributions are deductible from employment income. Donations to Slovak organizations for the purpose of, for example, financing science and education are deductible up to a maximum of 10% of total taxable income, provided the total value of the donations is at least SKK500. From January 1, 2002, it is possible to donate 1% of the taxpayer's personal tax liability to eligible organizations by request to the tax authorities.

Personal allowances/A basic allowance of SKK38,760 per annum is available to all individuals. A further SKK12,000 per annum is available to taxpayers supporting a spouse in a joint home, provided the spouse's income does not exceed SKK38,760 per annum. An allowance of SKK16,800 per dependent child is available, and further allowances are available for disabled dependents. The allowances are deducted from the tax base. Spouse and child allowances are not available to individuals who do not have a permanent abode in the Slovak Republic.

Tax credits

A credit for foreign tax paid on foreign-source income taxable in the Slovak Republic is available up to the amount of tax that would be payable on that income in the Slovak Republic.

Other taxes

Social security taxes/Individuals employed by a Slovak entity must pay social and health insurance contributions totaling 12% of gross salary, calculated on a maximum monthly threshold of SKK24,000 for health insurance and SKK32,000 for social security contributions. Employers must pay corresponding contributions totaling 38% of gross salary. The employees' contributions are deductible from salary for income tax purposes. Neither foreign individuals nor their employers are required to make contributions if they are employed by a foreign company under foreign law.

Private entrepreneurs must contribute to social security and health insurance at the rate of 50% of half of the prorated monthly tax base from their business activities. This half cannot be lower than SKK3,000 and should not exceed SKK24,000.

Local taxes on income/There are no local taxes on income.

Tax administration

Returns/If annual income is in excess of SKK10,000, a return must be filed by March 31 following the calendar year-end. A request to extend the filing deadline to June 30 may be submitted at the latest by March 31. The deadline may be extended to June 30 if the personal income tax return is prepared by a registered Slovak tax adviser under a power of attorney. It is also possible to file a request with the tax authorities for an extension to September 30, for example, if the taxpayer has income from sources abroad, but in this case the extension is based on the decision of the tax authority, which has 30 days to notify the taxpayer of the actual decision.

Husbands and wives must file separate income tax returns.

A tax return does not have to be filed if all income received has been subject to tax at source in the Slovak Republic. This also applies if the employment income paid by a Slovak employer is the only source of income of an individual and the individual did not change its employer or was not employed by two entities during the year.

Payment of tax/Income tax is withheld monthly at source from employment income for employees of a Slovak company or branch, for employees of a foreign company assigned to work in a Slovak branch or permanent establishment of that foreign company, and for employees assigned to work in a Slovak company.

For income from all sources that has not been liable to Slovak tax at source, individuals are responsible for making advance tax payments on the basis of their previous year's tax liability, unless their only Slovak-source income is from a dependent activity, in which case the taxation is administered through a Slovak payroll.

Tax rates

Personal income tax

Taxable income			Tax on Column 1	Percentage on excess
Over	Not over			
(Column 1)				
0	SKK 90,000	....	—	10
SKK 90,000	180,000	....	SKK 9,000	20
180,000	396,000	....	27,000	28
396,000	564,000	....	87,480	35
564,000		....	146,280	38

INDIVIDUAL TAX CALCULATION

Calendar year ending December 31, 2002

Assumptions

The individual is a foreigner who is employed by a non–Slovak-resident employer and assigned to work in the Slovak Republic for a period of more than 183 days in a calendar year. The individual is married, supports a spouse and two children. No social security liability arises. Accommodation is directly provided by the employer. The individual was resident in the Slovak Republic for the financial year.

Tax computation

Income from employment:		
Salary	2,000,000	
Accommodation	245,000	
Company car (1)	96,000	SKK 2,341,000
Less—Personal allowance		38,760
Taxable income		SKK 2,302,240
Rounding		SKK 2,302,200
Tax due (146,280 + 38% of 1,738,200)		SKK 806,796

Notes:

1. 12% of purchase price (including VAT) of SKK800,000.
2. Exchange rate of the Slovak koruna as of December 31, 2002: US$1 = SKK40.036.

PwC contact

For additional information on taxation in Slovenia, contact:

Nada Drobnic
PricewaterhouseCoopers
Parmova 53
1000 Ljubljana
Telephone: (386) (1) 475 01 00
Fax: (386) (1) 475 01 09
e-mail: nada.drobnic@si.pwc.com

Significant developments

There have been no significant tax or regulatory developments as regards individual taxation in the past year.

Territoriality and residence

Both resident and nonresident persons are liable to individual income tax.

Residents, that is, individuals with permanent residence in Slovenia, are liable for tax on their Slovenian-source income as well as—in certain cases—on their worldwide income (e.g., income from property, dividends, interest).

Nonresident individuals who have a temporary domicile in Slovenia are also subject to tax, but only on their Slovenian-source income, which may arise from payments for an activity performed in Slovenia or from payments made in Slovenia for an activity performed abroad. Nonresidents are exempt from tax on income if so stipulated by an international treaty ratified by the Republic of Slovenia. Nonresidents are obliged to submit annual tax return if they are present in Slovenia for at least six consecutive months in a calendar year.

Taxable income

Individuals are subject to tax under the Law on Personal Income Tax, which entered into force on January 1994.

Individuals are taxed at progressive rates on their income received in one calendar year, which is classified into the following six categories.

1. Income from employment, pensions, and other receipts.
2. Income from agriculture.
3. Income from private business or professional activity.
4. Capital gains.
5. Income from property.
6. Income from property rights (royalties).

The annual taxable base is the aggregate of the taxable bases of these different types of income.

Income from employment, pensions, and other receipts/The first category of income includes salaries, salary compensation, and other income from employment, income in the form of incentive and benefits (compensation for work-related expenses are exempt from the tax base up to a certain level as determined by the government regulations) less social security contributions; pensions; gross income earned under contracts for temporary work or for the execution of services and jobs on other bases reduced by expenses in a lump-sum amount (10% of the income) or actual expenses; and other receipts, including prizes.

The taxable benefits that form a part of the personal income tax base include the following items:

1. Payments made by the employer for noncompulsory old-age pension and health insurance, other personal insurance, lodging expenses; and educational expenses unrelated to employment.
2. The value of any gifts provided by the employer if, in the month in which the gifts are received, their value exceeds 5% of the average salary of all employees in the Republic of Slovenia in the previous month.
3. The difference between the interest charged on the basis of growth of retail prices and the lower interest charged by the employer on a loan given to an employee.
4. Cars provided by an employer for the personal use of an employee. Two percent of the vehicle's net book value is included in the employee's monthly tax base, taking into consideration the straight-line depreciation method and an annual depreciation rate of 15%.
5. The amount of the discount granted to the employee on products, commercial goods and services of the employer.

Income from agriculture/Cadastral income of farmland and woodland under the regulations on ascertainment such income.

Income from private business or professional activity/Profit derived by a sole proprietor whose sole activity is the independent performance of a profit-making activity and the profit derived from the professional activity of writers, painters, professional athletes, and so on. The profit is determined by deducting expenditures from income for a given calendar year.

Capital gains/Capital gains are defined as the gain achieved by selling real estate and/or securities and other shares in capital.

Taxes paid by the taxpayer in connection with real estate are deducted from the taxable base.

Income from property/Income from property is defined as income from participation in profits; interest from loans; and income from renting land and buildings.

Income from participation in the profits of legal persons, that is, dividends, is subject to a lump-sum deduction of 40%. Income from participation in profits of partnerships, that is, income received by a limited partner, is not subject to this 40% deduction.

Income from interest on loans is determined by subtracting the interest calculated on the basis of the growth of retail prices from the interest received.

Income derived from rental property (except land) is subject to either a lump-sum deduction or the actual expenses incurred. The lump-sum deductions that may be claimed are as follows.

1. For renting accommodation, buildings for business purposes and garages—40%.
2. For renting furnished accommodations with equipment—60%.

If a lump-sum deduction is claimed, no other expenses may be deducted.

Allowable deductions from income derived from renting land are those expenses actually incurred, including any taxes.

The taxable base for income derived from the renting of equipment and other property is arrived at after deduction of the actual expenses for investment and current maintenance.

Income from property rights/Income from property rights is defined as income from copyrights; income from inventions, trademarks and technical innovations; and income from inherited intellectual and industrial property rights, whether or not they are protected by relevant legislation.

Income from property rights is subject to lump-sum deduction (40% of the income) unless the taxpayer chooses to calculate actual expenses.

Deductions

The consolidated taxable base can be decreased by allowable deductions, which are as follows.

1. General allowance—11% of the annual average wage in Slovenia for all taxpayers.
2. Disabled person's allowance—Full annual average wage in Slovenia if the taxpayer is a 100% disabled person (one deduction per year).
3. Student allowance—40% of the average wage if the taxpayer is a student (only when he derives income from his work as a student).
4. Seniority allowance—8% of the annual average wage if the taxpayer is above 65 years of age.
5. Special deductions—Certain expenses may be deducted from the aggregate taxable base up to a limit of 3% of the taxable base for the purposes specified in the law.
6. Family allowances—These are granted to taxpayers who are supporting their children, as follows:
   a. 10% of the annual average wage for the first child or any other dependent family member;
   b. 15% of the annual average wage for the second child;
   c. 20% of the annual average wage for the third child, and so on; and
   d. 50% of the annual average wage for a disabled child.

Tax credits

Payments of foreign tax may be credited against the Slovenian tax liability.

Other taxes

Special tax for certain receipts/The payer is obliged to pay the special tax at a rate of 25% of the amount payable to individuals who are employed by the payer (legal entity or natural person) on temporary contracts. The tax payment should be made within three days of the payment to the individuals.

Payroll tax/The Law on Tax on Payroll entered into force on July 1, 1996. The taxpayers are all legal entities and individuals who are obliged to pay social security contributions, usually those employing people on a permanent basis and are paying out salaries. The taxable base is gross salary.

The taxable base is taxed as follows.

Taxable base (In tolars)	Tax %
Up to 130,000	0.0
130,001–400,000	3.8
400,001–750,000	7.8
Over 750,000	14.8

Social security contributions/Contributions for pensions, health insurance, and unemployment are paid by employers and by employees. In both cases, the payment of the contributions is administered by the employer, on its own behalf and on behalf of its employees. The contributions amount to 38.2% (16.10% paid by employer and 22.10% by employee) and are as follows.

1. Pension and disability insurance—paid to the Pension Fund at 24.35%.
2. Health care—paid to the Health Fund at 12.92%.
3. Unemployment insurance—paid to the state budget at 0.20%.
4. Maternity benefit—paid to the state budget at 0.20%.
5. Injury and illness—0.53%.

The tax base is the amount of the gross salary. The contributions are deducted monthly from the employee's salary.

Tax administration

Returns/The tax year is the calendar year. All income received must be included in the annual tax return, as well as all compulsory contributions and advanced taxes paid during the tax year.

All taxpayers must submit the annual tax return in the prescribed form to the Ministry of Finance by March 31 of the following year.

Payment of annual tax/Tax due (calculated as the difference between the total tax payable and the total amount of advance payments) must be paid within 30 days from the day the written order is submitted. When the total sum of advance payments exceeds the tax payable, a refund can be requested.

Advance tax rates/There are two tax schedules (one for income from employment and pensions, one for income from private business or professional activity) containing income brackets and progressive tax rates, which are revalued each period according to the movement of the average wage in Slovenia in the relevant previous period and different flat advance tax rates depending on the category of income.

With respect to employment income, income of professional activities (if the taxpayer is a registered person) and royalty income, the employer or the payer is required to calculate and withhold tax from the gross payment and remit the tax withheld to the tax administration office.

The amount of advance payment of income tax, which is automatically withheld from salaries by the employer, is as follows.

Annual tax rates

An individual's annual income is aggregated and the total amount is taxed according to the special annual tax schedule, containing six income tax brackets and the following progressive tax rates: 17%, 35%, 37%, 40%, 45%, and 50%.

Taxable income		
More than (AMW)*	Up to (AMW)*	Advance tax
0	50%	17%
50%	100%	50% AMW x 17% + 35% over 50% AMW
100%	150%	50% AMW x 52% + 37% over 100% AMW
150%	200%	50% AMW x 89% + 40% over 150% AMW
200%	300%	50% AMW x 129% + 45% over 200% AMW
300%		50% AMW x 219% + 50% over 300% AMW

* AMW is the average monthly salary of employees in the Republic of Slovenia in the month before last.

Notes:

1. The rate of advance tax on income earned under contracts for temporary work or for the execution of services and on other receipts, including prizes, is 25%.
2. The rate of advance tax payment on income from property and income from property rights is 25%.
3. The rate of advance tax payment on capital gains is 30%.
4. In the case of income from agriculture, the rates of advance tax are as follows:
   a. 0% of taxable base below 30% of the average annual wage in Slovenia in the preceding year;
   b. 8% of taxable base exceeding 30% of the annual wage in Slovenia in the preceding year;
   c. 17% for nonresidents.

Note

Exchange rate of the Slovenian tolar at December 31, 2003: US$1 = SIT189.3674.

Solomon Islands

PwC contact

For additional information on taxation in the Solomon Islands, contact:

Wayne Morris
PricewaterhouseCoopers
City Centre, First Floor
Mendana Avenue
P.O. Box 70
Honiara, Solomon Islands
Telephone: (677) 21851
Fax: (677) 23342
e-mail: wayne.f.morris@sb.pwc.com

Significant developments

There have been no changes to the Income Tax Act during the last three years.

Territoriality and residence

An individual who was present in the Solomon Islands for a period or periods exceeding in the aggregate six months of the tax year is deemed to reside in the Solomon Islands for income tax purposes.

Gross income

Employee gross income/Employee gross income includes wages, salary, leave pay, sick pay, payment in lieu of leave, fees, commissions, bonus, gratuity, or any other allowances or perquisites or other benefits. Most benefits in kind are taxable, including the value of free or subsidized housing, vehicles supplied by employers, and education allowances paid by employers. There are no concessions for short-term residents.

Capital gains and investment income/There is no capital gains tax. Short-term residents are not subject to tax on capital gains and investment income from outside the country.

Deductions

Business deductions/Individuals are allowed work-related deductions for transport, entertaining, or other expenditure where the Commissioner is satisfied it was necessarily incurred in gaining income.

Nonbusiness expenses/Interest on maximum borrowings of SBD20,000 for a principal residence in the Solomon Islands can be deducted.

Personal allowances/Individuals are allowed a basic exemption of SBD7,800 regardless of whether they are single or married.

Tax credits/Tax credits are given to resident individuals for withholding tax deducted. The basis of assessment of foreign income and the calculation of available tax credits is the same as for corporations. The Solomon Islands tax payable is computed as the average rate applicable to total income.

Other taxes

Social security taxes/A National Provident fund provides social security benefits to residents on retirement. Employers are required to contribute 7.5% of employees' salaries or wages; employees are required to contribute 5% (minimum). Income tax deductions apply to these contributions (within limits), and proceeds on retirements are tax-free. Expatriate employees are required to contribute unless approval to contribute to a nonresident scheme has been granted. Benefits withdrawn on final departure from the Solomon Islands are tax-free.

Local income taxes/There are no local income taxes, but local Councils are permitted to charge a head tax on individuals, which is known as the basic rate. Employers are required to withhold this tax from employees' salaries and wages and to account to the Council by June 30.

Tax administration

Returns/December 31 is the standard year-end, but an alternative date may be adopted by business taxpayers. Provisions do exist to aggregate the income of married individuals in certain circumstances.

Payment of tax/A pay-as-you-earn (PAYE) system of taxation applies to all income from employment or services rendered.

Tax rates

Resident individuals are subject to tax only on taxable income accruing in, derived from, or received in the Solomon Islands. Income tax rates are the same for residents and nonresidents.

A PAYE system of taxation applies to all income from employment or service rendered.

The tax payable on total income less personal exemptions and deductions is as follows.

Taxable income		Tax on	Marginal
Over	Not over	Column 1	rate
(Column 1)			
0	SBD 15,000	—	11
SBD 15,000	30,000	SBD 1,650	23
30,000	60,000	5,100	35
60,000		15,600	40

INDIVIDUAL TAX CALCULATION

2004

Salary	SBD 410,250
Interest income	10,000
	420,250
Less—Basic deduction	7,800
Taxable income	SBD 412,450
Tax payable	SBD 156,580

Note:

Exchange rate of the Solomon Islands dollar at December 31, 2003: US$1 = SBD7.6161.

PwC contact

For additional information on taxation in South Africa, contact:

Mark Badenhorst
PricewaterhouseCoopers
Private Bag X36
Sunninghill 2156, South Africa
Telephone: (27) (11) 797 4641
Fax: (27) (11) 209 4641
e-mail: mark.badenhorst@za.pwc.com

Significant developments

The past year has, once again, seen a large volume of amendments to the tax legislation of South Africa (SA). Many of these changes were aimed at clarifying the uncertainties regarding the residence basis of taxation and the capital gains tax that were introduced during 2001. Further developments include the exemption of qualifying foreign dividends for years of assessment commencing on or after June 1, 2004, and the ring-fencing of assessed losses incurred from carrying on certain trades.

Territoriality and residence

SA residents are taxed on their worldwide income. Credit is granted in SA for foreign taxes paid. Residence has not historically been a major factor in the SA tax system, but the switch to a residence tax basis following the relaxation of exchange controls has changed this. A natural person will be resident in SA who is ordinarily resident in SA, or if who is physically present in SA for a specified period.

Nonresidents are taxed on their SA-source income. The same rates of tax are applicable to both. Residence of less than 183 days in a fiscal year may give rise to exemption from tax under double taxation agreements. In addition, nonresidents who are physically absent from SA for at least 183 days in aggregate during the year are exempt from tax on interest earned in SA in certain circumstances.

Gross income

Employee gross income/Taxable remuneration includes all cash amounts received for services rendered, including bonuses, allowances, tax reimbursements, and most benefits in kind, such as the use of assets and soft loans. There are no special concessions for short-term residents, except under double taxation agreements.

Capital gains and investment income/25% of net capital gains realized are taxed at the normal income tax rates. A natural person is entitled to an annual exclusion of R10,000 in determining the net capital gain for the year. However, a gain may be treated as noncapital income, and subject to income tax, if it arises from a profit-making scheme. Following the recent replacement of the source basis of taxation with a residence basis, all foreign income of a SA resident is included in the SA tax net.

Local dividends are exempt from tax. Foreign dividends accrued to or received by SA residents on or after February 23, 2000, as well as foreign dividends that accrued to a SA resident before that date but were received after it are subject to tax. However, qualifying foreign dividends received or accrued during years of assessment commencing on or after June 1, 2004 will be exempt. The first R10,000 of taxable interest and dividend income not otherwise exempt from tax will be exempt (R15,000 for taxpayers over 65) for the tax year ended February 28, 2004; however, only R1,000 of the exemption may be used against non–SA-source interest and foreign dividends.

Deductions

Business deductions/A taxpayer may deduct expenses not of a capital nature incurred in the production of income, such as business-related travel, automobile and entertainment expenses. There are no blanket or standard business expense deductions.

Nonbusiness expenses/A taxpayer may deduct certain expenses, including pension fund and retirement annuity fund contributions, where such funds are registered in SA (subject to certain maximum limits) and donations to certain approved public benefit organizations involved in, inter alia, community development, education- and AIDS-related activities (up to a maximum of 5% of taxable income). Taxpayers over the age of 65 may deduct all their medical expenses, handicap medical expense in excess of R500 are deductible while there are fairly limited deductions for medical expenses incurred by other taxpayers. Mortgage and other personal interest expenses are not deductible.

Losses from trade/Subject to certain provisions, assessed losses incurred by a taxpayer from certain trades during years of assessment commencing on or after March 1, 2004 are ring-fenced, and hence cannot be set off against other income earned by the taxpayer. Such amounts may, however, be carried forward and claimed against taxable income from that trade in future years.

Personal allowances/A taxpayer is entitled to personal allowances in the form of tax rebates, which are deducted from tax payable. For the 2004 tax year, the following rebates apply:

1. Primary rebate—R5,400 for all natural persons.
2. Additional rebate—R3,100 if the taxpayer is age 65 or over.

Tax credits

A rebate is allowed for taxes paid on foreign income that is taxable in SA. Personal allowances (see above) take the form of tax rebates.

Other taxes

Donations tax/Donations tax is payable by SA-resident individuals. Exempt donations include those between spouses. Donations by natural persons in excess of R30,000 in aggregate per tax year, are subject to donations tax at a flat rate of 20% of the value of the property donated.

Estate duty/Estate duty is levied on the "dutiable" amount of a deceased person's estate. An abatement of R1,500,000 is deducted from the net value of the estate in order to determine the dutiable amount, on which estate duty at a flat rate of 20% is calculated. Persons who are not ordinarily resident in SA will be subject to estate duty only on assets located in SA.

Regional services levies/Individuals who trade in their own names or practice a profession are liable to regional services levies comprising a payroll levy at the rate varying between 0.25% to 0.4% of remuneration paid to employees and a regional establishment levy varying between 0.1% and 0.2% of turnover (plus 14% value-added tax (VAT) on both). Partners' drawings are regarded as remuneration for purposes of the payroll levy.

Employers are obliged to make contributions for all employees to a State Unemployment Insurance Fund at the rate of 1% of gross remuneration. The contributions are currently limited to either R88.36 per month or R1,060.32 per annum.

Skills Development Levy/A compulsory levy to fund in-house education and training is also levied on an employer's payroll. The Skills Development Levy consists of 1% of an employer's payroll per month.

Workmen's compensation/Employers are liable for workmen's compensation, calculated by applying to the employee's earnings varying rates depending on the employer's industry.

There are no other social security taxes.

Tax administration

Returns/The tax year for individuals ends at the end of February or, in few exceptional cases, June. Spouses are taxed separately and must submit separate returns.

The date for the filing of returns is fixed each year, which is usually in May or June. Reasonable extensions may be obtained upon request.

Payment of tax/Pay-as-you-earn (PAYE) withholding tax is withheld on salaries. Standard Income Tax on Employees (SITE) is an alternative method for determining liability for normal tax of persons earning net remuneration not exceeding R60,000. Where PAYE deductions are made from remuneration, these deductions constitute nothing more than advance payments toward liability for normal tax. The main objective of SITE is to ensure that taxpayers who earn salaries of less than R60,000 per tax year need not file tax returns; for them, SITE represents the full and final amount of income tax they will pay. For other taxpayers, SITE constitutes the minimum amount of income tax to be paid.

Tax rates

Natural persons/Taxable income is taxed at progressive rates. Taxable income in excess of R255,000 per annum is taxed at R74,100 plus 40% of the excess above R255,000.

Taxpayers other than natural persons and companies (e.g., trusts)/Taxable income is taxed at 40%. The tax rates on the taxable income of special trusts (e.g., a trust created solely for a person who suffers from a "mental illness") are at the rates used for individuals. Trusts do not qualify for the tax rebates referred to above.

Tax payable/The formula for calculating the tax payable is as follows.

Gross income	
(Total receipts and accruals less receipts and accruals of a capital nature)	XXX
Less—Exempt income	(XXX)
Less—Deductions and allowances	(XXX)
Add—Taxable capital gains (effective October 1, 2001)	XXX
Taxable income	XX
Tax thereon calculated per tables	XX
Less—Rebates	(X)
Tax payable	X

INDIVIDUAL TAX CALCULATION

Year of assessment 2003/2004 (based on year ending February 29, 2004)

Assumptions

Husband and wife under 65 years, one spouse earns all the income; number of children irrelevant.

Tax computation

Receipts:		
Salary		R 280,800
Interest income		12,000
Long-term capital gain		30,000
Total receipts		322,800
Less:		
Capital item—Long-term capital gain	30,000	
Exempt income—Standard interest exemption (limited to 10,000)	10,000	40,000
		282,800
Less—Deductions:		
Donation to an approved public benefit organization	1,000	
Pension fund contribution (maximum 7.5% of income from employment)	21,060	22,060
Taxable income before taxable capital gains		260,740
Add—Taxable capital gain		5,000
Total taxable income		R 265,740
Tax thereon:		
On 255,000		R 74,100
On 10,740 at 40%		4,296
		78,396
Less—Primary rebate		(5,400)
Tax payable		R 72,996

Notes:

1. Capital gains tax calculation:

	R
Proceeds	50,000
Less—Base cost	20,000
Gain	30,000
Less—Annual exclusion	10,000
Gain	20,000
Taxable gain (at 25% inclusion rate)	5,000

2. Exchange rate of the rand at March 18, 2004: US$1 = R6.7.

Spain

PwC contact

For additional information on taxation in Spain, contact:

Jose Félix Gálvez
PricewaterhouseCoopers
Paseo de la Castellana, 53
28046 Madrid
Telephone: 00 34 91 568 45 30
Fax: 00 34 91 568 46 72
e-mail: jose.felix.galvez@es.pwcglobal.com

Significant developments

Personal income tax is levied only on available income, calculated as income received reduced by personal and family minimum figures. The Personal Income Tax Act attempts to bring taxation into line with the taxpayer's actual capacity with respect to the taxable base, rather than through deductions from tax payable. This has given rise to major changes in the overall tax structure.

General note

This entry also covers the Canary Islands.

Territoriality and residence

Personal income tax is regulated by two laws, one for residents and another for nonresidents, and persons are liable to Spanish income tax either as residents or nonresidents.

1. Resident—Persons who reside in Spain for more than 183 days in a calendar year or have Spain as their center of economic interest are considered to be resident for tax purposes. A person can also be liable to tax whose family unit is in Spain and the members opt for the joint taxation system. In such cases, worldwide income, capital gains, and wealth are subject to tax. Joint taxation is maintained as the basic system for the taxation of the members of the family unit if the spouse does not receive any income. However, this system is no longer compulsory, and it is possible for each individual to file separately.
2. Nonresident—Persons who do not reside in Spain for more than 183 days in a calendar year or do not have Spain as their center of economic interest are not considered to be resident for tax purposes. In such cases, Spanish-source income and capital gains and wealth in Spain are subject to tax.

For the purpose of calculating the period of residence, temporary absences abroad are taken into consideration unless it can be proved that the taxpayer has been resident or domiciled in another country.

In determining the permanence period of more than 183 days in the Spanish territory, temporary visits to Spain that derive from contractual obligations under cultural and humanitarian collaboration agreements with the Spanish Public Administration without remuneration will not be counted.

Gross income

Employee gross income/Taxable income includes all types of remuneration, such as salary, living allowances, housing allowances, bonuses, tax reimbursements, and remuneration in kind (e.g., schooling and rent-free housing). Withholdings and advanced payments on account are required on wages and salaries and on benefits. Leaving indemnities, as stipulated by law, are not taxable. Income derived from the delivery of courses, conferences, seminars, and the like is regarded as gross earned income, as is income from literary, artistic, or scientific works when the rights to the exploitation thereof have been transferred. Income from involvement in humanitarian or welfare activities organized by not-for-profit entities is also regarded as gross earned income.

Capital gains and investment income/Capital gains can arise on all transfers inter vivos, but not mortis causa. The new law has eliminated the updating ratios that were applicable under the previous legislation with regard to capital gains. These are retained only for transactions involving real property.

Short-term capital gains (i.e., generated in one year or less) are included with other ordinary income in the "general part" of the taxable base and are taxed at the general rate. In contrast, capital gains from assets held for more than one year are included in the "special part" of the taxable base and are taxed at 15%.

The capital gains bases arising in 2004 from transfers of assets or rights acquired before December 31, 1994 are reduced by 14.28%, 25.00%, or 11.11%, depending on the type of assets, for each year the assets or rights have been held between the acquisition date and December 31, 1996 for more than two years. The law provides that no tax is due if these assets have been held for more than 8, 5, and 10 years, respectively.

Capital gains derived from the sale of participations in investment funds will not be taxed at the moment of sale if the total sale value is reinvested in the acquisition of other participations in investment funds.

Capital gains or losses arising on inheritance are not taxed under the personal income tax regime.

Profits or losses deriving from the transfer of assets used in the taxpayer's business activity are now subject to personal income tax and taxed as other capital gains. The capital gain obtained from the sale of a taxpayer's home is exempt in the same proportion as the amount that is reinvested in a new home, provided the new home is purchased within two years.

Disposal by a nonresident of a property located in Spain is subject to capital gains tax. The purchaser is required to deduct and pay to the local authorities 5% of the actual consideration if the property has been held for less than 10 years at December 31, 1996. This withholding is treated as an advance payment of capital gains tax for the vendor. The nonresident vendor must be formally represented through a lawyer or legal representative.

The following investment income items are taxable: dividends, interest, pensions, notional rent, royalties, fees, actual rent, annuities, alimony, and income deriving from insurance contracts. The amount declared is generally the gross amount received. Any withholding at source is available as a tax credit against the final tax liability.

When urban property is rented or subleased by the taxpayer, the amounts actually received from the tenant or subtenant are included in taxable income. However, in the case of property rented for habitual dwelling, the net amount calculated would be reduced by 50%. With regard to the taxpayer's real property, no tax is paid as a "profit" obtained from the taxpayer's habitual dwelling, but tax is paid in respect of other nonhabitual dwellings owned by the taxpayer that have not been let. The tax payable in this case is 1.1% or 2% of the ratable value, depending on whether this value has been reviewed after January 1, 1994.

Capital losses/Capital losses arising from the transfer of assets held for more than one year can be offset only against capital gains generated in more than one year. If the result of the offset is negative, it may be offset only against capital gains generated in more than one year, arising in the following four years. Capital losses arising from the transfer of assets held for no more than one year can be offset only against capital gains generated in no more than one year. The excess losses can be offset against other types of regular income, limited to 10% of such income. Further unused losses may be carried forward four years.

Deductions

Business deductions/Only expenses that are necessary to obtain income are deductible.

Nonbusiness expenses/The nonbusiness expenses listed below are deductible.

1. Social security contributions.
2. Legal defense expenses, up to a maximum of €300, in relation to earned income.
3. In relation to investment income, the expenses necessary to obtain the income and deterioration suffered due to use or the passage of time.

Legal reductions/As follows.

1 Personal minimum figure, which in general amounts to €3,400. For joint filing, the personal minimum is €6,800.

2. Reduction on income from employment—This reduction will depend on the net salary obtained:
   a. If net income is lower than €8,200—€3,500;
   b. If net income is higher than €13,000—€2,400;
   c. If net income is between €8,200.01 and €13,000—€3,500 – ((net income – €8,200) x 0.2291).

   If the taxpayer is handicapped, these reductions would be increased.

   Other reductions are as follows:
   a. The reduction on income from employment could be increased by 100% if the taxpayer is 65 years old and is still an active worker;
   b. The reduction on income from employment could be increased by 100% if the taxpayer was unemployed and has accepted a job that obliges him to change his habitual dwelling to another municipality;
   c. Reduction for children under three years old—€1,200;
3. Reduction for age—When the taxpayer is over 65 years old, the taxable base will be reduced by €800. For every ascendant over 65 years old, or handicapped, who lives with the taxpayer and does not obtain income over €8,000, the taxable base will be reduced by €800.
4. Reduction for assistance—When the taxpayer is over 75 years old the taxable base will be reduced by €1,000. For every ascendant over 75 years old who lives with the taxpayer and does not obtain income over €8,000, the taxable base will be reduced by €1,000.

5. Reductions for handicap—In addition to the reductions described above, the following reductions would be applicable:
    a. Handicap of taxpayer—€2,000; if the degree of handicap is equal to or higher than 65%, the tax reduction would be €5,000;
    b. Handicap of ascendants or descendants—If they generate a right to the reduction, the taxable base would be reduced by €2,000. If the degree of handicap is equal to or higher than 65, the tax reduction would be €5,000.
    c. For assistance—If the taxpayer needs assistance of a third person, or has reduced mobility, or a degree of handicap equal to or higher than 65%, the taxable base will be reduced by €2,000. Additionally, for each ascendant or descendent who has a right to the reduction and who needs the assistance of a third person or has reduced mobility or a degree of handicap equal to or higher than 65%, the taxable base will be reduced by €2,000.

    In these cases, it will be understood that a person is handicapped when he proves that he has a handicap degree of at least 33%.
6. A family minimum figure of:
    a. €1,400 for the first single descendant under 25 forming part of the taxpayer's household;
    b. An additional €1,500 for the second descendant;
    c. An additional €2,200 for the third descendant.
    d. €2,300 for any more such descendants.
7. Taxpayers' annual contributions to pension plans up to a maximum of €8,000 per annum. If the employer makes contributions to a pension plan on behalf of the employee, this limit will increase by another €8,000. These amounts may be increase by €1.250 for every year of age that the taxpayer exceeds of 52. Additionally, contributions made to the spouse's pension plan when he/she does not obtain income higher than €8.000 are also deductible, with a limit of €2.000.
8. Alimony or maintenance payments under court order.
9. Reduction in the taxable base when income has been generated over more than two years or in a clearly inconsistent manner over time. This reduction is applied to the gross income and may be 40% or 75%, depending on the kind of income involved and the length of time over which it was generated. Nevertheless, the gross income from employment derived from stock option plans that could benefit from the reduction of 40% has a limit. This limit is the result of applying 40% on the result of multiplying the taxpayer's median annual salary by the number of years in which the income has been generated. In the case of income obtained over notably irregular time periods, the number of years will be five. The average annual salary for 2003 is €17,900. This limit could be doubled if the shares acquired are held for at least three years from the exercise date, and the offer has been made under the same conditions for all the workers of the company, group, or subgroup of the company.

Personal allowances/Under the new Act, the number of deductions has been reduced in favor of the personal and family minimums referred to above.

Corporate tax incentives/Such incentives will be applicable to individuals who carry on business, professional, and artistic activities, with the same rates and limits.

Tax credits

Withholding taxes and payments on account are credited against total tax due.

Credits are granted for the following expenditures.

1. Acquisition of main residence—15% to 25% to 20% of expenses, as follows:
   a. Without loan—15%, up to a limit of invested amount of €9,015.18.
   b. With loan (if certain requirements are met)—For the first two years of investment 25% and 15% of the amounts paid, up to a limit of invested amount of €9,015.18. The 25% is credited on the first €4,507.59 and 15% on the excess up to €9,015.18.

   For subsequent years of investment credits amount to 20% rates 15% of the amounts paid, up to a limit of invested amount of €9,015.18. The 20% is applied on the first €4,507.59 and the15% on the excess up to €9,015.18.
2. Donations—10% or 25 % of the amount, depending on the type of the donation.
3. Dividends received on which corporate tax has been paid—40% of dividends received.
4. A new maternity deduction has been introduced, under which women with children under three years old who work and are registered with Social Security can deduct €1,200 from their tax liability. There is a possibility for these women to request this tax deduction from the Spanish tax authorities in advance, in which case this amount would not be deducted in the personal income tax return.

Nonresidents with a permanent establishment in Spain can claim the credits for taxes withheld, dividends received, and corporate tax incentives when applicable.

In addition to the credits listed above, credits are available for foreign income tax paid, provided it is not greater than the Spanish tax on the income.

Other taxes

Social security taxes/Social security contribution rates are applied on basic salaries ranging from €537.30 to a maximum of €2,731.50 per month, depending on the individual's category. The general percentage contribution rates as from January 2004 are 6.35% or 6.4% for employees, depending on the type of contract and 30.6%, 31.3%, or 32.3%, depending on the type of contract for employers.

Local taxes on income/For residents, income regional taxes are levied at rates varying from 5.94% to 15.84% of taxable earned income. These rates, together with the central tax rates, will constitute the total personal income tax rates applicable to taxpayer.

Wealth tax/Resident individuals are subject to wealth tax on worldwide wealth; nonresident individuals are subject to this tax on wealth in Spain only. Wealth of individuals is computed by adding all assets and deducting liabilities. A tax-free allowance of €108,182.18 is available for residents. Additionally, the habitual dwelling is tax exempt up to €150,253.03. Nonresidents do not receive tax-free allowances. However, nonresidents who were considered tax residents in the previous year can choose to file their wealth tax return as tax residents in Spain.

Wealth tax rates are as follows.

Taxable base		Tax on	Percentage
Over	Remainder	Column 1	on excess
(Column 1)			
0	€ 167,129.45	0	0.2
€ 167,129.45	167,123.43	€ 334.26	0.3
334,252.88	334,246.87	835.63	0.5
668,499.75	668,499.76	2,506.86	0.9
1,336,999.51	1.336,999.50	8,523.36	1.3
2,673,999.01	2,673,999.02	25,904.35	1.7
5,347,998.03	5,347,998.03	71,362.33	2.1
10,695,996.06		183,670.29	2.5

Tax administration

Returns/Returns must be filed and tax paid between May 2 and June 30. The tax period is the calendar year.

Payment of tax/Withholding taxes are imposed on investment income at the rate of 15%. Capital gains generated from the transfer or redemption of equity shareholdings or holdings in collective investment institutions are subject to an 15% withholding. For the letting and subletting of property, there is a withholding rate of 15%.

Withholding taxes are credited against total tax due.

Tax rates

The following rates apply for 2003.

Central tax

Taxable base		Tax on	Percentage
Over	Remainder	Column 1	on excess
(Column 1)			
0	€ 4,000	0	9.06
€ 4,000	9,800	€ 362.40	15.84
13,800	12,000	1,914.72	18.68
25,800	19,200	4,156.32	24.71
45,000		8,900.64	29.16

Regional tax

Taxable base		Tax on Column 1	Percentage on excess
Over (Column 1)	Remainder		
0	€ 4,000	0	5.94
€ 4,000	9,800	€ 237.60	8.16
13,800	12,000	1,037.28	9.32
25,800	19,200	2,155.68	12.29
45,000		4,515.36	15.84

Notes:

1. For the tax year beginning January 1, 2003 the taxpayer's income deriving from joint and individual returns must be declared, and it will be divided into two parts. From the total taxable income, 64.80% goes to the central government, while 35.20% is allocated to the regional government of the area in which the taxpayer resides. The tables above give the details.
2. For residents, the 2004 rate is restricted to a maximum cumulative rate of 60% when considered together with the wealth tax.
3. For nonresidents, general income is subject to a flat rate of 25%; capital gains are subject to a flat rate of 35%, and dividends and interests at a flat rate of 15%.
4. Exchange rate of the Euro at January 2, 2004: US$1 = €0.79.

PwC contact

For additional information on taxation in Sri Lanka, contact:

Hiranthi Ratnayake
PricewaterhouseCoopers
100, Braybrooke Place
Colombo 2
Sri Lanka
Telephone: (94) (11) 2304282
Fax: (94) (11) 2304286
e-mail: hiranthi@pwc.lanka.net

Copies of all inquiries regarding entry advice and related tax issues in Sri Lanka should be sent to the above address.

Significant developments

- Threshold for personal income tax raised from Rs240,000 to Rs300,000, and rate bands widened from tax year 2004/2005.
- Threshold for taxation of retirement benefits increased to Rs3.5 million from tax year 2004/2005.
- The scope of employment income has been widened to include, as an employment benefit, the profits derived by an employee from the sale of shares given to him by his employer or on behalf of his employer at no cost or at a price below the prevailing market value of such share, either directly or through a share option scheme.
- Effective from April 1, 2004, an upfront tax of 10% will be imposed on the divisible profits and other income of a partnership. The tax can be set off against the proportionate individual tax liability of each partner up to a maximum of his tax payable, but with no carry over provision.

Territoriality and residence

Individuals physically present in Sri Lanka for 183 days or more during any tax year are treated as resident in Sri Lanka throughout that year. Those persons treated as resident for two or more consecutive tax years are treated as resident until absent from Sri Lanka for an unbroken period of 365 days; when so absent, they are treated as nonresident from the commencement of the tax year in which the absence commences. Where a person is deemed nonresident, any presence in Sri Lanka for 30 days or less will be treated as spent outside the country.

Upon being employed in Sri Lanka, an individual who is not a citizen of Sri Lanka is treated as nonresident for a period of three years, calculated from the date on which employment commences in Sri Lanka. However, if the individual is employed by a company in which the foreign investment is not less than US$50 million or its equivalent in another foreign currency, the employee is treated as nonresident for five years from the commencement of employment. Resident individuals are subject to income tax on their worldwide income. Nonresident individuals are taxed on Sri Lanka-source income only.

Gross income

Employee gross income/Employment income is computed gross and comprises all items of remuneration received in the course of employment; the value of any benefits to the employee and to the employee's spouse, child or parent; and payments to third parties for the benefit of the employee, spouse, child, or parent. Also included in gross employment income are payments made upon termination of employment, such as retirement gratuities, monies accumulated to the credit of the employee in an approved provident fund and compensation for loss of employment, as well as the rental value of a residence provided rent free by the employer and the benefit from use of an employer-provided automobile.

The rules for determining the statutory income from a trade, business, profession, or vocation are the same as those described for a company (see the Sri Lanka entry in *Corporate Taxes—A Worldwide Summary*). Deductions are given only for remuneration accrued but not paid (treated as bad debts) and for contributions made to an approved provident fund by an employer on the employee's behalf.

Exempt income/Certain items of income are exempt in the hands of an individual, including the following.

1. Non-Sri Lanka-source income and official emoluments of certain residents, such as foreign diplomats and members of their staff who are citizens of the countries represented by these diplomats; experts, advisers, technicians, or officials who are brought to Sri Lanka by the government through the United Nations Organization (UNO) but are not paid by the government; foreign trainees sent to Sri Lanka under the aegis of the UNO or the Colombo Plan Organization; and officials of the UNO who are not citizens of Sri Lanka.
2. Official emoluments of resident Sri Lanka citizens employed by the UNO or any of its specialized agencies.
3. The values of travel warrants and passages granted to expatriates serving in Sri Lanka or to their spouses and children to enable them to travel between their home countries and Sri Lanka.
4. Travel, subsistence, and lodging allowances granted to employees for travel abroad in connection with their employment.
5. Emoluments and pensions earned in foreign currency and paid in Sri Lanka or remitted to residents or their spouses for employment services, past or present, that they have rendered outside Sri Lanka.
6. Capital sums paid as gratuities or compensation for death or injuries.
7. Sums paid as compensation for loss of office under a uniform voluntary retirement scheme approved by the tax authorities or under a retrenchment scheme approved by the labor authorities.
8. Income from scholarships, exhibitions, or bursaries enjoyed by students in educational establishments.

The emoluments paid to persons serving the public sector will, from April 1, 2003, form part of the statutory income of the persons concerned. However, through a credit mechanism, that part of the tax attributable to such emoluments will be excluded from the tax payable.

Capital gains and investment income/The taxation of capital gains has been abolished. Dividends, interest, annuities, and royalties are computed gross without any deductions.

A schedular system applies to taxation of dividends. A resident company pays income tax at 10% on the amount of dividends distributed to resident and nonresident shareholders; the tax is withheld at source. The tax withheld represents the final tax payable by shareholders; thus dividends on which tax has been withheld does not form part of the shareholder's assessable income. Foreign dividends received by a resident are subject to income tax at 10%.

A limited form of schedular taxation also applies to interest income. Tax on interest income derived from deposits with banks and financial institutions, treasury bills and bonds, and corporate debt securities is withheld at source at 10% and represents the final tax on such income payable by an individual taxpayer. Tax will not be deducted on interest from banks and financial institutions where the interest income does not exceed Rs9,000 per month or Rs108,000 per annum on all deposits held in a bank or its branches, or where the interest income is the sole or primary income (i.e., more than 90% of total income) of the depositor or the total income of the depositor for the relevant tax year including any exempt income does not exceed Rs300,000. Interest from foreign currency deposits is exempt.

Any royalty or annuity payable to a nonresident individual is subject to a withholding tax at 20%. However, if the individual is a resident in a country with which a double taxation treaty is in force, a lower rate of 10% is generally applicable. The tax withheld is, in such cases, the final income tax due.

Rental income from land and improvements is computed on the gross rent received or receivable. Deductions are allowed for rates and for 25% of the balance for repairs, to the extent the owner bears their costs.

Deductions

In computing taxable income, a deduction is allowed for a tax-free allowance of Rs300,000 (resident individuals only), donations to approved charities; and contributions in cash or kind to the government. Furthermore, an employee can deduct any annual contributions to an approved provident fund and premiums paid on a life or medical insurance policy However, the total deduction for donations (except cash donations to the government), contributions to an approved provident fund, and payment of insurance premiums cannot exceed 10% of statutory income or Rs75,000, whichever is lower. Donations in kind to the government may be deducted up to a limit of Rs2 million. Additional deductions are allowed to an individual in respect of any amount spent on the construction purchase of a first house after April 1, 2001, up to 10% of statutory income or Rs100,000, whichever is lower.

Donations to the government can be deducted without limit, and any unrelieved excess can be carried forward indefinitely. In the case of housing, the unrelieved excess can be carried forward for set off against statutory income in the next succeeding nine years.

A deduction is allowed for interest paid on business borrowings and other interest paid on any loan obtained from a bank, financial institution, or other institution recognized by Commissioner General of Inland Revenue.

Withholding tax rates

Source of income	Resident individual	Nonresident individual
	%	%
Dividends	10	10
Interest	10	20
Royalty	15	20
Service fees	5	5
Nonresidential rents	10	—
Rewards to informants, and lottery prizes of not less than Rs500,000	10	—

Tax credits

If a double taxation treaty applies, residents with foreign-source income are entitled to a credit equal to the income tax levied on that income in the foreign country. This credit cannot exceed the Sri Lanka income tax imposed on that income.

If no tax treaty is in force, the foreign tax paid is allowed as a deduction in computing the profits from the applicable source for Sri Lanka income tax purposes.

Other taxes

Local taxes/Taxes (commonly called "rates") are currently assessed and collected annually from the owners of land and buildings by the local authorities of the areas in which the properties are located. These authorities also impose and collect annual license fees from certain businesses as well as "taxes" based on the annual gross takings of certain businesses such as hotels.

Employees Provident Fund/Employers and employees are required to contribute specified percentages (employer, 12%; employee, 8%) of each employee's monthly emoluments to the Employees Provident Fund (EPF) established by the government. Alternatively, employers and employees must contribute to certain private provident funds approved by the labor authority.

Employees Trust Fund/Employers are also required to contribute a specified percentage (currently 3%) of each employee's monthly emoluments to the Employees Trust Fund established by the government.

Tax administration

Returns/A tax year is any period of 12 consecutive months commencing on April 1 and ending on the March 31 following. An individual is required to file an income tax return in a prescribed format (with financial statements and supporting schedules, if applicable) on or before November 30 immediately following the end of the tax year.

Spouses are taxed separately on their individual incomes. The statutory income of a child (under 18 years of age, unmarried, not illegitimate), whether natural or legally adopted, is aggregated with the father's income if the marriage subsists. If the parents are living separately, either under a court decree or in circumstances that are likely to be permanent, the income is aggregated with the income of the parent who maintains the child.

Payment of tax/Under the pay-as-you-earn (PAYE) tax system, employers are required to deduct from the monthly emoluments of each employee income tax computed on the basis of statutory tables. In general, where employment is an individual's only source of income, the tax deducted by the employer and paid to the tax authority is the final income tax due from the employee. Individuals with high employment income or income from other sources are entitled to set off the annual income tax deducted by the employer from the overall income tax payable.

Under Sri Lanka's pay-and-file system, individuals other than employees are required to pay tax in installments on or before August 15, November 15, and February 15 of the tax year and the May 15 immediately following its end. If each installment is not less than one-quarter of the income tax payable for the immediately preceding tax year, the balance of any income tax payable may be paid without incurring penalties on or before September 30 immediately following the end of the tax year.

Tax rates

Tax rates are as follows.

Taxable income	Rate
Rs	%
First 300,000	0
Next 240,000	10
Next 240,000	20
Balance	30

Concessionary tax rates apply to retirement benefits paid to an employee on cessation of employment, by way of compensation, commuted pension, retirement gratuity, accumulated employers contribution to an approved or regulated provident fund, and contributions to the Employees Trust Fund. A tax-free threshold of Rs3.5 million is granted.

The rates are as follows.

Taxable income	Rate
Rs	%
First 3,500,000	Nil
Next 500,000	5
Next 500,000	10
Balance	15

Compensation paid under a uniform scheme of voluntary retirement approved by the tax authorities or under a scheme of retrenchment approved by the labor authority is exempt from tax (see item 8 under "Exempt income" above).

Income from agriculture, nontraditional exports, fisheries, tourism, livestock, and construction activities qualifies for a rate of not more than 15%.

A concessionary rate of 10% is accorded to emoluments and fees earned in foreign currency by an individual or partnership in respect of services rendered in Sri Lanka by such individual or partnership to persons outside Sri Lanka in the course of carrying on any profession or any vocation in the field of literature or fine arts.

An expatriate who commences employment in Sri Lanka is taxed on Sri Lanka-source income at a flat 15% for a period of three consecutive years from the commencement of employment and at 15% of Sri Lanka employment income for the next two years.

However, if employed in an enterprise with a total investment of not less than US$50 million or its foreign currency equivalent and for which a tax holiday has been approved by the Board of Investment (BOI), the tax rate is 15% for the duration of the expatriate's employment within the tax holiday period, even if it exceeds five years.

INDIVIDUAL TAX CALCULATION

Tax year 2004-2005

Assumptions

Resident and nonresident individuals; nonresident resides in treaty country.

Tax computation

	Resident individual	Nonresident individual
	Rs	Rs
Employment income	6,000,000	Nil
Dividends	100,000	100,000
Fixed deposit interest	200,000	Nil
Loan interest		100,000
Royalties	100,000	100,000
Total statutory income	6,400,000	300,000
Less—Deductions from statutory income:		
Dividends (1)	100,000	100,000
Fixed deposit interest (1)	200,000	Nil
Tax-free allowance	300,000	Nil
Contribution to Employees Provident Fund	75,000	Nil
Taxable income	5,725,000	200,000
Tax on royalty and interest (2)	Nil	20,000
Income tax		Nil
	1,645,500	20,000
Less—Tax credits:		
Employment income	(1,615,500)	Nil
Loan interest	Nil	(10,000)
Royalties	Nil	(10,000)
Balance tax payable/(refundable)	30,000	Nil

Notes:

1. Income tax at 10% withheld at source is the final tax.
2. Taxed at no more than 10% under presumed treaty.
3 Average exchange rate (buying/selling) of the Sri Lanka rupee at December 31, 2003: US$1 = Rs96.50.

PwC contact

For additional information on taxation in Swaziland, contact:

Theo Mason
PricewaterhouseCoopers
MTN Office Park
Smuts Street
P.O. Box 569 or 2513
Mbabane, Swaziland
Telephone: (268) 40-43143, 40-40658, 40-42861
Fax: (268) 40-45015, 40-43142
e-mail: theo.mason@sz.pwcglobal.com

Significant developments

There have been no significant changes as regards individual taxation in the past year.

Territoriality and residence

Residence is not specifically defined, but effectively anyone in employment or business in Swaziland will be regarded as resident for tax purposes. Work permits are required for noncitizens to take up employment in Swaziland, and, as such, expatriates who work under a permit held by their employers or who are self-employed are deemed to be resident for tax purposes.

Gross income

Employee gross income/Income tax, as for companies, is levied on all income derived from a source within or deemed to be within the country, irrespective of whether the recipient of the income is actually resident in Swaziland.

Standard valuations apply for various benefits-in-kind and are included in the taxpayer's gross income for tax purposes. These include the following.

1. Noncompany-owned housing (i.e., where rental is paid to a third party). The taxable benefit is 20% of the rental. Where the calculated benefit falls below the amount specified in the table (this depends on size and location) then the table rate applies, and not the smaller calculated amount. This benefit will be phased out over the next four years.
2. Noncompany-owned vehicle. The annual motor vehicle allowance may not exceed 30% of the value of the motor vehicle. The taxable benefit of this allowance is deemed to be 30%. (Changes to this method are proposed for 2005.)
3. Entertainment and travel expenses: The benefit is the amount paid by the employer, less justifiable expenses incurred by the employee.
4. Free or subsidized fuel supplied by the employer for the employee's transport.
5. Provision of personal services:
   a. Electricity and telephone: E840 per annum for each service or 20%, whichever is the greater. In order for these amounts to qualify for this tax treatment, the service providers must be paid directly. These allowances are to be phased out over the next four years.
   b. Gas, coal, water, etcetera: E390 per annum for each service and as above.

6. Children's educational benefits are taxable in full.
7. Domestic servants:
   a. Household (cooks, maids, etc.): E954 per annum per servant; or 20%, whichever is the greater. In order for these amounts to qualify for this tax treatment, the members of staff must be paid directly. These allowances are to be phased out over the next four years.
   b. Gardeners: E476 per annum per servant, or 20%, whichever is the greater. In order for these amounts to qualify for this tax treatment, the members of staff must be paid directly. These allowances are to be phased out over the next four years.

Income from farming on traditional land is exempt from tax.

Capital gains and investment income/There are no capital gains or estate taxes.

A rate of 10% applies to dividends received by or accrued to or in favor of an individual or a company.

Deductions

Business deductions/For the purpose of ascertaining the taxable income of any person, the following may be deducted from the income of that person.

1. Expenditure and losses actually incurred in Swaziland by the taxpayer in the production of income, as well as such expenses incurred outside Swaziland in the production of taxable income as the Commissioner may allow, provided the expenditure or losses are not of a capital nature.
2. Expenditure actually incurred by the taxpayer during the year of assessment for repairs of property occupied for the purpose of trade or in respect of which income is receivable and sums so expended for the repair of machinery, implements, utensils, and articles employed by the taxpayer for the purposes of the taxpayer's trade.
3. Such sum as the Commissioner may think just and reasonable as representing the diminished value by reason of wear and tear during the year of assessment of any plant, machinery, implements, utensils, and articles used by the taxpayer for the purposes of the taxpayer's trade.

Nonbusiness expenses/The following maximum deductions apply for the tax year to June 30, 2004.

1. Pension fund contributions: Up to E1,750 per annum by persons holding appointed office or employment.
2. Retirement annuity fund contributions: Contributions during the year of assessment by members of the fund, with the sum of these contributions not to exceed:
   a. 15% of the taxable income accruing to the taxpayer from the trade carried out by the taxpayer, provided the allowable deductions do not exceed E5,000;
   b. E3,000, less contributions made by the taxpayer to a pension fund; or
   c. E1,750.
3. Mortgage interest paid to an approved financial institution at commercial rates (self or spouse):
   a. Where the gross income of the taxpayer or spouse does not exceed E15,000—200% of the interest paid during that year of assessment;

b. Where such gross income exceeds E15,000 but not E60,000—100% interest paid during that year of assessment;
c. Where such gross income exceeds E60,000—50% of the interest paid during that year of assessment.

However, the interest for the purposes of this subsection is limited to the lower of (1) interest payable on that portion of the amount of the loan, mortgage, or similar financial arrangement that does not exceed E60,000 or (2) E9,000.

No deduction is allowed for medical expenses.

Personal allowances/rebates/General rebates for married and unmarried persons are incorporated into the marginal tax rates.

Tax credits

See "Personal allowances/rebates" above.

Other taxes

There are no social security taxes or local taxes on income. There is a graded tax (poll tax) of E1.50 per month for all employed persons.

Stamp tax on a sliding scale rising to 6% is payable on transfers of real estate, mortgages, leases, and transfers of shares.

Tax administration

Returns/The tax year runs from July 1 to June 30. All persons liable to taxation, whether personally or in a representative capacity, are required to file returns within 30 days of June 30. The Commissioner may allow an extension of time as deemed appropriate.

There is no differentiation in the taxation of husband and wife.

Payment of tax/Individuals in paid employment are subject to pay-as-you-earn (PAYE).

Every provisional taxpayer is required to submit to the Commissioner on the prescribed form an estimate of the total tax payable for the year of assessment. The estimate of taxable income for provisional tax purposes should not be less than the taxable income assessed for the latest preceding year of assessment for which an assessment has been issued not less than 21 days before the date the current estimate is made, unless the taxpayer can satisfy the Commissioner of Taxes that the taxable income for the current year will be less than that for that preceding year.

A provisional taxpayer is rendered liable to a penalty if the estimate of taxable income for the purposes of the second payment of provisional tax is found to be less than 90% of the taxable income as finally determined and is also less than the taxable income as assessed for the immediately preceding tax year.

For individuals, the first payment must be made by December 31 and the second payment by June 30, and if a third top-up payment is required, this should be paid by December 31 of the following year, that is, one year after the first provisional tax payment.

Tax rates

The following rates apply for the tax year to June 30, 2004.

Taxable income				
Over	Not over		Tax on Column 1	Percentage on excess
(Column 1)				
0	E 14,000	....	—	0
E 14,000	20,000	....	0	12
20,000	30,000	....	E 720	19
30,000	36,000	....	2,620	26
36,000		....	4,180	33

INDIVIDUAL TAX CALCULATION

For year ending June 30, 2004

Tax computation

Salary		E 200,000.00
Benefits in kind (1):		
House	9,600	
Car	27,000	36,600.00
Bank interest—Now taxed at source		—
		236,600.00
Deduct:		
Mortgage interest of 9,000 per annum (restricted) (2)	4,500	
Pension contributions (maximum)	1,750	6,250.00
Taxable income		E 230,350.00
Tax payable		E 68,315.50
Graded tax (poll tax) payable		E 18.00

Notes:

1. Benefits in kind are based on a four-bedroom executive house in Mbabane (capital) and a rental of E4,000 per month and a 2,500cc engine capacity car costing E300,000.
2. Mortgage interest relief is restricted to the lower of 50% of interest on a maximum mortgage amount of E60,000 or E9,000.
3. Exchange rate of the emalangeni at February 3, 2004: US$1 = E6.55.

PwC contact

For additional information on taxation in Sweden, contact:

Anders Assarson
Öhrlings PricewaterhouseCoopers
Kungsgatan 18
S–113 97 Stockholm, Sweden
Telephone: (46) (8) 555 33 000
Fax: (46) (8) 555 33 002
e-mail: anders.assarson@se.pwcglobal.com

Significant developments

There have been no significant tax or regulatory developments as regards individual taxation in the past year.

Territoriality and residence

The amount of income subject to national and municipal income taxes depends on the individual's residence status. Persons staying in Sweden continuously for more than six months are deemed to have gained taxable residence and become liable to pay income taxes on income from all sources worldwide. Individuals present in Sweden for less than six months are usually liable to pay taxes only on Swedish-source income.

Residence status at year-end determines whether an individual is liable to net wealth tax on all taxable property worldwide or only on taxable property in Sweden. However, foreign citizens who are staying temporarily (for no more than three years) in Sweden have limited tax liability.

Five-year rule/Citizenship affects the residence status of Swedes only. Swedish citizens, as well as foreigners who have been resident in Sweden for ten years, are deemed resident in Sweden for tax purposes until they can prove that all important ties with Sweden have been broken. Five years after a taxpayer leaves Sweden, the burden of proof is reversed and the tax authorities must prove that ties still exist between the individual and Sweden.

Six-month and one-year rule/Swedish residents who have been assigned to work abroad or who have taken up employment abroad with a planned duration of not less than six months are not liable to Swedish income taxes on income from this employment, provided the income is taxed in the country of employment and you do not spend more than 6 days per month or maximum 72 days per 12-month period in Sweden. If no tax is payable in that country because of exemptions under domestic legislation, the income is tax exempt in Sweden only if the assignment or employment is intended to last for at least one year.

Gross income

Employee gross income/All remuneration from employment, whether in cash or in kind, is treated as taxable income, including directors' fees, bonuses, commissions, pensions, annuities, and all kinds of allowances. Tax equalization payments are taxable. The rental value of free housing, the estimated value of free automobiles and the value of free meals are the major taxable benefits in kind.

Reimbursement from a Swedish employer to a nonresident individual is taxed at a flat rate of 25% at source, that is, foreign citizens temporarily in Sweden without attaining tax residence are taxed at the flat rate of 25% on their salary. The same rate applies when a pension is paid by a Swedish source to a person not tax-resident in Sweden.

Foreign experts and key personnel are only liable to tax on 75% of the income earned during their first three years in Sweden. Some benefits, like school fees, moving allowances, and home travel allowances, are tax exempt. These regulations apply to foreign personnel employed by a Swedish company with a permanent establishment in Sweden. The employment and residence in Sweden must be limited in time (not exceeding five years), and the employee cannot have been a resident in Sweden prior to the employment. To qualify for this exemption, the employee must obtain a ruling from the National Tax Board.

Loans from an employer to an employee at low or no interest are deemed to generate a taxable benefit. However, the taxable benefit is deductible as ordinary interest paid.

Capital gains and investment income/Individuals resident in Sweden are taxed on capital gains realized during the period of residence.

Nonresident individuals are not taxed on Swedish-source capital gains, except for capital gains on Swedish situs real estate. For private real property and tenant owner's apartments, the maximum taxable profit is two-thirds of the profit. However, it is possible to roll the tax payment over when buying new private real property.

The taxable gain on the sale of shares is the net profit, that is, the sales price less the average purchase price for all shares of the same kind. Only 70% of the calculated loss may normally be deducted.

Special rules apply to the taxation of capital gains from the sale of shares of small companies. Those rules are very complicated, and it is therefore recommended that Öhrlings PricewaterhouseCoopers be contacted if consideration is to be given to selling such shares.

Gains on the sale of personal assets are taxable only if they exceed SEK50,000 per year. The acquisition cost of personal assets is either the real purchase price or, optionally, 25% of the sales price. Other assets are taxed on the net profit without the mentioned limitations.

The taxable portion of the capital gains is taxed as capital income.

All current income from bank savings, financial instruments, claims of different kinds, and dividends received by a resident person is taxable as capital income.

Deductions

Business deductions/In principle, all expenses incurred during the fulfillment of the employment agreement are deductible, for example, travel expenses, automobile expenses, living allowances on business trips, necessary literature, and tools of the trade. The deduction related to cost-of-living allowances is, however, limited.

Nonbusiness expenses/The most common deductions are listed below.

1. Under certain conditions, expenses for travel between home and place of work, based on the cheapest means of public transport or, if a private car or a company car is used, on a fixed amount per kilometer. Only the part of the cost exceeding SEK7,000 is deductible.

2. Interest paid, when calculating capital income.
3. Management costs for the administration of investments, to the extent the costs exceed SEK1,000.
4. Personal pension insurance premiums and contributions to restricted pension savings, to a limited extent.

Personal allowances/From the aggregate taxable income, a basic allowance of SEK11,000 to SEK26,400 (for 2004) or one-twelfth of SEK11,600 per month or part of a month the person has been resident in Sweden is granted.

Treatment of losses/Losses from earned income and business may be set off against future earned income and business profits without time limitation. This will be done only within each individual source of income. For losses incurred on income from capital, a tax credit of 30% of the loss is granted against tax on earned income for losses not exceeding SEK100,000 and 21% for losses in excess thereof. However, when calculating the final loss, losses from the sale of private real property, securities, and so on, are in general deductible only up to 50% or 70%. The tax credit may not be carried forward.

Tax credits

Foreign tax credits are available.

Other taxes

Social security taxes/Social security charges of 32.70% (2004) of total remuneration in cash and in kind are levied on the employer. A pension fee of 7% of gross earned income up to SEK340,900 (i.e., a maximum fee of SEK23,900) for 2004, is payable by the employee, 25% of which is deductible for income tax purposes.

Local taxes on income/Municipal income taxes are assessed together with the national income tax and vary between 29% and 37% according to municipality (Stockholm—30%). They are not deductible for national tax purposes.

Wealth tax/Wealth tax is paid by individuals owning assets with a net value in excess of SEK1,500,000 and (SEK2,000,000 for families) at December 31. The tax rate is 1.5%.

Real estate tax/Real estate tax is paid by the owner. The tax rate is 1% of the taxable value of the real estate for houses and for a block of flats. For persons resident in Sweden, real estate tax is payable for real estate (as well as flats) situated abroad if the property is held for private purposes.

Tax administration

Returns/Individuals file a tax return for the calendar year. For most individuals, the filing date is May 3. The tax authorities assess income taxes by applying the appropriate tax rates to the aggregate taxable income from the various sources. Spouses are taxed separately, except on wealth.

Payment of tax/Preliminary taxes must be withheld by a resident employer. In the case of a nonresident employer, tax payment must be submitted to the tax authority by the employees themselves. A final tax bill will be issued to the individual between August and December in the year after the income year. Income taxes not covered by the preliminary taxes withheld must be paid by the individual 90 days after the final tax bill is issued.

Tax rates

Income year 2004

Employment income tax/As follows, on rounded taxable income amounts.

Taxable income	National income tax	Municipal income tax*
	SEK	%
From 0 to SEK291,800	200	31
From SEK291,800 to SEK441,300	200 + 20%	31
Over SEK441,300	200 + 25%	31

*This rate equals the average municipal tax rate.

Capital tax/Flat rate of 30%.

Wealth tax/Flat rate of 1.5% on net wealth in excess of SEK1,500,000 for single taxpayers and SEK2,000,000 for families.

INDIVIDUAL TAX CALCULATION

Income year 2004

Assumptions

The taxpayer is resident in Sweden and does not own real estate in Sweden or abroad.

	SEK
Salary	800,000
Capital income:	
Interest received on bank deposit	10,000
Dividends received	25,000
Interest paid	150,000
Loss on sale of shares	20,000

Tax computation

Income from employment (earned income) taxation

Salary for year		SEK 800,000
Add:		
Sickness allowance received under the National Insurance Act	8,000	
Travel allowance granted by employer	8,800	
Other remuneration in cash or kind:		
Telephone	3,000	
Newspaper	1,600	21,400
		821,400
Deduct:		
Business travel expenses	4,400	
Travel costs from home to office (8,000 – 7,000)	1,000	5,400
Net income from employment		816,000
Deduct:		
Private pension insurance premium	39,300	
Pension fee (7%) of which 25% is deductible	6,000	45,300
		770,700
Less—Basic allowance		11,600
Taxable income for national and municipal tax (1)		SEK 759,100
National income tax		SEK 109,350
Municipal income tax (2)		227,930
Pension fee		23,900
Less—Tax reduction, 75% of pension fee (rounded down)		(17,900)
Total tax on income from employment		SEK 343,280

Income from capital (unearned income) taxation

Interest received on bank deposit	SEK 10,000
Dividends received	25,000
Interest paid	(150,000)
Loss on shares (70% x 20,000)	(14,000)
Total loss	SEK (129,000)
Tax credit:	
(30% x 100,000)	SEK 30,000
(21% x 29,000)	6,090
Total tax reduction	SEK 36,090

Total tax

On income from employment	SEK 343,280
Less:	
Tax credit on unearned income	(36,090)
Special tax reduction for year 2004	(200)
	SEK 306,990

Notes:

1. Swedish income taxes are always computed on the taxable income rounded off to the next lowest SEK100.
2. Assuming a rate of 30%.
3. Exchange rate of the krona at March 1, 2004: US$1 = SEK7.3850.

Switzerland

PwC contact

For additional information on taxation in Switzerland, contact:

George Ladner
PricewaterhouseCoopers AG
Stampfenbachstrasse 52
8035 Zurich, Switzerland
Telephone: (41) (1) 630 11 11
Fax: (41) (1) 630 45 15
e-mail: george.ladner@ch.pwc.com

Significant developments

In the canton of Zurich the taxation of stock options has significantly changed. Traditionally, taxation at grant was the general rule. As an exception, exercise taxation could be negotiated with the Cantonal tax authorities. Now, in the canton of Zurich, the stock option is considered a taxable benefit in the hands of the employee at the time the stock option becomes an irrevocable right (i.e., grant, vesting or exercise). To determine the moment at which the stock option becomes an irrevocable right the stock option plan, subplans, and individual agreements need to be analyzed.

Territoriality and residence

Switzerland taxes its tax residents on their worldwide income and wealth. An individual is considered a tax resident under Swiss domestic tax law who:

1. Intends to exercise a gainful employment for more than 30 days in Switzerland, or;
2. Stays more than 90 days in Switzerland without exercising a gainful employment.

Tax residents who are Swiss citizens pay federal income taxes, cantonal/communal income, and wealth taxes by means of filing a Swiss tax return.

Only foreign tax residents are subject to wage tax withholdings on their employment income. If the foreigner's income or wealth exceeds a threshold, a Swiss tax return needs to be filed as well.

Each of the 26 cantons has the freedom to set its own tax rates and tax deductions. The communities located within a canton have different tax multipliers resulting in different tax liabilities. Consequently, the amount of income and wealth taxes payable through filing a Swiss tax return can be significantly different between cantons and communities.

Nontax residents are subject to Swiss tax on only limited sources of income, such as:

- Employment income derived by physically working in Switzerland.
- Director's fees received from a Swiss company.
- Dividends and interest paid out from Switzerland.
- Swiss real estate.

In nearly all cases Swiss taxes are paid by means of withholding taxes, and a Swiss tax return cannot be filed. Depending on the canton, worldwide income is considered when determining the applicable tax rate.

Especially worth mentioning are the flat withholding tax rates that apply to directors' fees, which can vary from 16% to 25%. The exact withholding tax depends on the canton in which the Swiss company is seated.

Gross income

Employee gross income/An employee is taxed on all salary and benefits in kind. Special tax concessions for qualifying expatriates are granted by various cantons.

Although they are based on a federal ruling, the expatriate concessions accepted by the tax authorities in practice can differ from canton to canton. In general terms, the following tax deductions or tax-free reimbursements should be accepted:

1. Transportation—Actual moving costs to Switzerland (e.g., transportation of household) as well as the moving costs upon return to their home country are deductible for expatriates. The same applies for travel expenses for expatriates and their families at the beginning and at the end of the assignment.
2. Housing—If an expatriate maintains a foreign apartment or house during the period of assignment in Switzerland, the costs of additional housing in Switzerland are deductible. Depending on the canton the housing deduction might be limited.
3. School fees—International school fees for primary and secondary education are tax deductible where public schools do not provide education in the mother language.

In Geneva a lump-sum 10% tax deduction to cover various expatriate expenses can be applied for.

Capital gains and investment income/Capital gains on movable property realized by tax residents are normally tax-exempt throughout Switzerland. The capital gain realized on the sale of Swiss real estate is, however, subject to a communal capital gains tax, the rate of which is different in each canton that levies it.

Deductions

Business deductions/A tax resident may deduct several deemed business expenses or claim the actual expenses as a tax deduction, if actual expenses exceed the deemed business expenses. Tax residents and nontax residents may claim expatriate tax deductions.

Nonbusiness expenses/A wide variety of deductions are allowed, such as:

- Paid social security contributions.
- Payments made to recognized pension schemes.
- Paid interest on debts/mortgage.
- Donation to qualifying Swiss charities.
- Extraordinary medical expenses.

Certain conditions need to be fulfilled to claim one or more of the listed deductions and limits apply to tax deductions (e.g., the tax deduction for interest payments is limited to the total of the received private investment income, deemed rental income or actual rental income plus CHF50,000).

Personal allowances/Personal allowances are granted according to individual circumstances, as shown below.

	Direct federal tax	Zurich cantonal tax	Geneva cantonal tax
	CHF	CHF	CHF
Married taxpayer	—	—	27,500
Single taxpayer	—	—	15,000
Single, divorced, or widowed taxpayer living with dependent children or other dependents	—	—	27,500
For each dependent child	5,600	5,400	6,500
For each additional dependent child	—	—	6,500
For each dependent other than wife or child	5,600	2,400	6,500
For each additional dependent	—	—	6,500
Day care expenses		3,000	2,500

Tax credits

Pursuant to the provisions of a double taxation treaty concluded between Switzerland and another country, income is exempted or a tax credit is given by Switzerland to avoid double taxation.

Generally speaking, a tax exemption applies in cases where foreign employment income, foreign director's fees, or income from foreign real estate is subject to taxation abroad. In accordance with the Swiss tax progression system the foreign income is, however, taken into consideration to determine the applicable Swiss tax rate at which the nonexempt income is taxed.

A tax credit normally applies to foreign interest and dividend income to avoid double taxation.

Other taxes

Social security tax/If an individual is subject to the Swiss social security system. The following social security contributions are payable:

Insurance	Contribution rate		Contribution base
	Employer	Employee	
Old age, survivors', and disability insurance............	5.05%*	5.05%*	Entire salary
Unemployment insurance............	1%	1%	Salary up to CHF106,800
Children allowances..........	1%–3%	0%	Entire salary
Occupational accident insurance............	0.17%–13.5%	0%	Salary up to CHF106,800
Medical insurance............	Private insurance	Private insurance	
Occupational pension scheme...............	Private insurance	Private insurance	

*In Geneva, as from January 1, 2003, an additional compulsory maternity insurance contribution of 0.15%, with no ceiling, is also applicable. The same rate of contribution applies to the employer

Cantonal and communal taxes/Most of the cantons levy a church tax to support the three recognized churches (Protestant, Roman Catholic, and Christian Catholic). For individuals who belong to another faith or who are not a member of any faith, the tax is not levied. In the canton of Zurich, it is important to indicate religious denomination clearly on the registration form at the town hall when first entering Switzerland, as this will serve as the basis for assessing church tax. In the canton of Geneva, payment of the parish or church tax is not compulsory.

Wealth tax/All cantons levy a wealth tax based on the balance of assets minus debts. Net assets include all assets (real estate property, net business assets, securities, receivables, deposits, surrender value of life and similar insurance policies) Debts include: loans, tax debts, mortgages, and private borrowings). Depending on the canton a personal allowance is deducted from the taxable base. The amount of the personal allowance depends on the canton.

Personal tax/A personal tax of CHF24 (CHF48 for joint filing) in Zurich and CHF25 in Geneva is levied on each return.

Tax administration

Returns/Married couples file a joint Swiss tax return and are assessed jointly.

An individual who is obligated to file a Swiss tax return must file the Swiss tax return by March 31 of the following calendar year. A tax-filing extension can be applied for.

Foreign employees with no permit to settle permanently in Switzerland and whose employer is resident in Switzerland are usually taxed at source. However, they are obliged to file a tax return if their gross annual salary exceeds CHF120,000 or their private income exceeds a threshold (for the canton of Geneva, CHF500,000 and/or the fulfillment of four other conditions

Payment of tax/Swiss citizen tax residents pay their taxes by way of filing the Swiss tax return.

A foreign tax resident is subject to wage tax withholdings on employment income. If the foreign employee is obligated to file a Swiss tax return, the final tax liability is assessed on the basis of the filed Swiss tax return.

As it can take up to two years to settle the final tax bill, provisional tax bills are issued prior to the final tax settlement. Voluntary tax payments can also be made to reduce the interest charges that are calculated up to issuing the final tax bill.

As a general rule, nonresidents pay their taxes by way of withholding taxes. The withheld tax is the final tax liability. As an exception, a Swiss tax return needs to be filed to report the income derived from, and the value of, Swiss real estate.

Tax rates

Direct federal tax on income

I—Married

Taxable income		Tax on Column 1	Percentage on excess
Over	Not over		
(Column 1)			
CHF 0	CHF 24,900	—	—
24,900	44,700	—	1
44,700	51,300	CHF 198	2
51,300	66,200	330	3
66,200	79,400	777	4
79,400	91,000	1,305	5
91,000	101,000	1,885	6
101,000	109,300	2,485	7
109,300	115,900	3,066	8
115,900	120,900	3,594	9
120,900	124,300	4,044	10
124,300	126,000	4,384	11
126,000	127,700	4,571	12
127,700	788,400	4,775	13
788,400		90,666	
788,500		90,678*	

*11.5% of total income (11.5% being the maximum rate applicable).

II—Single

Taxable income			Tax on Column 1	Percentage on excess
Over	Not over			
(Column 1)				
CHF 0	CHF 12,800	....	—	—
12,800	27,900	....	—	0.77
27,900	36,500	....	CHF 116.25	0.88
36,500	48,600	....	191.90	2.64
48,600	63,800	....	511.30	2.97
63,800	68,800	....	962.70	5.94
68,800	91,100	....	1,259.70	6.60
91,100	118,400	....	2,731.50	8.80
118,400	154,700	....	5,133.90	11.00
154,700	664,300	....	9,126.90	13.20
664,300		....	76,394.10	
664,400		....	76,406.00*	

*11.5% of total income (11.5% being the maximum rate applicable).

Zurich cantonal tax

III—Income Tax

Table A—Married/Single parent

Taxable income			Basic tax on Column 1	Percentage on excess
Over	Not over			
(Column 1)				
CHF 0	CHF 11,000	....	—	0
11,000	16,400	....	—	2
16,400	23,200	....	CHF 108	3
23,200	31,400	....	312	4
31,400	40,900	....	640	5
40,900	53,100	....	1,115	6
53,100	80,300	....	1,847	7
80,300	107,500	....	3,751	8
107,500	148,300	....	5,927	9
148,300	197,200	....	9,599	10
197,200	250,200	....	14,489	11
250,200	311,400	....	20,319	12
311,400		....	27,663	13

Table B—Single

Taxable income Over (Column 1)	Not over	Basic tax on Column 1	Percentage on excess
CHF 0	CHF 5,500	—	0
5,500	9,600	—	2
9,600	13,700	CHF 82	3
13,700	20,400	205	4
20,400	28,600	473	5
28,600	38,100	883	6
38,100	49,000	1,453	7
49,000	63,900	2,216	8
63,900	92,500	3,408	9
92,500	121,000	5,982	10
121,000	165,900	8,832	11
165,900	224,300	13,771	12
224,300		20,779	13

IV—Wealth Tax

Table A—Married/Single parent

Taxable wealth Over (Column 1)	Not over	Basic tax on Column 1	Percentage on excess
CHF 0	CHF 136,000	—	0.00
136,000	340,000	—	0.05
340,000	680,000	CHF 102.00	0.10
680,000	1,223,000	442.00	0.15
1,223,000	2,039,000	1,256.50	0.20
2,039,000	2,854,000	2,888.50	0.25
2,854,000		4,926.00	0.30

Table B—Single

Taxable wealth Over (Column 1)	Not over	Basic tax on Column 1	Percentage on excess
CHF 0	CHF 68,000	—	0.00
68,000	272,000	—	0.05
272,000	612,000	CHF 102.00	0.10
612,000	1,155,000	442.00	0.15
1,155,000	1,971,000	1,256.50	0.20
1,971,000	2,786,000	2,888.50	0.25
2,786,000		4,926.00	0.30

The effective cantonal and communal income and wealth tax is determined by multiplying the basic rate of tax listed in the tables by the tax multiplier set by the canton and community. For Zurich, the effective 2004 cantonal tax is 100% of basic tax.

Zurich communal tax/Each commune levies its taxes as a percentage of basic cantonal tax. For 2004 the effective communal tax of the city of Zurich is 122% of basic tax.

Church tax/Church tax is levied as a percentage of basic cantonal tax. For 2004 the following percentages are applicable in the city of Zurich.

	%
Protestant	10
Roman Catholic	11
Christian Catholic	14

Geneva cantonal tax

V—Income Tax

Table A—Single

Taxable income	**Base cantonal tax (*)**	**Tax rate before tax discount**
CHF	CHF	%
20,000	1,600.05	8.00
30,000	2,858.95	9.53
40,000	4,201.70	10.50
50,000	5,592.30	11.18
75,000	9,211.70	12.28
100,000	12,995.50	13.00
150,000	20,958.10	13.97
200,000	29,328.75	14.66
300,000	46,888.95	15.63
500,000	83,689.75	16.74
1,000,000	178,214.60	17.82

*Before cantonal/communal multipliers, personal tax discount and 12% communal taxes rebate.

Table B—Married Taxpayers and Taxpayers Living with Children in Own Household

Taxable income	Base cantonal tax (*)	Tax rate before tax discount
CHF	CHF	%
20,000	1,068.20	5.34
30,000	2,060.70	6.87
40,000	3,200.05	8.00
50,000	4,430.10	8.86
75,000	7,751.75	10.34
100,000	11,374.60	11.37
150,000	19,257.55	12.84
200,000	27,621.25	13.81
300,000	45,180.90	15.06
500,000	81,981.70	16.40
1,000,000	176,506.50	17.65

*Before cantonal/communal multipliers, personal tax discount and 12% communal taxes rebate.

VI—Wealth Tax

Table A—Basic Tax

Taxable wealth		Maximum tax for the band	Percentage
Over	Not over		
CHF 1	CHF 103,403	CHF 180.95	0.175
103,404	206,805	232.65	0.225
206,806	310,208	284.35	0.275
310,209	413,611	310.20	0.300
413,612	620,416	672.10	0.325
620,417	827,221	723.80	0.350
827,222	1,034,026	775.50	0.375
1,034,027	1,240,832	827.20	0.400
1,240,833	1,551,040	1,318.40	0.425
1,551,041			0.450

Table B—Supplementary Tax on Basic Tax

Taxable wealth		Maximum tax for the band	Percentage
Over	Not over		
CHF 1	CHF 103,403	0	0
103,404	206,805	CHF 11.65	0.01125
206,806	310,208	14.20	0.01375
310,209	413,611	31.00	0.03000
413,612	620,416	67.20	0.03250
620,417	827,221	108.55	0.05250
827,222	1,034,026	116.35	0.05625
1,034,027	1,240,832	165.45	0.08000
1,240,833	1,551,040	263.70	0.08500
1,551,041	3,102,079	1,744.90	0.11250
3,102,080			0.13500

The above tax rates are basically applicable to taxpayers filing a tax return. Effective cantonal income and wealth tax is determined by multiplying the basic tax by the multiplier applicable for the tax (calendar) year in question, which is 147.5% for tax year 2003, and then by adding the supplementary tax on wealth.

Geneva communal tax/Each commune levies its taxes as a percentage of the above tax. For 2003 the effective communal tax of the city of Geneva is 45.5% of basic tax.

INDIVIDUAL TAX CALCULATION— CANTON AND CITY OF ZURICH

Calculation for direct federal tax and cantonal and communal taxes, canton and city of Zurich—2004.

Assumptions

1. Married with two children, member of the Protestant Church and living in Zurich.
2. Employment income is CHF175,000 (net of social security taxes and pension fund contributions).
3. Compensation as director CHF3,200.
4. Deemed business expenses CHF7,000 per annum.
5. The value of the securities and savings accounts total CHF140,000 and the income there from CHF4,000).
6. Living in own apartment, the assessed municipal value is CHF180,000 and the deemed rental value CHF12,500.
7. The mortgage loan is CHF100,000 and the paid mortgage interest totals CHF5,000 per annum.
8. Surrender value of life and annuity insurances total CHF5,000.
9. Motorcar with market value of CHF25,000.

Computation of Swiss income taxes

	Federal tax—2004	Zurich tax—2004
	CHF	CHF
Gross income:		
Employment income	175,000	175,000
Director's fees	3,200	3,200
Deemed income from real estate property	12,500	12,500
Income from securities and bank accounts	4,000	4,000
Total income	194,700	194,700
Deductions:		
Deemed business expenses	7,000	7,000
Deemed paid insurance premiums	4,500	7,000
Paid mortgage interest	5,000	5,000
Personal allowance	11,200	10,800
Total deductions	27,700	29,800
Total taxable income	167,000	164,900
Swiss income taxes:		
Federal income tax	9,884	
Cantonal income tax		11,259
Communal income tax		13,736
Church income tax		1,126
Personal tax		48
Total Swiss income taxes	9,884	26,169

Computation of Swiss wealth taxes

	CHF
Assets:	
Real estate property	180,000
Securities and bank accounts	140,000
Surrender value of life and annuity insurances	5,000
Motorcar	25,000
Total assets	350,000
Debts:	
Mortgage loan	100,000
Other debts	0
Total debts	100,000
Total taxable net wealth	250,000
Cantonal tax	57
Communal tax	70
Church tax	6

INDIVIDUAL TAX CALCULATION— CANTON AND CITY OF GENEVA

Calculation for direct federal tax 2003 and cantonal and communal taxes, canton and city of Geneva—2003.

Assumptions

1. Foreign executive transferred by an international group to Switzerland for a maximum period of five years; married with two children (aged more than 12); one spouse earns all the income. Member of the Protestant Church, living and working in the city of Geneva.
2. Employment income, net of social security taxes and pension fund contributions.

	2003
	CHF
Base salary	153,000
Residency allowances	22,000
Total	175,000

3. Compensation as director CHF3,200.
4. Securities and savings accounts total CHF140,000; income thereon CHF4,000 (including interest on savings accounts of CHF2,200).
5. Living in own apartment, assessed value of CHF180,000; estimated net deemed rental income of personally used real estate property CHF12,500 for Geneva cantonal and federal tax purposes; mortgage CHF100,000; mortgage interest CHF5,000.
6. Sickness and accident insurance premiums CHF2,000 per annum. Life insurance premiums CHF2,300 per annum; surrender value of life insurance CHF5,000.
7. Motorcar with market value of CHF25,000.

Determination of taxable income

	Direct federal tax 2003 (1)	Geneva tax 2003 (1)
	CHF	CHF
Determination of net income		
Gross income:		
Income from employment	175,000	175,000
Secondary income—director's fee	3,200	3,200
Net income from real estate property	12,500	12,500
Income from securities and receivables	4,000	4,000
Total	194,700	194,700
Deductions:		
Lump-sum representation expenses	8,750	8,750
Travel to and from work (depending on distance)	840	840
Federal lump-sum meal expenses	3,000	
Authorized tax deduction:		
Lower of 10% of gross employment income or residency allowances (2)	17,500	17,500
Sickness and accident insurance premiums	2,000	2,000
Life insurance premiums and interest on savings accounts	2,500	4,500
Medical bills (Note 3 for Geneva tax and Note 4 for direct federal tax)	—	—
Interest on mortgage	5,000	5,000
Total	39,590	38,590
Net income:		
Total of gross income	194,700	194,700
Total of deductions	(39,590)	(38,590)
Less—Portion of charitable donations deductible (Note 5 for Geneva tax; Note 6 for direct federal tax)	—	—
	155,110	156,110

Notes:

1. Income of 2003.
2. As per 2003 practice. Changes to come, probably by 2004.
3. Only the part exceeding the 1% of net taxable income.
4. Only the part exceeding the 5% of net taxable income.
5. Cash donations to charities up to 5% of net taxable income.
6. Cash donation to charities up to 10% of net taxable income.

Determination of taxable income

	Direct federal tax 2003	Geneva tax 2003
	Income of 2003	Income of 2003
	CHF	CHF
Net income	155,110	156,110
Tax-free amounts (social allowances):		
For married persons	—	
For dependent children	(11,200)	
Taxable income	143,910	156,110

Determination of taxable wealth

(Geneva tax, December 31, 2003)

Determination of net assets

	CHF
Assets:	
Real estate property	180,000
Securities and receivables	140,000
Surrender value of life insurance	5,000
Car	25,000
Total	350,000
Liabilities:	
Mortgage	100,000
Total	100,000
Net assets:	
Total assets	350,000
Total liabilities	(100,000)
	250,000
Taxable wealth:	
Net assets	250,000
Tax-free amount (social allowance):	
For married persons with two children	(150,000)
Taxable wealth	100,000

Tax computation

Direct federal tax		
Income tax on taxable income of 143,900 (rounded off)		CHF 6,881.50
Cantonal and communal tax		
Computation of basic tax:		
Income tax on taxable income of 156,100	16,997.70	
Wealth tax on taxable wealth of 100,000	175.00	
Basic tax	17,172.70	
Total tax liability		
Cantonal tax—147.5% of basic tax (rounded off)	25,329.75	
Less—Reduction of initiative 111—12% of cantonal tax (1)	(3,008.60)	
Supplementary cantonal tax—1% of basic tax	170.00	
Communal tax—45.5% of basic tax	7,813.55	
Supplementary wealth tax on 100,000	—	
Personal tax	25.00	
Real estate cantonal tax (0.1% of CHF180,000)	180.00	33,251.60
Total of taxes payable in canton of Geneva		CHF 40,133.10

Notes:

1. Discount on cantonal income tax only.
2. Exchange rate of the Swiss franc at January 1, 2004: US$1 = CHF1.24070.

Tahiti

Pwc contact

For additional information on Tahiti and French Polynesia, contact:

Christophe Parion
PricewaterhouseCoopers–Fitec
Centre Vaima
BP 608 – Papeete
Tahiti
Telephone: (689) 50 86 00
Fax: (689) 43 99 31
e-mail: coopers@mail.pf
Att: Christophe Parion

Absence of taxation

Income tax is not imposed on individuals in Tahiti or French Polynesia.

Note

Exchange rate (selling) of the Pacific franc at December 31, 2003: US$1 = XPF95.18. The Pacific franc is pegged to the Euro at €1 = XPF119.33.

PwC contact

For additional information on taxation in Taiwan, contact:

Wen-Horng Kao
PricewaterhouseCoopers
International Trade Building, 23th Floor
333 Keelung Road, Sec. 1
Taipei 110, Taiwan, ROC
Telephone: (886) (2) 2729 5209
Fax: (886) (2) 8780-0342 (Tax)
e-mail: wen-horng.kao@tw.pwc.com

Significant developments

There have been no significant developments regarding individual taxation in the past year.

Territoriality and residence

Taiwan taxes its citizens, as well as aliens whose period of stay in Taiwan is more than 90 days in a calendar year, on compensation attributable to Taiwan situs services and other Taiwan-source income. An alien whose period of stay is not more than 90 days is taxed on income paid in Taiwan.

Aliens who reside in Taiwan for 183 days or more in a calendar year are considered residents. Those who were resident in the previous year and continue to reside in Taiwan are also considered residents in the current year, regardless of their period of residence during this year. An alien who resides in Taiwan for less than 183 days is considered a nonresident.

Gross income

Employee gross income/An alien who is present in Taiwan for more than 90 days is taxed on salary, bonuses, and commissions earned for work done in Taiwan, regardless of where payment is made, but is not taxed to the extent that the compensation relates to services performed outside Taiwan. Such an individual is also taxed on fringe benefit reimbursements, such as housing, living, education, and transportation allowances. However, many major fringe benefits, such as housing, rent and utilities, automobile purchase and operating costs, and compensation for servants, are not taxed if provided directly by the employer without cash payment to the employee.

Income tax concessions to expatriates/If a nonresident individual holding the position of director, manager, or technician of an enterprise that invests in Taiwan in accordance with the Statute for Investment by Foreigners/Overseas Chinese stays in Taiwan to perform investment, plant construction, or market survey operations for a period of less than 183 days in a taxable year, the salary for such work paid by the overseas employers will not be deemed to be Taiwan-source income.

Capital gains and investment income/Gains from the disposal of capital assets are included in an individual's taxable income with the exceptions listed below.

1. Gains from the sale of land and household furniture.
2. Gains from the sale of marketable securities (for both listed and unlisted securities) are liable to securities transaction tax at a rate of 0.3% on the gross

proceeds from sale of stocks and 0.1% on the gross proceeds from sale of debentures and government-approved bonds.

3. Income tax on gains from the sale of an owner-occupied house may be refundable if the taxpayer purchases another house for occupation (at an amount greater than the selling price of the old house) within two years from the date of sale. The income tax on the gain can be refunded up to the amount by which the cost of the new house exceeds the sales price of the old house. The tax reduction is also available if the new house is purchased before sale of the old house.

Capital losses are deductible only against capital gains; unused losses may be carried forward for three years.

Imputation tax system/The main purpose of the imputation tax system is to eliminate double taxation on earnings of a corporation. Corporations are taxed at 25% on profits. (An additional 10% tax that is imposed on any undistributed current earnings.) This tax can be distributed to the resident individual shareholders to offset their individual income tax. Any excess tax credits will be refundable to the resident individual shareholders.

As for nonresident individual shareholders, only the 10% tax on undistributed retained earnings can be claimed by foreign corporate shareholder as tax credit to offset the 20% withholding income tax on dividend distribution. No refund would be available to nonresident individual shareholders.

Income on investments outside Taiwan is not taxed. Investment income earned in Taiwan is taxable. The first NT$270,000 of certain types of interest income and dividend income from a listed company is exempt from tax. This NT$270,000 special deduction does not apply to dividend income received from a listed company.

Deductions

Business deductions/No deduction of business expenses is allowed to individuals.

Nonbusiness expenses/Taxpayers have the option to claim either a standard deduction or itemized deductions for their income deduction purpose. These deductions are as follows.

1. Standard deduction—The deduction for single taxpayers is NT$44,000. A husband and a wife filing a joint return are eligible for a standard deduction of NT$67,000.
2. Itemized deductions—Itemized deductions include charitable contributions, insurance premiums (maximum NT$24,000 per person), medical expenses, calamity and losses, and interest (maximum NT$300,000) paid on loans for the purchase of an owner-occupied house, or rental expenses (not for business use and up to a maximum of NT$120,000 per household). There is no ceiling on the itemized deduction total.

Nonresident aliens are not eligible for any deductions.

Personal allowances/A resident alien is eligible for a personal exemption of NT$74,000. Additional NT$74,000 exemptions are available for a spouse and for each dependent, and an exemption of NT$111,000 applies to the taxpayer, his/her spouse and dependents who are over 70 years old. In addition, taxpayers may deduct NT$75,000 of their income from salaries or wages.

A handicapped person is eligible for a deduction of NT$74,000. Tuition for children attending college can be deducted up to NT$25,000 per family.

Losses from disposal of properties can be deducted to the extent of gains resulting from the disposal of properties in the same tax year.

The amounts for exemptions, the standard deduction, the special deduction of income from salaries or wages, and the special deduction for handicapped persons are to be revised triennially to reflect the inflation rate.

A nonresident alien is not eligible for any personal allowances.

Tax credits

According to the Statute for Promotion of Industries Upgrading, aliens may be entitled to an investment credit. Individuals subscribing to or underwriting important high-tech enterprises or venture capital enterprises may claim 10% of the investment amount as a tax credit.

Other taxes

There are no social security or local income taxes in Taiwan.

Tax administration

Returns/Husbands and wives must file joint returns if both the husband and wife are tax residents in Taiwan in a calendar year. A spouse has the option to calculate the taxes due on that spouse's salaries or wages separately. Total tax liability for the joint return consists of the taxes due on the spouse's salaries or wages and the taxes due on all other joint income.

Nonresidents who are in Taiwan for not more than 90 days are not required to file an income tax return, since tax is withheld by the employer on compensation paid in Taiwan.

Income tax returns must be filed on a calendar-year basis between May 1 and May 31 of the following year.

Payment of tax/There is income tax withholding on locally paid salaries. Additional tax due must be paid at the time of filing.

Tax rates

Tax rates are as follows.

1. A nonresident alien residing in Taiwan for not more than 90 days is subject to 20% withholding tax on remuneration received from a Taiwan-registered entity. Remuneration received from an entity registered outside of Taiwan is not taxable.
2. A nonresident alien residing in Taiwan for more than 90 days but less than 183 days is subject to a 20% income tax rate on Taiwan taxable income, regardless of where paid.
3. A resident alien is subject to progressive tax rates as shown below.

Taxable income		Rate of tax	Less progressive difference
From	To		
		%	
0	NT$ 370,000	6	0
NT$ 370,001	990,000	13	NT$ 25,900
990,001	1,980,000	21	105,100
1,980,001	3,720,000	30	283,300
3,720,001		40	655,300

Note:

The progressive difference is subtracted from taxable income times the tax rate to determine income tax due.

INDIVIDUAL TAX CALCULATION

Assumptions

Resident alien husband and wife, two children; one spouse earns all the income.

Tax computation

Gross Income:		
Salary		NT$ 2,700,000
Dividend income		100,000
Interest income		400,000
Total gross income		3,200,000
Less—Itemized deductions:		
Insurance premiums (maximum deduction—24,000 per person)	96,000	
Medical expenses	42,000	
Charitable contributions	8,000	
Calamity	10,000	156,000
Less—Personal exemptions (74,000 x 4)		296,000
Less—Special deductions:		
Salary or wages	75,000	
Savings and investment	270,000	345,000
Taxable income		NT$ 2,403,000
Income tax		NT$ 437,600
Less—Tax credits derived from dividend received		(25,000)
Net income tax payable		NT$ 412,600

Notes:

1. Tax imputation system (Investee corporation), calculated as follows.

	NT$
Income before tax	100,000
Income tax of 25%	25,000
Net income	75,000
Distributable earnings	75,000
Tax credits distributable to shareholders	25,000

   The investee corporation can distribute NT$75,000 of dividend and NT$25,000 of tax credit to the shareholders under the new tax imputation system.

2. Exchange rate of the New Taiwan dollar at December 31, 2003: US$1 = NT$33.92.

Tanzania

PwC contacts

For additional information on taxation in Tanzania, contact:

Vinoo Somaiya
David Tarimo
PricewaterhouseCoopers
International House
Garden Avenue
P.O. Box 45
Dar es Salaam, Tanzania
Telephone: (255) (22) 2133100
Fax: (255) (22) 2133200
e-mail: vinoo.somaiya@tz.pwc.com
david.tarimo@tz.pwc.com

Significant developments

In the 2003 Budget speech, the Minister for Finance announced that a new Income Tax Act was to be introduced with effect from January 1, 2004. He requested stakeholders to make representations on the Act before it is tabled in Parliament. The latest draft of the Income Tax Act 2004, which is set out in a bill dated January 30, 2004, has gone to Parliament for a first reading and the commencement date is now set for July 1, 2004. As the new Income Tax Act 2004 has yet to be passed into law and as the current Income Tax Act 1973 continues to apply for years of income starting prior to commencement date, the information below relates to the current Income Tax Act 1973.

Territoriality and residence

Residents, including short-term residents, are taxed on their worldwide income. Nonresidents are taxed on their income accrued in or derived solely from sources within Tanzania.

An individual who fulfills one of the following criteria is considered resident.

1. Has a permanent home in Tanzania and is present in Tanzania during any part of a tax year.
2. Spends more than 183 days in Tanzania in any one tax year.
3. Spends an average of more than 122 days per year over 3 tax years.

Gross income

Employee gross income/Income from employment or services rendered includes salaries, wages, leave pay, sick pay, payment in lieu of leave, fees, commissions, bonuses, gratuities, and any allowances (excluding those expended wholly and exclusively in the production of income from employment or services rendered), as well as benefits-in-kind, for example, the value of residential accommodation provided by employer; furniture; private use of a car provided by employer; school fees; and gas, electricity and water supplied at the expense of the employer.

Capital gains and investment income/Capital gains tax was reintroduced at a rate of 10% as of July 1, 1999. Interest income exceeding the first TShs150,000 on monies saved in any bank operating in Tanzania and dividend income are taxed only at the appropriate resident withholding tax rates for such income.

Investment income derived by residents from sources outside Tanzania is taxable.

Deductions

Business deductions/Business expenses that are deductible from income derived from employment or services rendered are not specifically listed, but an individual may claim a deduction for expenses incurred wholly and exclusively in the production of such income. No blanket or standard deductions are available.

Nonbusiness expenses/No deductions are allowed for mortgage or other interest, social security contributions, taxes, or charitable contributions. There are no standard deductions.

Tax credits

The following tax credits are available to resident individuals, including short-term residents.

1. Any tax paid in another country in respect of income derived from that country.
2. Any tax paid in a country with which Tanzania has concluded a double taxation treaty, in respect of income derived from that country.

Other taxes

Social security taxes/Every employer must contribute to the National Social Security Fund. The contribution is 20% of the employee's gross employment earnings. The employer is entitled to recover up to half of this from the employee.

Tax administration

Returns/Taxpayers file both provisional and final returns, as follows.

1. Provisional return:

   Individuals are required to furnish a provisional return, containing an estimate of their chargeable income. Tax is payable thereon in four quarterly installments from the beginning of the year of income or the accounting period to which the return relates.
2. Final return:

   Individuals are also required to file a final return of income containing a statement of their income from all sources chargeable to individual income tax in Tanzania within 30 days from the date of service of the notice requiring them to furnish this return. In case of a person carrying on business who has made a provisional return of income, the return is due for submission within six months from the end of the year of income or the accounting date to which the return relates.

An individual whose income is derived solely from employment and whose employment income has been fully subjected to pay-as-you-earn (PAYE) deduction is not obliged to furnish a provisional or final return of income.

Joint filing of returns applies only where the wife derives income from any employment in any business carried on by her husband or with any partnership firm in which her husband is a partner. Otherwise, spouses file separate returns and are liable to tax on their respective incomes.

Tax years not coinciding with the calendar year are permitted in relation to income from any source other than employment or services rendered.

Payment of tax/Payroll withholding of individual income tax operates under the PAYE scheme.

Tax rates

Tanzania/The following table is applicable to residents of Tanzania.

Annual taxable income		Tax on	Percentage
Over	Not over	Column 1	on excess
(Column 1)			
0	TShs 600,000	—	—
TShs 600,000	2,160,000	—	18.5
2,160,000	4,320,000	TShs 288,600	20.0
4,320,000	6,480,000	720,600	25.0
6,480,000		1,260,600	30.0

Zanzibar/Individuals who are ordinarily resident in Zanzibar and whose income is accrued in or derived from Zanzibar are liable to tax at the rates given below.

Monthly taxable income		Tax on	Percentage
Over	Not over	Column 1	on excess
(Column 1)			
0	TShs 25,000	—	—
TShs 25,000	45,000	—	7.5
45,000	65,000	TShs 1,500	10.0
65,000	85,000	3,500	12.5
85,000	105,000	6,000	15.0
105,000	125,000	9,000	17.5
125,000	145,000	12,500	20.5
145,000	175,000	16,600	22.5
175,000	205,000	23,350	25.0
205,000	235,000	30,850	27.5
235,000	265,000	39,100	30.0
265,000		48,100	35.0

INDIVIDUAL TAX CALCULATION

2003

Tanzania resident

Assumptions

1. Resident employee, gross income TShs64,000,000 per annum.
2. Housing provided by the employer.
3. Benefits provided by employer:
   a. Car.
   b. Payment of electricity, telephone and water bills aggregating to TShs3,000,000.
   c. Domestic servant with annual salary of TShs500,000.
4. Bank deposit interest: TShs3,000,000.
5. Mortgage interest: TShs1,000,000 (no deduction permitted).
6. Capital gain: TShs3,000,000.
7. Dividend income: TShs2,000,000. (Assumption: not listed on Stock Exchange).

Tax computation

Salary income		TShs 64,000,000
Benefits in kind:		
Utilities	3,000,000	
Domestic servant	500,000	3,500,000
		67,500,000
Housing benefit (15% of salary plus benefits)		10,125,000
		TShs 77,625,000
Tax thereon:		
On the first 6,480,000	1,260,600	
On the remainder (71,145,000) at 30%	21,343,500	TShs 22,604,100
Tax on dividend income of 2,000,000 at 10% (resident withholding tax rate) (1)		TShs 200,000
Tax on bank interest income (3,000,000 – 150,000) at 15% (resident withholding tax rate) (1)		TShs 427,500
Capital gains tax on 3,000,000 at 10%		TShs 300,000

Zanzibar resident

Assumptions

1. An employee, married with two children, gross income TShs64,000,000.
2. Benefits provided by employer: car; payment of electricity, telephone and water bills aggregating to TShs300,000; and domestic servant annual salary TShs360,000.
3. Bank deposit interest: TShs300,000.
4. Mortgage interest: TShs84,000 (no deduction permitted).

Tax computation

Salary income		TShs 64,000,000
Benefits in kind:		
Utilities	300,000	
Domestic servant	360,000	660,000
Chargeable income		TShs 64,660,000
Tax thereon:		
On the first 3,180,000	577,200	
On the remainder (61,480,000) at 35%	21,518,000	TShs 22,095,200
Tax on bank interest income (300,000 – 150,000) at 15% withholding tax rate (1)		TShs 22,500

Notes:

1. Taxed at withholding tax rate. Withholding tax is final tax.
2. Exchange rate of the Tanzanian shilling at December 31, 2003: US$1 = TShs1,064.

PwC contact

For additional information on taxation in Thailand, contact:

Janist Aphornratana
Bangkok City Tower, 15th Floor
179 South Sathorn Road
Bangkok 10120, Thailand
Telephone: (66) (2) 286 9999
Fax: (66) (2) 286 2666
e-mail: janist.aphornratana@th.pwcglobal.com

Significant developments

There have been no significant developments to tax on personal income in the past year.

Territoriality and residence

Thailand taxes its residents and nonresidents on their assessable income derived from employment or business carried on in Thailand, regardless of whether such income is paid in or outside Thailand. Residents, defined as persons residing in Thailand at one or more times for an aggregate period of 180 days or more in any tax year (calendar year), who derive income from abroad are taxable on that income if remitted into Thailand in the year in which it is received. Short-term residence is not defined under Thai tax regulations.

Gross income

Employee gross income/Both resident and nonresident individuals who receive assessable income by virtue of hire of service performed in Thailand, including salary, bonuses, gratuities, pensions, the monetary value of rent-free housing, the employer-paid income tax, or any other money, property or benefits derived by virtue of hire of service, are subject to tax in Thailand, regardless of whether the income is paid within or outside Thailand. There are no concessions to foreigners or short-term residents.

Capital gains and investment income/Most types of capital gains are taxable as ordinary income, except that (1) capital gains from the sale of shares in a company listed on the Securities Exchange of Thailand and from the sale of investment units in a mutual fund are exempt and (2) in respect of gains from the sale of government bonds, debentures, bills, or certificates of indebtedness issued by a corporate entity, an individual may elect to bear only withholding tax at a flat rate of 15% and exclude the gains from assessable income in the computation of personal income tax at the end of the year.

Capital losses may not be offset against capital gains.

Capital gains and investment income earned by a resident from sources outside Thailand are not taxable unless remitted to Thailand.

Interest received from bank deposits, loans made to finance companies, government bonds, debentures, and bills issued by a corporate entity is subject to withholding tax at a flat rate of 15%. Individuals may choose to exclude such interest income from other income, in which case they pay the 15% withholding tax, or they may choose to include such interest income with other income and pay tax according to the personal income tax rates, in which case the tax withheld at source is credited against the tax liability.

A dividend received from a company incorporated in Thailand is subject to withholding tax at a flat rate of 10%. A resident who receives dividend income from a company incorporated in Thailand may elect to exclude this income from the computation of income tax and waive the tax credit mentioned below.

Deductions

Business deductions/There are no business deductions.

Nonbusiness expenses/Donations to specified charities are deductible up to 10% of taxable income after all other allowances are deducted. Life insurance premiums paid by a taxpayer or spouse to a Thai insurer are deductible up to a maximum of Bht50,000 each. However, if one spouse does not earn income, an allowance of only Baht10,000 is allowed for that spouse. Contributions to an approved provident fund in Thailand may be deducted up to a maximum of Bht300,000. Mortgage interest incurred for the purpose of purchase or construction of a residential building in Thailand may be deducted up to a maximum of Bht50,000. Contributions to the Social Security Fund (see below) may be deducted.

From January 1, 2003, income from the sale of a taxpayer's main residence is tax exempt, provided the taxpayer has resided in it for more than one year and buys a new one within a year before or from the date of such sale. The income exemption will be equal to the value of such property, but cannot exceed the value of the new property. The value of immovable property will be based on the government-appraised value for the purpose of collecting fees for transfer registration under the Land Code.

Personal allowances/A standard deduction of 40%, with a limit of Bht60,000, is permitted in respect of income from employment. In addition, there is a personal allowance of Bht30,000 each for the taxpayer and the taxpayer's spouse, Bht15,000 for each child, and an additional Bht2,000 for children studying in government-recognized institutions. A nonresident is allowed spouse and child deductions only if they are resident in Thailand.

Tax credits

Persons domiciled and residing in Thailand can elect to take income tax withheld at source from dividends received from Thai-incorporated companies as a credit against their tax liability. In this case, a credit to take into account the underlying corporate income tax paid on the profit being distributed is added to dividend income, which is then aggregated with other types of income. Tax at the personal income tax rates is calculated on the total taxable income; the value of the tax credit is then deducted from the tax so calculated.

Foreign taxes cannot be taken as a credit against Thai taxes unless permitted by treaty.

Other taxes

Social security taxes/Starting from January 1, 2004, all employers are required to contribute an amount equal to 5% of each employee's salary (maximum of Bht750 per employee per month) to a social security fund. The government and employees are also required to contribute an equal amount of 5%. However, the government portion of the contribution has been reduced to 2.75% (maximum of Bht412 per employee per month).

Other taxes on income/No other taxes are levied on income.

Tax administration

Returns/There is no reduced tax rate for a joint return filed by husband and wife. Where a joint return is filed, all income is attributed to the husband. Separate returns may be filed for income in the form of salaries and wages only, but, in this event, special rules apply concerning the allocation of income allowances and deductions between husband and wife.

The taxable year is the calendar year. All persons liable to taxation are required to file a return no later than March 31 of the following year.

Payment of tax/There is income tax withholding from salaries and other benefits and some other categories of income. The balance of any tax due for a calendar year is paid at the time of filing the annual tax return. Individual tax rates are shown below.

Tax rates

Individual tax rates are shown below:

Taxable net income		Accumulative tax	Percentage on excess
Over	Not over		
(Column 1)			
0	Bht 80,000	—	0
Bht 80,000	100,000	Bht —	5
100,000	500,000	1,000	10
500,000	1,000,000	41,000	20
1,000,000	4,000,000	141,000	30
4,000,000 up		1,041,000	37

INDIVIDUAL TAX CALCULATION

Calendar year 2003

Tax computation

Salary		Bht 3,750,000
House rent paid by employer		960,000
Tax paid by employer on house rent		517,409
Total assessable income		5,227,409
Less—Deductions:		
40% standard deduction, but not exceeding 60,000	60,000	
Personal allowances:		
Self	30,000	
Spouse	30,000	
Two children in school	34,000	
Charitable contributions	10,000	
Social security contribution	2,700	166,700
Total taxable income		Bht 5,060,709
Income tax thereon		Bht 1,434,962
Payable by employee		Bht 917,553
Payable by employer		Bht 517,409

Note:

Exchange rate of the Baht at December 31, 2003: US$1 = Bht39.44.

PwC contact

For additional information on taxation in Trinidad and Tobago, contact:

Peter R. Inglefield
PricewaterhouseCoopers
11–13 Victoria Avenue
Port-of-Spain, Trinidad
Telephone: (1) (868) 623 1361
Fax: (1) (868) 623 1512
e-mail: peter.inglefield@tt.pwc.com

Significant developments

The 2004 Budget removed the 5% tax on interest income earned by resident individuals on funds invested with a bank or other financial institution in Trinidad and Tobago.

Territoriality and residence

Individuals who are domiciled and resident in Trinidad and Tobago are taxed on their worldwide income whether or not such earnings are remitted to Trinidad and Tobago. A nonresident is taxed on income arising from employment in Trinidad and Tobago wherever received, subject where applicable to the provisions of double taxation treaties. Individuals are considered resident for tax purposes if they are in Trinidad and Tobago for more than 183 days in any calendar year. An individual who is in Trinidad and Tobago for some temporary purpose only and has actually resided in Trinidad and Tobago at one or more times for a period of less than six months in the year of income is considered to be temporarily resident in Trinidad and Tobago. A temporary resident is not taxed on any income arising outside of Trinidad and Tobago.

Gross income

Employee gross income/An individual is taxed on income received for services performed in Trinidad and Tobago whether or not such income is received in Trinidad and Tobago. For tax purposes, the term "income" includes all benefits and allowances derived from employment, including the value of board and lodging provided by the employer.

Sole traders and self-employed individuals are also subject to a business levy on income exceeding certain levels.

Capital gains and investment income/Only gains on the disposal of an asset within 12 months of its acquisition, or disposal and reacquisition within 12 months, are taxable. Gains on the disposal of any security in Trinidad and Tobago are excluded; also excluded are gains on automobiles and household goods disposed of for TT$5,000 or less. Taxable gains are included with other income and are not separately taxed. Capital gains realized outside Trinidad and Tobago by individuals who are resident but not domiciled in Trinidad and Tobago are not taxable.

See "Other taxes" below for the taxation of interest and dividends.

Income arising outside Trinidad and Tobago paid to an individual who is resident but not domiciled is taxable in Trinidad and Tobago only to the extent that such income is received in Trinidad and Tobago.

Deductions

Business deductions/An employed individual is not entitled to any blanket or standard deductions. Such an individual may claim a deduction only for unreimbursed travel expenses incurred wholly, exclusively, and necessarily in the course of employment. Where the individual is self-employed and is carrying on a trade, business, profession, or vocation, the expenses incurred wholly and exclusively in the production of the income are deductible, as are capital allowances.

Promotional expenses incurred by sole traders or persons employed in agriculture in the expansion of existing markets or the creation of new markets for the export of locally produced goods are tax deductible as an expense at 150% of the actual outlay. Other tax allowances available include the training allowance of 150%; apprenticeship allowance of 200%; and a local entertainment and education production allowance of 100%.

Nonbusiness expenses/A deduction in respect of mortgage interest for owner-occupied property is granted up to an amount of TT$18,000. This allowance may also be used in respect of expenses incurred for tertiary education of the taxpayer or the taxpayer's spouse or children.

Residents who are first-time homeowners can claim an allowance of TT$10,000 for each of the first five years for the purchase of a house. Resident individuals are also entitled to an allowance of the amount invested, up to a maximum of TT$10,000, on shares purchased in a society registered under the Co-operative Societies Act, whereby there is a net increase for the year of income in the nominal value of the shareholding.

Income received on an annuity purchased by an individual over 60 years of age is exempt from tax.

Personal allowances/A personal allowance of TT$25,000 per taxpayer is granted. For persons aged 60 years and older, the personal allowance is TT$40,000. The allowance of TT$40,000 also applies to an individual who is not resident in Trinidad and Tobago who is in receipt of income accruing in or derived from Trinidad and Tobago.

Tax credits

Credit is granted to residents for taxes paid in foreign countries for doubly taxed income on the bases set out in existing double taxation treaties for the particular type of income.

Other taxes

Tax on interest/Interest received by a resident individual on all classes of savings or other accounts with banks, financial institutions, or other forms of deposit-taking institutions is exempt from tax

Tax on dividends/Dividends, excluding preference dividends, received from investments in resident companies are now exempt from tax in the hands of resident individuals. Distributions other than interest received from a mutual fund established in Trinidad and Tobago are also exempt from tax in the hands of a resident individual.

Tax on insurance premiums/A tax on general insurance premiums at the rate of 6% is imposed. Excluded are long-term (life) insurance business, commercial insurance relating to ships and aircraft, loss of or damage to goods in international transit, risks arising outside Trinidad and Tobago, and reinsurance. The 6% tax is collected from policyholders and paid over to the Board of Inland Revenue by the insurance company.

Social security taxes/There is a social security tax, referred to as National Insurance, which is deducted at source at varying rates. The maximum rate is TT$87.87 per week (of which TT$29.29 is paid by the employee and TT$58.58 paid by the employer) for monthly income over TT$1,000. Seventy percent of the employee's contributions may be deductible in arriving at taxable income.

Health surcharge/A health surcharge is deductible at source for all employees, in accordance with the income tax regulations. The maximum rate is TT$8.25 per week for monthly income over TT$470.

Business levy/A business levy of 0.20% is applicable to sole traders and self-employed individuals having gross income or receipts in excess of TT$200,000 per annum.

Tax administration

Returns/Tax returns must be filed by April 30 of the year following the calendar or accounting year-end. A six-month grace period is allowed, following which a penalty of TT$100 for every six months or part thereof accrues. Tax returns are filed for income earned in a calendar year (which coincides with the tax year) except in the case of a sole trader or partnership, where filing is done according to the accounting terminal date.

Each individual must file a separate tax return. There is no provision for joint filing by husband and wife.

Payment of tax/Income tax is deducted at source on all employment income under the pay-as-you-earn (PAYE) system. Any shortfall of taxes deducted at source should be settled by the due date, that is, April 30 following the year of income.

Tax rates

The tax rates currently in force for 2003 are listed below.

Taxable income			
Over (Column 1)	Not over	Tax on Column 1	Percentage on excess
0	TT$ 50,000	—	25
TT$ 50,000		TT$ 12,500	30

INDIVIDUAL TAX CALCULATION

Year of income 2004

Assumptions

1. Individual (resident but nor domiciled) with salary of TT$340,000, with a nonworking spouse and two children attending school.
2. Individual is resident for more than 183 days in a calendar year and therefore is able to claim personal allowance.
3. Individual owns a residential property and is able to secure a mortgage in Trinidad and Tobago.

Tax computation

Salary		TT$ 340,000
Deduct:		
Mortgage interest (25,000, but restricted)	18,000	
National insurance contributions (335 x 70%)	234	18,234
Subtotal		321,766
Deduct—Personal allowance		25,000
Taxable income		TT$ 296,766
Income tax thereon:		
On first 50,000	12,500	
On remainder (246,766) at 30%	74,030	86,530
Less—PAYE withholding		(86,500)
Balance payable		TT$ 30

Note:

Exchange rate of the Trinidad and Tobago dollar at January 1, 2004: US$1 = TT$6.30.

PwC contact

For additional information on taxation in Turkey, contact:

Adnan Nas
PricewaterhouseCoopers
Basaran Nas Yeminli Mali Müsavirlik A.S.
BJK Plaza, Suleyman Seba Caddesi, No. 48
B Blok, Kat 9 Akaretler
Besiktas 34357
Istanbul, Turkey
Telephone: (90) (212) 326 60 60
Fax: (90) (212) 326 60 50
e-mail: adnan.nas@tr.pwc.com

Significant developments

Between 1998 and 2003, salaries that have already been taxed by way of payroll withholdings in Turkey need not be reported on an annual tax return. However, for salaries received by Turkish tax residents after January 1, 2003, in the event that the employment income is received from multiple employers, the salaries will need to be reported on an annual tax return unless salaries received from the second and consecutive employers do not exceed the declaration limit applicable for the year (TL14 billion for 2004) and where such income has already been taxed through withholdings in Turkey,

Turkish Income Tax Law allows for a deduction from taxable employment income for a certain portion of rent, health, clothing, food, and education expenses incurred in Turkey, provided they are adequately substantiated. For individuals paying their taxes through payroll withholdings in Turkey, the deduction takes the form of a tax credit to be offset against next year's payroll taxes. Effective from January 1, 2004, the same expenses, up to the individual's tax base, still qualify for deduction (or for those taxed on the payroll, as tax credit). However the allowance will be calculated as per a new threshold, which would apply as 8% for the first TL3 billion, 6% for the second TL3 billion, and 4% for the remaining amount.

Effective from calendar year 2004, income from immovable and movable property that is neither subject to Turkish withholdings nor any exemptions is not required to be reported if the total amount is below the declaration limit applicable for the year (TL750 million for 2004).

Until December 31, 2006, interest income and capital gains derived by individuals from government bonds and treasury bills issued between July 26, 2001 and December 31, 2004 are exempt from income tax subject to a threshold (TL156,5005 million in 2004).

For gains generated in 2003 calendar year and onward, half of the dividends received from Turkish-resident corporations, which are subject to corporate withholding taxes within the body of the distributing company, are exempt from income tax for the Turkish-resident recipients. A tax credit is also available for corporate withholding tax applied by the resident corporation. Note that transition provisions apply to dividends relating to accounting periods ending December 31, 1998 and before, and to dividends corresponding to exempt earnings generated during or before the accounting periods ending December 31, 2002.

In 2004, interest income is not subject to taxation, provided it has already been taxed through withholdings in Turkey. Additionally, rental income from property let out as residence is not subject to declaration if the total income does not exceed the exemption limit (TL1,800 million in 2004).

Effective from January 1, 2004, the Turkish annual income tax return is due by February 15 of the following year for income derived exclusively from trade activities subject to the simple method of taxation, and by March 15 in all other cases. The taxes will be payable in two equal installments, one in the month of filing and one in the third month thereafter.

Territoriality and residence

Turkey taxes its residents on their worldwide income, whereas nonresidents are taxed on Turkish-source earnings only. Residents are persons with legal residences in Turkey or who intend to settle in the country. Persons with uncertain residence status are considered to be resident if they have lived in Turkey uninterruptedly for more than six months in one calendar year.

Residents are treated as full taxpayers. Individuals who do not have a residence in Turkey or do not reside in Turkey for more than six months in a calendar year are treated as limited taxpayers. In general, those who stay in Turkey for more than six continuous months exclusively for the fulfillment of specific and temporary assignments are not considered as resident, and they will still be treated as limited taxpayers.

Gross income

Employee gross income/Taxable income includes all amounts, whether in cash or in kind, arising from an office or employment in Turkey. In addition to salary, any bonuses and commissions, overseas adjustments, housing allowances, education payments, and home leave payments are also considered as employment income.

Resident individuals are taxed on salary earned for work performed anywhere in the world, regardless of where payment is made and regardless of whether it is remitted. Nonresidents are taxable on remuneration for work performed in Turkey, but may be exempted under double taxation treaty provisions.

Capital gains and investment income/As of January 1, 2003, gains on shares that have been held for at least three months and traded on the Turkish stock exchange markets are exempt from tax. Gains on the sale of shares in Turkish resident companies are also exempt from taxation, provided that they have been held for more than a year. Additionally, both residents and nonresidents are exempt from tax on the first TL12 billion of their capital gains in 2004 calendar year after inflation adjustment. Individuals are not required to file tax returns for the following income generated in Turkey in 2004, which is taxed at source through withholding.

1. Interest on bank deposits.
2. Dividends paid by marketable securities investment funds.
3. Repo (repurchase order) income.
4. Employment income received from one employer.

Until December 31, 2006, the interest and capital gains of individuals derived from government bonds and treasury bills issued between July 26, 2001 and December

31, 2004 are exempt from income tax, subject to a threshold (TL156,505 million in 2004), which ranges from 20% to 45%.

Both residents and nonresidents are taxed on investment income at the same rates.

Indexation of cost and inflation allowance/Two alternative mechanisms are available to adjust the capital gains and other investment income meeting certain conditions for the effects of inflation. Depending on the type of income, inflation adjustment is performed by either increasing the purchase price according to the WPI (Wholesale Price Index determined by the State Statistical Institution) or by reducing the income by the discount ratio announced by the Ministry of Finance (57.5% for 2003).

Deductions

Business deductions/For individual employees, no business deductions are permitted.

Nonbusiness expenses/Nonbusiness deductions are possible within defined limits for donations to specific institutions. Personal insurance premiums (for self, spouse, and/or children) and pension contributions are deductible. However, the deduction cannot exceed 10% for pension contributions, and 5% for insurance premiums, of the individual's monthly gross income. Furthermore, the annual cumulative deduction cannot exceed the annual minimum gross wage. Contributions to social security may also be deducted.

Additionally, there is a special deduction regime for employees. According to Turkish Income Tax Law Recurring Article 121, it is possible to deduct a certain portion (limited to the annual cumulative tax base) of the education, food, health, clothing, and residential rent expenses incurred in Turkey by the employee, spouse, and children from the employee's income tax base provided that the expenses are adequately substantiated. The deductible portion corresponds to 8% for the first TL3 billion, 6% for the second TL3 billion, and 4% for the remaining expense amount. After the deduction is made, the income tax withheld previously is adjusted and the difference is offset against the employee's income tax liability in the coming months or refunded in cash if the employee is no longer working. In the absence of a local employer, related expenses are directly offset against the income tax base reported by the individual on the annual tax return.

Personal allowances/There are no personal allowances.

Tax credits

Residents may deduct from their income tax liability foreign taxes assessed on foreign income. However, the deductions may not exceed the rate of tax assessed for similar income earned in Turkey.

Other taxes

Social security taxes/Social security premiums, which are calculated on salary limits, effective from January 1, 2004, of a minimum of TL18,321,000 and a maximum of TL91,605,000 per day must be paid by the employer and the employee at rates defined according to labor categories. For Turkish nationals, the general rates are 19.5% for the employer and 14% for the employee.

A foreign national who remains covered under the social security system of his home country is not required to pay Turkish social security premiums, provided proof of foreign coverage is filed with the local social security office. The employee's portion of the social security contributions is deductible in determining taxable income.

Unemployment insurance/Unemployment insurance premiums are calculated over an upper earnings level of TL91,605,000 per day. The premiums are paid by the employee, employer, and the state at the following rates.

	%
Employee	1
Employer	2
State	1

Foreign nationals qualify for this insurance on condition of reciprocity between Turkey and their home countries.

Local taxes/There are no local taxes or national wealth taxes apart from some minor transaction charges and immovable property tax imposed and collected by municipalities.

Tax administration

Returns/The annual tax return for the year has to be filed by February 15 of the following year if income is derived exclusively from trade activities subject to the simple method of taxation, and by March 15 in all other cases. No extensions are available.

Payment of tax/Income tax is withheld every month from salaries paid through a Turkish payroll. Except for taxable remuneration received directly from abroad or for remuneration exceeding certain thresholds received from multiple employers, no further declaration is necessary for employment income.

The tax, when a return is filed for any outstanding liability under the aforementioned principles, is paid in two equal installments: in the month of filing and in the third month thereafter. Nonresidents leaving Turkey must settle full liability within 15 days before departure.

Taxpayers filing income tax returns for their commercial or professional income must pay advance income tax (under the title of "temporary tax"), calculated as 20% of their cumulative income as at the end of each quarter during the calendar year. The tax return is due by the 10th of the 2nd month following the end of the related quarter and tax must be paid by the 17th of the same month. Tax paid in advance is credited to income tax computed on the annual tax return for the same year.

Tax rates

The following rates apply from January 1, 2004 through December 31, 2004 for employment income.

Individual income tax

(In TL '000s)

Taxable income			
Over	**Not over**	**Tax on Column 1**	**Percentage on excess**
(Column 1)			
0	TL 6,000,000	—	15
TL 6,000,000	14,000,000	TL 900,000	20
14,000,000	28,000,000	2,500,000	25
28,000,000	70,000,000	6,000,000	30
70,000,000	140,000,000	18,600,000	35
140,000,000		43,100,000	40

The following rates apply from January 1, 2004 through December 31, 2004 for all other income.

Individual income tax

(In TL '000s)

Taxable income			
Over	**Not over**	**Tax on Column 1**	**Percentage on excess**
(Column 1)			
0	TL 6,000,000	—	20
TL 6,000,000	14,000,000	TL 1,200,000	25
14,000,000	28,000,000	3,200,000	30
28,000,000	70,000,000	7,400,000	35
70,000,000	140,000,000	22,100,000	40
TL 140,000,000		50,100,000	45

INDIVIDUAL TAX CALCULATION

Calendar year 2004, income year 2004

Assumptions

Resident alien on a local company's payroll. Total compensation is TL100,000,000,000 per annum. Employee is assumed to be a national of a country with which Turkey has a social security agreement, without social security coverage in his home country.

Tax computation

			(In TL '000s)
Base salary		TL	85,000,000
Add:			
Housing allowance	9,000,000		
Tuition for dependents	2,000,000		
Year-end bonus	4,000,000		15,000,000
Total employment benefits			100,000,000
Less:			
Social security premiums (2,748,150 x 14% x 12)	4,616,892.00		
Unemployment insurance premiums (2,748,150 x 1% x 12)	329,778.00		4,946,670
Taxable income		TL	95,053,330
Tax thereon:			
On first 70,000,000		TL	18,600,000
On remainder (25,053,330 x 35%)			8,768,665
Total income tax		TL	27,368,665
Stamp duty (0.6%) (1)		TL	600,000
Net salary		TL	67,084,665

Notes:

1. 0.6% stamp duty applies on gross income paid through a local payroll.
2. Exchange rate of the Turkish lira at December 31, 2003: US$1 = TL1,395,835.

PwC contact

For additional information on taxation in Uganda, contact:

Russell Eastaugh
PricewaterhouseCoopers
Communications House
1 Colville Street
P.O. Box 8053
Kampala, Uganda
Telephone: (256) (41) 236018
Fax: (256) (41) 230153
e-mail: russell.eastaugh@ug.pwc.com

Significant developments

There have been no significant changes as regards individual taxation in the past year. The information in this entry is based on the Income Tax Act (CAP 340).

Territoriality and residence

Individuals are taxed on worldwide income. A resident individual is a person who meets the following criteria.

1. Has a permanent home in Uganda.

   or

2. Is present in Uganda for 183 days in any 12-month period that commences or ends during the year of income or has been present for an average of 122 days per year of income for the current and the two preceding years of income.

Gross income

Employee gross income/For pay-as-you-earn (PAYE) purposes, the Income Tax Act is applied with effect from January 1, 1998, that is, the middle of the fiscal year. All information set out below is based on the new act.

Gross income of an employee includes wages, salary, leave pay, fees, commissions, bonuses, gratuities, compensation for the termination of a contract, all allowances except security, and any other income derived by an employee from employment. Where housing is provided by the employer, the benefit is calculated as the lower of the market rent or 15% of employment income including the market rent.

Major exclusions from employment income are the following.

1. Cost of passages on appointment and termination of contract for noncitizens recruited or engaged outside Uganda.
2. Cost of any medical services provided by the employer.
3. Allowances for accommodation, travel and subsistence when traveling, provided the allowances do not exceed actual cost.
4. Meals provided in staff canteens if all full-time employees have access to the canteen on equal terms.
5. Any contribution or similar payment by the employer made to a retirement fund for the benefit of the employee or any of his or her dependants.

Capital gains and investment income/All income not included in employment income is taxable except for capital gains.

Rental income/Rental income derived by individuals is taxed separately from other income at the rate of 20% on 80% of the gross rental income provided it exceeds UShs1,560,000.

Deductions

Business deductions/No business deductions are available against employment income apart from graduated tax.

Personal allowances/None.

Nonbusiness deductions/Graduated tax (see below) is an allowable deduction. A limited possibility to make allowable donations to eligible organizations is available.

Tax credits

Foreign tax paid is creditable up to the average Ugandan tax rate.

Other taxes

Social security taxes/Employers are required to contribute 15% of salaries and are entitled to recover 5% from the employees. Employees are entitled to a refund of the total contributions upon retirement plus interest at a stipulated rate (currently 6%).

Graduated tax/Graduated tax is payable by every individual over the age of 18 with income from farming, business, or employment. The rate is progressive, with a maximum of UShs101,000 per annum. The tax is an allowable deduction for income tax purposes.

Tax administration

Returns/Resident individuals are required to submit provisional estimates and final returns, except those who have no income other than from employment and who believe that the whole of the tax payable will be recovered by deduction by the employer.

Unincorporated businesses may apply to be taxed on the income of their accounting period ending with another date than June 30, which is the normal tax year. It is no longer necessary to obtain the Commissioner's written permission before a "small" taxpayer (with gross turnover of less than SHS 50 million) can make a normal return of income. A provisional estimate is due within three months from the commencement of the accounting period. A final return is due four months after the end of the tax year.

Payment of tax/Employers are required to deduct tax on a monthly basis from any taxable emoluments paid to an employee.

Tax, as per the provisional estimate, is payable in four equal installments due 3, 6, 9, and 12 months after the commencement of the accounting period. If the final tax charge exceeds the provisional estimate, the excess is payable within 45 days from the service of the notice of assessment.

Tax rates

Resident individual tax rates

Taxable income				
Over (Column 1)	Not over		Tax on Column 1	Percentage on excess
0	UShs 1,560,000	....	—	—
UShs 1,560,000	2,820,000	....	—	10
2,820,000	4,920,000	....	UShs 126,000	20
4,920,000		....	546,000	30

Nonresident individual tax rates

Taxable income				
Over (Column 1)	Not over		Tax on Column 1	Percentage on excess
0	UShs 2,820,000	....	—	10
UShs 2,820,000	4,920,000	....	UShs 282,000	20
4,920,000		....	702,000	30

Rental income tax rate/Rental income derived by an individual is taxed at the rate of 20% on 80% of the gross income provided it exceeds UShs1,560,000.

INDIVIDUAL TAX CALCULATION

Year ending June 30, 2004

Assumptions

The taxpayer is a resident individual.

Tax computation

Gross income:		
Salary		UShs 120,400,000
Interest		2,000,000
Dividends		1,000,000
		123,400,000
Less—Deductions:		
Dividends, interest	3,000,000	
Charitable donations	500,000	
Social security taxes		
Graduated tax paid	80,000	3,580,000
Taxable income		UShs 119,820,000
Tax payable:		
On first 4,920,000		UShs 546,000
On balance of 108,880,000 at 30%		34,470,000
		UShs 35,016,000

Note:

Exchange rate of the Uganda shilling at December 31, 2003: US$1 = UShs1,950.

PwC contact

For additional information on taxation in Ukraine, contact:

Jorge E. Intriago
PricewaterhouseCoopers
5th Floor, 38 Turgenevska
Kyiv 01054
Ukraine
Telephone: (380) (44) 490 6777
Fax: (380) (44) 216 4558/244 5571
e-mail: jorge.e.intriago@ua.pwc.com

Significant developments

The following information on individual taxation in Ukraine is accurate as of April 1, 2004. For subsequent developments, refer to the contact above.

Ukraine is currently in the process of revising its tax legislation. The following significant developments in Ukrainian legislation governing individual taxation took place during 2003.

1. New Law "On Personal Income Tax" was adopted in 2003 and became effective from January 1, 2004. The new law completely revised the Ukrainian legislation governing taxation of individuals. The previous scale of rates (from 10% to 40%) was replaced by a 13% flat tax rate.
2. The Law "On Mandatory State Pension Insurance" was adopted in 2003 and became effective from January 1, 2004. The new law has not significantly changed the procedure for calculation and payment of mandatory pension contributions, however, the procedure for calculation of the state pension benefits has been revised considerably.
3. As of June 1, 2003, the cap on the taxable base for social contributions (both employer's and employee's) has been increased from UAH2,200 to UAH2,660 per individual per month.

Territoriality and residence

Tax residency/The tax status of individuals is defined according to their residence status. Residents are individuals who have their place of abode in Ukraine. If an individual has a place of abode in another country as well, the individual is deemed to be resident of Ukraine if he/she has a permanent place of abode (domicile) in Ukraine. If an individual has a domicile in another country as well, he/she is deemed to be a resident of Ukraine if he/she has a center of vital interests in Ukraine. A sufficient but not exclusive ground for determining country of individual's center of vital interest is place of permanent abode of individual's family members. In the event an individual's center of vital interests cannot be determined or the individual has no domicile in any country, he/she is deemed to be a resident of Ukraine if he/she stays in Ukraine at least 183 days during the tax year (calendar year).

If residency status cannot be determined based on the above rules, an individual shall be deemed to be resident of Ukraine if he/she is a citizen of Ukraine.

Nonresidents are individuals who do not qualify as residents of Ukraine.

Residents are liable to Ukrainian income tax on their total worldwide income received during a calendar year unless protection under a double taxation treaty is available.

Nonresidents are subject to Ukrainian tax only in respect of their income from sources in Ukraine, which is defined as any income received from any activity performed in the territory of Ukraine. The main items specified in the nonexclusive list of Ukraine-source include:

1. Income received by a taxpayer from his/her employer (either resident or nonresident) in respect of employment exercised in Ukraine.
2. Interest, dividends, and royalties paid by residents.
3. Investment profits from transactions with securities and corporate rights.
4. Income from renting out or disposal of movable and immovable property.
5. Prizes (except for prizes from the state lotteries).
6. Gifts.
7. Charitable donations.
8. Assets received as inheritance if the assets or source of payment are located in Ukraine.
9. Income received by the members of the Board of Directors or Supervisory Board of Ukrainian companies.
10. Income from entrepreneurial or independent professional activity in Ukraine.

Gross income

Employee gross income/All income received from employment in monetary form or in kind during a calendar year is subject to personal income tax. This includes all basic pay, overtime pay, supplemental pay, awards and bonuses, compensation for unused vacation, all other monetary amounts, and additional benefits granted by employers to employees, including the following main items:

1. Tangible or intangible assets provided for employee's use free-of-charge except for certain items specifically exempt from tax (see "Tax-exempt income" below).
2. Value of goods and food provided to employees free of charge, except for value of special clothing, uniforms, and food provided to employees within the norms established by the Cabinet of Ministers of Ukraine.
3. Amounts of reimbursements of employee's expenses or losses, except for items specifically exempt from tax.
4. Financial assistance granted to employees, including debts cancelled by a creditor.
5. Value of goods, services provided free of charge and value of discounts in respect of goods and services sold to employees at a price lower than market price.

Taxable income of foreign nationals who are residents of Ukraine is determined in the same order as for Ukrainians.

Capital gains and investment income/There is no separate capital gains tax. Instead, gains from the disposal of property and assets are subject to personal income tax at the standard rate.

The following types of income are generally taxable in Ukraine.

1. Interest income from deposits placed with banks and nonbanking financial institutions and from saving certificates. Exemption from tax is available for year 2004.

2. Income from disposal of property. In year 2004 income from the sale of real estate is exempt from personal income tax, provided the respective sale-purchase agreement has been duly notarized, and the relevant of stamp duty has been paid. Income from disposal of a car, motorbike, yacht, or boat with engine is exempt from personal income tax if the seller pays the stamp duty (1% if sale is to spouse, parents, or children, 5% in other cases) upon notarization of the sales agreement.
3. Dividends on shares and other financial assets
4. Income from leasing property, both in Ukraine and abroad.
5. Investment profits from transactions with shares and corporate rights.
6. Royalties in respect of intellectual property rights.

Tax-exempt income/The main types of tax-exempt income are as follows.

1. Accommodation provided by the employer to employee free-of-charge is not taxable where such free-of-charge provision is a condition for performing of labor functions by employee or is provided by an employment contract or legislation within limits specified therein.
2. Benefit in form of use of vehicles does not constitute taxable income if this benefit is granted by a resident employer who qualifies as corporate profits tax payer.
3. Income from investments in securities issued by the Ministry of Finance and prizes from state lotteries.
4. Alimony received from residents.
5. Shares received from capitalization of undistributed profits provided that allocation of shares between shareholders remains unchanged.
6. Premiums paid by employer in respect of long-term life insurance or nonstate pension insurance of its employees within the limit equal to 15% of employee's monthly salary but maximum 1.4 times the subsistence minimum (currently UAH510) per month.
7. Amounts received from employers in respect of certain types of medical treatment and services. Income from sale of a car, motorbike, yacht, or boat with engine, provided the seller pays the stamp duty upon sale.
8. Amounts paid by employers to educational institutions for training/re-training of employees within limits of 1.4 times the subsistence minimum (at present UAH510) per month of education. If the employee terminates employment during education or prior to the end of the second calendar year following the year when education was completed the cost of education should be taxed as additional benefit.
9. Interest income from deposits placed with banks, nonbanking financial institutions, and from saving certificates (exemption is available for year 2004 only).
10. In year 2004 income from sale of real estate is exempt from personal income tax, provided the respective sale-purchase agreement has been duly notarized with payment of stamp duty.
11. Social security contributions (see below) made by the employer per Ukrainian tax legislation are not included in the taxable income of the individual.

Deductions

Business expenses/In general, bona fide expenses incurred by individuals in the course of business or trade can be deducted from taxable income. Individual entrepreneurs may deduct business expenses and depreciation charges subject to the rules established by the Corporate Profits Tax Law. If actual expenses of an individual entrepreneur cannot be documented, then a specific standard deduction may be applied (rates ranging from 5% to 60%, depending on the type of activity).

Nonbusiness deductions/A taxpayer can claim a limited deduction from his/her annual taxable income for the amount of documented expenses incurred in the reporting year in respect of:

1. Interest (certain portion) on mortgage. This deduction will be available after January 1, 2005.
2. Secondary professional or higher education of taxpayer or family members (spouse, parents, parents-in-law, children). Deduction is limited to the amount of up to 1.4 times the subsistence minimum (currently UAH510) per month of education;
3. Certain types of medical treatment of taxpayer or his/her family members. This deduction will be available in the year following the year when the law on mandatory medical insurance is introduced.
4. Premiums on voluntary long-term life insurance or nonstate pension insurance. Deduction is limited by the amount of up to 1.4 of subsistence minimum per month of the insured period in case of self insurance and ½ of this amount in case of insurance of taxpayer's family members. Deduction for expenses on nonstate pension insurance will be available after January 1, 2005.
5. Donations to charity and not-for-profit organizations in the amount from 2% to 5% of individual's taxable income.

Total amount of deductions cannot exceed amount of taxable income received in the form of salary. Amounts not deducted from income of the reporting year cannot be carried forward.

Employees' pension or social security contributions are deductible from employment income.

Personal allowances/Low-income individuals (with monthly income of less than 1.4 times the amount of subsistence minimum for able-bodied individuals (currently UAH510) can claim a Social Tax Allowance (STA).The amount of STA equals the statutory minimum wage for ordinary taxpayers and 150% to 200% of minimum wage for some privileged categories. For 2004 the amount of STA is UAH61.50.

Tax credits

Tax residents are allowed to credit foreign taxes paid on income received abroad against their Ukrainian tax liabilities (an official confirmation issued by the relevant foreign tax authority is required) provided there is a double taxation treaty between Ukraine and the relevant foreign state. The amount of foreign tax credit is limited to the amount of Ukrainian tax that would arise from the equivalent income in Ukraine.

Other taxes

Social security taxes/Employers (including representative offices of foreign companies in Ukraine) are required to pay the following social security taxes in respect of their employees based on gross salary.

1. Pension Fund—32%.
2. Social Security Fund—2.9%.
3. Unemployment Insurance Fund—1.9%.
4. Accidents at Work Insurance Fund—From 0.2% to 13.8%. (The rate should be determined by Fund's authorities specifically for each entity and depends on the level of accident risk of the entity's industry sector.)

Employees' contributions (withholding requirement applies) are as follows.

1. State Pension Fund—2% (1% if the monthly salary is up to UAH150).
2. Social Security Fund—0.5%.
3. Unemployment Insurance Fund—0.5% (for Ukrainian national employees only).

Social contributions (both employee's and employer's) are not due on the income that is not subject to personal income tax. The taxable base subject to such contributions, both employer's and employee's, is currently capped at UAH2,660 per individual per month.

Employee's contributions, in general, are deductible for personal income tax purposes.

Foreign nationals temporary employed by a Ukrainian entity are not subject to unemployment insurance in Ukraine. Therefore, they are not required to contribute to the Unemployment Insurance Fund. However, the employer should pay contributions to the Fund in respect of such employees.

Foreign nationals remaining on the foreign payroll are not liable to pay social contributions in Ukraine.

Individual entrepreneurs, except for those paying taxes under the "unified tax" regime, must contribute 32% of the annual tax base to the Pension Fund. In order to have the right to enjoy social security benefits, individual entrepreneurs may contribute voluntarily 3.4% of the annual tax base to the Social Security Fund and 2.4% to the Unemployment Insurance Fund. The tax base is determined as gross income less deductions. The tax base is currently capped at UAH2,660 per month.

Gift and inheritance tax/There is no gift or inheritance tax in Ukraine. However, gifts and inheritance will be subject to personal income tax under special rules effective from January 1, 2005. In addition, stamp duty is payable by individuals, both Ukrainian and foreign nationals, on transfers of certain properties (e.g., real estate, cars) situated on the territory of Ukraine, whether the transfer is by way of gift or inheritance. Rates vary from 0.1% to 5%, based on the value of the transfer and depending on the relationship of the transferor and transferee.

Tax administration

Returns/An individual who received during a reporting year only income from tax agents, which are obliged to file reports on personal income tax, is not obliged to file a personal income tax return.

An individual, either resident or nonresident, who received any taxable income from entities/sources other than tax agents individual will be required to a file personal income tax return with the local tax authorities (where the individual resides in Ukraine). Tax resident individuals, including those whose income was subject to final taxation at source, also have the right to file a tax return, if they wish to claim a tax credit (deduction) in respect of certain expenses incurred during the year and/or claim a foreign tax credit in Ukraine. The tax return must be filed before April 1 of the year following the reporting one and the tax due must be paid before April 11.

In cases of departure from Ukraine, a tax resident individual must submit a "departure tax declaration" no less than 60 days prior to departure and settle the tax due based on the assessment issued by the tax authorities.

Ukrainian nationals engaged in entrepreneurial activities are generally required to file quarterly tax returns within 40 days following the reporting quarter and file a year-end tax return by February 9 of the next calendar year. Private entrepreneurs who pay tax under the "unified tax" regime are required to file quarterly reports by April 5, July 5, and October 5 of the current year and January 5 of the year following the reporting one.

Payment of tax/Employers and other business entities that pay income to individuals are defined as tax agents who are responsible for withholding the tax and state pension and social insurance contributions from income payable and remitting it to the state and appropriate authorities. Tax agents should pay tax to the state at the date of payment of income to individuals. Tax in respect of income that is accrued but not paid to the individuals should be transferred to the state within 20 calendar days following the end of reporting month.

If income is paid in-kind, tax agent should remit the tax to the state on the next banking day following the day of payment. Tax agents who failed to withhold tax from income paid to individuals are responsible for payment of tax liability (plus fines and interest); in this case, the individual concerned is free from obligation to settle the tax liability. Tax agents should file quarterly reports on income paid to individuals and amount of tax withheld from such income.

Personal income tax must be paid in Ukrainian currency (Hryvnia).

Individual entrepreneurs are required to make quarterly advance payments of the estimated liability for the year before March 15, May 15, August 15, and November 15. Payments of the "unified tax" by private entrepreneurs are due in advance, generally on a monthly basis.

Final settlement of any tax liability must be executed within one month after receipt by the individual of the assessment issued by the tax authorities.

Tax rates

For 2004–2006 the standard tax rate for tax residents is 13%; from January 1, 2007 the tax rate will be 15%. The standard rate is applicable to most types of incomes, including salary income, dividends, royalties, investment income, and gifts (with certain exceptions).

Income in the form of prizes (except for prizes from the state lottery in cash) is taxed at double the standard rates (26%/30%).

Interest income from deposits placed with banks and nonbanking financial institutions and from saving certificates is not subject to personal income tax in year 2004.

Income earned by nonresidents from sources in Ukraine in form of interest, dividends, and royalty is taxed at the same rates as for residents (see above).

The PIT Law provides that any other income earned by nonresidents from sources in Ukraine is taxed at double the standard rates. However, the PIT Law is unclear whether standard or double rates apply to salary income earned by nonresidents. In accordance with the tax clarification issued by the State Tax Administration of Ukraine, income paid to nonresident individuals by a Ukrainian employer is to be taxed at standard rate.

Note

Exchange rate of the Hryvnia at April 1, 2004: US$1 = UAH5.4796.

United Kingdom

PwC contacts

For additional information on taxation in the United Kingdom, contact:

Personal taxation

Clive Mackintosh
PricewaterhouseCoopers
1 Embankment Place
London WC2N 6RH, England
Telephone: (44) (20) 7804 3000,
804 5614 (direct)
Fax: (44) (20) 7403 5265
e-mail: clive.mackintosh@uk.pwcglobal.com

Expatriate taxation

Stephanie Phizackerley
PricewaterhouseCoopers
Plumtree Court
London EC4A 4HT, England
Telephone: (44) (20) 7804 3000,
804 1765 (direct)
Fax: (44) (20) 7378 0647
e-mail: stephanie.phizackerley@uk.pwcglobal.com

Significant developments

1. The launch of a new Child Trust Fund (CTF) providing children born from September 2002 with an endowment at birth. The CTF will be introduced from April 2005 to benefit children across the United Kingdom by:
   a. Providing an initial endowment at birth for every child of £250, rising to £500 for children from low-income families who qualify for full Child Tax Credit;
   b. Allowing additional contributions to be made by parents, family members and friends up to an annual limit of £1,200.
2. The capital gains tax rules for determining whether assets (other than shares or securities), qualify for taper relief purposes are to be extended so that a wider range of assets will qualify. The new extended definition will have effect for periods of ownership from April 6, 2004.

Territoriality and residence

The United Kingdom taxes its residents on their worldwide income and capital gains and taxes nonresidents on their U.K. income (but not generally on capital gains). The non-U.K. investment income and capital gains of a person resident but not domiciled in the United Kingdom are generally taxed only if they are received in the United Kingdom.

The domicile of individuals is generally the country or state in which they have their permanent homes. However, for inheritance tax purposes only, individuals are also regarded as domiciled in the United Kingdom at any time if they have been resident in the United Kingdom for tax purposes for not less than 17 out of the 20 tax years before that time or were domiciled in the United Kingdom during the three years before that time.

Persons are resident in the United Kingdom for a particular tax year if they are present for more than 183 days in that year or have made, or intend to make, regular and extended visits over a period of years.

However, persons who come to the United Kingdom for a purpose which will mean that they remain here for at least two years are treated as resident from the day of arrival to the day of departure. If they come for less than two years or do not know the length of their time of stay, they will be treated as resident for the year only if the normal conditions dealt with above apply.

Similarly, a person who leaves the United Kingdom to work full time abroad under a contract of employment or for self-employment is treated as not resident and not ordinarily resident in the United Kingdom from the day after departure until the day before returning to the United Kingdom at the end of the period of overseas employment/self-employment, provided that certain conditions apply.

1. The absence from the United Kingdom and the employment/self-employment abroad last for at least a whole tax year; and
2. During the absence, visits to the United Kingdom are less than 183 days in any tax year and less than 91 days on average (the average is calculated over a maximum period of four years).

A paper entitled "Reviewing the residence and domicile rules as they affect the taxation of individuals: a background paper" has been published. This followed an announcement by the Chancellor of the Exchequer in the 2002 Budget indicating that the Government would begin a review of the residence and rules. The review is continuing. It seems probable that if changes are to be made to the U.K. tax rules in this area they are most likely to be focused on "long term U.K. residents" rather than an abolition of the favourable tax rules entirely.

Gross income

Employee gross income/A non–U.K.-domiciled but U.K.-resident individual is taxable on worldwide emoluments (salary, personal expense allowances and reimbursements, and benefits), except in the instances noted below.

1. A short-term resident is taxable on emoluments for work performed outside the United Kingdom only if they are received in the United Kingdom.
2. Other residents are taxable on the emoluments of a separate employment carried on wholly outside the United Kingdom for a nonresident employer only if the emoluments are received in the United Kingdom.

A non-United Kingdom-domiciled person who is not resident in the United Kingdom is taxable only on emoluments for work performed in the United Kingdom but may be exempted by a double taxation treaty.

Capital gains and investment income/Capital gains are taxable on persons resident in the United Kingdom and on nonresidents if the gains are realized on U.K. trading assets. Generally, gains realized on non-U.K. assets by a United Kingdom-resident but non-U.K.-domiciled person are taxable only if the gains are received in the United Kingdom. Gains realized in the tax year of arrival in or departure from the United Kingdom may, in certain circumstances, be taxable even if realized before arrival or after departure. From March 17, 1998, an individual who leaves the United Kingdom for a period of nonresidence of less than five tax years and has been resident for at least four of the seven tax years prior to the departure is taxed on the disposal, while nonresident, of any assets that were acquired before ceasing to be resident. The assets are treated as disposed of in the year of return to the United Kingdom.

Capital gains are taxed at rates equivalent to the rates of income tax that would apply if gains were treated as the top slice of the individual's "savings" income, but there are numerous reliefs available, including an allowance for inflation (up to April 5, 1998), annual exemptions, exemptions for certain assets (including a principal private residence), and deferrals for certain types of gifts.

The amount of gain that is taxable (after reliefs and the offset of losses but before the annual exemption) is reduced by a "taper" factor based on the length of ownership after April 5, 1998. For business assets held for two or more years after April 5, 2000, and disposed of after April 5, 2002, only 25% of the gain is subject to tax, the taper factor being 75%. For assets held for less than two years, the taper factor is 50% after one year of ownership. For nonbusiness assets, the taper is less generous. There is no reduction for assets held for less than three full years after April 5, 1998; thereafter, the taper factor is 5% per full year until the asset has been held for ten or more years, only 60% of the gain then being taxable. Where the nonbusiness asset was owned on March 17, 1998, the ownership period for taper purposes is increased by one full year.

Gains and losses arising on the disposal of assets held on March 31, 1982, are computed as if the assets were acquired at their market value on that date. The costs to be deducted from gross proceeds on the disposal of an asset are the market value of the asset on March 31, 1982, and the costs of any improvements made after that date, or the costs of acquisition and subsequent improvements if the asset was purchased after March 31, 1982, plus indexation. Indexation represents an uplift in the above costs based on the percentage rise (if any) in the U.K. retail prices index (RPI) over the relevant period, that is, from March 31, 1982, the date of acquisition, or the dates the improvements were carried out, as appropriate, to the date of disposal or April 5, 1998, whichever is earlier. See the tax calculation below, "Capital gains tax." There are various exceptions to these rules, in particular where using market value produces a greater gain or a greater loss than that arising from using historical cost and insofar as indexation cannot create or increase a capital loss.

A non–U.K.-domiciled individual resident in the United Kingdom is taxable on all U.K. interest, dividends, rents, and royalties and on any overseas investment income received in the United Kingdom. The tax liability on U.K. investment income of a non-U.K. resident is often reduced or eliminated by a double taxation treaty. Even where there is no such treaty relief, the U.K. tax liability of a nonresident on certain "excluded income" cannot exceed the tax (if any) withheld or deducted at source or treated as deducted at source. "Excluded income" includes dividends from U.K. companies, interest income, and certain social security benefits.

Deductions

Business deductions/Necessary business expenses (restrictively defined) can be deducted from employment income and are not taxable if paid for or reimbursed by the employer. Travel to and from work is not regarded as a business expense.

Reimbursements for business entertainment and for removal and relocation expenses of up to £8,000 are not normally taxable.

Nonbusiness expenses/Contributions to qualifying employee pension schemes of up to 15% of total earnings are eligible for tax relief. However, for these purposes, where a scheme was set up on or after March 14, 1989, or a new member joins an existing scheme after May 31, 1989, earnings in excess of a permitted maximum are disregarded so that there is no relief for contributions in excess of 15% of the limit. For the year ending April 5, 2005, the permitted maximum is £102,000. (The maximum is generally increased annually in line with the retail prices index.) For those not in pensionable employment and who contracted a qualifying retirement annuity policy prior to July 1, 1988, tax relief is available for premiums up to a limit of 17.5% of total earnings (higher limits apply for those over 50 years of age). Whether or not they are in pensionable employment, from June 30, 1988, individuals may alternatively make contributions to personal pension schemes for which, generally, contributions up to a limit of 17.5% of total earnings are eligible for tax relief; higher limits apply for contributions made by those over 35, but in all cases, tax relief for contributions made to personal pension schemes is subject to the permitted maximum of earnings of £102,000 for the year ending April 5, 2005. Tax relief at the basic rate is given at source, and for higher-rate taxpayers, a claim for further relief can be made through their self-assessments (see below).

With effect from April 6, 2001, the earnings "cap" will apply to individuals who contribute to a stakeholder pension. Stakeholder pensions are available to any U.K. resident who is under 75, in receipt of U.K. taxable earnings, and not a member of an occupational scheme. Contributions of up to £3,600 can be made without any reference to the individual's earnings. Tax relief at the basic rate is given at source. Higher-rate taxpayers can claim further relief through their self-assessments.

From April 2006 a new regime for relief for pension contributions to all registered plans will be introduced. Relief will initially be allowed for contributions of up to £215,000 in a year, provided the overall value of an individual's pension plan does not exceed £1.5 million; this limit increases each year, to £1.8 million by 2010). For final salary schemes the plan is valued at 20 times the expected pension, and the contributions limit operates by reference to increases in the value of the plan on that basis.

Relief is available for gifts to U.K. charities under approved payroll deduction schemes and also by way of outright money gifts and charitable payments made under deeds of covenant. No relief is available for medical expenses, social security contributions, council tax, other U.K. taxes, or insurance premiums (except for qualifying life insurance premiums on policies issued before March 14, 1984).

Personal allowances/Apart from the married couple's and other linked allowances, personal allowances are fully deductible in determining taxable income. Every individual who is under 65 throughout the year of assessment ending April 5, 2005, is entitled to a tax allowance of £4,745.

Those over 65 but under 75 at any time during that tax year, £6,830; and those 75 and over at any time during that tax year, £6,950. Married couples are also entitled to a married couple's allowance of £5,725 where either member of the couple was born before April 6, 1935; the allowance is £5,795 where either is 75 or older. The increased age-related allowances are reduced by £1 for every £2 of income in excess of £18,900. Relief for the married couple's allowance is given at a rate of 10%. The couple may elect to divide the married couple's allowance between them equally or to allocate it wholly to either one.

Children are taxable in their own right unless their income derives from gifts by the parent.

From April 6, 2003 the children's tax credit was replaced with the Child Tax Credit (CTC). The CTC can benefit individuals where family income is up to £58,000 (£66,000 in the year of a child's birth).

Tax credits

Either by double taxation treaty or by U.K. unilateral relief, U.K. residents are entitled to a credit for foreign taxes paid against the U.K. income tax or capital gains tax payable on overseas income or gains. Alternatively, the taxpayer may elect for the foreign tax to be deducted from the taxable amount rather than be taken as a credit.

Other taxes

Social security taxes/National insurance contributions apply to salary (excluding benefits) up to £610 per week. On the first £91 per week, no contributions are payable; thereafter, between £91 and £610 per week, contributions amount to 10%, with a further 1% levied on earnings in excess of that figure. In situations where the employees are in contracted-out employment (broadly, where they are not entirely covered by the state pension scheme), an abatement is given. Persons not domiciled but resident in the United Kingdom are in some circumstances exempt from contributions during the first year of their stay if they are employed by a non-United Kingdom-resident employer.

Self-employed persons pay a flat-rate contribution of £2.05 per week. There is an additional contribution on earnings between £4,745 and £31,720 per annum of 8% of the excess over £4,745. Any profits above £31,720 attract an additional 1% contribution.

All the rates quoted above are for the year ending April 5, 2005.

As noted, relief against income tax is not available for social security contributions.

The United Kingdom has treaties with many countries with regard to social security.

Other taxes on income/There are no other taxes on income. Other taxes are raised in the form of customs and excise duties on certain goods and on air travel, value- added tax (VAT) on the purchase of most goods and services, inheritance tax on certain gifts and on estates, and insurance premium tax.

Local taxes on income/There are no local taxes on income as such. Local authorities are financed partly by the imposition of council tax, a property-based tax levied on the occupier of a domestic dwelling at a flat rate per dwelling. Unoccupied dwellings are also taxed on the property's owner. The remainder of local authority finance comes from the imposition of the uniform business rate on business property and from central government grants.

Tax administration

Returns/Returns must be filed for each tax year ending April 5, but only a quarter to a third of taxpayers are required to file a return, since most liabilities are collected by withholding at source. Married couples are independently responsible for their own affairs, and each spouse files his or her own return. The taxable year for individuals is always the year commencing April 6 and ending on the following April 5.

The United Kingdom has a self-assessment tax system. Returns for 2004-2005 will be due by January 31, 2006, if the taxpayer self-assesses and pays the balance of tax due with the return. Alternatively, the taxpayer may elect to have the Inland Revenue compute the liability, in which case the return must be filed by September 30, 2005, the tax still being due by January 31, 2006. If a tax return has not been issued, the taxpayer must notify the Inland Revenue of significant capital gains and new sources of income by October 5 following the end of the tax year.

Payment of tax/Income tax is normally withheld from salaries under the pay-as-you-earn (PAYE) system. Income from most other U.K. sources is received after the savings-rate tax has been deducted. Under the new self-assessment regime, any tax not collected through withholding is paid through payments on account on January 31 in the tax year and July 31 after the end of the tax year, with any final balance due at the latest by January 31 after the end of the tax year.

Employers are required to notify the revenue authorities of total pay, benefits, and expenses paid or reimbursed, and the employee then makes a claim for allowable business expenses.

Tax rates

Tax rates for the tax year ending April 5, 2005 are as follows.

Income tax

Taxable income		Other income	Dividends	Savings income
Over	Not over	%	%	%
0	£ 2,020	10	10.0	10
£ 2,020	31,400	22	10.0	20
31,400		40	32.5	40

Dividends are treated as the top slice of income (and carry a tax credit that covers the 10% rate), "savings income" as the next slice, and other income as the lowest slice. The most common form of "savings income" is interest, but certain other forms of income are also included.

Capital gains tax

Taxable gains		Tax on Column 1	Percentage on excess
Over (Column 1)	Not over		
0	£ 8,200	Nil	—
£ 8,200		—	—*

*Gains are taxed as the highest part of income and gains.

INDIVIDUAL TAX CALCULATION

Based on income in the year to April 5, 2005

I—Income tax

Assumptions

Non-U.K.-domiciled married man; husband and wife under 65, with U.K.-resident employers; tax computation.

Tax computation

	Husband	Wife
	£	£
Salary	50,000	12,000
Car benefit (based on carbon dioxide emissions)	5,250	—
Gasoline benefit (based on carbon dioxide emissions)	2,880	—
Total earned income	58,130	12,000
Dividends from U.K. companies (Husband, 2,700 plus tax credit of 300; wife, 900 plus tax credit of 100)	3,000	1,000
Loan interest received—Husband, net 800 plus 200 tax withheld; wife, net 160 plus 40 tax withheld	1,000	200
Total income	62,130	13,200
Less:		
Mortgage interest paid (2,600)	—	—
Personal allowance:		
Husband	4,745	—
Wife	—	4,745
Taxable income	57,385	8,455
Income tax thereon:		
Husband:		
On first £2,020 at 10%	202	
On next 29,380 at 22%	6,436	
On dividends—3,000 at 32.5%	975	
On remaining 22,985 at 40%	9,194	
	16,807	
Wife:		
On dividends—1,000 at 10% (1)		100.00
On interest—200 at 20% (2)		40.00
On first 2,020 of other income at 10% (1)		202.00
On remaining 5,235 at 22%		1,151.70
Total tax liability (3)	16,807	1,493.70
Less—Credits/withholding on dividends and interest	(500)	(140.00)
	16,307	1,353.70

Notes:

1. Dividend income is taxed only at 10%, except for taxpayers who pay tax at the highest rate. This 10% liability is satisfied by the tax credit for such income, although the credit cannot be repaid to nontaxpayers. Dividend income that is taxable in any event at 10% will not be treated as using part of the general 10% rate band.

2. Savings income—normally interest—is taxed at only 10% or 20%, except for taxpayers who pay tax at the 40% rate. Tax is normally deducted at source at a rate of 20% and can be repaid to nontaxpayers.
3. The total liabilities as calculated above are discharged partly by withholding at source and partly by direct tax payments.

II—Capital gains tax

Assumptions

In September 2004, a non-U.K.-domiciled but U.K.-resident individual disposes of a non-U.K. asset acquired in April 1994 and realizes a capital gain (net of indexation allowance—see above) of £4,000. Of £10,000 proceeds of sale, £2,000 is received in the United Kingdom. The individual also sells a taxable U.K. business asset for £200,000 in September 2004 that cost £25,000 in July 1980. As at March 31, 1982, the asset had a market value of £35,000. The individual is liable to U.K. income tax at the higher (40%) rate.

Tax computation

1. U.K. business asset:		
Proceeds of sale		£ 200,000.00
Market value at March 31, 1982		35,000.00
Total gain		165,000.00
Indexation allowance:		
RPI March 1982	79.44	
RPI April 1998	162.60	
Value at March 31, 1982 (35,000 x 1.047)		(36,645.00)
Taxable gain before taper		128,355.00
Taper—Disposal of business asset owned for more than two complete years—Business asset taper of 75%		(96,266.25)
Taxable gain		£ 32,088.75
2. Overseas asset:		
Taxable gain = (Proceeds received in United Kingdom ÷ Net proceeds) x Total gain		£ 4,000.00
Less—Taper relief (six complete years owned since April 5, 1998, but treated as seven years' ownership since held before March 17, 1998. Nonbusiness asset taper of 25% is available)		(1,000.00)
Total gain		£ 3,000.00
Taxable gain—(2,000 ÷ 10,000) x 3,000		£ 600.00
3. Total taxable gains		£ 32,688.00
Less—Annual exemption		(8,200.00)
Taxable amount		£ 24,488.00
Capital gains tax payable January 31, 2006 at 40%		£ 9,795.20

Note:

Exchange rate of the pound sterling at December 31, 2003: US$1 = £0.6114.

United States

PwC contact

For additional information on taxation in the United States, contact:

Michael Budnick
PricewaterhouseCoopers
1301 Avenue of the Americas
New York, NY 10019
Telephone: (1) (646) 394-3156
Fax: (1) (813) 329-5356
e-mail: michael.budnick@us.pwc.com

Significant developments

There have been no significant developments regarding individual taxation in the past year.

Territoriality and residence

The United States taxes its citizens and resident aliens on their worldwide income. Nonresident aliens are generally taxed only on their U.S.-source income, as discussed below. The determination of an alien's residence status is subject to a set of relatively objective tests. These rules generally treat the following individuals as residents:

1. All lawful permanent residents for immigration purposes ("green card" holders), and
2. Those who meet a "substantial presence test" (present in the United States for at least 31 days in the current year and a total of 183 equivalent days during the current year and prior two years). For the purposes of this 183-equivalent-day requirement, each day present in the United States during the current calendar year counts as a full day, each day in the first preceding year as one-third of a day and each day in the second preceding year as one-sixth of a day.

Special rules apply to the determination of the portion of the year an individual will be treated as a resident or nonresident in the first and last years of residency. Income tax treaties may also modify an individual's residency status.

Gross income

Employee gross income/Nonresident aliens are taxed on compensation earned for work performed in the United States, regardless of when or where payments are made, absent a treaty or Internal Revenue Code provision to the contrary.

Resident and nonresident alien employees are generally not taxed on reimbursements for either personal living expenses (i.e., food and housing) or for other travel expenses while on "travel status." However, reimbursements for similar expenses of a spouse or dependent are taxable. Unlike the tests for determining U.S. residence status described above, being in travel status requires a temporary absence from an individual's tax home. Assignments for more than one year in a single work location are not considered to be temporary, regardless of any other facts and circumstances.

Capital gains and investment income/Capital gains of a resident alien are included in worldwide income and subject to U.S. taxation. Investment income of a resident alien is treated in the same manner.

Nonresident aliens may be taxed at 30% on U.S.-source net capital gains if they are in the United States 183 days or more during the taxable year in which the gain occurs. The operation of this provision is limited to situations where an alien is not otherwise taxed as a resident under the substantial presence test above. Capital gains from U.S. real property interests are taxable regardless of U.S. presence.

Nonresident aliens' U.S.-source interest, dividends, rents, and royalties are generally subject to a flat 30% tax rate (or lower treaty rate), usually withheld at source. However, a nonresident alien can elect to report real property rental income net of expenses, subject to tax at graduated rates. In addition, certain "portfolio interest" earned by nonresident aliens is generally exempt from tax.

Deductions

Business deductions/Resident and nonresident aliens can generally deduct, to the extent not reimbursed, travel or personal living expenses while on "travel status"; ordinary and necessary business expenses, including those for business-connected moving; and meals and entertainment expenses, subject to certain limitations. The deductible amount for meals and entertainment expenses is limited to 50% of actual costs. Additionally, all business expenses of an employee are deductible only to the extent that, when added to other miscellaneous itemized deductions, they exceed 2% of adjusted gross income (AGI). Unreimbursed moving expenses are not subject to this 2% floor and are deductible in arriving at AGI. Reimbursements for moving expenses may be eligible for exclusion from an employee's income; if reimbursement of moving expenses is so excluded, the expenses are not deductible by the employee. Nonresident aliens in travel status may deduct commuting expenses; however, resident aliens generally may not, because they are typically not in travel status.

Nonbusiness expenses/Resident aliens can deduct as itemized deductions qualified residence interest; most state and local income and property taxes; certain expenses incurred in producing income to the extent that they and other miscellaneous itemized deductions exceed 2% of AGI; and, subject to limitations, medical expenses, casualty and theft losses, and charitable contributions. No deduction is allowed for personal interest.

There is a limitation on these otherwise deductible itemized deductions (other than medical expenses, casualty and theft losses, and investment interest) for taxpayers with an AGI exceeding certain thresholds. In 2004 these thresholds are $142,700 for married taxpayers filing jointly, single taxpayers and head of household taxpayers and $71,350 for married taxpayers filing separately. These amounts are adjusted annually for inflation.

Such otherwise allowable itemized deductions are reduced by 3% of the amount of AGI in excess of the threshold amounts. In no event is the total of these otherwise allowable deductions reduced by more than 80%.

Interest paid on investment debt is deductible, but only to the extent there is net investment income (i.e., investment income net of investment expenses other than interest). Disallowed excess investment interest expense may be claimed as a deduction in subsequent years to the extent of investment income in such years.

Nonresident aliens may deduct, subject to limitations, casualty and theft losses incurred in the United States, contributions to U.S. charitable organizations, and state and local income taxes.

Instead of itemizing deductions, resident aliens (i.e., those who are residents for the entire tax year) may claim a standard deduction. The standard deduction for 2004 is $9,700 for married individuals filing a joint return, $4,850 for single individuals, $7,150 for heads of household, and $4,850 for married individuals filing separate returns. These amounts are adjusted annually for inflation. Nonresident aliens may not claim a standard deduction.

Taxpayers who are blind or age 65 or over, including resident aliens, are entitled to a higher standard deduction. For 2004 they may increase it by $950 if they are married filing a joint return or by $1,200 if they are single or married, filing separately. If they are blind and age 65 or over, they may increase their standard deduction by $1,900 and $2,400, respectively.

Personal allowances/Resident aliens are allowed a personal deduction (exemption) for themselves, for their spouse (subject to exceptions) and for each of their dependents (who must be citizens or residents of the United States, Canada, or Mexico).

Nonresident aliens are entitled to only one personal exemption (except for those from Canada, Japan, the Republic of Korea, or Mexico).

For 2004 the personal exemption amount is $3,100. The personal exemption is adjusted annually for inflation.

The deduction for personal exemptions is phased out by 2% for each $2,500 or fraction thereof ($1,250 for married persons filing separate returns) by which a taxpayer's AGI exceeds a certain threshold. For 2004 these thresholds, which are adjusted annually for inflation, are $214,050 for joint return filers, $178,350 for head-of-household filers, $142,700 for single filers, and $107,025 for married persons filing separately.

Tax shelters/Tax reform has limited the use of tax losses derived from so-called tax shelters ("passive" losses) to offset other taxable income. Passive losses may not offset income from other sources, such as earned income and portfolio (i.e., interest and dividend) income. Such losses can be used to offset passive income only. Similarly, credits from such investments can be used only to offset tax on net income from these investments. Disallowed losses can be carried forward to offset income from tax shelters in future years and, when the investment is sold or otherwise disposed of, income from other sources.

Tax credits

Resident aliens may claim a credit against their tax liability (subject to limitations) for income taxes paid or accrued to foreign countries or foreign governmental units. Alternatively, foreign taxes may be deducted from taxable income. Nonresident aliens are generally not entitled to a deduction or credit for foreign taxes. Resident aliens may claim a child credit if the child is a resident of the United States, subject to limitations.

Other taxes

Social security and Medicare hospital insurance taxes/For 2004 a resident or nonresident employee's share of social security taxes (old-age, survivors and disability) is 6.2% of the first $87,900 of wages, plus Medicare hospital insurance taxes of 1.45% on all wages. The social security tax for self-employed individuals is equal to 12.4% of the first $87,900 of net self-employment income plus Medicare hospital insurance tax of 2.9% on all net self-employment income. Self-employment tax (i.e., social security and Medicare hospital insurance tax) is imposed on residents. Nonresidents are not generally subject to self-employment tax. Social security and Medicare hospital insurance taxes are not deductible in determining an employee's taxable income. However, a deduction is allowed for an amount equal to one-half of the combined self-employment social security and Medicare hospital insurance taxes imposed.

State and local income taxes/Most states and a number of municipal authorities impose income taxes on individuals working or residing within their jurisdictions.

California

The 2003 California personal income tax rates range from 1% to 9.3%. The top marginal rate of 9.3% applies to California taxable income in excess of $78,267 for married individuals filing joint returns and $39,134 for single individuals and for married individuals filing separate returns.

New York State

The New York State personal income tax rates range from 4% to 7.7% for 2004 returns. When New York State taxable income exceeds $500,000, the tax rate is a flat 7.7% on total taxable income.

In addition, New York City imposes a tax on its residents in 2004 at graduated rates from 2.907% to 4.45%. When New York City taxable income exceeds $500,000, the tax rate is a flat 4.45% on total taxable income.

Tax administration

Returns/Husbands and wives may generally file a joint return only if each is either a citizen or a resident. However, where only one spouse is a full-year or part-year citizen or resident, a joint return may be filed if both spouses agree to be taxed as full-year residents on their combined worldwide income.

Generally, joint filing will result in a lower tax liability than separate filing. However, with the phase-out of the personal exemptions and the limitation imposed on the deductibility of itemized deductions, this determination can be made with certainty only after a thorough review of the taxpayers' facts and circumstances. Married nonresident aliens (i.e., where both spouses are nonresident aliens such that an election to file jointly is not available) may not file joint returns and must use the tax table for married persons filing separate returns. Nonresident aliens may not file as heads of household.

Payment of tax/Income tax is withheld from employee compensation. Resident and nonresident taxpayers with significant income not subject to withholding (e.g., self-employment income, interest, and dividends) must generally make quarterly payments of estimated tax due April 15, June 15, September 15, and January 15. Nonresident aliens who do not have any income subject to payroll withholding tax make three estimated tax payments (rather than four) due June 15, September 15, and January 15, with 50% due with the first payment.

Tax rates

Effective 2004

Married taxpayers

Joint return (1, 2, 3)

Taxable income Over (Column 1)	Not over	Tax on Column 1	Percentage on excess
0	$ 14,300	—	10
$ 14,300	58,100	$ 1,430.00	15
58,100	117,250	8,000.00	25
117,250	178,650	22,787.50	28
178,650	319,100	39,979.50	33
319,100		86,328.00	35

Separate return (1)

Taxable income Over (Column 1)	Not over	Tax on Column 1	Percentage over
0	$ 7,150	0	10
$ 7,150	29,050	$ 715.00	15
29,050	58,625	4,000.00	25
58,625	89,325	11,393.75	28
89,325	159,550	19,989.75	33
159,550		43,164.00	35

Unmarried taxpayers

Single (1)

Taxable income Over (Column 1)	Not over	Tax on Column 1	Percentage over
0	$ 7,150	0	10
$ 7,150	29,050	$ 715.00	15
29,050	70,350	4,000.00	25
70,350	146,750	14,325.00	28
146,750	319,100	35,717.00	33
319,100		92,592.50	35

Head of household (1, 3)

Taxable income		Tax on Column 1	Percentage over
Over	Not over		
(Column 1)			
0	$ 10,200	0	10
$ 10,200	38,900	$ 1,020.00	15
38,900	100,500	5,325.00	25
100,500	162,700	20,725.00	28
162,700	319,100	38,141.00	33
319,100		89,753.00	35

Notes:

1. The maximum federal tax rate on capital gains is 15% for assets held for more than 12 months. The graduated rates of tax apply to capital gains from assets held for 12 months or less. The 15% tax rate also applies to qualifying dividends, generally dividends paid by U.S. companies.
2. Joint return rates may be used by a qualifying widow(er).
3. As noted, nonresident aliens may not take advantage of head of household status or joint return rates.

Alternative Minimum Tax/In lieu of the tax computed using the above rates, the Alternative Minimum Tax (AMT) may be imposed under a two-tier rate structure of 26% and 28%. The 26% rate applies to the first $175,000 ($87,500 for married individuals filing separate returns) of a taxpayer's alternative minimum taxable income (AMTI) in excess of an exemption amount; thereafter, the 28% rate applies. The exemption amount for 2004 is $58,000 for a joint return or qualifying widow(er), $29,000 for married filing separate returns, and $40,250 for other taxpayers. If, however, AMTI exceeds $150,000 for married taxpayers filing jointly ($75,000 for married filing separate returns and $112,500 for other taxpayers), the exemption is reduced by 25% of the excess amount.

Alternative Minimum Tax is payable only to the extent it exceeds the regular net tax liability. The foreign tax credit is available for determining AMT liability to the extent of the foreign tax on the foreign-source AMTI, subject to certain limitations. No more than 90% of AMT liability may be offset by foreign tax credits.

Alternative minimum taxable income is generally computed by starting with regular taxable income and adding tax preference deductions (claimed in the computation of regular taxable income) and making special adjustments to some of the tax items that were used to calculate taxable income. For example, the taxpayer must add back all state and local income taxes claimed in computing regular taxable income.

For nonresident aliens with a net gain from the sale of U.S. real property interests, the AMT is calculated on the lesser of their alternative minimum taxable income (before the exemption) or the net gain from the sale of the U.S. real property interest.

INDIVIDUAL FEDERAL TAX CALCULATION

Calendar year 2004

Assumptions

Resident alien husband and wife with two children; one spouse earns all the income, none of which is foreign-source income. A joint return is filed. AMT liability is less than regular tax liability.

Tax computation

Gross income:		
Salary		$ 120,000
Interest		9,500
Qualified dividends		5,000
Non-qualified dividends		1,700
Long-term capital gain (on assets held for more than one year)		1,250
Total gross income		137,450
Adjustments		0
Adjusted gross income		137,450
Less—Itemized deductions:		
State and local taxes	9,000	
Charitable contributions	2,000	
Unreimbursed business expenses (exclusive of 50% of meals and entertainment costs)—1,500 (1)	0	
Phaseout of itemized deductions (2)	0	11,000
		126,450
Less—Personal exemptions: 4 x 3,100 (3)		12,400
Taxable income		$ 114,050
Tax thereon:		
On taxable income of 107,800 (114,050 less capital gain of 1,250 and qualified dividends of 5,000) at joint return rates		$ 20,425
On 1,250 capital gain and qualified dividends at 15%		938
Total tax		$ 21,363

Notes:

1. Must exceed 2% of AGI ($137,450), or $2,749, to be deductible.
2. Phaseout begins when AGI ($137,450) exceeds $142,700.
3. Phaseout begins when AGI ($137,450) exceeds $214,050.

PwC contacts

For additional information on individual taxation in Uruguay, contact:

Leonardo Decarlini
Patricia Marques
PricewaterhouseCoopers
Cerrito 461, Piso 4
11000 Montevideo, Uruguay
Telephone: (598) (2) 916 0463
Fax: (598) (2) 916 0605, 916 0653
e-mail: leonardo.decarlini@uy.pwc.com
patricia.marques@uy.pwc.com

Significant developments

There have been no significant regulatory or tax developments in the past year.

Absence of income tax

Income tax is not imposed on individuals in Uruguay.

Other taxes

Social security taxes/The Uruguayan social security system is comprehensive, covering retirement pensions, health insurance, sick pay, and unemployment insurance. Social security contributions are compulsory, based on the salary earned, including bonuses and commissions, and are borne by the employer and the employee.

The employer contributes an amount equivalent to 18.625% and withholds from 18.125% to 36.125% from the employee, as follows.

	Employer contributions	Employee contributions
	%	%
Retirement contributions	12.5 or 0 (1)	15
Health insurance	5 or 2.5 (2)	3 (2)
Payroll tax	1	0, 3, 7.5, 9, 10, 13, 14, 15, 17, or 18 (3)
Labor restructuring	0.125	0.125

Notes:

1. The 0% rate is applied to salaries earned by workers of industrial plants.
2. There is no health insurance contribution for corporate directors. The 2.5% rate is applied to salaries earned by workers of industrial plants.
3. The rate depends on the amount of the employee's salary. The 18% rate is applicable to remuneration exceeding approximately US$2,100 per month. Salaries above UYP34,240 (approximately US$1,100) are not subject to the retirement contribution on the excess over this amount. Health insurance and payroll tax are applicable on the whole salary.

Capital tax/Individuals who own capital not related to industrial and commercial activities exceeding UYP1,370,000 are subject to capital tax, which is applied on net worth (assets located in the country less certain liabilities). The tax is levied at progressive rates varying between 0.7% and 3%.

Note

Exchange rate of the peso at December 31, 2003: US$1 = UYP29.29.

PwC contact

For additional information on taxation in Uzbekistan, contact:

Abdulkhamid Muminov
PricewaterhouseCoopers
5 Ivlev Street
Tashkent 700090, Uzbekistan
Telephone: 998 71 120 6101
Fax: 998 71 120 6645
e-mail: abdulkhamid.muminov@uz.pwc.com

Significant developments

Legislation in the Republic of Uzbekistan is constantly evolving during the period of economic transition from the preindependence socialist economy. The information presented below is based on laws, regulations, and practices as of March 15, 2004.

Significant changes in the tax and regulatory legislation are effective from January 1, 2004, and include further reduction of the top personal income tax rate to 30% (down from 36% to 33% in 2002 and further to 32% in 2003).

Territoriality and residence

Both residents and nonresidents are subject to tax in Uzbekistan. Residents are taxed on their worldwide income, whereas nonresidents are taxed on income from their activities in Uzbekistan. An individual is a resident if one of the following two tests is met.

1. The individual resides in Uzbekistan on a permanent basis.
2. The individual is present in Uzbekistan for 183 days and more during any 12-month period beginning or ending in a calendar year.

Gross income

Gross income of an individual includes the following items.

1. Income from employment, including:
    a. Salary and other payments for work performed, as envisaged by labor or civil contracts;
    b. Negative difference between the prices at which goods (work, services) are provided to employees and the costs of acquisition of these goods (work, services);
    c. Reimbursement of employee's expenses not related to business activity;
    d. Employee's debts to an employer forgiven by the employer;
    e. Employer's expenses in relation to nonobligatory life and health insurance;
    f. Amounts subject to withholding from an employee, but paid by an employer;
    g. Other expenses of an employer constituting, directly or indirectly, income of an employee.
2. Income from property (interest, dividends, and rent income).
3. Income from entrepreneurial activity.

Capital gains taxes/Capital gains generated from entrepreneurial activity are subject to income tax.

There are no specific concessions offered to foreigners in the personal income tax legislation with the exception of diplomats.

Exempt income/The following income items are not subject to personal income tax.

1. Statutory social security allowances, unemployment allowances, dismissal payments, maternity payments, aid payments received from charity and ecology funds (sick leave allowances are not exempt).
2. Child support received.
3. Scholarships within statutory limits.
4. Statutory pensions.
5. Income from disposal of personal property (if the disposal is in the course of entrepreneurial activity, the income is taxable).
6. Gifts from legal entities valued at less than six times the statutory minimum monthly wage during a year (approximately US$33).
7. Money and property received in the course of inheritance.
8. Insurance proceeds.
9. Bank interest from Uzbek banks.
10. Material support (if related to natural disaster—exempt in full; in other cases—limited to 12 times the statutory minimum monthly wage during a year (approximately $65 per year).
11. Dividends used for the purchase of shares of a company from which the dividends were received. Recent changes in legislation introduced five-year exemption for dividend income received from shares of companies created on the basis of privatized enterprises.
12. Income from intellectual property.
13. Reimbursement of business expenses (business trips), within statutory norms.

Deductions

There are no standard deductions under Uzbek law. The only deductions available relate to income derived from entrepreneurial activities and represent expenses and mandatory payments and charges associated with such activities.

Certain categories of individuals are also either fully exempt from personal income tax (e.g., diplomats) or provided with an additional monthly deduction of four amounts of the statutory minimum monthly wage (approximately US$22 per month), including veterans, disabled people, widows/widowers with children, and women with many children, among others.

Local income taxes

There are no local income taxes.

Tax credits

According to the tax code, a credit is provided for foreign taxes paid to countries with which Uzbekistan has a double taxation treaty.

Tax administration

The tax period is the calendar year. A tax return must be submitted by the individual to the tax authorities at the location of the individual's registration in Uzbekistan on or before April 1 of the year following the reported year.

Tax rates

The tax rates are as follows.

Taxable income	Tax rate
	%
Up to 5 times the minimum annual wage	13
From 5 to 10 times the minimum annual wage	21
More than 10 times the minimum annual wage	30

The minimum annual wage (MAW) is UZS65,280. As mentioned above, the annual wage deduction has been abolished.

INDIVIDUAL TAX CALCULATION

As of January 1, 2004 (1)

	US$	UZS
Salary	80,000	78,400,000
Interest from a foreign bank	5,000	4,900,000
Taxable income	85,000	83,300,000
Tax base	85,000	83,300,000
Tax thereon:		
5 x MAW at 13%	43	42,432
5 x MAW at 21%	70	68,544
Balance at 30%	25,300	24,794,160
Subtotal	25,413	24,905,136
Less—Foreign tax paid (2)	(10,000)	(9,800,000)
Tax due	15,413	15,105,136

Notes:

1. Assumes an exchange rate of UZS980 per US$1 (actual rate as of January 1, 2004).
2. In theory, only foreign tax paid in a country with which Uzbekistan has a double taxation treaty can be credited against Uzbek tax.
3. Capital gains from the disposal of nonbusiness property are not included to taxable income (e.g., sale of premises, cars, etc.).
4. Official exchange rate of the soum at January 1, 2004: US$1 = UZS980.

PwC contacts

For additional information related in Venezuela, contact:

Luis Fernando Miranda
Valentina Boccardo
Espiñeira, Sheldon y Asociados
Edificio Del Rio
Avenida Principal de Chuao
Caracas 1061-A, Venezuela
Telephone (58) (0212) 7006124, 7006251
Fax (58) (0212) 7006280
e-mail: fernando.miranda@ve.pwc.com
valentina.boccardo@ve.pwc.com

Mailing address:
Espiñeira, Sheldon y Asociados
c/o Jet International-M347
P.O. Box 020010
Miami, Florida 33102-0010
U.S.A.

Significant developments

The following information is updated as of March 8, 2004. During the past year there have been no significant tax developments.

Territoriality and residence

Changes to the Income Tax Law effective as of January 1, 2001 have broadened the territoriality regime, establishing a system based on taxation of worldwide income, as follows.

1. Resident individuals are subject to tax on their total worldwide income.
2. Individuals domiciled abroad with a permanent establishment in Venezuela must pay taxes on their income of national or foreign source attributable to said establishment.
3. Nonresident individuals will pay taxes on their income whenever the cause or origin of such income lies within Venezuela.
4. Resident individuals, as well as individuals domiciled abroad with a permanent establishment in Venezuela, may credit the income tax paid abroad for income of extraterritorial source.

Individuals are considered to be residents in Venezuela for tax purposes when they spend more than 183 days in Venezuela in aggregate during a fiscal year or if they have spent more than 183 days in Venezuela in the preceding year. Thus, an individual who spends 184 days in Venezuela will be deemed to be a resident for tax purposes.

According to the Organic Tax Code, individuals will be considered resident in Venezuela for tax purposes if they establish a residence or home in Venezuela, unless they have stayed in another country more than 183 days and demonstrate, by evidence issued by the corresponding tax authorities, that they are tax resident in that other country.

Venezuelan citizens are presumed domiciled in Venezuela unless they can prove otherwise.

Gross income

Employee gross income/Resident and nonresident individuals are taxed on salaries and wages and on any other remuneration for personal services such as meal allowances, pensions, profit sharing, and other similar remunerations, regardless of the place of payment or currency used. Employees are not taxed on pensions and termination benefits as set forth in the Labor Law or collective contracts (employer/union) and interest thereon, or income from trusts established to administer employer contributions to the related funds.

Foreign-source income will be taxable for tax-resident individuals unless an exemption or tax treaty applies.

Tax units/The 1994 amendment to the Income Tax Law established the concept of a tax unit (TU) to reduce the negative effect of inflation on the determination of the tax rates. The Tax Code established the initial TU at Bs1,000 with annual basis adjustment based on the variation of the consumer price index (CPI) from the previous year. In March of each year, the tax unit value is adjusted for inflation that occurred in the preceding fiscal year.

For the 2004 the tax unit value will be Bs24,700.

Capital gains and investment income/Capital gains are taxable as ordinary income. Individuals are taxed on any Venezuelan source income, including income derived from industrial and commercial activities, earnings derived from the sale of personal property or services, and royalties and interest.

Income earned by individuals investing in the local stock exchange (sale of shares) are subject to a flat tax of 1% (via withholding). Profits and losses related to the same activity can not be taxable or deductible against ordinary taxable income.

Dividend tax is levied at a flat rate of 34% on the positive difference between book income and fiscal income generated after 2001. To determine this difference, the LIFO method applies. The 34% (domestic) rate can be mitigated under tax treaties to 10%, 5%, or even 0%. The withholdings are to be made at the moment a dividend is declared or credited (to an account of the recipient).

Dividends obtained from companies incorporated or domiciled abroad or incorporated abroad and domiciled in Venezuela are excluded from the dividend tax system. However, these dividends will be taxed at 34% flat tax income tax rate.

Income received in the form of interest, royalties or proceeds from the sale of real estate is taxable when paid. Interest earned from Venezuelan saving deposits or saving funds is tax exempt.

Deductions

Business deductions/Resident individuals who are not employees can deduct expenses allowed by law, using the same guidelines applicable for corporations. Taxable income does not include properly documented travel expense reimbursements and limited representation allowances. Business deductions from salary income are not allowed.

Nonbusiness expenses/In determining taxable income, Venezuela residents can deduct the following expenses.

1. Educational payments made in Venezuela for the taxpayer and for dependent children under 25 years of age.
2. Life, surgery, hospitalization, and maternity insurance premium payments.
3. Medical, dental, and hospitalization payments.
4. Rent or interest payments on loans granted for the acquisition or enlargement of the taxpayer's home. The authorized disencumbrance might not exceed 1,000 TU for the fiscal year in the case of interest on loans, or 800 TU for the fiscal year in the case of payments associated with the leasing of main or permanent housing.

Taxpayers should attach the invoices, with the *Registro de Infomacion* (RIF) number (taxpayer number), to the tax return.

Special deductions/Taxpayers have the option to claim a special (single) deduction of 774 TU. No documentation is necessary. Taxpayers who choose the special deduction cannot claim the deductions indicated above.

Personal allowances/Residents receive a personal tax credit of 10 TU for the taxpayer, spouse, and any dependent.

Tax credits

Resident Individuals may take credit for income tax paid abroad in regard to extraterritorial source income.

Other taxes

Social security taxes/Social security taxes are 4% of salary, up to a maximum salary of Bs247,104 per month.

Unemployment benefit program/Funds to finance this program are obtained from contributions paid by both the employers and the employees. The rate is 2.2% of the salaries earned by employees, of which 1.7% must be paid by the employer and 0.5% by the employee through monthly withholdings.

Mandatory housing savings plan/Special legislation aimed at creating funds for financing construction for low- to medium-priced housing requires employers and employees/workers to make a monthly contribution to personal accounts opened by employers on behalf of their employees. The employer must contribute 2% and the employee/worker 1% of salary.

Other taxes on income/Municipal tax authorities impose taxes on commercial activities conducted by individuals within their jurisdiction. An individual carrying out business activities can deduct these taxes in determining their Venezuelan income tax.

Tax administration

Returns/Spouses must, in principle, file joint returns even if they have personal income arising from their own activities. They will be considered as a single taxpayer. Husbands and wives can file separate tax returns only when the following conditions apply.

1. There was a mutual agreement for separation of property.
2. They both are reporting salaries, wages, and professional fees and choose to declare separately.

Individual taxpayers must file their returns on a calendar-year basis. Exceptions are permitted (for instance, when an individual leaves Venezuela or ceases all business).

Payment of tax/Income tax is withheld from salaries, professional fees, royalties paid to nonresidents, and certain other payments received by nonresidents.

Individuals other than employees must file estimated returns only if, during the year immediately preceding fiscal year, they received income exceeding 1,500 TU from commercial, credit, leasing, or subleasing activities involving movable or real property or salaries exceeding 1,000 TU.

The estimated tax is based on 75% of the tax that would result from applying full rates to the estimated income declared (80%). The prepaid tax resulting from the estimated returns must be paid in either a single installment or in three equal installments.

Final tax returns must be filed within three months following the end of the tax year. Tax resulting from the filing of the final tax returns must be paid in a single installment or in up to four equal installments.

Tax rates

Resident individuals are subject to tax using graduated rates, with the marginal rate reaching 34% on annual income above approximately US$ 72,000 in 2004 (using an exchange rate of US$1 = Bs1,608.63).

Income for nonresident individuals arising from nonbusiness professional activities is subject to tax of 34% on 90% of the gross payments. Salary and other income received by nonresidents for services performed in Venezuela are subject to a flat 34% tax, withheld at source.

The annual income tax, before credits, is calculated using the following tax rate table (Tariff No. 1).

Range of taxable Income (in TU)		Tax rate	Deduction
Over	**Not over**	**%**	**TU**
0	1,000	6	0
1,000	1,500	9	30
1,500	2,000	12	75
2,000	2,500	16	155
2,500	3,000	20	255
3,000	4,000	24	375
4,000	6,000	29	575
6,000		34	875

Note:

Exchange rate of the Bolivar at March 8, 2004: US$1 = Bs1,920.00.

PwC contacts

For additional information on taxation in Vietnam, contact:

Richard J. Irwin
Tax and Consulting
PricewaterhouseCoopers (Vietnam) Ltd.
4th Floor, Saigon Tower
29 Le Duan, District 1
Ho Chi Minh City, Vietnam
Telephone: (84) (8) 823 0796
Fax: (84) (8) 825 1947
e-mail: r.j.irwin@vn.pwc.com

Significant developments

Effective from July 1, 2004, the personal income tax (PIT) rates for Vietnamese taxpayers will be significantly reduced under the amended PIT Ordinance which was passed on March 19, 2004. For foreigners, the highest rate of 50% is now removed. However, foreigners who stay in Vietnam less than 30 days, who were previously exempt, will now also subject to PIT in the same manner as nonresidents.

The PIT rates reflected in this summary are effective for foreigners only. For other tax (including personal tax on Vietnamese employees) or regulatory developments, please refer to the contact above.

Territoriality and residence

Residence is determined as follows.

1. Foreigners are considered to be resident in Vietnam and are taxable on their worldwide employment income if they live and work in Vietnam for an aggregate of 183 days or more within a period of 12 months. Tax is computed at progressive rates (see “Tax rates” below).
2. Nonresident foreigners who spend less than 183 days working in Vietnam are taxed only on Vietnam-sourced employment income, and the tax rate is a flat 25%. Individuals who are tax resident of countries which have a double taxation agreement with Vietnam can obtain a tax exemption if they are nonresident for Vietnam tax purposes and certain additional conditions are met.

Gross income

Employee gross income/In general, tax applies not only to employment income but to all forms of income received by an individual. Regular income includes salaries, wages, directors' fees, allowances, and bonuses. Employer-provided housing, electricity, and water are taxed.

Technically, all noncash benefits are taxable. However, there are exceptions, including school fees for expatriates' children, home leave for expatriates, and education/training fees for employees, provided these payments are paid directly by the employer to the suppliers.

The taxable value of employer-provided housing is limited to 15% of gross wages or salary if this is less than the actual housing cost.

Where an employee is remunerated on a net basis (i.e., net of tax) this net income is required to be grossed up to determine gross income subject to PIT.

Irregular income (e.g., gifts from overseas; lottery prizes; fees or commissions for technology transfer, industrial design or technical construction design; and royalties from cultural works, conducting technical seminars or scientific research) is taxed separately on each transaction at rates different from those applicable to regular income. Business income would normally be subject to business income tax and not PIT.

Capital gains and investment income/Under the tax regulations, certain capital gains and investment income are temporarily not taxable; these include interest on bank deposits, bank savings and loans; profits from purchases of bonds and shares; income derived from investment in stocks; and gains from purchases and sales of stocks.

Deductions

Business deductions/Business income and deductions are dealt with under the rules for business income tax, not personal income tax.

Nonbusiness expenses/No deductions are allowable.

Personal allowances/Certain types of allowances are treated as nontaxable, including specific hardship, night-shift, and fixed meal allowances. There are no personal allowances.

Tax credits

Vietnam has no unilateral tax credit relief for foreigners or Vietnamese nationals, however, relief or exemption is available where tax treaties apply.

Other taxes

Social security taxes/Employers contribute 15% and employees 5% of the employee's total salaries for social insurance purposes every month. Expatriates are exempt.

Health insurance/Health insurance is payable by employers at the rate of 2% of the employee's wages. The employee contributes an additional 1%. Expatriates are exempt.

Contributions to Social Insurance and the Health Insurance Fund from employees' salaries and wages are tax deductible.

Tax administration

Returns/PIT returns can be filed on an individual or company basis. Tax on regular income is finalized annually or upon termination of the employment contract. Employers or employees are required to file monthly provisional PIT returns. The tax year is the calendar year, and annual tax returns of employees are to be finalized with the tax authorities by February 28 or within 30 days of the termination of the contract.

Payment of tax/There are two options: the employee can pay the tax personally each month or the employer can withhold tax monthly and pay it to the authorities on behalf of the employees within 25 days of beginning of the following month. An employer that withholds the PIT and remits to the tax authorities receives a commission (0.5% of tax payable) for being the withholding agent.

The monthly payments are provisional and will be finalized at the end of the year.

Tax rates

Regular income/Rates for resident foreigners applicable from July 1, 2004, are as follows. Note that even for finalization of annual PIT returns the employee's income is converted to a monthly basis and tax is calculated accordingly.

Monthly income		Tax on	Percentage
Over	Not over	Column 1	on excess
(Column 1)			
0	VND 8,000,000	—	—
VND 8,000,000	20,000,000	—	10
20,000,000	50,000,000	VND 1,200,000	20
50,000,000	80,000,000	7,200,000	30
80,000,000		16,200,000	40

The rate for nonresident foreigners is a flat 25% in the first year on the Vietnam-source income. In subsequent years the provisional tax rates for foreign residents apply, but only on the Vietnam-source income.

Irregular income/Rates on such income, applied to each individual transaction, are as follows.

Monthly income		Tax on	Percentage
Over	Not over	Column 1	on excess
(Column 1)			
0	VND 2,000,000	—	—
VND 2,000,000	4,000,000	—	5
4,000,000	10,000,000	VND 100,000	10
10,000,000	20,000,000	700,000	15
20,000,000	30,000,000	2,200,000	20
30,000,000		4,200,000	30

In the case of fee income from technology transfers, the rate is a flat 5% per transaction (nil for income of less than VND2,000,000).

For lottery winnings, the rate is a flat 10% per event (nil for winnings of less than VND12,500,000).

In the case of gifts from overseas, the rate is a flat 5% (nil for items less than VND2,000,000).

INDIVIDUAL TAX CALCULATION

For regular income earned by foreigners, for the calendar year 2004.

Assumptions

Annual gross income is VND1.08 billion (VND90 million per month), that is, annual income of US$71,933 and monthly income of US$5,994.

No housing is provided by the employer.

Tax computation

Gross monthly taxable income	VND	90,000,000
Income tax thereon:		
On first 80,000,000	VND	16,200,000
On remainder (10,000,000) at 40%		4,000,000
	VND	20,200,000
Annual equivalent (12 x 20,200,000)	VND	242,400,000

Note:

Average exchange rate of the Vietnamese Dong at January, 2004: US$1 = VND15,697.

PwC contact

For additional information on taxation in Zambia, contact:

Eileen Duncan
PricewaterhouseCoopers
National Savings and Credit Bank Building
Seventh Floor
North End, Cairo Road
(P.O. Box 30942)
Lusaka, Zambia
Telephone: (260) (1) 228809–10, 220782, 220778
Fax: (260) (1) 220768
e-mail: pwclsk@zamnet.zm, offices@zm.pwcglobal.com
Attn: Eileen Duncan
Eileen.duncan@zm.pwcglobal.com

General note

This entry is repeated from the 2003/2004 edition. For more up-to-date information consult the contact listed above or Jacqueline Collette at jacqueline.collette@us.pwc.com.

Significant developments

There have been no significant developments regarding individual taxation in 2002. The information in this entry is current as of January 2003. For subsequent developments consult the contact listed above.

Territoriality and residence

Zambia taxes income received by individuals from a source within Zambia and foreign interest and dividends received by citizens and residents (including expatriates). For the purposes of Zambian taxation, individuals are not treated as resident if they are visitors with no intention of establishing residence in Zambia and have not actually been resident for a total of 183 days in any tax year. An alien person taking up employment in Zambia under contract enters Zambia on a work permit and is classified as an "expatriate."

Gross income

Employee gross income/An employee is taxed on total emoluments and benefits (other than those detailed below), regardless of where payment is made and regardless of whether it is remitted. Inducement allowances to expatriates are subject to tax in their hands. The cost of inducement allowances is allowed as a deduction in determining the employer's taxable income.

The gratuity up to 25% of the basic salary or inducement allowance for a minimum period of two years under a written contract of employment is taxed separately. Any amount in excess of 25% is added to the salary and other emoluments and taxed normally.

An employee is not taxed on the following items:

1. Accommodation provided by the employer directly or for which rent is paid by the employer to the landlord. However, the housing benefit to be disallowed in the

employer's tax computation is 30% of the taxable income paid to an employee per annum, regardless of whether the housing is employer-owned or rented.

2. A car benefit. However, the Commissioner of Taxes has determined that the value of noncash fringe benefits for cars that are also used personally by the holder is disallowed in the employer's tax computation. For this purpose, two categories have been set up:
   a. Luxury cars—Those with an engine capacity of 1800 cc and above. The fringe benefit for these cars is assessed at ZK200,000 per month.
   b. Other cars—Cars with an engine capacity that is below 1800 cc. The fringe benefit for these cars is assessed at ZK120,000 per month.
3. Terminal benefits paid by way of ex gratia payments or compensation for loss of office. The first ZK5 ,000,000 is exempt, and the balance is taxed at a flat rate of 10%. Any ex gratia payment in respect of a deceased employee or payment for termination of employment on medical grounds are exempt from tax.

In addition to the above, an expatriate is not taxed on economy-class commencement and terminal passages made by the individual.

The exemption relating to an education passage for each child for each consecutive period of four months was removed with effect from April 1, 2002, and no longer applies.

Approved share option schemes were introduced in 2002. However, the legislation is still at the infancy stage and is under development. Sale proceeds from the shares acquired under an approved share option scheme in Zambia or on the termination of services will be deemed to be income of the individual; relief from income tax will be provided, subject to certain conditions.

Capital gains and investment income/Currently, capital gains are not taxable. Dividends received by an expatriate outside Zambia are aggregated with Zambian income. Relief for any tax withheld by the foreign country is subject to the provisions of any tax treaty between the two countries. Rental income received from outside Zambia is exempt from Zambian tax.

With effect from April 1, 1999, interest earned by a resident on any sum deposited in Zambia is subject to a final 25% withholding tax. Foreign bank interest received by a resident in Zambia is liable to tax at the normal rate for individuals, which is currently 30%.

Deductions

Business deductions/Every person can deduct pension contributions to an approved fund (subject to limitations) and, to the extent not reimbursed, subscription fees for membership in technical/professional associations.

Nonbusiness expenses/An expatriate can deduct premiums paid under an approved annuity contract (not exceeding ZK180,000) and approved charitable contributions (restricted to 15% of assessable income). Alimony and maintenance payments are not deductible and are not subject to tax in the hands of the recipient. Insurance premium payments are not allowable as deductions. No other standard deductions are available.

Tax exemption/With effect from April 1, 2002, the individual tax credit for every individual taxpayer was removed and replaced by a tax-free sum of K1.8 million per annum. This means that an individual with an annual income of ZK1,800,000 or less is not liable to tax for the year involved.

The tax credit for individuals with disabilities has been increased from ZK1,200 per annum to K18,000 per annum.

Tax credits

Resident taxpayers can take income taxes paid to foreign countries as a credit against their Zambian tax liability, subject to the provisions of a tax treaty.

Other taxes

Social security taxes/Social security contributions are deductible for a resident taxpayer. Expatriates are not eligible to contribute to the Social Security Fund.

Local taxes on income/Apart from the personal levy, which is negligible, there are no local taxes on income.

Tax administration

Returns/For all persons, annual self-assessment returns are required to be filed by September 30 of each year for the previous fiscal year ended March 31. Outstanding tax liabilities should be settled by that date. There is a penalty for failure to submit tax returns on or before any specified due date.

Husbands and wives can file separate returns even if both are resident in Zambia. The earned and investment income of the wife is taxed on her separately. As a result of a change in the tax law with effect from April 1, 1996, the wife's investment income is no longer assessable on the husband.

Payment of tax/Income tax is withheld from salaries (pay-as-you-earn (PAYE)). A taxpayer who has a sizable income not subject to PAYE is required to make quarterly payments of estimated tax on a current-year basis. All unsettled income tax liabilities must be paid by September 30 of each year (i.e., within six months of the March 31 fiscal year-end).

Tax rates

Expatriate employees may be paid remuneration in two parts, a local salary and an inducement allowance, which are both liable to income tax at unified rates (however, see "Gross income" above).

With effect from April 1, 2002, there is now one tax rate. Income below ZK1,800,000 is not subject to tax. Income above this amount is taxed at a flat rate of 30%.

INDIVIDUAL TAX CALCULATION

For fiscal year ending March 31, 2003

Assumptions

Resident husband and wife, two children; husband earns all the income.

Tax computation

Salary (including inducement allowance)		ZK 10,000,000
Add:		
Zambian-source bank interest	100,000	
U.K.-source bank interest	50,000	
Cash allowances	400,000	550,000
		10,550,000
Less—Deductions:		
U.K. National Insurance contributions (social security)	5,000	
Charitable contributions	50,000	55,000
Taxable income		ZK 10,495,000
Tax liability		ZK 2,608,500
Add—Bank interest subject to 25% (1)		25,000
Tax due (2)		ZK 2,633,500

Notes:

1. Bank interest is now subject to tax at 25% with no exemption applicable for individuals.
2. Normally, tax amounting to ZK2,608,500 on the salary and cash allowances would have been deducted by the employer under the PAYE system.
3. Exchange rate of the kwacha at March 25 2003: US$1 = ZK4,896.

PwC contact

For additional information on taxation in Zimbabwe, contact:

Manuel Lopes
PricewaterhouseCoopers
P.O. Box 453
Harare, Zimbabwe
Telephone: (263) (4) 307213 19
Fax: (263) (4) 332724/332495
e-mail: manuel.lopes@zw.pwcglobal.com

General note

This entry is repeated from the 2003/2004 edition. For more up-to-date information consult the contact listed above or Jacqueline Collette at jacqueline.collette@us.pwc.com.

Significant developments

There have been no significant tax or regulatory developments as regards individual taxation in the past year.

Territoriality and residence

The Zimbabwean income tax system operates mainly on a territorial basis, and income is as a general rule taxable in Zimbabwe if the source is within Zimbabwe. Individuals who are not ordinarily resident are taxable only on income from sources in Zimbabwe. Individuals who are regarded as being ordinarily resident in Zimbabwe are subject to tax on employment income earned during temporary absences from Zimbabwe (up to 183 days in a tax year) and on foreign investment income. Income for services performed outside Zimbabwe is deemed to be from a Zimbabwean source if the services are incidental to employment in Zimbabwe.

There is no definition of "ordinarily resident" in the legislation, and no hard and fast rules apply for determining whether a person is ordinarily resident in Zimbabwe. The question must be decided on the particular circumstances of each case. A foreign employee who has been present in Zimbabwe for two years or more and who has been joined there by spouse and family would be regarded as being ordinarily resident in Zimbabwe for the period of stay. However, employees who have been in Zimbabwe for six months to a year and who have left their families at home would probably not be treated as ordinarily resident.

Gross income

Employee gross income/Expatriate employees are taxable on salary and on any overseas allowances, irrespective of the place of payment and whether or not these monies are remitted to Zimbabwe. Living and housing allowances, tax reimbursements, and the value of benefits such as free accommodation and the use of motor vehicles, as well as the deemed value of interest-free or low-interest loans, are included in taxable income. There are no tax concessions in favor of short-term residents, and all income relating to services rendered in Zimbabwe is taxable.

Any bonus received by an employee (to the extent that it does not exceed Z$20,000 or 10% of annual remuneration after excluding the amount of the bonus, whichever is lower) is exempt from income tax.

A foreign employee who was present in Zimbabwe on a short-term contract for a very limited period (one year or less) and who was not ordinarily resident would have a reasonable chance of successfully claiming that the provision of accommodation did not constitute a taxable benefit. This would be on the basis that the accommodation was for the purpose of the employer's business and that the foreign employee continued to maintain a family establishment in the home country. As with ordinary residence, there are no strict rules, and taxability of benefits must be decided on the basis of individual circumstances.

Capital gains and investment income/Zimbabwe-source capital gains are taxable at the rate of 20%. Tax is levied on the gain after deduction of acquisition costs and a 50% annual allowance on these costs. The tax is confined to disposals of immovable property (real estate) and marketable securities, which include, as the most important items, stocks and shares. (Shares quoted on the Zimbabwe Stock Exchange are exempt.) The intent is to exclude gains on foreign real estate and foreign stocks and shares from Zimbabwean capital gains tax. Residence in and of itself has no bearing on liability for capital gains tax.

Dividends payable to resident individuals by Zimbabwean corporations are subject to a 20% withholding tax but are exempt from income tax. Dividends from corporations quoted on the Zimbabwe Stock Exchange are subject to a reduced rate of 15% withholding tax.

Withholding tax at a rate of 20% applies to interest (including discount instruments and treasury bills) payable by a Zimbabwean bank, discount house, financial institution, or building society to a resident. The interest is exempt from normal income tax and the 20% withholding tax is final. Interest from local foreign-currency-denominated accounts is exempt. All other taxable interest from Zimbabwean sources is taxed at normal tax rates. Interest and dividend income on foreign investments is taxable in Zimbabwe if the recipient was ordinarily resident in Zimbabwe at the time of accrual of the income.

Short-term residents regarded as ordinarily resident in Zimbabwe are taxable on such income. Interest is taxable as ordinary income, but foreign dividends are taxed at a special flat rate of 20%. Foreign rents and royalties are not taxable in Zimbabwe except for royalties paid for the use of the property or rights in question in Zimbabwe. Zimbabwe-source interest and dividends (other than dividends from shares listed on the Zimbabwe Stock Exchange) payable to nonresident individuals are subject to withholding taxes of 10% and 20%, respectively, unless reduced by a double taxation treaty. Dividends from shares listed on the Zimbabwe Stock Exchange are subject to a withholding tax of 15%, again subject to the provisions of any double taxation treaty.

Deductions

Business deductions/No business-related expenses are deductible unless they are incurred as a condition of employment or for the purpose of producing the employee's income, such as in circumstances where the expenditure can be shown to influence the level of the employee's income. An employee remunerated on a commission basis could be in this position. Moving and travel expenses are not deductible. Entertainment expenses are prohibited as a deduction, and business entertainment and travel allowances provided by an employer are taxable to the extent that they are not expended for the purpose of the employer's business. There are no standard or blanket deductions except a nominal deduction for tradesmen's tools where the tools are provided by the employee. Subscriptions to business, trade, technical, or professional associations are deductible.

Nonbusiness expenses/Contributions to approved pension funds (to a maximum of Z$90,000) are deductible, including contributions to approved social security schemes of other countries. Credits are allowable on medical expenses (if the taxpayer is ordinarily resident in Zimbabwe).

No allowances are available for mortgage and other interest payments, taxes and charitable donations (except to a few specified institutions). There are no standard deductions for nonbusiness expenses.

Personal allowances/No personal credits are available.

Tax credits

Unilateral relief from double taxation is available where income from foreign sources is deemed to be from a Zimbabwean source. The relief takes the form of a foreign tax credit up to the amount of the tax brought about by inclusion of the foreign income in the Zimbabwean assessment.

Other taxes

National Social Security contributions are payable by all employees (to a maximum of Z$5,400 for the fiscal year ended December 31, 2003). No local income tax is payable in addition to central government taxes.

Tax administration

Returns/Married taxpayers file tax returns separately. Filing of joint returns is not permitted. Taxpayers must adhere to a calendar year.

Payment of tax/A pay-as-you-earn (PAYE) system, under which income tax is withheld from remuneration payable to employees, is in operation. From the year ending December 31, 2002 this will be the final tax for employees who are employed by the same employer throughout the year and who have no other source of income. Such employees will not be required to file tax returns.

Tax rates

Income tax/In the case of income from employment, with effect from January 1, 2002, there are graduated taxes of tax up to Z$1.5 million of taxable income. The tax on this amount is Z$488,000. Thereafter, the maximum rate of 45% applies. In addition there is an AIDS levy of 3% of the tax chargeable, giving an effective rate of 46.35%.

Any taxable income accruing to an individual from any trade, investment, or other activity (excluding employment or pension) is taxed at a flat rate of 30% plus an AIDS levy of 3% of tax chargeable, giving an effective rate of 30.9%.

INDIVIDUAL TAX CALCULATION

Assumptions

A foreign national is on a three-year contract and is regarded as ordinarily resident in Zimbabwe. Income and deductions for the year ending December 31, 2003 are as shown below.

	Z$
Salary	2,350,000
Overseas allowance	400,000
Net local bank interest (withholding tax, Z$1,800) (1)	840
Proceeds from sale of private residence in Zimbabwe (purchased in February 1999 for Z$800,000)	2,900,000
PAYE deductions from salary	1,090,000
Contributions to company pension fund	97,000

Tax computation

Income tax computation

Salary	Z$ 2,350,000
Overseas allowance	400,000
	2,750,000
Less—Pension fund contributions (maximum)	90,000
Taxable income	Z$ 2,660,000
Income tax on 2,660,000 (rounded)	Z$ 1,010,000
3% AIDS levy	30,300
	1,040,300
Less—PAYE	(1,090,000)
Net income tax refundable	Z$ 49,700

Capital gains tax computation

Proceeds from sale of residence		Z$ 2,900,000
Less:		
Cost of acquisition	800,000	
50% on acquisition costs for each tax year involved	2,000,000	2,800,000
Capital gain		Z$ 100,000
Capital gains tax payable at 20%		Z$ 20,000

Notes:

1. Bank interest from which tax has been withheld at source does not figure in the income tax determination.
2. Exchange rate of the Zimbabwe dollar at January 1, 2003: US$1 = Z$57.145.